W. B. YEATS

Also by Stephen Coote

BYRON – The Making of a Myth
WILLIAM MORRIS
A SHORT HISTORY OF ENGLISH LITERATURE
A PLAY OF PASSION – The Life of Sir Walter Ralegh

W. B. YEATS

A Life

Stephen Coote

Hodder & Stoughton

First published in 1997
by Hodder and Stoughton
A division of Hodder Headline PLC

British Library Cataloguing in Publication Data

Coote, Stephen
W.B. Yeats: a life
1. Yeats, W. B. (William Butler), 1865–1939 – Biography
2. Poets, Irish – 19th century – Biography 3. Poets, English
– 19th century – Biography
I. Title
821.8

ISBN 0 340 64710 8

Typeset by Palimpsest Book Production Limited,
Polmont, Stirlingshire
Printed and bound in Great Britain by
Mackays of Chatham PLC, Chatham, Kent

Hodder and Stoughton
A division of Hodder Headline PLC
338 Euston Road
London NW1 3BH

For
Jessica,
Rebecca and Louise

'the spreading laurel tree'

Acknowledgements

During the writing of this book I have incurred many obligations. Those to academic specialists are acknowledged in the footnotes and the bibliography. The staffs of the British Library, the London Library, and the University of London Senate House Library were, as always, unfailingly helpful. In the matter of illustrations, I would particularly like to thank Anna MacBride White, Rex Roberts and Colin Smythe, as well as the staffs of those institutions listed below. My agent, Anthony Goff, helped make some rough places plain; while my editor, Roland Philipps, and his assistant Angela Herlihy, were unfailingly supportive.

Among personal friends, Frances Campbell offered me a vital insight into Yeats's psychology, and afterwards invited me to talk to the Oxford Psychotherapy Society on some aspects of Yeats and Jung. I would like to thank that attentive and enthusiastic audience. Sally Johnson was, as always, a great and supportive friend. David Warner offered unstinting companionship to an often distracted author.

This book is dedicated to my sister and her daughters as a token of my profound esteem for their courage.

Note: For the reader's convenience, autobiographical works published during Yeats's lifetime are often referred to as *Autobiographies*. I have, in addition, in all but one instance, regularised the erratic spelling in Yeats's letters and other personal writings.

Contents

CONTENTS

List of Illustrations

Illustration credits: British Library: 25; Philip Goodman Esq: 40; Irish Tourist Board: 36, 54; Anna MacBride White: 18, 19, 21, 37; National Gallery of Ireland: 6, 7, 19, 26, 31, 32, 33; National Portrait Gallery: 10, 17, 30, 34, 39, 47, 48; University of Reading: 11, 13, 24, 29, 38; Rex Roberts: 1, 2, 3, 4, 5, 15, 16, 35, 41, 42, 43, 44; Colin Smythe: 27, 28, 45, 49, 50, 52, 53; Theosophical Society: 12.

Preface

Reminiscing about his early manhood in 1919, Yeats declared that 'one day when I was twenty-three or twenty-four this sentence seemed to form in my head, without my willing it, much as sentences form when we are half-asleep: "Hammer your thoughts into a unity." For days I could think of nothing else, and for years I tested all I did by that sentence. I had three interests: interest in a form of literature, in a form of philosophy, and a belief in nationality.'[1] From these three interests Yeats hoped to create the unity of his being, and they are the three principal themes I have chosen to discuss in this biography – my means of getting to the heart of this titanic man.

To trace Yeats's interest in nationality is to place him against Ireland's struggle to find both its political independence and its cultural identity. It is to tell the story of the birth of a nation and to see Yeats himself discovering in an ancient golden age of Celtic achievement the ideals that might have built a future. It is to see literature taking on a quite exceptional importance as it preserved national consciousness through years of defeat, but it is also to trace a poet's gathering disillusion as the social and political realities of his newly independent land fell short of his imagined ideal. As Sean O'Casey wrote after Yeats's death: 'his greatness is such that the Ireland which tormented him will be forced to remember him for ever'.[2]

Yeats's interest 'in a form of philosophy' is a theme of comparable scale. The political man trying to fashion a concept of nationhood was also the man seeking a fully spiritual life after the loss of conventional Christian belief. In a search that was to take him from the circle of Madame Blavatsky, through the occult practices of the Golden Dawn, to the spiritualist experiments that were to culminate in *A Vision*, Yeats was seeking ultimate assurances, a structure of belief. He was engaged in the heroic task of preserving a spiritual life amid materialism. As he told his mentor John O'Leary: 'the mystical life is the centre of all that I do and all that I think and all that I write'.[3] It also lay near to the heart of two of the most important relationships in Yeats's life. His long love affair with Maud Gonne, interpreted by them both as a 'mystic marriage', was in part the means by which each hoped to contact occult powers that might give spiritual life to Ireland and strength to their own endeavours. Yeats's late marriage to George Hyde-Lees and their discovery of her spiritualist faculty was the inspiration for Yeats's creation of a philosophy which, however curious and even dangerous it might appear, yet seemed partly to fulfil a deeply felt need by joining man to the cosmos and explaining his destiny.

Finally, it was the merging of these two themes – Yeats's search for national consciousness and spiritual revelation in human love – which he tried throughout his lifetime to merge with his art, creating with John Synge and Lady Gregory especially a literary renaissance in Ireland as well as a body of his own work which is one of the pinnacles of late-nineteenth- and early-twentieth-century achievement. Both Yeats's poetry and his drama deal constantly with the most fundamental ideas and show, I think, that his search for unity, for integrity, was a continuous and often painful struggle, constantly checked by reverses and doubt, constantly under threat from events. Hammering his thoughts into a unity was a great poet's lifelong endeavour in which euphoria often doubled with despair. In this lies its profound human interest and an explanation of one of Yeats's last and greatest insights: 'Man can embody the truth but he cannot know it.'4

PART ONE

'That Toil of Growing Up'

The ignominy of boyhood; the distress
Of boyhood changing into man;
The unfinished man and his pain
Brought face to face with his own clumsiness.

I

The Ignominy of Boyhood
(1865–1881)

I
The Yeatses and the Pollexfens

When William Butler Yeats was born in Dublin on 13 June 1865, the doctor in attendance congratulated his parents on producing a son with a fine, broad forehead and so great a fund of natural strength that, he assured them, the baby could be left 'all night on the windowsill' without any harm coming to him. On the surface all seemed well. A healthy child had been born, while the Yeatses themselves were a young Anglo-Irish couple who seemed set for social and professional success. Susan Yeats was a daughter of the prosperous Pollexfen family of Sligo, while John Butler Yeats, who was currently reading for the Bar, was a well-connected landlord who could number among his friends some of the most talented men of his generation. The birth of his first child further increased his happiness by opening in him a vein of unsuspected paternal feeling so deep that he 'hated to see any stranger, even the nurse', touching his son.[1] Such a concern was to last through a long lifetime and exerted an influence on the growing boy equalled only by what John Butler Yeats himself insisted were the very different characteristics the child inherited from his mother.

The relationship between the young father and his wife's family dated back to John Butler Yeats's boyhood, the earliest years of which he remembered as an idyll of domestic affection. He recalled particularly that, on most evenings when the Ulster rectory at Tullylish was quiet and the servants had gone to bed, his father, the Reverend William Butler Yeats, would sit by the fire in the kitchen smoking 'a new clay pipe' and talking to him of books and memories. The parson was a lively and intelligent man, firm in his belief that in the house of an Anglo-Irish gentleman everything should be settled by cultivated feeling. The parson felt as a matter of quiet certainty that he and his kind were 'socially the equals and the superiors of most', and he was determined that his offspring should carry into the

3

second half of the nineteenth century habits of sympathy, intelligence and social refinement.

Many generations of the parson's family had encouraged him to such views, since the history of the Yeatses for more than 150 years had been the history of the Anglo-Irish themselves. Some time in the late seventeenth century, a certain Jervis Yeats had emigrated from Yorkshire to Dublin, where he set up as a wholesale linen merchant. Such entrepreneurial people, thriving in the wake of the English victory over the native Catholics at the Battle of the Boyne, were viewed by Swift as the backbone of the nation. Two generations followed Jervis Yeats into the linen trade until his grandson Benjamin married Mary Butler, a member of a leading and ancient house connected to the Dukes of Ormonde. Butler was now to become a name regularly used in the family, and with this hint of an aristocratic connection went over 560 acres of land in County Kildare, an estate which helped support the family when Benjamin's business eventually failed.

Mary Butler's pension from the War Office also helped her family pass easily from the hazards of trade to the greater security of the professional classes. Trinity College and Dublin Castle, the great centres of English Ascendancy power in Ireland, were now open to them. After graduating from Trinity, Mary and Benjamin's son married the daughter of a Castle official and was soon promoted to the comfortable living of Drumcliff in County Sligo. During the first half of the nineteenth century, the scholarly 'Parson John' enjoyed an income of £4000 a year and a local reputation for his family's being 'the best blooded in the county and no impudence about them'. But there was kindness here, and tact too. It was said that Parson John would rattle his keys before entering a room where he feared he might find two servants in a compromising position, but it was only on his death in 1846 that it was discovered how this good man had had a relish for the pleasures of life which extended to his building a secret liquor cupboard in his Drumcliff rectory and stocking it at the cost of £400 in credit.

The Reverend William Butler Yeats promptly paid his father's debts and settled to a comfortable domestic life. In 1835 he had taken as his wife Jane Grace Corbet, a descendant of one of Marlborough's generals, and a woman who showed her high spirits on the day of her marriage when she delighted her husband by challenging their postillion to race another bridal couple down the road. William Butler Yeats himself, tall and redheaded, had been the finest horseman at Trinity College and remained so enthusiastic that his first rector good-humouredly complained that he had 'hoped for a curate but they sent me a jockey'.[2] But, for all that the Reverend William Butler Yeats was an enthusiastic sportsman, he tempered his vigour and pride with a faith which taught him to see it as his duty 'to follow closely in the footsteps of Jesus, to be like him sympathetic and like him affectionate, and like him courteous'. Apparently safe in the values of the established

Anglican Church of Ireland, the Reverend William Butler Yeats was able to maintain easy relations with his Roman Catholic neighbours (even while looking askance at the dour creed of the local Presbyterians) and to prove his faith by performing acts of charity when cholera struck Ulster in 1845.

Nonetheless, although the man who sat with his son in the kitchen could confidently wave away the tobacco smoke curling about him, subtle problems were beginning to crowd round his kind, and their gradual focussing was to show that the Anglo-Irish were an increasingly anomalous people belonging fully neither to England nor to Ireland itself. For the moment, much seemed to disguise this. The industrialisation of England had made Ireland a ready market for mass-produced goods. Belfast became part of the modern British economy. English fashions, English sports, English literature and, above all, the English language triumphed over a nation of Gaelic-speaking and Roman Catholic people soon to be decimated by famine, eviction and the emigration that followed these.

And what industrialism prompted, legislation secured. Efforts by Wolfe Tone in the wake of the French Revolution to assert Irish independence were savagely crushed and then supposedly ended by the Act of Union in 1800. Grattan's parliament surrendered its powers to Westminster. But, as the nineteenth century wore on, what seemed to bind the Anglo-Irish to British protection left them increasingly isolated among a resentful indigenous population. Daniel O'Connell, the first modern Catholic to take a seat at Westminster, headed early-nineteenth-century demands for the repeal of the Act of Union and the re-establishment of the Irish parliament, while the Young Ireland movement, campaigning through the *Nation*, urged physical force in the pursuit of an independent country. The bases of Anglo-Irish power were being challenged and, when the Reverend William Butler Yeats sat in the kitchen at Tullylish recounting stories of his days at Trinity College, one of the main characters he recalled was Isaac Butt, a man who was eventually to adopt the great nineteenth-century cry of Irish Home Rule.

For the young John Butler Yeats the happy days of early boyhood came to a sudden close when, in 1849, his father decided he could no longer teach him at home but would have to send him to a school near Liverpool run by the Davenport sisters. Family love was replaced by a religion of fear. The children slept with bibles under their pillows and were frequently punished as a foretaste of the notion that 'we were so wicked that even if we got to heaven we should not enjoy ourselves'. John Butler Yeats noticed, however, the hypocrisy with which the teachers touched up his drawings for the 'edification' of his parents, and he began to wonder if there was any point in praying for letters from home when the time for posting them had long gone by. In such ways, childhood miseries sowed the seeds of later religious doubt.

After two years of such treatment, John Butler Yeats was deemed ready to go on to Atholl Academy on the Isle of Man. Here the puritanism of the Davenport sisters was made more dismal by the regime inflicted on the school by the headmaster, William Forrester, who prowled the corridors in carpet slippers eagle-eyed for wickedness he could punish with a rubber cane. John Butler Yeats was too intelligent, however, not to see the virtues that underlay his teacher's beliefs, and he came in time to respect him for his insistence on hard work and clear thinking. As he wrote in his unpublished memoirs, Forrester 'was an able and honest man of great natural force and he loved his boys, not of course as they were but as he intended to make them. He believed that in every boy were the seeds of intelligence and virtue – only they needed the rod.' John Butler Yeats himself rose to the top of the school, despite his problems with arithmetic, and, as he did so, he began to look with fascination at those of his Irish fellows he so far excelled. In particular, his attention was caught by two boys from Sligo, Charles and George Pollexfen, who were forever at the bottom of the class.

Neither was an attractive boy, each being sour, repellent and slow. 'They were not the sort to be interfered with,' John Butler Yeats wrote, and he attributed their lack of charm to their upbringing in a household where commerce and an austere puritanism were all important. Nonetheless, as if reaching out to embrace his opposite, he was intrigued by George Pollexfen especially, for although the boy made little attempt to return his friendship, John Butler Yeats thought he detected in him qualities he found alluring. While he himself might amuse his schoolfriends with his highly proficient drawings and cartoons, George Pollexfen could, when all the boys were in the dormitory, hold them spellbound with stories shot through with a poetry, a closeness to nature and a stirring primitive quality 'presented without philosophy, without theories, without ideas, in a language that recalled the vision of Chaucer'. George Pollexfen 'talked poetry though he did not know it', and in such ways the tastes of a lifetime were formed.

On leaving Atholl Academy, John Butler Yeats spent an agreeable half-year living with his retired father next to Sandymount Castle, the eighteenth-century Dublin home of his Uncle Robert Corbet, with its beautiful tree-lined vistas looking out across the mountains and the Bay. Here he prepared himself for entrance to Trinity College and enjoyed his uncle's considerable hospitality while mixing with such notable Dublin figures as Sir William Wilde, the father of the poet and playwright, and his wife, the 'Speranza' of Irish poetic nationalism. For the moment, John Butler Yeats was barely attracted to the latter's views. His Tory, Unionist Uncle Robert had made his fortune in politics and 'in those happy times', he wrote ironically, 'the Protestants owned everything (of course it was only right) and despised the Catholics for being so poor (which was also quite right)'.

Nonetheless, if John Butler Yeats was still politically unawakened, he was beginning to be assailed by questions about his faith. The doubts unwittingly sown by the Davenport sisters and nurtured by the brutality of Atholl Academy were beginning to mature. He turned naturally enough to his father, who recommended he read Bishop Butler's *The Analogy of Religion*, but the work that was the foundation of the pastor's belief proved the undoing of his son's. John Butler Yeats put the book aside convinced it showed Christianity to be merely 'myth and fable'. He was facing a crisis experienced by many young men of his generation and, like them, he turned to the great modern philosophers for guidance. He became an assiduous reader of John Stuart Mill, while, under the influence of Comte especially, he developed a scepticism which drove him to reduce all phenomena to general terms. As he himself wrote: 'I came in time to recognise natural law and then lost all interest in a personal God, which seemed mainly a myth of the frightened imagination.' For John Butler Yeats, there was now no reality beyond the compass of a man's mind and heart, and this was a way of thinking that was profoundly to affect his son, who was to spend a lifetime in the quest for ideals he believed more spiritually nourishing.

The sceptical glance John Butler Yeats cast on religion was cast with equal rigour on life at Trinity College. He gradually came to feel that, as a conservative outpost of the English establishment, it 'turned away from Irish aspirations' and worked to discourage real controversy and intellectual speculation. Although some of the students were keen nationalists and even mounted a protest against the new Lord Lieutenant's entry procession into the city, the majority seemed merely 'noisy and monotonous' young men, and there were compensations for him in the fact that the state of his father's finances made it necessary for him to live at home rather than in College itself. Because of a bout of rheumatic fever, John Butler Yeats graduated without honours in the spring of 1862. Although his tutor encouraged him to stay on, he had resolved on becoming a barrister and he enrolled at King's Inn for the following autumn. In the meantime, he entered the College competition in political economy. He was the only candidate and, having satisfied the examiner of his ability, was awarded the £10 prize. It seems that he had also fallen in love. The name of the young woman has not been preserved, but, although John Butler Yeats remembered the affair as 'beautiful' and 'delightful', his suit was unsuccessful. In his disappointment, and with the £10 prize in his pocket, he resolved to set off for Sligo and visit his old schoolfriend George Pollexfen.

The beauty of the Sligo coast put the unhappiness of Dublin out of his mind. The Pollexfens themselves were holidaying at Rosses Point and, finding George in an unusually talkative mood, John Butler Yeats went with him on an evening walk along the seashore, glancing up from time to time towards the glorious mountains of Knocknarea to the south and Ben Bulben to the north, which were later to enter so deeply into the Yeats mythology. But there were other attractions in the Pollexfen household for a young man recently crossed in love. George's sister Susan was a slight girl whose prettiness was made the more attractive by her strongly contrasted eyes, one of which was blue and the other brown, and each of a 'decided' colour. Over the course of the next few days the couple grew closer and, on a family excursion to Bundoran, they went to explore some caves where Susan 'timorously' returned her suitor's kisses. Later, she agreed to marry him. On the rebound of passion, John Butler Yeats claimed he was drawn to Susan by her very defects, her tendency to petulance and sourness and that absence of humour which had first attracted him to her brother. These were qualities which, he believed, masked a deep, instinctive poetry, a oneness with the natural world of Sligo about her. 'If you were to lose those faults,' he told Susan, 'you would lose your individuality.' In his naivety, he was marrying less the woman he saw than the woman he half guessed at.

Meanwhile, John Butler Yeats found his fiancée's qualities multiplied in the family about her. Their sombre Sundays concentrated the natural Pollexfen gloom. 'It was', he wrote, 'puritanism without religious ecstasy or exaltation – a dark cave with its one lamp extinguished though still smoking.' The young suitor observed the family members gathered together in mutual dislike, the heavy silence broken only by the turning of a page of an improving book, a sigh or 'the creaking of someone's brace'. Most solemn of all was the family patriarch. William Pollexfen, powerful and prosperous, broadly built and scowling at the world with vividly blue eyes, was a man of iron will who through sheer force of character had risen from being a Devonshire sailor lad to owning, in partnership with his brother-in-law William Middleton, the milling firm of Middleton & Pollexfen, along with the Sligo Steam Navigation Company. As a man who had so conspicuously got on in the world, William Pollexfen despised literature and poetry as being a part of the idleness he feared would lead to moral and financial disaster.

The weight of such opinions hung heavily in the Sunday parlour and stifled the natural fascination his family had for verse and the things of the imagination, a taste which for some male members of the household at least found an outlet in active freemasonry. Nonetheless, while John Butler Yeats was intrigued by the family's gift 'for being dismal', the Pollexfens regarded him with a more practical satisfaction. Here was a young man whose family had long been part of the Anglo-Irish Ascendancy and whose members had for generations been in the professions rather than trade. John Butler Yeats himself could look forward to a career of eminent respectability and eventually to inheriting a Dublin house and properties in County Kildare.

That inheritance came to him surprisingly quickly. John Butler Yeats had barely begun his study of the law when, on 26 November 1862, his father died. Eventually, when probate was cleared, he found he was possessed of a sufficient if not ample annual income of £379.0.6. With the lack of interest in matters of practical detail which was so disastrously to characterise his life, John Butler Yeats at once asked his Uncle Corbet to act as his agent. Although he was himself diligently studying the law, a day-to-day interest in the business of tenancies and agreements was irksome to him. The drawing, which he had never abandoned since his schooldays, and the conversation of such college friends as the Dowden brothers and John Todhunter, were altogether more agreeable. And, above all, there was the thought of Susan. 'I long to be married to you,' he wrote, 'because when vexed about anything, instead of brooding about it I will go to you with it, and we will share it together.' For the moment, he saw his future wife as a source of comfort and tranquillity. Eventually, on 10 September 1863, they were married at St John's church, Sligo.

The couple set up home at Georgeville in Sandymount Avenue, a comparatively modest house close to Uncle Corbet's castle and furnished largely from auctions. John Butler Yeats continued to make pages of notes from 'quantities of very big books' on the law, but, although he was the most distinguished member of his class, conversations with his friends were beginning to show him the true nature of his character: the subjectivity, the delight in ideas and the relish for the close contact of excited intellects that underlay his scepticism. Religion indeed formed a principal topic of conversation. John Dowden was a firm believer who eventually became a bishop. His brother Edward, a clever and tactful man who would suavely make his way to a position as contemporary Ireland's most distinguished literary critic, was altogether more ambiguous, relying on generalisations at once acceptable but vague. The Quaker Todhunter was more openly critical of received ideas, but all three recognised JBY, as they called him, as their intellectual leader, the man whose mental vigour was so abundant they could use the word 'genius' of him without it sounding false. JBY was, besides, so variously talented. His mind encompassed the law with little difficulty. He had been elected auditor of the King's Inn debating society and, at the time of the birth of his first son, was preparing the lecture he would give with such brilliant effect. In addition, his talent as a draughtsman was becoming more and more evident, and it was now that he set about a pen-and-ink sketch of his sleeping child. The rounded baby form of William Butler Yeats lies under a blanket, his square head on a pillow, his broad forehead clearly visible as his cheek rests on a tiny clenched fist.

In public meanwhile JBY was telling the cream of Dublin society gathered to hear his talk that they should make use of 'mind coming into collision with mind' so that their lives would no longer be directed by 'dead dogmas or corrupt prejudices but [by] living energies, moulding the whole character into conformity with themselves'.[3] This was the ideal in which JBY would rear his sleeping son, for the formation of the whole character, the harmonious expression of the complete individual, was becoming his faith and his means of greeting the energies constantly awakening in his own mind.

Besides such ideas as these, the practice of the law was a cramped and paltry thing. At the beginning of 1866, John Butler Yeats was admitted to the Bar, but attendance at a notorious trial concerning a disputed will impressed him merely as a display of high intellect demeaning itself for gain. He poured his exasperation into his sketchbook, covering sheets with cartoons of the mendacious and complacent faces gathered in the courtroom. His sketchbooks indeed were becoming altogether more important to him than his legal studies. On a family holiday to Sligo he made a fine drawing of the shore and the local fishermen mending their nets. Nonetheless, John Butler Yeats now had a growing family to support. On 25 August 1866, Susan gave birth to a delicate and premature baby who was christened Susan Mary and nicknamed 'Lily' by her mother. But the burden of looking after her children told on Susan's nerves and she was, besides, worried by her husband's preference for art and talk over the business of the law.*

His ideas and aspirations were of no interest to a young mother reared among the Pollexfens and now she looked on suspiciously. Although his father's old friend Isaac Butt offered to help in his career and although he conscientiously tried to succeed, John Butler Yeats felt his professional efforts undermined by a second and deeper self, 'another will', whose force was altogether more powerful. As a gentleman he might despise the worship of getting on in the world, and might even define a gentleman precisely as one who disdained such things. 'A gentleman', he would say, 'is simply such because he has not the doctrine of getting on and the habit of it. The contest is not against material things, but between those who want and those who don't want to get on, having other important things to attend to.' JBY's reluctance to fight for rewards among his legal peers was thus more than the carapace of class feeling. He accepted that his disinclination could be seen as a fault, a lack of 'practical businesslike energy', but it was also the necessary accompaniment to his deepest beliefs, his conviction that life should be not a battle for money and social prestige but an unfolding of those qualities at once aesthetic and ethical by which a man such as he revealed his fullness. John Butler Yeats was slowly advancing towards the idea that it is the artist – the artist not as producer, not as careerist, but as the most complete and various perceiver of the world – who embodies the greatest human potential.[4]

For a young barrister, this was a dangerous position and its effects were revealed in the most striking way. Despite the pleas of his friends, JBY continued to draw in court and his cartoons were regularly passed around. Their malignant accuracy was such that once, in the middle of an

---

* That Susan was the victim not just of her own temperament but of contemporary male attitudes is suggested by a small anecdote. Around this time she developed a cataract. On seeking the advice of Sir William Wilde, she was told: 'You are married, leave it alone; but don't forget to ask your husband when his uncle Thomas is going to send me those fishing rods.'

important case, they threatened to interrupt the majesty of the proceedings. John Butler Yeats went home that evening making, as he described them, 'new resolutions'. He had already sent a packet of his work to a magazine editor in London and now, when he received a favourable reply, the decision towards which he had been slowly moving was suddenly and decisively made. To the consternation of all concerned, he told his wife and family that he was throwing up the law and leaving Dublin for London and a training at an art school.

Susan and the children would have to stay with the Pollexfens in Sligo until he had found a place for them to live. The visit there was made particularly painful by the fact that the Pollexfens themselves had recently moved to a large eighteenth-century house whose spaciousness seemed only to emphasise the foolhardiness of John Butler Yeats's plans. The contrast between the bourgeois and the bohemian created an atmosphere the would-be artist described as 'awful'. The contemptuous and bitter gloom seemed even to affect the twenty-one-month-old Willie. His aunts thought they saw a natural seriousness in the child but also noted how the swarthy infant bore a marked resemblance to his irresponsible father. It was not like their family to behave in so feckless a way, and when Willie felt they were carping he began pitifully to cry. 'I remember little of childhood but its pain,' he would write,[5] but that pain and, with it, the complex Pollexfen temperament were familiar to him from years beyond his conscious recall.

II
London

In July 1867, Willie, Lily, their mother (now in her third pregnancy) and her young sister Isabella were summoned to London. John Butler Yeats had found a house for them at 23 Fitzroy Road near Primrose Hill.[6] Here, for the next five and a half years, they would endure increasing financial hardship as JBY's career as an artist came to nothing. The magazine illustration with which he had started was soon given up for a feverish attempt to learn the Pre-Raphaelite techniques of Watts, Millais and, above all, Rossetti. The crude transference of designs to woodblocks required by the magazines was replaced by the scrupulously accurate depiction of nature on a white canvas worked over inch by inch.

JBY was well placed to develop these interests. Leighton came to lecture at Heatherley's art school, while the Madox Browns were neighbours. But John Butler Yeats seemed to shy away from men who might advance his career, fearful perhaps that their more practised energy would diminish his own. When Rossetti sent his brother to see him the invitation was never taken up, partly because JBY's interests were by then beginning to veer away from Pre-Raphaelitism towards an altogether looser style derived from the French school. A lively correspondence, meanwhile, was maintained with friends in Dublin, and it was to Edward Dowden, quietly advancing his career in distant Trinity College, that JBY confessed what he saw as the real cause of his plight. 'I am a Celt', he wrote, 'and therefore enamoured of beauty – but too eager, too restless, wanting in concentration, and therefore ineffective.'[7]

Susan Yeats, obliged to live in hated London, watched the decline of her hopes in morose silence. The birth of Elizabeth Corbet Yeats, or 'Lollie' as she was always called, worsened the nervous strain of handling her children, and she knew that she could not look to her husband for help. John Butler Yeats's full love for his offspring would only be clearly shown when they were beyond the tiresome state of babyhood. Nonetheless, while he recognised that 'Susan could not have boiled an egg' and feared what might happen every time he left the house, he was sufficiently unscrupulous to put aside any doubts he might have had over securing a further mortgage on his properties against her jointure. A harassed Susan meanwhile, perhaps hoping life would return to her expectations, listed her husband's profession on Lollie's birth certificate as 'barrister'.

In addition to nurturing such futile hopes, Susan had also to endure her husband's new friends. The future satirist Samuel Butler (always referred to deferentially as 'Mr Butler') was one of his fellow students and, where the Pollexfens were staunchly Unionist, Butler began to stir JBY's incipient nationalism. Events both at home and in England were to stimulate this. On St Patrick's Day, 17 March 1858, James Stephens had founded the Irish Revolutionary Brotherhood, later renamed the Irish Republican Brotherhood, the IRB. A year of secret meetings as he travelled across the island had helped convince Stephens that only revolutionary activity could relieve the abject humiliation of the native Irish people. The great Famine of ten years before had decimated the population, and, while many emigrated to America to avoid the anguish of mass suffering and a squalid interment in a mass grave, those of the living who remained were told by the leaders of English imperialist opinion that 'the great evil with which we have to contend is not the physical evil of the famine, but the moral evil of the selfish, perverse and turbulent character of the people'.[8] The Famine, in other words, could be seen as God's punishment on a race easily looked on as barely human. To counter this savage myth, Stephens fostered an altogether more profound one of his own: the belief that England was a satanic power and that a morally superior and independent Ireland was deeply impressed on his countrymen's souls and evoked a commitment of mystic intensity.

For such beliefs men and women were prepared to die. Believing that a combination of native and American Irish could foment a successful Nationalist revolution, Stephens swore his Fenian followers to a secret oath in which they promised to 'do my utmost at every risk while life lasts, to make Ireland an independent democratic republic'.[9] Effective ardour soon lapsed into procrastination, fantasy and sporadic violence, but when Stephens himself was arrested and then escaped to France he became a national hero. He had helped focus Nationalist resentment and, through his stridently republican newspaper the *Irish People*, inspired such young men as John O'Leary, who, on his return to Ireland after years of imprisonment and exile, was to have a profound effect on William Butler Yeats, the youthful poet.

In the meantime, the IRB was condemned to acts of violence which ensured that the reputation of the Irish in England continued to be that of an ignorant and vicious people to be condemned variously as buffoons and monsters. In 1867 for example, when an attempt by Fenian terrorists to rescue some of their number from Clerkenwell Jail went wrong and their bomb killed twenty innocent passers-by, outraged British opinion enthusiastically branded the whole Irish nation as barbarians. No man in JBY's position could remain indifferent. Although his politics were always moderate, he was beginning to see 'how insolently the English and all the smug tribe of the Pharisees have trampled on the poor Irish, the miserable Irish, the dirty papist, the scum of the earth'.[10]

If such political views were alien to his wife, the briefly assembled members of 'The Brotherhood' – JBY's friends J. T. Nettleship, George Wilson, the nineteen-year-old Edwin J. Ellis and John Butler Yeats himself – filled the house late into the night with conversation Susan neither trusted nor understood. The alleged genius of Ellis especially was deemed sufficient to excuse his ill-mannered behaviour towards Susan, who never entered a studio or went to an exhibition. She might object to Ellis, and her husband might even see the justice of her complaints, but no practical compensations appeared. Finished and saleable work failed to materialise. Ellis himself meanwhile could decry 'the Mrs Yeatses' of this world as the enemies of art, while JBY could warn Todhunter that marriage itself was a 'fatal mistake', a cause for repentance, sackcloth and ashes. He himself, although an upholder of monogamy, drifted into a brief affair at this time with a woman he never named and which he later regretted.

Amid such problems, JBY nonetheless felt he was freeing himself from the destructive mill of convention. He believed he was becoming more consciously an individual, more surely his own man. Nor was this mere bohemian irresponsibility. Making an early visit to Fitzroy Road, Todhunter was astounded by the quality of the conversation there. It seemed like 'pure Oxygen' after the stuffiness of Dublin, and he reported back to Edward Dowden that JBY thought Dowden himself was sinking into an intellectual sleep from which only emigration could save him.[11] Dowden was more circumspect. He feared that London, and by this he meant the conversation of JBY as much as anything else, would prove a fruitless confusion of ideas to a man such as he who worked best by 'calmly brooding' over a few notions. Besides, he knew that he had comfortable emoluments to protect and that if he surrendered these he would have to work for his bread.

JBY was naturally critical of such an attitude, and in a letter to his friend began to outline his ideas on art and personal development. 'Art', he told Dowden, 'has to do with the sustaining and invigorating of the Personality.' In poetry, Whitman and above all William Blake were now his guiding lights, and it was partly under their influence that JBY at one point refused to let Susan teach her children the prayers of the Church of Ireland in which she had been brought up. Blake's anti-clericalism was an influence on Yeats's life from his earliest days, and it was he who would later work with his father's friend Ellis on a major edition of Blake's work. For the moment, however, he could only look up at the strange man and ask: 'Are you related to Cinder Ellis?'

Ellis's departure for Italy temporarily removed a problem from Fitzroy Road, but his absence only slightly lessened the burdens that fell on Susan. By early 1870 she was heavily pregnant again, and in the February of that year JBY executed a pencil drawing of her which is a sad comment on the state of their marriage. Susan sits huddled on a chair, one hand across her lap, while, with her other, she presses a handkerchief to her mouth. Her head is bent slightly forward, so that the focus of interest is on her eyes. These are heavy and withdrawn. The delicacy of the observation and the proficiency of the technique suggest that JBY had at last found what was to be perhaps his most successful form of creativity – the pencil portrait – but the sketch shows the price that had to be paid for this. The work is a picture of marital misery in which pity is not far removed from guilt.

The child Susan was bearing, Robert Corbet or Bobby Yeats, was born on 27 March 1870, but, for all the joy he may have brought, his presence must have increased Susan's domestic cares. Then, soon afterwards, JBY fell ill and began spitting blood. London, he realised, was destroying the health and happiness of both himself and his wife. Any artistic progress he might have made was being held back, while both parents feared the prospect 'of being some day left penniless' in an alien city. Then, in the middle of such troubles, Willie caught scarlatina. His mother, already so burdened, was never sympathetic to the illnesses of others and could only enforce on her children the stoic philosophy by which she herself survived. For Willie and the other children in Fitzroy Road, there were few kisses and little warmth, and this lack of maternal affection – the persistent, haunting sense of being deprived – was to have a profound effect on Yeats's development and his relationships with women especially.

But there was not, it seemed, any prospect of an immediate escape from London. There were family holidays to Sligo every year, but there was no opportunity of quitting the London house permanently until the lease ran out in the middle of 1873. Income on JBY's own Irish properties meanwhile continued to fall. Tenants were variously bickering and unreliable. Disputes led to the wounding of JBY's bailiff, while Uncle Matthew Corbet had to take over as agent when Robert Corbet, himself now fallen on hard times, was found to have creeping paralysis. He was eventually to commit suicide by jumping off the ferry to England, having first deposited on the deck his rings, watch and chain. Such problems with money were exacerbated by JBY's own failure to make an income. Although an illustration to a Browning poem was praised, it was sold at a loss, while the birth of a fifth child – John Butler or Jack Yeats – kept Susan away from Sligo in the summer of 1871, and the wearing anxiety of the following winter was such that JBY realised it would be cruelty to keep her in London any longer. London life, he confessed, was 'injuring our characters as well as our physical strength'.

Plans were loosely made for Susan and the children to go on an extended stay with the Pollexfens in Sligo. When they set off on 23 July 1872, Willie was just seven years and a month old. This was the last time he was to know 23 Fitzroy Road as a home, but even his parents were probably unaware that, among all its domestic unhappiness, it had left one other indelible impression on him. In the first part of his *Autobiographies*, Yeats recalled staring out of the window and watching some boys playing in the street. One was wearing a uniform, perhaps that of a telegraph messenger boy. When Willie turned to ask the servant who the boy might be, the woman, with memories of the recent Fenian bombings in mind, told him the lad intended 'to blow the town up'.[12] Willie went to sleep that night in terror. The political violence, the vision of anarchy that was to move the centre of his mature vision, scarred even his childhood dreams.

III
Sligo

The visit to Sligo was to last for twenty-seven months, the impressionable period between Willie's seventh and ninth years. He emerged into boyhood with the beauty of the western Irish coast and the shadow of his Pollexfen inheritance so deeply imprinted on him that London and Sligo were ever afterwards to remain antimonies, contrasted worlds whose opposition helped define his own.

To make the voyage to Sligo, the family had first to go to Liverpool. There, when the hansom cab dropped them at the Clarence Basin and sailors employed by the Sligo Steam Navigation Company hurried forward to collect their luggage, Willie was surrounded by soft Irish accents. If the attentions of 'an old woman who had come to Liverpool with crates of fowl made me miserable by throwing her arms around me', the sailors intrigued Willie and he tried to imitate their rolling walk.[13] Later during the course of the thirty-hour crossing he might be invited up on to the bridge where the elderly captain, famous for his fights and daring seamanship, talked of shipwrecks narrowly avoided or joked about the timorous mate who claimed he had seen the coach-a-baur or fairy death coach bowling along a road until it was hidden by a cottage and never reappeared. The peasant Ireland of magic and myth was drawing close, and sometimes, if the steamboat had made a particularly slow crossing, the lobster fishermen who came alongside as it passed the great cliffs of Donegal could be seen 'blowing on a burning sod to draw our attention'. The ship then sailed up past Rosses, past the large figure of the Metal Man pointing to the deepest channels, and on to the Sligo quays. Here Ellie Connolly, one of the Pollexfen servants, would cry out through the darkness in greeting: 'The Lord love you, Master Willie.'

Merville, the Pollexfens' house set in its sixty acres, was the centre of Willie's Sligo life and there he had to make his own discovery of his Pollexfen relatives. His grandfather especially, old William Pollexfen, was simplified into a sacred monster by Willie's childhood awe, and was to remain for him always 'the silent and fierce old man'. Stories of his daring seamanship were frequently told, and Willie knew that his grandfather kept a hatchet by his bed to ward off burglars and that he took a revolver with him to church in case of Fenian trouble. There was a great scar on his hand made by a whaling hook. He had travelled to almost unimaginable parts of the world, and in a cabinet in the dining room were some of the treasures he had brought back: coral, water from the Jordan, Chinese pictures on rice paper and an Indian ivory walking stick 'that came to me after his death'. So frightened were the Yeats children of their grandfather's roaring, his constant state of irritation, that they would try to see him only at mealtimes when, with the cunning of infants, they would contrive to sit on the same side of the table as him so he would be less likely to see them taking too much sugar and throw them one of his terrifying, silent stares.

His wife Elizabeth had learned both to fear and to manage him. By long habit, she would, when his temper was worse than usual, blink nervously. Her husband would then look at her, utter a short laugh and fall silent. It was Grandmother Pollexfen who brought such grace and tact to the house as it possessed, and Willie loved her as she went about simply but correctly dressed in rustling black silk and real lace, dispensing charity to neighbours, tending her garden, making exquisite pictures of flowers – the only art that Merville knew – and checking the rooms at night to see that no burglar prowled there in danger of her husband's hatchet.

But Elizabeth Pollexfen had only a limited influence on the household. The values her husband espoused, his dour religion and, above all, his reverence for money and class stifled the poetry and imagination of the whole family and obliged their energy to run in channels where it would not naturally flow. His disparaging temper reached out to his children, and Willie was aware of aunts and uncles coming and going at Merville in moods of sourness or harsh material ambition. 'All was serious and silent, no merry talk at meals, no running to and fro.'[14] The strain would tell on nearly all of them. Both Aunt Alice and Aunt Elizabeth were to suffer breakdowns sufficiently severe for them to require special care. George Pollexfen, with his wistful eyes peeping out 'like stars in the early twilight', became a hypochondriac and depressive, while William Middleton Pollexfen, who had trained as an engineer and designed the Sligo quays, was now occupied with writing a pamphlet which explained that he was inventing an unsinkable warship with a solid wooden hull. He was actually going mad and had eventually to be put in a mental home.

Depressive mania thus haunted the fringes of the Pollexfen family, and the Yeats children were not immune. Willie began to experience moments of melancholia that seemed to connect themselves to the religious atmosphere in the house. 'I think I confused my grandfather with God,' he wrote, 'for I remember in one of my attacks of melancholy praying that he might punish me for my sins.'[15] Sometimes Willie would pray for several days together that he might die and then, fearful that he was indeed dying, would pray again that he might live. Once he thought his soul was lost because he could not hear what somebody described to him as the voice of conscience. Eventually words sprang spontaneously to his mind and he felt as grateful as he did when he heard his great-uncle William Middleton say: 'We should not make light of the troubles of children. They are worse than ours because we can see the end of our trouble and they can never see any end.' The terrors lurking in the puritan psyche tormented the boy, making him vulnerable to that need for spiritual reassurance which would characterise his entire adult life.

But boyhood troubles were not confined to moments of spiritual fear. At seven years old, Willie still did not know his alphabet. The Pollexfens were appalled. The fact that the boy could not read was a reproach to their sense of striving for success, and with the nastiness that came so naturally to them they even wondered if the short-sighted little boy was not in some way mentally deficient. They began to brand him as a failure or, in his father's words, 'unsuccessful and therefore wicked'.[16] Such callousness showed itself in other ways too. Willie was a mere seven or eight when he was woken one night by one of his uncles who needed to borrow a railway pass. It went without saying that William Pollexfen would not lend his, and Willie was obliged to get out his pony and, secretly leaving Merville, ride six miles in the dark to the house of a cousin who might be prevailed on to lend his pass. Willie did not return until the small hours, when he found old Scanlan the stableman waiting up for him, the only figure perhaps who appreciated the courage he had shown.

JBY's absence had a predictable effect on his wife and children. Susan sent dismal letters from Merville listing childhood ailments – Lily's breathing troubles and Lollie's fits of gloom – as well as expressing her worry over her sisters' treatment of her eldest son. The latter concerned JBY particularly, for he knew how badly Willie might be affected. His father recognised that he was an 'intensely affectionate' boy who would develop fully only if swathed in love. Willie was, he wrote, 'sensitive, intellectual and emotional, very easily rebuffed', and he thought it of the greatest importance that the child should be protected from his aunts.

On his occasional visits to Sligo,* JBY resolved to do what he could, but even so his presence frightened Willie. His father, who in his letters at least showed that he knew how badly the boy needed affection, appeared to him now as a black-bearded and only partly familiar man who walked up and down the nursery floor with 'one cheek bulged out with a fig that was there to draw the pain out of a bad tooth'. Nor did the boy find it easy to impress him. He had learned a little hymn at the local dame school but when he sang it for his father it at once became obvious that Willie was tone deaf. JBY wrote to the school insisting his son 'never be taught to sing again'. Willie also hated going to church and, noting that his father did not attend, was told that he need not go either. Instead, his father would teach him to read, but this first of many parental eruptions into Willie's education was not a success and ended with an 'angry and impatient' father flinging the book at his son's head. Willie went to church the following Sunday, but his father persisted with the lessons during the week, trying to coach a boy whose own thoughts were always more interesting to him than mere educational grind. 'I was difficult to teach,' Yeats confessed in his *Autobiographies*, and eventually he continued to be sent to the local dame school for spelling and grammar lessons. Again, these were only a moderate success, and to the end of his life Yeats's spelling was at best idiosyncratic.

JBY nonetheless took pleasure in reading to his children, hoping to awaken an interest in literature by stimulating their appetite for narrative. He would take Willie and Lily (who were close to each other at this time) to a place between Sligo and Rosses Point where he read them Macaulay, Chaucer and *The Lay of the Last Minstrel*, which gave Willie a first taste of his lifelong obsession with magicians, the magus whose powers can alter the world. At other times JBY told them the plots of Shakespearean comedies

---

* JBY crossed to Ireland not just to see his family but also to paint portraits. His ill luck continued to dog him, however. He worked on a portrait of the bride of one of the Herberts of Muckross, but the girl ran away from her husband, the portrait was no longer wanted, and JBY felt that he could not charge for the work. The canvas was eventually bought by Dowden.

and Balzac's *Peau de Chagrin*. Eventually such encouragement brought its rewards. One of JBY's pencil drawings from this time is a portrait of his eldest son. Willie is shown sitting astride a chair, a soft-haired little boy in knickerbockers smiling in delighted concentration as he stares at a book.

Contact with the ordinary local people was another boyhood pleasure. The Yeats children had a room with four windows, two of which looked out over the stable yard. Here the constant comings and goings fascinated them. Old Scanlan the coachman let them watch him shave and was always careful to see that each was given a turn to ride on the coach beside him. His stout, untidy wife lived in the gatehouse with him and kept her snuffbox hidden deep in her bosom 'among the folds of many little shawls'.[17] The stableboy, Johnny Healy, became a particular friend of Willie's (who partly unconsciously picked up his accent) and together in the hayloft they would read Johnny's volume of the Protestant political lyrics of the Orangemen. When rumours of Fenian troubles came to Merville, Willie began to imagine himself the Orange leader of a group of handsome athletes among whom he would die while fighting the enemy.

Servants such as John Healy played an important part in Willie's Sligo life, for, if the Pollexfens with their obsession with money and class inflicted ignominy on the boy and could never fully satisfy his imaginative and spiritual needs, some of the more ordinary people of Sligo had access to the remains of an ancient Celtic culture permeated by wonder and the supernatural. Despite the depredations wrought by famine, persecution and emigration – and despite, too, the large-scale efforts made to discourage the most ancient of western European vernaculars, the Gaelic language in which this knowledge was preserved – Celtic beliefs still survived around the farthest coasts of Ireland. Isolated from the mainstream of European development, such beliefs preserved within them the consciousness of an Iron Age civilisation at once local, poetic and pre-Christian.

The adult Yeats was to discover in this a world of high sophistication and learning whose sagas presented an image of Irish heroism and whose religion taught of gods, an afterlife and an immortal soul. To the boy, however, this Celtic world was most vividly present in the peasant beliefs of a local people living in the shadow of beautiful Knocknarea on whose cairn-crowned summit supposedly lay buried Maeve, Queen of the Western Sidhe.* There were, for example, stories readily told like that of the little old woman of nearby Ballisodare who had lived for seven years with the fairies and came back with no toes since she had danced them off. The Celtic world could be seen again in such simple, everyday actions as a peasant lifting his hat as

---

* Pronounced 'shee'. The diminutive *sidheog* (pronounced 'sheehogue') is Irish for a fairy. Maeve herself can be identified with Shakespeare's Queen Mab.

a whirl of leaves blew by and saying 'God bless them!' to the fairy powers who drove it.

These were moments charming enough perhaps to the eye of boyhood, but the memory of the poet was to store the sinister implications of such beliefs and recreate them as an image of the spiritual evil sweeping across Ireland when the country descended into civil war. Even now the dangers in the supernatural were evident. Where fairies danced, ghosts too might walk. As a middle-aged man, Yeats was to recall how one of the stable boys at Merville (perhaps Johnny Healy himself) met 'his late master going round the yard, and having told him to go and haunt a lighthouse, was dismissed by his mistress for sending her husband to haunt so inclement a spot'.[18] The Celtic mind moved easily and sometimes cruelly between the mundane and the magical, and Sligo itself was reckoned one of the most fairy-haunted regions of the entire country.

Indeed, Willie was so surrounded by talk of such things that it seemed quite natural to attribute to the fairies the fact that his carefully folded flag was one day found in a knotted heap. From time to time he would also visit his wealthy, easy-going Middleton relatives at Elsinore, their haunted home at Rosses where a ghostly smuggler's raps on the drawing-room window set the neighbourhood dogs barking. It was accepted as part of everyday life that Willie's cousin Lucy Middleton had second sight, while phenomena and premonitions even presented themselves to Willie himself. In later life he claimed that one day at Merville a fairy slid down towards him on a moonbeam but retreated when he tried to talk to it. He once dreamed that his grandfather had been shipwrecked and, the following day, William Pollexfen arrived back at Merville having barely escaped drowning. When Bobby Yeats died of croup, people said Susan Yeats had heard the banshee crying the night before. The supernatural was part of ordinary life in Sligo, existing with a spontaneity and ready assurance Willie would spend a lifetime trying to recapture.

Along with such intimations of the supernatural came Willie's awareness of family history. In a dark, creeper-hung house beyond the Sligo Channel lived Aunt Mickey. A tall woman and very thin, her arms were so long she could cross them behind her back and make her hands meet at her front. Delightfully eccentric, she would sometimes wander out of the house in the middle of the night to chase away the sheep 'her bones' told her were there. As Parson John's daughter, she was also a mine of stories about the Yeatses. While a boy, Willie was largely indifferent to these (only in later life did he come to see their poetic value to him) and for the moment he was more intrigued by Aunt Mickey's ancient table knives, so often cleaned they were 'pointed like daggers'. She also had a Jacobean cream jug with the Yeats motto and crest on it, while on her dining-room mantelpiece was a silver cup with the Butler crest, a piece old even in 1534 when some newlyweds' initials were engraved on it. A yellowed roll of paper inside gave a history of the generations who had owned the cup, but this was destroyed when someone used the paper as a spill to light their pipe.

Amid so much romance and history the influence of JBY was constantly active even if he himself was not always present. His father's scepticism had made Willie ponder the religious cast of mind he could never abandon as easily as his father had done. As he later wrote: 'my father's unbelief had set me thinking about the evidences of religion and I weighed the matter perpetually with great anxiety, for I did not think I could live without religion'.[19] At times Willie even wondered what religion the ants might have, and the matter perplexed him until he eventually thought he had found a proof for the existence of God. A cow had given birth, and because calves, like children, were the gift of God it was evident that such a hypothesis could be tested. The sceptical spiritualism of Yeats the man is evident in the boy. Willie vowed he would one day observe the process of birth, certain 'there would be a cloud and a burst of light and God himself would bring the calf out of the light'. For the moment his disquiet was settled, and it was only when an adolescent boy, sitting beside him in the hayloft, explained 'the mechanism of sex' that his illusion crumbled. Willie's new knowledge made him 'miserable for weeks', and a search through the long, difficult words of an encyclopaedia in the Merville library seemed only to confirm his worst fears. His disillusion was, he later declared, the first breaking of the dream of childhood.

IV
'I Shall Be a Famous Man'

Other disillusions followed fast upon it. By the autumn of 1874 John Butler Yeats had decided to summon his family back to artistic poverty in England. With the easy nastiness of the Pollexfens, one of his aunts told the departing Willie, now nine and a half years old: 'You are going to London. Here you are somebody. There you will be nobody at all.'

In a sense she was right. After the family moved into their new London home at 14 Edith Villas, West Kensington, JBY had no more professional success than before. Dowden tried to commission a picture from him, but the unfinished canvases continued to stack up. When JBY stood before his easel, self-doubt alternated with an obsessive perfectionism, and each led to paralysis. Besides, he was unsure about his evolving style. As Yeats himself wrote: 'my father began life as a Pre-Raphaelite painter; when past thirty he fell under the influence of contemporary French painting. Instead of finishing a picture one square inch at a time, he kept all fluid, every detail dependent on every other, and remained a poor man till the end of his life, because the more anxious he was to succeed, the more did his pictures sink through innumerable sittings into final confusion.' This was the story of JBY's artistic career, and some of his closest friends came to realise that a canvas by him had to be snatched from his easel if they were ever to own one of his works.

If JBY was experiencing difficulty with his artistic development, when he tried to take his son's lessons in hand the result was once more disappointment. In his worry and exasperation JBY tried to threaten Willie into some sort of excellence, shouting at him and telling him he was morally degraded. Then, attempting to make up for his harshness, he would indulge him. Willie and Lily were often ordered out of the house to get some fresh air. Sometimes they would walk to the National Gallery with a penny each to buy buns and rolls. At other times they would go to the Round Pond in Kensington Gardens. Here, Willie would sail his model yacht, a toy that was the object of some disparagement among the other children. His father seized on the opportunity, bought Willie the expensive *Moonbeam*, and had the satisfaction of seeing his son made commodore of the Model Yacht Club.

But although the return to London had had its excitement for the children, both Willie and Lily felt an undertow of homesickness for Sligo that was too painful easily to express. The spaciousness of Merville had been replaced by the cramped conditions of city living and this had its effect on relationships among the younger Yeatses. Jack was growing into an amiable child immediately liked by everyone but, as the baby of the house, he was too young to share the life of the others. Lollie, intelligent, gifted, but already showing the difficult signs of a manic–depressive temperament, was never to get on easily with her elder brother.

Willie and Lily were close, however, and now, as London hurled around them, its noise and crushing materialism emphasised how distant and even lost were the Sligo coast and the green hills running up to their beloved Ben Bulben. One day, by the drinking-fountain in Holland Park, brother and sister opened their hearts and spoke of their longing for Sligo. 'I know we were both very close to tears,' Yeats wrote, 'and remember with wonder, for I had never known that anyone cared for such mementoes, that I longed for a sod of earth from some field I knew, something of Sligo to hold in my hand. It was some old race instinct like that of a savage, for we had been brought up to laugh at all display of emotion.'[20] Indeed, Willie had been taught by his mother to despise public expressions of feeling. They were vulgar, she said, English, the sort of exhibition you could expect from 'Tow-rows' who ate skate and kissed in railway stations. Such comments suggest that the attitudes of Merville continued to make their mark even in London. Sligo itself may have seemed a distant dream, but 'every one I knew well in Sligo despised Nationalists and Catholics, but all disliked England with a prejudice that had come down perhaps from the days of the Irish Parliament. I knew stories to the discredit of England, and took them all seriously.'

But if Willie's tired and morose mother embodied such attitudes she made only a faint emotional impression on him, and in later years his memory of her at this time was dim. Susan's sense of her own personality was slowly disappearing amid her care for her children and her worries about money. In late August 1875 she had given birth to another daughter, Jane Grace, but the child fell ill and died at the start of June the following year. Her death was the most poignant of the family's many difficulties. Commissions still failed to materialise, while agents' fees ate up the small returns from JBY's inherited properties. It became more than ever important that he sell the Dublin house in Dorset Street but, when the sale was finally completed in the middle of 1877, the £600 it realised disappeared into his debts.

The artist himself meanwhile had quixotically set off on a new course, having decided to become a landscape painter, an idea that did not long survive under the pressure of his altogether more real abilities as a portraitist. While Susan and her younger children returned to Sligo and stayed on there, Willie was sent to be with his father, who was painting a study of a pond near Burnham Beeches. The picture became cruelly symbolic of John Butler Yeats's approach to his art. The painter began the work in the spring, toiled over it through the year, changing its details with the changing seasons, until he finally abandoned the canvas when he had painted the snow on the heath-covered banks. Willie knew that strangers called his father 'the painter who scrapes out every day what he painted the day before', and he was forcefully presented with a model of failure in the artistic world.

JBY was determined to have his son with him while he painted so that he should not be under the sway of his Sligo aunts, but he was also resolved once again to take Willie's education in hand. He was insistent that his knowledge should be broad and general, serving as the basis on which the boy might expand his personality and understanding. He bought him primers on geography and chemistry, and obliged him to attend to these with the greatest accuracy. Lessons began after breakfast and continued until half-past one or two in the afternoon. In the evening the boy had to repeat the lesson of the morning, and the thought filled him with misery 'for I could very rarely, with so much to remember, set my thoughts on it and then only in fear'. Willie was far happier exploring the countryside, watching the animals and capturing lizards which, much to the concern of the local landlady, escaped and could not be found again. As Willie wrote to his mother in one of the first of his letters to be preserved: 'My lizards walked off one night, Mrs Earl came in one morning to cettle [*sic*] the books on the top of the cupboard on which were the lizards but when she found them gone she was afraid to touch the books lest she should put [her] hand on them, we looked every where for them but have not found them yet.'[21]

But Willie's eyes had been opened to the natural world, and, however much he might fear his lessons, an interest in science had begun to stir in him.

His father knew that this sort of informal education could no longer continue, and when the family returned to Edith Villas at the start of 1877 Willie was sent to the Godolphin School in Iffley Road, Hammersmith. He tried to romanticise the Victorian gothic building and its surroundings, but in that part of his *Autobiographies* Yeats called *Reveries over Childhood and Youth* he confessed to its soul-destroying London ugliness. 'On one side, there was a piano factory of yellow brick, upon two sides half-finished rows of little shops and villas all yellow brick, and on the fourth side, outside the wall of our playing-field, a brick-field full of cinders and piles of half-burned yellow bricks.'[22] In this unattractive environment Willie would discover 'two things I had never known, companionship and enmity'.

He was now eleven and a half years old and he was forced suddenly to realise how very different his experience had made him to the normal run of English schoolboys. Amid 'the rough manners of a cheap school', Willie found boys who were interested only in how much his father earned. He was called names for being Irish and suffered from the other boys' crude aping of anti-Irish feeling. Once again, prejudice against the Irish seized on the violence endemic in their situation, and to this was added a fear of those characteristics seen among the many Irish crowded into the most wretched English slums: drunkenness, dirtiness and a suspect Roman Catholicism. Willie started to lash out at those who taunted him, involving himself in numerous fights which he usually lost, until, developing an early talent for manipulation, he got other and bigger boys to fight for him. He made a friend of the more athletic Cyril Vesey (a lad who also shared his interest in moths and insects) and eventually, under Vesey's tuition, became sufficiently confident to beat a boy who called him a 'Mad Irishman'. Indeed, he became so devoted to Vesey that he would follow him home at lunch times, missing his own meal, to be occasionally rewarded with leftovers which he climbed in through a window to collect.

But the feeling that he was different from the other boys in the playground went deeper than their taunts. 'I was divided from all those boys,' he wrote, 'not merely by the anecdotes that are everywhere perhaps a chief expression of the distrust of races, but because our mental images were different.' In this age of imperialism, the school's persistent emphasis on British national myths – on Crécy, Agincourt and the Union Jack – gave the other boys images whose potency Willie could not share. He would find the philosophy that went with them equally alien: the idea, expressed by a member of parliament in 1850, that the motivation to make the boundaries of empire ever wider sprang from the desire 'of spreading throughout the habitable globe all the characteristics of Englishmen – their energy, their civilisation, their religion and their freedom'.[23] Such were the beliefs of a people who now governed

24

a quarter of the earth's land surface and who, in Willie's thirteenth year, coined the word 'Jingoism' to express that type of coarse patriotism which ran through the crowded life of the cities particularly. To Willie, such beliefs were foreign, and even as a boy the cult of Empire marked him out as an Irish child among the English.

While Willie was unable to identify with the imperial ideal, he also found he was without those memories of such famous victories over the English as the Battle of the Yellow Ford which nourished the imaginations of Irish Roman Catholics. If he was Irish among the English, he was of Protestant stock among the Catholic majority. The ambiguous and isolated position of his kind of people was beginning to impinge on him and, in the search for symbols with which to identify, Willie's mind went back to Sligo, to Ben Bulben and to Knocknarea, the haunted mountain where Maeve, Queen of the Western Sidhe, had her legendary grave. In the middle of materialistic and imperial London, the myths of a free and ancient Ireland touched by magic were beginning to show Willie the sacred sites of a nation that had not yet forged its identity.

He was beginning to discover his myths, and the dreaming boy found such thoughts altogether more interesting than the lessons forced on him. His school report for the Lent term of 1877 placed him twenty-first in a class of thirty-one boys. His marks in classics were adequate, but he was in the bottom half for English and came twenty-seventh in mathematics. His performance was, as his form master declared, 'only fair'. The following summer his marks were much the same and JBY sensed that his son was really being described as 'amiable but hopeless'. Willie was known merely as a boy who collected moths and butterflies and got into 'no worse mischief than hiding now and again an old tailless white rat in my coat-pocket or my desk'.

In his secret life, however, Willie was beginning to explore those mysterious and not always attractive depths which, if he could keep them accessible but safe from commonplace familiarity, might yet be the springs of genius. On the surface, his intellect was often bored by routine, while his personality, protecting an innate shyness with an ever more obvious Pollexfen pride, often jibbed at the democratic rough-and-tumble of the playground. In his solitude, however, both intellect and personality revealed to him an incommunicable sense of promise. He was, he wrote, a schoolboy 'as proud of myself as a March cock when it crows to its first sunrise'. In an action which takes on something of symbolic force, Willie one day climbed to the top of a tree on the edge of the school playing-field and, looking down on his fellow pupils, reminded himself that as an artist's son he would have to make his work the whole of his life. He had already dedicated himself to a state of being and, in his excitement, could say: 'If when I grow up I am as clever among grown-up men as I am among these boys, I shall be a famous man.'

His parents nonetheless continued to see him chiefly as an ordinary and rather clumsy little boy. JBY would return from his landscape painting to hear from Susan a torrent of complaints about their eldest son. These so depressed him that sometimes he would beg her to wait till after supper before she recited her dismal list. Willie was becoming one of those preoccupied, awkward children who seem to be part of every domestic mishap. He got blamed for all that went wrong, and once, when someone else let the bath water overflow, he was found gleefully dancing about in the hall crying out: 'I didn't do it! I didn't do it!'[24]

The family had by this time made yet another move. They were now living at 8 Woodstock Road in the pretty Arts and Crafts colony of Bedford Park. Here was 'romantic excitement',[25] and Willie was delighted by the newness of everything around him, the empty houses where he could play hide-and-seek and the garden where he was allowed to plant a forest of sunflowers with an undergrowth of love-lies-bleeding.* His father had promised him a little haven protected by walls against newspapers and the infections of commerce, but, if this proved to be something of an exaggeration, Bedford Park offered Willie a sudden deepening of his aesthetic responses, a sense of beauty, well-being and community which he could set against the depersonalised ugliness of central London. Art, Pre-Raphaelite art especially, offered a solace and an escape for the imagination. 'We were to see De Morgan tiles', he wrote, 'peacock-blue doors and the pomegranate pattern and the tulip pattern of Morris, and to discover that we had always hated doors painted with imitation grain, the roses of mid-Victoria, and tiles covered with geometrical patterns that seemed to have been shaken out of a muddy kaleidoscope.'

The family and its problems intruded nonetheless. JBY's friend Todhunter and his aggressively intellectual new wife had moved in close by, and JBY himself wondered if he could now complete his old circle of friends by inviting Dowden for a visit. Somehow Susan managed to suggest to Dowden that if the young professor were to come he might like to consider contributing the purely 'nominal' sum of fifteen shillings to the household expenses. Kept in ignorance of this, JBY was puzzled by Dowden's letter of reply and eventually wrote an embarrassed response excusing his wife's request. He begged Dowden to come all the same, but the tactful don postponed his visit and, in the end, desperate for the chance to paint lucrative portraits, JBY went to stay with him in Dublin.

Just before his departure in the autumn of 1879, and because of the severe famine conditions prevailing in rural Ireland especially, JBY sent his family

---

* Unsuccessfully, it seems. Lily recalled that 'Willy had dreams and plans, a forest of sunflowers with an undergrowth of love-lies-bleeding. A few sunflowers did come up. I don't think any of the undergrowth did.'

on a holiday to Branscombe in Devon. The children drew talented vignettes of the local scenery and characters, and watched delightedly as the fishermen pulled their catch from 'the mackerel crowded sea'. Willie's fascination with language was also beginning to develop and for days he would repeat to himself, intrigued by the grammar and accent, the words of a local boy who came up to him and said: 'I saw thee and the little brother and the maids at church.' Nonetheless, despite such moments of content, the family was ever more pressed for money. Commissions were not coming in, and, while half the dwindling revenue from JBY's properties went in settling debts, the bills mounted. By 1880, the butcher in Bedford Park was owed £26 and it was feared he would no longer extend the Yeatses credit. Loans from friends helped day-to-day survival, but it was clear something drastic would have to be done. The lease on Woodstock Road was due to expire in the middle of 1881 and, once they were free of that, the family could return permanently to Ireland.

In the meantime, in 1880, they went for a late-summer holiday to Sligo. Willie went climbing in the mountains with Johnny Healy and riding with his father, who complained about his slack horsemanship. Left to himself, however, Willie let his pony ramble to such places as his great-uncle Matt's house where he and the other children played with little toy boats. But, at fifteen, he was getting too old for this sort of pastime and often, at night, he would go herring-fishing with Henry Middleton, even when the seas were rough and their boat was in danger of running aground by that cleft in the Ballisodare rocks where a murderous monster lived, his presence known from his constantly buzzing like a bee. Willie had given up shooting when he heard the death-squeals of a rabbit, but fishing was to remain a lifelong pleasure. Besides, the sailors and the other boys who went with him told him such stories that 'the world seemed full of monsters and marvels'.

But it also began to cloud with shame. 'The great event of a boy's life', Yeats wrote, 'is the awakening of sex.'[26] Willie now began to take a new pleasure in his body and its energies. He went swimming off Rosses Point and, when he came out of the water, lay down and covered himself with warm sand. The weight of the sand gave him an erection, but it was only after he had reached orgasm and his mind went back to the encyclopaedias in which he had despondently verified the facts of life that he fully realised what had happened. 'It was many days before I discovered how to renew that wonderful sensation,' he wrote, or to feel, once again, the nervous exhaustion that always accompanied it. From then on, his days became a continuous struggle against masturbation (the excessive indulgence of which was widely believed to lead to physical decline, insanity and death) and gave him his first inkling of the sexual torment that was to fill so much of his life.

The family returned to London after their holiday, and at Easter 1881 Willie left Godolphin School. Paradoxically, he was just beginning to be successful there. Science was becoming a fashionable subject, and Willie's reading and butterfly collecting stood him in good stead. 'Of exceptional ability' appeared on reports which were, his father declared, written in rose-water. Although JBY was still worried that his eldest son, while not naturally idle, was averse to dull routine and found it hard to settle to work, he saw a great future opening before him. 'He will be a man of science,' he said to himself, adding: 'It is great to be a man of science.' But this was a career Willie would have to pursue in Dublin if at all. By the close of 1881, while Jack was sent off to live with his grandparents, Susan, Willie, Lily and Lollie were moving first to Balscaddan Cottage in Howth, just across the Bay from Dublin, and then, six months later, into a nearby house called Island View.

V

Fairytales, Fossils and Fantasies

Despite their lack of funds, the Yeatses' time at Howth was a happy period. Howth was much cheaper than London, but the choice of location was made partly for Susan's sake. Here, among the crooked lanes and the tarry fishing luggers, was a place where her incipient poetry could at last be nourished. Susan had never pretended to feelings she did not have or tried to win over people she did not greatly care for. Now, among the fishermen's wives, and with Willie sometimes beside her, she could enjoy the humour and sudden intensities of 'stories Homer might have told'.[27] Tales of fairies and ghosts especially – of Mrs Arbunathy visited by one of the good people or the luck of the herring-sellers when they slept in the haunted room – showed the ancient and supernatural Celtic world to be authentically alive.

London and English ways seemed out of place here. When Cyril Vesey, Willie's athletic friend from Godolphin School, came on a visit, his discomfort at missing his lunch while the boys were out on a sailing expedition seemed merely ridiculous.* Nor was Cyril's boyish interest in butterfly collecting any longer acceptable. If Willie was enthralled as he and his mother listened to the local people reciting their folklore, his enthusiasm for natural science had begun to stir his powerful need for system and explanation, and the opportunity of harnessing these to his particular interests. The intensity of his intellectual ambition was awakening. He was already planning a book on the yearly life cycle of a rock pool and had even elaborated a theory (subsequently forgotten) on the coloration of sea anemones.

---

* Yeats and Vesey were to meet again as adults when the latter returned from India. However, they were disappointed to find that they had nothing to say to each other.

28

To this end, Willie now immersed himself in the works of Darwin, Wallis, Huxley and their commentators. By so doing, he became naively familiar with the most troubling dilemma exposed by nineteenth-century thought: the discovery that the universe is ruled neither by the God of Genesis nor by man but instead appears set on a purposeless course where chance alone ensures the survival of the fittest. For a while, fired with adolescent radicalism, Willie could revel in pulling the old structures down. He was, he recalled, 'hot for argument in refutation of Adam and Noah and the Seven Days' of creation. He even took pleasure in taunting a pious geologist who came to look for fossils along the Howth cliffs, telling him that the existence of what the man sought disproved the bible in which he placed his faith. The geologist begged Willie not to raise the question again for he had considered the implications far more deeply than Willie himself and felt that in a godless world it would be impossible to lead a moral life.

But if Willie had destroyed his belief in the old biblical order of creation, the world he left himself could not always satisfy his imaginative needs. He went out with his green butterfly net but, through the growing power of his imagination, he began sometimes to change it into a magician's wand. By its power, the Howth cliffs where Druids once gathered became no longer just a primer in natural science but a place of enchantment in whose caves he could camp out at night, feasting on eggs and cocoa, and imagining himself as Byron's Manfred or, more potently still, as one of Shelley's death-bound heroes. 'I had many idols,' he recalled,

> and as I climed along the narrow ledge I was now Manfred on his glacier, and now Prince Athanase with his solitary lamp, but I soon chose Alastor for my chief of men and longed to share his melancholy, and maybe at last to disappear from everybody's sight as he disappeared drifting in a boat along some slow-moving river between great trees. When I thought of women they were modelled on those in my favourite poets and loved in brief tragedy, or like the girl in *The Revolt of Islam*, accompanied by their lovers through all manner of wild places, lawless women without homes and without children.[28]

And, just as there was a potential conflict between Willie's interest in science and folklore, so his euphoric sexual fantasies were accompanied by their obverse. He was becoming cruelly afflicted by the self-consciousness of adolescence. He began to make blunders when he went on social visits and was told by a woman who had known him as a child that he had 'changed for the worse'. When he was on his own, self-recrimination made him feel yet more gauche. The ideal he treasured of being wise and eloquent, an ideal gathered from reading lives of the scientists, seemed cruelly unattainable. A conflict was opening in Willie's mind between his given, natural self and an altogether more polished being, a mask to be created, as he later thought, out of a deliberate act of imagination and will. His mind was full of adolescent confusion and contradiction, and under the sway of every powerful influence it encountered.

None of these was greater than his father, with whom he now travelled into Dublin each day by train. JBY had taken a large, handsome room in a York Street tenement-house for his studio, and there, over breakfast, he would read to Willie passages from his favourite poets. In earlier days, JBY had tried to move his son's literary interest through the pleasures of narrative. Now his readings were selected to influence him in the direction of his own deepest concerns. The generalised, the abstract and the didactic were all shunned. 'He never read me a passage because of its speculative interest, and indeed did not care at all for poetry where there was generalisation or abstraction however impassioned.' JBY concentrated instead on poems and plays at their most passionate moments, reading out, for example, the opening passages of *Prometheus Unbound* where all appeared as intensity, 'an idealisation of speech'. JBY himself saw such ambitious intellectual striving as typically Irish, writing proudly that 'with us intellect takes the place which in the English home is occupied by the business faculty'.[29] Certainly, his father's influence over Willie was now at its height and, in the presence of this hapless but brilliant conversationalist, Willie was encouraged to see how the finest poetry – the work of Shakespeare, Keats, Shelley, Byron, Rossetti and William Morris especially – appealed through emotion, intellect and style to that most treasured of all JBY's values: the personality, to what he once described as man in harmony with himself and 'alive and glowing like a star'.[30]

2

Growing into Man
(1881–1887)

I
'A Kind of Super-Boy'

His father told Willie to enrol himself as a pupil at the Erasmus Smith High School in Harcourt Street, a few minutes' walk away from the studio. At sixteen, Willie was a handsome boy, tall, with black hair falling over his forehead and the distant, slightly aloof air of one with short sight. To the other pupils, this last feature seemed to emphasise his stand-offish nature, the Pollexfen traits in his personality which adolescence brought to the fore. A contemporary much later recalled that 'there was something quietly repellent in his manner at school which affected even his relations with the masters'.[1]

It was also seen that there was something 'queer' in this student with his background of wide general culture and familiarity with the dangerous ideas of the evolutionists. For all the poetic fantasies Willie projected on the Howth cliffs, he still retained his interest in science, even seeing school life as 'an interruption of my natural history studies'. In a school which disparaged such hobbies, Willie was known to the other pupils as the 'insect collector', and it was seen that he carried on him little cardboard boxes filled with his victims. When one of these escaped and a crowd of boys seemed about to crush it, he called out to the master: 'Oh stop them! Stop them! It's my bloody-nosed beetle.' The incident caused such a commotion that Willie was sent up to the headmaster, who gave him a stiff imposition.

If Willie was not regarded by the general run of boys as an attractive figure (he kept himself aloof, for instance, from the hurley games in the playground), the more discerning recognised his qualities. William Kirkpatrick Magee (later known as the writer 'John Eglinton') recalled Willie as 'a kind of super-boy', at moments riding freely above the values of his peers. Routine tasks might bore him, while his weakness at mathematics was as evident as ever, but if he hid a crib inside his classical texts (a tacit admission of a lifelong difficulty with foreign languages) Willie's interest in history far outshone the other boys'. The Erasmus Smith School was an intensely ambitious institution and the pupils were worked hard. Nonetheless, the rigidity of the curriculum was inimical to Willie, and while the future bank managers and solicitors dutifully got down to learning their Virgil, 'I, who, it may be, had tried to find out what happened in the parts we had not read, made ridiculous mistakes.' By the greatest of paradoxes, 'I was worst of all at literature, for we read Shakespeare for his grammar exclusively.'

Poor spelling and bad handwriting meant that Willie never won a prize for his essays, but it was the content rather than the execution of these that threatened to cause a scandal. They were, noted a contemporary, 'full of imagery and fancy', and, when Willie read them out with the same orotund voice with which he declaimed the classics, the power of his performance was such that none of the other pupils presumed to laugh. Perhaps they waited in suspense for the next daring idea, for the impress of his father was everywhere on these works, and the conventionally minded masters were shocked by the ideas expressed in essays on such topics as Evolutionary Botany. JBY in his turn was appalled by the complacent themes on which his son was told to write. When he discovered that one title set was 'Men may rise on stepping-stones of their dead selves to higher things', he broke out that it was precisely by absorbing such notions that boys were made 'insincere and false to themselves' and he told Willie to write instead on the Shakespearean theme 'To thine own self be true'. Such proceedings naturally made Willie unpopular with his teachers, and an exasperated headmaster once told him that he was going to set him an imposition simply because he could not get at his father and set him one.

The morning conversations in the studio continued meanwhile, Yeats's schoolfriend Charles Johnson later recalling 'the long room, with its skylight, the walls pale green, frames and canvases massed along them; a sofa and a big armchair or two; the stout iron stove with its tube; and, filling the whole with his spirit, the artist stepping forward along a strip of carpet to touch his work with a tentative brush, then stepping back again, always in movement, always meditating high themes'. He talked to his son, for example, on the relation of villainy to genius. 'The same surcharge of energy makes both,' JBY said. 'You must have a high positive force to be a successful pirate; a change in environment would have made the same man a great creative artist!' Willie, 'brushing the shaggy black hair from his eyes, and still hovering in thought between science and art', broke out: 'Transmutation of energy!' 'Precisely! That's it exactly!' cried Mr Yeats, enthusiastic over his son's phrase; 'And now let's have some tea!'

At other times talk turned to literature, JBY insisting that dramatic poetry, flowing over with life and individual feeling, was the finest form of literature since it was the least didactic. Willie absorbed such lessons but, spending much of his free time in a secret gathering of trees on the Howth promontory, was now inspired to form his own aesthetic. 'The thicket gave me my first thought of what a long poem should be,' he wrote in his *Autobiographies*. 'I thought of it as a region into which one should wander from the cares of life.' Here, in imagination, he could mingle with shadowy characters who, crossed in love, could be presented with all the rich and sad harmoniousness of a Pre-Raphaelite dream:

> When to its end o'er ripened July nears
> One lurid eve befel mine history—
> No rime empassioned of envenomed years
> Or the embattled earth – a song should be
> A painted and be – pictured argosy
> And as a crew to guide her wandering days
> Sad love and change yea those that sisters be
> For they upon each others eyes do gaze
> And they do whisper in each others ears always.[2]

The youthful Yeats was attracted, like the youthful Keats, to the slow, rich stanza of the greatest Anglo-Irish poet of the renaissance, Edmund Spenser. Again like Keats, Yeats saw poetry at this time as a means of escape from the world, a little region of the imagination in which to wander. The landscape and those who populate it are, nonetheless, wholly conventional. The important discovery is not of new insight but of the apprentice poet finding his powers by copying his masters. If Spenser and Keats were two of these, then William Morris and, above all, Dante Gabriel Rossetti were others. Nonetheless, the adolescent listlessness of such work is contrasted in other poems to proud and solitary heroes staring contemptuously at the changing crowd from the isolation of their own superiority. Keats and Spenser give way to Byron:

> They say I am proud and solitary yes proud
> Because my love and hate abideth ever
> A changeless thing among the changing crowd
> Until the sleep, an high soul changeth never.[3]

JBY's insistence on the superiority of dramatic verse is clear in these attempts at passionate soliloquy. Nonetheless, as he himself discovered when he began to read Willie's work, his son had as yet only an imperfect knowledge of scansion.* It was obvious, however, that Willie wrote for the spoken voice rather than the eye, and that the foundation of his poetry was

---

* This was, curiously, to remain a lifelong problem and suggests perhaps that Yeats was gifted with too subtle an ear to subdue it to a mechanical exercise. Certainly, even in old age he felt bound to confess 'how bothered I am when I get to prosody, because it is the most certain of my instincts, [but] the subject of which I am most ignorant'.

the speech of a youth genuinely moved. The lessons learned in JBY's studio were beginning to be put into effect and were merging with the instinctive, brooding intensity of Willie's Pollexfen inheritance. His boyish verses had what JBY recognised as their own wild and strange music, and he proudly declared that by marriage to the Pollexfens he had given 'a tongue to the sea-cliffs'. Willie was deeply touched.

The cliffs of Sligo themselves meanwhile continued to feed his imagination. The family still spent their summers with the Pollexfens, despite the fact that old William Pollexfen himself was now experiencing financial difficulties. His partner had died, there had been legal trouble, and 'he was no longer the rich man he had been, and his sons and daughters were married and scattered'.⁴ His temper remained as fiery as always, however, and the sight of a mismanaged mud-lighter would throw him into a rage. But age gave him other preoccupations. Although he could still steer a steamship with 'all his old skill and nerve', William Pollexfen had become morbidly obsessed with death. Disdaining to lie near his Middleton relatives, he spent much of his time supervising the building of his burial place, believing that 'if he had not looked after the tomb himself the builder might have added some useless ornament'.

Willie himself meanwhile was drawing closer to his uncle George Pollexfen, now ensconced in an ugly house in Sligo and running his father's part of the business. The relationship between them was to deepen over the ensuing years, enhanced by the family traits they shared. JBY's old schoolfriend was now a well-to-do middle-aged bachelor, a diligent and methodical man who had unostentatiously won the respect of the local people through his reserve and ceremony. He still had his measure of the Pollexfen gloom and was slowly curtailing activities he had once enjoyed such as hunting and the racing which, as JBY declared, transformed his habitual puritanism into a momentary display of benevolence, grace and strength.

George had also become a hypochondriac. His woollen clothes had always to be weighed and had always to be the same number of ounces on such a day as they were in other years. Morning depression would descend on him, and when his nephew tried to cheer him up he would merely respond: 'How very old I shall be in twenty years.' Nonetheless, with the Pollexfen gloom went the suppressed Pollexfen imagination. He enjoyed Tennyson and could beautifully embroider a trifling tale. The boy who had held his schoolfriends spell-bound with his stories still had a mind full of pictures and a sympathy with nature such that he had learned two cries of the lapwing, one that drew the birds to where he stood and one that made them fly away. Uncle George also had the sympathy some of the other Pollexfen children showed for the supernatural, and George himself was later to become an occult adept. Meanwhile, his servant Mary Battle had second sight and was a mine of stories and folk legends.

But it was with his cousin Lucy Middleton that Yeats now had an experience of the supernatural. As he recalled in his *Autobiographies*, Lucy and another went out for a late-evening walk past a graveyard and a village that had been destroyed in the wars of the seventeenth century. 'Suddenly we all saw a light moving over the river where there is a great rush of waters. It was like a very brilliant torch. A moment later the girl saw a man coming towards us who disappeared in the water. I kept asking myself if I could be deceived.' Yeats wondered if what he had seen was someone walking in the water with a light. As he continued to stare at the flame, however, so it began to ascend the slope of Knocknarea seven miles away. With that scientific attitude which so often accompanied Yeats's approach to the supernatural, 'I timed it on my watch and in five minutes it reached the summit, and I, who had often climbed the mountain, knew that no human footstep was so speedy.'

The supernatural affected him ever more profoundly, and from this time onwards Yeats not only began to wander about the raths and fairy hills, questioning old men and women about their experiences of the fairy world, but began 'telling people one should believe whatever had been believed in all countries and periods, and only reject any part of it after much evidence, instead of starting all over afresh and only believing what one could prove'. The supernatural was slowly moving towards the core of those religious beliefs Yeats was attempting to construct as a shelter against the oppressive world of nineteenth-century scientific materialism.

If the supernatural intrigued Yeats, sex remained an embarrassing and sometimes tormenting mystery. Sexual passion seemed to be something variously romantic and squalid. One day when he was out sailing with his cousin, the boy who was their crew 'talked of a music-hall at a neighbouring seaport, and how the girls there gave themselves to men, and his language was as extravagant as though he praised that courtesan after whom they named a city or the Queen of Sheba herself'. Other servants gave him other views of the subject. 'A young jockey and horse-trainer, who had trained some horses for my uncle, once talked to me of wicked England while we cooked a turkey for our Christmas dinner, making it twist about on a string in front of his harness-room fire. He had met two lords in England where he had gone racing, who "always exchanged wives when they went to the Continent for a holiday".'

The youth was later sacked for impropriety, and there were times when the adolescent Yeats thought that if only he could conquer 'bodily desire and the inclination of my mind towards women and love' then he could live amid nature seeking wisdom as Thoreau had done. Indeed, *Walden* had a great influence over him at this time and, with his uncle's permission, he once set out from Sligo at about six in the evening to walk to Slish Wood, from where he planned to spend the night looking out over Lough Gill and the beautiful island of Innisfree which seemed to float in its waters. Yeats had planned for himself a night of romantic reverie, but found he was so frightened at the thought of being caught by the wood-ranger that he was unable to get to sleep and eventually got home the following day 'unimaginably tired and sleepy, having walked some thirty miles partly over rough and boggy ground'. When he arrived at George Pollexfen's house a servant there refused to credit his story. 'She believed I had spent the night in a different fashion and had invented the excuse to deceive my uncle, and would say to my great embarrassment, for I was as prudish as an old maid, "and you had good right to be fatigued".'

II
'Words Alone Are Certain Good'
———

In the autumn of 1882, when he had returned to Dublin, Willie had his first experience of calf love. He was climbing a hill at Howth when a pony and trap drew up beside him driven by a pretty girl with lovely red hair. Her name was Laura Armstrong and she was a distant cousin, three years older than Willie himself. She had in her 'a wild dash of half-insane genius' which sometimes showed itself in religious excesses.5 She was also involved in an unsatisfactory engagement and, needing Willie as a confidant, allowed him to fall in her love with her. His passion, he recalled, woke him from 'the metallic sleep of science'. A correspondence was begun, she naming herself Vivien, he Clarin. It was with Laura in mind that Willie wrote his heavily melodramatic play *Vivien and Time* at the beginning of 1884 when he was eighteen and a half. The play was rehearsed and perhaps even given an amateur performance at Howth, Laura Armstrong (the Vivien of the love-letters) playing the part of the proud but lovely queen subdued to mortality. By the end of the year, however, Laura herself had married and Willie would look back on her merely as 'a pleasant memory'.

But with new inspiration went the old hardships. The family's financial affairs worsened through the following two years. At the close of 1883 JBY moved out of his York Street studio and set up in Stephen's Green, next to a grocer's shop. Intellectual Dublin came there to enjoy his conversation and noted the canvases stacked against the walls and supposedly hiding a little kitchen and a tea-table. JBY was not inclined to paint people who did not interest him, while his prices were reckoned too low to attract wealthy and exclusive patrons looking for works to enhance their prestige. His career was still floundering, and the artist was often behind with the rent, even after he had moved his family from Howth to a dull house in suburban Ashfield Terrace. Worried letters were sent to relatives asking for loans. Susan had promised immediate payment of £20 to the butcher who had refused to supply them, while in November 1883 Willie was sent, despite an illness, to get money from Uncle Matt. Setting aside his father's request that he be allowed to stay overnight, Willie returned by train to Dublin, resolved to hear Oscar Wilde lecturing on 'The House Beautiful' and proclaiming that it was the spiritual ministry of art to sanctify everything it touched.

Such aesthetic ideals were far removed from the practical circumstances of life in Ashfield Terrace, if not from its hopes and aspirations. Economies were so necessary that in the evening the family gathered round the light of a single oil lamp while Willie did his homework and then began murmuring over his verses. Eventually such murmuring grew louder until it filled the whole room and his sisters would call out and ask him to stop composing. His voice would be temporarily lowered until, rising once again to a shout, a second lamp would be found and lit for Willie in the kitchen, where he could speak his verses to his heart's content.

By early 1884, JBY felt sufficient confidence in his son's efforts to show his work to Dowden. He was delighted by the critic's praise. He excused Willie's metrical problems by referring to his oral method of composition and was sure his work showed powers of thought, however rudimentary these might as yet be. Some day, he believed, Willie would have something important to say, and he confessed: 'that he is a poet I have long believed, where he may reach is another matter'.[6] Willie himself was certain he could reach further than Dowden. The scholar's comments had pleased him, but meetings with Dowden in his father's studio and elsewhere convinced him that JBY was right when he said his old friend had failed in life because he would not trust his own nature. The man who described *Prometheus Unbound* – that sacred text – as merely Godwin's philosophy versified, and who then admitted that he was tired of his many years' work on a biography of Shelley, was guilty of crass philistinism in Willie's eyes. Those around him, even the most eminent, would from now on be weighed in the exacting scale of his often carping judgement.

With the easy fertility of adolescence, plays continued to tumble from Willie's hand and to mix violence, escapism and melodrama with a growing sense of the conflicts he was coming to see as particularly his own. *Love and Death* allied a child's murder of its father to a perception of the potentially tragic struggle between the mortal and immortal natures within mankind, while in *Mosada* the battle between the materialists and the supernatural was suggested by the conflict between the magician and the inquisitors, between imagination and the forces of organised religion. An important change was ever more clearly taking place within Yeats. The cocksure boy refuting Genesis with arguments gathered out of Darwin and Huxley was giving way to a youth homesick for spiritual experience.

But if Yeats had now conceived a 'monkish hatred' for science, he was left vulnerable by what he had relinquished. While the works of the evolutionists showed him a grey and mechanistic world, they destroyed the Christian belief that might have reanimated it. Yet the child who had known religious fear and even wondered what faith the ants might have could not, in adolescence, deny his need for a spiritual life. Yeats was approaching, however tentatively, the fundamental question of his life: is mankind related to something infinite or not? Biblical Christianity and the rituals of the recently disestablished Anglican Church of Ireland had failed to satisfy him. Was he therefore left to his own resources – to the stance of mind adopted by his father – and the pursuit of merely finite ends? Or were there proofs of the divine and means of experiencing its influence? Yeats was beginning to glimpse the challenge made by the contemporary world to his deepest instincts and, in starting his search for spiritual experience, was finding his essential concerns.

Events and encounters were to hurry him along sometimes confused avenues. JBY had hoped his son would follow family tradition and enter Trinity College, but Yeats himself, aware that his classics and mathematics were too weak to guarantee his matriculation, decided to enrol instead at the Metropolitan School of Art. All the Yeats children had drawn from infancy and, though Yeats himself showed little more than average ability, time spent at art school would at least give him the opportunity to develop his late-adolescent self in a fairly unhindered way. For, despite the ideas stirring in him, Yeats was still in the stage between boyhood and manhood. Sometimes he caught himself striding along the Dublin streets with steps imitated from a performance of *Hamlet*. He would stop to look at himself in shop windows and examine 'my tie gathered into a loose sailor-knot and . . . regret that it could not always be blown out by the wind like Byron's tie in the picture'.[7]

Adolescence also showed itself in other ways. Willie's difficulties with his art suggest there was a conflict brewing with his father. Yeats himself wanted to paint in the Pre-Raphaelite manner JBY had abandoned. He longed for an art strong in pattern and allied to poetry. 'In my heart I felt that only beautiful things should be painted, and that only ancient things and the stuff of dreams were beautiful.' His father's portraits with their realistic, humanitarian insight and interest in personality displeased him. He yearned to free himself from material reality and to live in a world sanctioned by dreams. The work of Dante Gabriel Rossetti especially had shown him one way of doing this. Once in Liverpool, as he was travelling to Sligo, Yeats had stopped to look at *Dante's Dream*, and now Rossetti's women – 'The Blessed Damozel' warming the bar of Heaven with the weight of her breasts or his numerous studies of sloe-eyed 'stunners' with their heavy, kiss-bruised lips – filled his teenage imagination. A flight from the weariness of doubt, anxiety, paternal pressure and the material world characterises much of his earliest work, and if Rossetti pointed in one direction, memories of Sligo pointed in another:

> Come away, O human child!
> To the woods and waters wild
> With a faery, hand in hand,
> For the world's more full of weeping than you can understand.[8]

But, for all this longing, Yeats as a painter at least was too timid either to break decisively with his father's style or to ignore completely the tame academic studies pursued by the majority of the students around him. The work he was set bored him, and only one young man, a tall, thin painter, carelessly dressed in Donegal tweed and enveloped in a silence occasionally broken by a torrent of wild and stuttering speech, seemed to float above the mediocrity around him. His name was George Russell, later known as the poet A.E.[9] The other students regarded him with the respect due to a 'holy fool' and looked on with puzzled envy as, without the help of any preparatory sketch, Russell put down on his canvas compositions that not only showed great technical mastery but glowed with his visionary imagination. Here was a student, not quite two years younger than Yeats himself, who seemed to embody what Yeats was grasping for. He was determined to win Russell's friendship. To his delight, he discovered that some few months previously Russell had found that in wild and lonely places the scenery would change as unknown, beautiful people moved among the rocks and trees. 'The visible world became like a tapestry blown and stirred by the winds behind it,' Russell wrote, and he believed that if its folds were raised for only an instant he would be in paradise. But the visions would not stay and it was in his art that he recorded his glimpse of what Yeats called 'the woods in veils of violet weather'.

Yeats himself was too sceptical to approach his friend's work with complete credulity (he was aware that Russell was to some degree influenced by the paintings of Gustave Moreau) but the friendship between them deepened. Russell, with his 'great overcoat flying open', would come on evening visits to Yeats at Ashfield Terrace where, in the kitchen and with the oil lamp burning, they would write, chant verses to each other, or let the conversation range over such supernatural topics as thought transference or 'what cosmic sounds make mushrooms grow'.* Dressed in their flowing, French artists' ties (Yeats's was scarlet to offset his sallow face) they were two young men united against the material world and, if their

---

* Their eccentricities were not unique. Russell lent a theosophical work to a student who wore a daisy chain round his neck and was told, on receiving the book back, that he would 'drift into a penumbra'.

enthusiasms sometimes seemed merely silly, there underlay them a steely dedication.

Yeats was now discovering some of his most important early motifs. In particular he was fascinated with an image of the sea-wandering Forgael yearning to escape from himself. Surprising a galley with a beautiful woman on board, Forgael thinks love might offer him transcendence and he casts a spell over the lovely Dectora only to find (with great psychological insight) that he has merely projected on to her a shadow of himself. In the early version, a depressed Forgael seeks the world of the immortals alone. This very potent myth, which Yeats was later to refashion into *The Shadowy Waters*, was to undergo numerous transformations to become his most constantly revised play.

Yeats himself was impressed by Russell's pictorial ability, while the painter was won over not just by the poems Yeats was writing but by the self-discipline he brought to refining his craft. Russell discovered that Yeats was now giving an hour or two every day to the writing of verse, regardless of whether he felt inclined to or not. The amateur scansion and adolescent lack of focus seen in Yeats's earliest work were being transformed by a rigour which drew on the deep resources of his will and his altogether more mysterious need for form, for perfection of the work. Poems of escape from the melancholy world of doubt and materialism, invocations of dreams and Arcady, were wrung from an anguish of concentration but seemed as spontaneous as falling dew:

> Where the wave of moonlight glosses
> The dim grey sands with light,
> Far off by furthest Rosses
> We foot it all the night,
> Weaving olden dances,
> Mingling hands mingling glances
> Till the moon has taken flight;
> To and fro we leap,
> And chase the frothy bubbles,
> While the world is full of troubles
> And is anxious in its sleep.[10]

Russell, in love with such passages as with his friend, would never deny the feelings Yeats's early work roused in him, despite the later difficulties in their association. For these allies against materialism were markedly different characters, and their reactions to a momentous but seemingly casual event focussed this. In April 1885, Willie's Pollexfen Aunt Isabella sent him a copy of a book called *Esoteric Buddhism*. The title suggested an atmosphere of spiritual initiation and secrecy likely to appeal to two such youths as Yeats and Russell, and this was an impression the author, A. P. Sinnett, was keen to enhance. His book claimed to offer a secret doctrine (the sacredness of which had hitherto been concealed from the profane herd) that originated in mystic India and had at first been revealed only to such members of the Theosophical Society as himself. Sinnett's work now promised all those wishing to learn 'the absolute truth concerning Nature, Man, the origin of the Universe, and the destinies towards which its inhabitants are tending'.[11]

To Yeats the disillusioned evolutionist, *Esoteric Buddhism* and the teachings of Theosophy appeared a partial answer to his spiritual confusion. Evolution did not, as the followers of Darwin proclaimed, lead merely from ape to man. The Mahatmas and Arhats of the East taught that the soul was a spark of the unknowable and boundless Absolute which should evolve back to godhead. This it could do through a series of eight hundred incarnations in seven rounds, each round being led by the Avatar of a higher round until the seven principles of the personality (the mystical mathematics of the scheme was part of its allure) was so attenuated as to become the Universal Self or Atman. This process of bodily, mental and spiritual evolution, spread over many lives both past and to come, constituted a man's karma and, just as the individual evolved, so did the race he belonged to and humanity in general. *Esoteric Buddhism* proceeds through a series of such parallels to proclaim that all the great religions of the world originate from the supreme source which Theosophy proclaims, a 'secret doctrine' preserved in its purest form by the Tibetan masters who delivered it to the as yet mysterious Madame Blavatsky, the founder of Theosophy itself.

Yeats later claimed that his reaction to this heady mixture of the spurious and the profound was guarded by the scepticism acquired from his father, but it is clear the book made a deep impression on him and that it did so in a way similar experiences in the future were to do. Yeats became no simple convert to Theosophy, happy to answer questions with rote-learned dogma, rather did his mind and imagination feel their way towards what the book could touch among his deepest needs. *Esoteric Buddhism* supported his intimation of the supernatural and gave him less a creed than a manner of thinking to which he could bring his originality. The cycles of history outlined by Sinnett, for example, suggested how history itself could be fitted to that type of model at once spiritual and geometric which, in his maturity, Yeats would forge for himself in *A Vision*. Sinnett's sense of cataclysm and renewal again helped suggest the bearings of Yeats's moral and historical view. But above all Theosophy gave him its gathered wealth of tradition and, as Yeats came to read more widely in its works, so he began to discover the immense variety of esoteric teaching which, through a lifetime, he would try to harness to his purposes. As Sinnett himself wrote: 'at whatever age a boy or a man dedicates himself to the occult career, he dedicates himself to it, be it remembered, without any reservations and for life'.[12] In saying this at least, he was a certain guide.

Yeats showed Sinnett's work to Russell and his erstwhile schoolfriend Charles Johnston. The latter was immediately enthusiastic, so enthusiastic indeed that Yeats's old headmaster was worried that this star pupil was giving his time to mysticism rather than work for his examinations. Russell, too, was impressed by *Esoteric Buddhism*, but in a different way. He found many of the book's ideas more attractive than the narrow Christianity in which he had been reared, but he read the work in part for its moral exhortation. He was already beginning to show the asceticism of the mystic, that earnest suppression of ambition and desire which in time would separate him from Yeats. For Yeats himself was coming to believe that the alliance of religion and morality was a stifling thing compared to the marriage of religion and art. He was developing into a poet who read religious texts less for their moral content than for their images and symbols. He delighted, for example, in the thought of Madame Blavatsky's mentors as enormous shapes seated on the Himalayas, their hair unrolled along the summits and filled with unnumbered birds. The monastery of the mahatmas was less an actual place than a state of the soul. Lhasa lay within, and, while Russell veered towards austerity, Yeats was the young man who, in his own phrase, hoped to light his every 'cigarette at the stars'.

It was such a difference that in part prevented Russell from joining Yeats immediately in the newly formed Dublin Hermetic Society. Yeats's own membership of this group, however, was his initiation into a pattern that was to characterise much of his spiritual and eventually his artistic and political life: his joining small, elite and more or less secret societies centred around ideas of transforming spiritual revelation. One of the dominant motifs of his career was this being sounded and, at the group's inaugural meeting on 16 June 1885, Yeats was elected president. This suggests the growing power of his personality and points to the fact that the dreamy poet was also a natural organiser. Indeed, over the course of time and schooled by some bitter disappointments, Yeats was to develop into a formidable committee man.

He was also acquiring the skills of a public speaker, and his introductory talk to the Hermetic Society stressed that its name, although sanctioned by Madame Blavatsky, suggested that its concerns should be wider than the study of Theosophy alone. With the eclecticism that characterised his entire approach to spiritual matters, Yeats suggested that the young Hermeticists take the whole of literature as their province, for 'whatever the great poets had affirmed in their finest moments' was, he would eventually say, the closest man came to an authoritative religion. The imagination was the measure of the spirit, and Yeats was moving towards that position where he could write of himself:

> I am very religious, and deprived by Huxley and Tyndall, whom I detested, of the simple-minded religion of my childhood, I had made a new religion, almost an infallible Church of poetic tradition, of a fardel of stories, and of personages, and of emotions, inseparable from their first expression, passed on from generation to generation by poets and painters with some help from philosophers and theologians.[13]

The other members agreed only briefly and reluctantly to such an approach. They needed parameters for their security and, by early 1886, Johnston had obtained a charter signed by Sinnett himself for a newly reconstituted and renamed Dublin Theosophical Society. Yeats did not rejoin. The spiritual had to be more vibrant than mere scholasticism.

Yeats was nonetheless briefly drawn back to the Dublin Theosophists by the arrival in the city of Madame Blavatsky's emissary, the gentle Brahmin Mohini Chatterjee, 'a handsome young man with the typical face of Christ'.[14] Yeats was immediately attracted to this teacher as he sat making little gestures with his delicate hands and expounding his philosophy with great clarity and breadth of knowledge. Basing his ideas on those of the eighth-century seer Sankara, Mohini Chatterjee taught that the material world is an illusion. When we think that people, objects and processes are real we are like the bewildered man who mistakes a coiled rope for a snake. The doctrine of reincarnation seemed to prove this. When Yeats asked Chatterjee what words he should mutter before going to sleep, he was told to say: 'I have lived many lives. It may be that I have been a slave and a prince. Many a beloved has sat upon my knees, and I have sat upon the knees of many a beloved. Everything that has been shall be again.' The social and historical personality is an illusion. Only the inmost Self is real, and contemplation of the Self is our only valid activity. We must reject, Chatterjee taught, the insubstantial shadow world and, along with it, desire – even the desire for immortality. Man's goal must be the inner world of the passive contemplation of beauty and, drawing on the doctrines of Pater (Chatterjee had brought a copy of *Marius the Epicurean* with him to Dublin) he set out to prove that 'art for art's sake' was the one sinless doctrine for the artist to follow.

Here was a heady combination of the most ancient ideas with the most modern. Just as Chatterjee believed that only aestheticism could perceive 'the shadow of the world as it exists in the mind', so Pater, convinced that modern evolutionary thought showed life to be a continuous and evanescent process of change and refinement, urged the supreme value of beauty in the face of death. Constant flux ensured that man lived in a wholly relative world where knowledge could be nothing more than a series of flickering and unstable impressions playing across an individual's mind. Art, Pater taught in his *Studies in the History of the Renaissance*, was the most potent means of conveying this elusive effect, but since art had been sundered from morality it could no longer have a didactic purpose: 'for art comes to you professing frankly to give nothing but the highest quality to your moments as they pass, and simply for the moment's sake'. To many Victorians, such wholesale relativism was an appalling and decadent threat. To others, to be open to such experiences as Pater described, 'to burn always with this hard gem-like flame, to maintain this ecstasy, is success in life'. Pater's doctrine of art for art's sake – his freeing art from the burden of moral teaching – marked a fundamental divide between an older world of received earnestness and a newer one of free experiment. Yeats recognised this and paid tribute to it near the end of his life when he printed Pater's famous description of the Mona Lisa as *vers libre* at the opening of his *Oxford Book of Modern Verse*.

Meanwhile, in the last of his early plays, Yeats offered his youthful view of man's predicament as Pater and Chatterjee had revealed it to him. *The Island of Statues* is an Arcadian fairy tale in which, in an important Yeatsian image, an enchantress turns to stone those who seek immortality. The yearning for a state beyond flux, in other words, is a yearning for death. When the enchantress herself dies, the statues are brought back to life and given the choice of remaining in Arcady or returning to the world. They choose Arcady in preference to the mundane, relishing dreams and the subjective life over an existence dominated by the 'Grey Truth' of modern scientific rationalism:

> The woods of Arcady are dead,
> And over is their antique joy;
> Of old the world on dreaming fed;
> Grey Truth is now her painted toy;
> Yet still she turns her restless head:
> But O, sick children of the world,
> Of all the many changing things
> In dreary dancing past us whirled,
> To the cracked tune that Chronos sings,
> Words alone are certain good.[15]

Poetry and vision, Yeats suggests, reveal more than any telescope, and subjectivity is infinitely to be preferred to the world of deeds. Only the poet's art can offer and perhaps even briefly make for man the spiritually nourishing life he craves. Language and the imagination, it is hinted, create their own evanescent reality, and 'Words alone are certain good'. 'The Song of the Happy Shepherd', as Yeats called this tailpiece to his play when he published it separately, sparely yet sensitively conveys the extreme passivity of much of his earliest work, the all but disembodied quality of disillusion hankering after vision. The piece now stands as the first lyric in Yeats's collected poems, the introductory statement of a young man who had placed himself at the frontier of contemporary thought and was acutely aware of the burden of modernity.

III

The Contemporary Club

In these doctrines of passivity, art and imagination won from Pater and Chatterjee, Yeats found the first elements of his vision but, in so doing, he also found a form of belief at variance with his father's insistence on personality. In his long conversations with Mohini Chatterjee, Yeats discovered an intuitive and spiritual ideal to set against JBY's dominant mind forever running over with Mill, Comte and humanitarianism. Here was a way of making art that, unlike JBY's portraits, was not dependent on material reality. The challenge Yeats had failed to make to his father in the studio could perhaps be made in his poetry. To win this struggle was to begin to establish his independence, and the psychological element in Yeats's thought is clear. The pursuit of a mystic state of being beyond desire was in part motivated by deep if subterranean feelings. As he later confessed in his *Autobiographies*: 'it was only when I began to study psychical research and mystical philosophy that I broke away from my father's influence'.

JBY was naturally worried by his son's new concerns and disapproved of what he considered their irrationality, just as he was disapproving of friends like Russell who were involved in them. The occult was both an affront to his intellect and something which, he feared, might stir the dangerous, depressive Pollexfen traits in his son's personality. These differences were to become a source of conflict, but JBY recognised that the poetry Willie was now writing had quality and, because he loved him, was determined to help him. One of JBY's closest friends was the painter Sarah Purser, known as the wittiest woman in Dublin. She told JBY at one of her dinner parties that he was a fool to apprentice his son to an art school when he could have made him a doctor for fifteen shillings a week. JBY determined to defend his son's apparently aimless course not by pointing to his pictures but by reading them one of his poems. Miss Purser replied that she would listen, but not with any sympathy. When JBY finished reading Willie's 'The Priest and the Fairy', her mind was entirely changed. She and her family became the boy's allies and, as JBY later wrote in his unpublished memoirs, 'his passports were made out and he was free to enter the kingdom of poetry, all because of a little poem . . . in which these infallible critics had found the true note'.

It was necessary others should find it too. In the close-knit world of the Dublin intelligentsia, it was a comparatively easy matter to approach one of Dowden's colleagues, Charles Hubert Oldham, and arrange publication of some of Willie's poems in the newly founded *Dublin University Review*. 'Song of the Fairies' and 'Voices' were printed in the issue for March 1885, and five other issues for that year also contained works by him, including *The Island of Statues*. Their reception was not wholly uncritical – Dowden thought his friend's son was a youth precariously balanced 'between genius and (to speak rudely) fool' – but it was becoming clear to everyone that the tall young man who wandered about Dublin muttering to himself, smoking his cigarettes and wearing a pair of black trousers reputedly cut down from his grandfather's, was not Yeats the art student but Yeats the poet – a youth of promise.

That promise was still underscored by personal insecurity, the shyness and occasional gaucheness that had troubled Yeats since the onset of adolescence particularly. He was determined to master this and, if needs be, to create a mask of worldly competence with which to cover his timorous features. The publication of his poetry offered him the opportunity. In addition to organising the *Dublin University Review*, C. H. Oldham had begun to invite friends to his Trinity College rooms on Saturday evenings to discuss the issues of the day. Oldham himself was an advocate of Home Rule, and the regular gathering of those of a similar persuasion so alarmed the College that meetings had eventually to be held above Ponsonby's bookshop in Grafton Street. Here, constituted as the Contemporary Club, the seventy-five members and their guests enjoyed vigorous and uninhibited conversation liberally spiced with Dublin malice.

JBY was a regular attender at the Contemporary Club, but while he spent much of his time sketching the lively personalities gathered there, his son threw himself into the debates. Here, if he was to make a career for himself, were the people he would have to influence. They were a daunting assembly and, to an often awkward young man, a potentially threatening one. Yeats approached them with deliberate policy. 'I wished to become self-possessed,' he wrote later, 'to be able to play with hostile minds as Hamlet played, to look in the lion's face, as it were, with unquivering eyelash.'[16] The image he presented would be neither shy nor naively spontaneous. Yeats would make his mark through the exercise of will power and, where necessary, manipulation. But the process was neither as easy nor as successful as he hoped. He could speak fluently enough until strongly attacked by a figure like the forceful orator John F. Taylor, when he would either hesitate and fall into confusion or wildly exaggerate his ideas until he got carried away. Just as with his earlier social blunders, he would then spend hours in recrimination and self-criticism, putting right in imagination what he had got wrong in combat.

He made an impression nonetheless. As the literary historian Stephen

Gwynn recalled: 'some of us were recognised as counting for something and likely to count for more. But every one of us was convinced that Yeats was going to be a better poet than we had yet seen in Ireland.' Then he added: 'the significant fact is that this was not out of personal liking'.[17] The quality of repelling others noted by Yeats's schoolfellows persisted. He was far from being at his ease, and was protecting both his shyness and his sense of his own superiority under a mask at once sour-faced and aggressive. In such ways the student of Theosophy was tentatively trying to become the public man and, if this conflict brought out unattractive traits in Yeats's personality, it is clear that he was also beginning to discover altogether more profound aspects of his psyche, insights he was to develop through a lifetime into a philosophy of art, religion and history.

The teenage Yeats was coming to realise that he belonged both to the withdrawn, esoteric world of Mohini Chatterjee and to the abrasive public domain of the Contemporary Club. He was uncovering in himself a dualism, the fact that it was less stable certainties than dynamic opposites which appealed to his mind and that it was from the confrontation of these that the most vibrant forms of consciousness flowed. From this shrewd and courageous awareness would develop some of Yeats's most fundamental insights: his belief in what he called the 'antithetical man' exploring his polarities, his concern with the mask as a way of living out those aspects of life that have been hidden or repressed, the subtle and curious antimonies later to be explored in *A Vision*, and the extraordinary vigour of his last and greatest poems in which a heroic Yeats rejoices in a life tossed exultantly between spirit and flesh, art and nature, euphoria and defeat.

IV
'Celtic Passion'

And now, as always, Yeats had to face the historical realities of his country. Politics formed a major but not exclusive topic of debate at the Contemporary Club, and by the middle years of the 1880s a number of significant developments had taken place. The activities of the Fenians that had once troubled the dreams of the infant Yeats had been curtailed by British coercion. The desire for independence had not been repressed, however, and the Reverend William Butler Yeats's old friend Isaac Butt had now founded the Home Rule Confederation of Great Britain. It was thus the Anglo-Irish who still appeared to lead the movement for liberty, even if Butt himself seemed largely ineffective. He believed that the cause of Ireland would be best advanced by the gentlemanly pursuit of reason, an argument that had the support of JBY, who in 1876 painted Butt's portrait.

More passionate groups disagreed. The Famine of 1879 and its attendant economic hardships had led under James Daly and Michael Davitt to the setting up of what eventually became known as the Land League and, with this, the outbreak of the Land War with its mass meetings, civil disobedience and boycotts. The League was outlawed in 1881, but in May the following year a secret society known as the Invincibles ensured that the violence which was never far below the surface of Irish political life once again became brutally evident. As Lord Frederick Cavendish, the new Lord Lieutenant, was walking across Phoenix Park with his Permanent Undersecretary Thomas Burke, they were attacked by a small band of men and stabbed to death with surgical amputation knives. When a declaration purportedly issued by the Irish Republican Brotherhood attempted to justify the crime, many repudiated it.

Among these was the man who now defeated Butt and took over his leadership, the great nineteenth-century Irishman Charles Stewart Parnell. Uniquely able to draw together the complex residues of Nationalist feeling, Parnell, a master of parliamentary management, ensured wide support at home partly by advising the peasant farmers to withhold rents and services from their landlords. The English sought to master the situation with a series of Irish Coercion Bills which, inflaming the situation, led them eventually to arresting Parnell and throwing him into Kilmainham jail at the close of 1881. The Crimes Bill passed after the Phoenix Park murders was yet another way of suppressing Irish political aspirations, but by the middle years of the 1880s, when Yeats first started to attend meetings of the Contemporary Club, supporters of Irish Home Rule had once again reached a pitch of excitement.

With Parnell now released, with the Irish Parliamentary Party behind him and supported by large numbers of a newly enlarged electorate, Home Rule seemed set for success. Parnell himself, drawing ambiguously on Fenian feelings and playing off Liberal against Conservative with great adroitness, was bringing pressure to bear on Gladstone to convince him of the necessity for Home Rule. By this Parnell meant the establishment of that state of affairs whereby a Dublin parliament would exercise authority over an important range of domestic matters while Westminster retained control over issues affecting the Crown, defence and foreign affairs. To the champions of Home Rule such a change appeared much more than a modest measure of devolution. It was, in the words of one, the 'filing through the last link of the chain that binds our country to the chariot wheels of England'.[18]

Into this excited atmosphere came a figure who was to have a profound influence on Yeats. On 19 January 1885, the Fenian leader John O'Leary returned to Dublin after nineteen years of imprisonment and exile. Such experiences had not changed O'Leary's views, only tempered them. He was still sympathetic to those who sought independence through physical force and still believed that only a wholesale repeal of the Act of Union would set Ireland free. He declared that 'a people who are not prepared to fight in the last resort rather than remain slaves will never be made free by any sort of Parliamentary legerdermain'.[19] He was, nonetheless, cautious. 'Better wait another century for the right sort of Home Rule than take an altogether wrong sort in a much shorter period.' O'Leary belonged to the old-fashioned school of Nationalists who associated patriotism with morality and public life with tolerance. Expediency and gratuitous violence offended his view of Irish dignity. He believed such things would not secure the cause of his people's freedom and, in their place, he urged a policy Yeats was to make his own.

On the evening of his arrival in Dublin, O'Leary gave an address to a vast audience in the Rotunda. Looking back to the work of the original leaders of the Young Ireland movement, to men like the poet Thomas Davis, O'Leary claimed that while their political aims had come to nothing they had had an incalculable influence on all subsequent agitators by providing and disseminating literature on nationalist themes. He encouraged the current members of the Young Ireland Society to do the same, to set aside political debates for literary meetings and to extend their activities by founding libraries across the land in which there should be a plentiful supply of Irish books. No nation, O'Leary believed, could be truly independent until it had an image of its own identity, and that image was most vividly seen in its literature. In lectures around the country and in conversations at the Contemporary Club, O'Leary praised such Irish writers as Davis and Gavan Duffy, Mitchel, Standish O'Grady and George Sigerson. His own library of these men's works had been slowly built up from the Dublin bookstalls (during his exile his sister Ellen had guarded 'John's treasures' as she called them), and study had made O'Leary familiar with their strengths and weaknesses. These writers had done much but, as O'Leary told an audience in Cork, 'it is one among the many misfortunes of Ireland that she has never yet produced a great poet. Let us', he added, 'trust that God has in store for us that great gift.'

Yeats was strongly drawn to O'Leary. His 'noble head', which he thought worthy of a Roman coin, remained with him as a lifelong image of Irish dignity. Tall and ascetic in appearance (even if the flask from which he refreshed himself was not, as he claimed, filled with cold tea), O'Leary was an intensely romantic figure. The story of his being a member of the Young Ireland movement at eighteen, his helping edit a revolutionary newspaper and his subsequent imprisonment was bound to impress. But Yeats also discovered in O'Leary an heroic decorum, a 'moral genius' which had no trace in it of bitterness towards his captors. It was almost certainly under O'Leary's influence that Yeats allied himself to the aims of the Irish Republican Brotherhood, the secret body of 'physical force' Nationalists, although like O'Leary himself he did not actually swear their oath. To Yeats, O'Leary was reminiscent of a figure out of Plutarch, a man of conservative views who, Yeats was later exaggeratedly to claim, nurtured a patrician and even feudal hatred of democracy.

In fact, as an old-fashioned Fenian, O'Leary had an affectionate respect for the poorer classes, who needed, he thought, the leadership of an enlightened intelligentsia. What he really despised (and here his influence on Yeats was to be immense) was a middle class led by 'the lowest motifs' of prudence and materialism – the hereditary enemy, in fact, of the romantic rebel. Yeats was to absorb such attitudes and, in conversations at the Contemporary Club, he fell increasingly under the spell of O'Leary's personality. The old Fenian himself, meanwhile, staring out with his sad, vulnerable eyes, started to notice the tall, sallow youth with his stub of beard whom he referred to as 'Mr Yeets'. He began to see in him a protégé and even, perhaps, the son he never had. Above all, O'Leary divined Yeats's real qualities. 'Young Yeats', he prophesied to the Contemporary Club, 'is the only person in this room who will ever be reckoned a genius.'

Yeats began to call on his new mentor in his lodgings in Leinster Road. On an early visit he found that O'Leary was not at home. His sister persuaded Yeats to wait and invited him to join a card game she was playing with friends. Yeats lost a sixpence he could ill afford, but when Ellen O'Leary offered him a glass of sherry in compensation the drink went to his head and apparently took several days to wear off. Other visits were of a more serious nature. O'Leary gave Yeats the run of his library, and here he began to discover a native Irish literature written in English or translated into it. A decade of voracious reading was opening and, with this, a lifetime's commitment. As Yeats wrote in his *Autobiographies*, from debates, from O'Leary's conversation 'and from the Irish books he lent or gave me has come all I have set my hand to since'.

As Yeats pursued his studies in O'Leary's library, it became clear to him that the work he was reading followed two broad approaches. The first was written by literary nationalists, men like Thomas Davis and his Young Ireland followers. 'Educate that you may be free,' Davis had declared, and the didacticism and political content of this verse took precedence over aesthetic refinement. O'Leary's taste had detected this fault – 'patriotism', he opined, 'seems to take a peculiar delight in the manufacture of bad verse' – and Yeats agreed with him. Both men recognised, however, the sincerity with which this verse had been written, and Yeats was briefly if genuinely touched by such clumsy lines as those describing the shores of Ireland as seen by a returning, dying emigrant.

The second tradition Yeats discovered was scholarly, a literature not of nationalism but of patriotism. Its roots lay in the eighteenth century when studious Anglo-Irish men and women began to recover the traces of a culture which others of their caste had, over the centuries, tried to destroy. Antiquarians and literary translators set out to preserve what they could of indigenous Irish literary culture written in a language more remote from contemporary Gaelic than is Anglo-Saxon from current English, and to publish their findings. Such activities were intended as a contribution to a widespread interest in ancient European cultures. The process was still continuing in the 1880s with the publications of the indefatigable patriot and scholar Sir Samuel Ferguson, and such works as Standish O'Grady's two-volume *History of Ireland*.

O'Grady indeed was to influence Yeats profoundly for he was a man who could not only reveal 'the wonder-world of Irish heroic myth and romantic literature' but could connect this to a concept of an elite cultural nationalism which in turn moulded his political views. Fundamental to his beliefs was the idea that the Irish lived through the eye of the imagination. In Ireland, the writer was not hopelessly subdued to 'positive history and unyielding despotic fact'. In such declarations lay not just an appeal to native ideals (powerful though that was) but a more specific attack on English commentators and, in particular, Matthew Arnold. In his essay *On the Study of Celtic Literature*, Arnold had written of how alienated he felt from the habits of mind he detected in his subject and urged a rigorously objective analysis of what clearly baffled and intrigued him.

O'Grady, by contrast, not only exalted the subjective but saw in its powers an Irish superiority over English materialism. In this he again exerted a powerful influence over Yeats, who also came to adopt O'Grady's belief that it was the Ascendancy aristocracy that could best defend these values against 'the wolf of democracy'. Patriotism and anti-popularist values had characterised the thoughts of many Nationalists from the eighteenth century onwards, and throughout the 1880s O'Grady warned his readers that 'the day of absolute democratic power in Ireland draws nigh – the day of reckoning and vengeance'. His *Toryism and Tory Democracy* revealed a pressing fear that, in an image often repeated by the mature Yeats, the peasantry would one day invade the great houses and commit larceny on their cultural inheritance. Taking his cue from Carlyle, O'Grady urged against this alleged catastrophe the necessity of preserving 'the feudal feeling' which, he argued, was 'one of the most natural and instinctive in the heart of man'. Although O'Grady himself was to change his views and eventually declare that the failure of the landlords meant that 'the future of Ireland is with the people', Yeats was to become ever more sympathetic to O'Grady's patrician Toryism and later extolled him as 'a man whose rage was a swan-song over all that he held dear, and to whom for that very reason every imaginative writer owed a portion of his soul'.

For the moment, however, in the purely historical and literary works of such people, Yeats found the intense imaginative appeal of a Celtic culture at once ancient, heroic and steeped in mythology. Here was the historical basis of an authentic Irish civilisation untouched by Christianity, by English conquest or by a baleful scientific materialism, a culture of the magical and the supernatural whose remains he had glimpsed among the Sligo peasantry. The Celts had once enjoyed, he discovered, a European-wide culture of immense antiquity for, in addition to spreading through Spain, France, England and the Danube valley, they had fully settled in Ireland by at least 500 BC. In Ireland at least, where they largely escaped the attentions of the Roman Empire and the cultural devastation that followed its fall, the Celts were a tribal people ruled by numerous petty kings. Their learning was vested in the Druids, who, as Julius Caesar noted, committed great amounts of poetry to memory (there was no written language), as well as having a wide knowledge of the stars 'and of the powers and spheres of action of the immortal gods'.

There were well over a hundred of these gods in the Celtic pantheon, chief among them, according to Lucan, being Esus – the god of arts, crafts, trades and travellers – along with Taranis, Teutatis and a harvest deity known as Lugh who was later to have a special resonance for Yeats and who, through the subtleties of cultural transmission, gave something of his qualities to the Arthurian Lancelot. The earth itself meanwhile was worshipped as a mother, a provider and a protector, while many rivers, streams and trees were venerated as divine. Nature, in the Celtic world, was thus alive with occult vision rather than being the spiritless automaton familiar to Yeats from his reading in nineteenth-century science. Celtic religion, he discovered, also taught of an afterlife and the immortal nature of the soul which was reincarnated after death.

The society that practised these beliefs was divided into three broad but rigid groups of aristocrats, freemen and slaves. Warriors, judges and Druids belonged to the aristocracy, as did historians and the poets or *fili*. Yeats was particularly pleased to discover that poets were given an honoured place in Celtic society. 'The bards', he wrote, 'kept by the rules of their order apart from war and the common affairs of men, rode hither and thither gathering up the dim feelings of the time, and making them conscious.'[20] He believed that the bards, with a knowledge deeper than fancy or mere intellect, touched the universal emotions, that knowledge which was 'created out of the deepest instinct of man, to be his measure and his norm'. The young occultist and Nationalist was beginning to discover his own notion of the poet's role through an idealised version of his nation's past, and, with this discovery, went his reading of the four great surviving cycles of bardic sagas. Of these, the Mythological Cycle offered an account of waves of invaders culminating in the Danaans, whose four treasures – the Lin Fail or coronation stone, an inexhaustible cauldron, a magic sword and a spear – were to enter deeply into Yeats's own mythology. The Ulster or Red Branch cycle contained the great masterpiece of this literature, *The Cattle Raid of Cooley*, whose hero Cuchulain became a symbol of heroic resistance not just for Yeats himself but for the whole Irish people. Finally, the King and Fenian cycles mingled history with myth and offered a view of a Celtic civilisation passionately involved with the arts, warfare, law and human wisdom.

For Yeats, these great surviving cycles of bardic sagas were 'a wild anarchy of legends' full of dreams and beautiful shadows, heroes and women as lovely as the desolate and queenly Deirdre. He described these works as murmuring with the sound of lamentation like a dark sea, and he thought that through them all there throbbed one impulse: 'the persistence of Celtic passion'. Here was a poetry of the greatest cultural and political significance, for Yeats claimed that such legends were the mothers of nations and that it was the duty of every Irish reader to study them deeply 'for in them is the Celtic heart'. Here was the imaginative world that could answer to his needs. 'Ireland fierce and militant', he wrote, 'is Ireland poetic, passionate, remembering, idyllic, fanciful, and always patriotic.'

In thus allying the literature of a golden age with a romantic and poetic desire for national identity, Yeats was not simply following O'Leary's ideas but making his own contribution to a European-wide movement. Culture and politics were merging in a powerful and often provocative way. Across Europe, Poles, Hungarians, Serbs and Croats to the east, Finns to the north, and Basques and Catalans in the south all sought – as did the inhabitants of such divided states as Italy – a sense of ethnic renewal and communal assertion. Ireland in this was no exception, for, quite as profoundly as class, gender or religion, national identity was now becoming a form of collective consciousness which drew to itself (as it still does) a complex of aspirations to freedom and self-expression. What Yeats was discovering in O'Leary's library was the call of a homeland where shared myths, shared history and a shared culture could give a sense of solidity and renewal – a sense of belonging to an albeit repressed community possessed of a glorious if largely unrecognised past which might yet lead to an equally glorious future.

Conversations at the Contemporary Club also bore in on Yeats the necessity for Home Rule and finding an answer to what he was now ready to call the more than dubious moral achievements of 'British civilisation'. That civilisation continued everywhere to disparage native Irish life. On the crudest level this led to such popular racism as Tenniel's cartoon of 'The Irish Frankenstein', a creature of hideous and mindless violence supposedly fabricated by Parnell. Even among such allegedly informed people as the dons of Trinity College, the great inheritance of Irish literature was openly condemned, and in such a situation Yeats felt ever more keenly a profound need for ethnic self-renewal, for the restoration of collective and personal faith through Irish national regeneration.

He also believed that those who threatened this should be exposed, and the death in August 1886 of the historian Sir Samuel Ferguson roused Yeats to his first prose publications. The leading obituaries had claimed Ferguson for Britain. Yeats, knowing the man had devoted his life to Celtic interests, was determined to claim him for Ireland. At the close of the year he published in the *Dublin University Review* an expanded version of an earlier essay on Ferguson's poetry. This was Yeats's first major statement of his literary ideas and in it he declared himself a man who stood for Irish epic literature, for 'fatherland and song'.[21] Ferguson himself was extolled as the greatest poet Ireland had produced because he was the most Celtic. He was the true bard whose 'spirit had sat with the old heroes of his country'. In praising what he thought of as the heroic simplicity of Ferguson's translations especially, Yeats was asserting an Irish poetic ideal over current English practice. The bardic voice was not one weakened (as it is implied the voices of Wordsworth, Tennyson and Arnold had been) by 'tepid emotions and many aims'. In Ferguson's work, such personal perplexity has been ousted by 'noble sorrow and noble joy'.

Why then had Ferguson's poetry not met with the praise Yeats thought its due? With a subtlety greater than his critical judgement, Yeats realised that a proper audience did not yet exist for such works. His own essay was aimed at creating one, at providing 'young men clustered here and there throughout our land' with the grammar of a new and even redemptive enthusiasm. But the essay was also concerned to identify the enemy. He lurks, Yeats suggested, in the complacent comfort of Trinity College. Here, editing and writing on English texts, he is happy to think what his neighbours think and protect his emoluments by praising George Eliot rather than his countrymen. His name is Professor Dowden. JBY's friend, whom the artist himself tolerated for the faults he saw, has here been publicly and rather nastily exposed. The battle for Ireland was in part at least the struggle of the son against the father.

V

Irish Themes

O'Leary meanwhile was determined to encourage his protégé and enable him to set up as a poet and writer for Ireland. To this end he encouraged Yeats to contribute to the *Gael*, the magazine of the strongly nationalist Gaelic Athletic Association, and also fostered his relations with his literary contemporaries. Douglas Hyde, for example, had been born in Yeats's Sligo but moved when seven to County Roscommon. Here, unlike Yeats himself, he had learned to speak Irish from the local people and was now writing poems in the Irish language. Keeping Gaelic as a living tongue was a major aim of Hyde's life, and partly to this end he immersed himself in Irish folklore. This was an interest both he and Yeats were to share, but Hyde's advocating a vernacular Irish literature and Yeats's necessary insistence on English suggests what was later to become an important rift.

Another friend was the poet Katharine Tynan. She was nearly five years older than Yeats, a plain, lively and affectionate woman with red-gold hair who, like Yeats himself, suffered from short sight. Her first volume of poems had been sufficiently well received to run to a second edition, but under the influence of O'Leary especially she turned her Catholic muse to Irish themes and was now at work on a volume called *Shamrocks*. A friendship developed between the two young people which Yeats was to value highly, and, if poetry was one bond between them, an interest in the supernatural was another.

Together they attended a Dublin seance. The medium 'fell asleep sitting upright in his chair', the lights were turned out, and Yeats experienced a twitching in his shoulders and hands.[22] When this became violent he managed to stop it and he sat motionless for a while until his whole body suddenly moved with the violence of an 'unrolled watch-spring' and he was thrown back against the wall. He returned to sit at the table, but the medium, who was now in a state of trance, stood up and began walking round the room and pushing with his hands as though he was trying to remove an obstacle. Yeats too felt he was in the grip of the supernatural. He tried to pray, but because he could not remember any prayers he was obliged to repeat the opening lines of *Paradise Lost*. 'Then I saw shapes faintly appearing in the darkness, and thought "They are spirits"; but they were only the spiritualists and my friend at her prayers.' Yeats was clearly disturbed by the experience, and it would be many years before he again attended a seance and began to make spiritualism the centre of his occult life.

While Katharine Tynan had also been frightened by her experiences of the occult, she was clearly attracted to Yeats as a youth who was 'so beautiful to look at, with his dark face, its touch of vivid colouring, the night-black hair, the eager dark eyes'. Yeats for his part was to fear that she was falling in love with him. He was probably unaware that Katharine Tynan actually found aspects of his personality so exasperating that she would sometimes invent imaginary errands for him to go on when she wished him out of her way. She also had to accept such unexpected arrivals as the time when Yeats appeared at her father's house wet through from a snowstorm and needing food and warmth. Katharine Tynan was, however, a figure in whom Yeats could confide and from whom he could expect a sympathetic hearing for the difficulties and delights of his vocation.

For literature was now becoming firmly established as Yeats's major preoccupation. He left the Metropolitan School of Art in April 1886 and in October, *Mosada*, his first publication in volume form, was issued with a frontispiece portrait by his father. The book's commercial and critical success was inconsiderable (the text was offset from the *Dublin University Review* for what was probably a run of less than one hundred volumes) and JBY gave many copies away. Father Matthew Russell, editor of the *Irish Monthly*, where, along with the *Irish Fireside*, Yeats published some of his earliest work, hailed the appearance of 'the voice of a new singer of Erin, who will take a high place among the world's future singers', but others were less enthusiastic. One of the recipients of a copy of Yeats's work was the English Jesuit priest Gerard Manley Hopkins, who was unimpressed. 'This *Mosada* I cannot think highly of,' he wrote. 'It was a strained and unworkable allegory about a young man and a sphinx on a rock in the sea (how did they get there? what did they eat? and so on). People think such criticisms very prosaic; but commonsense is never out of place anywhere.'[23]

But Yeats himself had already begun to grow out of such work. The exotic locations of his early verses had started to be replaced by Irish settings and Irish themes. A political poem called 'The Two Titans' shows those traits of the strained and improbable Hopkins was quick to notice, but now, as Arcady and India gave way to Ireland under O'Leary and O'Grady's influence, so Yeats was beginning to discover how the myths and folksong of his native land could be turned to his purposes. As he declared near the end of his life: 'because of the talk of these men, and the books the one lent and the other wrote, I turned my back on foreign themes [and] decided the race was more important than the individual'. Now, in 'The Madness of King Goll', the tale of an Irish hero offered Yeats the possibility of exploring an hallucinatory combination of refinement and insanity. When the work was published in *The Leisure Hour*, the first English magazine to print Yeats, it was accompanied by a fine illustration of his father's which shows the bearded poet himself as the hero tearing at the strings of his harp as madness descends on him.

'Down by the Salley Gardens' shows a wholly antithetical approach. Reconstructed from a memory of an old woman singing in Sligo, the artifice of the age of Swinburne gives way to a timeless simplicity:

> In a field by the river my love and I did stand,
> And on my leaning shoulder she laid her snow-white hand.
> She bid me take life easy, as the grass grows on the weirs;
> But I was young and foolish, and now am full of tears.[24]

Here once again was an expression of Yeats's romantic nationalism, a recreation of the ancient arts of poetry 'as they were understood when they moved a whole people and not a few people who have grown up in a leisured class and made this understanding their business'. Indeed, so perfectly do these lines capture the manner of authentic folksong that they entered the traditional repertoire and, by 1935, the Free State Army was marching to a tune composed to them. Now, however, as Gladstone's Home Rule Bill was narrowly defeated and English dominance over Irish affairs seemed ever more assured, the young man who had abandoned all for literature began his first work of real importance: the Irish and mythological *The Wanderings of Oisin.**

VI
William Morris and Madame Blavatsky

Yeats was to work on this poem from October 1886 to November 1887, a year of intense labour and deepening family difficulties. Although JBY had painted a number of excellent portraits in Dublin, he had as always failed to handle his financial affairs in a way that guaranteed him and his family an adequate income. In addition, the sympathetic Uncle Matt, who had for a long time acted as the agent for JBY's properties, died in August 1885. When his successor presented his accounts, it was found that nearly £200 was owed in arrears of rent while there were charges against the estate itself of over twice that sum. Greatly though it hurt him to do so, JBY decided to take advantage of the newly passed Ashbourne Act and allow his tenants to purchase their holdings from public funds. Vainly believing that by realising his capital he would provide himself with an income which he could then augment by work in illustration, JBY moved back to London. His family followed him there in April 1887.

The following month Yeats confessed to Katharine Tynan that he found London 'hateful'. The pleasure of living alone in lodgings quickly palled when he was assailed by headaches, colds and more worrying attacks of nervousness which prevented him doing as much work as he wanted to. When he finally moved into 58 Eardly Crescent, South Kensington, the house JBY had found for his family before going off to paint in Oxford, his depression was made worse. The rooms were dark and dirty, while the noisiness of the area was increased by the regular sound of gunfire issuing from Earl's Court, where Buffalo Bill and his Indians were staging a circus. Then in the late summer, trapped in the close and dismal house, Susan Yeats had a stroke. She was so ill she could not be moved before the end of the year, and since JBY was having little success with selling either his illustrations or his estate, the family was financed partly from Yeats's meagre earnings as a reviewer.

He read, wrote his articles and polished his poems in the Art Library of the South Kensington (now the Victoria and Albert) Museum. The air blowing in through the open windows from the chestnut trees outside made this appear the one pleasant place in a London which was otherwise full of crowds and wretched individuals broken, as Yeats told Katharine Tynan, either by their

---

* Pronounced 'Usheen'.

wealth or by their poverty. The poet, the mystic and the patriot was living once again in the greatest commercial city in the world where a foreign parliament held the reins of his homeland. On 6 May 1887, Yeats went to the House of Commons to hear the Irish MP Timothy Heeley give a defence of the Home Rule Party. Heeley rightly charged that a series of vicious articles in *The Times* on 'Parnellism and Crime' was mere sensationalism designed to boost the newspaper's circulation. The Irish cause, he declared, would endure for ever, and Yeats thought his 'rugged oratory' the most human moment in the whole debate.

But, if London was the seat of alien political power, it was also the place where a young writer could hope to make contacts. By the middle of May 1887 Yeats had met the industrious editor Ernest Rhys, 'a not brilliant but very earnest Welshman', who promised to introduce him to members of the Fellowship of the New Life, a socialist group from whose ranks the Fabian Society would later spring. The most important socialist figure Yeats was to get to know in this period, however, was William Morris.

Yeats had first met Morris at the Contemporary Club, where he had come 'to preach us into Socialism'.[25] The lecture was not sympathetically received but Yeats was impressed by Morris's explanation of declining artistic standards and asked him if he would lecture in Dublin on Irish poetry. Morris told Yeats he would gladly do so except that Dubliners appeared to know too little about it. Now the young people of the Socialist League gathered about Morris in London were trying to remedy the defect. Morris's amanuensis and future son-in-law H. H. Sparling was editing an anthology entitled *Irish Minstrelsy*, and in June 1885 Yeats heard him give a lecture on 'Irish Rebel Songs' at one of Morris's Sunday gatherings. He was afterwards introduced to Sparling's financée and Morris's daughter May, who impressed him with her strange beauty and intelligence, but of Sparling himself he was unsure. He lumped him together with the pallid talents he thought typical of young literary men in London, and he told Katharine Tynan that their existence made him captious. He did not add that he was himself alone, struggling and perhaps jealous of Sparling's position and even of his engagement. Yeats's virginity was becoming a burden to him.

Sparling angered Yeats by the way in which he appeared to fawn on Morris. Yeats himself soon had an opportunity of seeing this since as a talented and ambitious young man he quickly became one of those who joined Morris for supper after the Sunday meetings, sitting 'round a long unpolished and unpainted table of new wood in a room where hung Rossetti's *Pomegranate*, a portrait of Mrs Morris, and where one wall and part of the ceiling were covered by a great Persian carpet'. The company could be a difficult one. May Morris had become engaged to Sparling partly to spite those around her, while Sparling himself eagerly took Morris's opinion as a final word on all subjects. His marriage would not be a success, while that between Morris and his own restless and beautiful wife was notoriously unhappy.

Partly in compensation, an immense quantity of once highly influential poetry flowed from Morris (he was sometimes capable of composing seven hundred lines a day) in which ancient narratives were reclothed in exquisite Pre-Raphaelite draperies. *The Life and Death of Jason* showed this particularly clearly, and it was a young Henry James who accurately defined its appeal. 'To the jaded intellects of the present moment,' James wrote, 'distracted with the strife of creeds and the conflict of theories, it opens a glimpse into a world where they will be called upon neither to choose, to criticise, nor to believe, but simply to feel, to look, and to listen.' Yeats too could at times be beguiled by such soporifics, but it was Morris's next work, the collection of tales he called *The Earthly Paradise*, and, in particular, 'The Lovers of Gudrun', which helped show Yeats how a great heroic story from the northern European Dark Ages could be refashioned into a Victorian narrative. Morris thus provided a model for the work of Celtic revivalism Yeats himself was hoping to create in *The Wanderings of Oisin*.

But Morris, the 'idle singer of an empty day' as he termed himself, the man whose *Earthly Paradise* had inspired Pater to his paean on the aesthetic life, was more than a poetic mentor. Gluttonous at table and occasionally as frighteningly irascible as old William Pollexfen, he was the opposite to the usual image of a Pre-Raphaelite poet and the difference – this living embodiment of the antithetical man – fascinated Yeats. He later wrote how 'William Morris, a happy, busy, most irascible man, described dim colour and pensive emotion, following, beyond any man of his time, an indolent Muse'. But if Yeats was flattered to be part of this company and to be asked to contribute an article he never wrote on the Irish question to Morris's *Commonweal*, he was not uncritical. Socialist conversation was not invariably agreeable to his temperament, nor did he think that such people's work, 'good' though it was, could be his own. Nonetheless, Yeats was for a while a frequent visitor to Morris's Kelmscott House, and he would come to find Morris himself increasingly important to his ideas on the nature of the poet.

Yeats was also a visitor to a very different London house at this time. In May 1887, Madame Blavatsky returned to London and was now living in Upper Norwood.[26] The woman Yeats found there, vast and shapeless in body and perpetually smoking her hand-rolled cigarettes, reminded him of Morris. She was equally unpredictable, equally suffused with immense human energy. These qualities had carried her through a bizarre career and, though Yeats was willing to be impressed, he now knew enough about Madame Blavatsky to be on his guard. His longing for the occult was as always checked by his scepticism.

In 1878, Madame Blavatsky's restless travels had taken her to India where, after years of table-rappings, spiritualism and study of the occult, she and Colonel H. S. Olcott founded the international headquarters of the Theosophical Society. Madame Blavatsky had by then published *Isis Unveiled*, the work she described as a master-key to the mysteries of ancient and modern science and theology. Her Tibetan masters had allegedly given her a comprehensive insight into the religions of the East. Now, in *The Secret Doctrine*, Hindu and Buddhist ideas melted into Hermeticism, neo-Platonism and other European creeds. The late nineteenth century was a period when immense scholarly efforts were put into synthesising the world's spiritual traditions, and Madame Blavatsky's volumes were a part of this.

In fact, Madame Blavatsky's attempts at synthesis were often more apparent than real for, in her exposition of the individual's path to freedom and the state of Nirvana, she drew with oppressive and seemingly random eclecticism on the widest range of sources in the attempt to illustrate the universality of her 'Wisdom Knowledge'. Some of the most profound spiritual traditions lay heterogeneously side by side, fragments of insight in a wilderness of words. Madame Blavatsky taught, however, that treading the Path to wisdom – 'the Great Work' – was a process whereby the inner nature of the individual was developed and transformed. She also believed that the Path was long and arduous, and that traversing it would take many lives. Her system appears a scrupulously demanding one (which was part of its attraction) and it was only when her handyman in India levelled charges concerning her integrity that the Society for Psychical Research despatched an investigator to India.

The investigator found that Madame's occult experiments particularly relied on sliding panels and other trickery, and when Yeats visited her in Upper Norwood he already knew that she had been condemned as 'one of the most accomplished, ingenious, and interesting impostors in history'. This was hardly an auspicious introduction and, while Yeats was kept waiting, he was surprised by the cuckoo in Madame Blavatsky's clock springing out and suddenly calling at him even though 'the weights were off and lying upon the ground'. He too started to look for sliding panels, but Madame Blavatsky called out that the cuckoo often hooted at strangers and that he was not to break it. Was there a spirit in it? Madame Blavatsky did not know.

When Madame herself finally appeared, Yeats was suitably impressed. Her imposing presence drew him, while the aims of her Society, despite its disrepute, seemed to come close to answering his needs. The stout Russian émigrée could offer much to the tall and volatile young Irishman, and the sustaining effects of Madame's teaching were redoubled by her personality. 'She made upon me an impression of generosity and indulgence,' Yeats wrote. Madame Blavatsky was used to having such young men among her 'chelas' and knew how to handle them. Sometimes she could be quite severe. Yeats confessed to her, for example, that he had attended a seance in Dublin, and Madame Blavatsky, who now found spiritualism abhorrent, soundly rebuked him for the error of his ways.

The only other person who might have done this and still retained Yeats's regard was his father, but if Madame Blavatsky had this degree of authority she also had the sort of insight into anxious youths that for a while at least could make them dependent on her. 'I remember how careful she was', Yeats wrote, 'that the young men about her should not overwork. I overheard her saying to some rude strangers who had reproved me for talking too much, "No, no, he is very sensitive."' The image of an over-excited young Yeats is telling, as is Madame Blavatsky's quiet tact. This she was obliged to use more imaginatively on another occasion when Yeats read the Theosophical Society a dull paper which the members received with a certain coldness. Madame Blavatsky called across the room to him and said: 'Give me the manuscript. Now you go back and say your say about it.' Yeats did so with greater success and was always grateful for Madame Blavatsky's intervention.

VII

The Wanderings of Oisin

Yeats was partly drawn to Madame Blavatsky's teaching by its suggestion that the study of myth and folklore might lead to the discovery of long-lost but important secrets. Here was a means of combining the influence of O'Leary with that of the Theosophists, and in August 1887 Yeats returned to Sligo in order to have congenial surroundings in which to complete his mythological and nationalist poem *The Wanderings of Oisin*.

As he was often to do in the future, Yeats stayed first with his uncle George Pollexfen at Rosses Point. The Sligo earth, he wrote to Katharine Tynan, put him in good spirits. 'Down at Sligo one sees the whole world in a day's walk,' he declared. Climbing Ben Bulben, passing the tracks of hare, sheep and deer to see the legendary spot where Dermot died, Yeats could perhaps imagine himself in the setting of the first Book of his work. In this, the Fenian warrior Oisin begins to confess to St Patrick the events that followed his falling in love with the beautiful Nimah. Patrick, the Christian and ascetic, the 'man of croziers', is fashioned by Yeats into a figure wholly subdued to external discipline, to service. His faith circumscribes the limits of his imagination. For him, there are no dreams. His realities are sin and damnation. He extends his chilling rule not just over Nimah, whom he sees as a personification of wickedness, and over Oisin, whom he tries to humble into penitence, but over the whole Irish world. As so often in Yeats's work, figures wrested from the deepest resources of myth have an historical role, a political dimension. As the man who brought Christianity to Ireland, St

Patrick is the figure who led that moment in its history when the age of heroes passed and a weakened, submissive age of discipline ensued.

The meeting between St Patrick and Oisin suggests that turning point and is a confrontation between what Yeats would later call the 'objective man' and objective periods in a country's history, on the one hand, and the heroic, 'antithetical man' and periods of rich cultural achievement, on the other. If St Patrick's world in part suggests contemporary Ireland's plight – 'a small and feeble populace stooping with mattock and spade' – then the Oisin of legend suggests the golden age of its past on which Yeats believed the future could be built. Oisin is the heroic embodiment of the creative ideal, and his meeting with Nimah reveals the conflicts in the mind of the truly antithetical man. So far, Oisin has been content with the active, warrior world of the Fenians. Now the subjective world is opened to him as he meets the embodiment of beauty:

> A pearl-pale, high-born lady, who rode
> On a horse with a bridle of findrinny;
> And like a sunset were her lips,
> A stormy sunset on doomed ships;
> A citron colour gloomed in her hair,
> But down to her feet white vesture flowed
> And with the glimmering crimson glowed
> Of many a figured embroidery;
> And it was bound with a pearl-pale shell
> That wavered like the summer streams,
> As her soft bosom rose and fell.[27]

Yeats was to confess at the end of his life that such an image of aristocratic sexuality, virginal and dangerous, mysterious yet physically present, was created out of his own frustrated desire. This is surely so. But his Celtic enchantress appears in Pre-Raphaelite guise, a seductress from a Rossetti canvas. Like so much in Pre-Raphaelite art, she is also reminiscent of Keats, in particular the innocent yet destructive Lamia who seduces her lover into a fantasy world where pleasure seems sundered from pain. Nimah offers a similar temptation. The three islands to which she takes Oisin appear to provide an unending indulgence in what Yeats regarded as man's three deepest desires. As he told Katharine Tynan in February 1889: 'there are three incompatible things which man is always seeking – infinite feeling, infinite battle, infinite repose – hence the three islands'.

As Oisin succumbs to these desires, so the warrior discovers a subjective side to his being which seeks vision and creativity – the paradise of the first Book of the poem, for example, where beautiful boys and girls move for ever through the rose thicket by the sea in a dance of joy. One of Yeats's abiding images of life and art is here beautifully presented in the manner of a long and sensuous Burne-Jones dream. But it is only a dream and, as twice more in the poem, its satiety points to the paralysis of fantasy. A broken lance floats by and Oisin recalls that he is a Fenian and a man: 'Remembrance, lifting her leanness, keened in the gates of my heart.' The visionary longs once more for the world of men, for that human state which knows it must die. But Yeats's dying Oisin, the antithetical man, will not accept St Patrick's proscriptions, old and broken though he is. In the pride and glory of his spirit, he refuses to go down in penitence to a Christian hell. At the moment of his death, Oisin asserts a fierce and even tragic joy as he resolves to 'dwell in the house of the Fenians, be they in flames or at feast'. A specifically Christian form of religious culture is shown to have failed, and the social desolation it has wrought is particularly clear in the poem. New principles, new mythologies, new energies must replace it and, by searching the heroic past for these, Yeats suggests that for his nineteenth-century audience life-giving forces lie not in the contemporary world but in the values of a shared past, a past that is imagined as being at once heroic and subjective, a world of combat and reverie.

And it is the nature of the reverie that most clearly shows Yeats's debt to current literature. Reviewing the poem, Oscar Wilde praised its 'nobility of treatment and nobility of subject matter, delicacy of poetic instinct, and richness of imaginative resources'. He pointed out, nonetheless, the as yet immature ambition in a poet set on '"out-glittering" Keats'.[28] Tennyson too, the Tennyson of 'The Lotus-Eaters' especially, contributed to the narcotic sibilance of many passages, just as, in the last Book, the long rhythmic lines are clearly an attempt to challenge the metrics of Swinburne. But it is the Pre-Raphaelites above all who supply the bulk of the work's English debts: its pictorial surface, its moments of exquisite detail and the unworldly lassitude which subdues consciousness without ever becoming vision. Nonetheless, in the characters of Oisin, St Patrick and Nimah, the archetypal figures of Yeats's imagination were beginning to assemble. He believed that 'our intellects at twenty contain all the truth we shall ever find', and the antithetical hero, the saint and the woman of mysterious and threatening beauty embody areas of experience to which Yeats was to return over a lifetime.

3

The Troubling of his Life
(1888–1891)

I
Antithetical Masters

Yeats returned to London on 26 January 1888. The city oppressed him as always. Writing to Katharine Tynan, he imagined his letter being carried across the fields in a postman's basket and delivered to her house in the countryside round Dublin. He wished he was folded up with it. But, in sailing from Ireland, Yeats had once again put native, close-knit communities behind him. Now he was more than ever obliged to face the fact that London was a swelling population of strangers (it would double its size in forty years to reach more than six million by the turn of the century). In its 'horrible numerosity',[1] it was the unchallenged focus of English national culture, the centre of commerce and communication, the city from whence came the newspapers, journals and books which formed the ideas of the nation at large and the vast hinterland of the Empire that supported it. But sometimes only ugliness stood out. Certain old women's faces filled Yeats with horror as they passed by, fat and blotched above double chins and coarsened by excess. In Dublin, such figures belonged to romance. In 'abhorred London' they were part of teeming, material reality.

And the very vastness of the crowd brought with it its own danger. Impersonal and anonymous, enforcing consensus at the expense of individuality, the crowd was indifferent to the intellectual, apparently rendering powerless and even futile serious imaginative effort. In time, Yeats was to see it as a principal enemy. Even now a disorientating isolation closed ever more tightly round him, and it was amid such an atmosphere that he would hunt out those little groups that sought the imaginative life in art, marginal politics or occult mystery.

One such group offering at least a partial solace was the community gathered in Bedford Park. JBY had resolved to move his family back there once Susan returned from a stay in the house of a sister, where she had suffered a second stroke. She and Lily moved into 3 Blenheim Road on 13 April, a few days after the rest of the family. Here Susan would live out her remaining years as a sometimes difficult invalid, slowly moving to the edges of her existence and passing her time reading or feeding the birds on the windowsill. The rest of the family meanwhile were in their own ways variously discontented. Something had clouded Yeats's boyhood memories of Bedford Park, dulled his recollection of De Morgan tiles, peacock-blue doors and the pomegranate patterns on the Morris fabrics. Such village characters as JBY's old friend Todhunter and a new acquaintance, York Powell, the bluff Oxford professor of history, provided stimulus. There was much lively talk in Bedford Park, especially at the local club, the Calumet, while conversation at home also maintained an energetic level, Lollie writing of JBY's discussions with his son that 'sometimes they raise their voices so that a stranger might fancy they were both in a rage. Not at all. It is only their way of arguing. I suppose it is because they are natives of the Emerald Isle.'[2] Yeats himself, however, needing to escape, often walked the mile or so to William Morris's house by the river in Hammersmith, an intense young man and, as he described himself in his *Autobiographies*, as volatile as 'an old-fashioned brass cannon full of shot'.

At Kelmscott House, and despite his shyness and the unattractive aggression with which he sought to hide this, Yeats met craftsmen such as Walter Crane and Emery Walker, along with political figures such as H. M. Hyndman of the Social Democratic Foundation, and the gentle, scholarly anarchist Prince Kropotkin, who told him in an influential conversation that the French Revolution had swept away ancient peasant customs and so left the people at the mercy of capitalism. Bernard Shaw was also a visitor. An obscure man for the moment, still writing novels rather than plays, Shaw was drawn to Morris as a naturally aristocratic figure who, with his developed sense of life, could help further Shaw's aim of using art in the service of socialism. Yeats harboured ambiguous feelings towards his fellow Irishman, admiring him for his malice but mistrusting him for his antipathy to romance. He told Katharine Tynan that Shaw's stories were as good as everyone said they were, but wondered if his wit showed a mind somewhat 'wanting in depth'. Neither Shaw nor Yeats himself, however, was excused the down-to-earth views of the working men who came to Morris's Sundays. One of them once told Yeats he had talked more nonsense in an evening than the man had heard in the whole of his life. Thirty years later, the rebuke still rankled.

Some of these young socialists planned a tour to France and arranged to take French lessons in Morris's coach-house. Yeats joined them and, for a while, was an ideal pupil. Clearly proud of himself, he told his father about his progress and JBY insisted that Willie get his sisters admitted. Yeats was resentful. He feared Lily and Lollie might see that he was not quite the 'model student' he claimed to be and resented this family intrusion into what he needed as his own territory. JBY insisted, however, the girls were admitted, and Lollie watched with sisterly amusement as Yeats stumbled over pronunciations he invariably got wrong. Willie himself soon left the class, but Lily stayed on at Kelmscott House and became, under May Morris's acid direction, a skilled embroideress and a welcome breadwinner for her family.*

JBY also obtruded in another way on Yeats's involvement with Morris. Once Yeats had enjoyed reading his father's copy of *The Earthly Paradise* and, to a lesser extent, *The Defence of Guenevere*. He thought *The Man Who Never Laughed Again* the most wonderful of tales until JBY accused him of preferring Morris to Keats and his pleasure was spoiled. Carping gradually took the place of delight, and eventually Yeats ceased to read Morris's verse widely. Now, however, as he began to know the man better, it was less Morris's poetry that influenced him than his personality and the form his resistance took to nineteenth-century materialism. Here was a man who understood Yeats's horror amid the London crowds, who taught him to see the vulgarity their wealth produced, and to understand how their commercial drives sundered class from class, so dividing the nation.

When Yeats asked Morris who had led him to Marx and socialism, Morris characteristically replied: 'O, Ruskin and Carlyle, but somebody should have been beside Carlyle and punched his head every five minutes.'[3] Differences of opinion apart, the great Victorian prophets exposed Morris to the fact that England's unprecedented wealth had brought poverty and exploitation to the vast crowds thronging the workshop of the world. To the great majority of people, socialism meant either the Paris Commune or anarchism and nihilist bombings. To Morris it meant education, manners and breeding fostered independently of the wealth of a person's parents. Morris believed that no one was to have money except as wages for work done. There should also be adequate leisure and a science devoted to inventing machinery that eliminated the soul-destroying ignominy of 'unmitigated slavish toil'. It would then be possible for the craftsman to produce genuinely wholesome and modest work rather than the sordid vulgarity that characterised much Victorian mass production. As Morris himself declared: 'what I mean by Socialism is a condition of society in which there should be neither rich nor poor, neither master nor master's

---

* Lollie described 8 December 1888, when Lily brought home her first pay packet of ten shillings, as 'a red letter day'. Her earnings rose rapidly to seventeen shillings a week by the start of the new year. Lily rapidly became an extremely competent needlewoman and was eventually employed on embroidering the famous curtains for Morris's bed at Kelmscott Manor. However, virtually all she earned was poured into the 'swalley-hole', as the Yeats family called their debts. It is suggestive that in January 1889 she gave over five shillings for a carpet in Yeats's study, which Lollie thought 'a great improvement'.

man, neither idle nor overworked, neither brain-sick brain workers, nor heart-sick hand workers'.4

Morris's concern about the destruction of a wholesome life was a cause for anger that Yeats could share. Morris himself had once believed that only a revolution could heal the damage. Writing to a friend in 1885, he rejoiced at the thought that a sick civilisation was doomed and that barbarism would flood the world, bringing with it 'real feelings and passions'. Morris himself, however, was now tempering his ideas. He had recently experienced the horrors of Bloody Sunday, 13 November 1887, when a vast crowd of people converging on Trafalgar Square to protest, among other things, against the arrest of an Irish MP had been roughly dispersed by the police. Social insurrection would clearly not prevail. The revolution was not at hand and, as the Social Democratic League floundered towards acrimony, Morris's own dreams of how the world might be were set down in a series of prose romances beginning with *News from Nowhere*.

These were among the few books Yeats himself wished might never end. In them he found a dream of natural happiness, of rest and of beautiful things created without strain. The prose romances, Yeats believed, offered a vision of the natural world in its perfect form, free from morbid fancies and the greed and materialism of modern man. Here was a life of bounty and acceptance, of loose-limbed, uncomplex men and women at one with the abundance of the fresh well and the green tree. In imagination at least the blight of contemporary materialism had been overcome and the vision was to have a lasting influence over him. It was to work its way into Yeats's developing nationalism as he began to imagine an Ireland where 'the people live according to a tradition of life that existed before commercialism, and the vulgarity founded upon it'. It was also to reappear in some of the most euphoric images in his later poetry.

Yeats remained intrigued that so pacific a vision came from a man so 'extremely irascible' that he once threw a badly baked Christmas pudding out of the window. Here indeed was the antithetical man of Yeats's mature philosophy, a man of immense energy who nonetheless called himself 'the idle singer of an empty day'. What particularly fascinated Yeats was the way Morris himself seemed unaware of the paradox and hence appeared content. Yeats was coming to see him as the one modern writer who could combine his antithetical roles without self-doubt. He was a man in unity with himself, 'the happiest of poets'. Yeats often claimed that Morris was the one figure with whom he would willingly exchange his own existence, and he remained for him always his 'chief of men'.5

But Yeats did not see the vision in the prose romances develop at first hand, for he ceased going to Kelmscott House. At one of the Sunday debates, a fierce row broke out between Yeats and one of the working men over the speed with which the revolution would come. Yeats, arguing 'with all the arrogance of raging youth', believed it would advance with astronomical slowness and that the required change of heart could be effected only by religion. Religion, however, was anathema in these atheistic circles. Morris rang his chairman's bell and rang it again before Yeats would sit down. He gently told him over supper that he had done this not to silence him but to close a debate in which the young man was not being understood. He also intimated that the necessary change of heart might come more quickly than Yeats supposed.

An insulted Yeats claimed he never returned to Kelmscott House, although he was to see Morris at least once more. Just before their parting, he left a copy of *The Wanderings of Oisin* in Hammersmith and, meeting Morris by chance in Holborn, the older man praised the volume as 'my sort of poetry' and added that he would review it in the *Commonweal*. Yeats believed that Morris would have said more had he not just then caught sight of a new and ugly cast-iron lamp post. Here was a symbol of the commercial society Morris had spent his life fighting and he proceeded to wave his umbrella at it in a frenzy. The incident shows Morris as both poet and activist, dreamer and warrior. Yeats's ideal of the antithetical man again stands revealed.

Morris was not the only influence on Yeats at this time. A second and very different man he regularly visited was the journalist and versifier W. E. Henley. Henley had led a life of chronic illness. In 1865 he had had to endure the amputation of his left leg. He then spent two more years in hospital for the treatment of a tubercular infection in his remaining foot. After a period working as an editor, Henley returned to freelance journalism, and there now gathered at his house in Richmond a group of young literary men he referred to as his 'lads' and Max Beerbohm (who was not one of them) called the 'Henley Regatta'. They were drawn partly by the fascination of Henley's robust and domineering personality. He could also get them work on such papers as the *National Observer*, for which Yeats wrote his 'first good lyrics and tolerable essays'.[6]

Yeats admired the force rather than the content of Henley's opinions. He felt that his personality was the antithesis of his maimed body. With his powerful head, disordered hair and steady eyes, Henley seemed to Yeats like a great actor 'pressed and pummelled' into readiness for a role life never gave him the opportunity to play. Power seemed to flow from his crippled body and to search subconsciously for conflict. Afflicted himself, Henley attacked anything that seemed to smack of weakness or self-indulgence. He was strongly opposed to the Pre-Raphaelites and Ruskin, for example, and he would later encourage virulent attacks on what he saw as *fin de siècle* decadence. Yeats believed it was in these flashes of anger that the real man stood revealed. He wrote of Henley that 'half his opinions were the contrivance of a consciousness that sought always to bring life to the dramatic crisis and expression to that point of artifice where the true self could find its tongue'.

Here was an influence based on opposition. 'I disagreed with him about everything,' Yeats wrote of Henley in his *Autobiographies*, 'but I admired him beyond words.' On his Sunday evening visits to Henley's house, feasting from his table of cold meats, Yeats heard how to talk for victory. He also realised how Henley got the best out of his 'lads' and saw that they accepted him as the judge of their work since he was a man whose opinion could be neither softened nor deflected. Although he did not care for Henley's verse, Yeats allowed him to correct his lyrics. He did not always accept the changes made as final, but was comforted by the knowledge that Henley also rewrote Kipling, and was gratified by such moments of generosity as when Henley declared of one of Yeats's early pieces: 'See what a fine thing has been written by one of my lads.'

When Yeats first met Henley in 1888 the older man had been recently converted, partly under the influence of Kipling, to the doctrines of Imperialism. Soon Henley was to found what Yeats called 'the declamatory school of imperialist journalism' and, as a consequence, and despite an admiration for Gaelic culture, he was strongly opposed to Irish Home Rule. As he told Yeats: 'They say Ireland is not fit for self-government, but that is nonsense. It is as fit as any other European country, but we cannot grant it.' It was Henley's view that the pride and prestige of the imperial crown would be seriously compromised if England ever acceded to Irish Home Rule. Others of his visitors rejected such ideas. The Empire had brought immense riches to some but: 'With all your pomp and wealth and art you don't know how to live – you don't even know that.'[7] This is the less familiar voice of Oscar Wilde.

Yeats was immediately attracted to Wilde. He felt that the wit and insight of his conversation were given their force by the perfect rounding of his sentences. Here, Yeats believed, was the triumph of artifice over nature. Despite the fact that Wilde may have seemed at this time to be lying fallow (his American tour was behind him and the great comedies were still to come) Yeats himself reckoned this was his most contented period, and Wilde was, besides, preparing those essays that would shape the future direction of the Aesthetic Movement.

Conversation turned to Pater's *Studies in the History of the Renaissance*. 'It is my golden book,' Wilde declared, 'I never travel anywhere without it; but it is the very flower of decadence: the last trumpet should have sounded the moment it was written.'[8] Some dull guest volunteered a question. 'Would you not have given us time to read it?' 'O no,' was the retort, 'there would have been plenty of time afterwards – in either world.' There was a deft frivolity in this that reminded Yeats of a renaissance *magnifico*, but it was the sort of comment that displeased Henley. Although the two men found each other mutually intriguing, Wilde described the basis of literary friendship as 'mixing the poisoned bowl', and Henley was already gathering the hemlock that would be offered to Wilde at the time of his trials.

But Wilde's excessive praise of Pater hints at the idea that he already felt the need to go beyond him. Pater's mannered suggestions of the aesthetic life seemed pallid now, vulnerable to Wilde's greater vitality as well as being an inhibition on the energies newly released by the discovery of his particular type of socialism and the frank acceptance of his homosexuality. Reviewing a book by Edward Carpenter, a man who had found his own way of combining these needs, Wilde wrote that 'to make men Socialists is nothing, but to make Socialists human is a great thing'. He would build an aesthetic around such ideas and, looking for converts, he asked to his house a series of clever young men he could dazzle and even seduce by the daring of his intellect. Robby Ross, André Raffallovich, Richard Le Gallienne and Bernard Berenson all visited and, at the close of 1888, Yeats was invited for Christmas Day.

The house in Tite Street impressed him even while he mistrusted it. Back in Dublin, Wilde's parents were notorious for an haut-bourgeois dirtiness, and wits declared that the fingernails of the famous eye surgeon were so black because Sir William Wilde had scratched himself. In the son's house, however, everything was decorous and modern. There was no hint of Pre-Raphaelitism. Peacock blue had been replaced by Whistler whites. White panels in the drawing room had Whistler etchings let into them, while the whites in the dining room were contrasted to a diamond-shaped red tablecloth on which stood a terracotta statuette lit by a red-shaded lamp. Searching again for the antithetical man, Yeats wrote that Wilde 'perpetually performed a play which was in all things the opposite of all that he had known in childhood and early youth'. But he also thought the house a little too perfect and felt himself a slightly ungainly intruder there. When he was asked to tell Wilde's son a fairy story, the child ran screaming from the room. When, now or on another occasion, Yeats turned up in shoes of fashionably unblackened leather, Wilde observed them with the sort of surprised disapproval that permanently alters a young man's self-esteem.

After their dinner, and perhaps as a form of Christmas present, Wilde read to Yeats from the proofs of *The Decay of Lying*. Here was a work designed to take the breath away from artistic twenty-year-olds. Wilde began by disparaging Victorian realism, the belief that literature justified itself by the close imitation of surface appearance. The true uses of the imagination are wholly different, and in presenting them *The Decay of Lying* opened up areas of argument and discovery of the greatest importance to the modern movement in literature and to Yeats in particular. Poetry is now seen as having broken away from the old idea of the poet engaging in a dialogue with his audience. Art has nothing to do with teaching or representing the material world. As a consequence,

'Art finds her own perfection within, and not outside of, herself. She is not to be judged by any external standard of resemblance.' Art does not express the age in which it is created, nor should it try to. Consequently, 'the two things that every artist should avoid are modernity of form and modernity of subject-matter'. An ideal might be the timeless and all but disembodied art of Byzantium where, in his maturity, Yeats was to place his Golden Bird, or the rich and lofty language of Elizabethan drama, far removed as it is from the speech of everyday life.

To these ideals Yeats would add the ancient traditions of Gaelic culture, a concern with the Celtic imagination Wilde, as a fellow Irishman, shared. As he was to write in *The Critic as Artist*:

> we have got rid of what was bad. We now have to make what is beautiful. And though the mission of the aesthetic movement is to lure people to contemplate, not to lead them to create, yet, as the creative instinct is strong in the Celt, and it is the Celt who leads in art, there is no reason why in future years this strange Renaissance should not become almost as mighty in its way as that new birth of Art that woke many centuries ago in the cities of Italy.

This was to be an ambition Yeats himself was central in realising but, in addition to disparaging realism and insisting on the autonomy of creation, Wilde urged a third thesis: the belief that life imitates art. 'Things are because we see them, and what we see, and how we see it, depends on the Arts that have influenced us.' We recognise the beauty of the sunset because Turner has shown it to us. We feel our various moods because literature has invented them. 'Schopenhauer has analysed the pessimism that characterises modern thought, but Hamlet invented it. The world has become sad because a puppet was once melancholy.' At this point Yeats interrupted. Why had Wilde written 'melancholy' rather than repeating 'sad'? A surprised Wilde said he wanted a full sound at the close of the sentence, but to Yeats this seemed an example of the 'vague impressiveness' he thought marred Wilde's prose.

But, for all his refusal to be over-awed, Yeats was greatly influenced by Wilde. The belief that art creates life moved to the centre of his poetic faith, as did the notion that the poet is not tied to material reality but should follow the direction his work suggests to him. This would almost certainly mean leaving the crowd behind and, as Wilde showed in *The Soul of Man under Socialism*, evolving an elite individuality. The general run of people would have to try and catch up if they could. The modern poet, pursuing the purposes given to him by his craft and indifferent to wide public acclaim, is here being made. Deliberate and conscious artifice is the keynote, and Wilde showed Yeats how this applied to both the artist and his work.

'Man is least himself when he talks in his own person,' he declared in
The Critic as Artist, adding in a phrase of the greatest significance to the
development of Yeats's own thought: 'give him a mask, and he will tell you
the truth'.

II

Remembering Innisfree

Wilde also told Yeats that he should not try and make a living by writing
up literary tittle-tattle for the newspapers. This was not a fit occupation for
a gentleman. He complied, even though such pieces 'give me very little
trouble and are fairly profitable'. He had received £7 for work published
in the *Leisure Hour*, but the question of earning an income exercised him
nonetheless. 'I was greatly troubled because I was making no money,' he
wrote. 'I wanted to do something that would bring in money at once, for
my people were poor and I saw my father sometimes sitting over the fire in
great gloom, and yet I had no money-making faculty.'[9] Writing to Katharine
Tynan on 12 February 1888, he expressed the hope that regular work would
bring him peace of mind, 'but Papa sees all kinds of injury to me in it'. He
wondered if losing his mental liberty to routine would be harmful, and JBY
was relieved when he decided not to take a post on the Unionist *Manchester
Courier* recommended to him by York Powell. Besides, Yeats himself did
not want to become a miscellaneous writer subduing his mind to other
men's truths. Ernest Rhys's offer of editing a book called *Fairy and Folk
Tales of the Irish Peasantry*, however, poorly paid though the work would
be, seemed ideally to combine Yeats's Irish and occult interests. He would
also be working on a living mythological tradition that could influence his
poetry.

To compile the book Yeats read extensively in the field, studying a
wide range of translations and scholarly interpreters. But the historical and
philological aspects of the subject were of less interest to him than its intrinsic
imaginative appeal, and the belief that Irish folklore preserved remnants of
ancient and secret doctrines once known to all peoples. This was, he believed,
a wisdom desperately needed in the modern world, and he laboured hard
to present it. That *Fairy and Folk Tales of the Irish Peasantry* was no hastily
produced anthology is suggested by the range of Yeats's sources and the care
he gave to identifying the different types of fairy, a taxonomy still respected
by folklorists today.

His own preference was for the more extravagant folktale – Teig O'Kane
surrounded by ghosts while trying to bury a corpse presented by the fairies
was a special favourite – but it is also clear that he edited his material to ensure

directness and pace. He wanted to present a world that was imaginatively beguiling, serious and spiritual. Here was not, as the British often thought, a culture to be laughed at or condescended to. It was dignified, melancholy and, on occasions, tragic. Above all, it was timeless and profoundly satisfying. As Yeats himself wrote:

> Here at last is a universe where all is large and intense enough to almost satisfy the emotions of man. Certainly such stories are not a criticism of life but rather an extension, thereby much more closely resembling Homer than that last phase of 'the improving book', a drama by Henrik Ibsen. They are an existence and not a thought, and make our world of tea-tables seem but a shabby penumbra.

In Irish folklore was an inherited subject matter far removed from modern materialism and the realistic literature that followed in its wake. Working in the heart of London, Yeats could reveal a magical world of great antiquity which not only offered far more than the contemporary sterility about him but which allowed him to exalt his own nation and compare its imaginative life to the ancients. To support these views, Yeats was beginning to construct an ideological system he hoped would combine his literary, spiritual and nationalist interests. He was hoping to forge that unity he would spend a lifetime elaborating. He wanted a literature which, turning its back on the 'impurities' he found in the work of such Victorian poets as Tennyson, Browning and Arnold, those 'curiosities about politics, about science, about history, about religion', would be a 'pure work', something 'half-anonymous' like the Border Ballads or the medieval Arthurian romances.[10] This search for something at once integrated and impersonal was in part a reaction to what he thought of as the hideously fractured state of contemporary culture, his conviction that the world was now 'but a bundle of fragments'. It was also an attempt to replace such aimless confusion with a literature that expressed a fully rounded and balanced humanity rooted in tradition. 'Nations, races and individual men', he wrote much later, 'are unified by an image, or a bundle of related images, symbolical or evocative of the state of mind which is, of all states of mind not impossible, the most difficult for that man, race or nation; because only the greatest obstacle that can be contemplated without despair rouses the will to full intensity.'

Yeats harked back to an 'age where poet and artist confined themselves gladly to some inherited subject-matter known to the whole people'. He strove after an ideal of a Unity of Culture in which art and literature were cohesive and organic rather than specialised and divisive. He believed that the renaissance especially had shattered this ideal and had fostered what he could not endure, 'an international art picking stories and symbols where it pleased'. Such a process inevitably spoiled individuals and nations alike, for it spoiled the images that gave imaginative cohesion and the urge to the fullest possible expression of unified national consciousness. Perhaps Ireland alone of all the nations of Europe had the spiritual and literary resources that could yet be salvaged for its national redemption. As Yeats wrote in his *Autobiographies*:

> We had in Ireland imaginative stories, which the uneducated classes knew and even sang, and might we not make those stories current among the educated classes, rediscovering for the work's sake what I have called 'the applied arts of literature', the association of literature, that is, with music, speech, and dance; and at last, it might be, so deepen the political passion of the nation that all, artist and poet, craftsman and day-labourer would accept a common design?

As he worked on his first and later anthologies, Yeats's nationalist and spiritual interests were once again being made to coincide.

But poverty and over-work took their toll. Sometimes in the British Museum Library, Yeats felt too delicate to lift the heavy volumes of the catalogue. Money was so short that he would try and save the pennies for his afternoon coffee and roll by making the long journey between the library and Bedford Park on foot. But at home he was again surrounded by straightened circumstances. A diary kept by Lollie from this time shows the family living in something considerably less than genteel poverty. Meat, as always, was obtained on credit. There was often no butter and too little marmalade to go round. If money did come in, it immediately disappeared into paying bills. When guests arrived, desperate strategies had to be resorted to. Todhunter called, for example, and Yeats quietly asked him for the loan of three shillings, slipped out of the house and went to buy tea, sugar, butter and jam so that the visitor could unwittingly eat at his own expense. A few days later, when JBY's tax bill arrived, it was met from his son's slender earnings.

Feelings between father and son were understandably running high. JBY's professional failure was made the more obvious by Yeats's own efforts to establish himself in London literary circles. Not only did JBY fail to sell his paintings, illustrations and occasional short stories, he also miscalculated what he would be paid for the sale of his Irish properties and found he would be left with nothing after his debts had been cleared. His despair ran close to breakdown. Sometimes York Powell could talk him round, but JBY's humiliation had its unpleasant side. Energetic high talk sometimes degenerated into rows with his elder son, and a violent disagreement about Ruskin led to his father 'putting me out of the room' with such fury that he 'broke the glass in a picture with the back of my

74

head'. On another occasion, JBY followed Yeats into the room he shared with Jack and demanded a fight. Yeats disdained to lay a hand on his father, but Jack, who had been woken up by the incident, lost his temper. JBY fled without speaking and Jack turned to his brother and said: 'Mind, not a word till he apologises.' It was some days before the quarrel was made up.

Jack himself was currently studying at art school and, during his vacations, spent much of his time in his beloved Sligo. Lollie called him 'the Baby' because of his sleepy blue eyes, and it is clear that Jack was an attractive young man blessed with far more 'ordinary good nature' than his elder brother, who largely disregarded him. Jack would arrive back from Sligo with shrimps, pickled herring and plums for his needy family, showing the sort of thoughtfulness Yeats himself would not so readily have revealed. This open-handed nature mysteriously coexisted with a reserve that few, even his attentive sister Lily, could penetrate. As she wrote later: 'Willy gives you all that is in his mind, spreads it all out, work, plan, thoughts. Jack keeps all to himself.'[11] He was extremely guarded about work in progress, never allowing people to see it or (despite his considerable literary production) to let others know that he was writing. Jack was also discovering his commercial bent. He offered to sell menus to Lady Gore-Booth at the great Sligo house of Lissadell and, by the end of the decade, was earning nearly £20 a year. Lily was not so happy. Her employer May Morris was a 'she-cat' who, while paying her thirty shillings a week, allowed her no holidays or money when she was ill. Lollie, unable to work until a second servant was found to look after her mother, was, despite her increasing tendency to depressive mania, a busy, observant young woman who read, drew and carefully recorded her family's trials in her diary, noting especially her father's continuing professional humiliations.

By May 1889, however, when the entries in her diary become less regular, Lollie had resolved on pursuing her own career. She attended the Froebel School as an unpaid student teacher, passing her certificates and emerging as a well-trained art teacher, eventually teaching both privately and in a number of institutions such as the Chiswick High School and the Central Foundation Schools. She also developed her own techniques for brushwork painting (partly out of her enthusiasm to see that her pupils got immediate results rather than labouring over a drawing) and eventually published three books on the subject. In such ways, and despite her easily strained and increasingly annoying temperament, Lollie became for many years the family's chief bread-winner, her more irksome qualities somewhat hidden for the moment because 'she was away all day, had her own friends and went away every holiday'.[12]

The situation was a distressing one, even so, and near the end of his life

JBY ruefully described the contribution his daughters especially made to a household he was incapable of supporting himself. He wrote of:

> Lily working all day at the Morrises, and Lollie dashing about giving lectures on picture painting and earning close on 300 pounds a year, and one year more than 300, while both gave all their earnings to the house. And besides all this work, of course, they did the housekeeping, and had to contrive things and see to things for their invalid mother – and all this while quite young girls, and cut off from living like other young ladies of their age and standing. They paid the penalty of having a father who did not earn enough and was besides an Irish landlord.[13]

What JBY was pointing out was how dependent Yeats himself had been on his sisters' hard work and generosity while he was a young man.

For his part, Yeats himself found his father's failure to achieve professional success extremely aggravating. Not only did he have to help support him when he could ill afford it – a situation that was to continue for many years – he had also to endure his father's criticism of the efforts he himself was making. Yeats felt he was trapped in a drifting and hopeless family, and Pollexfen traits of haughty superiority stiffened his resentment. These are particularly clear in a pencil drawing of him made by JBY in about 1888. A besuited Yeats sits upright in a chair reading what may be a galley-proof. The air of aloof concentration, the carefully clipped hair and neat beard, all suggest a volatile superiority, that coldness many were to note throughout his life. His own prospects remained poor and, despite O'Leary's advice and help from Todhunter, who hoped to find him a post in a library, Yeats was still eking out a living as a freelance journalist.

Such poverty, fatigue and anger were compounded with the hatefulness of English life, and at times only Yeats's fantasies could sustain him. He was obliged occasionally to accept the most menial work, going to Oxford for example to copy out rare renaissance texts in the Bodleian for a publisher. He survived for several days on tea and buns, as proud as a prophet living off locusts and wild honey. As he inked over his socks to prevent them peeping too obviously through the holes in his shoes, he planned 'some great gesture' in which the might of his soul would outweigh the world. Oxford itself, however, pleased him, as it was to do periodically throughout his life. Despite his diet, Yeats told Katharine Tynan on 14 August 1889 that he had managed a sixteen-mile walk, 'going to the places in Matthew Arnold's poems'. He claimed that the city and the countryside helped him to understand English poetry better, but he felt a stranger all the same. 'How very unlike Ireland the whole place is – like a foreign land (as it is).'

Back in London, the miles of stone buildings oppressed him as the expression of an immoral materialism, 'and as I walked the streets I used to believe that I could define exactly the bad passion or moral vacancy that had created, after centuries, every detail of architectural ugliness', he recalled in his *Autobiographies*. Yeats often turned to fantasies of escape. Sometimes, to ease his sexual frustration, he imagined 'adventurous love stories with myself for hero'. At other times he tried to stifle his desires by imagining an austere life like Thoreau's to be led in the Sligo countryside. Walking down Fleet Street one day and passing a tinkling little fountain in a shop window, the sound of water recalled to him how in his teens he had dreamed of living on an island in the middle of Lough Gill called Innisfree:

> I will arise and go now, and go to Innisfree,
> And a small cabin build there, of clay and wattles made:
> Nine bean-rows will I have there, a hive for the honey-bee,
> And live alone in the bee-loud glade.[14]

The lyric became, and probably remains, Yeats's most popular poem. Among its early admirers was R. L. Stevenson, who wrote from Samoa to praise a work 'so quaint and airy, simple artful, and eloquent to the heart'.* Yeats would never allow his publishers to use this quotation in their advertising, probably because he himself was soon dissatisfied with the work. He was already concerned that *The Wanderings of Oisin* was 'confused, incoherent, inarticulate'. He felt there were clouds in his details and hated such vagueness and softness. 'The Lake Isle of Innisfree' was an attempt to escape from rhetoric into a more personal sense of rhythm, but Yeats had to admit that 'arise and go' was a conventional archaism and that he did not yet understand – or only occasionally understood – that he would not succeed unless he used nothing but the plainest syntax. Beneath such doubts lay the immense personal cost of leading a fully imaginative life. As so often at this time, Yeats wrote about his problems to Katharine Tynan. He knew he was no mere dilettante, he told her, and confessed that he had put his life into his works. While others appeared to be enjoying themselves, Yeats believed he had 'ground himself down in a mortar' in order to write at all. He felt he stood on the edge of life as an observer and that his poems were merely works of 'longing and complaint' when his aim was 'insight and knowledge'. With a touch of melodrama, he told Katharine Tynan that he had buried his youth and raised over it 'a cairn built not of stones but of clouds'.

---

* The immediate reception of the work was not so enthusiastic. When Yeats had finished drafting it he immediately wanted to recite it to Lily, Lollie and a visiting friend, Helen Acostos. All three women were busy at the time with their art work, and when Yeats finished reading the poem Miss Acostos merely turned to the sisters and said, 'May I have my paintbrush?' She had not even pretended to listen and thus assured a very minor immortality by missing out on a memorable moment in the history of English-language literature.

There is a sense of Yeats's vulnerability in this comment, but, regardless of what he himself later called his 'incredible timidity', his ambitious nature would not allow him to succumb. Despite his shyness, he sought to influence and organise, to explore the antitheses of his being. Irish literature again gave him the opportunity, and O'Leary offered tireless support. While his protégé was in London, O'Leary canvassed to raise subscriptions for the publication of *The Wanderings of Oisin*. To secure him some additional income, he used his influence with the American Irish to open for Yeats the pages of the Boston *Pilot* and the *Providence Journal*. Articles which broadly reflected O'Leary's opinions duly appeared. In 1888 a small volume called *Poems and Ballads of Young Ireland* was also issued. O'Leary had inspired it, and the book was dedicated to him. His influence is clear throughout. The Nationalist tradition of Thomas Davis has been replaced by legend and folk material carefully crafted. Among the poets represented were Katharine Tynan, Douglas Hyde and Yeats himself.

O'Leary's influence was also clear in Yeats's work with the Southwark Irish Literary Club. When he first went there in 1888, Yeats immediately caught the attention of at least one of the members, W. P. Ryan, who described him as 'tall, slight, and mystic of the mystical. His face was not so much dreamy as haunting . . . He spoke in a hushed, musical, eerie tone: a tone which had constant suggestions of the faery world.' His work on Irish fairy stories reinforced this impression and when he took these tales as a subject for a talk he made a deep impression. As one of the audience recalled: 'some of us thought we had a tolerable acquaintance with the ways and doings of the Irish fairies, but Yeats's first lecture (of course it was on the good people) was something of a revelation to us – in fact he spoke as one who took his information first hand'.[15] This power to impress on the lecture rostrum, despite his nervousness, was a skill Yeats was to develop until he became one of the great lecturers of his generation.

But the Southwark Literary Club itself was failing in intellectual stamina and, for all his withdrawn appearance, Yeats was determined to revive its fortunes and make it a platform for his beliefs. The necessity for this was more than ever urgent since the hopes of Irish Nationalists were now under threat. Parnell was being destroyed not by the lies printed in *The Times* – those had been exposed as forgeries – but by his own way of life. He had long been having an affair with Kitty O'Shea, the wife of a colleague. At the close of 1889, Captain O'Shea sued for divorce and the social embarrassment ensuing was the wedge that split the party. Inspired by O'Leary, Yeats saw the growing importance of a strong literary culture to support Ireland's sense of identity, but, if O'Leary motivated the changes Yeats would soon make to the Southwark Club, he also arranged for him to meet an ardent young Fenian sympathiser who was to have the most profound influence on his life. Her name was Maud Gonne.

III
'Overpowering Tumult'

Maud Gonne's fame and notoriety preceded her. Yeats already knew something about 'a beautiful girl who had left the Viceregal Court for Dublin nationalism'. Now, because of her political activities, hostile newspapers were publishing pictures of Maud at the time of her presentation at court. It was clear even from these that she was astonishingly beautiful: tall, with abundant light-coloured hair and large, deep, Pre-Raphaelite eyes. For her debut she had worn a dress of white satin that was sewn with iridescent beads and 'flowed like a fountain'. She had danced first with the Duke of Clarence, who trod on her toes and who was busy telling her there were no pretty women in Dublin when his father, the future Edward VII, pushed him aside and led Maud in triumph to the royal dais. It was this woman who had now thrown herself into radical politics and had recently campaigned so vigorously in a safe Conservative seat that the Irish Parliamentary Party candidate had won by a comfortable margin. On 30 January 1889, Maud Gonne took a hansom cab from Belgravia to Blenheim Road. Yeats's sisters watched her arrival from an upstairs window. Lollie later noted with amazement that she kept the cab at their door for the entire time of her stay. Lily observed that, with delicious casualness, Miss Gonne was still in her slippers.

She sat in the Yeatses' parlour smoking her innumerable cigarettes and insisting that Ireland must be freed, if necessary by physical force. JBY was vexed. His politics had always been temperate, and to hear such talk from a young woman was particularly shocking. For all his bohemian life, he had grown up in a world where such people were broadly expected to prepare themselves for a marriage in which they would work to provide the domestic bliss that would nurture their husbands' moral excellence. By the 1890s, however, advanced people were rejecting such constrictions. The New Woman disdained a chaperone and, as a sign of her freedom, often smoked in public. More importantly, she sought equality in the realms of education, money, sex and politics. As Maud told the Irish parliamentarian Tim Harrington: 'I know women can do some things better than men, and men can do some things better than we can; but I don't like this exclusion of women from the National fight, and the fact that they should have to work through back-door influence if they want to get things done.'[16] Yeats eagerly defended Maud to his father. She was like one of the Shelleyan heroines who had stalked his teenage dreams. She stirred the passions that had led him to associate himself with the IRB. She had read and praised the newly published *Wanderings of Oisin*. She was, besides, at twenty-two, 'so beautiful and so young'.

But, if Maud Gonne was the New Woman, she had about her the ancient and timeless beauty which, Yeats felt, belonged 'to famous pictures, to poetry, to some legendary past'. The tresses of her gold-brown hair wound so luxuriously round his imagination that they would be a constant theme in his poetry. Her height too awed him. She was nearly six feet tall, 'a stature so great that she seemed of a divine race' and the grace of her deportment as she moved round the room led him to understand why poets in antiquity would write of a beautiful woman that 'she paces like a goddess'. He thought too of Blake, for he saw that Maud Gonne had that beauty which Blake called the highest because it changes least with time. But, though Maud might belong among the ancient archetypes, the bloom of her complexion held her delicately in the present. It reminded Yeats of the apple blossom which, with a trick of memory, he later thought was arranged in a vase in the room although it was only January. In the coming months, he would sleep with apple blossom on his pillow in the hope of conjuring Maud into his dreams. He was twenty-three years old and, as he later confessed in his posthumously published 'Autobiography', 'the troubling of my life' had begun.*

Maud asked him to dine with her that evening in her rooms in Ebury Street. Yeats went, and the invitation was repeated for the next nine evenings of her London stay. Where the household in Bedford Park was often hungry, in Ebury Street food came with easy abundance. Yeats noticed too – he could hardly avoid it – that Maud's lodgings were filled with her menagerie. She travelled constantly between France, England and Ireland with the animals to which she could give her unconditional love. One of her favourites was her monkey. In Dublin, Sarah Purser painted a portrait of Maud leaning against a column, her arms generously folded round a forlorn and irritable little monkey poised as if about to scratch itself. As Yeats wrote to John O'Leary: 'monkeys are degenerate men'. Maud had called one of hers her Chaperone.

Yeats also told O'Leary that he found Maud not just handsome but clever too, even if her politics were 'a little sensational'. In his 'Autobiography' Yeats was to recall something declamatory and even unscrupulous in her talk. Maud 'spoke of her desire for power, apparently for its own sake, and when we talked of politics spoke much of mere effectiveness, or the mere winning of this or that election'. He was troubled, for so strident a note seemed in harsh counterpoint to what she had told him about her work

---

* The 'Autobiography' was first printed, along with a full version of Yeats's 'Journal' by Denis Donoghue in the volume entitled *Memoirs* (1972). It should be distinguished from the publicly intended volumes of reminiscences brought together in *Autobiographies*.

among the peasantry in Donegal and her hopes of easing the plight of the
Fenian prisoners in Portland jail. To a young man who had hardly known
other women beyond his secluded mother, Maud's abundance, her selfless
generosity, conflicted with something strident, an 'opinionated mind' Yeats
would in time grow to hate. But to her he was an innocent, deeply enamoured
youth with, as Maud recalled, 'dark eyes behind glasses, over which a lock
of dark hair was constantly falling, to be pushed back impatiently by long
sensitive fingers'. His imagination, which intrigued her, knew nothing of the
reality of her life, and it would be years before he truly knew her mind.

How much she told him of herself is less clear than what she held back.
Since the age of four Maud had been looked after by a series of relatives and,
from time to time, by her army father, whom she idolised. He was often away
but, as she grew older and he shared his periods of leave with her in England
or on the Continent, so 'Tommy' moved to the centre of Maud's life. They
roamed across Europe playing up to people's dangerous illusion that they
were a honeymoon couple. Tommy's encouragement strengthened Maud's
unconventional mind and his beliefs became her own. When he was posted
to Dublin as part of the huge force garrisoned there to keep the peace, Maud
had a natural place among the glittering Ascendancy. On visits to the houses
of the great Anglo-Irish families, however, she saw the cruelty of the evictions
forced by landlords as a hapless peasantry were turned out of their hovels
and cattle replaced less profitable crops. Maud was deeply shocked, while
Tommy was beginning to understand that his military role was an abuse of
power. He kept his troops in their barracks when the Land League marched
through Dublin. Eventually, he resigned his commission in order to stand as
a Home Rule candidate. He had given himself to the Irish cause and, when
soon afterwards he suddenly died, a grieving Maud assumed the mantle of
his ideals.

She had not yet reached her majority, and when English relatives discour-
aged her activities she left their house to earn her living as an actress. She
had had some training and performed in amateur theatricals, but when the
hard life of the professional actress wore down her health she was obliged to
convalesce in France. Here, while recuperating, she was introduced to Lucien
Millevoye, a fervent right-wing nationalist whose mistress she became. She
saw their relationship as an 'alliance'. He would help her breach the wall
of silence England had built round Irish affairs by publishing her cause in
the French press. She would assist him in efforts to regain for France the
territories of Alsace-Lorraine. When she came of age and inherited her share
of the family money, Millevoye summoned Maud to Paris prior to sending
her to St Petersburg with documents sewn into her travelling dress. The
couple were to be apart for many months, and for Maud the political rather
than the sexual basis of their alliance was the factor of greater importance.
Millevoye, experienced, opportunistic and married, was useful to her. He

could show her how a rebel might work. As she threw herself into political activity, Maud was having to face her deep-seated fear of physical sex. Tommy had marked her, it seems, more deeply than perhaps she knew.

Maud returned to Dublin where, despite mistrust of her being an English gentlewoman, she braved the Contemporary Club on C. H. Oldham's arm and so conquered that captious crowd that it was not until the early hours that she was escorted home by J. F. Taylor and John O'Leary. Although O'Leary himself disagreed with many of her beliefs he realised what an enormous propaganda influence so beautiful a woman might have. She read his books and attended Young Ireland meetings. Writers and Fenians came to her salon in her rooms in Nassau Street. She asked an enthusiastic Douglas Hyde to teach her Gaelic.

This was much, but it was not enough. Longing for action, Maud went to London, won over Tim Harrington of the National League, and crossed back with his encouragement to Donegal. There, with her cousin May to help and Dagda her great dane to protect them, she found her immense gift for organising and working with people. The distress caused by the evictions stirred her pity. Penniless children, unable to pay their fines, were being imprisoned for cutting a little turf to warm their hovels. Great wooden battering rams slammed at other doors. Helpless old women were carried out on mattresses clutching their rosaries. Young mothers sank exhausted into ditches. Many died of the winter cold. Others Maud sheltered in her hotel room. She doled out soup. She wrote to the press. She raised funds and comforted the hopeless. Among them all, this strange, tireless and exotically beautiful woman became a legend. She was woven into Celtic myth. Maud was now the 'Woman of the Sidhe', that spirit who rode a white horse through Donegal bringing hope to those in abject despair.

Something of this she told Yeats as he sat at her dining table in Ebury Street. Then, as he walked his poor man's way home, it seemed to him that her presence was 'a sound as of a Burmese gong, an overpowering tumult' annihilating in its intensity. Only in the fading resonance could he capture something of what he had experienced. They had talked not only of her efforts for Ireland, but of his too. He had suggested to her how his art was given to Ireland's cause and, seeing *Les Contemplations* on her table, said disingenuously that he wanted to become an Irish Victor Hugo, a declamatory nationalist. Because she had once been an actress, she asked him to write her a play on an Irish theme. She seemed to bring to life all the usable past of his country, and from his work on Irish fairy stories Yeats recalled a tale that seemed wholly appropriate for Maud. It was a simple, powerful study of good and evil. During a famine the Devil ensures that there is no way left to relieve the people's suffering. His followers, disguised as merchants, offer to buy their souls, but a beautiful lady – the spirit of Ireland herself – sells her own soul to ransom theirs. In the play, she would be adored by a young poet. Yeats would call his play *The Countess Cathleen*.

He knew he could offer little else to Maud beyond his poetry. He had seen her generosity and courage, and he had seen too that her mind was without peace. He was in love, he confessed in his 'Autobiography', 'but had not spoken of love and never meant never to speak' of it. With the gravest consequences for his happiness, Maud became the more adorable for being unattainable. Yeats tried to rationalise his feelings into abeyance, asking himself 'what share she could have in the life of a student', a life like his. But this was in part the narcissism of a young man's passion. Yeats saw only his own plight, for he was largely ignorant of hers.

IV

'Quit the Night and Seek the Day'

Maud and Yeats had talked of Ireland and poetry and found, too, that they had a shared interest in Theosophy. Maud had joined the Dublin Lodge of the Society and now Yeats took her to meet Madame Blavatsky, newly settled in Kensington. Maud was not impressed. She recalled there was a blockage in the pipe of the gas chandelier which made it flicker badly. 'Spooks in the room,' said Madame, glancing up from her baize-covered patience table. Then she whispered to Maud: 'They are all looking for a miracle.'

So, in his way, was Yeats. His struggle against materialism was still unresolved, and by the close of 1888 he had joined the Esoteric Section of the Theosophical Society in the hope of enlightenment. Somewhat to his surprise, Madame Blavatsky agreed to set up a group that would prepare for a study of the arcane relationship between the natural and divine worlds. Russell was concerned that Madame Blavatsky was moving the Theosophists away from a study of the godhead to 'proving the phenomena of spiritualism, table-rapping, and the evocation of spirits', but she told him that the classes were intended merely for instruction in magic rather than its practice. She herself meanwhile insisted on loyalty to Theosophy and to herself. The latter especially caused Yeats some difficulty, but the matter was solved when each member promised obedience 'subject to the decision of his own conscience'. Yeats also agreed, again with some difficulty, to swear to a belief in Madame Blavatsky's teachers. He had already rejected the fraud theory, but his attempt to preserve some measure of objectivity in such matters is suggested by his wondering if the mahatmas were living occultists, Madame's unconscious dramatisations, spirits or the 'principle of nature expressing itself symbolically'.[17]

Madame's warning that great and sometimes painful changes would occur in the occult student's soul might, for Yeats, have been an encouragement, but the tensions in a society already attacked from without and fractious within – a state Yeats was to become painfully familiar with over the ensuing years – is clear from a diary he kept. From this, his critical eye for others' shortcomings is also evident. The young man who described a fellow student as having the intellect of 'a good sized whelk' cannot have been an easy associate. Nor, despite sleeping with talismans under his pillow, did the hoped-for miracles occur. Yeats also believed, as he confessed in his *Autobiographies*, that 'if you burnt a flower to ashes and put the ashes under, I think, the receiver of an air-pump, and stood the receiver in the moonlight for so many nights, the ghost of the flower would appear hovering over its ashes'. He had pressed hard for such experiments, but the patience of the Theosophists was finally overstretched and Yeats himself, exhausted from his efforts and suffering from a mild heart complaint, was eventually asked to resign.* His comment to the official who came to him is revealing of the tenor of his thought. 'By teaching an abstract system without experiment,' the man was told, 'you are making your pupils dogmatic, and taking them out of life.' The official had to admit the justice of this remark, but Yeats's leaving Theosophical circles was perhaps made easier by Madame's prediction that 'no more supernatural help would come after 1897'.

By now, however, still captivated by a search that had fascinated him since earliest youth, Yeats had found other ways of pursuing occult studies. While working in the British Museum Library, he had been intrigued by the gaunt, determined appearance of an athletic man in his middle thirties dressed in a brown velveteen coat. His name was Samuel Liddell Mathers (Yeats was to know him better as MacGregor Mathers) and he was an authority on the arts of war and ritual magic.[18] In 1887 Mathers published a translation of *The Kabbala Unveiled* and was now gathering material on the occult from ancient texts and medieval *grimoires* or books of spells. In this he had been particularly encouraged by W. Wynn Westcott, a member of the masonic Societas Rosicruciana in Anglia, and the owner of an allegedly ancient German cypher manuscript detailing rituals of a masonic type. The manuscript (which suspiciously, considering its origins, transliterated into English) was supposedly superscribed with the name of a certain Frau Anna Sprengel of Stuttgart. With his wide learning and strong imagination, Mathers was particularly fitted to this editorial task, while his other patron, Annie Horniman, had got him appointed curator of her father's collection of ethnographia in South London.

When Yeats went to visit Mathers there, he discovered that his host was

---

* Madame Blavatsky had told Yeats at the close of 1889 when, at Jack's suggestion, he had shaved off his beard that he would have an illness within six months because of the loss of the mesmeric forces gathered in it.

not simply an authority on magic but a practising magus as well. Mathers persuaded Yeats to stare at cut-out coloured symbols, to close his eyes and bring the symbol before his imagination. He was then encouraged to let his reveries drift under the influence of the symbol and describe what he saw. Yeats had a vision of a 'desert and a black Titan raising himself up by his two hands from the middle of a heap of ancient ruins'. What he had almost certainly been encouraged to participate in was a tattwa experiment. In this form of vision raising, one of the five elemental signs – the yellow square of earth, the blue circle of air, the red triangle of fire, the silver crescent of water, and the black egg of the spirit – is stared at so intensely as to make a gateway to various parts of the astral world. 'Thought seeing' rather than seeing with the eyes fills the inner vision as, vibrating the Hebrew names of God and the angels of the chosen element in his throat, the skryer is encouraged to pass through the symbol itself into the world of vision. Elemental inhabitants of the astral plane now allegedly appear and must be greeted with fearless self-control and deference. Here, it seemed, was the melting away of the material world into the immaterial, and Yeats was so impressed by this and other encounters with Mathers that in March 1890 he was admitted to the Isis-Urania Temple of the secret society Mathers, Westcott and others had founded three years earlier, supposedly under the auspices of Frau Sprengel. Its name was the Hermetic Order of the Students of the Golden Dawn.

In approaching this secret society, Yeats was allying himself to the great nineteenth-century rebirth of occult studies and to those people who, through ceremony and symbolism especially, believed they could make contact with what the contemporary world apparently denied them: a shared, instinctual and numinous experience of life which could be genuinely felt as a spiritual release. The rational discovery of the physical world was set aside for the ritual exploration of the divine. Science and measurement were eschewed for symbols of the infinite and, in their search for a language to express this, the occultists turned to the enquiries of pre-scientific man: to the renaissance revival of Hermetic philosophy, to Rosicrucianism and alchemy, and to what one of the history lectures of the Golden Dawn itself called 'the vastly older wisdom of the Quabilistic Rabbis and of that very ancient secret knowledge, the Magic of the Egyptians, in which the Hebrew Pentateuch tells you that Moses the founder of the Jewish system was "learned"'.[19]

MacGregor Mathers's studies in the Kabbala were particularly important in this respect, for the Kabbalists had attempted a remarkable synthesis of their understanding of the cosmos and its relation to man's soul in their symbol of the Tree of Life. Issuing from the region of Infinite Light, the Tree of Life extended downwards to the world and held out to mankind its ten Sephiroth or Holy Emanations, the foci of spiritual evolution through which the believer could progress as he traversed the Tree's twenty-two connecting Paths or branches until he was once again brought back to the

Light and that spiritual experience of a unity of being from which all has been manifested and to which all must return.

The Order's initiation ceremony, which took place in the studio of MacGregor Mathers's fiancée Moina Bergson, offered Yeats a glimpse of this process and of the Order's rich panoply of symbolism.* Every item, every officer and even the positions the officers took up had significance. The officers urged Yeats to 'Quit the Night and seek the Day'. He was to pass beyond the Gates of the Land of Night and free himself from the bonds of materialism. Those involved represented the three parts of the mind that would assist in this: reason, intuitive consciousness and the will. The 'hierophant', seated on his Eastern throne, represented the divine in man. He appeared as Osiris glorified through trial, perfected by suffering, and, as he came down from his seat, he also embodied the descent of supernal splendour to the world below. His speech, uttered as he held out his wand, pointed to the core of the mystery: 'I come in the power of the Light. I come in the Light of Wisdom. I come in the Mercy of the Light. The Light hath healing in its wings.' A great transformation was now envisaged as sweeping over 'the chaos, the darkness, and the Gate of the Land of Night'. Divine Light could be brought down to irradiate mankind's spiritual wasteland while man was allegedly assumed into the godhead and glimpsed a new heaven and a new earth. In the words of the Golden Dawn rituals themselves, their purpose was: 'by the intervention of the symbol, ceremonial and sacrament, so to lead the soul that it may be withdrawn from the attraction of matter and delivered from the absorption therein, whereby it walks in somnambulism, knowing not whence it cometh nor whither it goeth'.

Here, perhaps, was the possibility of spiritual rebirth, and it was during this introductory Neophyte Ceremony that Yeats himself was initiated into the Order under the name *Demon est Deus Inversus* or 'The Devil is the Inverse of God'. Now it would be his task to work through the ensuing grades of the Golden Dawn and so awaken the elements of his being that they could be purified, harmonised and consecrated to the Great Work, thereby becoming a fit temple for the Light. As Yeats passed through the rites of Earth, Air and Water towards the challenging region of Fire (in Kabbalistic vocabulary, as he worked his way through the Sephoroth Malkuth, Yesod, Hod and Netzach), so he was being obliged

---

* Wilde had accurately pointed out in *The Decay of Lying* why ceremony and ritual were so important for the late-nineteenth-century imagination. 'I cannot conceive anything better for the culture of a country than the presence in it of a body of men whose duty it is to believe in the supernatural, to perform daily miracles, and to keep alive that mythopoeic faculty which is so essential for the imagination.' This is perhaps the place to comment that those who flinch from the rituals of the Golden Dawn as either ridiculous or repellent or both are rarely troubled when presented with similar experiences in Mozart's *The Magic Flute*. To draw a musical parallel, the ceremonious seriousness of the Golden Dawn initiation ritual might be seen as having the emotional grandeur of 'O Isis and Osiris, welche Wonne!'

to explore regions of his unredeemed being and to understand more fully his spiritual needs.

In terms of the teaching of the Golden Dawn, Yeats was coming to learn that only when his elemental chaos had been returned to balance, only when his earthly kingdom had found order and integration, would he be able to glimpse the promised beatitude, redeem his fallen Adam and defeat the hydra-headed dragon coiled round the Tree of Life. This done (and the Order made clear how strenuous a process of self-examination this was) Yeats would be ready for the birth of his higher consciousness, for his glimpse of the Sephirah of Tiphareth or Beauty where, with the help of the important symbol of the Red Rose on the Golden Cross, he might devote himself fully to the Great Work of enlightenment and experience a vision of those powers in the universe which would profoundly affect his poetry.

V

Transparent Lamps and Spiritual Flames

Meanwhile, the knowledge of symbolism required of the members of the Golden Dawn was important to another of Yeats's activities at this time. On a visit to his father's old friend Edwin Ellis, he was shown a scrap of paper on which Ellis had interpreted a poem by Blake in terms of the four Zoas, or the mythological embodiments of the four elements and the forces of life.[20] So intrigued was Yeats with this that by early 1889 the two men were at work on a complete edition of Blake, a monumental undertaking which would need four years to complete and which, when it was eventually published by Quaritch in 1893, would again have a profound effect on Yeats's poetry.

Ellis himself was both a poet and a painter. Yeats did not greatly care for his pictures but, if he had a qualified regard for his poetry, he was impressed by Ellis's critical powers. Indeed, he found his mind fascinating, just as his father did. Ellis had an almost psychic sensitivity to other people's thoughts and an ability with abstract and symbolic arguments that was the most remarkable Yeats ever encountered. His mind, Yeats wrote, 'was constantly on the edge of trance'. Sometimes, indeed, Ellis's conversation was so rapid and so dense as to defy comprehension. His home life was equally bizarre. Ellis was widely experienced sexually and Yeats, who was constantly troubled by his virginity, dreaded conversation turning to the topic, as it frequently did. Ellis's 'half-mad foreign' wife, however, lived on the edge of insanity and so dominated her husband that she would sometimes refuse to let him out of her sight for days at a time. Ellis had come to accept this state as normal, but Yeats, with a young man's arrogance, tried to protect Ellis from his wife so that they might work on Blake undisturbed. Sometimes Mrs Ellis ordered him out of the house, saying Yeats was casting a spell on her husband. She would then forgive him and present unpalatably rich cakes as a peace-offering. At other times the two men had to arrange clandestine meetings in the ABC café near the British Museum. In these less than ideal circumstances they shared their discovery of Blake's mystic truths.

Much labour was required to gather these. Yeats went to Oxford to copy out *The Book of Thel* and to Redhill where the descendants of Blake's patron John Linell had many manuscripts, including a barely studied version of *Vala, or the Four Zoas*. These they guarded with extreme care, the old man who sat in the room ostensibly to sharpen Yeats's pencils probably being there to ensure that he and Ellis did not steal the papers. But the Linells were generous people, offering their guests fine port for lunch and eventually presenting Yeats himself with a set of Blake's illustrations to Dante, on which he would write a fine essay. The academic value of the edition itself remains disputable, however. Experts have emphasised the worth of the commentaries and the exposition of the symbolism, but have pointed to the large number of inaccuracies in the transcriptions of the texts themselves. While some of these were intentional alterations, many are merely mistakes made while copying and were in part due to Yeats's weak eyesight. This had been poor from childhood onwards, and he was eventually diagnosed as having a conical cornea in his left eye and an astigmatism in the right. Such complaints were tiring, and in 1898 he told Lily that 'when reading I have to rest a minute or two every twenty minutes'.

But it was an over-zealous imagination rather than physical weakness that led to the work's most egregious error: the assumption that the ancestry of so mystical a poet as Blake must be Irish. Swinburne, whom Yeats had seen fit to attack for weaknesses in his commentary on Blake, seized on this when his own work was reprinted and wrote that such alleged ancestry might indeed account for the extravagance of *Vala*, where 'fever and fancy take the place of reason and imagination'. Yeats's subsequent denunciation was bitter. Swinburne was 'that turgid and monotonous poet, with his intellectual underbreeding and inferior kind of pride'. He was, Yeats declared, an 'aristocratic cad' whose notorious private life showed him to be a 'man without a sweetheart, wife or mistress'.[21]

Such acrimony was the carapace around Yeats's exultant regard for Blake. While the Linells were narrowly orthodox Christians, and were concerned that Blake himself 'did not believe in the historical Jesus', to Yeats this was an aspect of his glory. Blake was the poet who had taught that the truly imaginative artist is Christlike, leading his audience into the life of the spirit. In a magnificent sentence that is quite as applicable to Yeats himself as to Blake, Yeats wrote of him that Blake was 'a man crying out for a mythology, and trying to make one because he could not find one to his hand'.[22] In his reshaping of Christianity, Blake taught that the imagination itself is divine, and Yeats believed that Blake, by announcing this religion of art, heralded the modern world in which people create their souls not by going to church but by exposure to great works of the imagination.

Here was the true theology, one 'not made by men of action, drudges of time and space, but by Christ when wrapped in the divine essence, and by artists and poets, who are taught by the nature of their craft to sympathise with all living things'. Art was the revolt of the soul against materialism. It was vision and could most truly express this through symbols such as Blake's own tiger burning in the forests of the night. As Yeats declared: 'the symbol is indeed the only possible expression of some invisible essence, a transparent lamp about a spiritual flame'. Although Yeats himself found Blake on occasions an over-literal transcriber of the symbolic imagination, he believed that he was the first modern writer to explore the marriage of art with symbol, and in both this and in his creation of his own mythology Yeats would follow him.

But, if Yeats was looking for the future in the past, he was also determined to know his peers and to fashion his poetry on contemporary models. Many years later he remembered saying to Ernest Rhys: 'I am growing jealous of other poets and we shall all grow jealous of each other unless we know each other and so feel a share in each other's triumph.' [23] He was already friendly with some of the men associated with the Morris-inspired *Century Guild Hobby Horse* magazine, including Herbert Horne, Selwyn Image and their lodger Lionel Johnson. Now, probably in May 1890, Yeats, along with Rhys and T. W. Rolleston, founded the Rhymers' Club so that more contemporaries could meet and discuss their work. For four years members gathered monthly at the Old Cheshire Cheese pub off Fleet Street. Those in funds dined at seven, then the whole company moved to a room on the second floor where some smoked long churchwarden pipes as readings and criticism took place. Yeats himself appeared dressed in the role of the poet, wearing 'a brown velveteen coat, a loose tie, and a very old Inverness cape, discarded by my father twenty years before'. The decorous and sometimes rather dull atmosphere was sharpened from time to time by Yeats's own forceful expression of theoretical views most of the others did not share, and 'a gloomy silence fell upon the room' when he began to speak in his 'broad-vowelled brogue'. For all the growing sophistication of Yeats's ideas, there was still about him an air of provincial brashness.

Among those who regularly gathered were Lionel Johnson, Ernest Dowson, Victor Plarr, Ernest Radford, John Davidson, Richard Le Gallienne, T. W. Rolleston, Selwyn Image, Edwin Ellis and John Todhunter. Arthur Symons and Herbert Horne were less frequent visitors. Oscar Wilde occasionally attended when meetings were held in private houses. These were all men with common interests rather than a common cause, and as Yeats once told them in words as revealing of his own temperament as of the Rhymers themselves: 'None of us can say who will succeed, or even who has or has not talent. The only certain thing about us is that we are too many.' But three figures were to influence Yeats particularly – Ernest Dowson, Lionel Johnson and Arthur Symons – and it was chiefly around these men that Yeats was later to weave his explanatory myth of artistic alienation and self-destructiveness summed up in his phrase 'the tragic generation'.

By the close of 1889, Ernest Dowson had already met 'Missie', the thirteen-year-old daughter of a Polish restaurant keeper, and fallen in love. Dowson was a highly sexed man, and the painful tensions arising from his infatuation heightened his need for the sublimities of religious ritual (he converted to Catholicism in 1891) as well as for drink and dissipation. Sober, his concern was only for the little girl, but drunk he found relief with any woman who came his way. Lionel Johnson lectured him on chastity out of the writings of the Church Fathers, but as he did so each drank heavily, for Johnson too was a deeply riven man.

Yeats was to record that Johnson 'became for a few years my closest friend, and what drew me to him was a certain elegance of mind that seemed to correspond to his little, beautifully formed body'. To this physical and intellectual fascination was added the influence of Pater especially. Johnson 'had taken from Walter Pater certain favourite words which came to mean much for me: "Life should be a ritual", and we should value it for "magnificence", for all that is "hieratic"'. In pursuit of this fascination, Yeats would visit Johnson at his lodgings, where he had a very large library for a young man newly down from Oxford. Indeed, so many books lined the brown-papered walls that Johnson wondered if he could somehow suspend more shelves from the ceiling. He gave an impression of severe intellect, of retreat from the world and of a personality manufactured in the silence of study. From this partial truth sprang fantasies of familiarity with great men, fantasies repeated with such consistency that they were generally taken for fact. His alcoholism seemed at first mastered by his self-control, but it was a destructive element in a torn nature. Johnson had failed to mature physically and gave every appearance of being a beautiful fifteen-year-old with a Grecian profile. He had been homosexual since his schooldays, and at Oxford was the unwitting angel of destruction who introduced Wilde to Lord Alfred Douglas. His own sexuality was increasingly a matter of guilt to him, a problem deepened by his conversion to Catholicism.

Like Johnson, Arthur Symons was also indebted to Pater. Symons was largely self-educated and it was a sign of his considerable professional flair that he sent an early study of Browning to Pater. He recognised the importance of contacts, as Yeats did, and won not only Pater's support and his suggestion that he follow principally the calling of a prose writer, but the attention of Ernest Rhys and Havelock Ellis, who offered him editing work. It was with Havelock Ellis that Symons made his first trip to France, where he met such leading figures as Rodin, Mallarmé, Verlaine and Huysmans. More than any other of the Rhymers he had a first-hand knowledge of the French avant-garde, of the Decadent movement and, above all, of the French Symbolists. Yeats was growing aware of the somewhat narrow nature of his own culture, and Symons would become a deepening influence over him. As Yeats himself wrote: 'my thoughts gained in richness and clearness from his sympathy'.

Such contact with French poets among the Rhymers suggests why certain members at least were opposed to the sentimental and didactic elements in Victorian verse, but there was another feature that bound many of them in loose association, and that was their Celticism. John O'Leary occasionally attended meetings and a number of members like Todhunter were also associated with the Southwark Irish Literary Club. Rhys was Welsh, Davidson a Scot, Symons a Cornishman, and Lionel Johnson claimed Irish relatives. As Yeats himself wrote to Irish-Americans in the *Pilot*: 'it is only among the sociable Celtic nations that men draw nearer to each other when they want to think and dream and work'. Such journalism also suggests how the Rhymers managed to get a hold on English literary pages and publishing houses. Richard Le Gallienne, for example, secured contacts with John Lane's Bodley Head and with Elkin Matthews. By 1891 he was also literary editor of the *Star*, writing under the appropriate name 'Log-Roller'. Such anonymity made mutual 'puffing' easier, but the inevitable complaint arose when it appeared that the book pages of the *Daily Chronicle* had become all but the private preserve of the Bodley Head. Nor was such a publicity machine infallible. When *The Book of the Rhymers' Club*, an anthology of members' work, appeared, the reviews were not invariably favourable.

Yeats claimed that this anthology had been his initiative but he was also working on a considerable quantity of prose. This focussed exclusively on his literary and Nationalist interests, and he followed up his work on Irish folklore with *Stories from Carleton* and *Representative Irish Tales*. The Irish peasant as a noble and visionary being was now becoming a figure of interest to Yeats in his own right. He admired Carleton particularly as a peasant who hated and loved with his class, and it was these qualities Yeats emphasised in his selections rather than the more familiar themes of politics, religion and a degrading anti-Irish humour.

In line with this literary nationalism, Yeats was also generous in his support of young Irish poets, although his help was not always without its risks. He felt obliged to write to Elizabeth White on 31 January 1889, for example, apologising 'for the slight damage to your M.S. My study window was open and the wind blew your M.S. into the fender where a red-hot coal somewhat charred one corner'. His criticism of her work was generous and attentive, however, and, along with recommending her to the Reverend Matthew Russell of the *Irish Monthly*, he gave her general advice which clearly reflected his own interests. 'You will find it a good thing to make verses on Irish legends and places and so forth,' he told her. 'It helps originality – and makes one's verses sincere, and gives one less numerous competitors – Besides one should love best what is nearest and most interwoven with one's life.'[24] The balance of conviction and shrewdness in this is a sure indication that by the start of 1889 when he wrote the letter Yeats had made himself into a literary professional.

In addition to his work as an editor and adviser, Yeats was also composing *The Countess Cathleen* and concentrating his thoughts on drama generally. In 1886, Todhunter had mounted a lavish London production of his 'oratorical Swinburnian play' *Helena of Troas*, which Yeats himself 'thought as unactable as it was unreadable'. Four years later Todhunter presented his *Sicilian Idyll* in Bedford Park, a work which Yeats again 'never rated very high as poetry' but which nonetheless showed him that in such pieces 'poetical culture may be more important than professional experience'.[25] The melodious voice of the actress Florence Farr impressed him particularly, though it was a while before she had a direct influence on his writing. But the production itself had caused Yeats to ask himself some fundamental questions. 'When our political passions have died out in the fulfilment of their aims', he wrote in *United Ireland*, 'shall we, I wonder, have a fine native drama of our own?' He thought it 'very likely'. Todhunter had been obliged to write 'for an English public in the very last stages of dramatic decadence', but the choice of a true Irish theme, the avoidance of 'an international art, picking stories and symbols where it pleased,' might yet allow a great poet to write a new *Prometheus Unbound* from the legends of Patrick, Columcille, Oisin or Finn. Drama, in other words, might become an effective way of giving poetic expression to Nationalist sentiments.

In the meantime, Yeats was experimenting with prose narratives. JBY had suggested he write a short work of fiction, but when the mythological *Dhoya* failed to please him, Yeats followed up his father's suggestion that he write about real people. *John Sherman* is a realistic and sometimes lyrical account of a young man moving between materialistic London and an Irish town modelled on Sligo. The contrast between the two is deeply felt. Where London is sterile, anonymous and dirty – a place where nature is sometimes no more than the fourteen dead flies spotting the ceiling of a commercial office – the description of Ballah evokes the Celtic world with all the emotional precision of an exile:

As he went through the streets his heart went out to every
familiar place and sight: the rows of tumble-down thatched
cottages; the slated roofs of the shops; the women selling
gooseberries; the river bridge; the high walls of the garden
where it was said the gardener used to see the ghost of a former
owner in the shape of a rabbit; the street corner no child would
pass at nightfall for fear of the headless soldier; the deserted
flour store; the wharves covered with grass. All these he watched
with Celtic devotion, that devotion carried to the ends of the
world by the Celtic exiles, and since old times surrounding their
journeyings with rumour of plaintive songs.[26]

Character, as Yeats told Katharine Tynan, is more important than incident
in the work, and when John Sherman finally leaves London and the superficial
Margaret Leland for Ballah and the gentle Mary Carton, he is shown fulfilling
the law of his own being. He rejects worldliness for a life of dreaming and
the imagination set amid the beauty of Ireland. The book was published in
Unwin's Pseudonym Library under the name 'Ganconagh' and earned Yeats
a much needed £40.

VI
White Birds

By July 1891 Yeats himself had returned to Ireland. The country was once
again in a state of acrimonious self-division. Seven months earlier the verdict
had been awarded against Parnell in the O'Shea divorce case and his party
was in crisis. The issue of Home Rule was now confused by the forces of
moral opprobrium. Parnell was deemed unfit by some for public life and
Gladstone withdrew Liberal support. Parnell refused to step down and his
party fractured into those who stood by him and the anti-Parnellites, who in
the end succeeded in voting him out. He married Kitty O'Shea and, although
a sick man, fought to regain his power. By the time Yeats arrived in Dublin,
however, three of his candidates had been defeated and Parnell himself was
near to physical collapse.

In such an atmosphere Maud Gonne, the half-English woman turned
Irish nationalist, was for many a figure of scorn. Now she had returned
to France, it was said, she wore a green dress embroidered with shamrocks
as if Home Rule were just a question of fashion. John O'Leary disowned
her as a disciple because she had gone to the inauguration of a new town
simply, he said, to show off her hat. Sarah Purser, whose portrait of Maud
Yeats loathed for its superficiality, said to him archly: 'So Maud Gonne

is dying in the South of France.' She then told Yeats she had lunched with her in Paris and dwelt on the fact that Maud had been accompanied by a tall Frenchman. There was also a doctor in the party and he told Miss Purser that both Maud and the Frenchman would be dead in six months. Yeats wrote to Maud in the greatest agitation, enclosing in his letter his poem 'A Dream of Death'. Maud was amused to receive her epitaph when she was in fact getting better. Now, however, Yeats heard she was back in Dublin. He went to see her in the Nassau Hotel and, as she came through the door, her great height seeming to fill it, he was overwhelmed with pity. Her beauty had vanished, her face was wasted, her manner seemed lifeless. 'She hinted', Yeats wrote, 'at some unhappiness, some disillusionment.'[27]

Maud could not tell Yeats everything that had happened to her in the year since they had met. She had gone back to Ireland, been smuggled out and then returned ill to France when the British issued a warrant for her arrest. With the support of Millevoye she had thrown herself into political activities and become an early female journalist as she propagandised for the cause of Ireland. In this she was remarkably successful. The wall of silence around Irish affairs was breached and Maud was quoted in newspapers from Cairo to St Petersburg. Then, in early 1891, she bore Millevoye a son they named Georges. But the child who might have focussed the happiness in their relationship only increased the stress it was under. Millevoye's hero, General Boulanger, had fled to Brussels. The movement to annex Alsace-Lorraine collapsed, and Millevoye's own aspirations were in tatters. He promised Maud he would get a divorce and marry her, but it seems that in his confusion he also urged her to offer her sexual favours to those who might help him. Maud herself, convinced now that sex was justified only by child-bearing, retreated to Ireland unable either to stay with her son and his father or wholly to leave them.

Yeats, ignorant of this and seeing Maud grown gentle and indolent in her sorrow, felt himself in love again. Perhaps she sensed he wanted desperately to give her the protection and peace he felt she craved. 'Yet,' wrote Yeats, 'I left Dublin next day to stay somewhere in Orange Ulster with the brilliant student of my old Dublin school Charles Johnston.' He later attributed this curious action to a belief that he was not yet altogether Maud's captive, but the fact that he, Johnston and Johnston's elder brother spent the next few days in heedless boyishness chasing home-made fire balloons across the countryside suggests a different story of escape and even relief.

It seemed that Yeats had let himself get too close and then recoiled, but when a letter arrived from Dublin he went at once to Maud's side. In her loneliness and anxiety she had found the exact note with which to call him. She had had a dream, she wrote. In her dream they were brother and sister. They had been sold into slavery and forced to traverse mile after mile of sand. Almost at once, and hardly looking at her or thinking of her beauty, Yeats proposed marriage. As he described the scene in his 'Autobiography': 'I sat there holding her hand and speaking vehemently. She did not take away her hand for a while. I ceased to speak, and presently as I sat in silence I felt her nearness to me and her beauty. At once I knew that my confidence had gone, and an instant later she drew her hand away.' No, she said, there were reasons why she could not marry, would never marry. All unaware, Yeats and Maud had set the pattern of their relationship, a pattern which would be reduplicated over the next decades with the compulsive repetition of a neurosis. They would come close, flinch from an intimacy they both feared, and then, usually at Maud's prompting, come close once again on what they both hoped was a higher, spiritual plane, a sublimated world where occult and nationalist sentiments mixed, and an agonised Yeats would find much of the material for his poetry.

Such anguish was even now productive. The day after their reconciliation they went to Howth and wandered along the cliffs where each had played in childhood. Here Maud had always been happiest, believing the Howth coast more beautiful than the Mediterranean. There were two gulls diving in the air and riding the foam that afternoon. Maud told Willie that, if she had the choice of being any bird, she would choose to be a gull above all. Her somewhat obvious remark was transformed into the poem beginning 'I would that we were, my beloved, white birds on the foam of the sea', which Yeats sent her three days later. They then visited the little cottage where Maud's retired nanny lived and Yeats heard the old woman ask if they were engaged to be married. In the evening he found to his concern that the day had cost him fully ten shillings, which he could ill afford. This earned a reproach from O'Leary who, as so often, had lent him some cash, but Yeats told him Maud always paid her share. She had insisted on that in London. Now, as they met day after day, Yeats read her drafts of *The Countess Cathleen* until, suddenly, Maud was called back to France. The Boulangistes, she said, demanded her immediate presence. In fact, little Georges was seriously ill with meningitis.

Yeats was thrown back on the company of his friends. For part of the time he stayed at 3 Upper Ely Place, where George Russell lived with an eccentric band of Theosophists and visionaries. Many people dropped in to discuss philosophy and the arts in the language of 'the vague Platonism that all there talked'. The host was 'a black-bearded young man with a passion for Manichean philosophy', while at the top of the house lived a medical student who read Plato and took hashish as well as a young Scotsman who owned a vegetarian restaurant. 'On a lower floor lived a strange red-haired girl, all whose thoughts were set upon painting and poetry, conceived as abstract images like Love and Penury in the *Symposium*; and to these images she sacrificed herself with Asiatic fanaticism'.[28]

There was much dispute among the various spiritual factions in the house, Yeats himself quarrelling frequently with Russell because he wanted his friend to examine his visions more rigorously and admit that they were symbolic rather than direct revelations of the divine. There were also expeditions to less respectable spiritual groups. Yeats now discovered in Dublin 'a whole colony' of black magicians 'of the most iniquitous kind', he told Lionel Johnson. While 'good Theosophists' were known to 'shake in their shoes at the mention of their name', Yeats claimed he was amused by their 'hideous costumes' and worship of Isis. The tone of his letter admirably captures his scepticism. 'The black magicians have invited me to drop in on an incantation now and again as a compliment to my knowledge of the black art. They have not got enough in the way of soul left to cover an old sixpence but that does not matter much for the present.' Yeats's critical faculty was not always so in evidence, however. In the house of Dr Sigerson, Yeats the occultist experimented with hypnotism and a crystal ball in which a seer (who was probably Mrs Sigerson) claimed to see a vision of a gigantic figure waving his arms around some golden letters. Yeats was wildly excited until Dr Sigerson pointed out that what the seer could actually see was the reflection of a man cleaning the windows by the sign on the Medical Hall opposite.

But the visionary absurd could sometimes run parallel with the poetic sublime. Even while he was conducting experiments that had in them more than a little of the ridiculous, a profound reordering of Yeats's deepest imaginative concerns was taking place. He was to write many years later that when he was twenty-three or twenty-four 'this sentence seemed to form in my head, without my willing it, much as sentences form when we are half-asleep: "Hammer your thoughts into a unity." For days I could think of nothing else, and for years I tested all I did by that sentence.'[29] Three elements in his thought especially were being brought together. Yeats had dedicated himself to a form of nationalism in which the spiritual regeneration of his people was his upmost concern. His experiments in Theosophy and occult magic meanwhile had begun to convince him that he could participate in a spiritual reality altogether more profound than the oppressive materialism that seemed to hold the contemporary world in its grip. Now he sought a symbolic poetry in which these concerns could merge in a new form of art. In early August 1891 he began writing the 'Rosy Cross Lyrics'. These are the verses in which the lover, the magus, the poet and the political man started to bring his desires into focus and live his imaginative life by the all-encompassing sense of mystery and wonder suggested by the mystic rose:

Red Rose, proud Rose, sad Rose of all my days!
Come near me, while I sing the ancient ways:
Cuchulain battling with the bitter tide;
The Druid, grey, wood-nurtured, quiet-eyed,
Who cast round Fergus dreams, and ruin untold;
And thine own sadness, where of stars, grown old
In dancing silver-sandalled on the sea,
Sing in their high and lonely melody.
Come near, that no more blinded by man's fate,
I find under the boughs of love and hate,
In all poor foolish things that live a day,
Eternal beauty wandering on her way.[30]

With these words Yeats evoked his central symbol in 'To the Rose upon the Rood of Time'. Many elements are fused here, and it is in their fusion that the vision lies, for this is a truly symbolic poetry which draws deeply on the shared unconscious energies of mankind to express feelings at once imprecise, tumultuous and profoundly alive. Incidentals rise into the universal. A rose impaled upon a cross was, for example, a sacred lamen worn across the heart during the inmost rites of the Golden Dawn. The crucifixion of the four-leafed, female rose on the male and sacrificial cross was seen as a mystic marriage which gave birth to a fifth and supernatural element. Here was an image of the magus passing beyond the trembling veil that divided the mundane from the immaterial. The rose could also be seen as intellectual, spiritual and eternal beauty impaled upon the world and suffering with mankind as transcendence becomes immanence. But if the rose was the ultimate symbol of the spirit it was also the special beloved. The rose was Maud Gonne, whose presence worked in her poet his longing for divine beauty. And, in life as in art, it was impossible for Yeats to separate Maud from the cause of Ireland. Ireland too was a rose of mystery suffering in the material world but redolent of an ancient spiritual and heroic life far richer than contemporary materialism. Yeats was here beginning to create a poetry which stood on the very edge of contemporary awareness and which gathered into itself longings for spiritual exaltation and political freedom, doing so in a way that was the expression not merely of one man's feeling but of a nation's deepest yearnings. The petals of the rose thus folded around a host of suggestion and, as the 'Rosy Cross Lyrics' developed, so they began to explore ever more subtly Yeats's fundamental preoccupations, each running into each.

Such a synthesis was created at great nervous cost. Here was a wholly new way for a poet to envisage the unity and the complexity of his world.

Katharine Tynan, with whom Yeats was staying during part of August 1891, wrote to a friend that she found him an extremely tiresome visitor. 'He thinks all the rest of the world created to minister to him, and there is no rebuffing of him possible. I did nothing while he was here, nor should I if he was here a twelvemonth.' Such were the effects of genius extending its range, but internal agitation was not in itself enough to inspire great poetry. Events, too, played a decisive role.

Yeats now received an unexpected letter from Maud Gonne that was wild with sorrow and hinted at a half-truth. Avoiding all mention of her real relationship to little Georges, she said that a child she had adopted three years since had died. Maud wrote of a bird of ill-omen that had perched on the nursery windowsill the day the infant was taken ill and of how she had sent for doctor after doctor to no avail. Tragedy in the private world was then matched by disaster in the public sphere. On 6 October 1891, exhausted by his labours and defeats, Parnell died in Brighton of a heart attack. His body was brought back to Ireland on the same ship that carried a deeply grieving Maud. Yeats was on the quayside as the ship docked, and now, as Parnell's mighty funeral procession wound its way through Dublin and the skies over the cemetery parted to reveal a falling star, so an era in Irish history ended.*

Political hope seemed over, and the Home Rulers would soon fall into faction and paralysis. Maud sensed the uselessness of this and realised that constitutional efforts to win Irish freedom would have to be replaced by more extreme methods. To Yeats, it seemed that literature alone could keep the nation's dignity alive. As he was later to write of the forthcoming renaissance: 'the literature of Ireland, and indeed all that stir of thought which prepared for the Anglo-Irish war, began when Parnell fell from power in 1891. A disillusioned and embittered Ireland turned from parliamentary politics; an event was conceived; and the race began, as I think, to be troubled by that event's long gestation.'[31] Yeats was determined to be in the vanguard and to influence that event – the liberation of his homeland. Devoted equally to the cause of Maud and Parnell, Yeats the occultist, the patriot and the lover would now begin to emerge as the poet of the rose who sang 'to sweeten Ireland's wrong'. He would start to make himself a national figure.

* Yeats, disliking crowds, did not attend the funeral and poetically could manage only the unfortunate elegy 'Mourn – and Then Onward'.

PART TWO

The Secret Rose

I, too, await
The hour of thy great wind of love and hate.
When shall the stars be blown about the sky,
Like the sparks blown out of a smithy, and die?
Surely thine hour has come, thy great wind blows,
Far-off, most secret, and inviolate Rose?

4

Celtic Twilight
(1891–1894)

I
The New Irish Library

On 28 December 1891 Yeats held a meeting in his study in Bedford Park to help determine the future of Ireland's literature. Earlier attempts to unite the various groups back home into a Young Ireland League had come to nothing and now Yeats resolved on a less ambitious approach. He invited the active members of the Southwark Irish Literary Club to meet T. W. Rolleston, a fellow Rhymer and editor of the *Dublin University Review*, with the aim of revivifying the Club's original energies. It quickly became clear, however, that Rolleston's organising abilities were considerably more practised than Yeats's own, although the degree of his deviousness was not yet apparent. Soon virtually every London-Irish writer was involved in the newly renamed Irish Literary Society, and, the following May, Rolleston was acting as secretary, Yeats and Todhunter had been appointed to the committee, while the distinguished elder statesman Sir Charles Gavan Duffy was asked to become president. Taking up John O'Leary's ideas, the Society then set about launching a magazine, encouraging scholarly editions of Gaelic texts, arranging lectures and promoting the idea of a popular series of books to be called the New Irish Library.

In Yeats's commitment to this initiative there was 'much patriotism and more desire for a fair woman'.[1] He was determined that Maud Gonne should be involved in his plans. When she returned to Dublin, her grief and vulnerability were so evident that Yeats resolved to find her work into which she could throw her energies. She had spoken to him of little Georges' death without, however, making clear to him that she was the boy's mother. In her distress, she had temporarily lost her ability to speak French and was now taking chloroform to help her sleep. One evening she and Yeats were joined by George Russell, who, as Yeats wrote, had 'given up art and was now an accountant in a draper's shop, for his will was weak and an emotional occupation weakened it still further'. Despite such carping comments, Russell had a reputation as a caring and sympathetic man of visionary insight. Talk turned to reincarnation, and Russell gave it as his opinion that a dead child might be reborn to the same family. Earnest and gentle behind his thick glasses, Russell made so profound an impression on Maud that Yeats felt obliged to silence his scepticism about Russell's too easy assumptions. Nonetheless, when Maud told Yeats of a ghostly 'grey woman' who had haunted her thoughts since childhood he resolved to use techniques learned from the teachings of the Golden Dawn to make the spirit manifest itself. He believed that it was this figment of evil who created what he thought of as Maud's unhealthy desire for power and he felt that, if she confronted it, she could exorcise it.

Both Yeats and Maud recorded that the spirit was indeed manifested and claimed to be an ancient Egyptian priestess who once sold false oracles. Now her soul was split from her personality and she was condemned to a half-life as a shadow who wanted to be united with Maud. Luridly fascinated by this and by the power it seemed to give him, Yeats persuaded Maud to cross with him to London and consult with the Matherses. Without describing the apparition, Yeats arranged a seance with Moina Mathers as seer. The grey woman again appeared and, according to Maud, wrung her hands in grief over killing her child. Maud felt her own guilty feelings confirmed and, while Yeats and the Matherses believed the woman was what the ancient Egyptians called a Ka or that aspect of the personality which survives death, Maud in her grief and anguish resolved to join the Golden Dawn. On 16 November 1891, she underwent the Neophyte Ceremony and adopted the name and motto *Per Ignem ad Lucem* ('Through Fire to Light'). Her natural intensity was thus given symbolic expression.

Although, in a sentence deleted from his 'Autobiography', Yeats wondered if the manner of his involvement in Maud's troubles smacked of evil, he felt, along with his vague guilt, the thrill of 'a hunter taking captive some beautiful wild creature'. He began to dream of a married life in which he and Maud would devote themselves to mystic truth like the medieval magus Nicholas Flamel and his wife. A chaste and sexless relationship based on shared occult insight was to become increasingly important to both lovers as they struggled with an attraction constantly undermined by powerful psychological inhibitions. Such a way of constructing their closeness suggested intimacy and exclusivity without the physical commitment they both found so troublesome, and in time they would believe they had solemnised a 'mystic marriage', a union blessed by the divine powers who thereby provided them with the inspiration to work for Ireland. The fruit of their marriage would be a free nation. Even now, magic and politics were becoming increasingly the vehicles for a displaced passion, and, as Maud herself returned to France for some months, Yeats felt not only that he had an occult hold over her but that he could further secure her interest by getting her to work for the cause of Irish literature. Perhaps in this way nearness would lead to love.

There was much in the literary movement that might attract Maud. The publicity surrounding the new Irish Literary Society in London, for example, and the suggestion that London rather than Dublin was the true intellectual capital of the country, had led to an announcement in the columns of *United Ireland* that plans for a National Literary Society were now in hand. An inaugural meeting was held on 24 May 1892, shortly after Yeats himself returned to Dublin, but the acrimony that was to characterise the movement was evident from the start. Yeats felt he had to prevent Rolleston from making the Society a learned rather than a popular one, and he threw himself into a movement which, with the decline of Irish hopes after the death of Parnell, commanded wide support. Yeats even became a well-known figure and, much to O'Leary's disapproval, spent many hours canvassing support and talking to all and sundry about his plans.

Influential people began to flock to Yeats's cause. John O'Leary himself (in whose house Yeats was lodging) was a loyal if truculent supporter, an indispensable man. Yeats and his allies 'made him the President of our Society, and without him I could do nothing, for his long imprisonment and longer exile, his magnificent appearance, and, above all, the fact that he alone had personality, a point of view not made for the crowd's sake, but for self-expression, made him magnetic to my generation'.[2] With his reputation enhanced by his gravity O'Leary felt he could dispense wisdom, and he told Yeats, 'There are things a man must not do to save his nation.' When Yeats asked what these were, O'Leary said, as Yeats recorded, '"To cry in public", and I think it probable he would have added, if pressed, "To write oratorical or insincere verse."' O'Leary also advised Yeats how important it was to secure the support of the Fenians. But age had made O'Leary suspicious of innovation, while his mistrust of democracy and his distaste for propaganda often made him an obstinate ally.

His 'disciple', J. F. Taylor, with whom Yeats had clashed at the Contemporary Club, was even more fearsome, a personification of Dublin's acrimonious divisiveness. He was, Yeats declared, 'a gaunt, ungainly man, whose mind was perpetually occupied with an impassioned argument, to which he brought vast historical erudition, upon the justice of the national cause'. His mind had become abstract as a result. 'He saw the world, as it were, in mathematical forms, and, being incapable of compromise, hated and would always hate the actual leaders of Ireland.' Standish O'Grady attracted Yeats by the rancour that seemed to give music to his style, while Lionel Johnson, drinking heavily but now at the height of his powers, was to be the movement's official critic. Such men were difficult supporters but, since Ireland itself seemed to Yeats 'like soft wax', it was with just these people that he could hope to mould it into a new and noble shape.

These hopes were threatened partly by the facts and partly by Yeats's own temperament. The literature with which he aimed to shape the soul of his people – and his aim was nothing less – had to be of the utmost refinement. He treasured the belief 'that certain wavering rhythms . . . are nearer to the soul than the resolute rhythm of political oratory'. In a country where rhetoric was often politics, where words were deeds, this was an untenable sophistication. Nor, of course, did it come close to the popular view. The general taste was for the Nationalist verse of Davis and his followers, and Yeats was to comment sardonically that Irish books were expected to have harps and shamrocks on their green bindings. Such narrowness depressed him greatly, for he believed it destroyed true imaginative literature. Davis and his followers 'had sought a nation unified by a political doctrine alone, a subservient art and letters abetting', Yeats wrote in his *Autobiographies*. The result was merely crude propaganda in which 'all the past had been turned into a melodrama with Ireland for blameless hero and poet; novelist and historian had but one object, that we should hiss the villain'. Here, among the catcalls, was no large audience for *The Wanderings of Oisin*, no nation to be readily enfolded in the petals of a mystic rose.

Events were to confirm this. In July 1882, Sir Charles Gavan Duffy arrived in Dublin. An unprepossessing figure with a rash temper, Duffy was a man whose achievements carried such authority that his presence leached Yeats of much of his recently acquired influence. Duffy, a Catholic Nationalist, was now in his seventies. It had been he, along with Blake Dillon and Thomas Davis, who back in 1842 had founded the influential weekly the *Nation* to support the Young Ireland cause. Duffy's fiery journalism had eventually led to his being elected an MP but, in despair over Ireland, he had emigrated to Australia, where he became Prime Minister of Victoria. Despite such an absence and his acceptance of a knighthood, Duffy's Davisite volume *Ballad Poetry of Ireland* ensured that he remained a household name.

It was with such a man that Yeats in his naivety hoped to work on equal terms. Instead he found a veteran of 'domineering obstinacy and an entire lack of any culture' who was determined to carry all before him. Duffy was particularly concerned to be sole editor of the New Irish Library and to provide the Irish people with books chosen 'to fill up the blanks which an imperfect education' had left them with. Yeats was determined that such a series should not founder in dreary didacticism and he bitterly opposed Duffy's initiative. The acrimony even spilled over into the newspapers, with Yeats urging the formation of a committee to check the partiality of Duffy's list of books, while supporters of Duffy's cause such as J. F. Taylor suggested that Yeats was merely an ambitious and manipulative young man who was looking to take the series over.

Yeats later admitted he had behaved with 'the impatience of youth', and his fissile elders, believing he had detracted from the compliment they wished to pay an elder statesman, were clearly angry. Yeats's conduct certainly showed much of the haughtiness and sourness that were the psychological props for his idealism. His position had, nonetheless, something to recommend it and he was unprepared for the degree of deceit his enemies were now to employ. Yeats himself had approached his new publishers (T. Fisher Unwin, who had recently taken over the rights to *The Wanderings of Oisin*) with an idea for a series of books on Irish themes. Rolleston was aware of this and, when Duffy's plans began to founder, revealed the approach to the older man. Duffy at once began his own negotiations with Unwin and successfully cut Yeats out. Greatly hurt but realising that, if he protested too much, Unwin would drop the whole project, Yeats tried to bring pressure to bear through the London and Dublin Literary Societies. This was largely unsuccessful (there were few who would seriously challenge Duffy) and when Duffy's New Irish Library launched with a dry historical work by Thomas Davis the relative failure of the series seemed assured.

It was not simply such complex squabbling that distressed Yeats's nerves. The frustrating presence of Maud Gonne drove him to distraction. The part he hoped she would play in the revival of Irish literature had been clear to him from the start. She would use her great practical talents to found libraries across the land. She had shown herself enthusiastic, and by 14 June 1892 had been appointed, along with Yeats himself, to the Library Sub-Committee of the National Literary Society. During the autumn she helped raise money for the scheme by lecturing in France, and in the winter she returned to Ireland where, despite her doubts about whether the people needed books more than food, she founded three of the seven libraries set up by the Society. As Yeats saw, Maud was now acquiring that mastery over popular feeling that Irish MPs had lost after the fall of Parnell and in this lay a danger to him, a powerful and subtle rival to his love.

Others continued to disparage Maud's achievements, O'Leary seeing her merely as a beautiful woman in search of excitement. Sarah Purser dismissed her as little more than a society belle. Torn by his private thoughts about her and challenged over her in public, Yeats strove to defend Maud and tackle the complexity of his own feelings. The divisions he perceived in Maud's mind distressed him. The woman who lived surrounded by animals and the old people who came to seek her help was benevolent and patient, 'the woman I had come to love'. Maud was still Queen of the Western Sidhe. But alongside this was another woman longing for political involvement and the opportunity to give vent to that oratory which had about it, Yeats thought, so much of 'emotional temper' and uncontrollable self-expression, so much of a lust for the extreme. He longed to bring Maud into peace with herself and to refashion her after his own image of feminine self-content.

That Maud seemed responsive to his art encouraged Yeats to think he might gain influence over her imagination. He tried to woo her with his occult symbols, declaring that he was 'always seeking to bring her mind by these means into closer union with the soul, and above all with the peace of the soul'. Yeats conjured up for her a vision of an angel which, he wrote in his 'Autobiography', showed her the three circles of spiritual happiness to which she might one day aspire from her hell of guilt and grief. Maud would say, sometimes, that in such ways Yeats had saved her from despair, but she nonetheless forgot her visions and it seemed to them both that the grey lady and her evil harassed Maud ever more cruelly. Yeats even wondered if Maud had 'a subconscious conviction that her soul was lost', and the intimacy that allowed him to think this, the very closeness that they had fragilely achieved, splintered in quarrels.

These arose all too frequently from the literary work in which Yeats had hoped to ensnare his muse. Maud could not believe, as Yeats so passionately did, that the future of Ireland was at stake in the Literary Society's choice of texts. She found his attitude to popular poetry elitist and listened sympathetically to J. F. Taylor's arguments and to Gavan Duffy's case, seeing the power that lay in common, popular goals. Fearing he was losing her through the very means by which he had sought to entrap her, Yeats sat bitterly in Maud's rooms in Nassau Street, his jealousy of Taylor rising to a fury until the older man's more vigorous temper forced him into ridiculous over-statement or yet more ignominious, confused retreat. Yeats was fast losing ground. He had begun his literary campaign believing he could save his nation's soul. Now it seemed he had alienated the older men, alienated Maud and even alienated the men of his own generation, who began to subvert his plans for provincial libraries. John O'Leary put blame on Yeats's attempt to be a popular leader, a talker in pubs and private houses. He should, he said, have kept himself aloof. This was a lesson dearly learned and was to strike deep roots.

But as 1892 drew to a close it became clear that Yeats's failure to establish the precedence of an elite literature in Ireland was only one part of a much wider campaign for national identity. Other intellectuals were also aware that the country's sense of itself was in danger of slipping away, and the failure of politics after the death of Parnell exposed ever more starkly the range of English influence in Ireland, the decline of traditional ways of life and the steady disappearance of the Gaelic language. English assumptions could be seen as a powerful contamination, and it had to be asked if there really could be, as Yeats supposed, a true Irish literature that was not written in the Irish language. An enthusiasm for Gaelic could now be seen as a touchstone of Nationalism and when, on 25 November 1892, Yeats's friend Douglas Hyde delivered his lecture on 'The Necessity for De-Anglicising Ireland' he very ably put the case for a Gaelic revival inspired by Nationalism. Hyde would soon be made the first president of the Gaelic League, and Yeats watched with dismay as a man he thought of as a great poet and folklorist gave himself increasingly to such ideals.

When, in mid-December 1892, Yeats himself left for England, the complex and bitter forces inherent in literary Nationalism were beginning to become clear, and he knew he would achieve a position of influence only with difficulty. But, if his public position was a fraught one, his private life was under continuous stress. Money was one major problem. 'It was growing increasingly hard to earn a living,' he confessed.

> I never spent more than a pound a week, but I could now scarcely earn so much and was growing anxious. My work was interfered with by lack of money, and I had to allow the London society to do things I objected to because I could not afford my ticket to London. As a result of the split in the Irish party that followed the fall of Parnell, there were two newspapers for every one before it, and papers that had but half their old circulation could not pay for verse or even for reviews.[3]

And to poverty was added the frustration of his love for Maud Gonne. 'I was tortured by sexual desire,' from which there seemed no release. Pride, lack of opportunity, idealised passion and deep-seated fears imprisoned Yeats in his 'unctuous celibacy'. As he wrote of this time in his 'Autobiography': 'when I returned to London in my twenty-seventh year I think my love seemed almost hopeless, and I knew that my friends had all mistresses of one kind or another and that most, at need, went home with harlots. Henley, indeed, mocked at any other life. I had never since childhood kissed a woman's lips.' But the temptation Yeats glimpsed all around him proved to be no temptation at all. 'At Hammersmith I saw a woman of the town walking up and down in the empty railway station. I thought of offering myself to her, but the old thought came back, "No, I love the most beautiful woman in the world."' Idealism was the armour with which to ward off experience, just as poetry would become the means to explore his frustration.

II
The Vault of the Adepti

Harassed in these ways, Yeats, in a response typical of his antithetical mind, turned to the world of mystic reverie. Back in London during the winter weeks of early January 1892, he began to study in greater depth the rituals of the Golden Dawn. He had already discovered that, whereas meetings of the Theosophical Society made his thoughts captious and abstract, the worlds opened up by MacGregor Mathers gave him an imaginative strength which stimulated his work for Ireland. Now, however, just as Irish literary politics were riven with discord, so the first divisions were beginning to appear among the English occultists. These were precipitated by what was emerging as Mathers's disturbed personality.

Early in the previous year Mathers had had a row with Annie Horniman's father and lost his job as curator of his collections. For a while he and Moina lived in cheap lodgings off the Tottenham Court Road where, in his frustration and despite a secret subsidy from Annie herself, Mathers began to review his career. London no longer seemed to him a satisfactory base, and in the summer of 1891 he went to Paris to seek further occult enlightenment. He realised that if the movement in England were to develop, more advanced rituals than Yeats as yet knew would have to be formulated. Mathers was growing ever more determined to have the Order wholly under his control and would be soon making plans to oust some of its leading founder members. He claimed that in Paris he was contacted by a Higher Adept, one *Frater Lux E Tenebris*, who apparently gave him the materials to construct the Second Order ritual for which Yeats was now studying. Mathers also claimed that the so-called Secret Chiefs required him to transfer his operations permanently to Paris. There was some sense in this. Paris was much cheaper than London, it was the true European centre of the occult movement and the Paris libraries had excellent holdings of medieval *grimoires*, while the struggles there between rival factions of Rosicrucians meant that a man of strong personality could yet make his mark. Mathers and Moina eventually left for France in May 1892 but, before they did so, their benefactress was initiated into the Second Order of the movement she had so generously funded.

Annie Horniman was to have a great influence on Yeats, both through the Golden Dawn and in other ways. Born the elder child of the Horniman tea heir, Annie was educated at home by her brothers' tutor and showed a keen interest in history and foreign languages. Always independent, she defied her Nonconformist family's disapproval of the theatre by slipping out at thirteen to see a production of *The Merchant of Venice*. By the 1880s she was an avid theatre-goer and a passionate Wagnerite, travelling to Bayreuth in 1884 on the first of many visits. During her travels, many of them made on her bicycle, she acquired a wide knowledge of the European avant-garde theatre and of the serious and often subsidised drama that seemed to her so much more interesting than the commercial persiflage of London's West End. She had by this time enrolled as a student at the Slade School of Art, where she soon struck up a friendship with the eighteen-year-old Moina Bergson and her fiancé MacGregor Mathers.

Annie herself eventually came to realise the limits of her artistic talent, but she believed in Moina's ability and was at first suspicious of the occultism to which her friend was so committed. What was probably the disappointment of a failed love affair drew Annie closer to Moina, however, and by the close of 1889, having received many kindnesses and much instruction from Moina and Mathers, she joined the Golden Dawn under the name *Fortiter et Recte* ('Bravely and Justly'), a motto she would try genuinely to live up to as she strove to be the movement's patron. It was this emotionally intense, plain and energetic woman, dressed in loosely flowing Pre-Raphaelite gowns, who now provided the Matherses with an income of £200 a year and paid for the decoration of the Vault of the Adepti in Clipstone Street.* There, on 20 January 1893, Yeats himself was initiated into the Second Order of the Golden Dawn, the *Ordo Rosae Rubeae et Aureae Crucis*, or the 'Order of the Red Rose and the Golden Cross'.

The Portal Ceremony which introduced Yeats to the Second Order was intended to give him a glimpse of a supernatural world which lay beyond what, in a symbol of the greatest importance to the Yeats of the 1890s, was called the Paroketh or 'the Veil of the Temple' trembling between the mundane and the supernatural worlds.[4] His earlier progress through the elements of Earth, Air, Water and Fire had supposedly integrated and balanced his primal self and this would now be symbolically sacrificed and offered to the Higher Genius. As *Demon est Deus Inversus*, Yeats stood at the Portal in a state of intense mystical excitement. He was on the threshold of a spiritual rebirth, and, as he prepared himself for the first sub-grade in the rank of Adeptus Minor, his meditations on the Order's symbolic pictures of the growth of the soul to new life, his understanding of his place in mankind's evolution, and his learning to stand outside himself to see how his 'mask' or lower self appeared to others, all encouraged him to spiritual self-knowledge. He was urged particularly to reflect on the power of words, his obsession with them and their effect. He was brought to the position where he fully realised what a Golden Dawn document called 'the tremendous miracle of words, the magic both good and evil of human communion'. With his mind thus prepared, Yeats could undergo the Adeptus Minor ritual, his symbolic death and resurrection in the seven-sided Vault of the Adepti.

At the centre of the Vault itself stood a copy of the tomb of the founder of the Rosicrucian Order, Father Christian Rosenkreutz, where, as a medieval document held, the body of this wise and careful alchemist had lain uncorrupted for many years until discovered by the faithful few. On the lid of the tomb Moina Mathers had painted Adam, the partially illuminated man, rescuing the fallen kingdom of his natural self through personal sacrifice.

---

* Annie Horniman was quietly generous to many members of the Golden Dawn, and Yeats especially would pass cases of hardship to her. The following instance of one 'B' suggests that charity and broadmindedness were often-practised values. 'She has left word that all bills are to be sent to her and will I think look after her until she gets well . . . My mystics will not bemoralise her, which her other friends seem to have been doing vigorously.'

Above him stood the radiant figure of a saved Adam entered into the glory of his potential godhead. In these illustrations, and in the symbolism of the Vault as a whole, was an image of mankind's resurrection from the dark tomb of mortality into the power of the spirit. For Yeats, a new era was about to dawn. 'I cannot get it out of my mind that this age of criticism is about to pass,' he wrote in 'The Body of the Father Christian Rosencrux'. Scientific materialism had run its course and now, in a little rented room in Clipstone Street, an age of imagination, emotion and revelation was about to supersede it. The external world was no more the standard of reality and mankind would 'learn again that the great passions are angels of God'.

The Second Order rituals of the Golden Dawn enacted this process of apocalyptic revelation. Yeats was led in, arrayed in his insignia and badges and calling himself by his magical name. He was warned that he should approach the mysteries in a humble rather than vainglorious spirit, and was stripped of his insignia before being bound to a large wooden cross dressed only in a simple black gown. He was about to undergo the redemption of his personality, to do battle with 'the poisonous Dragon' and rise anew in his potential divinity. He was, in other words, a type of the 'dying god' familiar from Frazer's *The Golden Bough*, an Osiris, a Christ, an Adonis about to return to godhead. Here was a rite of passage leading to the inner and eternal world of illumination and, once illuminated, Yeats could utter the daring Obligation of the first Adeptus Minor grade: 'I will from this day forward apply myself unto the Great Work, which is so to purify and exalt my spiritual nature that with the Divine Aid I may at length attain to be more than human, and thus gradually raise and unite myself to my higher and divine Genius.' The means by which Yeats would do this was Ceremonial Magic.

There was nothing in this practice of the self-surrender, the patient and humble waiting on the divine associated, for example, with conventional Christianity. The magical invocations of the Golden Dawn were not prayers uttered by the powerless to the godhead. They were a summons, and what were summoned were the forces allegedly inhering in the symbolic world of the *anima mundi* or Great Memory, that collective unconscious of the initiated. Here lay the magus's power, and to meditate on the mystic Rose, for example, was a means of making that power operative in the world. People could be drawn into its aura and, in such ways, their lives might be changed. Since it was also a widely held belief among the occultists that language created that which it expressed, the art of poetry, the most refined and potent use of words, could convey the images gleaned from the magician's symbolic world with unique effect. There is little doubt that Yeats's interest in the Golden Dawn derived in part at least from his belief that its rituals offered him symbols that had a magic power over his readers, a spiritual potency which led beyond materialism and into the deepest recesses of the psyche. It was for this reason that Yeats could inform a querulous John O'Leary that 'the mystical life is the centre of all that I do and all that I think and all that I write'.[5] Yeats was, he believed, in the vanguard of a great renaissance, which he described as 'the revolt of the soul against the intellect'.

III
'The Celtic Heart'

It was also once again, and in part at least, the revolt of the son against the father. With a quick, defensive instinct, Yeats realised that John O'Leary's doubts over his magical interests had probably been raised by JBY's discoursing on them from 'the immense depths of his ignorance'. The phrase betrayed the competitive sourness that still existed between the unsuccessful father and the ambitious son who, at twenty-seven, continued to live for much of his time at home. This situation brought out the unpleasant traits in both men, but, if JBY was genuinely worried over what he considered the dangerous silliness of his son's occultism, the poems gathered into the collection Yeats called *The Rose* show the exceptional subtlety of his occult concerns.

Here is no merely triumphant irrationalism. The poems have the range of feeling, the richness and occasional doubt more usually associated with conventional religious lyrics. In *The Rose*, Yeats's occult world suggests the experience and suppleness of a seasoned faith. For all the euphoria with which, as an initiate, he might have stood before the Portal of the Vault of the Adepti, the poet was more subtle, more circumspect. Yeats's literary occultism was both radiant and questioning. While he was convinced that the artist must indeed be inspired by those 'moods' which were for him 'the labourers and messengers of the Ruler of All, the gods of ancient days still dwelling on their secret Olympus', he was aware of the dangers inherent in their service. The careful shaping of the collection works to this end. Moments of insight are woven into a sequence that has an authority greater than the individual lyrics that compose it. By presenting his work in this way, by orchestrating an elaborate internal debate, conscious artifice provides a complexity that is both subtle and emotionally satisfying.

The range of these works is suggested by the opening poem, 'The Rose upon the Rood of Time'. Here, the manifold suggestiveness of the crucified Rose is shown as inspiring Yeats's use of Irish mythology, and the two poems that follow tell the stories of Cuchulain and Fergus. Building on such ideas, the Rose is then evoked as a symbol of eternal beauty illuminating and absorbing all earthly things until it becomes 'The Rose of the World', that archetype of loveliness which hovers over history connecting the fate of individuals and nations to the eternal. Yeats suggests that the Rose unfolded its petals above Helen of Troy and Deirdre, even as it now finds its reflection in the face of Maud Gonne, who herself briefly becomes 'The Rose of Peace'. In a glorious celebration of romantic idealism, Maud's beauty is seen as the ultimate reconciler of cosmic conflict.

But, if the loveliness of the Rose is briefly extolled as the maker of world harmony, it is suggestive both of the collection's range and of Yeats the antithetical man that the Rose of Peace, the reconciler of opposites, can also become 'The Rose of Battle', inspiring man to struggle against his fate in unequal combat. As the Rose stretches down to toiling man, so the desire it raises is infinite and can lead to dissatisfaction, defeat and the annihilation of endeavour:

> Rose of all Roses, Rose of all the World!
> You, too, have come where the dim tides are hurled
> Upon the wharves of sorrow, and heard ring
> The bell that calls us on; the sweet far thing.
> Beauty grown sad with its eternity
> Made you of us, and of the dim grey sea.
> Our long ships loose thought-woven sails and wait,
> For God has bid them share an equal fate;
> And when at last, defeated in His wars,
> They have gone down under the same white stars,
> We shall no longer hear the little cry
> Of our sad hearts, that may not live nor die.[6]

In the final poem in the collection, 'To Ireland in the Coming Times', Yeats argues that because the Rose is so profoundly implicated in history – is that ideal towards which men strive even as the Rose herself strains to reach down to them – the Rose is a wholly suitable subject for political poetry. Indeed, more than this, such art as Yeats's own is the creator of history. Yeats suggests that by staring deep into his heart and the *anima mundi* he has brought forth the great images that must by their very nature inspire men to action. In terms of English literary romanticism Yeats stands with Shelley, who, he wrote, 'in *A Defence of Poetry* . . . will have it that the poet and the lawgiver hold their station by the right of the same faculty, the one uttering in words and the other in the forms of society his vision of the divine order, the Intellectual Beauty'. Yeats is not, he claims, the remote and ineffective mystic but a poet who, like Davis and Ferguson, can cause men to act and inspire events to take place. Such men, he wrote, 'had one quality I admired and admire: they were not separated individual men; they spoke or tried to speak out of a people to a people; behind them stretched the generations'. The measured lines of Yeats's art thus contain within them the immeasurable power of eternal vision and historic nationalism, and, because life imitates art, Yeats's poetry of mystic insight can be seen as a powerful force in the world:

> Nor may I less be counted one
> With Davis, Mangan, Ferguson,
> Because, to him who ponders well,
> My rhymes more than their rhyming tell
> Of things discovered in the deep,
> Where only body's laid asleep.
> For the elemental creatures go
> Around my table to and fro,
> That hurry from unmeasured mind
> To rant and rage in flood and wind;
> Yet he who treads in measured ways
> May surely barter gaze for gaze.
> Man ever journeys on with them
> After the red-rose-bordered hem.
> Ah, faeries, dancing under the moon,
> A Druid land, a Druid tune![7]

This is ceremonial magic in action and the reason why Yeats could tell O'Leary that his interest in magic was wholly compatible with his nationalism. Art, mysticism and politics have combined. Yeats's interests have been forged into a unity, and the magus and the patriot are at one with the poet. Yet for all the power and idealism of such assertions there is in these works – and it is in this that the subtlety of the sequence partly lies – a complex relation between the mundane and the supernatural. Yeats was acutely conscious that in summoning the infinite suggestiveness of the mystic Rose he might, even in inspiring his countrymen, lose touch with reality and so drift along a confusing path of purely subjective intuition. He feared especially that he might:

> no more hear common things that crave;
> The weak worm hiding down in its small cave,
> The field-mouse running by me in the grass,
> And heavy mortal hopes that toil and pass;
> But seek alone to hear the strange things said
> By God to the bright hearts of those long dead,
> And learn to chaunt a tongue men do not know.[8]

There is a haunting fear in these lines which suggests that, even as he celebrated the power of the Rose, Yeats was acutely aware that its force threatened his spiritual serenity. Time would show that these worries were justified.

The occult patriotism of *The Rose* is seen again in another project from this time. While Yeats was deeply involved in Ceremonial Magic and the rituals of the Golden Dawn, he still maintained his interest in the superstitions and folklore of the peasantry that had surrounded him since his childhood in Sligo. Now, rather than using published sources, he was collecting the stories he himself had heard at first or second hand into a volume called *The Celtic Twilight*. This title would become synonymous with the entire literary movement Yeats was heading. Folklore was coming into its own as a literary genre, and *The Celtic Twilight*, Yeats's anthology of stories revealing 'the vast and vague extravagance that lies at the bottom of the Celtic heart', shows how successful he could be in combining the roles of the artist and story collector, a man concerned to exhibit the beliefs of a still elemental people in touch with the ancient mysteries of a pre-Christian world.[9]

Something of the allure of the fairy world of 'the untiring ones' is suggested in the story of that title where Yeats contrasts the mixed human life of joy and pain, 'this entanglement of moods which makes us old', with the existence of the Sidhe, whose love and hate are clear, distinct and life-enhancing. Their untiring joys and sorrows are at least half their fascination, Yeats suggests. 'Love with them never grows weary, nor can the circle of the stars tire out their dancing feet'. It is this magical energy that the Irish peasant, so much more fortunate despite his poverty than the modern city-dweller, knows as he bends over his spade or sits by his fire at night to tell tales. More modern men, living 'in a time out-worn', can also find spiritual refreshment in thoughts of such immaterial reality and, in so doing, pay tribute to the eternal youthfulness of 'mother Eire'. Yeats seems much closer here to his peasant sources than in his earlier work, and it is partly the character of the peasant, the blend of joy and tragedy he detected in these people, that led him to create sympathetic portraits of such tellers of tales as George Pollexfen's servant Mary Battle.

Yeats himself also figures in the volume, nowhere more interestingly than in the narrative entitled 'Regina, Regina Pigmeorum, Veni'.[10] Here Yeats presented himself walking the Sligo coast at night with two companions, who were almost certainly his uncle George Pollexfen and his cousin Lucy Middleton, a young woman 'who was reported to be enough of a seeress to catch a glimpse of unaccountable lights moving over the fields among the cattle'. Conversation turned to 'the Forgetful People' – another name for the Sidhe – and when the companions came to a shallow cave among the rocks which they knew to be a notable fairy haunt Yeats pictures himself asking the girl if she can see anything. He then describes her passing into a trance so deep that she becomes oblivious of her surroundings while Yeats (and it is he who takes the initiative throughout the incident) calls out the names of the greater fairies.

At this point Yeats's other companion interrupted to say he could hear the laughter of children behind the rocks. He too, however, was beginning to fall under the influence of the spirits of the place, and Yeats's friends now claimed to hear music and the stamping of feet. A bright light then appeared out of the cave, and the young girl saw 'a quantity of little people, in various coloured dresses, red predominating, dancing to a tune which she did not recognise'. When Yeats asked the girl to summon the Fairy Queen he was at first disappointed, but when he repeated the words aloud the girl described a tall and beautiful woman emerging from the cave.

Yeats's position in all this is ambiguous. He suggests that he can call spirits from the vasty deep (or at least from their cave beside the sea), but when he calls they manifest to others. He is neither completely lapped in vision nor wholly the objective observer. Rather has he fallen into what he calls 'a kind of trance', a state of suspended will learned from MacGregor Mathers in which the imagination allegedly moves of its own accord. He admits to being able to see only an impression of gold ornaments and dark hair rather than the precise, Richard Dadd-like vision described by the girl. Yeats thus places himself scrupulously on the border of an experience he nonetheless claims to control, for it is he who now bids the girl ask the fairies to line up in serried ranks. At first they refuse to comply, and 'I found as before that I had to repeat the command myself.' Once again, the fairies obey Yeats's voice but become visible only to others:

> The beings then came out of the cave, and drew themselves up, if I remember rightly, in four bands. One of these bands, according to [the girl's] description, carried boughs of mountain-ash in their hands, and another had necklaces made apparently of serpents' scales, but their dress I cannot remember. I asked their queen to tell the seeress whether these caves were the greatest fairy haunts in the neighbourhood. Her lips moved, but the answer was inaudible. I bade the seeress lay her hand upon the breast of the queen, and after that she heard every word quite distinctly.[11]

Yeats then asked through his intermediary if the fairies carried mortals away and, if so, whether they put another soul in the place of the one they had stolen. 'We change the bodies,' the Fairy Queen said and then told him that some of her kind were indeed born into mortal life. When Yeats asked for examples of who such people might be he was told that it was not lawful for him to know. He then asked if the fairies were merely dramatisations of human moods, a question the Queen claimed she did not understand, saying that her kind were similar to human beings and did many things that humans did. But eventually Yeats's persistent questioning began to make her cross and she wrote out on the 'sands of vision' the stern warning: 'Be careful, and do not seek to know too much about us.' Realising that he had offended her, Yeats thanked the Fairy Queen and allowed her to return into her cave. He had learned little that was not commonplace fairy-lore and the whole episode, despite its charm, is cunningly constructed to suggest more than it actually offers. The sceptical magus again stands adroitly pitched on the edges of vision.

IV
'A Serious Quarrel'

The first edition of *The Celtic Twilight* was assembled out of miscellaneous pieces of Yeats's journalism. He was working extremely hard during these years to make a precarious living out of further anthologies such as *A Book of Irish Verse*, as well as publishing articles and reviews for such leading journals as the *Spectator* and the *Bookman*. He reviewed among other works the poems of Wilfred Scawen Blunt, Oscar Wilde's *Lord Arthur Savile's Crime*, Todhunter's poems and Douglas Hyde's *Love Songs of Connaught*. He also reviewed works on Celtic history and wrote articles and miscellaneous pieces on a wide range of subjects, including the Irish Literary Society in London, an exhibition of works by William Morris and a book on the Ainu, a group of primitive Trans-Siberian people who he found had analogies with the ancient Celts. But while these efforts were almost always tied to his patriotic interests, Irish literature demanded other platforms. On 19 May 1893, Yeats delivered to a Dublin audience his lecture on 'Nationality and Literature'.[12]

Part of Yeats's purpose in this talk was to show that literature in England had reached an extreme cosmopolitan complexity while Ireland, alone perhaps among the nations of Europe, was still in its epic age and capable of being fed by such beliefs as those revealed in *The Celtic Twilight*. Yeats feared, however, that narrow provincialism might stunt the growth of this literature and he urged the study of the best Continental models so that Irish writing might become genuinely European and strong in a sophisticated technique. Nonetheless, if the emphasis of his lecture was on the epic possibilities for a nation still in the infancy of consciousness, Yeats's own understanding of the far reaches of modern literary sophistication pointed to the path he was already taking in *The Rose*. The lecture argued forcibly that with 'advancing subtlety poetry steps out of the market-place, out of the general tide of life and becomes a mysterious cult, as it were, an almost secret religion made by the few for the few'. Poetry and the occult had become identified, and the direction of Yeats's increasingly elitist concerns is clear.

These interests remained a source of friction between himself and Maud Gonne. Not only had Maud listened sympathetically to such enemies of Yeats's as J. F. Taylor, she was now inviting to her rooms in Nassau Street representatives of a younger generation, enthusiastic Catholics from working-class families like William Rooney and Arthur Griffith. These men saw the importance of uniting the factions divided by the fall of Parnell but also realised the place of literature in forming the opinions of their people. National consciousness would not any longer be the prerogative of the minority Anglo-Irish community. A subtle and profound change was taking place in Ireland, and Rooney in particular was playing an important part in this. He had helped found the Celtic Literary Society, which was now issuing a journal for the ordinary working people of Dublin. Maud's democratic spirit approved of such initiatives. Her 'headquarters' in Nassau Street became a centre for all sorts and conditions of Nationalists and a place where her philosophy of life was applied to art and politics. In contrast to Yeats, 'I never willingly discouraged either a Dynamiter or a constitutionalist, a realist or a lyrical writer,' Maud wrote.[13] 'My chief preoccupation was how their work could help forward the Irish Separatist movement.' Yeats would have to take his place among these others. When he complained, Maud called him a snob, and by the early summer of 1893 the tension between them had exploded in 'a serious quarrel'.

Almost immediately afterwards, Maud fell ill. A cold developed into congestion of the lungs and she was ordered to bed. Dr Sigerson, with whom Yeats had disagreed over the New Irish Library scheme, banned him from the sickroom and, to calm his worries, Yeats had to rely on news brought by a troublesome old woman who had inveigled herself into the role of Maud's nurse. Yeats arranged to meet this woman every night in a public garden, but she only increased his worries by telling him melodramatic tales. Yeats was to think no more of Maud Gonne, she said. She loved another – perhaps two others – for she had decided to hurry back to France to witness a duel between them. Yeats would not, the old woman told him, ever see his beloved again. Eventually, Maud's cousin May came to take her back to France. Maud was so weak that she had to be carried to the train, despite Sigerson's insistence that she not be moved at all. The wretched nurse, meanwhile, let Dublin know what had really happened behind the closed curtains in Nassau Street. Excited by the power of her fantasies, she said that Yeats had been Maud's lover, that he had made her pregnant and that he had even been present when she underwent an illegal abortion. The falsehoods were soon circulating everywhere and, by the end of May, Yeats himself left a gossip-ridden Dublin for the relative anonymity of London.

V

'The Land of Heart's Desire'

Here, in his confusion and wretchedness, Yeats visited the Vault of the Adepti in Clipstone Street as often as three times a week. He sought consolation in the occult and also in poetry. By the close of August, he had begun the small white notebook in which he drafted many of the poems later to be published as *The Wind among the Reeds*. Soon afterwards, restless and unhappy, he returned to Dublin and busied himself with plans for an Irish literary magazine, with meetings of the National Literary Society, and with a speech given to the Young Ireland League. In December, *The Celtic Twilight* appeared and then, towards Christmas, he returned to London. Still deeply concerned about Maud, he was asked by a near neighbour, the actress Florence Farr, to write for her a one-act play in which her niece, a little girl of eight or nine, might make her first stage appearance. In this way, Yeats was brought into contact with the professional theatre, and he now determined to write a drama in which he could explain to himself the cause of Maud's defection.

The circumstances surrounding the invitation to write the play were less transparent than Yeats supposed. In May 1890, he had seen Florence Farr play the part of the moon goddess Selene in Todhunter's *A Sicilian Idyll*. He had been greatly impressed by her beauty, by her subtlety of gesture and, above all, by the power of her voice. As Yeats wrote in his *Autobiographies*, 'she had three great gifts, a tranquil beauty like that of Demeter's image near the British Museum Reading-Room door, and an incomparable sense of rhythm and a beautiful voice, the seeming natural expression of the image'. Harnessing these powers, Florence Farr brought to Todhunter's indifferent verse what Yeats himself called 'a passionate austerity that made it akin for certain moments to the great poetry of the world'. When, soon after the production, Florence moved to lodgings near Brook Green, Yeats became a frequent visitor.[14]

Florence Farr had had a remarkable career. Five years older than Yeats, she had been educated at Cheltenham Ladies' College and, briefly, at Queen's College, London. Defiantly leaving university for the stage, her experience in 'low comedy' convinced her that an actress could succeed only if she was first-rate. 'She must be able to boss the show or quit.' After a lightning romance, she married Edward Emery, the weak and dissipated son of a long-established family of actors. Unable to tolerate either domestic life or what soon became a loveless marriage, Florence succeeded in persuading her husband (now mired in scandal) to depart on a theatrical tour of the United States. She herself then moved in with her sister and brother-in-law at Bedford Park, adding to her meagre resources by becoming an expert embroideress under May Morris. It was this attractive and resourceful woman, so close at hand and so sympathetic to his interests, whom Yeats now introduced to MacGregor and Moina Mathers. Florence's incantatory powers and her quick, eclectic intelligence – what Yeats would eventually describe as her 'insatiable, destroying curiosity' – might be of great help to the Golden Dawn. Recently admitted to the Order himself, Yeats encouraged

Florence's initiation and, in July 1890, she became one of the *sorores* under the name *Sapientia Sapienti Dono Data* ('Wisdom is a gift given to the Wise').

Simultaneously with these events, Florence was developing her relationship with Bernard Shaw. Shaw was later, and with more bad taste than accuracy, to make much of what he alleged to be Florence's promiscuity. What is more certain is that Shaw, a self-confessed philanderer, was attracted to this emancipated and hard-working actress who, under his influence, was soon to divorce her husband. It was she, however, who cut through Shaw's labyrinthine self-defences with a stark 'Let's get it over,' and by November 1890 they were lovers. Early in the following year, when Florence was playing the role of Rebecca West in the first English production of Ibsen's *Rosmersholm*, Shaw conceived the idea of fashioning her into his ideal actress. The woman with whom he was so closely involved was starring in a play by a writer who was profoundly to influence Shaw himself. He turned on Florence the full force of his critical genius, but Yeats, who reviewed her performance in *Rosmersholm*, felt that her exquisite gift for recitation was best displayed in poetic drama.

And in this lay the nub of Yeats's objection to Ibsen. He felt that *Rosmersholm* merely gave off 'a stale odour of spilled poetry'. Although he was too acute to miss the fact that both he and Ibsen had the same enemies – a bourgeois theatre audience fearful of anything that seriously challenged their preconceptions – he could not sympathise with Ibsen's realistic social criticism. While reviewers who saw Ibsen's work as 'an open drain: a loathsome sore unbandaged' could clearly be dismissed as philistine, Yeats could not side with those who, like Shaw, saw in Ibsen's work 'a vital truth searched out and held up in a light intense enough to dispel all the mists and shadows that obscure it in actual life'. For Yeats, enamoured of Celtic Twilight, Ibsen's was merely the sort of drama favoured by 'clever young journalists' who, in their love of abstraction, 'hated music and style'.[15]

Difficulties raised by the Lord Chamberlain over the staging of Ibsen's plays had shown to a number of those about Yeats how important it was, if England were to mount avant-garde drama, that there should be non-profitmaking minority theatres in which to perform it. Yeats's fellow Rhymer Arthur Symons argued for a London equivalent of the Parisian Théâtre Libre, while George Moore (soon to be an associate of Yeats) urged the need for a suitable playhouse for those three or four thousand people who, he reckoned, were interested in genuinely new literature. By 1891, the Independent Theatre Society was playing *Ghosts* and *Hedda Gabler*, while Florence Farr in 1892 had acted in the two matinée performances which were all that were given of Shaw's *Widowers' Houses*. When, in the following year, Florence's fellow Golden Dawner Annie Horniman received a substantial legacy from her grandfather, Florence was suddenly presented with the possibility of running her own subsidised season of new work. It was on the strength of Annie's money (and unknown to the playwrights themselves) that she could now turn to Shaw, to Todhunter and to Yeats and ask for new plays. 'And I,' Yeats recalled, 'with my Irish theatre in mind, wrote *The Land of Heart's Desire* . . . for I knew an Irish woman whose unrest troubled me.'

The reasons for that unrest were not altogether clear to Yeats when he visited Maud in Paris during February 1894. He believed that she was tired and ill when he watched her slowly climbing the stairs to a friend's flat but, although their row was patched up, Maud remained distant, a woman Yeats sensed he was on the point of losing. He was unaware that the turmoil in Maud's private life was not something she could yet fully confess to and he felt that some occult power was spiriting her away.

Depressed and ill, Maud had returned to France and saved Millevoye from the gloom into which the defeat of his political hopes had thrown him by urging him to take up the editorship of *La Patrie*. Here Maud published her own anti-English propaganda. By making herself and her lover so prominent, however, she had begun to attract enemies among the French themselves. None was more frightening than the leading politician Clemenceau, who, swaggering through a country racked by the corruption that fed the Dreyfus scandal, saw Maud and Millevoye as threats to his hopes for an English alliance. He vowed to break them. Maud, trailed as she knew by the British secret service, now found that her maid was in Clemenceau's employ. She sacked the woman and urged Millevoye to continue his campaign against Clemenceau. But Millevoye and his followers had drifted to the far right, and Maud saw the *belle époque* tarnishing about her. She was in some personal danger and had been obliged to confess to herself that while her physical desire for Millevoye had faded she still desperately wanted to have his child. Threatened by so many conflicts, the presence of Yeats in her apartment on the Avenue d'Eylau offered perhaps some measure of sympathetic distraction.

Yeats himself stayed in the altogether humbler flat rented by the Matherses on the Left Bank. Here the occult couple, planning the means by which they could propagate their beliefs, persuaded Yeats into four-handed games of chess in which Yeats partnered Moina while Mathers co-ordinated his moves with a spirit sitting invisibly in an empty chair opposite. Yeats believed the decay of Mathers's character had not yet set in, but saw that the magus was nonetheless under severe mental and physical strain. By the close of 1893, Mathers had begun to foresee traumatic changes in the world order and was announcing 'the imminence of great wars'.[16] Carnage, bloodshed and conspiracy filled his mind. He and Moina had decided that one of the principal aims of the Golden Dawn should be 'the Regeneration of the Race of the Planet', and now, to this end, they shut themselves away once a week and summoned their magic powers in an effort to rearrange the nations after their own grandiose fantasies.

The effort was so great that afterwards, Yeats observed, Mathers was seen to spit blood. But this frantic, chiliastic atmosphere had a profound effect on Yeats himself. He knew that across Ireland there were prophecies of the coming rout of her enemies in a battle to be waged in a certain 'Valley of the Black Pig'. He could see that such beliefs acted as a genuine political force on those people from among whom he had collected the stories gathered in *The Celtic Twilight*. During the next couple of years, Yeats's own thoughts were to be increasingly dominated by images of an Armageddon which, he believed, would extinguish all things in ancestral darkness as 'the blood-dimmed tide' began to encroach on the shores of the world.

Love, politics and magic enfolded Yeats in their often painful embrace, but while Paris stimulated his Irish and occult interests, it also offered him the wealth of its literary life. Yeats had been in Dublin when Verlaine came to speak to the London Rhymers, but now, aided by an introduction from Arthur Symons, he was invited to 'coffee and cigarettes plentifully' at the poet's tenement flat in the Rue St Jacques.[17]

The cigarettes and coffee were served by Verlaine's homely mistress, whose caged birds and sentimental lithographs, scattered between caricatures of the poet as a monkey, gave the room much of its character. Verlaine himself sat with one leg swathed in bandages and explained in an English that was much more fluent than Yeats's French that he had been 'scorched' by his profligate life in the city. His face, Yeats noted, had something of the 'voluminous tenderness' that was believed characteristic of the dissolute but, in this profoundly antithetical man, indulgence alternated with the joyous serenity of a poet who communed with spiritual ideas. Verlaine's great temperament, his Daimon, had, Yeats felt, been made uncontrollable so that his life could explore the sordid material his art demanded. The claims of the ideal had dissolved both sanity and morality, and the supernatural had been revealed to Verlaine in the midst of squalor even, Yeats noted, as the Incarnation had taken place in a stable.

The Christlike nature of the poet is hinted at, but the actual conversation was more down to earth. While another mute and curious visitor (a poor, unshaven man who reminded Verlaine of Louis XI) sat by the fire and played with his opera hat, the poet discoursed on writers he knew or admired. Tennyson, he said, was too noble, too English to translate and was, besides, overstocked with personal reminiscences. Hugo had all the mud as well as the flame of a volcano. Maeterlinck was a dear fellow but a bit of a mountebank. Verlaine offered Yeats an introduction to Mallarmé and, turning to the topical figure of Villiers de l'Isle-Adam, said he was 'exalté' but wrote the most excellent French. His new play *Axel* was meant to show, Verlaine believed, that 'love was the only important thing in the world', an interpretation Yeats considered somewhat narrow.

When Yeats called on Mallarmé he was eventually made to understand that the poet was lecturing in England. Mallarmé's daughter then wrote to her father of Yeats's visit, telling him of an unnamed young poet whom she described as 'a sort of Englishman' quite unable to speak a word of French. Despite this disqualification, Yeats had, with Maud's help, been toiling through many pages of Villiers de l'Isle-Adam's *Axel* and, on 26 February, they attended one of the two matinée performances of the work given at the Théâtre de la Gaieté. Despite the inordinate length of the play (the production ran for nearly five hours) Yeats, with Maud beside him to translate, was profoundly impressed.

Here was a work wholly contrasted to the spirit of scientific materialism which, Yeats believed, had led in the theatre to the realism and Ibsenism that in England were currently destroying older and yet more corrupt conventions. This process had already been completed in France, where the younger generation, tired of photographic impressions of the world, had 'returned by the path of symbolism to imagination and poetry, the only things which are ever permanent'.[18] In *Axel*, all the events were allegories and all the characters symbols of the ultimate truths of existence. While many of those crowded into the theatre could not appreciate this (during the third Act one critic turned his opera glasses from the stage to the pretty girls in the audience) Yeats believed the play showed that 'the infinite is alone worth attaining, and the infinite is the possession of the dead'.

His synopsis of the last scene illustrated this. Count Axel and the Medusa-like Sara meet in a vault full of treasure to avow their mutual passion. Axel then tries to kill his lover since she ties him to the world. Sara herself, having renounced the cloister, the active life and the passive existence of the Rosicrucian mystic, tries to seduce the Count with a line that was to haunt the lyrics of *The Wind among the Reeds*: 'Oh, to veil you with my hair, where you will breathe the spirit of dead roses.' Axel knows, however, that the world would contaminate so refined an ecstasy as this and, condemning all life, resolves with Sara on suicide. He is thus one of those 'creative persons from whom has fallen all even of personal characteristic except a thirst for that hour when all things shall pass away like a cloud'. His moods, glimmering, as Yeats wrote, as a flame glimmers behind the dusky blue and red glass in an Eastern lamp, place him among the mystic elite. Axel is an almost pure symbol and barely part of a world where, in a phrase Yeats was fond of repeating, 'as for living our servants will do that for us'.

A day or two after seeing *Axel*, Yeats returned to London inspired by the type of drama he was himself trying to write, a drama of poetry and symbolism which might evoke the spiritual basis of Maud's turning away from him. He could explain her remoteness only by telling himself she had some longing for 'an impossible life', a life of unvarying imaginative excitement like that aspired to by the heroine of his play, *The Land of Heart's Desire*.

In this short and sinisterly beautiful work Yeats depicted a woman who dies in the act of leaving the commonplace, Christian world of peasant Ireland for the lure of the Sidhe. He knew from his folklore studies that the fascination of this world was dangerous, an appeal to mankind's longing for immaterial freedom and a threat to his normal well-being. He had already partly explored this idea in his poem 'The Man Who Dreamt of Faeryland', where each of the central figure's deepest desires – his longing for money, vengeance and a quiet death – is destroyed by the inhuman world of magic and pleasure. Even love is so destroyed. The first stanza of the work portrays a young man who has 'known at last some tenderness' from the woman he adores. It seems that he has found contentment, but the faery world intrudes and suggests that his peace of mind is only a passing state, that as a human being he cannot know a world of permanently sated desire but must rather accept the truth of his condition, that 'entanglement of moods' which can be avoided only by denying his nature. The lure of fairyland becomes in this view a state of psychological paralysis, a neurosis that denies the humanity of those who feel its power.

The Land of Heart's Desire skilfully portrays this. The play opens in a hard peasant world where the heroine's mother is a cantankerous and jealous old woman who denies beauty and the subjective life, even as her husband seems content with his creature comforts. Their priest is a kindly representative of the world of Christian discipline. The young Shawn has a natural, tender love of physical pleasure, but the heroine Mary Bruin is a woman already committed to the lure of the Sidhe. The entry of the fairy child suggests the stealth with which the world from which she comes imposes on the human one. At first apparently charming and guileless, the fairy child seems to win over all those present. Nonetheless, as she accepts their milk and a place by their fire so, by folklore tradition, the humans put themselves in her power. When the child eventually persuades the priest to remove the crucifix, her victory is complete and she can spirit Mary Bruin away to fairyland, to a place:

> Where beauty has no ebb, decay no flood,
> But joy is wisdom, time an endless song.[19]

Here is a world of beauty that is less than human, and the heroine's being taken into it is a rapture over which blow cold winds of ambiguity. The occult world destroys commonplace content, and Yeats feared that Maud too was being carried on a tide of obscure longing. He felt he was losing her as surely as his heroine was stolen from the world of real human feeling. What he did not know was that, desperate for the reincarnation of little Georges, Maud had, some months before Yeats's visit to her in Paris, persuaded Millevoye to make love to her in the dead boy's mausoleum. She was now convinced that, by virtue of this rite, she had conceived the child she was carrying.

Yeats completed his play by the close of the first week of February 1894 when he wrote to John O'Leary to tell him that the effort had exhausted him and that now that his manuscript had 'gone to the typewriter for the actors I shall rest till rehearsals begin'. That rest was brief, for by late March the London billboards were covered with posters advertising *The Land of Heart's Desire* and Todhunter's Ibsenite drama *A Comedy of Sighs*. Designed by Florence's friend Aubrey Beardsley, the acidic yellow-green and cerulean blue posters were a masterpiece of Nineties design, proclaiming that the Avenue Theatre was now in the hands of the avant-garde. A delighted Annie Horniman boasted that even the cab horses shied at Beardsley's work. But the season advertised was fraught with problems both serious and absurd. Yeats, while walking to the first performance, lost his pince-nez down a grating in the Strand and was obliged to watch his play in a myopic mist. The work was comparatively well received, and he attended many of its subsequent performances. The impression Yeats himself made, however, was not universally favourable. George Moore, who had not then met Yeats, remembered him striding:

> to and fro at the back of the dress circle, a long black cloak dropping from his shoulders, a soft black sombrero on his head, a voluminous silk tie flowing from his collar, loose black trousers dragging untidily over his long heavy feet – a man of such excessive appearance that I could not do otherwise – could I? – than mistake him for an Irish parody of the poet that I had seen all my life strutting its rhythmic way in the alleys of the Luxembourg Gardens, preening its rhymes by the fountains, excessive in habit and gait.[20]

Nor was *The Land of Heart's Desire* a critical success. The audience, being accustomed to pantomime, 'felt themselves cheated of their expected entertainment'. But it was Todhunter's play that was the season's great disaster. Todhunter himself had conceived a passion for Florence Farr, and *The Comedy of Sighs* was a lame tribute to his image of the New Woman. Boos and catcalls greeted the work from its opening moments, and Todhunter felt obliged to sit in apathetic gloom as the voices of the actors were drowned out and the seats around him emptied of his friends. Yeats put much of the blame for the débâcle on Florence Farr. He believed there was an irksome and irresponsible side of her personality that was at war with her Demeter-like beauty. In the play, she was acting a role that ran wholly counter to her poetic gift, and the same urge had led her to try and shock the press in the publicity interviews she gave. But if *The Comedy of Sighs* proved a disaster, Florence Farr had an innate, tough resourcefulness. She contacted Bernard Shaw, urged him to finish his latest play and, after just a week of rehearsals, mounted a production of *Arms and the Man*.

Yeats was astounded by Shaw's mastery of the stage and the theatrical world. His play opens with crude melodrama and then turns to excellent farce. Those who came to laugh at the work soon found they were themselves being ridiculed. Yeats watched with a mixture of admiration and hatred. *Arms and the Man* embodied everything he stood against in the theatre, everything that had been suggested to him by the staging of *Axel*. The play was inorganic, logical and lacked both music and poetry. Nonetheless, Yeats could only feel aghast at its energy and watch Shaw himself become 'the most formidable man in modern letters'. As he walked home with Florence Farr (who was still running *The Land of Heart's Desire* as a curtain-raiser) Yeats expressed his bewilderment and later confessed to a poet's nightmare. *Arms and the Man* made him dream of a remorseless sewing machine that 'clicked and shone' and 'smiled perpetually'. By its power, it was Shaw rather than Yeats who conquered the literary world.

VI

'My Love Sorrow'

Yeats was now to contribute to another memorable event of the 1890s. In June 1894, John Lane issued *The Second Book of the Rhymers' Club*. The contents of this were as eclectic as those of its predecessor, and the inclusion of works like Ernest Radford's 'Song of the Labour Movement' suggests that these poems were not exclusively concerned with decadence and the alienated artist. Yeats himself contributed his subtle symbolist ballad 'Cap and Bells', but others were to offer works more characteristic of the Tragic Generation. Richard Le Gallienne's 'A Ballad of London', with its 'iron lilies of the Strand', evokes the metropolitan nightmare of London. Symons's 'Love and Art' juxtaposes a sharp awareness of sex – the 'odour of patchouli' – to the rigours of the poet's craft, a discipline Yeats was later to see as a fundamental characteristic of the Rhymers. Dowson's jaded but obsessive lover calling 'for madder music and for stronger wine' expresses the pain which, in Johnson's 'The Dark Angel', becomes an anguished believer's cry of 'aching lust'.

Johnson was of all the Rhymers the man closest to Yeats at this time, but the friendship was under increasing strain. Wilde might humorously describe Johnson reeling drunk every morning out of the Café Royal and hailing the first perambulator, but Yeats saw more clearly the squalor of an alcoholism which Johnson himself did not wish to have cured. A gloomy silence fell on him if Yeats refused him a drink while, as he drained glass after glass in cheap restaurants, his excited imagination reached out to those saints who had gelded themselves for the love of God. Johnson believed, Yeats wrote, the most terrible doctrines in order to keep down his own turbulence. Living in fantasies, crippled by guilt and lusting after the world he had almost renounced, Johnson was also the man who, in his more radiant moments, revealed to Yeats what he called the 'hieratic' nobilities of style and would discourse for hours at a time on the proper use of the semicolon. For Yeats, Johnson personified a lost generation. He was, he thought, a man in whom a disembodied soul, not yet ready for God, floated in a horrifying emptiness between the natural and supernatural worlds. 'When the soul turns from practical ends', Yeats wrote, 'and becomes contemplative, when it ceases to be a wheel spun by the whole machine, it is responsible for itself, an unendurable burden.'[21]

But, if Yeats and Johnson were drifting apart, Johnson was to perform for Yeats one more service. On 16 April 1894, Yeats was invited to the lunch at the Hotel d'Italia celebrating the launch of that quintessentially Nineties production, *The Yellow Book*. The impression of preoccupied intensity he made at this time was suggested by Arthur Waugh who accompanied him. He described Yeats as 'a tall, sallow, black-haired youth, with the jaw of a monk & a sort of catch in his voice – rather an interesting personality, tho' he would talk about the theory of poetry inside a 'bus, which seriously alarmed two homely old ladies and scandalised a City man'. At the lunch itself, Yeats was seated opposite a young woman of Grecian beauty whose look of sensitive distinction was offset by the cluster of old lace she wore at her breast. They were not introduced, but Yeats discovered the woman had enquired after him and that she was Lionel Johnson's married cousin Olivia Shakespear.

Olivia herself was accompanying the novelist Pearl Craigie, who, as 'John Oliver Hobbes', wrote fashionable and successful novels of marital torment based partly on her own experience and partly on her relationship with George Moore, whom she had met the previous year during her divorce suit. Moore himself was also present, a man with 'sloping shoulders, drooping moustache and short, flipper-like arms terminating in fat white hands'. Olivia Shakespear may have been present partly to shield her friend from Moore's attentions, but it is clear that, like many women, she found Yeats's 'weird' appearance intriguing and, in May 1894, Johnson arranged a meeting between them.

Mrs Shakespear had been so impressed by *The Land of Heart's Desire* that she had, she said, resolved to write to Yeats.[22] She was herself about to launch on a career as a novelist, and now, as they talked, Yeats began to be aware of the profound culture of this leisured gentlewoman. Yeats did not yet know how unhappily married Mrs Shakespear was but, as she began to reveal her knowledge of literature and of poetry especially, Yeats felt he was in the presence of a woman to whom he could confide. The role of the dolorous lover had become almost second nature to him and 'I told her of my love sorrow, indeed it was my obsession, never leaving by day or night.' Slowly, over the following months, the despair in this declaration would draw Yeats and Mrs Shakespear closer together.

5

Rosa Alchemica
(1894–1897)

I
Anima Mundi

Hard up and deeply frustrated, Yeats left London for Ireland at the beginning of October 1894 to stay with his uncle George Pollexfen.* Misfortune had crowded round the family. Two years earlier Yeats's grandmother Elizabeth Pollexfen had died, and Yeats, who attended her funeral at his father's request, was then asked to stay on in Sligo for the six weeks of his grandfather's final illness. Many of the younger Pollexfens meanwhile had their own problems to endure. William Pollexfen the engineer had been a patient in a mental home for well over ten years. Aunt Agnes too was placed temporarily under restraint, while her sister Elizabeth had to be similarly treated immediately after the funerals. The modest sum bequeathed by old William Pollexfen suggests that his business was failing at the time of his death, while his son George now confessed to having lost all of his money save for £10,000 tied up in the family firm.

A bookkeeper whom George had saved from drink was appointed to manage his accounts, but some time after Yeats's arrival in Sligo his hypochondriac uncle had other worries on his mind. There were rumours of smallpox in the mountains and George resolved to have himself reinoculated. Yeats, although indifferent to stories he did not believe, also agreed to be immunised. Both men caught some sort of poisoning as a result and, while Yeats himself merely felt poorly, his uncle became delirious. Two doctors were called, but when his uncle's fever reached its height Yeats had to attend to him alone. Uncle George thought the sickroom was visited by what he

---

* Precisely how hard up Yeats was at this time is suggested by a Christmas letter to Lily in which he wrote: 'a great many thanks for the handkerchiefs, and please convey my thanks to Lollie for the others – I am very sorry I have sent you nothing, but I possess nothing but a 2/- piece and a half-penny borrowed – and will be no wealthier until Methuen chooses to publish *A Book of Irish Verse*'.

described as 'red dancing figures', and Yeats, without telling the deluded man what he was doing, conjured up the kabbalistic names and symbols of water and the moon.[1]

This was almost certainly another tattwa vision, and Yeats had probably called up the water powers through the silver symbol of the moon itself. Then, passing through the doorway of vision, he had taken a small sliding step forward while raising both hands above his head, bringing them forward and thrusting out his fingers at the level of his eyes until he looked out between his thumbs. Now, with the doorway of vision behind him, he could vibrate the divine names of water, chanting them in the back of his throat in order to manipulate them and make them both more vivid and more safe. Soon George reported that he saw a river flowing through the room and sweeping away the red dancers in its current. Yeats then informed him of what he had done and, as he left the sick man to sleep, told him that if the dancers returned they could be banished in the name of the Archangel Gabriel. Yeats was mildly concerned at offering this advice since, although George had now joined the Order of the Golden Dawn (and was to become a considerably more able astrologer than Yeats himself), the name of Gabriel could only rightly be used by adepts of a higher degree than he had attained. The following morning George told the family doctor something of what had happened, and the bemused man of science put his patient's recovery down to 'a kind of hypnotism'.

In such ways Yeats began to acquire among the local people of Sligo a reputation for being a magician. It was said that by his powers he had sent his cousin Lucy Middleton out of her house and along the Rosses coastline, 'in the winking of an eye', a feat Yeats later claimed to have achieved through astral projection. Not all of his activities were so harmless, however. It was possibly at this time that a servant in the Middleton household gave notice after Yeats practised a water evocation and the woman had, she said, 'seen mermaids in the night who soaked her in sea water'. Visitors to Uncle George's house were also used as seers. A clerk from the local workhouse saw nothing of value, but, when Yeats tried to call up the last incarnation of George himself, Lucy Middleton had a vision of an Anglo-Indian she did not know of but who George dimly remembered as belonging to a branch of the Pollexfens that had separated from his own family a century before. A bank clerk was also inveigled into having a vision of Eden. Although in his normal life this young man had, Yeats supposed, the prosaic imagination he readily attributed to the Protestant Irish, he now saw apples with human faces hanging from the Tree of Knowledge. Eden itself, the young man reported, was a walled garden on a great mountain. But, if the guardian spirits could approach him in such moments of vision, his common-sense consciousness won out and he did not visit Yeats and his uncle again.

Yeats later found confirmation of the bank clerk's vision when he saw the Garden of Eden similarly depicted in Dante and a medieval manuscript illumination. This notion of the shared nature of visionary material, the idea that 'our memories are part of one great memory, the memory of Nature herself,' was, Yeats thought, central to 'what we have agreed to call magic'. The mild scepticism of his tone suggests his cautious efforts to be as objective as he could in such matters. Yeats wrote in his essay on 'Magic' that he believed in the evocation of spirits, though he did not know what they were. He was also sure that visions of truth rose from the depths of the mind when in reverie, yet in the same sentence he wrote of mankind's power to create 'magical illusions'. What Yeats partly perceived and partly desired was a community of the spirit, a universal experience of life free from the fetters of materialism: a proof, in other words, of the divine. He felt that all around him this was being lost. As he wrote so poignantly of what he saw as the plight of modern man: 'our souls that were once naked to the winds of heaven are now thickly clad, and have learned to build a house and light a fire upon its hearth, and shut-to the doors and windows'.[2] By practising ritual magic in Sligo, by seeking the supernatural on the very westernmost edge of Europe, Yeats believed he could force those doors and windows a little ajar.

Not that he thought such activities were parlour-trick proofs of the supernatural. If the *anima mundi*, the soul of the world, really did exist and was possessed of forces that could be communicated, then its power was both tremendous and subtle. If all people, especially really imaginative people, were a medium for its influence, then it had to be admitted that the shapes which floated up in the mind of a secluded seer hovered over politicians in their counsels, scholars in their studies, generals on the field of battle and poets struggling over their art. It followed from this, Yeats believed, that history itself would have to be rewritten, rewritten not in terms purely of economics, morality or the other conventions of the time, but in terms of the supernatural passing as invisibly and forcefully round the world as the wind. 'I am certainly never sure', Yeats wrote in his essay on 'The Symbolism of Poetry', 'when I hear of some war, or of some religious excitement, or of some new manufacture, or of anything else that fills the ear of the world, that it has not all happened because of something that a boy piped in Thessaly.' The artist and the adept might appear as people at the margins of contemporary life, but 'I doubt indeed if the crude circumstance of the world, which seems to create all our emotions, does more than reflect, as in multiplying mirrors, the emotions that have come to solitary men in moments of poetical contemplation.' The adept summons the Rose, the poet evokes her power, and the nature of the world can be changed.

Poets especially could cast their enchantment over those living in the benighted materialism of the cities. Poetry, Yeats believed, arose out of the sounds made by enchanters, and the fact that the highest praise poetry could receive was precisely its power to enchant the mind pointed, he thought, to its supernatural origins. A volume of verse – the lyrics Yeats was assembling for *The Wind among the Reeds*, for example – could be partly seen as a *grimoire*, a book of spells by which to enchant a nation. The experiments in occult politics Yeats had first conducted in *The Rose* were being continued.

In addition to working on these poems, Yeats was revising *The Countess Cathleen* in the light of his experience with *The Land of Heart's Desire* and was beginning to sketch out a version of *The Shadowy Waters*, a play which, after a long and difficult gestation, would be of importance to his dramatic development. He was also bringing his concentrated powers of self-criticism to bear on the earlier verses he would reissue as the *Poems* of 1895. Some works he simply excluded as not fitting with the general tone of the rest. In others the syntax was revised to approximate more closely to common speech, while throughout Yeats sought to eliminate the archaisms which he knew weakened his earlier poems. Although some critics, among them George Russell, would object to such revisions, Yeats felt he was achieving far more than mere technical improvements. Through the conscious exercise of craftsmanship he was refashioning his past, remaking himself, and this would become an impulse fundamental to his mature development.[3]

So much hard work was also beginning to ensure that Yeats was becoming a recognised name. By 1895, he had published or prepared seven books (four of them with American editions), edited or contributed to fourteen more, and published 173 essays, poems and letters in twenty-nine different periodicals. This was a formidable achievement for a man barely in his thirties and it brought with it a certain social cachet. Previous to this visit to George Pollexfen, Yeats's Sligo acquaintances had been restricted to members of the local merchant families. It was a convention that things should be so. Although there was respect between such people and the inhabitants of the nearby Ascendancy houses, long habit had set up a wall between them, and those who tried to climb it were not looked on favourably. 'But my going to the Gore-Booths was different.'[4] Yeats had written books, and it was natural for his readers to want to meet him. With his grandparents dead and his own life independent of their business, he felt he could now accept an invitation to the grandly neo-classical Lissadell set among its trees.

Yeats's short November visit to Lissadell in 1894 had a profound effect on him; he was, besides, fulfilling a boyhood ambition. Constance, one of the daughters of the house, was the 'acknowledged beauty of the county', and a focus of Yeats's teenage imaginings when he saw this glamorous tomboy, some three years younger than himself, sweeping by on her horse. Now, although she was much shorter than Maud Gonne, some slight physical resemblance and, above all, her low and modulated voice, reminded him of his love. There were, indeed, to be significant parallels between them, for Constance Gore-Booth was to play a wholly remarkable part in the struggle for Irish independence and, from her earliest days when she invited the bare-footed peasant children home for tea, she had shown her instinctive defiance of convention and sympathy for the poor. She grew up to be the wild Irish girl from the Big House, wearing a pet snake in her hair at parties and ordering a military suitor to throw his cap into the air to show him she was a crack shot. She was also well read in several languages, an enthusiastic gardener and a competent artist who, by 1893, had enrolled at the Slade.

But if Yeats in his sexual torment was reminded of the woman he could not attain, Constance's sister Eva was, for two happy weeks, a more sympathetic friend. Her 'gazelle-like beauty' reflected, Yeats thought, a mind more subtle than her sister's. Eva was a poet, but, though Yeats found her current work formless, her manner towards him was such that he felt that he could confess to her something of his love for Maud Gonne. When she listened, he felt so grateful that he almost believed he could say to Eva, in the words of William Blake, 'You pity me, therefore I love you.' But Yeats was sure the family would never accept so poor a suitor as himself and, to confirm his intuition, he consulted the tarot. He turned up the card showing the Fool and knew from this that nothing would happen. Harassed by memories of Maud, reminded of her by Constance, and confessing his unhappiness to an Eva to whom he dared come no closer, Yeats turned to replying to the many letters sent him by his London confidante Olivia Shakespear.[5]

She may well herself have sent him a copy of her novel *Love on a Mortal Lease,* a work which expresses her major literary theme: the truth that in late-Victorian middle-class society there was no escape for the woman and mother who has married the wrong man, and that her lot must be resignation. This was Olivia's own case. Her husband, Hope Shakespear, was a repressed and unsympathetic man and, although the sexual side of their marriage had now collapsed, it had lasted long enough for Olivia to become the mother of a girl, Dorothy. Olivia's fiction became a major outlet for her feelings and fantasies, and Yeats responded with both criticism and unwonted sympathy. 'I have never', he wrote on 12 April 1895, 'come upon any new work so full of a kind of tremulous delicacy, so full of a kind of fragile beauty.' Such praise, whether calculated or not, would be greatly welcomed in the unhappy household in Porchester Square.

Meanwhile, Yeats also turned his attention to Lissadell and its way of life, finding in its ordered grandeur something that impressed him deeply. The drawing room was as high as a church, and the great south-facing windows were to remain with him as an image of aristocratic ease and splendour. Here was an Ireland that had so far not deeply affected his imagination but which was now slowly to become an image of Anglo-Irish tranquillity and order, of an elite, patrician civilisation that might provide a stay against confusion and divided aims. Yeats was beginning his career as a courtier in ancestral houses. He also started to interest the Gore-Booths in the traditional peasant life about them, lecturing the local people on folklore and being introduced by the family itself to an old man who was a fount of stories. Yeats even attempted to inveigle Eva into writing on such themes and was delighted when the family bought his books.

But while Yeats was trying to build Lissadell into an image of Ascendancy Ireland at ease with itself, Constance and Eva had sensed its limitations. If Yeats had climbed the wall that once separated him from such people and found, as he thought, a place of relative tranquillity and innate good taste, the daughters of the house felt oppressed by what they saw as its complacent conservatism. The two beautiful girls 'in silk kimonos' were beginning to question an emptiness in their lives. Constance and Eva would soon leave the house and become suffragettes and socialists. They too were looking over the wall, and they believed they could see beyond it to the modern world.

II
The Castle of Heroes

If contact with members of the Ascendancy greatly influenced the future direction of Yeats's writing, his views on the proper work of an Irish man of letters had changed considerably in the months since his struggle with Sir Charles Gavan Duffy. The comparative failure of the New Irish Library made Yeats both regretful and angry. He still believed passionately that literature was one of the most profound influences over a nation, but now began to think that its business was not to quicken nationalism among the mass but to convert the educated classes – people like the Gore-Booths – and to urge intellectual temperance on fellow Nationalists. 'Ireland is terribly demoralised in all things', he wrote to a friend in September 1894, 'in her scholarship, in her criticism, in her politics, in her social life.' He would do what he could by honing the 'studied moderation' of his own style, but Yeats recognised that his increasing literary elitism could be certain of affecting only those few who were probably not in need of his efforts. Other approaches would have to be taken, and Yeats now tried to stir up controversies in the press to highlight the aims of Hyde, Rolleston, Johnson and his allies in the Irish Literary Revival.

One means of doing so was to attack Edward Dowden's sweeping condemnation of Irish literature given in a recent lecture. Dowden himself was accustomed to say that he 'knew an Irish book by its smell, because he had once seen some books whose binding had been fastened together by rotten glue'. Such Trinity College attitudes had to be rooted out. The institution 'desires to be English,' Yeats wrote and 'has been the mother of many verse-writers and of few poets; this can only be because she has set herself against the national genius, and taught her children to imitate alien styles and choose out alien themes, for it is not possible to believe that the educated Irishman is alone prosaic and uninventive.' Yeats and Rolleston now wrote to the Dublin *Daily Express* about such attitudes and lured Dowden into confessing that he was not opposed to Irish literature as such but only to its notes of false rhetorical technique and shrill patriotism. Yeats then pointed out that he and his friends had been opposing such faults for some years as well as trying to persuade their fellow Irish to read only the best in their own literature. Yeats claimed that Dowden got the worst of this fracas, and then went on to initiate a new campaign. He resolved to publish in the *Daily Express* a list of the thirty best Irish books – an inevitably contentious move – to stir controversy and so combat the twin enemies of indiscriminate praise and disillusioned indifference. When Dowden was once again lured into the combat, Yeats dismissed the Professor's rival list as an example of an academic's failure to understand what is truly creative.

With this campaign set in motion, Yeats left Sligo on 13 April 1895 to visit Douglas Hyde in County Roscommon. Here he would begin to shape another initiative which, he hoped, would bring together his literary and political interests, forging them into a unity with his occult beliefs. Yeats found that on a beautiful island in the middle of Lough Key there stood a comparatively recent, deserted but still habitable castle which, he thought, could be rented fairly cheaply. Here he hoped to establish an Irish Eleusis, a place of mystical initiation where the radical truths of received religion could be united to the spiritual beliefs of the Celtic world for the benefit of those young Irish men and women who longed for national and spiritual rebirth. In what Yeats came to call 'The Castle of Heroes', a shared Irish symbolism analogous to that of the Golden Dawn might encourage a school of poets and men of letters whose work would have the spiritual weight lacking, as Yeats believed, since the Middle Ages or even perhaps the days of Ancient Greece. 'For ten years to come,' he wrote, 'my most impassioned thought was a vain attempt to find a philosophy and to create ritual for that Order.'[6]

Yeats hoped his 'Castle of Heroes' would be an answer to some of his most searching criticisms of the contemporary world. His belief that commerce and manufacture had made that world ugly, and his feeling that the death of pagan nature-worship had robbed beauty of its holiness, showed Yeats the spiritual bankruptcy of his time. The activities of the adepts in his Castle might redeem this. 'Certainly,' he wrote, 'a thirst for unbounded emotion and a wild melancholy are troublesome things in the world, and do not make its life more easy or orderly, but it may be that the arts are founded on the life beyond the world, and that they must cry in the ears of our penury until the world has been consumed and become a vision.' In a way Yeats believed to be all but uniquely available to the Irish, his occultists in the Castle would revive the ancient forms of belief and so bring back the Celtic ways of a people who 'worshipped nature and the abundance of nature, and had always, as it seems, for a supreme ritual the tumultuous dance among the hills or in the depths of the woods, where unearthly ecstasy fell upon the dancers, until they seemed the gods or the godlike beasts, and felt their souls overtopping the moon'.

By means of such discoveries, contemporary existence would no longer be merely a 'bundle of fragments', the broken ends of a great culture haphazardly tied together. Through their knowledge of an ancient spiritual life, the adepts in the Castle of Heroes would slowly impose a unity of spirit and culture on an Ireland that was, for the present, painfully demoralised and at odds with itself. Such people would discover in individual and race alike that 'Unity of Being' which Yeats liked to compare to a perfectly proportioned human body. Living beauty and redemptive ecstasy would thus return to the world, and Irish myth would provide a new intoxication, a new beauty, that 'may well give the opening century its most memorable symbols'. But the process of discovering these symbols was as dangerous as it was futile. 'My rituals were not to be made deliberately, like a poem,' Yeats wrote in his *Autobiographies*,

> but all got up by that method Mathers had explained to me, and with this hope I plunged without a clue into a labyrinth of images, into that labyrinth we are warned against in those *Oracles* which antiquity has ascribed to Zoroaster, but modern scholarship to some Alexandrian poet: 'Stoop not down to the darkly splendid world where lieth continually a faithless depth and Hades wrapped in cloud, delighting in unintelligible images.'

Yeats was embarking down that 'path of the chameleon' where spiritual ambush lurked at every turn.

If the Castle of Heroes was Yeats's imagined means of bringing poetic and social salvation to Ireland, its occult mysteries might also provide a solution to the agonies of his private life. Yeats was convinced that his own magical abilities were not sufficiently powerful to be the bricks from which to build his Castle. Maud Gonne, however, had shown herself especially sensitive to the occult. Her violent outer nature, Yeats believed, hid a spirit so refined it seemed to touch the world with the tip of its finger alone, and he wondered if two people so complementary in their opposites had been brought together to complete the great task he imagined for the Irish adepts. Yeats knew – or thought he knew – that 'I, who could not influence her actions, could dominate her inner being.' By entering the Castle of Heroes, Maud might yet fall into Yeats's occult power. Now, in the ecstasy of sexual sublimation and with his art turned to redeeming his nation, Yeats believed he stood on the borders of revelation. Intense ardour shines through the great sentence in his autobiography where he recalls his feelings at this time:

I had an unshakable conviction, arising how or whence I cannot tell, that
the invisible gates would open as they opened for Blake, as they opened
for Swedenborg, as they opened for Boehme, and that this philosophy
would find its manuals of devotion in all imaginative literature, and set
before Irishmen for special manual an Irish literature which, though
made by many minds, would seem the work of a single mind, and turn
our places of beauty or legendary association into holy symbols.[7]

III
'The Dark Side of Progress'

With such euphoric ideals of mind, Yeats returned to London in May
1895 to find the English literary world thrown into the humiliating furore
of the Wilde trials. News had already reached Yeats in Sligo of Wilde's
troubles and he had at once said he thought Wilde would 'prove him-
self a man'.[8] He was now convinced that Wilde's dominating personal-
ity suggested a man of action – a soldier or a politician – who was a
writer only by chance. Nor was Yeats repelled by the notion of homo-
sexuality, his reading having dispelled any lingering prejudice. He was
now canvassing fellow Irish writers for letters of personal support for
Wilde (only Dowden conspicuously refused) and, at his father's sugges-
tion, he went to the house of Wilde's parents in Oakley Street. The
playwright himself was secreted in the home of some friends, but Yeats
handed his letters to Wilde's tearful brother, who asked if the correspon-
dents were advising flight. Yeats replied that he would not recommend
running away, and Willy Wilde, who was possibly a little drunk, con-
fessed that, although there was a yacht waiting, the family and Wilde
himself were determined 'to face the music, like Christ'. Willy Wilde's
wife then came in and, sitting down with an air of relief, said: 'It is
all right now, he has resolved to go to jail if necessary.' Deeply grati-
fied by the visit, Willy Wilde told Yeats that his brother would find the
letters an encouragement in the humiliation that was about to descend
on him.

Although Yeats never doubted that Wilde had made the right decision
and owed to his courage half his renown, the general response to the guilty
verdict was, as Yeats himself noticed, symbolised by the prostitutes who
danced in the streets. The newspapers declared that 'a dash of wholesome
bigotry' was to be preferred to easy toleration, and the *News of the World*
joyfully told its readers that 'the aesthetic cult, in the nasty form, is over'.
To the philistine mass, the Wilde trial suggested that advanced art and
literature were largely matters of the wickedness and madness so gloatingly

described in Max Nordau's *Degeneration*, where decadence itself is seen as a symptom of racial decline, a sickly emotionalism that is 'the dark side of progress'.

Others of Yeats's acquaintance were treading a less spectacular path of wretchedness. A year before, Henley's daughter had died of an illness connected with her father's venereal disease and the once dominant editor was now sunk in guilt and gloom. When Yeats called one evening, Henley's ne'er-do-well brother ridiculed him for his occult beliefs. Henley, less confident, said such activities were all the rage in Paris but, looking at Yeats across the table, asked him to confirm that they were all 'just a game'. Yeats was timidly evasive, and Henley then silenced the group with a comment charged with unfamiliar pathos: 'I want to know how I am to get to my daughter. I was sitting here the other night and she came in and played round the room, and it was only when I saw that the door was shut that I knew it was a vision.'9

If Henley's decline was something Yeats could observe directly, the troubles of his fellow Rhymer Ernest Dowson came to him largely by report. Frustrated love, drink and dissipation were rapidly taking their toll, and Dowson had become, Yeats wrote, a man whose life was burning to the socket in 'exquisite songs celebrating in words full of subtle refinement all those whom he named with himself "as the bitter and the gay"'. Drink was also destroying Lionel Johnson, and his friendship with Yeats was now drawing to a close. One night when Yeats visited him, Johnson seemed to talk perfectly logically if a little excitedly as he drew arguments from the Fathers to prove that the activities of the Fenian Dynamiters were always contrary to the teachings of the church. As he rose from his chair, however, Johnson fell drunk to the floor. 'From then on he began to lose control of his life,' drifting from Charlotte Street to Gray's Inn, and then to Lincoln's Inn Fields where the soured milk bottles on his doorstep gave mute witness to the greater squalor within.

For some days after his return from Ireland, Yeats was thrown into painful doubts about whether Johnson's cousin Olivia Shakespear might share what he saw as a family trait for dissipation and extremes. Olivia had told him that his replies from Sligo to her correspondence were 'unconscious love-letters', but she then spoke of her 'pagan life' in a way that suggested to Yeats that she had had many lovers and loathed her existence. The hint of immorality jarred with Olivia's dark and tranquil beauty, which had about it, Yeats thought, 'the nobility of defeated things'. He was both stirred and confused, while the burden of his virginity weighed on him ever more oppressively. Here was a woman who might offer him the physical comfort Maud Gonne consistently refused, and he thought there might be solace in devoting himself to another. But if Yeats's sexual hunger made him calculating, his feelings were a restraint. What could he, being poor, offer her? Besides, if the affair failed, Olivia might return to what Yeats imagined was her old way of life.

He agonised for a fortnight and then, resolved, asked Olivia to leave home with him. She was suffused with instant joy and, stirred by his delicacy, loved him the more for the merely brotherly kiss he gave her as he put his request. When Yeats then began naively to tell Olivia of the doubts he had harboured over the previous weeks, she was troubled and even ashamed. She had never had more than passing thoughts of adultery, she confessed. Yeats would be her first lover apart from her husband and, even now, with the extreme care they knew had to be exercised in such affairs, they determined not to sleep with each other until Olivia's elderly mother was dead. Each took a woman friend as confidante (Yeats probably chose Florence Farr) and for a year the couple met in railway carriages and art galleries, developing a taste for Watteau and Mantegna.

There was danger even in this degree of relatively innocent deception. Under the divorce laws as they were at the time, Olivia as the guilty party stood to lose custody of Dorothy together with all her property. Her father may well then have rejected her and she would certainly have been denied a position in respectable society. Yeats, for his part, could have been sued for damages, which would have ruined him. A separation would have entitled Olivia to some measure of financial support for her and her child, but if her husband could prove intimacy this plea would have evaporated. Even an affair conducted with the knowledge of 'sponsors' involved them in these risks, and under the prevarication runs the suggestion that Yeats himself was once again fearful of committing himself to a fully sexual affair. In his relationship with Maud Gonne he had, for all his desperate need, contrived to protect himself with a carapace made up from occult magic and a belief in a shared political mission. Maud, besides, had her own deep-seated inhibitions. Olivia Shakespear, however, was less troubled by such intricate defences and, when she took the initiative as she and Yeats were one day journeying to Kew, Yeats himself was startled and even a little shocked by his first experience of the long, passionate kiss of erotic love.

This element of fear is particularly present in the poetry, especially in a lyric Yeats wrote for Olivia originally entitled 'The Shadowy Horses'. This poem, later called 'He bids his Beloved be at Peace', portrays the tumult of the gathering horses of winter, Celtic beasts wild with the animal energies of death and disaster, as they circle round the half-sleeping lovers. The couple are protected only by the veil of the woman's hair, and the poet himself seems to be seeking from his love a comfort that is as much filial as sexual:

> Beloved, let your eyes half close, and your heart beat
> Over my heart, and your hair fall over my breast,
> Drowning love's lonely hour in deep twilight of rest,
> And hiding their tossing manes and their tumultuous feet.[10]

Cradled, protected and secure, the poet seems momentarily oblivious to personal anxiety and the altogether wilder forces of threatening nature.

IV

Bachelor Life

But a childlike dependence was more than an emotional metaphor. Although Yeats spent much of his time away from the parental home, it was a place to which he frequently returned and where he kept his books. In 1893 Katharine Tynan wrote a description of his study in Bedford Park, stating that it was:

> at the back of a quaint and charming house, in which, outside the poet's den, order reigns. It opens on a little balcony, twined about and overhung with Virginia creeper. He has generally a few plants there of which he is inordinately jealous . . . The fireplace is littered with papers. The mantelpiece is buried in layers of them. . . . The books cover a large range; but are mainly either poetry or books on occult subjects. . . . Of books, papers, letters, and proof sheets there is such a confusion that one wonders how he came to disentangle anything.[11]

Yeats was also becoming a notable local character. One night Lily came across him in the street 'in the agony of another lyric' and noticed that, as she walked home with him, the sympathetic eyes of the passers-by seemed to say that she was so nice a girl to be out with a mentally afflicted young man. There were also moments of comic exasperation, as when Lily hung fly-papers in the kitchen which the flies ignored but which her brother, clad in a 'marvellous' new coat, got stuck to and could only be separated from with difficulty. Lily was, however, also familiar with the acid and unpleasant side of her brother's character, and when a cousin telegraphed her to say she had gained her school certificate Lily thought it best to forge her brother's signature at the bottom of her note of congratulation.

His father's failure to develop his career still exasperated Yeats, but his brothers and sisters were, by and large, doing their best to earn a living and establish themselves. Jack, for example, had by 1892 found Mary Cottenham White ('Cottie'), the prosperous young art student whom he intended to marry. He went to Manchester to spend two years working on a newspaper, but by 1894 felt he was in a position to be married and, on 24 August, Yeats attended his brother's wedding at the Emmanuel church in Gunnersbury.

Lollie tried successfully to earn money by teaching her particular skill of brushwork painting, and the publication of her books on the subject seemed to make her happy. Nonetheless, her difficult temperament continued to trouble her and there were rows with her elder brother about such trivial items as an ink-bottle. Lollie was also in love with the much older scholar Louis Purser (the brother of the painter Sarah Purser), but for all that he might have seemed a good catch he was in fact too complacently contented in his life at Trinity College to countenance seriously the idea of marriage. Lily meanwhile continued to work with May Morris and to suffer under her bad temper, a sourness made worse by May's disintegrating marriage to H. H. Sparling. Eventually, when Lily's throat began to trouble her in 1894, her father suggested it was perhaps time to leave May's employment. Lily wrote a polite letter to May informing her of her decision but received such a curt reply that she decided to resign at once and eventually took up work in the South of France as unpaid governess to two Anglo-Indian girls.

JBY meanwhile, now fifty-six years old, was troubled with intense stomach pains which may have been of a psychosomatic origin. There were frequent testy conversations with his son and, eventually, in the autumn of 1895, aged thirty, Yeats felt himself obliged to leave home, moving into the flat at 2 Fountain Court, Middle Temple, rented by his fellow Rhymer Arthur Symons. Here, he boasted to Lollie, he could live on ten shillings a week. 'Let him try,' wrote Lily from Ireland, adding, in a sentence she only partly deleted, that if her brother could afford to live in the Temple then he could certainly afford to pay for bed and board at Blenheim Road.

Bachelor life now opened to Yeats. Symons was vaguely aware of his new affair and exercised great tact. He was out, for example, when his lodger finally asked Olivia and her confidante to tea. Yeats himself went to buy the cake but, as he returned home, his anxiety brought his deepest feelings to the surface. He could think only of Maud Gonne and, in his distracted state, found he had locked himself out. 'I had forgotten the key and I went off in a great fuss to find a locksmith and found instead a man who climbed along the roof and in at an attic window.'[12] That evening, around midnight, Symons returned and Yeats unburdened his heart, telling his friend not about Olivia but about Maud. The two men talked until early in the morning, Symons showing himself to be a great listener, patient and, as Yeats said, like a woman in his ability to take up what was said and flesh it out with sympathetic detail.

But if Symons was now privy to Yeats's intimate concerns, Maud herself also seemed to know what was happening. A couple of days after the tea at Fountain Court, Yeats received a wild letter from her. Was he ill? Had some accident happened? On the very day Yeats was entertaining Olivia Shakespear, Maud had seen him walk into her hotel room. 'At first she thought I was really there,' he recalled in his 'Autobiography', 'but presently on finding that no one else saw me knew that it was my ghost. She told me to return at twelve that night and I vanished. At twelve I had stood, dressed in some strange, priest-like costume, at her bedside and brought her soul away, and we had wandered round the cliffs [of] Howth where we had been together years before.' A long psychic torment was starting and, with it, 'all my old love had returned', Yeats wrote, 'and began to struggle with the new'.

V

George Moore and Arthur Symons

Meanwhile Yeats pursued his career, and the impression he made on London literary men at this time is suggested by an autobiographical passage in the writings of George Moore. The 'violent antipathy' Moore had formed towards Yeats when he first saw him stalking about at the back of the theatre during a performance of *The Land of Heart's Desire* was mollified when he happened to pick up a copy of *The Wanderings of Oisin* in J. T. Nettleship's studio. Nettleship was keen that Moore should meet Yeats, and the 'strain of genuine music' Moore detected in the volume he was reading made him enthusiastic.[13] A meeting was arranged at the Cheshire Cheese, where Moore and Nettleship found Yeats sitting abstractedly in front of a large steak. To get the conversation going, Nettleship told Moore that Yeats was working on an edition of Blake, and no sooner was Blake's name mentioned than Yeats forgot his food and began to engage Moore in a deep discussion about *The Book of Thel*.

Moore was to some extent familiar with Blake's illustrations but was less certain in his knowledge of the poetry. He was, however, a man of formidable conversational skill and believed he would have no difficulty in trouncing Yeats before Nettleship's eyes. But Yeats parried Moore's first blows so quickly and skilfully that Moore was immediately thrown on to the defensive, muttering to himself: 'a dialectician of the very first rank; one of a different kind than any I have ever met before'. As the conversation continued, Moore noticed that Yeats was sparring beautifully, avoiding his 'rushes' with great ease and clearly talking to tire him so that he would eventually be able to destroy him with a single stroke. When Moore tried to counter with an argument that had little substance to it, Yeats changed the subject. 'He was willing to do this, perhaps, because he did not care to humiliate me, or it may have been that he was wearied of talking about a literature to one that was imperfectly acquainted with it, or it may have been that I made a better show in argument than I thought for.'

Then, with his confidence shaken, Moore realised that what Yeats was really interested in was talking to him about the theatre. Yeats told him that he had written a four-act play in verse – *The Countess Cathleen* – and when Moore complimented Yeats on his poetry a smile of faint gratification trickled round his lips but seemed to Moore to be a little too dignified. He was also somewhat hurt that Yeats paid him no compliments on his own work. However, it was clear that Yeats wished to return to the topic of the theatre. Eventually Moore told him how his play *The Strike at Arlingford* had come to be produced, but if Yeats was hoping for an account of the production itself he was disappointed, for it was Moore's firm conviction that an author should never attend his own plays. Yeats by contrast believed that it was only by watching his plays in performance that a playwright could learn his craft. He politely consented to read *The Strike at Arlingford* and the meeting came to an end with Moore under the impression that Yeats looked upon himself as the more considerable author (despite his being ten years the junior) and that to be allowed to meet him at the Cheshire Cheese was a condescension on his part.

Moore was left with mixed feelings. The sheer quality of Yeats's conversation had managed to dissipate the awkward impression he first made, but if Moore disliked the fact that Yeats looked 'like a Bible reader and chanted like one in his talk', that talk had revealed to him an intellect of remarkable force. He began to think he wanted to see Yeats again and wondered if he should indeed send him a copy of *The Strike at Arlingford*. Nonetheless, Moore being an author who did not keep copies of his own books at home, he eventually realised that the trouble of obtaining one and then posting it to Yeats would be considerable. The volume was not sent, and Moore did not see Yeats again until he happened to call at the lodgings Yeats shared with Arthur Symons in Fountain Court.

Yeats's decision to move there had not been lightly made, for all that the area was an oasis in the heart of hated London. 'Mr Arthur Symons', wrote an anonymous critic in the *Pall Mall Gazette*, 'is a dirty-minded man, and his mind is reflected in the puddle of his bad verses.' This attack was prompted by the publication of Symons's volume *London Nights*, a collection much concerned with the innocence of fleshly love and containing one briefly notorious poem, 'Stella Maris', celebrating a chance meeting with a prostitute. The poems were turned down by several more reputable houses before being issued by the enterprising Leonard Smithers, a solicitor turned publisher, who was to play a small but vital role in the London literary life of the 1890s. Smithers was keen to attract Symons because his essay 'The Decadent Movement in Literature' and his close association with Verlaine appeared to make him the spokesman of the avant-garde. In the wake of the Wilde trials especially, Symons's sympathy with an intensely self-conscious literature, with French traditions of symbolism and impressionism, and the work of 'a civilisation grown over-luxurious, over-inquiring, too languid for the relief of action', made him a controversial figure. His being a reviewer of the music halls also gave him prominence and a certain notoriety. Verlaine, naturally, enthused over *London Nights*, and Yeats too congratulated Symons 'upon having written a book which, though it will rouse against him much prejudice, is the best he has done'.[14]

This circumspect praise was in marked contrast to Yeats's earlier view of Symons who, as a poet, had sometimes repelled Yeats by apparently seeing literature as nothing but a series of impressions of music halls and amorous adventures. Only in late 1893 when Symons, the hero of numerous liaisons, fell painfully in love with a young dancer now known only as Lydia did Yeats begin to admire the work of a man who 'tried for the expression of passion' and who had always recognised Yeats himself as the most talented of the Rhymers. It was probably Symons indeed who inspired Yeats's earlier comment that the typical young poets of the day were aesthetes who went slumming, hungry for the commonplace and the philistine. Now, however, with his own virginal priggishness under assault, Yeats could begin to appreciate that in Symons's poems on dancers especially this 'scholar of the music halls' revealed a vivid image of the isolated and the self-obsessed artist absorbed in a world at once beautiful and free from overtly moral purpose. Great popular dancers like Lolly Fuller and Jean Avril had for Symons 'the intellectual as well as sensuous appeal of a living symbol'. For Yeats too they were to be a central image of the modern artist justified only by the art which creates its maker.

Now, as Yeats came to know Symons better, this attentive and vigorous-minded man with his light hair, restless, blinking eyes and wet red lips, came to exercise a deepening influence over him. He saw in particular that for all Symons's compulsive eroticism – 'Oh Yeats, I was never in love with a serpent-charmer before' – he was in his way a fastidious man. While many of those around them were drinking to lethal excess, neither Yeats nor Symons felt the need to do so. From time to time their natural adherence to the temperate life Pater recommended troubled them, and there was a gloomy discussion one evening in Fountain Court about whether they were in some way lacking. They came to the conclusion that they would take two whiskies each night to see if they wanted a third. By the end of a fortnight, however, both men had returned to drinking tumblers of hot water (an indication of their frequent poverty)* and Yeats declared, half seriously: 'Symons, if we felt a tendency to excess, we would be better poets.'

Their sober evening colloquies, Yeats talking 'well and incessantly, moving his hands a good deal, and sometimes falling into a natural chant,' had the effect of greatly widening his range of culture. Symons would return from his visits to France with memories of conversations with the Goncourts and

---

* A scrupulous notebook entry confirms that Yeats was obliged to borrow threepence from Symons for a bus fare.

Mallarmé. In these lay the basis of the ideas he developed in his essay on the French symbolists especially, and, as he discussed their work with Yeats, so both men came to a more profound understanding of the European avant-garde.

Yeats himself was still working his way through *Axel*, his difficulties with French giving exaggerated importance to some passages and suffusing the whole with the appearance of a 'Sacred Book'. He later recalled that his conversations with Symons always seemed to centre around life at its most intense, those moments when talk of something supernatural seemed 'a stirring as it were of the roots of the hair'. Symons himself was making translations from Mallarmé and Verlaine, and the elaboration of their artifice was to affect Yeats's own work for many years. He longed for a poetry that was hieratic, ritualistic, free from everything contingent and various in the common world. Mallarmé in particular confirmed for Yeats what Blake and his own art had already shown him: that the poet could be the priest of the unconscious and that art itself was religion. Symons recalled that both he and Yeats were essentially in agreement about this and that their conversations led to a shared belief that symbolist poetry – Yeats's great lyrics to the Rose, for example – were attempts 'to spiritualise literature, to evade the old bondage of rhetoric, the old bondage to exteriority'. 'Description', Symons continued, 'is banished that beautiful things may be evoked magically.' And, in composing such poetry lay a great responsibility: 'for in speaking to us so intimately, so solemnly, as only religion has hitherto spoken to us, it becomes a kind of religion, with all the duties and responsibilities of the sacred ritual'.

Symons also knew that many of the French symbolists had been greatly influenced by Wagner, the power of whose music seemed to them to support a relationship between the conscious and the unconscious, mystical realms of the mind.[15] In resurrecting Germanic and Celtic myth, Wagner had also reared up a vision of an heroic past, juxtaposing it as Yeats wished to do in his own work to the grey world of industrial and scientific materialism. A transcendentally beautiful opera such as *Tristan and Isolde*, fusing love and death in redemptive eroticism, was profoundly influential on decadents and aesthetes alike. In an analogous way, Siegfried, the defeated national hero, showed how tragedy could be evoked in a work designed to oppose myth and magic to baleful materialism. Yeats was to absorb something of this from Symons for, in a London where Wagner-mania was epidemic, Symons had been an ardent Wagnerite since his eighteenth year. The opera house at Bayreuth (which he did not visit until 1897) became for him a potent image of the 'total work of art', that fusion of music, drama, dance, poetry, acting and design which Wagner derived from Greek tragedy. Yeats, too, was to think that 'the arts are but one Art', and would soon help establish in Dublin a theatre where the ritual dramatisation of Celtic myth might revive the spiritual power of the past to unite the Irish in an ideal future.

VI
The Savoy

In such ways Symons acted for Yeats as a focus for avant-garde thought, and no enterprise shows this more clearly than his work on the *Savoy*. Victorian London was richly provided with magazines that offered large numbers of readers a variety of fiction and social comment. Such journals were often unattractively produced, however, mass-market publications subsidised by ugly pages of advertisements and embellished with equally crude illustrations. In 1884, and in opposition to this approach, Yeats's acquaintance Herbert Horne and the architect Arthur Mackmurdo issued the *Century Guild Hobby Horse*, a work of beautiful and innovative typographical excellence, printed with wide margins on high-quality paper and clearly inspired by the work of William Morris's Kelmscott Press. By the close of the decade, the *Dial* was offering avant-garde, French-influenced writing in a similarly elegant format, but it was the publication of the *Yellow Book* in 1894 that marked in the most dramatic way the arrival of the aesthetic periodical. Although the magazine was seeking a balance between the conventional and the risqué, Aubrey Beardsley's striking cover of a voluptuous masked woman, Beerbohm's essay 'A Defence of Cosmetics', and Symons's own 'Stella Maris' ensured that the *Yellow Book* became an emblem of decadence. Some even asked for an Act of Parliament to make such publications illegal. The resulting publicity ensured healthy sales, despite the Wilde débâcle and the subsequent departure from the magazine of Aubrey Beardsley.

When, in April 1895, Leonard Smithers approached Symons to edit a rival magazine, Symons at once chose Beardsley as his chief illustrator, and it was Beardsley who suggested the *Savoy* as a title, fully aware of its association with the hotel that featured so prominently in the Wilde trials. To shock further, Beardsley then prepared an illustration for the prospectus which showed an imperial John Bull imperiously erect. Outraged prospective contributors managed to have the drawing altered, just as Smithers ordered the urinating Cupid on the magazine's first cover to be made more decent. The desire merely to shock was partly tamed, and the *Savoy* could now exemplify Symons's hopes for an avant-garde publication of the highest quality. 'We are not Realists, or Romanticists, or Decadents,' he declared. 'For us, all art is good which is good art.' To illustrate his thesis, he marshalled for the first edition work by Shaw, Beerbohm, Dowson, Image, Havelock Ellis, Whistler, Shannon, Beardsley, himself and, of course, Yeats. Yeats's 'The Shadowy Horses', along with a story entitled 'The Binding of the Hair' in which he gave a symbolic account of the dangers awaiting the artist who involved himself in the world, thus appeared in a diverse and brilliant context. 'We began', he wrote, 'a warfare on the British public at a time when we had all against us.'[16]

The response to the first edition was such as to merit a celebration, but, despite allowing his work to be published in the *Savoy*, Yeats considered Smithers 'a disreputable man' and made it a condition that he should never meet him after the launch party. This was an occasion that showed Yeats variously prickly and naive. The dinner was held in a private room at the New Lyric Club, where the gaudy Mrs Smithers, whom no one knew, was bravely determined to act as hostess. Beerbohm found her suburban, and when she drew Yeats's attention to the bamboo covering on the walls the reply was merely a courteous, lugubrious murmur. Things did not get better. Yeats felt he was in dubious company and perhaps for that reason had in his pocket two letters that confirmed his doubts. One was from T.W. Rolleston, the other from George Russell. Symons borrowed them both and, in a spirit of mischief, read them out. He was himself wary of Smithers, referring to him as 'my cynical publisher, Smithers, with his diabolical monocle', and Smithers at once fell into the trap. He demanded to be given the first of the letters but, as he shouted out that he would sue, so Symons backed away and read out Russell's letter, which described the *Savoy* as 'the organ of the incubi and the succubi'.

When matters had calmed down, Beardsley came up to Yeats and, looking at him with his elfin-like, tubercular face, began: 'You will be surprised at what I am going to say to you. I agree with your friend. I have always been haunted by the spiritual life. When I was a child, I saw a bleeding Christ over the mantelpiece. But after all I think there is a kind of morality in doing one's work when one wants to do other things far more.' Yeats was impressed. Beardsley had, he thought, that noble courage which Yeats himself believed the greatest of human faculties, and his way of talking had an icy realism, the wiry logic of his draughtsman's line. It also had an irony that was lost on Yeats. During the dinner, and perhaps thinking Beardsley's conversation implied that he was sympathetic to such matters, Yeats began to talk in deep, vibrant tones about what Max Beerbohm remembered him calling 'Dyahbolism'. Beardsley, obviously regarding the whole subject as ridiculous, merely interjected where he could: 'Oh really? How perfectly entrancing!', and 'Oh really? How perfectly sweet!' The tragedy underlying this self-possession was made clear, however, only at the end of the evening:

After the supper was over I wanted to go away. Symons said, 'No, we must go on to Smithers's flat. He will be offended if we do not; you need never go there again.' Smithers and Beardsley had gone on ahead of us, and when we arrived Beardsley was lying on two chairs in the middle of the room and Smithers was sweating at his hurdy-gurdy piano. His piano was at ordinary times worked by electricity, but at the moment his electricity had been cut off or he had not paid the bill and could only make music by turning the handle. Beardsley was praising the beautiful tone, the incomparable touch – going into the lavatory at intervals to spit blood – and Smithers, flattered, sweated on.[17]

But, for all Beardsley's evident bemusement at the supper-table, Yeats's occult interests provided an important contribution to the *Savoy*. He wrote, for example, an extended essay, published in parts, on 'William Blake and his Illustrations to the *Divine Comedy*'.[18] The concluding section of this work shows both the breadth of Yeats's Blake scholarship (the reward for his labours on editing the poet) and the acute originality of his art criticism. The bulk of the essay, however, is given over to drawing an extended contrast between Dante the Christian visionary and Blake the Christian mystic. In so doing, Yeats was attempting to work out some central problems of his own.

While the greatness of Dante is never denied, Yeats uses Blake to explore what both men regarded as a spiritual flaw in Dante's achievement. Dante's is the Christianity of high medieval scholasticism and is rooted in a theology which, however beautiful in its intellectual intricacy, had as its foundation a strict adherence to the laws of an external, institutionalised church, and thus a worldly philosophy 'established for the ordering of the body and the fallen will'. Blake, by contrast, believing the historical Jesus to be the supreme symbol of the artist living in the eternity of his imagination, poured scorn on external things and preached the sanctity of an inner church 'which has no laws but beauty, rapture and labour'. Where Dante is seen as the poet of adherence to outward things, Blake is the modern poet, the symbolist whose language, seeking to express the eternal and invisible essence of life, forms 'a transparent lamp about a spiritual flame'. This struggle between the inwardly rapturous and the outwardly conformist is again central to a short story Yeats published in the *Savoy*, the remarkable 'Rosa Alchemica'.

Yeats had for some time been publishing short stories on occult themes, being paid between six and ten pounds for each of these.* When in 1897

---

* The *Savoy* would eventually be a brief boon in this respect. As the ever indebted Yeats wrote to John O'Leary: 'I did not send the money before because Smithers, the publisher of *The Savoy*, was short of funds and asked me to wait, and now I send only £3.5.0 because I am short in my turn. . . . You shall have it almost at once however; I have I believe definitely turned the corner thanks partly to *The Savoy* which came in the nick of time to let me raise my prices until I get the new prices definitely established.'

he gathered them into a volume he called *The Secret Rose*, any sense of randomness his means of composition might imply was subsumed (in Yeats's original plan at least) to that harmonious and potent sense of order evident in all his purely imaginative volumes. As he wrote in his prefatory letter to George Russell, Yeats's theme in these stories was 'the war of spiritual with natural order', the subject in part of his Blake essay, but interpreted here in a purely Irish context. As Yeats carefully points out, his stories were not intended as a nationalist endeavour at romance designed to appeal to the mass of readers. They take their inspiration from 'that little, infinite, faltering flame that one calls one's self', and their Irishness lies in the visionary power such tending of the flame can give. Yeats's is the esoteric Celtic vision which, he claims, has died out in more materialist nations.

Because he also wanted to suggest the history of this vision, the ordering of his stories traces the cycles of Celtic mysticism from the pagan and monastic ages, through the seventeenth and eighteenth centuries, to the present day. Taking their manner of presentation in part from the immaterial world of Villiers de l'Isle-Adam and, in their 1897 version at least, their style from Pater (as so often Yeats was to revise these works as he reshaped himself) the stories gathered in *The Secret Rose* encapsulate Yeats's literary aims in the later 1890s. They create an occult and symbolic world for a national elite. As Yeats explained to John O'Leary, his volume was 'an honest attempt towards that aristocratic esoteric Irish literature, which has been my chief ambition. We have a literature for the people but nothing yet for the few.'[19]

How difficult this had been to achieve is suggested by George Moore's account in the autobiographical *Ave* of his visiting Yeats at Fountain Court one evening and discovering the manuscripts of the stories spread across the floor. Moore apologised for interrupting Yeats in his work, but Yeats told him he had come to a knot in one of the stories which he was for the moment unable to untie. When Moore suggested a solution to the problem that proved satisfactory he expected Yeats's face to light up, but was surprised that instead it remained impassive, 'hierarchic as ancient Egypt'. Moore asked himself what the difficulty could be, for Yeats being a poet would surely be able to find the right word. 'Not so much the right word,' Yeats interrupted, 'but the right language, if only I were sure of what language in which to put upon them.' Moore asked Yeats if he did not wish to write the stories in Irish. Once again, the Yeatsian smile trickled round his dark face and Moore heard him confess that he had no Irish. He was searching, however, for a style similar to that used by the Sligo peasants but realised it would take years to learn its effective usage. Moore said he thought Irish brogue was the ugliest dialect in the world. 'No dialect is ugly,' Yeats said; 'the bypaths are all beautiful. It is the broad road of the journalist that is ugly.' Moore was enchanted by the comment, not realising that in future years his own style would be damned by Yeats precisely for its journalistic qualities. For the moment, however, he felt as if a window had been thrown open and he could look down new and surprising vistas.

The glory and the shadow of the Rose – the exultations and defeats of the visionary life – hang over all the stories in *The Secret Rose*. Yeats concentrates remorselessly on the cost of the intrusion of the spiritual into the natural order. Visionaries are executed, misunderstood and harassed for their insights. For many the church is an alien and hostile force, while others are simply misunderstood. The memorable figure of the old knight in 'Out of the Rose', committed to divine vision in a world spiritually corrupted by those who worship external forms, is obliged to explain his mission to a simpleton. Hanrahan the poet, cursed by the Rose Woman he has rejected, lives an agonised life torn between natural desire and the unobtainable ideal that wrecks all his earthly pleasures. Only in his art can Hanrahan truly celebrate beauty but, in a way that would become central to the mature Yeats, his timeless images are wrested from his continuous desolation.

Hanrahan is punished for faltering before a complete embodiment of the spirit, the old knight believes he is living at the end of a spiritual era. Both motifs reappear in the separately published 'Rosa Alchemica' and, with the narrator of this story secluded in his aesthete's luxurious home, Yeats approaches his own time. There now bursts in on the life of his *fin de siècle* hero, the compelling figure of Michael Robartes, the wild-eyed, roughly clothed visionary wholly committed to the final overthrow of nineteenth-century materialism. He harries the narrator out of his little palace of art to an initiation ceremony in a Temple of the Alchemical Rose situated, as many of these works are, in a recognisable Sligo. Although the story is obviously more than anecdotal, Michael Robartes carries about him suggestions of MacGregor Mathers and, more directly, of George Russell. It is also possible to read 'Rosa Alchemica' as a comment on Russell's current state of mystical excitement.

Just as Yeats had fallen under the spell of MacGregor Mathers's chiliastic forebodings, so Russell had come to believe Madame Blavatsky's prophecies of an imminent spiritual revelation that would occur in 1897. Russell's recent volume of poems, *Homeward: Songs by the Way*, had been praised by Yeats as the work of an 'arch visionary', while an article in *The Irish Theosophist* had not only convinced him of Russell's interest in nationality, but shown him that Russell believed the Celtic legends contained sacred truths which would be embodied in their soon-to-be-reincarnated heroes. Russell was desperately keen that Yeats should join him in a popular revival of Celtic mysteries (money was already being raised for this in America) and he wrote Yeats many letters during the first half of 1896 in an attempt to enthuse him. The Celtic twilight, he declared, was about to break into dawn. 'The gods have returned to Erin and have centred themselves in the sacred mountains and blow the fires through the country.' Many had seen them in visions. Magic would soon awake everywhere, 'and the heart of the people will turn the old Druidic beliefs'.

Yeats was less enthusiastic. Russell's comments about the *Savoy* and his suggestions that Symons was a corrupting sex maniac had annoyed him and he was, besides, suspicious of Russell's popularist naivety and lack of analytical rigour.* Yeats had his own plans for a mystical revival and, if he was irked by the sense of competition, he also had a far shrewder and ultimately more humane understanding of the dangers lurking in the occult. He knew that the adept confronting supernatural powers risked the extinguishing of his identity, his sense of self – his humanity, in other words. In 'Rosa Alchemica' it is precisely this horror that provides the climax. Dancing in the Temple of the Alchemical Rose with a beautiful visionary woman, the narrator is suddenly aware of the psychic and sexual threat her wondrous but inhuman loveliness inspires: 'I remembered that her eyelids had never quivered, and that her lilies had not dropped a black petal, nor shaken from their places, and understood with a great horror that I danced with one who was more or less than human, and who was drinking up my soul as an ox drinks up a way-side pool.'[20] The narrator faints and wakes to find the temple is little more than a hut besieged by the local peasantry, those irate enemies of vision whose turbulent, blinded instincts have throughout the stories ensured 'the war of spiritual with natural order'.

The narrator of 'Rosa Alchemica' finally pictures himself as a man permanently torn between Christian consolation and the lure of supernatural vision. Yeats's adeptship too was both unsettled and unsettling, visionary but pained, euphoric but questioning. He longed for revelation but, as the conclusion of the introductory poem to *The Secret Rose* suggests, his ardour and his doubt were one:

> I, too, await
> The hour of thy great wind of love and hate.
> When shall the stars be blown about the sky,
> Like the sparks blown out of a smithy, and die?
> Surely thine hour has come, thy great wind blows,
> Far-off, most secret, and inviolate Rose?[21]

In this the last and perhaps the greatest of Yeats's poems to the Rose, the mystic fertility of the symbolic world is abundantly suggested, its power to evoke innumerable stories gloriously celebrated. Here indeed is a justification of the claims made by the Golden Dawn that 'by names and images are all powers awakened and reawakened'. Indeed, the idea that the Rose is best

---

* This did not prevent Yeats reusing this material much later in his career; see p. 422 below.

approached through occult invocation runs strongly through the poem, giving the impression that the seat of mystic power is more remote than in the earlier works. Transcendence seems to hover on the borders of immanence. The great moment of spiritual change is longed for, deeply felt and yet, in the end, ambiguous. The rhythm of the last sentence seems to lead to affirmation and triumph, but the silent final question mark destabilises the statement it closes.

Yeats was now to receive narrow-minded proof that the world did indeed not welcome visionaries. One of the illustrations published in the *Savoy* with the first part of his Blake essay was 'Antaeus Setting Vergil and Dante upon the Verge of Cocytus'. The nude figure of Antaeus worried the manager of W. H. Smith, who ordered the magazine to be removed from the shelves. An angry Symons went to remonstrate, and informed the manager that Blake was 'a very spiritual artist', but he was told: 'Oh, Mr Symons, you must remember we have an audience of young ladies as well as an audience of agnostics.' The withdrawal of the *Savoy* from so many outlets was a severe blow to the magazine, but while Yeats attributed its eventual demise largely to the presence of Beardsley (in particular the publication of his Rabelaisian fragment *Under the Hill*) Smithers's decision to go for monthly numbers rather than a quarterly appearance was a more likely cause, there being an insufficient market to cover the new capital that had to be raised.

But the sophistication of Yeats's recently published occult writings troubled him. The slow-moving, elaborate style of his work seemed far removed from earlier productions such as *The Countess Cathleen* and he feared that this threatened his hopes of spiritualising the Irish imagination. He sought the advice of Olivia Shakespear. Although she was not wholly familiar with the popular mysticism of the day, she had shown herself susceptible to Yeats's evocations and had insights close to those embodied in the teachings of the Golden Dawn. Now, when Yeats consulted her, she offered advice that, unintelligible to her, affected Yeats deeply. He was, Olivia said, 'too much under solar influence'. To counter this, he was 'to live near water and to avoid woods, which concentrate the solar power'.[22]

Yeats's affair with Olivia Shakespear had now advanced beyond its initial shyness, and their confidantes suggested they live together without more ado. Olivia, confessing now that her husband had soon ceased to make love to her, wondered about a separation. Hope Shakespear himself was so upset by this suggestion, however, that he retreated to bed, and Olivia turned to Yeats and said it would be kinder to deceive him. A love-nest was required, and early in 1896 Yeats moved into a tenement off the Euston Road known then as Woburn Buildings, which was to be his London home for quarter of a century. Here was both the raffishness and the squalor of bohemia. As Yeats's friend the poet John Masefield was later to write: 'there was a kind of blackguard beauty about Woburn Buildings at night. . . . The houses had come down in the world, and as it were gone on the streets. They seemed to screen discreet vice and secret crime. The court was quiet enough, behind drawn blinds and curtains; but in a street at the eastern end there were nightly rows and singings, and the children never seemed to go to bed.'[23] In such an area Yeats was known as 'the toff what lives in the Buildings'. He was also said to be the only man in the street who ever received letters.

In 1896, Yeats had only two rooms there on the second floor, the attic being occupied by a pedlar. Cooking was done in the front room while his back room was both scullery and bedroom. The windows were kept permanently closed and Yeats went out walking to get fresh air. But furniture was required, and Yeats, poor as always, bought such cheap items as he could afford and later dispense of without regret were he ever to become prosperous. A photograph from about this time shows him standing in his living room at Woburn Buildings, a cheap wicker chair and a bookcase behind him. There was, however, the problem of a bed. Olivia went with him to buy this from a shop on the Tottenham Court Road where an assistant hovered as the two lovers debated how large a bed they needed and could afford. 'Every inch', Yeats recalled, 'increased the expense.'

Yeats was thirty, living on his own at last, and about to sleep with a woman for the first time. So long a virgin and with his inhibitions now directly challenged, nervous excitement, as he confessed in his 'Autobiography', made him impotent. A meeting the following day in the British Museum seemed to show that the lovers' concern for each other had not faltered and when, a week later, Yeats's overwrought nerves again got the better of him and the couple merely sat in his room over cakes and tea, Olivia's feeling appeared to be all for him and she 'was only troubled by my trouble'. They were eventually to make love and share 'many days of happiness', but there was, nonetheless, an invisible, complex barrier to their intimacy. Although Olivia was gentle, beautiful and kind, a friend and companion, her very tenderness was a bar to the full expression of sexual passion. 'I could not', Yeats confessed, 'give the love that was her beauty's right.' And, behind their intimacy, loomed the altogether more forceful spectre of Maud Gonne.

VII
The Visionary Archer

Ireland also called, and in July 1896 Yeats and Symons departed for Galway, Sligo and the Aran Islands. The cost of this trip was partly covered by the advances Yeats was being paid for a novel he was trying to write called *The Speckled Bird*. Lawrence & Butler, the publishers of *The Celtic Twilight*, had agreed to pay him £2 a week for six months to cover his expenses. The projected novel would deal with mysticism, with Yeats's experiences of the Golden Dawn, and with the people involved in this, all lightly disguised. His hero would be autobiographical and would be shown trying to combine artistic ideals with those of an occult brotherhood. The strain of writing the book was beginning to tell, however, and the trip with Symons offered the chance of rest and research. Just before the two men left, a new friend of Symons's, the beautiful young Indian student Sarojini Chattopadhyay, knowing Yeats was accompanying him to Ireland, wrote asking if the gods spoke to the children of men in such places as the Aran Islands and wondering if 'beautiful demons lure mad poets to their destruction in that magical haunt'. Sarojini's affectionate teasing was harmless enough, but it pointed to experiences she could not possibly have foreseen.

Yeats and Symons spent most of August at Tulira Castle, the Galway home of a new acquaintance, Edward Martyn.[24] They had previously met Martyn in the Temple area around Fountain Court, where both Martyn and his Irish cousin George Moore had rooms. Yeats had not been initially impressed by a man whom he thought rustically uncouth, and as he and Symons approached Martyn's castle Yeats warned his friend to expect little more than a small, rough house where a 'bare-foot servant would wait upon us full of capacity and good will'. What they found was a vast neo-gothic pile built at the suggestion of Martyn's pinched and domineering mother after a previous building had been destroyed by fire. Edward Martyn himself ushered Yeats and Symons up the wide hall stairs and asked them to take their choice of rooms. Symons, slightly abashed by the factitious grandeur, was embarrassed when Yeats suggested they toss a coin to decide who slept where. 'The place, he thought, I suppose, should move one to ceremony.'

They found their host to be a life-hating man whose sourness and thwarted powers of imagination were a continuous fascination. Martyn himself loathed the house his mother had built as much as he despised the series of young women she was trying to marry him to. One of these was currently in residence, happy enough perhaps at the thought of being mistress of the vulgar furniture in the living room and sure in her contempt of what she took to be a Beardsley drawing but was, in fact, a magnificent Utamaro woodblock. Martyn had also collected works by Degas, Monet and Corot – moments of quality in a wilderness of bad taste – and on several evenings Yeats and Symons managed to persuade their host to extinguish all the lights save for a little Roman lamp and play the Palestrina he so loved on an ancient keyboard. As Yeats later recalled, Martyn 'drank little, ate enormously, but thought himself an ascetic because he had but one meal a day, and suffered, though a courteous man, from a subconscious hatred of women'. But he was also a generous patron of Irish causes and, in addition, had written a play called *The Heather Field*.

There were visits to the French novelist Paul Bourget at the nearby seaside house of the Comte de Basterot, a man crippled by the vices of his youth, while on 5 August Yeats, Symons and Martyn, joined now by George Moore, set off for the Aran Islands. This proved to be a crossing of nearly four hours but was rewarded with the sight of pearl-grey sands, a ruined fort and a local existence so primitive that Symons felt he had stepped into the world of Celtic dream and a consoling, immortal twilight where ancient warriors and fairy visions seemed almost tangible. 'I have never', he wrote, 'believed less in the reality of the visible world.' But, if the Aran Islands had both beauty and mystery, the people had an earthly reality that was to work its way into the Irish literary renaissance, enriching it with its ancient vocabulary, its Gaelic idiom and its humour. As one of the islanders told Yeats, speaking very slowly and with laughing eyes: 'If any gentleman has done a crime, we'll hide him. There was a gentleman that killed his father, and I had hid him in my own house six months till he got away to America.'[25] This anecdote was soon to acquire an immense significance in the history of Irish drama.

Yeats published no full account of the three-day expedition, although it was to affect him deeply and he had, besides, other problems on his mind. He was greatly concerned by Olivia Shakespear's warning about the harmful effects on him of solar energy. He believed that her enigmatic pronouncement had actually come from his own buried self speaking through her and, knowing from Mathers's teaching that solar forces suggested elaboration and rich artifice, he was resolved to turn this confused portion of his mind in a new direction. Hoping that a form of occult therapy might cure what he perceived as the defects of his art, Yeats resolved to conjure the names associated with the moon, thus summoning before his mind all that was 'simple, popular, traditional, emotional'. For nine nights Yeats climbed the winding staircase in Tulira Castle, crept through a secret passage and, in a vast, deserted room, invoked the forces of the moon. Eventually, having returned to his own room, and lying there in a state between sleeping and waking, he had a vision of a galloping centaur followed, a moment later, by the sight of 'a marvellous naked woman shooting an arrow at a star'.[26] Her flesh, Yeats recalled, made all earthly flesh seem sickly in comparison.

The following morning, Symons, unaware of his friend's activities, read Yeats the first poem he had ever written inspired by a dream, a vision of a clothed Diana which had visited him in the night. Conversation turned to such matters, and Comte Florimond de Basterot, who was also now staying at the castle, reported to Martyn that a couple of nights previously he had had such a vivid dream of Neptune, god of the sea over which the moon holds sway, that he had been obliged to get out of bed and lock his door. He also told his host that Yeats, with his swarthy complexion, broad nose and deep-set eyes, was clearly some sort of Finnish sorcerer. As a pious Catholic, the Count took such matters seriously, Yeats recalled, but his own excitement was now such that he could no longer keep his vision-raising to himself. Were not the visitors' shared dreams proof of minds in communication with the *anima mundi*? Their host was 'really angry'. The room in which Yeats had summoned his apparitions was directly over the chapel, and Martyn, whose austere faith drove him to long sessions of prayer, believed such activities threatened to obstruct the passage of his devotions.

At the end of August, Yeats and Symons left Tulira Castle to stay with George Pollexfen in Sligo. Uncle George cast Symons's horoscope, finding both imagination and violence in his aspects which prefigured, perhaps, his later nervous breakdown. They then moved on to spend three days by the slopes of Ben Bulben, where Symons wrote poems. But, if Yeats was back on his own territory, thoughts of the vision he had raised in Tulira Castle still preoccupied him. Later, when he returned to London, these thoughts were to become more pressing. It seemed that others too had shared his experience of the naked huntress. William Sharp, for example, a Scottish writer who published so persuasively under the name of Fiona Macleod that he managed to convince Yeats and others that his *nom de plume* was the actual name of a living woman, now composed a story called 'The Archer'. This had Yeats's vision of the mystic huntress at its core. It was unlikely that 'Fiona Macleod' had heard of the invocations at Martyn's castle directly, and even more unlikely that a child of one of Yeats's fellow members of The Golden Dawn had heard of it either. The child nonetheless ran to its mother crying out: 'Oh Mother, I have seen a woman shooting an arrow into the sky, and I am greatly afraid she has killed God.'

Yeats pondered the nature of this synchronicity. He wondered if some great event had taken place in the world of myth and if a few had been made privy to it. Had he experienced some ancient race memory, or had he merely had a fantastic dream that came to others by thought transference? A consultation with Olivia Shakespear left him more confused when, in a trance, she claimed that those who saw the vision would obtain 'wisdom older than the serpent' but that the child would die. Yeats went in his bewilderment to see Dr Wynn Westcott, the London coroner who, with Mathers and William Woodman, had founded the Order of the Golden Dawn. Westcott produced two crude watercolours from a drawer which showed the figure Yeats had seen. The images were, Westcott said, although Yeats could not have known this, figures found in the Christian Kabbala and representative of the elemental and divine spirit, of the straight path Samekh which, on the Tree of Life, joins the moon to the sun. As another initiate told Yeats, his vision pointed to wisdom achieved by deliberate intellectual effort. Yeats had been mystically advised to avoid the meandering road of the purely occult, the 'path of the chameleon'. To a worshipper of the Rose and the builder of a magic castle, however, this was a warning given in vain. So many seemed caught up in his vision, and one new friend in particular was, Yeats sometimes thought, brought to him by it too.

When he and Symons were staying at Tulira Castle, Martyn's near neighbour Augusta Gregory invited them to lunch.[27] After the gaudy splendour of his host's castle, Lady Gregory's plainer, Georgian house at Coole seemed a modest affair, despite the beautiful garden their hostess had created. Recently widowed and dressed in mourning black, Lady Gregory's love for her house was one of her ruling passions. In the effort to beautify its grounds and pay off the mortgage by the time her son Robert reached his majority, Lady Gregory had gone without comforts when staying in London where, in the summer of 1894, she had first glimpsed Yeats at a party. Now in her middle forties, she had been mildly intrigued rather than impressed by a young man who, she wrote, strove to look 'every inch a poet'.

Lady Gregory was familiar with such company. During the period of her marriage to Sir William Gregory, a diplomat nearly forty years her senior, many of the great and the good had attended her Hyde Park salon and signed their names on the ivory blades of her fan. Her politicians included Gladstone and Randolph Churchill, her painters Whistler and Millais, while among her literary men were Browning, Tennyson and the poet Wilfred Scawen Blunt, whose mistress she briefly became. As her early verse shows, Lady Gregory's views had been formed by such people, and Yeats's poetry may not at this time have been wholly to her taste. As she confided to her diary, 'his prose "Celtic Twilight" is the best thing he has done,' and this was a work that appealed to Lady Gregory not just as a lover of literature but as a woman who was undergoing a deepening sense of commitment to Ireland. Now, in the library after lunch, turning to him her plumply tranquil, intelligent face, Lady Gregory asked Yeats what work she could do to help further his literary movement. He remembered saying to her: 'If you get our books and watch what we are doing, you will soon find your work.' This mildly self-regarding reply was addressed to what Yeats probably considered to be no more than his hostess's momentary enthusiasm. He was perhaps as yet unaware that 'La Strega' (the Witch) as Symons called her would, as Symons himself knew, 'get' Yeats. Certainly, Yeats himself was not yet ready for a friendship which would eventually change the course of his life.

6

The Path of the Chameleon
(1896–1899)

I
Mysterium Coniunctionis

In December 1896 Yeats returned to Paris, 'the old lure', hoping to see both Maud Gonne and MacGregor Mathers. Maud, now the mother of a year-old daughter she called Iseult and whom, for the sake of propriety, she would always refer to as her adopted niece, had become disenchanted with Mathers's Golden Dawn. She discovered that some of the rituals were similar to those of freemasonry and these she associated with the British. She resigned her membership of the Order but still kept up her acquaintance with the Matherses and even maintained a lively interest in the occult. Mathers himself however feared that other occultists were slipping from his control, and in 1895 he appointed officers directly subordinate to him and required them to enforce his authority. Among these officers were Yeats's friends Florence Farr and Annie Horniman.

Florence herself was now deeply involved in the ritual magic of the ancient Egyptians and, in *The Speckled Bird*, Yeats offered a thinly disguised portrait of her communing with a mummy in the British Museum, where, Florence believed, she had been contacted by an Egyptian adept who convinced her she was one of the Secret Masters. The adept also gave her a vision of how world peace might be preserved as tension rose between Britain and the United States over boundary disputes in South America. Talk of war was in the air and, inspired by Mathers's prophecies of coming catastrophe, Yeats wrote to Florence wondering if 'the magical armageddon' had begun at last and telling her that he believed it would drag in half the world. Chiliastic vision increasingly preoccupied him:

> The dews drop slowly and dreams gather: unknown spears
> Suddenly hurtle before my dream-awakened eyes,
> And then the clash of fallen horsemen and the cries

Of unknown perishing armies beat about my ears.
We who still labour by the cromlech on the shore,
The grey cairn on the hill, when day sinks drowned in dew,
Being weary of the world's empires, bow down to you,
Master of the still stars and of the flaming door.[1]

Annie Horniman, meanwhile, enriched by another inheritance, continued to support the Matherses ever more generously. Nonetheless, when she went to visit them in Paris during the summer of 1895, she found their subsidy was nearly spent and that they had moved to an expensive flat near the Bois de Boulogne where they were entertaining one of the many spurious dukes who, with other royal pretenders, added colour to the Paris of the Nineties. Mathers himself, convinced that Armageddon would bring the collapse of the British Empire, was now a conspicuous member of the lunatic right and was planning to return a Jacobite king to the Scottish throne. When Yeats met him in Paris, he noticed that Mathers, arrayed in a kilt appropriate to the title he had assumed of Count MacGregor of Glenstrae, was drinking heavily. Mathers insisted that this was merely part of his political image but the truth was otherwise. He was giving way under psychological pressures, and a major rift was widening between himself and Annie Horniman which would reveal both her repressed sexuality and his megalomania.

Annie found the emphasis given to exotic love techniques by one member of the Order (Dr Edward Berridge or *Resurgam*) particularly upsetting and had written several times to Mathers insisting that something be done. She was irked by what she called Mathers's 'habitual lethargy', but was even more exasperated that she appeared now to be subsidising political interests which, as a convinced imperialist, she could not share. Annie felt her honour was at stake and, in July 1896, she terminated the Matherses' allowance. A little later, she resigned as sub-praemonstrix of the Isis-Urania Temple, although she continued to attend its ceremonies. Mathers, with his income drastically diminished, tried to eke out a living with translations and selling mystical tips to a gullible stockbroker, but by the close of October 1896 his persecution mania had become ever more apparent. He issued a manifesto requiring unquestioning obedience from the English occultists as a reward for the physical and mental strain he had endured while obtaining ritual insights from the Secret Chiefs. 'The sensation', he wrote, 'was that of being in contact with so terrible a force that I can only compare it to the *continued* effect of that usually experienced by any person close to whom a flash of lightning passes during a violent storm.' By such self-dramatising means Mathers was aiming at a control over the Order which amounted virtually to rule by divine right.[2] Annie Horniman refused to submit to his demands and, on 3 December 1896, just before Yeats arrived to visit him, Mathers expelled her from the Order amid allegations of insanity.

Yeats, hoping the Matherses might yet help with the rituals he sought for his Castle of Heroes, watched his old master descending into a world of phantoms. He was sympathetic to him nonetheless, and was still impressed by his powers. One morning over breakfast, for example, Mathers told Yeats he had last night seen a man wearing a kilt of the Macleod tartan. Later that day Yeats had a fever which for some reason he associated with the William Sharp who wrote under the name 'Fiona Macleod'. Mathers, making himself clairvoyant, declared that Sharp was in need. He turned to look for Moina and, as Yeats followed him to an inner room, so thoughts of Sharp and Fiona suddenly disappeared from his mind. Yeats expressed surprise, but Moina said: 'I have used a formula to send your soul away.' When Yeats wrote to Sharp, he eventually got a reply in which the author said Yeats's soul had indeed come to heal him during a fit of madness and he was now going to tell Fiona that he was better.

Yeats watched these bizarre events through a cloud of misery so intense that he sometimes wondered if he was himself going mad. Nearness to Maud had revived his love more sharply than ever, and he blundered through a world of illusion and pain. The imagery from his poems at this time suggests a pallid and desolate world drained of meaning, a limbo of exhaustion menaced by violence. 'Time drops in decay', broken things wrong the perfection of the Rose while an old woman labours to build a paltry fire, the chores of her meagre existence becoming the only focus of living attention. The best in such a world is 'sorrowful loveliness' and hope that the 'pearl-pale' muse will pay a brief moment of attention to a poet harassed by desire. But he remains the jester of 'Cap and Bells' singing to a queen who will not listen. Such a figure is, as Yeats wrote of his own relation to Maud Gonne, 'a romantic, when romanticism was in its final extravagance'. Perhaps by dying and leaving his beloved the trappings of his trade, the jester will gain a half-life in his beloved's heart. More often, however, the poet is merely a figure exposed to the merciless nullity of the wind:

> O curlew, cry no more in the air,
> Or only to the water in the West;
> Because your crying brings to my mind
> Passion-dimmed eyes and long heavy hair
> That was shaken out over my breast:
> There is enough evil in the crying of wind.[3]

Throughout these lyrics gathered into *The Wind among the Reeds* there is an agonising use of imagery that has at times a sado-masochistic intensity. In 'The Travail of Passion', for example, sexual consummation is equated with crucifixion. The world of natural energy is propelled by terrifying forces outside the poet's control and, in reaction, his feelings are reduced to passive longing.

Yeats told himself that if he went to Maud and proved his love 'by putting my hand into the fire till I had burned it badly' then surely she would realise his devotion was something she could not lightly discard. The thought repeated itself time and again as he made his way to her apartment, but the fear of actually going mad kept him from extreme displays, and instead he was obliged to wonder at Maud's revived beauty and the fierce energy of her idealism. He sat in her apartment in the Avenue d'Eylau in mingled awe and pity as he watched her in her Parisian dresses pacing the turkey carpets or sitting with her perpetual cigarette in a low chair by the little lace-covered table with its vase of expensive flowers.

But it was necessary for them both to preserve their distance. Maud talked to Yeats of Irish politics and the Irish occult, and the fervour between them was so great that he came in time to convince himself that these topics were in themselves the perfect link and could even restore their friendship after a quarrel. Maud drew out of him all the spiritual passion that burned under his abstracted, doleful appearance. Ireland, they both felt, was thronging with an invisible, mystical population. Here were those spiritual forces that could give strength when the nationalist movement seemed so weak. Together they read the Celtic studies of John Rhys and D'Arbois de Jubainville and began to feel that, 'if only we could make contact with the hidden forces of the land, it would give us strength for the freeing of Ireland'. They became familiar with the four talismans of the ancient Celtic peoples – the Sword, the Spear, the Stone and the Cauldron – legendary items around which Yeats hoped to construct his Order of Mysteries. Now, in their occult and political intimacy, Yeats was convinced that Ireland would be given new hope by the closeness to Maud he had so precariously achieved, by what he called 'a spiritual birth from the soul of a man and a woman'. Just as the alchemists whose lore helped shape the Golden Dawn had imagined a *mysterium coniunctionis*, a union of male and female which produced the noble and miraculously multiplying Philosopher's Stone, so might the sublimated relationship between Yeats and Maud lead to the conception of a golden and limitless force of national consciousness.

But Maud knew that action was also needed. She convinced Yeats that a Young Ireland Society should be founded in Paris and, on New Year's Day 1887, they held the first meeting of L'Association Irlandaise. Among the members were the Celtic scholar Richard Best, the journalist Arthur Lynch, Miss Barry O'Delaney and the classicist Stephen MacKenna. It was at this time too that Yeats met a friend of MacKenna's who was living in the garret of the hotel Yeats himself was staying at. This fellow guest was a melancholy young Irishman, interested in the literary revival and also in the works of Racine, on whom he hoped to write some articles. 'I liked him,' Yeats wrote, 'his sincerity and his knowledge, but did not divine his genius.' The young man's name was John Millington Synge, and he appeared virtually penniless.[4]

Yeats introduced his new friend to Maud, who, in her turn, arranged for Synge to work with her friend D'Arbois de Jubainville, whose lectures on Celtic literature Synge found of value. For a while he also allowed himself to be inveigled into L'Association Irlandaise, although he loathed extremism in politics. He soon began to distance himself from the Association on the grounds that he wished to work in his own way for Ireland, 'and I shall never be able to do so,' he wrote to Maud, 'if I get mixed up with a revolutionary and semi-military movement'. He had, besides, other plans. Yeats, who knew that Synge had learned Gaelic, advised him to return to Ireland, telling him particularly of Aran, where Synge would find a way of life that as yet lacked literary expression.

Other writers were also in Paris. Yeats found himself sitting in a café one day with two French-Americans, the German poet Dauthendey, who was seeking a poetry without verbs, and Strindberg, morosely searching for the Philosopher's Stone. Other occultists were more exuberant. The followers of the eighteenth-century mystic Saint-Martin, for example, invited Yeats to a party where wild dancing and wilder talk were stimulated by hashish. Drama, too, was swinging between extremes. The mystical introversion of *Axel* no longer held the stage. Instead, in Alfred Jarry's violent farce *Ubu Roi*, the actors imitated puppets while Père Ubu himself carried a lavatory brush as a symbol of his power. Yeats was depressed by this. Comedy and objectivity were replacing occult refinement. The subtle tones of Mallarmé and Verlaine seemed things of the past. But what could follow them? 'After us,' Yeats wrote, 'the Savage God.'

II
Politics and Protests

Yeats returned to London at the end of January 1897, where Maud soon followed him. She had set her mind on going to America to raise funds for a statue to be erected during the centennial celebrations for the great Irish patriot Wolfe Tone. The Dublin Wolfe Tone Committee refused to authorise her visit, however, and an angry Maud descended on Yeats insisting that, as the newly appointed President of the British and French branch of the Centenary Association (an organisation he had joined in pursuit of the political plans he was now nurturing), he give her his authorisation. This of course he arranged, while Maud herself also went to meet the socialist Keir Hardie, who asked her to help organise the protests planned to disrupt the Dublin celebrations of Queen Victoria's Jubilee. Although not over-impressed with the Independent Labour Party (her work, she said, was purely for the Irish people), Maud agreed. She was now committed to two projects designed to kindle a longing for freedom at the heart of the Empire and, inevitably, Yeats was drawn in.

But Maud's presence in London had another consequence. On her arrival she had, quite naturally, asked Yeats to dine with her. 'She certainly had no thought of the mischief she was doing,' he wrote, but now, even on his own territory, Yeats was wholly in her power, and the image of Olivia Shakespear was drained of such potency as it had.[5] One morning, when Olivia called on Yeats, he did not read love poetry to her as he usually did, but wrote letters instead. 'There is someone else in your heart,' Olivia said tearfully, and this was the breaking of their liaison for many years. The resulting poem has a terse, agonised pathos:

> Pale brows, still hands and dim hair,
> I had a beautiful friend
> And dreamed that the old despair
> Would end in love in the end:
> She looked into my heart one day
> And saw your image was there;
> She has gone weeping away.[6]

But Yeats himself was now carried by the political currents that always flowed about Maud. 'I discovered', he wrote, 'a situation that interested me,' and, in so doing, he prepared once more to reveal his antithetical nature. The occultist would once again immerse himself in politics. Yeats was aware that this posed a danger to his poetry, that in his enthusiasm he might be betrayed into the coarseness of propaganda, and he argued with himself to prevent this. 'Though a poet may govern his life by his enthusiasms,' he had recently written in his *Book of Irish Verse*, 'he must, when he sits down at his desk, but use them as a potter the clay.' It was essential that he strive 'to become a master of his craft, and be ever careful to keep rhetoric, or the tendency to think of his audience rather than of the Perfect and the True, out of his writing'. Now he would have to test this on himself.

Some while previously, Yeats had met T. W. Rolleston at a café in the Strand and been told by him of the 'new movement', the Irish National Alliance or the Irish National Brotherhood, which in 1895 had broken away from the Irish Republican Brotherhood. Yeats had been associated with the latter group since about 1886, but he persuaded himself that Dr Mark Ryan's new and secret party might further his literary and political aims by covertly influencing the Parliamentary Party and reviving the passions of the Young Irish movement. In a Dublin trapped in bitter political paralysis, anything, even extravagance, 'was better than that apathy or cynicism which were deep besetting sins'. Besides, here was a way of showing he could act independently of Maud as well as exorcising the demons of his own frustrated energy. As Yeats wrote of his joining the Alliance: 'I acted for the first time without any thought of her. I too had come to need excitement, forgetfulness.'

Yeats discovered that the Alliance itself was split into two violently opposed sections because of a murder that had taken place some years before. He believed that if he could get himself elected president of the English Centennial Committee then perhaps he could hold the Nationalist movement together. He succeeded in being appointed and, as the man at the head of the Centenary Association in England, he not only could issue Maud with the authority to travel to the United States, but could draw up his own political plans. These were advanced, if impractical. Yeats reckoned that the members of such a council as his, after a more careful form of election, could sit in permanent session and send delegates to Westiminster as their representatives when and only when an issue of importance to the Irish people arose. This would save money and, by freeing the delegates from English party allegiance, allow them to vote as they decided. Liberals and Conservatives in Westiminster would be unable to rely on the Irish vote and much uncertainty would thereby be caused. By letting it be understood that the delegates would also favour 'unconstitutional means' should these seem to their advantage, Fenians and more moderate Nationalists alike could join the party and the terrible swing of the pendulum between the two – that swing which brought 'death, defeat, and long discouragement' – might, Yeats thought, at last be stilled.

Yeats's 'grandiose plan' involved long and heavy hours of committee work which he never shirked, mastering the technicalities of such proceedings so that he could become the governing mind. Meanwhile, the day of Victoria's Jubilee was approaching. Among those determined to protest was the Irish Republican Party led by James Connolly, a short, stocky socialist whom Maud described as the bravest man she ever knew. She had already printed extracts from Connolly's speeches in her newspaper *L'Irlande Libre*. Now, and since Connolly's followers were barred from the more official anti-Jubilee protest, she agreed to speak at Connolly's demonstration. But when she saw she was billed as the principal speaker at a socialist rally she told Connolly she had changed her mind. Such an association might do harm to her wider cause. Connolly was bitterly disappointed and wondered how he could ever persuade his colleagues that he had once secured the support of the most glamorous agitator for Irish freedom. Yeats, seeing Connolly so downcast, persuaded Maud to change her mind. She sought Connolly and his family out in their desperate lodgings and, on the evening of 20 June, stood on a chair in College Green and addressed the crowd of his supporters. Yeats was there to hear Maud tell how the day before she had gone to decorate the graves of the Irish martyrs but had been turned back because it was a public holiday. 'Must the graves of our dead', she asked in her low, powerful voice, 'go undecorated because Victoria has her Jubilee?'

Plans for the great demonstration the following day were more elaborate. Maud arranged for a magic lantern to project from a window in the National Club slides giving details of the evictions and deaths from starvation that had occurred during Victoria's reign. Black flags were embroidered with the names of all those hanged for treason during the same period. A great crowd gathered and somewhere at the front of it was a coffin with 'The British Empire' printed on it. Yeats, who hated crowds, followed the procession and watched Maud striding with a triumphant, 'joyous' face among the people she had taken to her heart. As excitement rose, windows were broken. Yeats, who had lost his voice after a rowdy meeting earlier that day, tried to speak but could only whisper. He knew, however, that Maud would not try to contain the violence. Instead, as the swelling crowd surged through Dublin, the poet of the Rose 'resigned myself and felt the excitement of the moment, that joyous irresponsibility and sense of power'.[7]

The agitation became more extreme and a man eventually came rushing into the National Club where Yeats and Maud were taking tea crying: 'Oh it is awful; it is awful. Police are batoning the people outside.' Mounted police had in fact been summoned from Dublin Castle. They charged. Connolly was knocked down and arrested, having just managed to save the coffin of the British Empire from capture by telling the pall-bearers to throw it into the Liffey. Maud was determined to go out and do what she could. Someone said she would be hurt. Yeats ordered the locking of the Club doors to keep her inside. She stormed at him when he refused to let her go unless she explained what she meant to do. 'How do I know till I get out?' Yeats, now in a state of great tension, said he would himself go out provided Maud did not try to slip through the door. She would make no such promise. Two hundred people were being wounded and one woman was killed. 'You made me do the only cowardly thing of my life,' she wrote later. 'Our friendship must be strong indeed for me not to hate you.' The next morning, Maud went to Bridewell prison, paid Connolly's fine, got him breakfast, raised bail for the other prisoners and found all of them lawyers.

III

Lady Gregory

Yeats retreated to Tulira Castle, where a letter arrived addressed from the Grosvenor Hotel, Victoria Station. Maud wanted to make her feelings clear and define for them both the state of their relationship as she saw it. Their mutual political involvement particularly concerned her. 'For a long time,' she wrote, 'I had a feeling I should not encourage you to mix yourself up in the *outer* side of politics & you know I have never asked you to do so. I see now that I was wrong in not obeying this feeling more completely.' Had she done so, the old woman who had been killed during the police baton charge would not have died – 'this would not have happened if I had been able to do my duty', Maud wrote.[8]

There is an over-weaning self-confidence in this, as well as a suggestion of the guilt she felt for having given in to Yeats's insistence that she remain in the comparative safety of the National Club. Yeats was not, she said, a coward in himself, but he was cowardly when it came to caring for her. 'Do you know that to be a coward for those we love, is only a degree less bad than to be a coward for oneself? The latter I know well you are not, the former you know well you are.' This rebuke must have stung and was barely offset by Maud's telling him that as a poet he had 'higher work to do', while she 'was born to be in the midst of a crowd'. Maud's letter has much of the insight and more of the firmness of a leader whose crisp decisions are wholly and often unfairly subsumed in the cause they serve. Maud told Yeats that it was quite impossible for them ever to do any work together 'where there is likely to be excitement or physical danger & now let us never allude to this stupid subject again'. It was as if the conventional roles of lover and mistress had been reversed, and now, while Maud set off for Paris and politics, an exhausted Yeats settled in for a long stay in Galway.

When Lady Gregory came briefly to Tulira, bringing with her some fine trout for Martyn's Friday fast, she found Yeats 'white, haggard, voiceless, fresh from the Jubilee riots which he had been in the thick of'.[9] Her strong instinct to protect him was roused, but she was unable wholly to approve of what he had been doing. The Jubilee riots were not, Lady Gregory confided to her diary, 'a very dignified proceeding'. The comment says much about the patrician poise of the woman, but, while Augusta Gregory had her rightful place among the Ascendancy, she knew she belonged to a class that was under threat and could not look with any confidence to those politicians who had once attended her Hyde Park salon. One of the shrewdest of the Irish peers had told her that, with the passing of new Land Bills, the estates of the landlords would be slowly sliced away. However, as a widow with a mortgage to pay off and money to find for her son Robert's fees at Harrow, Ireland would have now to be Lady Gregory's home.

Ireland was, besides, the land where her heart was, and her instincts were increasingly to side with those about her, drawing landlord and peasant into a secure and independent sense of community. In this way the Irish might achieve self-respect and avoid the levelling excesses of democracy. Lady Gregory sensed, however, that she had little time. Her diary shows her squarely facing up to the facts. 'It is necessary as democracy gains powers,' she wrote in her diary for 8 April 1895, 'our power should go, & God knows many of our ancestors & forerunners have eaten – or planted – sour grapes & we must not repine if our teeth are set on edge.' History and current developments were both, she realised, against her. Nonetheless, 'I would like to leave a good memory & not a "monument of champagne bottles" & with all that, I hope to save the *Home*, house & woods at least for Robert.' A strong sense of her responsibilities as a landlord and a mother, of her innate dignity and commitment to duty, shine through this passage, its warmth fed by Lady Gregory's need to nurture, preserve and protect.

To go quietly along new ways needed courage and a measure of independent-mindedness. The Jubilee had given her the opportunity to display both. Much to the horror of her neighbours she had quietly declined to light celebratory bonfires at Coole, justifying herself by asking what the English Queen had ever done for Ireland. Henceforth, Coole would be a firmly Irish domain, the place where the leaders of Irish society could live in accord with the peasant farmers about them. Lady Gregory's diary records her increasing satisfaction that this stage of affairs was coming to pass, and forces both external and local helped to promote it. The now admitted over-taxing of Ireland united many against England, while the outbreak of the Boer War would show, despite the numerous Irish troops who volunteered to fight for England, how imperialism could war on dubious moral grounds fired by the crudest jingoism. The Gaelic League would with some justification portray the Empire approaching its decadence.

In the meantime, Yeats's literary work also had its effect on Lady Gregory's search for an Irish identity. When, on first inviting him to Coole, she had wondered what she could do to help further the Irish literary revival, her question had not been as idle as Yeats supposed. It is unlikely that he knew the small number of works she had published anonymously or guessed at the powers of an imagination not yet fully apparent even to Lady Gregory herself. However, when Yeats briefly returned to Coole after his trip from the west coast with Arthur Symons, Lady Gregory had begun to get into order the collection of Irish folklore she had been making and showed it to him.

The collecting of this material enthralled Lady Gregory and opened her eyes. It was, she wrote, 'the small beginning of a weighty change'. She had found a way of uniting her literary and patriotic instincts and, in so doing, discovered what she could think of as the soul of Ireland. 'If by an impossible miracle' she wrote in her *Visions and Beliefs in the West of Ireland*, 'every trace of Christianity could be swept out of the world, it would not shake or destroy at all the belief of the people of Ireland in the invisible world, the cloud of witnesses, in immortality and the life to come.'[10] She wrote up and published one of her stories anonymously in an English magazine, but soon, realising he needed the money more than she, she handed her material to Yeats for publication under his name. It was a gesture typical of her magnanimity and also of that subtle blend of pride and sometimes excessive self-effacement with which Lady Gregory conducted her life.

The round of entertaining by which the Ascendancy families of Galway maintained their contacts ensured that Lady Gregory met Yeats again a few days after her visit to Tulira Castle. She went to stay with Count de Basterot at Duras, his house by the coast, where Yeats and Martyn had also been invited. Sensing that the Count and Martyn had things to discuss in private, Lady Gregory took Yeats to the estate office where, with accomplished ease, she managed to draw him out. She had proved to him that her Irish literary interests were more than a passing whim and now, over tea and as the rain beat on the windows, she began to talk of a play Martyn had recently finished and which the Count had passed her to read. *Maeve* was, she thought, a fine work, although the London producers had not looked on it favourably. Martyn had wondered if he could have it produced in Germany. Conversation then turned to the idea of an Irish literary theatre, a long-treasured hope of Yeats's own, which he felt would never come to anything because of the difficulties of raising money in Ireland. He had spoken to Florence Farr about hiring some little London hall where he could perhaps produce plays, but again his idea seemed hopeless. Lady Gregory was less pessimistic. She encouraged Yeats to expand on his theme and he felt his sense of irresolution waning in the warmth of her greater practical strength. Although she had no knowledge of the theatrical world, she was intrigued. As Yeats recalled, 'we went on talking about it, and things seemed to grow possible as we talked, and before the end of the afternoon, we had made our plan'.

A short while later Yeats went over to Coole where, seated at her newly acquired second-hand typewriter, Lady Gregory took down from Yeats's dictation his plans for an Irish theatre. The prospectus would be signed by Martyn, Lady Gregory and Yeats himself, and proposed a three-year experiment during which 'certain Celtic and Irish plays' would be performed in Dublin to 'an uncorrupted and imaginative audience'. The stage Irishman of low English comedy, humiliating his countrymen by a gross stupidity that played up to an English sense of moral superiority, would be banished from the stage. His antics would no longer be an insidious model for imitation. The drama Yeats and his friends were proposing would show Ireland as 'the home of ancient idealism' and so offer an image of dignity that would give the audience a feeling of refined national identity that transcended the political differences that divided them.[11] Literature, as Yeats always hoped, would help forge a true Irish consciousness, and while Martyn – that generous if eccentric benefactor of Nationalist causes – guaranteed the costs of his own play *The Heather Field* and Yeats's *Countess Cathleen*, Lady Gregory contributed a further £25 and worked hard to solicit money from her friends and acquaintances.

Yeats was invited to stay at Coole for the close of July and he wrote explaining that he would come with George Russell, who was, he told Lady Gregory, the model for Michael Robartes in 'Rosa Alchemica'. A somewhat curious Lady Gregory waited at Gort Station for her new friend and the man he had described as having wild red hair, fierce eyes, rough clothes and looks 'something between a peasant, a saint and a debauchee'.* Yeats himself, however, was becoming concerned by these outward signs of what he increasingly considered the ineffective eccentricity of life at Ely Place. He felt that Russell should save his art by broadening his experience, and by the end of the year was successfully urging his friend to take up a post in Sir Horace Plunkett's newly founded Irish Agricultural Organisation Society in order, as he told Lady Gregory, 'to take him out of the narrow groove of Theosophical opinion'. To her relief, Lady Gregory herself found Russell quiet, harmless and above all able to draw out the best of Yeats's now formidable powers as a conversationalist. She confessed in the draft of her memoirs that she had found Yeats at this time 'a most brilliant, charming, lovable companion, never out of humour, simple, gentle, interested in all that went on'. There was something over-generous in this, however, and Lady Gregory later crossed out 'lovable' and 'simple'.

Above all, she could see that the carapace of sociability – the long evenings in the library, the amusing stories of the great and the drunk in literary London, the sudden galvanising idealisms – hid the troubles of a young man at the end of his tether and close to nervous collapse. Clearly Yeats told her something of the background to this, even if he did not feel able to confess to the pain of his broken affair with Olivia Shakespear, a married woman. A diary entry of Lady Gregory's makes clear that Maud Gonne was the focus of his revelations. 'He fell in love with her ten years ago,' she recorded, '& for 2 or 3 years it "broke up his life" he did nothing but write to her & see her & think of her – Then he grew stronger – and tho' still idealising her did not feel it in the same way – But lately, at the Jubilee riots it all came back to him – and he suffers tortures of hope & fear.'

But the white, haggard face Lady Gregory had seen at Tulira Castle expressed an anguish she was only partly privy to. Yeats's long years of intellectual and spiritual labour were taking their toll, their strain made the worse by the humiliating constraints of problems with money (George Pollexfen was currently providing him with a subsidy of a pound a week) and the fact that, as Katharine Tynan noted, Yeats was barely capable of looking after himself. The burden of incessant publication, his recent work with the fractious Centennial Committee, his loss of Olivia Shakespear and the agony of his unrequited love for Maud Gonne all tightened nerves already strained by his having lived so intensely on the perilous borders of occult revelation. Now, when the evenings in the library came to a close and Yeats retreated

---

* Russell himself had been greatly impressed by 'Rosa Alchemica', writing to tell Yeats he thought it 'a most wonderful piece of prose. Everything in it, thought and word, are so rich that they seem to be gathering in the temple of the mind thousands of pilgrim rays returning and leaving there their many experiences'.

to the master-bedroom Lady Gregory insisted he take, he was harassed in his sleep and his half-sleep by dreams that spun before him with the mad, all-mastering logic of association.[12]

Beautiful illuminated manuscript pages unfolded in front of his vision, their profound hieroglyphics luring him with the promise of meaning only to vanish and leave the memory of enigmatic wisdom. 'The secret of the world is so simple that it could be written on a blade of grass with the juice of a berry.' Once he dreamed of an initiation ceremony. He was lying in a stone trough in a great round house, a wind blew over him and currents of psychic power were directed at his body. These currents were painful and a voice said: 'We are doing this to find out if it is worth going on doing this.' On another night his soul was taken into realms of light to be shown its incarnations, but Yeats's vision of the mystic powers evaporated.

Sexual dreams, Yeats claimed, were rare, although one night a voice promised him a secret vision of life and death. The room brightened, the foot of the bed became a mass of precious stones that were at once jewels and the glass fruit he remembered from the lime-juice bottles of his childhood. The gathering brightness became associated with sex and, as it suddenly darkened, Yeats found he had ejaculated. The stones, too, became associated with passion, for when he tried to send his soul to Maud Gonne he was awakened by a shower of them falling on him. When Maud wrote, it seemed that she had shared these dreams and, in the desperate intensity of sublimation, Yeats thought he and Maud were united in purifying, eternal emotions – the world of precious stones. As his excitement died down, a figure who was both a man and a woman stood by his bed to join his other visitors: the sad, gentle lovers in olive green, the woman in the Elizabethan ruff, his mother holding a cup in her hand.

Yeats woke so exhausted he barely had the energy to dress himself, and Lady Gregory took to sending him bowls of broth with which to fortify himself. But the visions of the night often troubled him during the day. Walking in the Seven Woods of Coole and crossing a little stream in that 'landscape of mysterious and desolate beauty', Yeats felt a sudden sense of complete dependence on the divine will and told himself that this was the way Christians felt. In his waking as in his sleeping life, image called up image in an endless, exhausting procession. The radiant woman he had conjured in Tulira Castle, the huntress with her arrow, had, he believed, suggested to him the importance of rigorous intellectual effort. But he had not taken her warning and now, instead of clarity, Yeats felt he was wandering lost on that kabbalistic maze Mathers had once shown him, saying it was called Hodos Chameliontos (more properly Hodos Chamelionis) or the Path of the Chameleon. Now, as Yeats pursued this dangerous road, deep in the woods at Coole, so images of sexual desire and frustrated love lurked in the bends and the quiet places. 'My devotion might as well have been offered to an image in a milliner's window, or to a statue in a museum,' he wrote later. He felt it would be a relief to scream aloud and, as the phantom images of Maud beckoned to him, he repeated to himself time and again the last confession of Mallory's Lancelot: 'I have loved a queen beyond measure and exceeding long.' When the charm had no power and desire became unbearable, Yeats would break down and masturbate, the effort leaving him exhausted and ill.

He could tell Lady Gregory little of this and, when he did try to talk, Yeats found his words falling into confused silence. She sensed that he needed practical action, and difficulties over the founding of the Irish Literary Theatre seemed to offer this. Much had already been done. Money had been raised or promised, and *The Countess Cathleen* was ready for performance. However, under a system obsolete elsewhere, the two Dublin theatres held monopolies on all but charity performances and were booked by English companies for the best months of the year. The worst months were expensive, and it became evident that the only way to change the situation was by passing a Private Member's Bill at Westminster. Lady Gregory contacted an old friend of her husband's, the historian William Leckey, undertook a voluminous correspondence and eventually succeeded in having the regulation changed.

She could also see that Yeats was in need of work that was, in the local phrase, 'light upon the mind'. That summer she took him with her as she went among the cottages collecting folk material, an experience which inevitably brought him into contact with an everyday world of magic and superstition which occasionally came right up to the walls of Coole itself. As Yeats told Lily: 'a woman who came to mend chairs went a walk down the avenue with the housemaid last week and presently both came in a fainting state. They had seen three fairies – tall figures with black hats (Steeple-hats) and ruffs, evident Elizabethans'. The presence of the intense young man in black troubled the local people, however, who feared that Lady Gregory was bringing a missionary among them. As Lady Gregory herself wrote: 'Mr Yeats at that time wore black clothes and a soft black hat, but gave them up later, because he was so often saluted as a priest.'

She recorded other stories that were even wilder. 'I was told . . . that the curate of the Clare parish had written to the curate of a connaught parish that Lady Gregory had come over the border with "a Scripture reader" to try and buy children for proselytising purposes.' The local priest told one complainer not to be so foolish and, while Yeats and Lady Gregory discussed the balance of pagan and Christian beliefs in the material they found, both began to discover the power of the native spoken language. Here, for Yeats, was a way beyond the concentrated 'solar' artifice, the Paterian style of his first version of the stories in *The Secret Rose*. For Lady Gregory, making herself responsible for the writing down and typing up of some two hundred thousand words of dialect, the possibilities began to form of a studiedly simple style which she would later call Kiltartanese after the village of Kiltartan near Coole itself.

As Yeats and Lady Gregory worked together in these ways, so their mutual needs and contradictions, brought into fresher light by the respect and affection waking between them, gave each a new confidence. Emptinesses in their lives were being partly assuaged. For Lady Gregory, only just in her middle age, widowed, distant from her remaining family and with her closest relation an adolescent son, Yeats was an attractive younger man, intriguing, stimulating and at once forceful but vulnerable. She could offer him something of her need to mother and sustain and, in a way that touched her closely, could be his patron and his secretary. She was both the straight-backed Ascendancy lady in her domain and the woman who copied his letters. Yeats's imagination stimulated her intelligence, helped her further her place in Irish intellectual life, and offered the rewards of closeness to genius without the perils of sex.

For Yeats this last was an important factor. He could harbour for Lady Gregory – and he never addressed her as anything else – an almost filial regard which was returned by her always calling him 'Willie'. She was a woman who, like his mother, listened avidly to the folklore told in the cottages but, unlike the pitifully distant Susan Yeats, could offer an atmosphere of affection in which things could be made to happen. In Yeats's esteem for Lady Gregory there was something of the delight of childhood deprivations suddenly and miraculously made good. Her practical kindness and the unstrained reserves of her energy were, besides, qualities which, by their mere existence, calmed the fear and fever of his wandering the chameleon's path. Although he was in his thirties, there was an element of almost boyish dependence in Yeats's gratitude, and a need too of being noticed and admired when he burst in on her to tell her excitedly about his newest project. He told her that he needed her, in his father's phrase, as 'an anvil on which to beat out my ideas'.

These ideas centred increasingly around an Irish life in which a cultivated Ascendancy superiority drew on and lent dignity to the existence of the peasantry. The Big House was joined to an ancient Celtic world at once soil-conscious and spiritual. As Yeats and Lady Gregory drove back in her old phaeton from collecting folklore, so their journey symbolised the world they wished to create. They had sat in the local cottages and heard the stories which now, as they came by the long vistas of Coole and the clipped undergrowth of laurels, they would make into literature for the whole nation.

The modest grandeur of Coole – 'plain and box-like' as Yeats described it – began to embody for him the qualities he was finding in its mistress, and he came to adopt its ethos as a symbol of patrician comeliness.[13] At Coole he was far from hated London and close to his spiritual roots. The rented rooms in Bloomsbury with their cheap furniture – the wickerwork chair and the once embarrassing and now empty bed – could here be held at a distance, forgotten even. At Coole there was nothing of the isolation, the oppressive sense of being hard up, the smell of bachelor chops, the long evening walks alone forced on Yeats because his eyesight discouraged reading or writing by candlelight. The plumbing at Coole might be primitive, the horse-pumped water 'racy of the soil' and coloured by bits of weed, snail shells and even an occasional leech, but in such ways the life outside permeated the ancestral stabilities within.

Yeats was to become profoundly attached to these. Each generation had left its trace on the house, bringing back from the Grand Tour such items as the marble copy of the Venus de' Medici in the drawing room, the Canaletto, the Guardi and the Zurbaran. A Gregory had commissioned from Stubbs the portraits of the Arab horses, and many of the family had helped stock the library with finely bound volumes of the classics. Others had brought back from the Far East earthenware ewers, silver bowls and vivid Mogul miniatures. Round the walls of the breakfast room hung engravings that suggested other interests: portraits of Pitt, Fox, Wellington, Palmerston and Gladstone, and a letter from Burke to the Sir William Gregory who had been a high official in the East India Company. The eighteenth century did not as yet have for Yeats, still under the influence of William Morris, the great importance it was later to acquire. The carved and gilded picture frames were not to his taste. Nonetheless, he would in time be able to write that 'this house has enriched my soul out of measure because here life moves without restraint through spacious forms. Here there has been no compelled labour, no poverty-thwarted impulse.' Coole was to become an ideal by which the people of Ireland might yet stand firm and strong, a place of recuperation for both the public world and the private one. As Lady Gregory recorded in her diary at the end of Yeats's stay: 'I am bound to say that his healthiness of mind & body increased while at Coole – so that he wrote afterwards "my days at Coole passed like a dream – a dream of peace".'

IV

Visions and Divisions

There were also more active forms of politics to attend to. When Yeats left Lady Gregory in September it was with his energies sufficiently replenished to join Maud Gonne for the Wolfe Tone Centennial Convention in Manchester. During the previous months Maud had written to him on at least two occasions to tell him how she was 'galvanised by the great spiritual forces of Ireland'. Yeats's hope of winning her to occult nationalism was clearly being fulfilled, but what united them on the mystic plane was a threat to him in the material world. Inspired by his efforts, Maud said she had managed to communicate 'with the souls of those great & strong heroes who lived only for their ideal'. She received from such contact, she added, the strength to go on with her work. The Convention in Manchester would show how virulent and divisive that strength could be.

Menaced by conspiracies within the divided movement and threatened by the activities of the British secret service as well (there were, Yeats wrote, anonymous letters warning them to keep a bodyguard at the door), Yeats himself chaired noisy meetings and watched Maud with increasing awe and alarm. He deplored the 'raging abstraction' of her views but saw that even in extremes her mind was free, free with a joyousness that compelled others to her will. Her influence lay in this and in her beauty. 'Her power over crowds was at its height, and some portion of the power came because she could still, even when pushing an abstract principle to what seemed to me an absurdity, keep her own mind free, and so when men and women did her bidding they did it not only because she was beautiful, but because that beauty suggested joy and freedom.' Maud's great stature and distinguished looks had their own eloquence, yet there was about them Yeats thought something frighteningly impersonal. Her face was not simply that of a living woman but, 'like the face of some Greek statue, showed little thought'. Her whole body, he suggested, was less a thing of flesh and blood than 'a master work of long labouring thought, as though a Scopas had measured and calculated, consorted with Egyptian sages, and mathematicians out of Babylon, that he might outface even Artemisia's sepulchral image with a living norm'.[14]

This woman with her terrifying extremism moved eerily between the barely human and the absolute impersonality of the finest classic art, between the polarities of flaming passion and the chill of a marble form. Real affection could not touch her. 'She is', Yeats wrote to Lady Gregory, 'very kind and friendly, but whether more than that I cannot tell.' The only way he could reach her, it seemed, was through the occult. 'I have been explaining the Celtic movement and she is enthusiastic over it', Yeats reported, 'in its more mystical development.' Fire, stone and occult vision: passion reached out to all things in its contempt and fear of the body. Yeats served Maud in these aspects to the point of exhaustion and then, before she left for her onerous fund-raising trip to America, she wrote to him and said: 'I don't want you to give me so much place in your life.'

Yeats wrote to Lady Gregory expressing his fears for Maud's safety in America just before Lady Gregory herself came to London to see, in part, to his comfort. She visited Woburn Buildings, bought him a set of blue curtains and replaced the wicker chair with a large and comfortable leather one. Gifts of tinned fruit, wine and a fountain pen followed. 'How extremely good you are,' he wrote, 'nobody has ever shown me such kindness.' When she discovered how hard up Yeats was, Lady Gregory started to leave money behind the clock on the mantelpiece. 'Ought I to let you do all these kind things for me?' he asked. He was embarrassed and flustered, but he accepted her gifts.

Others were more wary of the Dame of Coole's patronage. Lady Gregory called on the Yeats family in Blenheim Road and found JBY sketching a pencil portrait of Edward Martyn. Realising how competently he worked in this medium, she at once commissioned portraits of George Russell, Douglas Hyde, herself and Willie. JBY's income for the year was considerably helped by this act of generosity but he was not, unlike his son, overwhelmed by it. JBY said it was not easy to like Lady Gregory. While he was not for the present unhappy that she had 'got' Willie and told her that she had the sort of courage that comes from absolute disinterestedness, what he really meant was that she was bossy. 'She is', JBY opined, 'so infernally haughty to lesser mortals – or whom she thinks lesser mortals.'[15] But, if Lady Gregory's hauteur was a fault, it was one she would learn to use to considerable advantage.

In the meantime she was determined to bring the rest of the Yeats household under her influence. The women, as always, interested her less than the men, and Lily was besides still suffering from the after-effects of the typhoid she had caught in France, an illness cruelly exacerbated by the fact that she was also suffering from an as yet undiagnosed thyroid complaint which caused her constant fatigue. As late as the spring of 1897 she could only go out in a bath chair for twenty minutes at a time. Lady Gregory was distant with Lollie, too, while around this time Susan Yeats had another stroke which left her so vague that JBY tried to stimulate her by asking for a daily letter. Each day Susan described the sky as seen from the parlour window. 'It was the only thing she ever wrote about,' JBY recalled, 'for everything else was only a worry.' But, if Lady Gregory had hoped to catch all the Yeats men, her haughty behaviour towards Jack's wife Cottie was perhaps responsible for the distance between herself and the young artist and writer, with his easy manners but steely inner reserve. Lady Gregory attended his first public exhibition at London's Clifford Gallery in late 1897; she enjoyed it, but when she lured Jack to Coole the following year he was as always reserved, preferring the company of the younger guests to that of his hostess.

Yeats himself, encouraged by hopes that his Irish Theatre was now coming to fruition, put aside his troublesome novel *The Speckled Bird* to continue work on his mystic and legendary play *The Shadowy Waters*. But he was still experiencing the difficulties engendered by his dramatic ideas. As he explained in January 1897 to Fiona Macleod: 'my own theory of poetical or legendary drama is that it should have no realistic, or elaborate, but only a symbolic and decorative setting. A forest, for instance, should be represented by a forest pattern and not by a forest painting. . . . The acting should have an equivalent distance to that of the play from common realities.'[16] These were notions that would in time be greatly elaborated but, for the moment, JBY declared the play 'absolutely unintelligible'.

Early in the New Year, Lady Gregory introduced Yeats to her old lover Wilfred Blunt, for whom he performed a vision. Blunt was unimpressed, although he found Yeats himself an 'interesting type'. But, if Blunt was unmoved by the occult, Yeats himself was now ever more deeply involved in his search for Celtic mysteries. He was still seeking help from the *fratres* and *sorores*, while also involving himself in the occult experiences of others. In particular, he began an extensive correspondence with W. T. Horton, whose artwork, much influenced by Blake and Beardsley, inspired the essay 'Symbolism in Painting'. Horton himself, who 'gave himself up to all kinds of amorous adventures', was to play a significant role in Yeats's later occult life and be the subject of a great stanza in one of the masterpieces of his maturity. Now, however, Yeats discussed with him the nature of the Golden Dawn.

The tone of the letter suggests the swift and assured mastery with which Yeats, himself still very much under the influence of Blake, could discuss the spiritual difficulties of others. 'Nor is our order anti-Christian,' he told Horton. 'That very pentagram which I suggested your using is itself as you would have learned, a symbol of Christ. I am convinced however that for you progress lies not in the dependence upon a Christ outside yourself but upon the Christ in your own breast.' The tone is that of a practised spiritual adviser, as is the intellectual range and the way it is tailored to an individual personality. 'I do not mean that you cannot progress outside the G.D. but that you should read and study in some unemotional and difficult school. Jacob Boehme is certainly the greatest of the Christian mystics since the Middle Ages and none but an athletic student could get to the heart of his mystery. You would, I think, find him consonant with your temperament.' As always, however, Yeats was aware of the dangers of the occult life. 'But no matter what school you study in you must expect to find progress beset by false intuition and the persecution of phantoms. Our past and its elementals, masked often as angels of light, rise up always against our future.'[17]

The danger was not all supernatural, however, for Golden Dawn itself was immersed in continuing turmoil, much of it provoked by Mathers. Having succeeded in removing Annie Horniman from the Order, he now had one of its founders and leading members in his sights.

Dr William Wynn Westcott, the magus who had helped Yeats interpret his vision of the star-shooting goddess, was a leading London coroner. It would be a matter of grave professional embarrassment for him if it came to be known that he was also a keen participant in occult practices, and Mathers, in pursuit of supreme power, almost certainly took advantage of this. In March 1897 he returned from Scotland, where he had been involved on some Jacobite errand, to Paris. On his way he stopped over in London where, on 13 March, he deliberately left in a cab a manuscript of magical practices conspicuously labelled with Westcott's name and work address. The manuscript was handed in to the police. Westcott himself was unaware of the ruse but, as he wrote to an acquaintance: 'It had somehow become known to the State officers that I was a prominent official of a society in which I had been foolishly posturing as one possessed of magic powers – and if this became more public it would not do for a Coroner of the Crown to be made shame of in such a way. So I had no alternative.'[18] Westcott resigned.

The role of Chief Adept fell to Florence Farr and, with it, a burden of administration. This, along with the constant intrigue and rumour-mongering, wore her down so greatly that a few months later Florence was thinking, she confessed, of 'chucking the whole thing'. But she did not, and, having that September attended the consecration of a new Vault at 36 Blythe Road, Hammersmith, she spent much of December and January helping Yeats construct his Celtic Order of Mysteries. With several other members of the Golden Dawn, she sat at a table on which were spread symbols of the four elements. Yeats himself evoked the Celtic gods through the cadenced repetition of the appropriate deity's name. Then, supposedly in the presence of the Celtic powers, those round the table prepared to leave Victorian London on a journey of astral projection.[19]

As Yeats recorded in his notebook, he and his fellow skryers went first to the Celtic Well of Knowledge in the Land of Youth, where flowed the waters of passion 'in which all purified souls are entangled'. By the side of the well grew a mountain ash which dropped its berries into the water like drops of blood. Descending into the depths of the well and protected only by the beams of Kusha from the 'utter passivity' of the watery element itself, the skryers then entered the dangerous world of lunar images. Here, in the palace of Mananan Mac Lir, Lord of the Sea, the god gave Yeats a wand made of mountain ash. With this he might lead his fellow adepts safely to the Land of the Heroes. Here, one by one, as Yeats himself stood like Aeneas in the Underworld, the great figures of legend passed before them: Deirdre, Conal, Conchubar, Fergus. Then, returning the way they had come, Yeats brought his friends back to London and, with a flourish of the Banishing Pentagram, the session ended.

V
'The Cry of the Sedge'

As Yeats came back from his carefully recorded trip to fairyland, Maud Gonne returned from the United States with £1000 to divide between the Executive Committee of the French and British Centennial Association and the group devoted to another of her major causes, the campaign to free Irish political prisoners. She found, however, as much acrimony as gratitude, and

Yeats was infuriated by the criticisms levelled against her, contrasting such a day-to-day debasing scrimmage with the muse of his own high imagining:

> They have spoken against you everywhere,
> But weigh this song with the great and their pride;
> I made it out of a mouthful of air,
> Their children's children shall say they have lied.[20]

Meanwhile, disaffected members of both the Prisoners Amnesty Association and the '98 Executive joined together under the MP Tim Harrington to form the so-called United Irishmen Centennial Association, 'in which all Irish Nationalists may be proud to take part'. Such shifts were to depress Maud increasingly as the Wolfe Tone celebrations neared. But, for the moment, a terrible famine in Mayo required her more urgent attention and she threw herself into relief work for the starving.

She then wrote to Yeats that she had seen a vision of a little temple of heroes which she proposed to build somewhere in Ireland once the Centennial was over and which she would make the centre of the literary and mystical movement. This was her way of furthering their spiritual relationship and the Nationalist strength she hoped might flow from it. Telling Russell of her plans, Yeats also asked how much it might cost him to live in the Irish countryside where he and Maud hoped to get 'the forms and shapes of the gods'. By January they were together in Sligo, where Maud's instinctive feeling for the country people and long experience of being with them allowed her to draw out much otherwise secret knowledge about where stone crosses could be found in groves and graveyards rich with memories of the Celtic heroes. Such thoughts, as always, gave back to Maud her resources of strength. These she now needed for, in her role as the Queen of the Sidhe, she was not only giving precise and very practical help to people too weak to bury their own dead, but was also urging on them the need to rise up against their oppressors. With James Connolly, Maud prepared a leaflet on 'The Rights of Life and the Rights of Property' which cited the Church Fathers in support of the idea that 'no *human* law can stand between starving people and their Right TO FOOD including the right to take that food wherever they find it'.[21] It was Maud's hope that such ideas might influence the people to an uprising when, later in the year, they celebrated the centenary of the great Irish patriot Wolfe Tone.

When Yeats told Lady Gregory that Maud was inciting the people to kill their landlords, she was appalled. She spoke 'very strongly' to her protégé, telling him there were other ways than murder with which to fight a famine and that it was the bounden duty of those with means and education to share all they had with the starving if needs be but to teach them to die with courage rather than live by theft. Did he not, she asked Yeats, realise the serious moral danger such wild ideas inflicted on the ordinary people?

Yeats replied, perhaps rather shamefacedly, that he did not. He had not thought about the people at all. His only concern was with the effect of her labours on Maud.

But Maud was not altogether pleased with Yeats either. In a letter from Dublin to Woburn Buildings written towards the end of February 1898 she reprimanded him for indiscretion and, after saying how pleased she had been to meet him, came to her most serious point. Clearly, Yeats had been pressing his suit while they were together in Sligo and Maud felt obliged to erect between them that physical embargo by which alone she felt she could protect both herself and their friendship. 'If you find that an absolutely *platonic friendship* which is all I can or ever will be able to give, unsettles you & spoils your work then you must have the strength & courage at once to give up meeting me.' Maud's distaste for physical contact again merged with her Nationalist idealism. She also told Yeats that she had to consider first and foremost what was best for his genius, for that genius belonged to Ireland. He owed it to Ireland, and 'you have no right to allow anything to injure it'.

Maud could not, however, entirely let him go. In a move characteristic of their entire relationship, she wrote that the intimacy she was unable to offer in the physical world might yet be shared in the occult one. In a letter of 16 March 1898 that was, by its very nature, ambiguously suspended between closeness and distance, Maud described how, while driving through Sligo, she had summoned Yeats's soul to be her guide. In the spirit world she could offer him a lover-like affection. 'I *went* to you,' she wrote, '& putting my hands on your shoulder asked you to come with me.' What followed could have been any lovers' evening stroll. 'We stood by that beautiful lake amid the twilight shadows, then you were on the car beside me driving among the mountains.' Out of such moments of spiritual intercourse might a 'mystic marriage' be made. 'All this sounds slightly mad, but you will not think it so & it is not at all – now please tell me exactly and truthfully were you conscious of any of this or not?' She begged him to write to her, but the postscript to her letter is a world away from reverie and shows the opposed forces warring in her soul: 'Try at any price to get the United Irishmen Centennial to unite with Exec. It is very important.' Vision and the suggestion of occult intimacy are drowned in a hail of commands, imperatives and the political squabbling which Maud was determined to master.[22]

The intimations of spiritual nationalism Maud had offered were profoundly influential all the same. Here was an experience of the occult at once personal and political, a drawing together of the ideals Yeats was pursuing in his poetry and his mystical life, and which could now provide a justification for his attacks on the baleful influence of English imperialism. For it was this – the British Empire and its materialistic pursuit of wealth and power – that Yeats was resisting. His enemy was an ideology more than a people.

In the spring of 1898, and in the pursuit of this cause, Yeats followed

Maud to Paris, where she had gone to rest and to see Iseult. He wrote to Lady Gregory, telling her that Maud had bronchitis and that because one of her lungs was affected she had to rest. 'She is unable to do any politics for the time and looks ill and tired.' She and Yeats passed their time with the Celtic mysteries instead. MacGregor Mathers was now hard at work on the rituals for these and had begun to puzzle out a form of initiation for the Castle of Heroes. Maud was invited to the Matherses' flat in the Rue Mozart to see visions and there was a keen anticipation of Fiona Macleod, whose presence would help make up 'a great Celtic gathering'.

In this last they were, of course, disappointed. Nor, when Yeats and Maud returned to Ireland in the early summer, were they any more successful in travelling to Newgrange where they had hoped 'to get the forms of gods and spirits and to get sacred earth for evocation'. Maud was overwhelmed with work and in June, while at the unveiling a memorial tablet, she was thrown from her carriage. She broke her arm, and her face was scratched and bruised. Yeats wrote in great concern to Lady Gregory but, finding Maud's hurt was not as bad as he at first thought, proposed delaying his trip to Coole merely for a few days 'to see if I can be of any use about political correspondence and the like'. When he finally parted from Maud, Yeats presented her with a copy of a journal in which were printed 'He thinks of those who have Spoken Evil of his Beloved' – his rebuke to Maud's political detractors – and 'He hears the Cry of the Sedge', his description of his sexual anguish:

> I wander by the edge
> Of this desolate lake
> Where wind cries in the sedge:
> Until the axle break
> That keeps the stars in their round,
> And hands hurl in the deep
> The banners of East and West,
> And the girdle of light is unbound,
> Your breast will not lie by the breast
> Of your beloved in sleep.[23]

The agony of unconsummated love is plain, and a few days later Maud wrote to Yeats to say: 'I read over & over again your poem until I didn't need the book to read it, it was so beautiful.' What she could not quite bring herself to say was that she had learned the poem by heart.

VI

J. M. Synge

When Yeats eventually arrived at Coole, Lady Gregory, who had recently returned from a folklore-gathering expedition to the Aran Islands, told him of a fellow writer she had met there. That writer was Synge and, when Yeats had sketched in something of his background, Lady Gregory insisted he be invited to Coole. In such ways would she make her house one of the great, inspiring centres of modern literature, a place where the continuous outpouring of mind and spirit would change people's views and encourage masterpieces. As Yeats himself later wrote, men of genius came like swallows to Coole, and the 'powerful character' of Lady Gregory gave certainty and direction to their aims. The greatest of them would be encouraged to carve their initials on the trunk of her copper beech tree, which became, in time, a visitors' book of unique interest.

But Synge, deeply reserved, desperately poor and inhibited, did not share Yeats's sense that here was a writer's earthly paradise. Coming from what was once a grand Ascendancy family, he had a more pessimistic and ultimately a more truthful view of the landlord class than that shared by Yeats and his hostess. He could see the insecurities that underlay a dying elite. He would, nonetheless, in his alliance with Yeats and Lady Gregory, find a means of releasing the as yet unexplored reaches of his genius and would soon contribute plays of world quality to the theatre they were devising. 'I think', Lady Gregory wrote, 'he got vitality from us.' That vitality would burn with great intensity until cancer killed Synge less than a decade later.

VII

'The Cloths of Heaven'

The high summer of 1898 saw the climax of the centennial celebrations for Wolfe Tone. In London there was a banquet at Frascati's and a public meeting the following day with Yeats in the chair and Maud and the Italian patriot Cipriani as principal speakers. The curious mixture of political radicalism and poetic suggestion in Yeats's politics at this time is clear from a speech he gave in which he decried 'the materialisms of England', urged an Irish patriotism inspired by the great leaders of the historic past, but reserved his most profound feelings for the heroes of legend. 'There is an old story', he declared, 'that tells how sometimes when a ship is beaten by storm and almost upon the rocks, a mysterious figure appears and lays its hand upon the tiller. It is Mannanan, the son of Lir, the old god of the waters. So it is with nations, a flaming hand is laid suddenly upon the tiller.' For all the enthusiasts gathered about him, the ship of state was still best guided by immortal powers. Cheers greeted the speech, and five days later the celebrations culminated in Dublin. Delegates from Australia, New Zealand and South Africa were present, but the promised contingent of American Irish were unable to attend due to their ships being requisitioned for troops needed in the Spanish – American War. The few who did come were more interested in tracing their roots than in public celebration and many were absent from the stone-laying ceremony itself.

For all that, the procession was a vast one. At the head went the Dublin Committee and their friends. Behind them, in a wagonette draped with a tricolour, rode Yeats, Maud and a small contingent of French visitors. Their appearance was the signal for great outbursts of cheering. Although Yeats himself was to believe that the procession was the occasion that marked the beginning of a rapprochement between the various factions of Irish politicians, acrimony and dispute were quite as in evidence as friendship. There was a quarrel between John Redmond and the leader of the anti-Parnellites and, at the last moment, Maud herself refused to appear on the platform in an empty display of unity with such men as the pro-British Lord Mayor of Dublin, Thomas Pile.

She stood instead among the crowds in Grafton Street, hearing the mutterings of discontent about the handful of French delegates who some had hoped would be an army, and listening to Yeats as he addressed the crowd. 'England', Yeats declared, 'had persuaded herself that Ireland, discredited by disunion, was about to submit – to accept a handful of alms. We have answered her today. She is no longer deceived. The people have made this movement.' Down in the crowd a voice cried out: 'No, no, it is Maud Gonne that has made it.' Maud herself would not, however, recognise such a claim. Thinking of what she had once hoped would flow from this occasion – uprising, death, Irish liberty – she felt only that a great opportunity had been lost. Even the laying of the foundation stone was a broken promise. No statue of Wolfe Tone was ever raised on it.

While Maud returned to her work among the starving people of the west, Yeats went to Coole where, in September, a parcel arrived for him containing the long-sought earth from Newgrange and a white bottle of water from the Boyne (gathered, Maud said, while the morning sunlight gleamed on the river), along with water from the holy well at Ballina. Maud urged Yeats to experiment with these items, touching his lips, eyes, ears and breast with them so that he should receive occult dreams of the heroic past. Such a request was in line with an essay he had published that June in the magazine *Cosmopolis*, where he once again asserted that if literature were not 'flooded with the passions and beliefs of ancient times' then it would dwindle to mere chronicle, fantasy or dry abstraction. Celtic belief, he asserted, was by far the most potent of the streams to feed European literature, and his propaganda

The infant Yeats asleep drawn by his father.

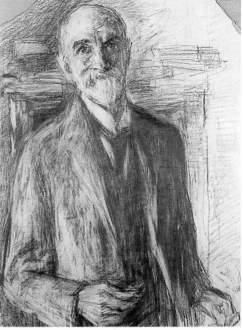

A study by John Butler Yeats for his unfinished self-portrait.

Susan Yeats in 1870.

Yeats as a boy pondering his reading

William Pollexfen circa 1862.

A pencil sketch of George Russell by JBY.

John O'Leary in 1904 by WBY.

William Morris in 1890.

An undated portrait of W. E. Henley.

Oscar Wilde in 1891.

MacGreggor Mathers portrayed by his wife.

Madame Blavatsky in Upper Norwood during 1887.

Lionel Johnson as Yeats first knew him.

· ARTHVR · SYMONS ·

A woodcut of Arthur Symons by Robert Bryden.

Yeats with an unidentified figure in the 1890's.

Yeats's uncle George Pollexfen.

Yeats in his early maturity photographed by Charles Beresford.

(*Clockwise from above*)

Maud Gonne at the time of her liaison with Millevoye.

Maud Gonne as Cathleen ni Houlihan by JBY.

Maud Gonne circa 1898.

Maude Gonne Macbride with Sean and Iseult.

(*Left*) Yeats in Woburn Place in 1904, photographed for the *Tatler*.

(*Above*) Florence Farr photographed for the *Pall Mall Budget* in 1891.

Eva and Constance Gore Booth at the time of Yeats's visit to Lissadell.

Olivia Shakespeare photographed for the *Literary Year Book* in 1897.

Lady Gregory in 1903 in a portrait by JBY

Lady Gregory beneath the catalpa tree at Coole.

Coole House.

The Abbey Theatre.

for Celticism was now to reach its apogee. In so doing, it would also lend itself to revision.

Yeats had praised Russell's poetry in the press, for example, highlighting its Celtic qualities, but in private he urged Russell to remove the poetic diction and archaisms which he had objected to in his own earlier work, seeing these now as a mannerism fostered by merely fashionable Celtic ideas. There was, however, a more profound consideration to this. 'Good writing', he told Russell, 'is the way art has of being moral, and the only way.' Scrupulousness created value, integrity. Russell was far from convinced, believing that ideas had a beauty apart from words. Yeats could not agree. 'If you want to give ideas for their own sake,' he commented tartly, 'write prose.' In poetry ideas must be subordinate to the beauty which is their soul. 'Isn't this obvious?'

The comment suggests far more than mere aesthetic interests. It hints at that subtlety of poise by which, in his art, Yeats brought his longing for revealed truth into balance with his scepticism. A life-enhancing idea – the concept of the mystic Rose, for example – should be held on to with sufficient strength to promote its worth but not so hard as to become a dogmatic belief. The poet was not a preacher or a recorder, but a discoverer releasing the potent essence of what he found by the art of his poem itself. And what the poet found, Yeats believed, were those archetypal states of mind that belonged at once to eternity and the individual. The ideal and the personal could thus be joined in a Unity of Being which spoke to the deepest intuitions of all people. Now, as Yeats left Coole for Sligo, so a public controversy obliged him to clarify these ideas.

His plans for an Irish Literary Theatre were being openly discussed, and an article by John Eglinton in the *Daily Express* attacked Yeats's work as a symbolist and visionary poet drawing inspiration from folklore. What Eglinton wanted was a nationalist drama that drew on the facts of daily life. Russell and the minor writer William Larminie got dragged in, and Yeats's eventual reply was his quintessentially Nineties essay 'The Autumn of the Body'.[24] Here, with a magisterial command of broad but emotive generalisation, Yeats (whose only modern language was a barely competent French) depicted writers across Europe struggling against 'that picturesque and declamatory way of writing, against that "externality" which a time of scientific and political thought has brought into literature'. He instanced the early poems of Shelley and the philosophical and scientific passages of Tennyson and Browning. 'We are about', he declared, 'to substitute the distillation of alchemy for the analyses of chemistry.' In what he guessed might be 'a crowning crisis of the world', art would turn to intuition, dream and vision. His friend Arthur Symons (whose *The Symbolist Movement in Literature* provided much of Yeats's background to French poetry) had explained that these ideas were central to Mallarmé and predicted that 'poetry will henceforth be a poetry of essences, separated one from another in little and intense poems'. The lyrics in *The Wind among the Reeds* exemplify this beautifully:

> Had I the heavens' embroidered cloths,
> Enwrought with golden and silver light,
> The blue and the dim and the dark cloths
> Of night and light and the half-light,
> I would spread the cloths under your feet:
> But I, being poor, have only my dreams;
> I have spread my dreams under your feet;
> Tread softly because you tread on my dreams.[25]

The original title of this poem, 'Aedh wishes for the Cloths of Heaven', provides a clue to Yeats's views on belief and style in poetry. Many of the lyrics in *The Wind among the Reeds* were first given to characters from *The Secret Rose*, where Aedh is a court poet of the heroic age whose severed head continues to sing of love after death. Aedh suggests, as Yeats wrote in the extensive note he first printed with the poems, 'the myrrh and frankincense that the imagination offers continually before all that it loves'. Absolute devotion, its reverence and association with death, are thereby brought together, and this contributes greatly to the desolation and awe in the volume, the sense of the autumn of the flesh and of meaning barely grasped from refined ecstasies of pain. Bringing to such a notion his occult interests, Yeats also saw Aedh as a self-consuming fire or the purity of the unchanging imagination. Such abstract structures can, however, be willed away (in subsequent printings Yeats removed them himself) and what abides is the scrupulous verbal music of the poem which suggests, as beautifully as anywhere in English literature, the all-spending ardour of a prostrate devotion, a sense both of wonder and abasement, the archetype indeed of the ever beseeching lover.

VIII
Mystic Marriage

At the close of 1898 Yeats returned from Sligo, where he had been experimenting with George Pollexfen on the Celtic mysteries, to spend time in Dublin with Maud Gonne. For all the psychological distance between them they were still the striking couple who caused the city to turn its gaze. Maud was as tall as a queen out of a saga, wrote one observer. She had a radiance as of sunlight. Yeats, 'that leopard of the moon', strode beside her restraining on its leash Maud's lion-coloured great dane, Dagda.[26] In public, they were a couple all but legendary, while in private, as *Demon est Deus Inversus* and *Per*

Ignem ad Lucem, they continued their occult studies, their visions drawing them ever closer on the supernatural plane as they probed the *anima mundi* for insight. A talisman Yeats developed gave Maud a vision of four Druids who told her that she and Yeats had already received the initiation of the cauldron and, in part, of the stone as well. Of the remaining jewels of the Tuatha de Danaan – the ancient Celtic objects that lay at the heart of their cult – Yeats told Maud he now felt sure that at least one was imminent. He sensed the powers of the spear hovering about him, and with these would come supernatural inspiration.

Yeats was careful to see that he and Maud stayed in separate hotels, and on the evening of 6 December, after he had left her for his own room near Rutland Square, he went to bed. At one-thirty the following morning he had a vision. Maud came to him in a red dress, its skirt full of flowers. She bent over him and they shared their first kiss. The following morning he went to her hotel in a state of high excitement. Joining him after breakfast, Maud asked if he had had a strange dream the night before. 'I dreamed this morning', he said, 'for the first time in my life that you kissed me.'[27] She made no answer and only returned to the subject later that evening. When dinner was over and Yeats was about to leave she said that last night she too had had an astral experience. Dressed in a white gown, she had gone to Yeats and been married to him by Lugh, the spear-wielding god of fire. Then, for the first time with her bodily mouth, Maud had kissed him. Here, in this celebration of their 'mystic marriage', was a moment of deep symbolic import to both of them, for Yeats now believed they were joined in holy service to the cause of Ireland.

But his excitement was short-lived. When he went round to see Maud the following day, he found her deeply depressed. 'I should not have spoken to you, in that way,' she said, 'for I can never be your wife in reality.' The previous night she had dropped her guard, and now she was desperate to rebuild her defences. Did she love someone else, Yeats asked? 'No,' she said and then, slowly, she added that there was someone else and that she felt it her duty to provide the moral substance for both their lives. She was referring to Millevoye, although the last stages of her affair with him were about to be played out.

Maud's violent swings of mood suggest an approaching psychological crisis. Beside the fire in the Nassau Street Hotel and in the vulnerability of her depression, exhausted from her work and with her failure to inspire an uprising perhaps still weighing on her mind, she confessed to Yeats the story of her life. In broken sentences, she told him of the affair with Millevoye, of the birth and death of little Georges, and of the conception of Iseult. It is clear that she could not prevent herself. There was no rational need for her to confess to what she did, but a few months before on 28 August 1898, she had written to Yeats that his friendship was 'such a charming restful thing &

I am sure so sure of it'. He was for her a small island of affection. In the last few days the occult mysteries had drawn them closer, their intimacy wearing away the distressed solitude of spirit, the seemingly squandered cost of the willed and ruthless distance from human touch Maud needed if she were ever to succeed in her father's work.

And amid her outpourings, driven by the terrible momentum of confession, she told Yeats of Tommy too. One night in Dublin years before, she said, sitting by the fire as she was now, she had wondered about her future life. She had longed to be the mistress of it. Looking at her father's bookshelves she had found a work on magic which, as she read it, made her think that the Devil, were she to pray to him, might help her. She prayed, asking for control of her life in return for her soul. 'At that moment the clock struck twelve, and she felt of a sudden that the prayer had been heard and answered.' Within a fortnight, Tommy was dead.

Yeats, in the paralysis of shock, told himself that if Maud were to come to him now then 'it must be from no temporary passionate impulse, but with the approval of her conscience'. But he was himself incapable of decisive action. He knew now with horrible certainty that the Rose of the World had been violated and that his mystic virgin was the mother of two illegitimate children. The woman whose bounty had been a revelation after the coldness of his mother had betrayed him at the deepest psychological level. In his abject confusion he wrote to the one person he felt could help him. He sent letters to Lady Gregory at her friend's palazzo in Venice. The letters reveal what, in the desperation of these days, made Yeats's anguish the more keen. It is clear that he and Maud were still deeply fond of each other. Maud had said to him, Yeats told Lady Gregory, and 'with every circumstance of deep emotion that she had loved me for years, and my love is the only beautiful thing in her life, but for certain reasons which I cannot tell you, reasons of a generous kind, and of a tragic origin, she can never marry. She is full of remorse because she thinks she has in the same breath bound me to her and taken away all hope of marriage.' This was true. Events had confirmed that Yeats was now indeed Aedh, the poet of ecstatic hopelessness.

But for Maud, even in a personal crisis, Ireland came first. When Yeats wrote his letter on 15 December she had gone briefly to Loughrea to deal with evictions and to address secret meetings. By the 17th of the month she had returned, and that evening she told Yeats that they were about to receive the long-expected Initiation of the Spear. As they sat in silence, Maud began to feel she was a great stone statue through which passed flame. Yeats felt himself to be that flame burning as he ascended a trunk of stone on which he could make no mark and from which he could evoke no response, even when he stared out of the statue's eyes and saw that the form about which the flames of his passion played was that of Minerva, the stern goddess who, at her birth, sprang fully armed from her father's head. 'Were the beings which stand behind human life trying to unite us,' Yeats asked, 'or had we brought it about by our own dreams?'

By this time Lady Gregory had arrived from Venice and was staying in the Nassau Street Hotel. When she and Maud met, the woman who was like a mother to Yeats could not see the beauty of the woman he was tied to by her refusal to be his lover. Lady Gregory saw only a death's head. Maud saw only a dumpy widow who reminded her of the detested Queen Victoria. For once, Lady Gregory was not quite sure what to say. She wrote that she and Maud got on 'amicably', but it is unlikely that this was Maud's view. When Lady Gregory asked the question she had hurried across half a continent to pose, Maud merely peered down from her imperious height and said: 'I have more important things to think about than marriage and so has he.' But, for all her sternness to others, Maud was gentle to Yeats in these last days of her visit, kissing him, safe in the knowledge that she would soon be gone. When, on the evening of her departure, Yeats finally spoke of marriage, she declined him as he surely knew she would, and then, with her hands clasped in desperation, she burst out with the painful and so long hidden truth: 'I have a horror and fear of physical love.' With that, she left for Paris, and when Lady Gregory offered Yeats money to go after her he merely turned aside and said: 'No, I am too exhausted, I can do no more.'

Yeats spent the rest of that month and much of January with his uncle in Sligo trying to gather together the shards of his self-confidence. In her apartment on the Avenue d'Eylau, Maud tried to do the same. She had shared with Yeats a partial Initiation of the Spear.[28] Now she wanted to see it plain. Recording her vision, she wrote how, with the Druids Semias and Estras on either side of her bed, she had trod the occult path to the place of the Sword where she had evoked Brighid and a reluctant Usces of the Black Hair. She then fell into a deep sleep and, when she awoke, knew she had been privy to some revelation.

Anxious to clarify what that revelation had been, Maud invoked Lugh himself, the god of the Spear. As she again entered a state of vision, she fell before the power of the god's weapon, grasped it and, rising through a mountain of fire, ascended in his chariot to a brilliant altar where lay a sun and a Rose. The god was so dazzling he was difficult to describe, but his face when he turned it a little aside was strong and proud. Maud gazed into his eyes, but the attendant Druid said she was unfit for initiation. Voices then cried: 'We need her, purify her, strengthen her and seal her lips for the work.' Fire rose within her, the god waved his spear, sanctified her and gave her his weapon to fight, as he said, the forces of Darkness, the enemies of Ireland. Confident in her power now, Maud could put Celtic mysticism behind her for a while at least. She feared such things might take her too far down the chameleon's path and away from the heart of Ireland's strength. To confirm her intentions, she resolved to sever her links with the Matherses and, using the most damning indictment available to her, wrote to Yeats saying the occult couple were English spies.

The truth was somewhat different. When Yeats arrived in Paris at the close of January, he discovered that the Matherses' flat in the Rue Mozart had been converted into a Temple of Isis. Here Mathers himself, dressed in a leopard skin whose spots supposedly symbolised the zodiac, invoked the goddess Isis, who appeared in the shape of Moina swathed in chiffon and crowned with a paper lotus. The couple were beginning to attract a following, and soon the rites of Isis were performed in a boulevard theatre and widely reported in the press. Wealthy and influential people were drawn to them, and Mathers gave his time increasingly to such projects. The Castle of Heroes fell into abeyance as Mathers approached the apogee of his occult success and was asked to build the Isis Temple for the Great Exhibition of 1900.

Maud attributed the heavy cold Yeats caught to the influence of a rival occultist, by whom she almost certainly meant Mathers himself. Although she allowed Yeats to see her, she was again distant with him. She needed time in which to establish her renewed sense of dedication, and her importunate lover must occasionally have been irksome. Yeats demanded nothing less than a surrender of all she stood for. He wrote to Lady Gregory, explaining in a sentence the tenor of his reproaches. 'Hers has in part been the war of phantasy and of blind idealism against eternal law,' he declared. Maud's extremism was a sort of spiritual and sexual trespass. Others tried to force the issue. Lady Gregory told Yeats not to leave Maud's side until she agreed to marry him. George Pollexfen had consulted the tarot and offered money for the wedding. Social pressure was added to private need, but neither could touch Maud. 'She will never', Yeats wrote, 'leave this life of hatred which a vision I made her see years ago told her was her deepest hell.' As always, he wanted to redeem her, to reshape her in his own image of content. He longed to show her 'the life of labour from the divine love', in which he believed she would find power. Maud did not care to look. She would find her own salvation in her work for Ireland, toiling for the evicted peasantry, making speeches and organising on an ever more impressive scale those groups that would give Ireland its political purpose and hope.

To further these aims Maud left Paris, and Yeats remained to wander the winter city on his own. He was a man leaving his youth behind. In the tension of despair, his long legs propelled a body so racked with torment that his shoulder blades seemed to press against his head. The path of the chameleon had brought him to the brink of despair. Those who encountered him recognised a terrible numbness but, deeper than this – untouchable, unappeasable and remote – lay that conviction of his destiny by which Yeats would recreate himself. It was now nearly a decade since Parnell had died and Yeats realised he had 'spent much of my time and more of my thought these last ten years on Irish organisation'. As the poet of the Rose he had also written poems so intricate that he feared he was losing 'my old country emotion'. Yeats had failed to reach and inspire a wide audience, and now, as he turned home to supervise the first production of *The Countess Cathleen*, so he would gather together and renew the sundered elements of his art, his occult studies and his hopes for Ireland. Yeats would indeed build his Castle of Heroes, but now it would be on the stage. 'If Ireland would not read literature,' he declared, 'it might listen to it, for politics and the Church had created listeners.'

PART THREE

Theatre Business, Management of Men

Players and painted stage took all my love.

7

Cathleen ni Houlihan
(1899–1903)

I
The Irish Literary Theatre

Yeats returned to London in February 1899 to arrange rehearsals for the Irish Literary Theatre with Florence Farr, Edward Martyn and George Moore. Moore left his own amusing and often malicious account of his involvement with the early stages of this project in the autobiographical *Ave*, where he described a visit made to his Victoria Street flat by Martyn and Yeats himself. The contrasted appearance of the two men immediately caused Moore to doubt the depth of their friendship. They were as fantastic to him as figures from a Japanese print, Martyn being a man of immense girth, a neckless owl blinking behind his glasses, while Yeats seemed 'lank as a rook, a dream in black silhouette on the flowered wall-paper'.[1]

When Moore's servant left the room and the two men unburdened themselves of their excitement, Moore's suspicion turned to amused pity as they talked of an independent theatre and their plan to set up in Dublin: 'Dublin of all cities in the world!' Moore's attitude suggests the reaction of a man who, ten years before, had left Ireland and its 'damp flaccid smell of poverty' to return to the Continent. His career had already involved him in the Aesthetic Movement and the realist school of Zola, where he made his most distinguished contributions as a novelist, before he showed an interest in Ibsen and eventually the Symbolists. Ireland, the country of 'abandoned dreams', he thought could offer him nothing. Martyn would have none of such attitudes. He had 'done' with London, he said, adding that 'Ninety-nine is the beginning of the Celtic Renaissance' and that Dublin would be its capital. The idea of Dublin as a new Florence left Moore incredulous but, as a man whose writings had covered an anthology of late-nineteenth-century styles, he felt there might be something new in the air. Determined not to be left out, he carefully said: 'I'm with you, but only platonically. You must promise not to ask me to rehearse your play.'

A few weeks later Martyn reported to Moore that rehearsals for *The Count-ess Cathleen* were going well while those for his own play *The Heather Field* were floundering. Moore at once suspected incompetent stage-management and, having been persuaded by his friend to break his vow and attend a rehearsal, he took a cab with him to the Bijou Theatre in Notting Hill. As they approached, Martyn pointed out the figure of Yeats swathed in a long black cloak, his manuscript sticking out of his pocket as he accompanied Florence Farr to the local bun-shop. Here they regularly went while rehearsals were in progress to discuss the finer points of verse speaking.

If such behaviour seemed to Moore amateur, Yeats was in fact beginning to develop ideas later embodied in his lecture 'The Reform of the Theatre'.[2] He longed for change, and his desire for change touched all areas of production. 'I think the theatre must be reformed in its plays, its speaking, its acting and its scenery,' he declared. 'That is to say I think there is nothing good about it at present.' These ideals were of a piece with Yeats's attempts to exalt the spirit and the imagination over the dead weight of nineteenth-century materialism. He hoped to create a drama which would reach out and strengthen those mystic qualities in his fellow countrymen on which he believed he could base his ideals of nationhood. In all areas of staging factitious realism was to be replaced by a hieratic, chastely beautiful and symbolic drama written for a discerning audience and drawing for its traditions on Greek tragedy, medieval morality and the conventions of English renaissance theatre. By striving after such formal beauty, Yeats believed he could have the stage once again move the imagination and the intellect, 'for imagination and intellect are that which is eternal in man crying out against that which is temporal and perishing'.

Instead of such crowd-pulling inventions as Beerbohm Tree's realistic sets complete with mechanical singing birds, Yeats declared that he saw in his imagination a stage where there would be both scenery and costumes, but scenery and costumes which would draw little attention to themselves and cost little money. But the practical advantages of this were a lesser consideration than the aesthetic gains. By imagining a stage which, while it appealed to the eye, nonetheless refused to dominate it, Yeats could create a drama whose fundamental appeal was to the ear – to poetry. He wrote that 'if we are to restore words to their sovereignty we must make speech even more important than gesture'. His work with Florence Farr was designed to achieve the state where an actor would understand how to discriminate cadence from cadence, and so to cherish the musical lineaments of verse or prose that he could delight the ear 'with a continually varied music'.

While this was criticism conducted on the highest level, Moore realised on entering the Bijou Theatre that, if performances were to take place at all, he would have to take charge of recasting the works. He promptly sacked the players and then took a terrified Martyn to the Green Room Club and found new actors for the Irish Literary Theatre's first season. Yeats could barely bring himself to bow in greeting to Miss Whitty, the new Countess Cathleen foisted upon him, but once Moore had convinced him that his own verse speaking had too much in it of the monotonous drawl of the Methodist preacher, Moore felt he could hand the stage management back to a competent professional and return to correcting the proofs of a new edition of his novel *Esther Waters*.

A while after Moore's first intervention a worried Martyn called on him again to say that Yeats had turned up that morning to a rehearsal and was now explaining his method of verse speaking to the actors while Florence Farr illustrated his intentions on a psaltery, a stringed instrument designed to accompany the quarter tones of the speaking voice and which would soon acquire considerable importance. Moore was appalled. Ordering Martyn to hail the nearest cab, he set off once again to put a stop to time-wasting experiments. Yeats eventually promised to desist and the rehearsal continued, in Moore's description, with Florence Farr rummaging ineffectively in her handbag to find her notes on stage-management while Yeats himself offered suggestions Moore and the professional cast found wholly unacceptable.

But, while high-minded experiments seemed to menace the season from within, open hostility was gathering outside. In March 1899, it suddenly seemed as if all the company's efforts would come to nothing. Yeats's play was under attack. The first version of *The Countess Cathleen* is a plain and often effective morality drama in which the heroine signs her soul away to a pair of demon merchants in order to feed her starving people. This was dangerous ground theologically and a rumour spread through Dublin that *The Countess Cathleen* was unorthodox. A priest declared it heretical, and the devoutly Roman Catholic Martyn, who was funding the season, immediately withdrew his support. Yeats, realising he was faced with a situation of the greatest delicacy, was determined at least to keep Martyn and Moore apart, unsure how Moore might take advantage. He was aware by now that, although the two men were cousins and inseparable friends, they were nonetheless bound one to another by mutual contempt. This last might break out at any moment and, having extracted a promise that Moore would not write to Martyn without first showing his letter to Lady Gregory, he arranged for two priests to read his own play through. Having received their *nihil obstat*, Yeats wrote to Martyn to tell him all was well.

But when Yeats went to visit Moore the novelist's face darkened. 'Oh Yeats,' he said when he heard the good news. 'What an opportunity I have lost! I had almost finished my article for the *Nineteenth Century*. I called it "The Soul of Edward Martyn".'[3] Indeed, so great was the temptation to disparage Martyn that Moore now recast his article as the previously embargoed letter and had it delivered as Yeats and Florence Farr went to engage Dublin's Antient Concert Rooms for their season. The following morning, a heavily perspiring Martyn arrived at their hotel as Yeats and

Florence were finishing breakfast to say that, because of Moore's letter, he had once again resigned from the project.

Yeats talked him round, but a more serious attack was now launched on the season by Frank Hugh O'Donnell, a clever but 'half-mad' politician who had been expelled from the Irish Party by Parnell himself and, while trying to get back into Nationalist life, had attacked the reputation of Michael Davitt so scandalously that Yeats and Maud Gonne had brought the matter to the attention of John O'Leary, who once again ostracised him. Now he wanted revenge. O'Donnell issued a pamphlet entitled *Souls for Gold* in which he quoted the words of the demon merchants from Yeats's play as if they were the author's own. The play, O'Donnell declared, was an insult to the Catholic piety of the majority of the Irish people, and this attempt to mobilise mass opinion was furthered when O'Donnell declared that the scene in which the starving women of the country barter their souls for money was an attack on the virtue of Irish womanhood. This was the first sounding of an important criticism, for a belief in the inviolable purity of such people was a staple of popular nationalism. O'Donnell's pamphlet was widely distributed, and Cardinal Logue, 'a dull, pious old man', as Yeats described him in his 'Autobiography', published a letter confirming that, though he had not actually read the play, no honest Catholic should attend a performance if O'Donnell had represented Yeats's views accurately.

The house for the first night of *The Countess Cathleen* on 8 May 1899, while not large, was on the whole friendly. Some of the female members of the audience, enthused by Celtic revivalism, turned up dressed in traditional cloaks and Tara brooches, with torques round their foreheads and other archaeological adornments. During the interval they sang patriotic songs. Others in the gallery, however, were determined to interrupt, and Yeats asked for police protection. Twenty or thirty officers arrived, but their sergeant explained that they could not act unless called upon to do so. Yeats asked a friend to stay by him for, he confessed, he had no experience of this sort of thing. The police smiled, and Yeats suddenly recalled a 'lying rumour' that it was he who had organised the Jubilee Riots, and that many people claimed to know just how much he had supposedly paid every rioter to appear.

When the merchants in his play commanded the Countess to sign her diabolical pact there were disturbances which were then drowned out by men from the Quays, brought along by Arthur Griffith to applaud everything the church might disapprove of. Yeats himself did not want his play turned into a mere anti-clerical demonstration. He wanted to offer a work in which the battle between good and evil was both a spiritual and a political conflict, a struggle between the materialistic and diabolical merchants with their suggestions of English imperialism and a heroine torn between saving her people and saving her soul. The play's alleged blasphemy, however, denied it a fair hearing, even if Yeats himself and some of those in the audience never

forgot the performance of Florence Farr as the poet Kevin (later renamed
Aleel) chanting the beautiful lyric:

> Who will go drive with Fergus now,
> And pierce the deep wood's woven shade,
> And dance upon the level shore?
> Young man, lift up your russet brow,
> And lift your tender eyelids, maid,
> And brood on hopes and fears no more.[4]

The loveliness of this is patent, but Yeats, his own severest critic, came to
regard *The Countess Cathleen* as ill constructed and he disparaged much of
its dialogue for 'turning aside at the lure of a word or metaphor'. Although
he was to alter the work at least five times after performances, giving it an
increasingly sumptuous Pre-Raphaelite texture, he could never regard it as
'more than a piece of tapestry' whose final scene, representing the people
of Ireland united in mystical community, could not be easily realised. The
enthusiastic Dublin theatre-goer Joseph Holloway confirmed this when
he wrote how he had been distracted at the close by a creaking door
and 'the too liberal use of palpable tin-tray-created thunderclaps'. Such
practical and aesthetic problems were now added to the literary and political
difficulties Yeats faced in his theatre, difficulties that were also affecting his
non-dramatic works.

Perhaps prompted by his father, Yeats changed his publishers, offering *The
Secret Rose* not to Fisher Unwin but to a family friend, the Elizabethan scholar
A. H. Bullen.[5] Bullen was to be unsuccessful with Yeats's work in Dublin,
however. Arriving in the city very drunk (an habitual problem with him) he
found that the booksellers refused to look at Yeats's texts. Unionists in the city
were opposed to a writer who had taken such a conspicuous part in disrupting
the Jubilee, while the church was opposed to Yeats's occult interests and the
whole cast of mind of the man who had written *The Countess Cathleen*. JBY
had also suggested that Yeats take his *Poems* of 1895 from Fisher Unwin
and offer it to Robertson Nicoll, a keen supporter of Yeats's and an editor
at Hodder & Stoughton. As JBY explained in a letter to his son,

> these practical men are in their way good guides – not only will Nichols
> make a good bargain with you (I hear he offers £100 down and
> royalties) but he commands and influences a very large and important
> public. . . . I may add that *York Powell* told me on Sunday that you
> should certainly do it. . . . It would be delightful for you to have
> suddenly (with the suddeness of a Fairy gift) £100 in your pocket
> – you would then be free to write at your own work without thought
> of writing reviews, etc. . . . Don't despise the nonconformists – They
> *do* read and do *think* – at least large numbers of them do.

Unwin, however, refused to part with the *Poems*, a comparatively lucrative volume which frequently reprinted and always provided Yeats with a modest royalty income, but Hodder & Stoughton would eventually be offered *The Shadowy Waters*, which Yeats would work on again that summer.

II
James Joyce

Meanwhile, one member of the original audience for *The Countess Cathleen* who had allowed himself to be impressed with the work was a young man who was soon to set 'Who Goes with Fergus?' to music and call it the best lyric in the world. He also refused to sign a letter of protest against the play. But the prickliness of his admiration for Yeats had already been shown when the two men had met in an interval of a rehearsal. Yeats had been forewarned by Russell. 'The first spectre of a new generation has appeared,' Russell told him. 'His name is Joyce. I have suffered from him and would like you to suffer.' Although Yeats invited Joyce to the Antient Concert Rooms, Joyce required that they meet by the National Library. Yeats went, and from there the two walked to a café where Joyce proceeded to challenge Yeats and amuse him with the self-conceit of his so far largely unrevealed genius. In particular, Joyce obliged Yeats to listen to the 'immature and eccentric harmony' of his recent prose 'epiphanies' and asked Yeats why he had concerned himself with folklore and politics. These were interests which, Joyce suggested, merely showed 'a cooling of the iron'. Yeats was told he was 'deteriorating'.

Once Yeats himself realised that Joyce was something more than the Catholic bigot he had at first supposed him, he treated him to a disquisition on the superiority of the folk imagination and the need for the true artist to draw on this as, he supposed, Joyce himself had done. Yeats later wrote that he concluded by saying:

'When the idea which comes from individual life marries the image that is born from the people, one gets great art, the art of Homer, and of Shakespeare, and of Chartres Cathedral.'

I looked at my young man. I thought, 'I have conquered him now,' but I was quite wrong. He merely said, 'Generalisations aren't made by poets; they are made by men of letters. They are no use.'

Presently he got up to go, and, as he was going out, he said, 'I am twenty. How old are you?' I told him, but I am afraid I said I was a year younger than I am. He said with a sigh, 'I thought as much. I have met you too late. You are too old.'[6]

That Yeats could take this in good part is suggested by the help which, prompted by Lady Gregory, he gave Joyce later in the year when he came through London on his way to Paris. Yeats also asked him to write a play for his theatre. Although himself only in his early thirties, Yeats was now aware that, with the advent of Joyce, a younger generation of Irish writers was 'knocking on my door'.

III
Yeats at Coole

During May 1899, and at the close of the first season of the Irish Literary Theatre, Yeats retreated to Coole, where he was to stay until November. It was clear that Martyn's *The Heather Field* had been the success of the run and arrangements were now made with the Gaiety Theatre for a second series of performances that would feature another of Martyn's plays. *The Tale of a Town* was a political satire and Martyn, despite difficulties with the plot, was determined to finish the script in Galway and then send it, as the rules of the theatre required, to Moore, Lady Gregory and Yeats himself. The arrival of Martyn's package at Coole, however, at once revealed the mistake that had been made in regarding him as the theatre's genius. The work, Yeats declared, had the crude violence to be expected from a not very bright child. When another copy of the script arrived in Victoria Street, Moore was equally taken aback, and he wrote to Martyn expressing his fears and suggesting that the problems might be sorted out during the two men's proposed pilgrimage to Bayreuth. Nothing effective was achieved, however, and, when the travellers returned to Tulira Castle, Martyn appeared increasingly defensive.

But *The Tale of a Town* was not the only formless play that hovered in the wings of the Irish Literary Theatre. Yeats had been working on *The Shadowy Waters* for many years, using it as a storehouse for innumerable symbolic and mythological ideas. The mythical elements were taken from the tale of Forgael, 'a Sea-King of ancient Ireland' who was promised by the souls of the dead (portrayed here as human-headed birds) a vision of 'supernatural intensity and happiness'.[7] Forgael could draw the birds to him by the power of a magic harp and, while his sailors and his lieutenant Aibric variously thought him mad or in search of something that can be found only after death, Forgael insisted they venture on. Presently they captured a ship, and found a beautiful woman upon it, and Forgael subdued her and his own rebellious sailors by the sound of his harp. The sailors fled upon the other ship, and Forgael and the woman drifted on alone, 'following the birds, awaiting death and what comes after, or some mysterious transformation of the flesh, an embodiment of every lover's dream'.

As Yeats described his deeper subject: 'the main story expresses the desire for a perfect and eternal union that comes to all lovers, the desire of love to "drown in its own shadow". But it also has other meanings. Forgael seeks death; Dectora has always sought life; and in some way the uniting of her vivid force with his abyss-seeking desire for the waters of Death makes a perfect humanity.' The spiritual union of the lovers, and its clear associations with Yeats's love for Maud Gonne, is seen as a unification of opposites, a spiritual rebirth, and the struggle of the artist to integrate the warring elements in his own mind. 'We make out of the quarrel with others, rhetoric,' Yeats wrote, 'but of the quarrel with ourselves, poetry.'

The wealth of the play's symbolism seeks to universalise these mythical and spiritual elements. For example, the sea where the action takes place represents (as in Blake) the waters of materialism, while Forgael's ship is the soul of man. When the vessels carrying Forgael and Dectora are joined by a rope, the act of piracy suggests the recognition of human physical desire from which they must cut free if they are ever to enter the world shown them by Forgael's harp and so experience that spiritual union which allows them to pass to the borders of the *anima mundi*.

By the time Moore arrived on the scene the play had already gone through several revisions and was so dense with additional symbolism that Yeats asked Moore to Coole, where he thought the problems presented by his text might be solved through a joint effort.[8] When Moore cycled over to the house, he found Yeats loitering by the lake amid the woods, dressed in a knee-length cloak and 'looking like a great umbrella forgotten by some picnic party'. It soon became apparent, however, that Yeats would resist all Moore's suggested changes but was nonetheless prepared to talk endlessly about the play itself as his 'febrile and somewhat hysterical imagination' evolved so many alterations that he became entirely oblivious to the beauty of the landscape about him.

The degree to which Lady Gregory was prepared to foster and indulge the obsessions of genius became apparent to Moore when he went back to Coole some days later. Lady Gregory herself had gone to church and, in her absence, Moore broached the topic of the problematic play. He was treated to a torrent of argument and explanation he found impossible to follow as phrase after phrase rose, turned and faded in Yeats's mind like smoke. When his ideas were finally exhausted, Moore mentioned the legend of Diarmuid and Grania. Did Yeats know it? The poet at once began to tell the tale, relishing its many variants, the dramatic possibilities of which only slowly became apparent to Moore himself. He knew, however, that he was in the presence of an imagination of exceptional fertility, and he was delighted when he was rewarded with Yeats's idea that they might collaborate on the suggested theme.

When Lady Gregory returned, her face clouded. She thought it unwise for Yeats to take on any more work at the moment, and later that afternoon confided to Moore that retreat to Coole was essential to his genius. 'We have been waiting for a new book from him,' she declared. 'Ever since *The Countess Cathleen* we have been reading the publisher's autumn announcement of *The Wind among the Reeds*. The volume was finished here last year; it would never have been finished if I had not asked him to Coole.' This proprietary note was embellished as Lady Gregory showed Moore how Coole itself had been arranged to serve Yeats's genius. In the back drawing room was his table carefully supplied with clean pens, fresh ink and a spotless blotter which it was Lady Gregory's special care every morning to attend to. She still looked askance, however, at a project for a joint play on the theme of Diarmuid and Grania, and, though she agreed that the subject was suited to Yeats's genius, she thought it would be better if Yeats wrote the work alone. Neither he nor Moore would benefit from a collaboration, she said, and then added, with a gentle but devastating little laugh, that Yeats would not benefit from Coole either if he escaped from London and people like Arthur Symons only to fall into the subtle traps laid by Moore. Moore made some clumsy reply and Lady Gregory whispered, not quite inaudibly, about a man of genius proposing to come together with a man of mere talent. The barb was barely noticed at the time, and Moore and Lady Gregory were talking about their responsibilities to genius when Yeats himself walked into the room.

Lady Gregory was pleased to be told that Yeats had written five and half lines that morning and that, after a stroll, he might return in the evening and achieve his daily maximum of nine lines. Moore and Lady Gregory then accompanied him on his walk, tramping the wet roads and fields in search of a ruined castle. As they descended the slippery stair of the castle, Moore's mind revolved means of persuading Lady Gregory to allow him to collaborate with her poet. He nonetheless decided to reserve his pleas for another visit, but when he tried to persuade Yeats himself to return to Tulira Castle, Yeats told him he could not leave his hostess on her own. She spent every evening reading to him, he said. Last summer they had worked their way through *War and Peace*, and now they were involved in a study of *The Faerie Queene*. Yeats was going to publish a selection from Spenser with an introduction, and he had to go back to Coole to listen to the seventh Canto.

There remained the troublesome issue of *The Tale of a Town*. When Yeats finally called at Martyn's castle he was asked if he had liked the new third act. The reply was blunt and to the point: 'No, no; it's entirely impossible,' he said. 'We couldn't have such a play performed.' Yeats then took off his cloak, ran his long hands through his hair and sank meditatively into a chair as Moore tried to argue him round. But Yeats's face took on a determined expression as he spoke. 'We are artists,' he said, 'and cannot be expected to accept a play because other plays as bad, and nearly as bad, have been performed.'

Impressed by the depth of such conviction, Moore asked Yeats to come over and start revising the work the following day. The resulting play was now renamed *The Bending of the Bough*, and Yeats provided the political material for a work he considered a microcosm of the last ten years of public life in Ireland. Inspired by the government's admitting that Ireland had for years been over-taxed, the play's hero Jasper Dean tries to recover harbour dues from a nearby town but, abandoning his cause for his English girlfriend, sees his party disintegrate in a struggle for leadership. Here was an allegory of the situation in Ireland after the death of Parnell, and Yeats prophesied that the work would 'make an immense sensation and our theatre a national power'.

The meetings at which Yeats and Moore rewrote the play were naturally difficult with Martyn hidden away in his tower and Yeats himself getting easily fatigued because of what might have been a trace of tuberculosis. Lady Gregory was certainly worried by his health and she sent a message that Yeats was not to be over-worked and that every two hours or so he should be served a glass of milk or, better still, a cup of beef tea. He was also to be provided with a glass of sherry and a biscuit half an hour after lunch. Under such conditions the collaboration continued, Yeats and Moore sometimes getting so carried away with their work that, if Yeats stayed on at Tulira for supper, he and Moore would unfeelingly discuss their revisions in front of Martyn, Yeats looking at his host as sternly as a schoolmaster if he was interrupted. But it was not only the interruptions that annoyed Yeats. He was also disturbed by Moore's frequently telling the disgusted Martyn stories of his amatory adventures, stories Moore repeated (much to Yeats's anger) in front of Lady Gregory's teenage son. If Moore was discovering in Yeats the tyranny of genius, Moore was beginning to appear to Yeats himself as a man who had sacrificed 'good breeding, honour, friendship, in pursuit of what he considered the root facts of life'.[9] The seeds of Yeats's future contempt were being sown.

IV
'The Famine Queen'

Yeats returned to London for Christmas where, on 3 January 1900, his mother suddenly and unexpectedly died. Both Lily and Lollie were away from home, but Yeats himself was staying in Blenheim Road, and it was he and his father who were roused by the maid when she feared Susan was having trouble with her breathing. The doctor gave the cause of death as 'general paralysis', and Susan was buried at Acton Rural Cemetery on 6 January. There was little conspicuous mourning, perhaps even a sense of quiet relief. Susan had lived on the edge of her family's lives for years, and her own disappointed existence, her reserve and outward coldness, had been absorbed into her illness until she was little more than a silent and anonymous invalid. As Yeats himself wrote to a friend some eight years later: 'my mother was so long ill, so long fading out of life, that the last fading out of all made no noticeable change in our lives'. It was Jack who took it upon himself to erect a plaque to her memory in St John's church, Sligo.

Late January and February meanwhile saw preparations being made for the second season of the Irish Literary Theatre. This was less distinguished than the first. The plays performed were *The Bending of the Bough*, now acknowledged by Moore, an inconsiderable piece called *The Last Feast of the Fianna* by Yeats's acquaintance Alice Milligan, and Martyn's poetic drama *Maeve*, with its well-received and influential inflammatory line: 'I am only an old woman but I tell you that Erin will never be subdued.' Martyn himself, however, was threatening once again to withdraw from the enterprise, although he travelled with the company to Dublin, where the Irish Literary Society gave a dinner in honour of the plays. A few days later, Moore, fired by his new Celtic enthusiasms, delivered a stirring speech about the Irish language which he himself had no intention of learning but which he obliged his nephew and heir to study.

The reviews of the season proved at best bland, and Lady Gregory, showing her quiet competence, invited the journalists to tea at her hotel and managed to extract promises of more favourable notices next time. Yeats meanwhile threw himself into aesthetics and Irish politics by writing to the newspapers on 20 January about a proposed statue to Parnell. He argued that a committee rather than a single politician should select an artist who would then be free to follow his own ideas. 'The good sculptor, poet, painter or musician,' Yeats wrote, 'pleases other men in the long run because he was first pleased himself, the only person whose taste he really understands.'

But issues of greater moment were now gripping Ireland, England and the Empire at large. The outbreak of the Boer War in the autumn of 1899 gave rise to the first great crisis of imperial identity.[10] The discovery of gold and diamonds in the Transvaal had drawn numerous British settlers from the Cape Colony with a resulting rise in tension between the treasure hunters and the long-settled Dutch Boers. Storr-Jameson's disastrous attempt to overthrow the Transvaal edged matters towards declared hostility, while the British authorities came to believe that a show of force would intimidate President Kruger. But in October 1899 the Boers seized the initiative and attacked the Cape Colony, inflicting so humiliating a series of defeats that the British felt the need to recruit soldiers from Canada, Australia, New Zealand and Ireland. Anti-Boer propaganda flooded the newspapers. 'Strike, England, and strike home!' wrote W. E. Henley.

Others were less certain about the morality of British involvement and, in the House of Commons, opposition to the Boer War united the Irish members. John Dillon spoke out fiercely against British supremacy in southern Africa. 'We know from long and bitter experience what that means,' he declared. The threat to the Boers made ever more obvious the suppression of Ireland by imperial England. 'Predominant race! That is what you are fighting for – to put the Dutch under your feet,' Dillon argued, and he assured the House they would never succeed. In Dublin, meanwhile, crowds gathered to cheer at the news of every English set-back. Arthur Griffith, newly returned from Johannesburg, began with his colleague William Rooney a newspaper under the respected title of the *United Irishman* in which he attacked the British presence in Ireland in ever more advanced Nationalist terms, arguing for an Irish state governed by Irishmen for the benefit of Irish people. Many contributed to the radical columns of the paper, including Russell, Moore, John Eglinton, Yeats and Maud Gonne.

Maud herself was particularly active in the Irish anti-war protests. She helped Griffith organise the Irish Transvaal Committee, for example, which had O'Leary as its president and Yeats among its members. She herself took the chair at the inaugural meeting and moved that congratulations and a patriotic flag be sent to a new Irish hero, 'Major' John MacBride, whose Irish Brigade had been with the first Boer commandos to cross the frontier of the Cape. Enthused by the response she received, Maud took her cause to the United States, where she succeeded in raising £1000 to support Griffith's *United Irishman* and the anti-imperial movement. When she returned, she worked hard to defeat British attempts to recruit Irish soldiers, having leaflets printed to explain that no man could be sent to the front unless he had personally volunteered for service. 'Ireland seems to be really excited,' Yeats wrote to Lily, 'and I am not at all sure that Maud Gonne may not be able to seriously check enlisting. She is working with extraordinary energy.'

Yeats was drawn into the issue with increasing enthusiasm. In his letter to Lily he wrote that 'the spectacle of John Bull amassing 70 or 100 thousand men to fight 20 thousand and slapping his chest the while and calling on the heavens to witness his heroism has not been exhilarating'. Casualties on the British side remained high, and the government resolved that the ageing Queen Victoria be sent to Ireland to stir enthusiasm among her subjects. As Yeats pointed out in a letter to the *Freeman's Journal*, Westminster had chosen a remarkable date for this visit – 2 April, the hundredth anniversary of the Act of Union. The symbolism stirred Yeats's deepest political feelings, and he proposed that a great meeting be held in the Rotunda under the chairmanship of O'Leary with all the Irish members of parliament in attendance. The meeting was convened, and those present protested against the Union and the presence of the Queen, and then resolved to 'disassociate Ireland from any welcome that the Unionists or the time-server may offer to the official head of the Empire in whose name liberty is being suppressed in South Africa, as it was suppressed in Ireland a hundred years ago'.[11]

Yeats also wrote a letter to the press timed to coincide with the Queen's triumphal entry into Dublin. This last occasion was reported by *The Times* as a massive propaganda success. As the royal procession passed Trinity College, the students struck up the National Anthem, while on Dame Street, 'for Unionists and nationalists alike, there was only one figure in that splendid array – the figure of the little lady in the fourth carriage who kept bowing to that huge concourse of surging humanity'. This unanimous admiration of the Queen–Empress was insisted upon. 'The Nationalists in front of the City-hall waved their hats and cheered themselves hoarse with just as much enthusiasm as the Unionists in the windows opposite.' Only a few people seemed to mar the festivities. In particular, 'Mr W. B. Yeats had sent a carefully-timed letter to this morning's papers in which he wrote: – "She (the Queen) is the offical head and symbol of an Empire that is robbing the South African Republics of their liberty as it has robbed Ireland of hers. Whoever stands by the roadway cheering for Queen Victoria, cheers for that Empire, dishonours Ireland, and condones a crime."' The passion in this is real and eloquent, but for *The Times* it was merely the tantrum of an ineffective spoilsport. 'In the presence of that Queen, who had come to pay a debt of personal gratitude to the Irish people, nobody considered either the Yeats [*sic*] or the Harringtons, and her Majesty passed down the Quays amid the cheers and blessings of a city whose jarring elements were united at least in their personal regard and affection for the greatest lady in the Empire.'

Yeats had his own response to this. He wrote in the *United Irishman* that the cheering crowds in Dublin were like those that greeted Louis XVI when he addressed the French Assembly after the fall of the Bastille. 'Everybody', he declared, 'knows what followed those cheers. Did the cheers that greeted Queen Victoria mean more than those that greeted Louis XVI? But for her fleet and her soldiers, and her great Empire, that watches over her, would she or any representative of English rule sleep easy under an Irish roof?' When the authorities in Dublin Castle then tried to suppress the *United Irishman* – 'the organ of Miss Gonne and the physical force party', because Maud had republished there her article on Victoria entitled 'The Famine Queen' – Yeats inveighed against the perils of censorship. He wrote to Lady Gregory: 'a number of her newspaper has been suppressed, to her great joy, as it will give a lift to the circulation'. He then published a further letter in the *Speaker* saying that 'it should be a principle of political life that all acts which involve public liberties should be done publicly'. Yeats's lifelong distaste for censorship was here being voiced.

The matter was only a part of Maud's activities at this time. She was now increasingly convinced that women should have a properly organised voice amid the rising cry of nationalism and, to this end, she helped found the Daughters of Erin.[12] The group worked against enlistment for the Boer War and, in particular, organised the Patriotic Children's Treat to reward those who had not attended Victoria's triumphal entry into Dublin earlier in the year. The procession was an enormous one, numbering some 30,000 schoolchildren. A clever exercise in revealing the innocent face of nationalism, the procession took two hours to pass and, as it did so, reinforced Irish aspirations by being accompanied by members of the Gaelic League, the Gaelic Athletic Association and the Celtic Literary Society. Many of those who took part remembered the occasion to the ends of their lives, but Yeats at least could see the potential dangers in such a display. 'How many of these children', he asked, 'will carry bomb or rifle when a little under or a little over thirty?'

But Yeats's sense of the moral risk in the events around him was sometimes clearer than his self-knowledge. While the cause of Irish nationalism stirred him deeply, the restraining influence of Coole and his own growing elitism gave some of his pronouncements an unpleasant edge. As he wrote to Lady Gregory on 10 April: 'in a battle like Ireland's, which is one of poverty against wealth, one must prove one's sincerity, by making oneself unpopular to wealth. One must accept the baptism of the gutter.' Soon, however, Yeats would find the 'gutter' an increasingly alien environment, while the stridency of Maud Gonne would become ever more problematic. Even now, the strongly imperialist Annie Horniman was advising him to be beware of 'a beautiful woman screaming from a cart'.

V

Disorders in the Golden Dawn

If Annie felt she should warn Yeats about the dangers she saw in Irish nationalism and Maud Gonne especially, she was to become increasingly dependent on him over the next few months in another matter that greatly concerned her: the future of the Golden Dawn.[13] On 18 October 1899, Annie received an unexpected letter from MacGregor Mathers offering to reinstate her as an honorary member of the Paris branch of the Order, because, as he said, he had overthrown all the opposition he believed she had raised against him and so thought 'you can now do me no further harm'. All that was required for this wealthy woman to be partly readmitted to the fold was her submission to Mathers's authority as the Head of the Second Order.

Annie at once sent a telegram saying she was awaiting a message from the Higher Chiefs. In a matter so important, mere human agency was insufficient. However, if she believed she was going to get occult guidance she was, Mathers's reply suggested, cruelly deceived. 'You have never known, as Westcott has never known, any chief higher than myself.' Mathers claimed he alone was in communication with the Higher Chiefs, and, when Annie wrote to Westcott, the embarrassed coroner attempted to keep his distance by confessing that he had indeed never claimed intimacy with such powers as Mathers knew. If Annie wanted her old position back, Westcott suggested, she should accept Mathers's terms. 'But I should advise you not to enter on a quarrel with him.' Mathers was, as Westcott recognised, an extremely dangerous enemy.

But if, for the moment, Annie remained outside the Order, Florence Farr was in a position to inform Yeats thoroughly of events now threatening the Golden Dawn. As Chief-in-Anglia and praemonstratrix of the Isis-Urania Temple, Florence had been exceptionally busy with her occult work. The Order itself was continuing to expand, and one particularly able twenty-three-year-old had been initiated at the close of 1890 under the name *Perdurabo* ('I Will Endure'). *Perdurabo* showed every sign of being a great magus. He advanced through the grades of the Outer Order at the rate of one a month and, when the rules required him to wait twenty-eight weeks for his elevation to Adeptus Minor, he went to Scotland, studied a particularly complex form of ritual magic, and had an affair with a married soror who ironically went under the name of *Fidelis* or 'The Faithful One'. Married women were not *Perdurabo*'s only interest, however. Rumours began to circulate of his homosexuality, and Yeats in particular took a strong dislike to the young man, finding his morals especially objectionable. With suspicions mounting against him, Florence decided it would be wiser to refuse *Perdurabo*'s request to join the Second Order. The young man she turned down went, in real life at least, under the name of Aleister Crowley.

Since the police were now actively hunting Crowley because of his homosexual activities, he fled to Paris where, on 16 January 1900, MacGregor Mathers initiated him into the Second Order. But, while Florence had refused the higher grades to Crowley, other members of the Second Order in England were increasingly dissatisfied with Mathers's remote and autocratic regime. They officially expressed a lack of confidence in him and perhaps even threatened mass resignation. Much of their loyalty, it appears, still flowed towards the unfortunate Westcott, who was, however, in no mood to get 'mixed up' with them again. Mathers now believed that Florence too was keen to work on Westcott and, when he wrote accusing her of trying to create a schism in the Order, she resigned as chief. Mathers was reluctant to accept her resignation, and on 16 February 1900 he wrote her a now famous letter.

In this he stated that while he was prepared to accept the resignation of certain officers, he refused categorically to close the Isis-Urania Temple and would receive Florence's resignation only with the '*very greatest regret*'. He recognised that she was a considerable occultist but, even more, he was afraid she might reform those about her into a heretical group working under the hated Westcott. In his increasing megalomania Mathers could not tolerate such a threat, and it was therefore essential to reduce Westcott in Florence's eyes to the level of an impostor. To do so – '(and understand me well, I can prove to the hilt every word I say here and more)' – he repeated to Florence the accusations he had previously made to Annie, namely that Westcott had never at any time been in personal or written communication with the Higher Chiefs of the Order. He said that the papers Westcott claimed to have received from Frau Sprengel were worthless, '*he having either himself forged or procured to be forged* the professed correspondence'. An oath of secrecy exacted by Westcott had hitherto bound Mathers's tongue, but now he felt obliged to reveal that '*every atom*' of occult knowledge the Order possessed had come through him alone.

Mathers felt encouraged to act in this way since Frau Sprengel herself (*Sapiens Dominabitur Astri* or 'Wisdom Shall Govern the Stars') had recently appeared on his doorstep in Paris in the form of an imposing American woman who, looking sixty, claimed to be in her middle forties. The name she went under in the daily world was Madame Horos and, in her wake, came one Dr Rose Adams and her own diminutive husband of thirty-five, Theo Horos. All three claimed they had come to help Mathers with his Isis movement, and Madame Horos herself, in addition to astounding Mathers with her magical name, revealed a detailed knowledge of the Order's grades (probably derived from a contact in the United States) as well as an uncanny awareness of Mathers's dealings with Madame Blavatsky. It is not altogether clear whether Mathers regarded Madame Horos as the real Frau Sprengel or a spirit incarnation of both her and Madame Blavatsky. But he was sufficiently impressed to introduce her to the Paris Lodge of his Order on the very day he wrote his damning letter to Florence Farr.

It was this state to which matters had come when Florence herself went over to Dublin to help Yeats with the second season of the Irish Literary Theatre. On her return, she retreated to the Kentish countryside to think over her position as the leader of a group of sincere people whose beliefs it was now suggested had been founded on forgeries and lies. She eventually called a committee meeting of the Second Order and read them Mathers's letter. The committee wrote to Mathers asking for proof of his allegations but, when he eventually responded, he refused to substantiate any of his claims. The matter was then placed before the whole of the Second Order, Mathers himself meanwhile having dismissed Florence from her post.

Three days later the committee met again, having by now contacted Westcott, who assured them that he saw no reason to believe that the original Frau Sprengel was not who she had claimed to be. He had, he said, her letters, but these were never produced as evidence. It is possible that Mathers might have brought pressure to bear on Westcott in the matter, but it is certain that Mathers himself now declared the committee void and threatened dire occult punishment for their disobedience. Above all, he instructed Aleister Crowley to appoint a new chief to the Temple, to seize the Vault and to obtain pledges of loyalty from each separately interviewed adept. Crowley was, in addition, to deal with Madame Horos should she reappear, for Mathers now realised she was a fraud who had stolen several of his ritual manuscripts. Crowley should seek her arrest for this since not only did Mathers want the return of his property, but he feared that others might fall under the sway of this powerful and destructive woman.

After a number of curious misfortunes, including the spontaneous combustion of his hansome cab and his mackintosh, Crowley arrived at the Vault of the Adepti in Blythe Road. He was unable to seize a property leased in Florence's name, however, and when he reappeared the following morning in a black mask and full Highland costume he was again forbidden entry while Yeats himself called a policeman. Yeats had been, he confessed, extremely worried by the whole business, and had only slept for a few hours each night while it was going on. The upshot was the suspension of Mathers from the English Golden Dawn, the eventual framing of a new constitution for the Second Order, and the reinstatement of both Annie Horniman and Florence Farr.

But this was not the end of the trouble. Yeats mentioned in his letter to Lady Gregory of 10 April that his fellow 'Kabbalists are hopelessly unbusinesslike and thus the minutes and the like are in complete confusion'. Much of the responsibility for this fell on Florence Farr, who, in addition to sloppy organisation, had for some time been resolved to ease the burden of the academic standards required for the grade examinations. She also wanted to set up her own 'Sphere Group'. When Annie took over as scribe, she was appalled by Florence's previous laxness, just as she was, like Yeats himself, angered by the thought of the Order splintering into sub-groups. Two very different temperaments were soon to clash, the one easy-going and tolerant, the other carping, officious and dogmatic.

By January 1901, acrimony had broken out. Florence wanted her Sphere Group (which used Egyptian techniques to harness the energy of the Tree of Life) to flourish freely, while Annie was resolved to outlaw it. A council meeting of 1 February proved bitterly divisive, accusations of occult dishonesty, incompetence and malevolence firing irreconcilable minds until, on a vote, only Annie and Yeats himself refused to allow the existence of sub-groups. Yeats and Annie were united in their dislike and fear of change, and each resisted the Order's apparent move away from the securities of regular discipline. Yeats in particular feared the tyranny of the purely instinctive and unconscious which he thought sub-groups implied. In a second letter he attacked Florence for a laxness he believed would eventually establish an autocracy as bad as that which Mathers had imposed as each of the proposed sub-groups looked for dominance over the other. His most profound feelings, however, were revealed in a letter of April 1901 entitled 'Is the Order of R.R. & A.C. to Remain a Magical Order?'[14]

This letter bears looking at in detail since the earnestness of the crisis Yeats was facing called forth some of his deepest instincts. His response to the threatened formation of sub-groups was to pit an ideal of community against what he saw as the anarchy of innovation and individualism. The problem as he saw it was to preserve unity, continuity and above all the organic life of the Order. He believed that the totality of the rites, each leading into each, was a truth far deeper than individual perception could attain to, and he argued that to shatter this was to destroy the spiritual integrity of the Order as a whole and surrender numinous wisdom to the vagaries of psychic research.

Yeats's love of system is felt throughout his letter, and with this went his increasing regard for hierarchy. The succession of grade examinations was for him like a ladder leading to heaven. The magical examinations whose rigour Florence Farr was trying to relax Yeats saw as far more than tests of knowledge. 'The passing by their means from one Degree to another is an evocation of the Supreme Life,' he wrote, 'a treading of a symbolic path, a passage through a symbolic gate, a climbing towards the light which it is the essence of the system to believe, flows from the lowest of the invisible Degrees to the highest of the Degrees that are known to us.' Hierarchy becomes a means of ordered aspiration to that truth which is itself a progressive revelation. The powerful imaginative and spiritual attraction the Order had for Yeats, the sense of decorous but awe-inspired communion between the spiritual and material worlds, here receives moving expression.

In custom, ceremony and decorum lay, Yeats believed, both truth and power. To humble the heart before the integrity of the Ancestral Light, to let its power and beauty and quiet flow through without end, was to create good magic and prepare for 'the change of thought that is coming upon the world'. If the Adepti only remained true, materialism might yet give way to revelation and the Adepti themselves would be disciples inspired by a true epiphany:

> If we preserve the unity of the Order, if we make such unity efficient among us, the Order will become a single very powerful talisman, creating in us, and in the world about us, such moods and circumstances as may best serve the magical life, and best awaken the magical wisdom. Its personality will be powerful, active, visible afar, in that all powerful world that casts downward for its shadows, dreams, and visions. The right pupils will be drawn to us from the corners of the world by dreams and visions and by strange accident; and the Order itself will send out Adepts and teachers, as well as hidden influences that may shape the life of these islands nearer to the magical life.[15]

In so far as the question was one of freedom, Yeats denied any substantial importance to the freedom to innovate for its own sake. Spiritual discipline and tradition were all. 'In our day every idler, every trifler, every bungler, cries out for his freedom,' he wrote, 'but the busy, and the weighty minded, and skilful handed, meditate more upon the bonds that they gladly accept, than upon the freedom that has never meant more in their eyes than the right to choose the bonds that have made them faithful servants of law.' Through being suddenly propelled into crisis by the threat posed to his spiritual life, Yeats was obliged to draw on some of his deepest impulses and to find that these were innately conservative. The letter to the *fratres* and *sorores* reveals aspects of Yeats's nature he would in time come ever more fully to express as these inherent predispositions to order and discipline stretched out to touch his social and political thought and, by extension, the nature of his art.

But, if the Golden Dawn provided Yeats with both a theology and a ritual, it now threatened him with embarrassment of a potentially extreme kind. In December 1900, the Horoses arrived in London, masquerading as Swami Vive Ananda and Mr Cornish. In September the following year they were arrested. The couple had placed advertisements in the newspapers by which young girls were lured to their house where Mr Horos and his 'mother' offered them the opportunity of 'spiritual advancement'. The Golden Dawn ceremonies and the papers stolen from Mathers provided a ready-made ritual, after the performance of which the young visitors were informed that 'the Spirit of Christ' was in Mr Cornish and that each young girl was to be his 'little wife'. When the sixteen-year-old Daisy Adams resisted these advances, Madame Horos held her down by her head while, on other occasions, she would join her husband in the act of rape. The Horoses had practised their vices through a trail of countries – the United States, Australia, France, South Africa – usually escaping to leave behind charges of theft, fraud and worse. Now, in England, they had been caught. As Theo Horos was sentenced to fifteen years' penal servitude and his wife to seven years in prison, the newspapers revelled in exposing the Order and its rituals, while membership declined sharply as the judge gave his opinion that its proceedings were blasphemous.

VI
John MacBride

While Yeats was struggling to maintain the integrity of the Golden Dawn, Maud was involved in problems of a different but equally melodramatic nature. Immediately after the Patriotic Children's Treat she had returned to

Paris with a delegation from the Dublin Transvaal Committee. Her purpose
was to revivify French antipathy to the cause of English imperialism. While
on a brief holiday to Switzerland afterwards, however, she read an article in *La
Patrie* which declared that Germany rather than England was the sole enemy
of France. The article, although it was not in his style, had been signed by
Millevoye and was a clear repudiation of the position Maud thought they
shared. She knew she had to confront him and, when she did so, her worst
suspicions were confirmed. It was true that Millevoye had not written the
piece, but he had allowed his name to be attached to the thoughts of a
young opera singer whom the sinister Clemenceau was using as a final and
effective means of breaking the relationship between the journalist and the
glamorous partisan. Their affair was now at an end and, years later, Maud
would recall how, at their parting in Chamonix, she gazed up 'at those cruel
snow mountains which were turning my heart to stone in spite of the scent
of flowers and the hum of the wild bees'.[16]

There was, however, to be one further difficult encounter with Millevoye.
Some while after their parting he demanded her presence in Paris where he
accused the IRB of betraying an officer in French military intelligence who
had been sent as a spy to London.[17] Maud had indeed supplied the man
with introductions to her Republican friends, and the fact of the Frenchman's
being sent home in disgrace, along with the strange disappearance of money
Maud had raised for the Transvaal Committee, seemed to point to an
informer among the IRB. Maud turned, in her confusion, to Yeats. Desperate
to help, Yeats discovered that their old enemy Frank Hugh O'Donnell was
now trying to buy his way into the ranks of the Parliamentary Party with
suspicious sums of money. When Maud confronted the head of the IRB in
England, Dr Ryan confessed that he had indeed entrusted O'Donnell with
information sufficient to expose the French spy and had paid him for doing
so out of money purloined from Maud's funds. Yeats himself confronted the
Parliamentary Party and insisted that Maud's money be returned. He was
relieved that Maud had the compassion to dismiss O'Donnell from her mind,
but, when she offered her resignation from the IRB, Yeats too withdrew his
sympathy from the organisation.

Maud herself meanwhile remained confident of the protection offered to
her by the spear and shield of Lugh. The cause of Ireland was still under
the aegis of the ancient gods and, to further this psychic involvement, Maud
now joined a women's group, the Fine, who burned herbs at the sacred sites
of Ireland in order that the wills of the living and the dead should be joined to
the strength of the elements and so free the land from bondage. As a special
symbol of the liberty they longed for, the members of the Fine implored the
deities to help them retrieve the Lin Fail, the sacred Stone of the Kings, now
lodged, it was believed, in the coronation chair in Westminster Abbey.

But, while magic was one means of working for Irish freedom, more familiar forms of propaganda were another. In December 1900, Maud went to Paris to welcome back the hero of the Irish Brigade in southern Africa, Major John MacBride. Standing on the platform of the Gare de Lyon, she saw 'a wiry, soldierly-looking man, with red hair and skin burnt brick-red by the South African sun'. Griffith called MacBride by his Afrikaaner nickname 'Rooinek' or 'Redneck', and a laughing MacBride said that the only nickname he had ever objected to was the one his schoolfriends had given him, 'Foxy Jack'. Maud invited both MacBride and Griffith to her flat for dinner, where the soldier recounted stories that moved him close to tears.

He told how the flag sent by the Dublin Transvaal Committee had become a sacred object to his men and how, by the light of the campfire, he had watched 'our lads go up and kiss its folds'. Stories of courage and suffering, of MacBride's own wounding at the Tugela river, of hardships, casualties and deaths, poured from the man as he sat by the fire and talked of how the guerrilla tactics employed by the Boers might be used against the English in Ireland. Maud, as a friend had warned her she might, fell immediately under his spell. MacBride was thirty-five and a hero in the Irish cause. More resolute, it seemed, than the vacillating Millevoye, he was also more obviously a man of action than Yeats.

Maud wondered what MacBride could do to satisfy his craving to support the Nationalist cause. His remaining in England, Ireland or France seemed ill advised for in the first two countries he was regarded as a traitor while in the last he could achieve nothing because of his lack of French. The most obvious course seemed to send him to America to stir the Irish there into support of the Boers. MacBride agreed but, looking up at Maud, said: 'You will have to write the lectures for me, then.' She did so and MacBride duly sailed for America. He was so bewildered by the metropolitan sophistication of New York and the terrors of public speaking, however, that he begged Maud to join him. He could not go on without her. She went, but matters did not improve. The New York audiences found MacBride amateur while, in the trains the couple took as they crossed the continent, Maud found MacBride's attentions irksome. Nor could she herself, it seemed, rouse the Irish-Americans to the heights of anti-English feeling she had once inspired. When Arthur Griffith wrote to tell her that his co-editor on the *United Irishman* was dying, Maud used her genuine concern to cut her visit short. But she was too tired and too ill to attend Willie Rooney's funeral on her return.

VII
Dramatis Personae

Yeats meanwhile continued struggling to build an Irish theatre. Collaboration with Moore on *Diarmuid and Grania* proved particularly difficult.[18] There was acrimony over detail and confusion over larger matters. At one point it seems as if this resulted in a plan whereby Moore would write *Diarmuid and Grania* in French, Lady Gregory would translate it into English, the English text would then be translated into Irish, and Lady Gregory would render this version back into Kiltartan dialect. So much confusion became for Yeats an image of frustrated effort, and in later years when some play grew more and more incoherent after months of work he would blame his difficulties on his experience of collaborating with Moore. It is hardly surprising that the finished work was barely satisfactory, for while Grania is a boldly drawn character (Yeats and Moore at least shared a fascination with strong and wilful women) the piece is little more than a modernised dramatisation of the original legend.

Other theatrical challenges were more rewarding. In January 1901 Ellen Terry's son Gordon Craig and his friend Martin Shaw revived their production of Purcell's *Dido and Aeneas*, presenting it along with *The Masque of Love* newly fashioned out of other pieces of Purcell's music.[19] The visual effects impressed Yeats deeply. Instead of the perspective backdrops common in the theatre of the time, Craig used a great purple cloth, dramatic and simple in itself, and an obvious challenge to the general standards of factitious realism. He enhanced the dramatic possibilities of his cloth when, in the last act, he projected a yellow light on to the stage, thereby turning the cloth itself blue while throwing a rich harmony of colour over the greens and scarlets of the draped robes worn by the singers. Here was a new and distinctly theatrical art which, Yeats realised, pointed the way to the future and chimed admirably with his own aesthetic. 'The staging of *Dido and Aeneas*', he wrote, 'will someday, I am persuaded, be remembered among the important events of our time.'

In late April 1901, Yeats visited Stratford to see F. R. Benson's company perform Shakespeare's history plays. The essay he wrote on the experience focuses many of his theatrical hopes in a Shakespearian context.[20] Yeats strove constantly through the essay to separate Shakespeare from nineteenth-century materialism, realism and imperialism, thereby refashioning him as a fresh and inspiring figure of immediate interest. The siting of the theatre in the market-town of Stratford itself was important in these respects, for Stratford is seen as the antithesis of metropolitan London. Yeats also believed that Shakespeare scholars like Professor Dowden (and here he revived a major disagreement between his father and his old friend) wished to see Shakespeare in imperialist terms. For them, Richard II was a weak and sentimental figure, perhaps even an embodiment of decadence, while Henry V is 'Shakespeare's only hero'.

Yeats believed that Shakespeare had altogether more important purposes than commonplace moral judgements based on nineteenth-century prejudices. Richard II, for example, is seen by Yeats as reaching into the archetypal imagination and touching something eternal. Nonetheless, in the inspiration Shakespeare provides, there is a hint of that falling away from the ideal which led to the barren confusion of the modern stage. Shakespeare is seen as a victim of the renaissance that created him. Had there been no renaissance, Yeats argued, English history might have attained a state comparable to that of myth in ancient Athens. It would have been the national expression of a people. But the renaissance brought with it a baleful cosmopolitanism, and 'I can never get out of my head that no man, even though he be Shakespeare, could write perfectly, when his web is woven of threads that have been spun in many lands.' The direction of Yeats's prejudice is clear. Just as the 'unearthly energy' of Shakespeare's history cycle reminded him of grey and elemental days on the Galway coast, so Ireland and Irish culture seemed to offer modern man an unsullied world where great dramatic art might yet again arise.

To do so effectively it needed Irish actors. Frank Fay first came to Yeats's attention in 1901 when he wrote articles in the *United Irishman* on Yeats's work for the theatre. Frank Fay himself was strongly nationalist in his views but, while he believed a true Irish theatre could express itself only in the Irish language, he recognised that for the moment at least plays would have to be written in English. But dramas such as those Yeats had so far written would not do. They were too polished, Yeats was 'too much the artist in words', and his dreamers were too reminiscent of 'exquisitely decorated corpses'. As Fay went on to declare: 'In Ireland we are at present only too anxious to shun reality. Our drama ought to teach us to face it. Let Mr Yeats give us a play in verse or prose that will rouse this sleeping land.'[21]

Frank Fay, who at this time had just entered his thirties, from his boyhood had nurtured a passionate interest in all aspects of the theatre and was familiar in theory at least with Continental developments. Both he and his brother Willie (the more easy-going of the two) had not merely an academic interest in the stage. They had set up the Ormonde Dramatic society and gave amateur performances in temperance societies and church halls. Convinced of the primary importance of speech among the actor's skills, and himself possessed of a somewhat light voice, Frank Fay had attended a Dublin acting school and studied the techniques of the great Italian voice coaches in order to make his own voice a strong and flexible instrument of beauty. All this was achieved while he was working for a firm of accountants, but, if Frank remained in his office, Willie Fay ran away to join a 'fit up' troupe touring the Irish provinces. Here he was obliged quickly to become a complete man of theatre, the sort of actor and director who could light a stage, paint a backdrop, play four or five one-act works a night and, when called upon to do so, perform a song-and-dance routine. In 1899, he returned to Dublin to earn his living as an electrician, but he continued to give his spare time to the Ormonde Dramatic Society and the W. G. Fay Comedy Combination.

If melodrama and farce were a staple of these companies, articles in the press kept both Fay brothers abreast of current developments in serious European drama. Contact with Maud Gonne's Daughters of Erin meanwhile put them in touch with the role of the arts in Irish nationalism. Drama was an important part of the educational curriculum of Maud's group, and she herself taught the subject whenever she had time. She also performed in a revival of Alice Milligan's *The Last Feast of the Fianna,* the curtain rising to show her seated in an ancient chair, a great book on her knees and two little medieval pageboys standing with candles on either side. Some of the future stars of Irish drama were enthralled, among them Maire nic Shiubhlaigh. In August 1901, Yeats himself was present when Willie Fay directed Alice Milligan's *The Deliverance of Red Hugh* and he 'came away with my head on fire'. The acting of Frank Fay in particular had shown Yeats how powerful Irish drama could be when performed by actors with real Irish accents, and now Yeats himself wanted above all to hear what in his *Autobiographies* he called 'Greek tragedy, spoken with a Dublin accent'.

By the autumn of 1901, Willie Fay had introduced himself to George Moore and was helping with the third and final season of the Irish Literary Theatre. Two plays were mounted on this occasion, the first being the collaborative *Diarmuid and Grania* with music by the young Edward Elgar. The hostile reviews this work received showed how passionately nationalism had entered the theatre.* The drama Yeats and Moore had written was, declared Standish O'Grady, a 'heartless piece of vandalism on a great Irish story'. George Russell, who was already greatly concerned that Yeats's interest in the theatre was robbing him of time better spent on lyric poetry, was also offended by the sexuality of the work – so offended, indeed, that he began a heroic play of his own on the legend of Deirdre. But Frank Fay was more perceptive about the cause of the work's failure. 'To my mind,' he wrote, 'the greatest triumph of the authors lies in having written a play in which English actors are intolerable.'

But the most aggressive critic was James Joyce, who had written his play *A Brilliant Career* for the Theatre but now flinched in horror at the values he saw shown in *Diarmuid and Grania.* Yeats himself had proclaimed in the movement's journal *Samhain* that 'we have for good and all taken over the intellectual government of our country'. In contrast to decadent England, 'we have, I think, taken up the wheel of life in our hands that we may set it to whirl on a new axle tree'. Joyce could not have disagreed more strongly and, in 'The Day of the Rabblement', tore into the ruinous compromise he considered *Diarmuid and Grania* to be.[22]

* Literally so. Synge recalled that during the interval of *Diarmuid and Grania* the young members of the Gaelic League who had been 'jabbering in very bad Irish', started to sing. 'It was the first time I had heard those melodies sung in chorus by young voices with the Irish words. I heard in the lingering notes an incredible melancholy, the agony of a nation.'

'The Irish Literary Theatre gave out that it was the champion of progress,' he declared,

> and proclaimed war against commercialism and vulgarity. It had partly made good its word and was expelling the old devil, when after the first encounter it surrendered to the popular will. Now, your popular devil is more dangerous than your vulgar devil. Bulk and lungs count for something, and he can gild his speech aptly. He has prevailed once more, and the Irish Literary Theatre must now be considered the property of the rabblement of the most belated race in Europe.

For the Fay brothers, however, the mounting of *Diarmuid and Grania* was a small matter compared to Willie Fay's staging of Douglas Hyde's *Casadh an t-Sugain* ('The Twisting of the Rope'). Here was an altogether more memorable event, for at last the Irish language had been heard on the stage of the principle metropolitan theatre. The Gaiety itself was crowded for the occasion, Fay noted, and among the audience 'Ireland's greatest daughter, Miss Maud Gonne, sat beside Ireland's greatest poet, Mr W. B. Yeats.' Yeats himself realised the historic importance of the moment and, quoting Victor Hugo, declared that 'it is in the Theatre that a mob becomes a people'.

The staging of these works brought to an end the three-year experiment of the Irish Literary Theatre. Martyn now resolved to pay for nobody's plays but his own and suggested the formation of a joint-stock company of Irish-speaking actors. Yeats was at first sympathetic to the idea, and Moore too favoured such an arrangement. But Moore's involvement with the Irish dramatic movement was now all but over, terminating inevitably with a row.

In a conversation with Moore, Yeats had outlined an elaborate plot for a play (originally prompted by an idea of Russell's) on which he suggested he and Moore might collaborate. As Moore withdrew from the Irish dramatic movement, Yeats wrote to tell him he thought he should himself develop the piece on his own. There was no answer for months and, after the two men met by chance, Moore telegraphed Yeats saying he had written a novel around the proposed scenario and would injunct Yeats if he used it. In fact, Moore had been unable to employ the plot as a novel and Yeats replied that he would certainly write on an idea he considered to be his own. In a state of intensely competitive ambition, Yeats went to Coole to ask the help of Lady Gregory, and she, Yeats and Douglas Hyde wrote *Where There Is Nothing* in a fortnight. The play was a study in anarchy and mysticism designed to illustrate the thesis that where there is nothing there is God. The text was then published in the *United Irishman* to establish copyright and, as Moore was one day coming out of the Antient Concert Rooms, he heard the newsboys shouting the supplement in the streets. Thereafter, as his interest in the Irish renaissance turned to irony, relations between him and Yeats were characterised by mutual mistrust.

VIII
'A Hard Service'

In October 1901, writing in *Samhain*, Yeats declared himself uncertain whether the type of drama he wished to encourage could now best be performed by the sort of Continental-style joint-stock company urged by Martyn and Moore or by building a wholly Irish theatre from a company trained by the Fays. He confessed that for his own part he would prefer to return to being a poet versifying the tales of the heroic age, but he nonetheless felt himself increasingly drawn to the sort of peasant life so successfully dramatised in Hyde's recent work. The same edition of *Samhain* in which Yeats wrote contained Lady Gregory's translation of this piece, now called *The Twisting of the Rope*, and the precision and earthiness of the peasant dialogue in her version were remarkable. Indeed, Lady Gregory's achievement marked the altogether unsuspected arrival of a considerable dramatic talent which would soon inspire, as she said, 'a theatre with a base of realism, with an apex of beauty'. This ideal is nowhere more evident than in the most important of Yeats and Lady Gregory's plays from 1901, *Cathleen ni Houlihan*.

The origins of this work suggest the closeness of the collaboration between them and, on Lady Gregory's part at least, the degree of her self-effacement. One morning in the summer of 1901 Yeats came down to breakfast at Coole and told his hostess he had had a dream 'almost as distinct as a vision, of a cottage where there was well-being and firelight and talk of a marriage, and into the midst of that cottage there came an old woman in a long cloak'.[23] Yeats had the impression this woman was 'Ireland herself, that Cathleen ni Houlihan for whom so many songs have been sung, and about whom so many stories have been told and for whose sake so many have gone to their death'. After breakfast, Yeats tried to turn his dream into a play but found he was unable to do so. He could not write peasant dialogue that sounded authentic. Eventually, he asked Lady Gregory to collaborate with him. The result was 'the first play of our Irish school of folk-drama', and a work of profound importance to Nationalist feeling.

Writing in one of the school exercise books she used for her folklore, Lady Gregory realistically created life inside a peasant cottage at the time of Wolfe Tone. Here the Gillanes enjoy their material success and look forward to their son Michael's wedding. The entrance of the poor old woman, however, Cathleen ni Houlihan, immediately suffuses the play with another atmosphere, a riddling, mysterious, highly charged feeling at once elusively metaphoric and emotionally telling. The woman says she is grieving for the loss of her 'four beautiful green fields'. She becomes at once pitiful and sinister as she tells of her loss and of how many have died for love of her. Michael Gillane himself is clearly intrigued, especially when the old woman refuses his mothers's offer of money and insists that anyone wanting to help her must give himself whole-heartedly to her cause. The old woman's metaphorical nature becomes more apparent and more enthralling as she sings of the self-sacrifice and death her cause entails, along with the assurance of immortality such devotion will win.

The high melodrama of the play's climax is especially effective. The lure of the Irish cause, of Cathleen ni Houlihan, is all the more powerful for never being made explicit, and when we are shown Michael in his fiancée's arms torn between happiness in the material world and the demands of a Nationalist vocation, the distant voice of Cathleen herself seems like a supernatural call to self-sacrifice. It is inevitable that Michael will tear himself from his girl's arms, reject the comfortable options of his daily world and join the Irish patriots in the rising of 1798. Cathleen ni Houlihan suggests the hard consequences of this decision in a speech which shows how effectively Lady Gregory had mastered a form of language at once colloquial and biblical in its resonance:

> It is a hard service they take that help me. Many that are red-cheeked now will be pale-cheeked; many that have been free to walk the hills and the bogs and the rushes will be sent to walk hard streets in far countries; many a good plan will be broken; many that have gathered money will not stay to spend it; many a child will be born and there will be no father at its christening to give it a name. They that have red cheeks will have pale cheeks for my sake, and for all that, they will think they are well paid.[24]

As Michael is won to the old woman's cause, we are told how Cathleen ni Houlihan herself is transfigured into a young girl who has 'the walk of a queen'.

The question of staging the piece now arose. At the close of 1901, the Fays were introduced to George Russell, part of whose *Deirdre* had recently been published. Russell agreed to finish his drama and let the Fays rehearse it. He also tried to persuade Yeats to let them have *Cathleen ni Houlihan* since *Deirdre* alone was too short for a full programme. Yeats was at first reluctant, partly because he considered Russell's play 'superficial and sentimental', but when it became clear that Martyn would no longer fund the Irish Literary Theatre and that a London production of the work also seemed out of the question, he agreed to hand the play to the Fays. What made him particularly happy to do so was the fact that Maud Gonne had agreed to play the title role.

The late summer of 1901 had seen a partial reconciliation between Maud and Yeats. Both were in London, where Maud herself was staying with her cousins in South Kensington. Her unhappily married sister Kathleen Pilcher and her children were also there. Yeats paid a call after dinner, arriving to find Maud still in her travelling clothes. The contrast between her unkempt beauty and the loveliness of the other women, carefully dressed in high Edwardian fashion, startled Yeats. Kathleen gently said that it was hard work being beautiful, while Maud tended to assume that her looks would take care of themselves. This idea of the work needed to create a seemingly effortless beauty became the subject of 'Adam's Curse':

> We sat together at one summer's end,
> That beautiful mild woman, your close friend,
> And you and I, and talked of poetry.
> I said, 'A line will take us hours maybe;
> Yet if it does not seem a moment's thought,
> Our stitching and unstitching has been naught.
> Better go down upon your marrow-bones
> And scrub a kitchen pavement, or break stones
> Like an old pauper, in all kinds of weather;
> For to articulate sweet sounds together
> Is to work harder than all these, and yet
> Be thought an idler by the noisy set
> Of bankers, schoolmasters, and clergymen
> The martyrs call the world.'[25]

A powerful change in Yeats's poetry is at once evident here. Pre-Raphaelite imprecision has been replaced by an exact sense of the daily physical world of work, pain and common things. These enter the poem in a metre that is determined but conversational. While Yeats achieves a fine, patrician confidence in this way, a sense both of dignity and ease, the final effect is to draw a telling contrast between the gracefulness of the drawing-room world and the hopelessness of high passion eclipsed, of something great irrecoverably lost:

> I had a thought for no one's but your ears:
> That you were beautiful, and that I strove
> To love you in the old high way of love;
> That it had all seemed happy, and we'd grown
> As weary-hearted as that hollow moon.[26]

The disillusion of the last line is especially poignant, and the following days were to show how far as always Yeats's passion was from being fulfilled. During a customary visit to Westminster Abbey to look at the Lin Fail, the Stone of Destiny embedded in the British throne, Yeats said to Maud: 'You don't take care of yourself as Kathleen does, so she looks younger than you;

your face is worn and thin; but you will always be beautiful, more beautiful than anyone I have known. You can't help that. Oh Maud, why don't you marry me and give up this tragic struggle and live a peaceful life? I would make such a beautiful life for you among writers and artists who would understand you.'[27]

There was much to back this heartfelt appeal. For all that he was still a poor man, Yeats had established a considerable position in the social life of literary and artistic London. The novelist Dorothy Richardson, living across the street from Yeats but never daring to visit the poet himself, watched the distinguished visitors who called on him for his 'Monday evenings': John Masefield and Robert Bridges among the poets, Mrs Patrick Campbell, Gordon Craig and Bernard Shaw from the theatre among others. Dorothy Richardson was intrigued as she looked into Yeats's rooms and saw his guests 'talking, talking, but in an inequality of communication'. Yeats, it seems, dominated such occasions with his 'tall, pervading figure, visible now here, now there, but always in speech'. That speech, had Dorothy Richardson been able to hear it, was as distinctive as every aspect of Yeats's appearance. 'His voice has almost a separate life of its own,' wrote one observer.[28] 'It is charged with the thousands of overtones of story, argument, song, anecdote, comment, and fable which have so richly freighted it. It is an intimate, quiet voice, with a touch of brogue and more than a touch of humour. It goes along swiftly, in grave sweeps of eloquence, and then hesitates, gropes – as if seeking the right word or waiting to be sure how his listener is following him.'

But it was not only the abundance of his talk that was attractive. As he entered his late twenties, Yeats impressed as an exceptionally handsome man an inch over six feet tall. Oliver St John Gogarty, the ebulliently talented surgeon and man of letters, meeting him at this time, saw Yeats's soft collar and flowing silk tie as offsetting with careful nonchalance a strong, russet-brown face with its firm jaw, aquiline nose and widely spaced eyes, one of which (the right) was noticeably lower than the other. 'His mouth was remarkable for the translucent lips that were soft and red like the berry of the yew.' Nonetheless, for all that Gogarty noted Yeats's 'charming voice with its mellow tones that quickened with his thoughts', the air of mystery, reserve and even coldness that had been apparent since Yeats's boyhood were still in evidence. Gogarty wrote that there 'was about him a strange aloofness – a remoteness – and he had a way of withdrawing into himself, the effect of which was as though someone had suddenly turned off a light'.

Those who were actually admitted to Yeats's lodgings at 18 Woburn Buildings left varying accounts of what they found there. Annie Horniman's comments were typically brisk and to the point. Although a Mr and Mrs Old were supposed to look after 'Yeaty,' as they called him, Annie was appalled by the moths in the curtains, the dusty books on the top shelves, the uncovered mattress and the dirty eiderdown and blankets. She was later to complain that while looking for Yeats's keys she had been obliged to open drawers where she found bits of fur rug which would encourage moths to attack his underwear. Naphthalene was required, she wrote.

Others were blind to these inconveniences or chose to ignore them, and one of the most memorable descriptions of Yeats's London home was left by John Masefield, who recalled the beautiful shadows of the plane trees that fell on the building when the streetlights were on and how a blind beggar was always loitering there with his little tray of matches and shoelaces. Yeats's name was engraved on a brass plate by the bell-pull and, once admitted, visitors were taken along the hall and up the stairs to the second floor where Yeats had a 'biggish' front sitting room and a small kitchen. His bedroom was now on the floor above. The sitting room was papered with brown paper and hung with an interesting collection of pictures. Masefield remembered a portrait of Yeats by his father and the beautiful *Memory Harbour*, an evocation of Sligo, by his brother Jack. Over the mantelpiece was an illustration to a Blake poem by JBY, along with Blake's own engraving of *The Whirlwind of Lovers*, one of the Dante illustrations given him by the Linells. There were, too, an engraving of Blake's head, an illustration from his *Job* and a print of *The Ancient of Days*. There were also two small pastels by Yeats himself of the lake and hills near Coole, and 'a beautiful pencil drawing by Mr Cecil French, of a woman holding a rose between her lips'. On the door leading into the kitchen hung Beardsley's poster for *The Land of Heart's Desire*. The whole effect, Masefield declared, was sombre, but the atmosphere was greatly enriched after Yeats's fortieth birthday when he was presented by his friends (led by Lady Gregory) with a copy of Morris's magnificent Kelmscott Chaucer, which he displayed on a dark-blue lectern between enormous candlesticks.

In such surroundings, Yeats gradually established a ritual of entertainment. On Monday evenings, from eight until two or three in the morning, he was at home to his friends, Masefield wrote. It was the rule that the last comer should always go down to let in the next comer, and 'that curved stair, lit by a lamp at the curve, was trodden by all that made our world.' The conversation was various and outstanding.

> On a good evening the sitting-room would be full, with perhaps a dozen men and women. All manner of things were discussed; some of the cleverest read their new poems or favourite poems; new methods of speaking verse were practised; occultists told of strange things done by magicians in simpler lands than this, or here, in simpler times; then, there were the new books; new plays; new paintings to talk of; or some gathered exhibition of paintings that then meant most to us. When these were our subjects, we were happy. We were, in the main, the last of the Pre-Raphaelite followers.

Maud, however, though she remembered enjoying such occasions, was not

to be won over to such a world. As Yeats asked her to join it permanently by
marrying him, she turned to him and said:

> 'Willie, are you not tired of asking that question? How often have I
> told you to thank the gods that I will not marry you. You would not
> be happy with me.'
> 'I am not happy without you.'
> 'Oh yes, you are, because you make beautiful poetry out of what you
> call your unhappiness and you are happy in that. Marriage would be
> such a dull affair. Poets should never marry. The world should thank
> me for not marrying you.'[29]

Such comments were shrewd and not unkind, but they gave no hint of the
fact that while rejecting her poet Maud was also being pursued by her soldier,
John MacBride.

But if Maud would not join Yeats in his private life she would nonetheless
play the part of Cathleen ni Houlihan, and she wrote excitedly to Yeats asking
for a copy of the script and saying how delighted she was that the Fays were
going to direct. Others were less pleased, and rehearsals proved a strain.
Edward Martyn thought the work 'a silly little play', while George Moore
considered the acting of the supporting roles provincial. He tried constantly
to interfere, something particularly irksome to the temperamental Willie Fay,
and also to Maud herself. The minor actors gathered from among Maud's
Daughters of Erin and George Russell's Hermeticists might endure this, but
Maud herself eventually decided to escape to the Wicklow Mountains to learn
her lines by a rushing stream, her grief for a dying friend (the poet Anna
Johnston) working its way into her interpretation of Cathleen's laments for
the heroes of Ireland.

Cathleen ni Houlihan was presented on the nights of 2, 3 and 4 April
1902. Crowds were turned away at the door of St Theresa's Hall. Inside,
'gleaming shirt-fronts mingled with the less resplendent garb of the Dublin
worker'. The footlights lit up a banner of the Daughters of Erin and
its motif of a golden sunburst on a blue ground. Even the aisles were
crowded with standing patrons. But the leading lady was nowhere to be
found, and it was only at the last moment that an appalled Frank Fay,
watching the auditorium through a peephole, saw Maud striding through
the hushed audience and preparing to mount the stage in the costume she
had chosen for herself: 'a beautiful untidy grey wig, a torn grey flannel
dress *exactly* like the old women wear in the west, bare feet & a big blue
hooded cloak'.[30]

Her performance was unforgettable. 'Never again will there be such a
splendid Kathleen,' wrote Willie Fay, and Maire nic Shiubhlaigh, who
was later to recreate the part, was convinced she had seen the definitive
interpretation. 'Watching her, one could readily understand the reputation

she enjoyed as the most beautiful woman in Ireland,' she wrote, 'the inspiration of the whole revolutionary movement.' And the role of Cathleen exactly suited this. 'In her, the youth of the country saw all that was magnificent in Ireland. She was the very personification of the figure she portrayed on the stage.' An enraptured Yeats told Lady Gregory that Maud played the part 'magnificently, and with weird power'. *Cathleen ni Houlihan* immediately became deeply rooted in the nationalist imagination. This showed in Arthur Griffith's face as the final curtain fell, and he was to write: 'we agree with Mr Yeats that nothing save a victory on the battlefield could so strengthen the national spirit as the creation of an Irish Theatre'. Constance Gore-Booth was to think of the work as a religious rite, and Stephen Gwynn left the theatre wondering 'if such plays should be produced unless one was prepared for people to go out and shoot and be shot'. Nor should it be forgotten that the play was performed repeatedly in the years after its first staging, thereby continuing to foment Nationalist opinion and reinforcing Yeats's idea when he said of Irish writers, 'it may be that it depends on us to call into life the phantom armies of the future . . . if we never allow ourselves to forget those armies, we need have no fear for the future of Ireland'. Politics and myth were powerfully coinciding and, after the Easter Rebellion of 1916, Yeats was to ask if his play had helped send out 'Certain men the English shot' – the martyrs of Irish liberty.

IX
'Not a Crumb of Comfort'

But if *Cathleen ni Houlihan* was a political rallying point, it also played a vital role in the Irish literary renaissance. A little while after the production, Yeats wrote to Willie Fay that a wealthy friend had advised him to 'work on as best you can for a year'. Then, 'at the year's end do what Wagner did and write a "Letter to my Friends" asking for the capital to carry out your idea'. The wealthy friend was Annie Horniman, who, as Yeats's unofficial secretary, also copied out the letter for him. Now, as the Irish National Theatre was formed under Yeats's presidency, so a patron was waiting to fund those productions in which Yeats himself would draw together his interests in dramatic poetry, nationalism and the occult. A great period in modern drama was being prepared.

The Irish National Dramatic Society was formally constituted on 9 August 1902, with Russell, Hyde and Maud Gonne as its vice presidents. The previous day a tiny hall in Camden Street was hired for a year at ten shillings a week as the Society's theatre. This hall was little more than a roofed-over yard at the back of a grocery shop. It could seat only two hundred people, while the stage was merely nine feet deep. There were no dressing rooms and performances had to be given against a background of noise from outside. Productions by the Society in the Antient Concert Rooms provided £60 for curtains and seating, and early in December 1902 the theatre opened with four plays, including Yeats and Lady Gregory's short comedy *The Pot of Broth*.

The impact made was best described by the enthusiastic Dublin theatre-goer Joseph Holloway, who found the acting 'so effective and unconventionally realistic, as to be startling'. Despite such praise, however, there were disagreements among the company from the start, and by the end of the year it was clear that three opposing factions had formed. The most intellectually powerful of these consisted of Yeats, Lady Gregory, Synge and the Fays, who wanted a national theatre fulfilling their own high aspirations for art. Against them was ranged a small but vocal Nationalist group led by Maud Gonne and Arthur Griffith, who wanted drama to be subservient to their political ends. The largest group, however, consisted of those mostly working-class members who hoped the Society could be kept as an amateur group dedicated to the promotion of local talent.

Trouble broke out when Lady Gregory submitted her one-act play *Twenty-Five*, a work named after the card game at its centre, in which a young lover returning from America willingly loses his savings to the impoverished husband of his erstwhile girlfriend. Maud Gonne vetoed the work on the somewhat flimsy grounds that the £100 with which Christie returns to Ireland might serve as an incentive to emigration, while the Fays had moral qualms about presenting a gambling scene on stage. At first it was decided to replace the work with Padraic Colum's *The Saxon Shillin'*, a stridently anti-British recruiting play that had recently won a prize. Willie Fay found the work melodramatic and difficult to stage, however, and, calling for revisions, was himself attacked by Maud and Arthur Griffith for over-stepping the bounds of his responsibility.

Yeats himself had recently joined with Griffith, Maud and others on a National Council consisting 'only of members who are opposed to the British Government of Ireland'. These people were the nucleus of what later became Sinn Fein, but while Yeats was associated with such groupings he would not, as an artist, follow the others into believing that only plays with a propagandist Nationalist message should be performed at the theatre. An important breach was widening, and Maud herself wrote in a fury to Yeats saying she could not remain vice president of 'an Association where I am told only the stage manager's opinion counts not only as to acting but as to altering cutting & choosing plays, & which may in this case involve a question of principle'. Maud was fighting, of course, to protect the ardent nationalism of *The Saxon Shillin'*.

A system for vetting plays was clearly called for and Russell, with the considerable administrative experience he had now gained from his work in agricultural reform, proposed that, while the nomination of plays should come from the board, their acceptance and casting should be decided on a three-quarters vote of the whole membership. This was a democratic move Yeats was soon to find intolerable, and even now there was bad feeling between him and Russell over the move. It is suggestive of Yeats's growing powers of manipulation that, once passed, he used the new rules to have *The Saxon Shillin'* withdrawn and a revised version of Lady Gregory's play put into rehearsal. But by the end of June 1903 it was clear that the procedures put in place by Russell were no longer adequate, and Yeats managed to persuade the Society to set up a reading committee in their place.

While Yeats was carefully establishing his position of power in the Society, Maud Gonne's involvement in its disagreements shows that passing time had brought no abatement to her political intensity. Yeats might notice that his 'well-beloved's hair has threads of grey' and could see that little shadows had begun to form about her eyes. For him, however, Maud remained both the embodiment and the victim of her heroic temperament, a woman as far as always from being his wife:

> 'No,
> I have not a crumb of comfort, not a grain.
> Time can but make her beauty over again:
> Because of that great nobleness of hers
> The fire that stirs about her, when she stirs,
> Burns but more clearly. O she had not these ways
> When all the wild summer was in her gaze.'[31]

Just how wildly the fire could indeed stir about Maud was revealed to Yeats with sudden and agonising intensity when, on her way back from Paris to Dublin, she stopped over in London and told him she had decided to become a Roman Catholic and marry John MacBride.

Yeats wrote to Maud three times from the depths of his despair.[32] 'I appeal to you in the name of 14 years of friendship to read this letter. It is perhaps the last thing I shall [write] you,' he cried. Yeats believed Maud was committing spiritual trespass against their love, against herself and against the cause of Ireland. His deepest thoughts tumbled over each other as he sought to explain and dissuade, to cajole, and to rescue Maud from 'the great betrayal'. Their mystic marriage had been sanctioned by Lugh himself, he argued, an ennobling, visionary, Irish deity and not the repressive God of the cosmopolitan Catholic Church. 'Your hands were put in mine & we were told to do a certain great work together. For all who undertake such tasks there comes a moment of extreme peril. I know now that you have come to your moment of peril.' By her conversion to Roman Catholicism, Maud was about to betray the great visionary truth she shared with Yeats. She was threatening 'the religion of free souls that is growing up in Ireland, it may be to enlighten the whole world'. She would do irremediable harm to the cause of mystic enlightenment by providing an easy victory for the priests. 'It was our work', Yeats wrote, 'to teach a few strong aristocratic spirits . . . to believe the soul was immortal & that one prospered hereafter *if one laid upon oneself* an heroic discipline.' With her capitulation to an outworn faith, Yeats believed, Maud now threatened the entire spiritual future of the nation she had fought for.

In addition to such heartfelt pleas, an earnest commitment to the elitism Maud so detested also runs through this letter and shows how little Yeats really appreciated the form that Maud's convictions took. He argued that ordinary people might 'need the priests or some other masters', but it was precisely because Maud was superior in social status to the suffering mass of Irish men and women that she had so powerful an effect on them. In sentences that suggest how far his patrician elitism had now come, Yeats wrote: 'You possess your influence in Ireland very largely because you come to the people from above. You represent a superior class, a class whose people are more independent, have a more beautiful life, a more refined life. Every man almost of the people who has spoken to me of you has shown that you influence him very largely because of this.'

It was precisely such arguments that Maud most despised Yeats for, and the brutal clumsiness of his despair is nowhere more urgent in the letter than when he turned on MacBride himself and told Maud that she was 'going to marry one of the people' and would therefore thrust herself down to their level. Yeats begged Maud to come back to herself, 'to take up again the proud, solitary, haughty life which made [you] seem like one of the Golden Gods'. But in begging her to raise herself to her divinity Yeats only persuaded Maud ever more surely into the arms of MacBride. On 21 February 1903, just before he was about to give a lecture, Yeats received a telegram informing him that Maud Gonne MacBride had married her soldier at a ceremony in Paris.

8

A Manly Pose
(1903–1907)

I
Emerging from the Twilight

On 26 February 1903, a great storm battered the British Isles. The oaks on Hyde Park fell like skittles, as did the elms in Dublin. Lady Gregory was in London reading John Synge's new masterpiece *Riders to the Sea* as news came that the 'Big Wind' had inflicted severe damage on the grounds at Coole. When she returned to the house, she saw the extent of the devastation. Ten lime trees were down between the house and the stables, the great oak on the front lawn had fallen, and large stretches of the Seven Woods were flattened. With the practical energy always at her disposal, Lady Gregory set about making good the damage, planting some 2500 saplings and setting up a sawmill to make use of the fallen timber. She then turned to look after the broken-hearted Yeats, who had been in Dublin producing *Twenty-Five* and his own one-act play *The Hour Glass*.

This last, especially in its original prose version, is a spare but not unattractive morality play in which a 'wise' agnostic is obliged to accept the reality of the spiritual life by recognising the validity of the antithetical world of the Fool – an important Yeatsian character – and his intimations of the supernatural. T. Sturge Moore's stage designs for *The Hour Glass* (developed from an idea by Lady Gregory's son Robert) also reveal the production as 'our first attempt at the decorative staging long demanded by Mr Yeats'. He was at last able to put his ideas into practice, and the resulting set, a simple and dignified suggestion of a scholar's study, was regarded by Holloway as profoundly impressive. That it was also the product of a fastidious eye and immense care is suggested by Yeats's note on the play in the 1908 Collected Edition. 'We always play it in front of an olive-green curtain', he wrote, 'and dress the Wise Man and his Pupils in various shades of purple. Because in all these decorative schemes one needs, as I think, a third colour subordinate to the other two, we have partly dressed the Fool in red-brown, which is repeated in the furniture.' Such effects as these, combined with the high quality of the acting seen in Frank Fay's Fool especially, made evident the reforms Yeats desired for his theatre, and Holloway declared that the first night of *The Hour Glass* was the turning point in the career of the Irish National Theatre Company, and had 'placed them on the wave of success'.

Lady Gregory meanwhile had spent the summer of 1902 revising *Twenty-Five*, along with writing up the Finn sagas to stand beside her version of the Cuchulain legend, but she also did much entertaining, giving Yeats especially the opportunity of getting to know well a man who was to have a considerable influence on him in the years after Maud Gonne's marriage, the American-Irish lawyer John Quinn. Quinn was a man of outstanding energy who was making his fortune in the law. He would soon set up on his own and, when he first came to Coole, Lady Gregory, now in her early fifties, felt herself immediately drawn to the tall, handsome bachelor of thirty-two with his decisive manner, classically crisp features, penetrating blue eyes and mobile mouth that constantly folded into a smile of high, sardonic intelligence. She took him, along with Yeats, Martyn and Hyde, to a celebration at the poet Raftery's grave, where they also met Jack Yeats, whose painting Quinn had read about in his hostess's reviews. What made Quinn himself particularly attractive to this already distinguished company was the fact that, in addition to his professional acumen, he was also acquiring a deep and well-informed love of contemporary Irish art and literature. This was a cause to which, sometimes with the greatest forbearance, he would offer unstinting support. The Yeats family, the Abbey Theatre and James Joyce were all recipients of his patronage.

The life at Coole made a profound impression on Quinn. Here was a world of high culture and artistic enterprise which proved beyond doubt what his fellow countrymen could achieve. He wrote that 'there seemed to be magic in the air, enchantment in the woods and the beauty of the place, and the best talk and stories I ever found anywhere'.[1] The brilliance and sparkle of the conversation, he recalled, never faded. Lady Gregory's interest in the people about her was untiring, and Quinn admired the routine she had quietly imposed of work in the mornings, walks and other out-of-door activities in the afternoons, and play-reading and discussion after dinner. Along with an impression 'of the gentleness and energy of this woman', Quinn also took back to America a second memory: 'the realisation of a unique literary friendship between the chatelaine and the poet Yeats'.

Once returned to New York, Quinn set about promoting, Yeats's genius in America. He founded a New York branch of the Irish Literary Society and proposed that it sponsor performances of *The Land of Heart's Desire*, *Cathleen ni Houlihan* and *The Pot of Broth*. Actors were assembled and, after only the briefest period of rehearsal, the plays were staged. Although the little season of his work was well received, Quinn was obliged to tell Yeats that no royalties would be forthcoming since the expenses had been heavy. He had also found it necessary to deal with the resignation of Archbishop Farley from the vice presidency of the Society, a move probably triggered by what the prelate considered to be the Protestant Yeats's heretical and anti-clerical views. As Yeats himself wrote in quiet self-justification on 14 July 1903: 'I am often driven to speak about things that I would keep silent on were it not necessary in a country like Ireland to be continually asserting one's freedom if one is not to lose it altogether.'

Quinn was in whole-hearted agreement, and this opposition to conventional Christianity was reinforced by a shared taste for the works of Nietzsche, which was particularly encouraged by Quinn when he sent Yeats his own copy of *Also Sprach Zarathrustra* along with translations of *The Case of Wagner* and *A Genealogy of Morals*. Although Quinn himself found Nietzsche's 'exaltation of brutality', his concept of the superman, 'abhorrent', he believed Yeats would enjoy the German thinker's 'wonderful epigrammatic style'. Yeats himself had probably first encountered Nietzsche in articles written by Havelock Ellis for the *Savoy*, but now he was to start finding in the philosopher's work ideas sympathetic to his own.

In May 1903, he sent Quinn a copy of his recently published volume of essays *Ideas of Good and Evil*. Yeats's publishers had accepted this work in lieu of his unfinished novel *The Speckled Bird*, urged to this partly by Yeats's new agent A. P. Watt and accepting the book the more readily because of the open hostility expressed about Yeats's occult work among the conservative Dublin booksellers. The new volume contained some of Yeats's finest critical writings, his essays on Morris and Shelley especially, but the poet himself realised that he was now moving beyond many of the ideas he had expressed in such works as 'The Autumn of the Body'. As he wrote to Quinn:

> The book is I think too lyrical, too full of aspirations after remote things, too full of desires. Whatever I do from this out will, I think, be more creative. I will express myself, so far as I express myself in criticism at all, by that sort of thought that leads straight to action, straight to some sort of craft. I have always felt that the soul has two movements primarily, one to transcend forms, and the other to create forms. Nietzsche, to whom you have been the first to introduce me, calls these the Dionysiac and the Apollonic respectively. I think I have to some extent got weary of that wild God Dionysus, and I am hoping that the Far-Darter will come in his place.[2]

Celtic Twilight was fading as the century turned, but the transition was far from smooth or painless. It was not simply a battle with an evolving culture, but of the internal conflicts fundamental to those who made that culture. As Yeats wrote to Russell of his world of the Nineties: 'this region of shadows is full of false images of the spirit and of the body. I have come to feel towards it as O'Grady feels towards it and even as some of my stupidest critics feel. As so often happens I am roused by it to a kind of frenzied hated which is quite out of control.' The antithetical man now required a new style to describe a new age, and Yeats, in the agonising period after the defection of Maud Gonne, was working towards that directness and physical awareness which were slowly to enter his writing and help make him a supreme lyric poet of the twentieth century.

II
Tarot Cards and a Psaltery

The month that saw Yeats sending his book of essays to Quinn also saw the London success of the Irish National Theatre. Five plays were produced in a matinée and evening performance at the Queen's Gate Hall, South Kensington. Yeats reported to Lady Gregory, who was on holiday in Italy, that he had never seen a more enthusiastic audience, and the immense success of the short season greatly enhanced the company's reputation. The *Times* critic A. B. Walkley was particularly impressed. The sheer pleasure of hearing English spoken with a genuine Irish accent (a pleasure that the reviewer insisted had nothing to do with Yeats's dramatic theories) was one of the principal delights. Here was no demeaning burlesque, no 'stage Irishman'. The effect, the reviewer continued, was one that 'ennobles our mother-tongue, brings it into relief, gives it a daintiness and a distinction of which, in our rough workaday use of it, we have never dreamed'.[3]

The reviewer also enjoyed the visual effects of the productions. The actors themselves were attractive, but it was the discipline of their posture and movements that particularly impressed. Yeats once fantasised about rehearsing his players in barrels mounted on castors to achieve this stillness, and Walkley noted that 'the speaker of the moment is the only one who is allowed a little gesture'. The changes Yeats had argued for in his 'The Reform of the Theatre' had clearly been achieved and were appreciated, while, with this simplicity and decorum of movement, went something else that greatly pleased the critic. 'Add that the scenery is of Elizabethan simplicity . . . this performance is a sight for sore eyes – eyes made sore by the perpetual movement and glitter of the ordinary stage.'

Some believed that the success of the season had been occultly predicted. On 1 March 1903, Annie Horniman, having spoken to Yeats of a current of energy she felt, laid out her tarot cards in four stacks, took the bottom card from each stack and began the intricate process of interpretation.[4] The cards, she thought, indicated that Yeats's theatrical plans would earn him fame once he had recovered from a loss. This first of several readings took place barely a week after Maud Gonne had announced her marriage. Annie's own life in the meantime had not been happy. Despite Yeats's standing by her in the tumultuous rows that had swept over the Golden Dawn, the Order itself had split, Yeats himself joining the new Stella Matutina group, with which he was to remain until at least 1923. Annie, however, resigned from a world where she felt she was not wanted and was now looking for a project into which she could throw much of her energy, her money and her enthusiasm for the world of avant-garde theatre. As she took the stack of tarot cards which contained her own significator, the Queen of Swords, and spread it into a horseshoe shape before her, so her future seemed to tell of a change from life to death and hinted that the disappearance of a brown-haired woman would surely bring new hope.

The brown-haired woman evidently referred to Maud Gonne. Her marriage removed a rival for the great poet whose correspondence Annie worked on when his eyes troubled him and for whom she might now do more. 'Work for love' appeared to have an occult sanction, but, although Annie might hope for success after initial difficulties, the cards told her that her hopes would not be completely fulfilled. Something of what she could expect, however, seemed predicted (and was, indeed, to a remarkable extent fulfilled) when she spread the stack of cards containing Yeats's significator, the Prince of Swords. It seemed that Yeats would 'remain anxious' about Maud Gonne but, as he slowly became reconciled to the situation, so he would experience the 'great violence of a new energy' bursting over his life and sweeping away obstacles with its power. When Annie consulted the cards for a second time on the day before the first London performance of the Irish National Theatre Society's season, she discovered that Yeats would experience a 'gain of authority about his dramatic affairs'. The undoubted success of the season seemed to fulfil the prediction, and Annie would soon ensure a generously funded alliance between dramatic poetry and the world of magical insight.

Another friend of Yeats's was also making an important contribution to his aesthetic at this time. Florence Farr was continuing her experiments with the psaltery.[5] Despite George Moore's exasperation, Florence's delivery of the lyrics in *The Countess Cathleen* had been praised, Yeats having previously advised the audience that these pieces would not be 'sung, but spoken, or rather chanted, to music, as the old poems were probably chanted by bards and rhapsodists'. Yeats contended that the modern sung delivery of lyrics often so submerged the subtlety of their verbal structure that there was sometimes a loss of intelligibility. Florence's art seemed to restore the balance.

At first she and Yeats had used a harp and piano accompaniment to suggest the notes and the pitch they sought. But this proved unsatisfactory, and it was only in October 1901, after they had enlisted the help of the distinguished musicologist Arnold Doletsch, that they perfected a form of notation and commissioned a mature form of the psaltery. A photograph of Florence shows her holding a lyre-shaped instrument with twenty-six steel and brass strings which covered all the chromatic intervals of the speaking voice. The effect enchanted Yeats, who cunningly replied to accusations that he was tone deaf with the argument that such a condition freed him from a concern with modern tonal music and so allowed his unencumbered ear to enjoy what he thought of as the sounds made by the ancient bards. In his essay 'Speaking to the Psaltery' he wrote: 'I have just heard a poem spoken with so delicate a sense of its rhythm, with so perfect a respect for its meaning, that if I were a wise man and could persuade a few people to learn the art I would never open a book of verses again.' For the first time for many centuries, the ear had reclaimed the literary lyric from the eye, and print had ceded to performance.

Yeats, who since adolescence had always composed for and by the ear, at once began to envisage an Order of Troubadours who would explore his 'new art' and for whom he would write all his shorter pieces, hoping especially to 'appeal to the worker who had no leisure to read, and the illiterate, who are not the less spiritually educated'. In fact, his appeal was, naturally enough, to a highly articulate elite. He and Florence gave over a score of recitals to London literary societies in the months after their successful debut at Clifford's Inn on 10 June 1902, when Florence and Dorothy Paget chanted Yeats's new lyric, 'The Players ask for a Blessing on the Psalteries and on Themselves'. In this Yeats suggested that the art he and his players espoused was something timeless and spiritually refreshing to set against the rhetorical blare of imperial London:

> Hurry to bless the hands that play,
> The mouths that speak, the notes and strings,
> O masters of the glittering town!
> O! lay the shrilly trumpet down,
> Though drunken with the flags that sway
> Over the ramparts and the towers,
> And with the waving of your wings.[6]

While performing to the psaltery furthered the aural refinement Yeats sought and was in some degree a riposte to the suggestion of material power, it was also involved with the other interests he was trying to forge into a unity: Irish nationalism and occult insight. The reasons behind this attempt to revive the art of the Celtic bard were most memorably expressed by Russell when he wrote that 'we are seeking for the old, forgotten music once heard in the dunes of kings, which made the reveller grow silent, and the great warriors to bow low their faces in their hands'. But for Florence

Farr, who, after the break-up of the Isis-Urania Temple, had severed her association with the Golden Dawn, the psaltery could be seen as part of her new interest in mysticism. By 1909, when she published her short book *The Music of Speech*, she had developed the idea that 'cantilating', as she called it, was 'the original art of the minstrels and the troubadours, the original art in which all love, religion, and history were once expressed'.[7] With her naturally low and beautiful voice, trained as it was in the skryer's art of vibration and developed by Yeats's insistence on the almost hypnotic power of quarter tones, she felt she could write of 'the magic of words that cast glamour, of "words of power" that opened doors', a power that lay also in witches' spells and bardic curses.

Meanwhile it was hoped that the money collected from the performances would fund a society called the Masquers. Chaired by Walter Crane and supported not only by Yeats but by Robert Bridges, Douglas Hyde, Arthur Symons, Gilbert Muray, T. Sturge Moore and others, the Masquers would create a 'Theatre of Beauty' and mount performances of plays, masques, ballets and ceremonies with that hieratic simplicity Yeats himself looked for in the performance of his own works. But the sheer busyness of the lives of most of those involved meant that the initiative came to nothing – Gilbert Murray wrote to Yeats saying how relieved he was, especially since they had managed to return all the subscriptions raised – and Yeats himself was obliged to accept that his theatrical future lay in Ireland.

III

Dublin

Yeats spent much of the summer of 1903 at Coole working in close collaboration with Lady Gregory. They wrote a little miracle play which was eventually performed as *The Travelling Man*, and there was more work on *The Shadowy Waters*, while Lady Gregory also helped remodel *The Stories of Red Hanrahan*. As so often Yeats was refashioning his past work in the light of new aims. The interest in form and clarity he had hinted at in his letter to Quinn meant the excision of much of the extravagant style he had learned from Pater. Yeats removed clumsily written peasant dialogue, replacing it with Lady Gregory's Kiltartanese. This was the style she had used for her *Cuchulain of Muirthemne*, a book Yeats extravagantly praised in his preface for rendering 'the beautiful speech of those who think in Irish . . . a speech as beautiful as that of Morris, and a living speech into the bargain'. Yeats himself was later to express veiled doubts about the success of the revised versions of his tales but, for the moment, he could write in the copy he sent to Quinn: 'Lady Gregory has helped me and I think the stories have the emotion of folklore. They are but half mine now, and often the beautiful idiom is the better half.'

Quinn himself returned to Ireland in August 1903, keen to develop his patronage of Irish writers and artists. He talked enthusiastically to Yeats about an extended American lecture tour, to which the poet agreed, but also gave time to promoting the efforts of the rest of his family. JBY and his daughters were now settled in Dublin, largely as the result of the initiatives of two remarkable women. Sarah Purser, who despite her talent for self-advertisement had long resented her native country's treatment of its artists, was especially angered when JBY's portraits were rejected out of hand by the 1901 hanging committee of the Royal Hibernian Academy. Resolved that she would help both him and another neglected artist, Nathaniel Hone, she set about organising a joint exhibition. She secured rooms in the Royal Society of Antiquaries, collected the artists' works, and prepared a catalogue and publicity.[8] Forty-four of JBY's canvases were exhibited, and when the artist, barely able to afford the fare, arrived in Dublin, he had unwittingly left Bedford Park for good. Now in his sixties, he found himself back on his native soil, made famous by the exhibition but still dogged by familiar penury.

The critical success of the exhibition brought JBY some important contacts. In particular, Lady Gregory's nephew, the successful young art dealer Hugh Lane, conceived the idea of commissioning a series of portraits of eminent contemporaries from JBY which he would then present to the nation. As so often, this hopeful project would end in disappointment, but another proposal of Lane's was eventually to involve Yeats himself in a way that focussed his engagement with the artistic life of Dublin. In 1904 Lane exhibited three collections of paintings in the city. One of these he proposed presenting to the public, while he also hoped to raise funds to buy the remaining works by Continental artists he had shown and thereby establish a free gallery for the enhancement of the cultural life of Dublin.* The issue immediately became contentious. Yeats, Lady Gregory, Russell and Hyde wrote a public letter in its support, while the Royal Hibernian Academy opposed the purchase of foreign work. But it seemed at first as if Lane's supporters would carry the day. The Corporation of the city voted £500 towards the project, the royal family offered further pictures, and Yeats along with such figures as Constance Gore-Booth (now Countess Markiewicz) and Sir Horace Plunkett were brought on to a committee to oversee the project.

Meanwhile, immediately after his exhibition and unable to raise the price of the ticket to London, JBY was living in cheap lodgings and eating at his

---

* Among the masterpieces were Renoir's *Les Parapluies*, Manet's *Portrait of Mme Eva Gonzales* and works by Monet, Degas, Ingres and Corot.

friends' dinner tables when a letter from Quinn arrived offering to buy three works, including a portrait of his famous son. In the first of many increasingly revealing letters he was to write to Quinn, JBY stated that the portrait of Yeats was available at £20. 'The other pictures you name are already disposed of,' he added. Quinn promptly bought the portrait of the poet, commissioned others of O'Leary, Hyde and Russell, and paid £20 for each of them without delay. 'You are a grand paymaster,' JBY wrote, 'and a prompt one.' Two decades of remarkable patronage had now begun.

Quinn had also visited Lily and Lollie while they were still living in Bedford Park, where early in 1902, and stimulated by her friend Augustine Henry, a second remarkable woman had appeared to help change the lives of the Yeats family. Evelyn Gleeson was a forty-six-year-old spinster and secretary of the Irish Literary Society in London.[9] Influenced by the ideas of William Morris, she was now resolved 'to find work for Irish hands in the making of beautiful things'. She proposed setting up a business where Lily would organise an embroidery department and Lollie, after a short course at the Women's Printing Society in London, would be in charge of a press producing limited-edition books. But, for all that the press especially was to play an important part in Irish cultural life, the personality and business conflicts which were to bedevil the enterprise were clear from the start. The Yeats sisters, unable to provide capital for the new venture but hungry for the work it seemed to provide, accepted Miss Gleeson's offer of a loan they had no hope of repaying. Here lay the first part of a mounting burden of debt – a debt that was intermittently to harass Yeats himself throughout his mature career – along with the serious misunderstanding that the sisters were the equal partners of Miss Gleeson rather than two women entirely beholden to her.

To compound this already dangerous position, Evelyn Gleeson and Lollie Yeats in particular were temperamentally antagonistic. The first appeared autocratic and over-dependent on drink, while now, as she entered the business world and came more closely into contact with her sister and her elder brother, Lollie's personal difficulties became ever more irksomely apparent. Lollie was a self-obsessed, physically attractive woman who, for all her undoubted energy and ability, dreamed of an escape into an easier life and vented her frustration and neurosis in endlessly excited chattering, lying and what an exasperated Yeats was to call her 'silliness'.

It was Lily who was chiefly to suffer under this onslaught, but Yeats himself was to be exposed to it too, particularly at times of crisis, which were frequent. There was no question but that his name was an advantage to the press, and Lollie went ahead with the project much relieved by her brother's offer to help her find suitable books to print at the newly named Dun Emer Industries. By December 1902, he was already able to see something of the press's first experiment: page proofs of a volume of his poems entitled *In the Seven Woods*. Finished copies were available by the following August in attractive half-papered boards with cloth spines and generous margins offsetting the type. Limited to 325 copies at 10s 6d each, the volume was reckoned a collector's item even if sales were slow. Yeats himself, keenly aware that books of poetry should be beautiful objects, was pleased, but his attitude to the press was made clear by his involvement in its next project: George Russell's *The Nuts of Knowledge*.

Yeats was displeased by some of the lyrics, ordered their removal and refused to let the press print those he had rejected. Both to protect his own name and in the ruthlessness of his genius's demand for excellence and professionalism,* he was showing that abrasive, possessive relationship to the press which, if it helped in the end to secure its enduring reputation, brought him into constant conflict with Lollie. For Yeats, his sister was essentially a manual worker. She, however, refused to accept a subordinate role. Mutually hostile family characteristics futher inflamed matters while, slowly and silently, the financial position of the press became ever more precarious.

While Yeats lent his energy and influence to the Dun Emer Press, he pointedly refused to concern himself greatly with his brother's work. An exhibition of Jack's watercolours and black and white drawings during the summer of 1902 had been praised as the output of a man of artistic ability and genius who chose to draw pictures of the rural poor in ways that broke new ground.† But Yeats made little effort to comment on them, while also refusing to rise to his father's championship of Jack's plays. JBY clearly considered Jack's *Flaunty* a drama more moving and better constructed than *The Shadowy Waters*, but Yeats's powerful, abrasive interest in the theatre was wholly focussed on his own ambitions and conflicts.

How serious those conflicts could be emerged at the end of the Coole summer of 1903. The Irish National Theatre Society was once again wracked by dissension, much of which was led by Maud Gonne, who, after the rapid collapse of her marriage, had returned to Ireland and the strident core of Nationalist politics. Although Maud's decision to marry MacBride had been partly inspired by her belief that they could work together for the Nationalist cause, the strains and absurdities that underlay their relationship were evident from the start. Their decision to honeymoon in Spain, for example, had been taken as part of a madcap scheme to assassinate Edward VII while he was on a visit to Gibraltar. Maud was supposed to act as decoy while MacBride himself would perform the assassination. MacBride got so drunk, however, that he was quite unable to commit the deed. Maud, who was horrified by

---

* Yeats insisted for example that all contributors to the press should be paid, else only 'amateurish' work would result. He himself received £31 10s for *In the Seven Woods*.
† Jack was to embark on his great oil paintings only after his return to Ireland in 1910. He and Cottie were currently living in Devon.

drunkenness, had been obliged to come to terms with the fact that she had married a jealous, alcoholic brute. A mere two months after her wedding she felt she had to confess to Yeats that she wanted to leave her husband, even while she recognised that an annulment was out of the question since she was by now pregnant.[10]

A dozen telegrams stirred her old acquaintances to action. 'Without fail be at my cottage, Rathgar, three o'clock tomorrow afternoon,' she wired. 'Meet Griffith, Martyn, Moore and others for most important conference. Maud Gonne'. The occasion for this conspiratorial meeting (from which George Moore at least excused himself on the ground that he was a man of letters and not a politician) was a threatened speech of loyalty to be given by the Irish Party on the occasion of Edward VII's imminent visit to Dublin. Maud proposed that some of the people assembled in her house attend a gathering of the Party and ask searching public questions about the rumoured speech. When Maud and 'four hulking fellows' invaded the stage of the Rotunda where the grandees of the Party sat 'banked in rows, like so many geraniums in a hot-house', her stately and commanding presence was like 'the sight of a stormy petrel'. Maud then seized a prepared statement from Martyn's plump and trembling hands and asked if the Party did indeed intend to welcome the English King to the Irish capital. Uproar broke out and, while loyalists stormed the platform, carefully placed Nationalists rose from the audience to protect the protesters as Maud herself was carried out of the building to safety.

Yeats himself was in sympathy with such views and had signed a National Council declaration which insisted that no Irishman 'can participate in any address of welcome to the King of England who can come only as the existing representative of the power responsible for all our evils'. He had also written on 13 July 1903 to the *Freeman's Journal* reminding its readers that royal visits to Dublin were often accompanied, as now, by promises of land reform and even whispers of Home Rule. As Yeats affirmed, however, the current Wyndham Land Purchase Act 'has not been given to us by English royalty but won by the long labours of our own people'. But it was Maud who was to mount the most telling protest against the gaudy entry of the royal party and its 20,000 soldiers. As she knew, Pope Leo XIII had recently died but would remain publicly unmourned while the head of the English Protestant church marched through the city. Maud the Catholic convert hung a black flag from her house instead of a Union Jack and the police were sent to tear it down. The following day a black petticoat on a broomstick appeared from Maud's window and, when the police again tried to remove it, another appeared, to be followed by another and yet more until the area was cordoned off and the police eventually allowed the black petticoat to flutter from the window for the duration of the King's stay.

But Maud and others believed that protest against the enemy without had to be matched by vigilance against what they saw as weakness within. The old and enduring argument between Maud and Yeats over art versus propaganda surfaced once again when the Irish National Theatre Society proposed to produce Synge's *In the Shadow of the Glen*. Between 1898 and 1902, while Synge travelled to the west of Ireland to collect material for his book *The Aran Islands*, he stayed repeatedly at Coole. He found Yeats and Lady Gregory's interest in the life and lore of the local peasantry greatly stimulating, just as their plays and Hyde's *The Twisting of the Rope* had shown him the possibilities inherent in dramatising such material. His own early play *The Moon Has Set* showed little promise, but the genius that in 1902 broke through with such fertility in *The Shadow of the Glen* and *Riders to the Sea* drew not simply on the early days of the Irish Literary Theatre but on Synge's own enigmatic personality. He had a character at once morbidly introspective and attracted to such remote places as the Aran Islands; he was a man capable too of intense curiosity about the human nature he found there and the 'fiery, magnificent and tender' imagination of the peasant which, he believed, lay at the root of Irish national consciousness.

Synge also had an ear more finely tuned than either Yeats or Lady Gregory to the ways in which peasant speech could be adapted for the stage. Partly translated from Gaelic and partly drawing on the seventeenth-century English spoken in the areas of Ireland he so loved, Synge created a stage dialogue in which 'every speech should be as fully flavoured as a nut or an apple'. Actors at first found this difficult, but, if Synge's language was a challenge, his approach to his material was seen by many as an affront. *The Shadow of the Glen* takes as its subject the problem of the arranged and loveless marriage. It shows the heroine admitting a tramp to the house while her husband lies apparently dead and she herself waits for her lover. When the lover arrives, the husband reveals his deception and gives the other man the choice of running off with his wife or remaining conventionally with him as his friend. The lover opts for the safety of convention, but when the tramp offers Nora the chance of sharing his life on the road, she chooses freedom rather than a stifling marriage: 'I'm thinking it's myself will be wheezing that time with lying down under the heavens when the night is cold; but you've a fine bit of talk, stranger, and it's with yourself I'll go.'[11]

All but the most liberal Dublin opinion was appalled. The issue of the unassailable virtue of Irish womanhood had once again been raised and there was a hot debate in the newspapers. 'Irishwomen are the most virtuous women in the world,' argued Arthur Griffith. Synge's play was 'nothing more or less than a farcical libel on the character of the average decently raised Irish peasant woman'. To impugn a national stereotype as Synge had done was to attack that nation itself and deal a blow to the sentimental image of superiority by which a subjected people could think themselves better than those who oppressed them. The *Irish Times* described Synge's play as 'excessively distasteful', while the *Irish Independent* launched a wholesale attack on Synge and Yeats himself.

We do not for a moment think that all the members of the Irish National Theatre Society can be held accountable for the eccentricities and extravagances of Mr Yeats and his friends. But once they are made acquainted with what is being done in their name, we hold that those who ambition the uprise of a dramatic art that shall be true, pure and National, should make their voices heard against the perversion of the Society's avowed aims by men who, however great their gifts, will never consent to serve on terms that never could or should be concealed.

Two of the Society's leading actors, Maire Quinn and her fiancé Douglas Digges, refused roles in the play and, with an outraged Maud Gonne, resigned from the Society itself. All three then attended the first performance only to walk out conspicuously in the middle.

In Maud's judgement, blinkered by Nationalist sentiment, Synge's plays could not rank among the works of Irish literature because the people themselves had objected to them. Yeats, deploring the tyranny of mass opinion, urged tolerance so that 'the half-dozen minds who are likely to be the dramatic imagination of Ireland for this generation may put their own thoughts and their own characters into their work'. He argued the case for genius and the free mind, while Maud put the case for a narrow provincialism: 'The best and truest writings of our greatest living poet, W. B. Yeats, are understood and appreciated by the people,' she woke on 24 October to the *United Irishman*. 'The poems and essays they do not understand are those touched by foreign influence, from which Mr Yeats has not altogether escaped, having lived long out of Ireland.'[12] The last was a stinging rebuke, but slowly the battlelines were hardening in a struggle over culture, national identity and the politics of literature. Arthur Griffith was now to revise Yeats's definition of a Nationalist as 'one who is ready to give up a great deal that he may preserve his country' by adding that 'unless he is prepared to give up all, we do not deem him a Nationalist'. The man who had insisted that the national theatre should only present Nationalist propaganda was now further extending his authoritarian ideas. The true Nationalist had no right to individual freedom of judgement, he implied, an attitude Yeats would fiercely oppose.

While *In the Shadow of the Glen* pointed to important issues of national consciousness, *The King's Threshold*, Yeats's new play for the October 1903 season, was to be of the greatest importance to the future of the Society itself, and thus to the remarkable flowering of twentieth-century drama in Ireland. Encouraged by a third favourable reading of the tarot, Annie Horniman was busy sewing rich and elaborate costumes for Yeats's play when she began to form a resolution. As she later recalled: 'I was thinking about the hard conditions in which they were working, and the idea struck me that if and when enough money were to turn up, I would spend it on hiring or building a little hall where they could perform in fair comfort.'

Annie, with her Pre-Raphaelite gowns and marvellous dragon pendant fashioned out of three hundred opals, was a lonely woman of forty-three looking for a purpose. Now she sensed opportunity. Maud Gonne had apparently removed herself from the circle of Yeats's legitimate affections, and the tarot appeared to promise some fresh joy in her own life. Besides, she had been allowed to design and sew costumes for the new play. The critics were by and large impressed by these, and the day after the first performance Annie wrote to Yeats: 'Do you realise that you have now given me the right to call myself "artist"? How I thank you!'[13] What she did not know was that Yeats and Frank Fay had tolerated what some in the company thought of as her 'incredibly graceless and ugly' creations because Yeats himself had hinted that with Miss Horniman lay the road to financial security. Now, encouraged by yet a further reading of the tarot, Annie, with her Hudson's Bay shares rising, resolved to build Yeats a theatre.

In this new building, Yeats would fight to establish a drama he considered worthy of his people, but now before he set sail for America and the extended lecture series organised by John Quinn he wrote two letters to the *United Irishman*.[14] These brought to an early climax his response to the opposition his work in the theatre had forced on him from the time of the attempt to subvert *The Countess Cathleen*. Both letters are deeply felt expressions of Yeats's belief in the importance of art to inspiring a national life that is vital, self-critical and creative, and these were qualities he feared were being lost in Ireland amid organised bigotry and the hatred of ideas. In a way that was to become increasingly important, he here began to pit what he saw as the elite and challenging euphoria of the truly creative against the life-denying mediocrity of the mass. In this dangerous but fertile ground he planted some of the seeds of his future greatness.

The theatre was central to Yeats's thinking on this issue at the time. The aesthetic innovations he was struggling for in the areas of staging and performance were accompanied by the whole-hearted moral conviction that drama was 'the most immediately powerful form of literature, the most vivid image of life' and he delighted in its power to stir up controversy. 'We cannot have too much discussion about ideas in Ireland,' he wrote in 1901, insisting that 'discussion over the theology of "The Countess Cathleen", and of the politics of "The Bending of the Bough", and now over the morality of "Diarmuid and Grania", set the public mind thinking of matters it seldom thinks of in Ireland'. Confrontation was both inevitable and desirable. It had, however, to be of comparable quality on both sides, and Yeats felt strongly that it was not. Dublin was not Athens, but a provincial capital ruled by an imperial government where indigenous ideas fell under the control of three enemies.

The first of these was 'the more ignorant sort of Gaelic propagandist' who could see no further than the columns in a book of grammar. Equally dangerous was 'the obscurantism of the more ignorant sort of priest' who, blind to the richness of his theological inheritance, narrowed his thoughts to proscribing anything that might trouble the unthinking conformity 'of farmers or artisans or half-educated shopkeepers', that part of the lower-middle-class population Yeats was to define as 'the mob' and who were to become increasingly the butt of his contempt. Politicians, 'and not always of the more ignorant sort', were another and more insidious danger, for it was this group that Yeats saw particularly as marshalling the people into unthinking 'squads' whose philistinism was reinforced by the brutality of a popular press such as Arthur Griffith's that reinforced a 'hatred of ideas'.

It was at this point that Yeats's argument suddenly and marvellously broadened into a great writer's vision of the perils of mass society. In the first years of the new century, Yeats was acutely aware of the most fundamental challenge that had to be faced: the problem of mass socialisation, mass politics and mass culture, the remorseless triumph of similar attitudes over everything distinctively individual, and the consequently ambiguous place of the intellectual within a crowd that threatened to swamp him. His vision was one of genuine horror. 'Certain generalisations', he wrote, 'are everywhere substituted for life. Instead of individual men and women and living virtues differing as one star differeth from another in glory, the public imagination is full of personified averages, partisan fictions, rules of life that would drill everybody into the one posture, habits that are like the pinafores of charity schoolchildren.' Here is a heartfelt cry against the tyranny of mass opinion. 'Life, which in essence is always surprising, always taking some new shape, always individualising is nothing to it, it has nothing to move men in squads, to keep them in uniform, with their faces to the right enemy, and enough hate in their hearts to make the muskets go off.' Behind the appalled vision, prompting its anger and despair, stood two poet-philosophers: Blake, whose Urizen forged the fetters of materialism, and Nietzsche, whose Zarathrustra tore them asunder. And Nietzsche, as Yeats claimed, completed Blake.

Quinn's kindling of Yeats's interest in Nietzsche came at a crucial period in the poet's development, and its effects were immediate and profound. In December 1902, Yeats apologised to Lady Gregory: 'I have written to you little and badly of late I am afraid, for the truth is you have a rival in Nietzsche, that strong enchanter.' It was from this absorption in Nietzsche's work that Yeats partly derived his view of the crowd and its values, an issue that was brought home to him not only by repeated attacks on his work in the press but by a particularly mean-spirited episode: the blackballing of George Moore from the Irish Literary Society. For all his disparagement of Moore, Yeats recognised that this attack on him by men of lesser stature augured badly. A Society that was narrowly content to be 'a court of opinions and morals' would soon 'reject on one ground or another almost every man of vigorous personality. The weak and the tame would alone speak through it.'

Writers had to stand against such a diminishing of public life, and for Yeats literature now became, as he wrote to the *United Irishman* on 7 December 1901, 'the principal voice of conscience'. He wrote eloquently of his belief that it is the duty of literature 'age after age to affirm its morality against the special moralities of clergymen and churches, and of kings and parliaments and peoples. But I do not expect this opinion to be the opinion of the majority of any country for generations, and it may always be the opinion of a very small minority.' Here, in Yeats's condemnation of the values of the 'herd' and his exaltation of the few lonely men of insight, the influence of Nietzsche – the Nietzsche of *Also Sprach Zarathrustra* – is particularly evident. It reappears once more in his praise of 'the beauty of the heroic life'.

By the middle of 1901 Yeats was, he told his father, trying to write narrative poems of the Irish heroic age. In July of that year he finished 'Baile and Aileen' and was planning other stories in a similar vein. Tradition, that increasingly important Yeatsian concept, would once again provide him with an image of the hero, but his letters suggest that the poet must in his own person fulfil this ideal too. The high striving after imaginative truth, the battling against accepted moral codes, is in itself heroic and constitutes the search for 'the voice of what metaphysicians call innate knowledge, that is to say, of conscience, for it expresses the relation of the soul to eternal beauty and truth'. It is with such discoveries as these that the poet as a type of the Nietzschean superman can go about his business of 'disordering the discipline of the squads' and so foster the deepest elements in the life of his countrymen. 'To me it seems', Yeats wrote, 'that ideas and beauty and knowledge are precisely those sacred things, an Ark of the Covenant as it were, that a nation must value even more than victory.'

It was on the stage that Yeats would now principally fight this battle. 'So long as I have any control over the National Theatre Society,' he wrote, 'no plays will be produced at it which were written, not for the sake of a good story or fine verses or some revelation of character.' The integrity of the poetic imagination had to be maintained, and Yeats's play *The King's Threshold* was a powerful presentation of this thesis. 'It was written', he declared, 'when our Society was having a hard fight for the recognition of pure art in a community of which one half was buried in the practical affairs of life, and the other half in politics and a propagandist patriotism.' The early versions of *The King's Threshold* are an attempt to illustrate the notion that poets are the acknowledged legislators of the world and should be crowned as such by those of merely kingly authority.

The early versions of this play (which are most satisfactorily studied in the revised text of 1906) made this idea explicit.[15] Seanchan the poet threatens to starve himself to death in protest at being excluded from the King's council. It is Seanchan who sees the correspondence between the earthly and supernatural worlds, who has imaginative vision, and so works to preserve the high ideals that could underlie the society that rejects him. The triviality and degradation of that society are revealed with considerable bitterness. The corrupt voices of materialism, expediency and limitation speak through the King, who dares not admit the poet and his imagination to his councils. Stupidity, self-interest and the corruption of institutions follow from this fatal decision and are embodied in the Mayor, just as the corruption of the church is revealed in the character of the Monk. The court ladies and the two princesses fail to preserve a world of culture and delight, being presented as merely frivolous women. Even Seanchan's beloved Fedelm cannot tempt him from his protest. His loyal servant Brian, however, preserves the imaginative integrity of the peasant and defends the poetic life, the power of which is also acknowledged by the Cripples. In the early versions of the play, the King is obliged to recognise it too, and he finally offers Seanchan his crown, thus giving power to the poet whose language makes the 'golden cradle' where the consciousness of his race can be nursed to maturity.

IV
Yeats in America

Part of the great influence his first visit to America was to have on Yeats was to show him a society that was altogether more vigorously pluralist than contemporary Ireland. He disembarked from the *Oceania* in November 1903 and stayed at Quinn's apartment in New York, where he found the walls covered with portraits of his acquaintances, many of them painted by his father. Quinn had put an immense amount of effort into organising the tour, assuring Yeats that he could always wire him for money should he run short and even giving him strict instructions about how he should arrange his laundry. He was not to be disappointed. Yeats lectured chiefly on 'The Intellectual Revival in Ireland', 'Heroic Literature', 'The Theatre' and 'Poetry', and received $75 for each appearance. Quinn himself went to a number of Yeats's lectures and found him 'incomparably capable and winning', declaring that no Irishman since Parnell's great trip had made so grand an impression.

Part of this success was due to Yeats's resolute professionalism. For instance, he did an immense amount of work to ensure that his 'big lecture' on 'The Intellectual Revival in Ireland' would be well received by the audience in Carnegie Hall. He wrote to Lady Gregory on 2 January 1904:

> I have already dictated the whole speech once; indeed, I have dictated some parts of it several times, and I am now going to go through it all again. Then I shall go down to the Hall and speak the whole lecture in the empty place. This is necessary, because I have found out that the larger the audience the more formal, rhythmical, oratorical must one's delivery be. My ordinary conversational happy-go-lucky, inspiration-of-the-moment kind of speaking gets all wrong when I get away from the small audiences I am accustomed to. Oratory does not exist, in any real sense, until one's got a crowd.[16]

Yeats was as good as his word, and when he arrived at what he thought was the empty hall, he was particularly keen to rehearse the old and tried device with which he had decided to wind up his speech. There was a large organ on the hall platform and, at the close, Yeats thought he would turn meditatively towards it and then, as if the idea had suddenly struck him, speak his carefully prepared peroration. It was this device he had just finished rehearsing when, out of the silence of a dark corner of Carnegie Hall, he heard applause from a single pair of hands. His perfomance had been watched and admired by the Irish caretaker.

So much preparation produced lectures that were both impressive and profound, and the effect of Yeats the public speaker was ably suggested by Joseph Hone, an acquaintance and Yeats's first biographer.[17] Yeats had, Hone wrote, 'the powerful lower lip which reveals the born orator and the born pugilist; a certain disdain, a certain pugnacity is necessary to both the pugilist and the orator'. Although Yeats was sometimes uneasy at the start of an appearance, striding up and down the platform 'before he attained to his natural distinction of bearing, his gravity of utterance and his rhythm', to hear him in full flow was to witness a great performance in which imagination and intellect were taken to the highest level. His delivery helped in this. Yeats's musical, melancholy voice at times rose, fell and lingered over words to create delicious cadences, while at other times 'he would introduce a harsh metallic note . . . like the clash of sword-blades'. Even his short-sightedness was brought into play, his myopic gaze seeming to turn inwards to the dark 'where, as he himself said, "there is always something"'. He held his audiences' attention by his seeming 'to be discoursing with himself rather than be persuading others'. Here, in Milton's phrase Hone noted, was 'the precious life-blood of a master-spirit, embalmed and treasured up on purpose to a life beyond life'. So, Hone concluded, Yeats 'was wont to handle the great themes which were his constant pre-occupation – his vision and renewal of the past – for his thought was always spiritual rather than personal, national in the highest sense, and among his countrymen he always assumed the voice and air of leadership'.

Such efforts were inevitably fatiguing, and Yeats could complain in his letters to Lady Gregory of the boredom of another month here, 'my heart at home all the while', but he was invariably punctilious, never missing his trains and for the most part nicely judging his audiences. His mammoth schedule sent him among other places to Yale, Smith College, Amherst, the University of Pennsylvania, Bryn Mawr and Vassar. There were excursions into Canada, as well as further lecturing in St Louis, Indianapolis, Perdue, Notre Dame, Berkeley, Stanford, Newark, Bridgeport and Connecticut. But there were many social duties as well as lecturing. Yeats naturally met a number of leading academics, among them the great Chaucer scholar F. N. Robinson, from whom he was obliged to borrow four dollars, and he had a lunch with 'the Colonel', as Quinn always called President Roosevelt.

He had to face, too, the hazards of being interviewed. As Yeats wrote to Lady Gregory: 'I had a long struggle with a woman reporter yesterday who wanted to print and probably will a number of indiscreet remarks of mine.'[18] She had asked him what he thought of Kipling. 'I shall say nothing whatever about Kipling if you please, I will say nothing about any living poet.' So far, so tactful, then Yeats added: 'If he would have the goodness to die I would have plenty to say.' He then looked aghast at the reporter. 'Good heavens, have you written that down?' The woman replied: 'Yes, it is the one Irish remark you have made.' Yeats asked her to rub it out and a ten-minute struggle ensued. As he wrote in his letter, he was still half expecting to see a banner headline reading 'Yeats desires Kipling's death', and he had sent urgent messages demanding to see the proofs. He had been painfully judicious for days, he explained to Lady Gregory, as the reporters had been Irish and asked about Ireland, but this woman asked about general literature and he was off his guard.

This comment suggests that, as might be expected, Ireland was one of Yeats's principal preoccupations during his tour. Emigration to the United States in particular was and continued to be the most obvious and dramatic fact of Irish social life. The means of transporting the many millions who made the great journey became increasingly sophisticated, and in the cities especially there were large and well-established communities of Irish-Americans, many of them prosperous and most of them Catholic. A strongly anti-British bias and a sense of racial purity were characteristic of these often highly organised groups, and their distance from their native land fostered a defensive and sometimes narrow love for what most of them had emigrated to preserve: the family farm. For it was not the farm-owners themselves who had gone to America, but their often numerous relatives, who sought there the liberty, money and opportunity which rural conditions at home denied them.

To such an audience as this, Yeats's anti-imperialist views were attractive, while in the land of Thoreau and Emerson he found people who would listen sympathetically to his social vision. In America he would present the obverse to the disillusion he increasingly felt at home. Instead of bitterness at the urban collective mind, he would develop ideas of a rural, pre-industrial benevolence much influenced by William Morris. He would, for example, tell an audience in New York that 'We Irish do not desire, like the English, to build up a nation where there shall be a very rich class and a very poor class. Ireland will always be in the main an agricultural country. Industries we may have, but we will not have, as England has, a very rich class nor whole districts blackened with smoke like what they call in England their "Black Country".'[19]

But now the size and diversity of America became a new and stimulating challenge for Yeats. Chicago delighted him particularly, for here was an open society very different to that he knew back home. He was 'delighted by the big merry priests of Notre Dame – all Irish and proud as Lucifer of their success in getting Jews and Nonconformists to come to their college'. As Yeats wrote: 'I have been astonished at one thing, the general lack of religious prejudice I have found on all sides here.' In his turn, he was lionised and sometimes spoke to audiences of upwards of two thousand people. He was honoured by the invitation to deliver the Emmet Lecture in New York, but he was also criticised. The scholar Paul Elmer More accused his work of confusing reverie with mysticism, of being imprecise and wallowing in 'a sense of failure and decay, rather than of mastery and growth'. Quinn was particularly concerned to refute this, describing the verse in *The King's Threshold* as 'like marble, as compared to the painting of the earlier poems'. He noted the 'brooding care' Yeats gave his most recent work, the craftsmanship which was leading to an increasing mastery of technique. 'The loosening of the verse structure', Quinn declared, 'instead of being a sign of decadence, is with Yeats the result of deliberate artifice and intention, and in this he is but following the best tradition of the last two hundred years.'

But Yeats himself was aware that his developing aesthetic was a matter more comprehensive than technique alone. Much of his published verse had taken subjectivity to an extreme and henceforth he wanted a poetry that showed 'delight in the whole man'. With his pleasure in antithetical extremes, passion, precision and ecstasy were his requirements now. In a passage that shows how resolutely Yeats was turning his back on shadows, he declared: 'we possess nothing but the will and we must never let the children of vague desire breathe upon it nor the waters of sentiment rust the terrible mirror of its blade'. The poet as warrior is no longer a Pre-Raphaelite knight but a man of willed energy. 'Let us have no emotions, however absurd, in which there is not an athletic joy.' The Yeats who now returned from New York with $3230.40 in the pocket of his astrakhan coat was searching to complete his being by putting on a mask of conspicuous self-sufficiency.

This was something Yeats had hinted at to Frank Fay when he wrote to him discussing the legendary Cuchulain as he had been refashioned for *On Baile's Strand*. Yeats wrote that in his portrayal of Ireland's great hero there was:

> a shadow of something a little proud, barren and restless, as if out of sheer strength of heart or from accident he had put affection away. He lives among young men but has himself outlived the illusions of youth. He is probably about 40, not less than 35 or 36 and not more than 45 or 46, certainly not an old man, and one understands from his talk about women that he does not love like a young man. Probably his very strength of character made him put off illusions and dreams (that make young men a woman's servant) and made him become quite early in life a deliberate lover, a man of pleasure who can never really surrender himself. He is a little hard, and leaves the people about him a little repelled.[20]

There is a great deal of the newly evolving Yeats in this passage, much of his wakening sense of disillusioned superiority, his remoteness, his attempt to harden his heart to romantic fallacy in the wake of Maud Gonne's marriage. But what is perhaps most interesting is the fact that Yeats was discussing a character in a play, a role to be acted, a mask to be worn.

V
The Abbey Theatre

That Yeats's new mask was in part at least fabricated from the less attractive Pollexfen traits in his personality, from those defences of sourness and arrogance on which he had always been able to call, was immediately apparent. It was not something new. The youth who had tried to domineer at the Contemporary Club and often made himself ridiculous was now, as a man, evolving an intellectual hauteur, an ability to 'ruffle in a manly pose', which he hoped was irresistible. Only the most perceptive realised that this mask depended to a degree on Yeats's inveterate shyness and the bitter confusions of middle age, but a number of people were sure it was something fabricated. As Wilfred Scawen Blunt shrewdly remarked: 'Yeats is just back from America, where they have made a great fuss with him, and he takes himself very seriously as a consequence. Though doubtless a man of genius, he has a strong touch in him of the charlatan.'[21]

Other observers were more generous and more subtle. Mary Colum, noting Yeats's habit of carefully dressing himself in blacks or browns, along with his cultivation of 'rhythmic speech' and carefully mannered gestures, felt bound to confess: 'I suppose there was a great deal that was studied about his appearance in those days, and the charge of posing that was often levelled at him had a certain foundation – that is, if one had not enough insight to take the whole personality into consideration.'[22] She saw that that personality was often isolated and, consequently, threatened. 'A good deal of his posing was due to the fact that he was not really very much at home with ordinary people, did not know much about life as lived by the rest of us and had not a great variety of friends.'* She saw too that Yeats's mask was also a protection. 'Human energy and human interest', she wrote, 'even in the most powerful personalities are limited, and unless people can put on some mask, the outstanding ones can be drained of energy by the demands upon them of people and of the world.' Certainly, such self-defensiveness could appear unattractive and many times gave offence. 'Yeats often gave an odd impression of being not only ill-mannered but insensitive,' she wrote. 'James Stephens once told me that he had cultivated this mask of insensitivity as a protection against the world and the slings and arrows that were so often launched against him.'

Michael Macliammoir agreed.[23] 'The people who dismiss him as a man by saying that outside his work he was a poseur whose rudeness and arrogance were unbearable', he wrote,

> are those who cannot have known him. Of course he could pose, of course he could be both rude and arrogant. He could indeed be anything he chose, and the ability to assume all these qualities at will is a bare necessity of life for him who would spend his time in Dublin, whose passionate and almost quixotic worship of mediocrity is coupled with an instinctive mistrust of the first rate, a permanent sense of discomfort in its presence, and a malicious determination to drown it in a storm of envy and belittlement.

These were indeed aspects of his mask that were to become increasingly important to Yeats, elements that were already a part of his embattled stand against those political and social forces which he saw as encroaching not simply on his own genius but on the possibility of living a high cultural life in Ireland at all. As such, the mask was part of Yeats's vocation. William Rothenstein recognised this clearly.[24] 'More than anyone I have known he stood for the dignity of the artist,' Rothenstein wrote, 'for the integrity of the arts. At a time when men give, often at little or no cost to themselves,

---

* The playwright Brinsley Macnamara illustrated this well. 'There's a story that Yeats once approached Fred Higgins [later managing director of the Abbey] and he said, "Higgins, do you know I have never been in a pub in my life and I'd like to go into a pub."' Worried friends tried to find a suitable bar. 'We decided on one pub, and Higgins went along with him there, and they called for some mild drink and Yeats looked around and he said, "Higgins, I don't like it. Lead me out again."'

ready sympathy for the proletariat, Yeats recognised the claims of those who had a right to power, since they had high courage, superior wisdom and, to Yeats an important aspect, fine breeding.'

None of these is a widely endearing quality – as Maurice Bowra was shrewdly to comment, Yeats was not in the least a 'cosy' man[25] – but if the mask was partly protection and partly an assertion of quality over mediocrity, it was also an essential aspect not just of Yeats's high claim for the true artist's worth but of his own creativity. As Padraic Colum realised, 'Yeats was a man who believed in style – or manner, if you like to call it that. "Art is art because it is not Nature", said Goethe, and Yeats often repeated that saying.' It was only when Yeats was able to forge a link between the mask and his occult interests, however – only when he had once again hammered politics, his art and his spiritual beliefs into a new unity – that the mask would take on the full richness of its significance.

In the meantime, Yeats's family were among the first to be shown the harsher aspects of his temper. To a man returned in triumph from a successful lecture tour, it was particularly exasperating to find his people little changed and, as always, importuning him for money and worldly support. It was clear that the pictures Hugh Lane had commissioned from JBY were not going well, and JBY felt he could not ask Lane for a further advance until he had more work to show for it. The letter he wrote to his son might have set anyone's teeth on edge: 'I am afraid you will think me very shabby in writing this just the moment when you have got together a few pounds, but I am quite sure that before very long I shall be in a position to repay you.'[26] JBY then asked for the unprecedented sum of £20. But if JBY felt he had to beg money from his son he knew he also had to protect the rest of his family from Yeats's increasing hauteur. He wrote beseeching him to be especially 'gentle with Lollie. If things go wrong and she gets much exasperated she gets quite ill.'

And things were going wrong. Miss Gleeson pressed the Yeats sisters for capital, and they in their turn pressed their brother, Lily writing a begging letter to him in America.[27] 'I have foreseen this moment all the while,' Yeats told Lady Gregory, 'but it is annoying.' To give too much in his sisters' support would inevitably be to lose more than he could afford, while to give too little would invite blame. 'Family duties,' Yeats opined, 'just because they are rather thrust upon one – leave me colder than they should.' But he would not renege on what he considered his responsibilities. He learned that rows about profits between the Yeats sisters and Miss Gleeson had become nastily involved with allegations about who did the more work. An attempt by George Russell to develop a businesslike compromise failed, and Yeats himself, with the proofs of his *Stories of Red Hanrahan* appearing interminably delayed, felt he had to intervene. The usually tranquil Lily wrote to their father about her brother's arrogance. He was, she said, 'full of "Do this,"

"You must do that," etc., "a press man is absolutely necessary", and so on . . . He even threatened us and bullied us generally.'

There were rows with Lollie, especially when she tried to assert a measure of editorial independence, and JBY again felt he had to intervene. His letters suggests how unpleasant matters had become, how offensive Yeats could be. 'You treat Lollie as if she was dirt. She is as clever a woman as you are, and in some respects much cleverer. She very naturally stands high in her own esteem as well as in that of other people, and she is entitled to be treated as a personage in her way.' Having tried to establish this point, JBY then went on to explain the practical aspects of the problem. 'When you advise about choice of books for the Press, it should be advice and not haughty dictation backed up by menaces. After all *the press is Lollie's business* and it means our means of living. And she has often other things to consider besides the literary excellence of a particular book. There are questions of convenience and commercial expedience and policy, matters for tactful consideration not to be decided offhand by a literary expert.' JBY suggested that his son ought to write a frank apology and then, having wondered if Yeats himself should resign his post as adviser, added a note saying that 'my own impression is that it would be best for all parties' if he did.

Lily maintained that Lollie and she stood their ground throughout such episodes, but this was not wholly true. A holiday down the Rhine in the middle of 1904 showed that the strain of running their business had caused Lollie to lapse into melancholia, the respite of a put-upon woman who could not stand intense worry and whose depressive temperament was of such concern to her father that he was sometimes concerned she might go mad. But, while JBY could do little, Lily braced herself to take on the responsibility for her sister, a responsibility she would shoulder for twenty years that were to be to her a 'torture'. She resolved that she would make no scenes, but this did not prevent an agonising inner dialogue. 'I said to myself she is incapable of realising what she is either saying or doing, but I also said to myself, "She is getting less and less sane, and she is gradually killing me." But again I thought, "I can do nothing as I have to live with her."' Meanwhile, their brother agitated for his proofs.

Yeats also had the business of his theatre to attend to and here his mask of authority would be particularly in evidence. While he was in America the company had put together a programme including Padraic Colum's *Broken Soil*. As a drama by a young working-class writer whose opinions of the peasantry clearly accorded with those of the Nationalists, the piece was well received. Yeats, who had turned down the first version of the work, was particularly pleased. Now, however, he found to his intense annoyance that while he had been away the Society had also been approached by Americans hoping they would perform at the 1904 St Louis Trade Fair. The actors themselves declined the invitation since it would have meant giving up their jobs, but the Americans then successfully approached the secessionists, who had quitted over the affair of *The Shadow of the Glen*, and Russell eventually gave these people permission to perform his *Deirdre*. A furious Yeats informed him that he had no right to give this and added that, since he considered a planned American tour of his own vital to the Society's finances, to send over plays performed by what he alleged were incompetent and disloyal actors was the height of folly. Tempers ran so high that Russell felt obliged to resign from the Society, and Yeats believed he was justified in accepting the resignation when the newspapers reported the failure of the Irish players in the United States.

But Yeats's own career in the theatre was not proceeding with undiminished success. While he had been in America the company had played with great success Synge's painfully emotional one-act play *Riders to the Sea*. Some of the audience were too moved even to applaud. A performance of the most recent version of *The Shadowy Waters* was far less enthusiastically greeted, however. As Synge wrote with chilling if unmalicious clarity: 'we had the "Shadowy Waters" on the stage last week, and it was the most *distressing* failure the mind can imagine – a half empty room, with growling men and tittering females'.[28] Synge then went on to explain his objections to the play. 'No drama can grow out of anything other than the fundamental realities of life which are never fantastic, are neither modern, nor unmodern, and as I see them rarely spring-dayish, or breezy or Cuchulainoid.' It was precisely this twilight world of the Nineties from which Yeats was trying to escape, and the revisions he made to *The Shadowy Waters* between now and 1907 suggest the heroic powers of self-criticism through which he refashioned his work, showing that in so doing 'it is myself that I remake'.

Such revisions were partly inspired by Yeats's deepening knowledge of stagecraft. His early insistence on seeing his work in performance in order to test its dramatic strengths and weaknesses was beginning to bear fruit. As he was to write in 1906: 'I have written a good many plays in verse and prose, and almost all those plays I have rewritten after performance, sometimes again and again, and every re-writing that has succeeded upon the stage has been an addition to the masculine element, an increase in strength of the bony structure.' This was an exacting and an exhausting process, and to follow Yeats's revisions in detail is to sympathise with his heartfelt outburst:

> My curse on plays
> That have to be set up in fifty ways. . . .[29]

Bare arithmetic shows how thorough this process could be.[30] The version of *The Shadowy Waters* Yeats issued in 1906 is some two hundred lines longer than the first but reuses merely forty lines of the original. On his return from America he told Frank Fay that he would not now write anything so remote and so impersonal as the first version of the play, and to search out its weaknesses he got it played again privately, and gave it to Florence Farr for a Theosophical convention in order that he might discover how to make a better play of it. He realised that the work must have bewildered and bored the greater portion of the audience and now, as he entered on his revisions, he resolved to make the groundwork simple and intelligible by highlighting the contrasts in his material. The sailors, 'lecherous with abstinence', become more comic and thus point up the contrast between vision and material desire. Aibric, the decent, ordinary man of action, becomes more personally involved in the moral dilemma posed by the struggle between the needs of his crew and the longings of his master, while Forgael is less of an imitation of a character out of Villiers de l'Isle-Adam or Maeterlinck, one of those 'faint souls, naked and pathetic shadows already half vapour . . . sighing to one another upon the borders of the last abyss'.

This new strength was achieved partly through a conscious change of style. The cloudy, figurative language of the Nineties was beginning to be replaced by an altogether more trenchant idiom. Once the sailors could ask, without any sense of the incongruous:

> How many moons have died from the full moon
> When something that was bearded like a goat
> Walked on the waters and bid Forgael seek
> His heart's desire where the world dwindles out?

The First Sailor of the revised version now asks:

> Has he not led us into these waste seas
> For long enough?

Doubts nonetheless remain about the success of these revisions as a whole. For all Yeats's striving to reshape, *The Shadowy Waters* remains a beautiful dream as remote from the stage as it is from life. As so often, Yeats was his own best critic. He confessed that in revising his play he had been obliged to learn an important lesson, namely:

> that all the finest poetry comes logically out of the fundamental action, and that the error of late periods like this is to believe that some things are inherently poetical, and to try and pull them on to the scene at every moment. It is just these seemingly inherently poetical things that wear out. My *Shadowy Waters* was full of them and the fundamental thinking was nothing, and that gave the whole poem an impression of weakness. There was no internal life pressing for expression through the characters.

Yeats's next work for the stage would show how much more conscious of the real needs of drama he had become and, as if to reinforce this, his new play would be presented in a new theatre, for Annie Horniman was now preparing to make her great public gesture.[31] In April 1904 she declared herself ready to take over the old Mechanics' Institute on Abbey Street and to use part of the £5000 she was prepared to advance for conversion and renovation, reserving the remainder for an annual subsidy. But the generosity of this was underscored by numerous problems. Support for a national theatre was coming from an English purse, Annie herself had an active dislike of Irish politics, while her prickly temperament was to create problems of its own. Difficulties immediately emerged when she took what in business terms was the sensible decision of refusing to allow sixpenny seats. This decision was reached because the actors, being amateurs, could perform for only one week a month and the building would therefore have to be rented out to other bodies for the rest of the time. Annie wished to ensure an adequate income from respectable uses which the presence of cheap seats might threaten, but the *United Irishman* immediately declared the move 'undemocratic' and 'unpatriotic'. Annie was accused of effectively barring the national theatre to the poorer members of the nation. The *Leader* thought she was plotting against the Gaelic League, while Maud Gonne MacBride told Yeats that many now considered him 'lost to nationalism' by his involvement in the decision.

There were difficulties too with acquiring a patent. The Lord Lieutenant was required to issue this only after an enquiry held by the Solicitor General. Other Dublin theatres opposed the application and, although a formula was eventually reached to minimise the degree of competition, because Annie Horniman herself was not an Irish resident the patent was applied for in Lady Gregory's name. Lady Gregory was later shrewdly to use this to her own advantage, but, despite her polite behaviour towards Annie at this time, it was clear she not only disliked being put under an obligation but nurtured an intense animus towards a woman she saw as a rival for her poet.

While Annie commissioned portrait sketches of Yeats, the Fays, the actress Maire nic Shiubhlaigh and herself from JBY to hang in the vestibule, work proceeded on the conversion, the ubiquitous Holloway, a practising architect, being in charge of the designs. The vestibule itself was lit by three stained-glass windows arranged by Sarah Purser to look like a tree in leaf. Steps led from here to the stalls, the pit and balcony, from where an audience of up to 562 people, sitting in scarlet leather seats, saw a proscenium arch twenty-one feet wide fronting a stage merely sixteen feet deep. Since the entirety of this depth was required for scenery, actors exiting on one side and re-entering on another had to dash round the lane at the back of the building. There was no scene-dock or wardrobe and, since there was not a workshop either, scenery had to be made on the stage, which inevitably caused problems while actors were trying to rehearse.

The conduct of Yeats in rehearsals was vividly recorded by Joseph

Holloway when, on the evening of 31 October 1904, he, Quinn and other favoured people were invited to watch Yeats at work. 'A more irritating play producer never directed a rehearsal,' Holloway wrote.[32] Yeats was for ever 'flitting about', interrupting actors in the middle of their speeches, 'showing them by illustration how he wishes it done, droningly reading the passage and that in monotonous preachy sing-song, or climbing up the ladder onto the stage and pacing the boards as he would have the players do'. The effect on the actors themselves can be readily imagined. 'Ever and always he was on the fidgets,' Holloway recorded, 'and made each and all of the players inwardly pray backwards. Frank Fay, I thought, would explode with suppressed rage at his frequent interruptions during the final speeches he had to utter.'

There were problems too with those not on the stage. George Moore, realising he had fallen away from a project now headed for success, tried to insinuate himself into favour with the Fays. Yeats would have none of it. With that talent for firmness and manipulation he was increasingly to show as affairs in the theatre grew more complex, Yeats wrote to Frank Fay that Moore's return to the theatre was out of the question. Then, having put his foot down, he cunningly added that among other reasons for this 'it is enough that he represents a rival tradition of the stage and would upset your brother's plans'. Yeats also considered it necessary to humiliate Annie Horniman, whose costume designs for Yeats's *On Baile's Strand* with which the theatre was to open were no more popular with the actors than her earlier efforts. On 16 November, and in the presence of the whole company, Yeats unrelentingly criticised her work. Annie may have paid for the theatre but she was not going to run it. As Yeats wrote to Lady Gregory: 'I am here, and for the moment at any rate master of the situation.'

On Baile's Strand reveals that Yeats was increasingly becoming the master of his new dramatic style. 'The first shape of it', he wrote of the play, 'came to me in a dream, but it changed much in the making, foreshadowing, it may be, a change that may bring a less dream-burdened will into my verses.' This was indeed the case. As the first version of 1903 (the version that was played at the opening of the Abbey Theatre) was reworked into the revised text of 1906, so the burden of dream was ever more completely purged until Yeats's heroic Cuchulain, loving, hating and fighting, is the antitype of his mystical Forgael drawn ever more obscurely from action to vision. *On Baile's Strand* offers a vivid Cuchulain who is at once a national symbol of the aristocratic heroic age, an embodiment of those ideals of Nietzsche's that Yeats was beginning to make his own, and a first essay too in a conception of the tragic hero which placed personality and passion at its core.

Personality, which Yeats distinguished from the comic elements of character, is that force which lies 'behind the momentary self, which acts and lives in the world, and is subject to the judgement of the world'. The tragic hero rises above the values of the many-too-many and reveals that 'which cannot be called before any mortal judgement seat'.[33] Exalted, inspired, noble in nature and purpose, the tragic figure is what 'a poet creates . . . from his own soul, that soul which is alike in all men. It has not joy, as we understand that word, but ecstasy, which is from the contemplation of things vaster than the individual and imperfectly seen, perhaps, by all those that still live'. Inevitably, such a figure is trapped and brought down by the world, but a heroic gesture made in defeat allows him to rise again to his moment of passionate intensity or 'tragic joy'.

Yeats's Cuchulain exemplifies this clearly. He is a type of the Celtic super-man dancing, hunting, quarrelling or love-making 'wherever and whenever I've a mind to'. Now, however, ageing himself, Cuchulain is obliged to face King Conchubar's world of the manipulative and the prudent. 'He ran too wild,' says one of the characters of the hero, 'and Conchubar is coming today to put an oath upon him that will stop his rambling and make him as biddable as a house-dog.' Cuchulain's first reaction to this suggests the abrasively sarcastic, domineering and haughty elements of the heroic character in which Yeats now took pleasure:

> And I must be obedient in all things;
> Give up my will to yours; go where you please;
> Come when you call; sit at the council-board
> Among the unshapely bodies of old men;
> I whose mere name has kept this country safe,
> I that in early days have driven out
> Maeve of Cruachan and the northern pirates,
> The hundred kings of Sorcha, and the kings
> Out of the Garden in the East of the World.
> Must I, that held you on the throne when all
> Had pulled you from it, swear obedience
> As if I were some cattle-raising king?[34]

Cuchulain and Conchubar, hero and pragmatist, the self and antiself, are brought together in a situation which fetters the heroic spirit and destroys the possibility of a heroic future by ensuring that Cuchulain slays his unrecognised and noble son. In the ecstasy of his anguish, Cuchulain goes out to fight with the sea. The waves overwhelm this last heroic gesture, and the world is left to the meanness of little people – the guileless Fool and the manipulative Blind Man whose thoughts can rise to nothing higher than planning petty theft.

The Abbey Theatre opened its doors to an audience for the first time on Tuesday, 27 December 1904, playing both Yeats's new work and *Cathleen ni Houlihan*, along with Lady Gregory's farce *Spreading the News*.[35] The house was full and the opening night was the most fashionable event of the year. Yeats, resplendent in evening dress, kept going back-stage to see how things were proceeding and, at the end of the evening, appeared in person to thank Miss Horniman for providing the actors with a building. She had, as Yeats suggested, done far more than this. She had given the Society the artistic freedom to ask, before putting on a play, '"Does it please *us?*" and not, until this was answered, the more usual question "Does it please *you?*"' Here indeed was artistic freedom unconstrained by a dominating concern with commerce. Four years later, Yeats was proudly to explain just what this meant. 'We are', he declared, 'the first subsidised theatre in any English-speaking country, the only theatre that is free for a certain number of years to play what it thinks worth playing, and to whistle at the timid.'

Their patent confined them to playing Irish plays on Irish subjects (foreign masterpieces were also allowed provided they were not English in origin), but this limitation they were determined to turn to their advantage. 'We are trying to put on the stage', Yeats explained, 'the life of this country, not a slavish copy of it as in a photograph, but a joyous, extravagant, imaginative image as in an impressionist painting.' This was, of course, the fulfilment of a long-treasured dream, but idealism of this order needed courage and, as Yeats addressed the Abbey audience on the theatre's first night, so he drew on the most revered of Anglo-Irish poets to declare that with Miss Horniman's help 'We will be able to be courageous, and can take as our mottoes those written over the three gates of the City of Love by Edmund Spenser – over the first gate was "Be bold", over the second "Be bold! Be bold! And Ever More Be Bold", and over the third "Be bold! And Yet Be Not Too Bold."'

Such courage would be needed, for audiences fell off drastically on the following nights and Joseph Holloway was minded to put a large part of the new theatre's difficulties down to the presence of Synge's work on the programme. *The Well of Saints*, first played on 4 February 1905, was a dark play whose repeated references to the deity disturbed the actors who performed it. The press was no more enthusiastic, wanting to believe that Synge was out of touch with those he wrote of and that his stage language was 'less Irish than Whitechapel Cockney'. Joseph Holloway put his finger on the nub of the difficulty, however. 'Making a jeer at religion and a mock at chastity may be good fun, but it won't do for Irish drama. If there are two things engrained in the Irish character above all else, they are their respect for all pertaining to their religious belief and the love of chastity, and these are the very subjects Mr Synge has chosen to exercise his wit upon.' Creating a modern national consciousness that was at once poetic and self-critical meant facing deep-seated moral inertia. In opening the doors of the Abbey Theatre, Yeats and his company had exposed themselves to the narrow-minded if sensitive prejudice Yeats himself so feared in the society about him. Soon he would be called upon to don the aggressive mask of the inspired Nietzschean superman defending the life-giving art he hoped to foster.

Meanwhile, at the close of 1905, Yeats began to develop a strategy whereby the loosely democratic organisation of the Society which George Russell had done much to promote would fall into what he considered safer pairs of hands and so enable the Abbey to become a fully professional organisation.[36] He and Lady Gregory proposed that the theatre should now be set up as a limited-liability company, votes being proportionate to shares that would be allocated rather than purchased. Yeats took a master tactician's pleasure in his powers of manipulation, writing to Quinn to say, 'I think we have seen an end of democracy in the theatre, which was Russell's doing, for I go to Dublin at the end of this week to preside at a meeting summoned to abolish it.' He nonetheless told Lady Gregory that they should 'leave as much as possible with Russell who now advocates everything we insisted upon'. Then, with something of machiavellian skill, Yeats arranged that the popular Russell should move the resolution which, as Yeats told Quinn, if all went well would see that 'Synge and Lady Gregory and I will have everything in our hands.' Things did indeed go well and Russell's motion was carried by fourteen votes to one. Control of the new company passed to the hands of its three principal playwrights, who were now empowered to appoint and remove stage manager, business manager and all other employees, fix their salaries and arrange their duites.

The move was extremely unpopular with a number of the leading players. Frank Fay sulked and wrote that 'since the Society turned into a limited company some weeks ago, things have not gone as smoothly as heretofore, and a big change in the personnel is likely to occur at any moment'. However, neither he, Maire nic Shiubhlaigh nor Sarah Allgood could leave right away since, just before the meeting that set up the limited-liability company, Annie Horniman announced she had decided to make an annual grant towards salaries, and each of these actors had given up their day jobs to accept her offer. Again, some reacted against this, lamenting the passing of the amateur ideal. But, for the moment, Yeats himself seemed safe. The theatre was in his hands and the best actors were tied by contracts. As he had told Florence Farr earlier, 'we have all the really competent people with us'. What he did not fully realise was that, by holding the new professional purse-strings, it was Annie Horniman who hoped to tighten them round the company in ways that she saw fit.

VI
Maud's Separation

The problems of the Abbey Theatre were not the only ones Yeats had to deal with at this time. With the rapid and distressing collapse of her marriage,

Maude Gonne MacBride turned to him for support.[37] The story she had to tell was one of consistent brutality. On Christmas Day 1903, MacBride had returned home with a friend drunk. A fight broke out between the two men, MacBride drew his revolver and, when Maud tried to intervene, he kicked her several times despite the fact that she was then heavily pregnant.

The child, Jean Seaghan (Sean) MacBride, was born on 26 January 1904, when Maud herself was thirty-seven. When she was strong enough she took the boy to Ireland to be baptised, returning to Paris in October, to face what she was thenceforth to call 'the hideous crash'. MacBride was still drinking heavily, and he and his friends assaulted the women of her household. MacBride himself raped Maud's ward and half-sister, Eileen, who was then speedily and forcibly married to MacBride's forty-three-year-old brother. Maud even hinted that MacBride had turned his attentions to her ten-year-old daughter Iseult. Though she knew that such a move would seriously damage her reputation, Maud felt she had no choice but to seek a separation. She tried at first to handle this in as discreet a manner as possible and asked a London lawyer recommended by Lady Gregory to draw up a separation agreement. But MacBride refused to sign this, and Maud was left with no option but to obtain a settlement through the courts. The case went before a French magistrate, who would hear the evidence *in camera*, but news of the proceedings inevitably leaked out to the press.

Yeats went to Paris to offer what support he could, but Maud's wretchedness disturbed him so greatly that he had to turn to Lady Gregory to relieve his feelings. 'I cannot bear the burden of this terrible case alone,' he confessed. 'I know nothing about lawyers and so on.' Maud's cousin suggested that Yeats contact Quinn to see what advice he could offer. The matter was, Yeats confessed, the most painful event he had ever had to deal with, and the cramped, ink-stained letter he wrote to Quinn indicates the degree of his pain. Quinn in his turn hired detectives in an effort to gather circumstantial evidence of MacBride's misconduct during his visit to New York, but the American-Irish, while sympathetic, closed ranks. Other friends were no more successful in helping. Even Annie Horniman was drawn in, offering to go to Westport to glean what information she could about MacBride's family and background. When she finally saw MacBride's brother, she wrote: 'he does not look a nice sort of person or rather not a pleasant character, but that without drinking would not be considered important'. And Annie could gather no hard facts about MacBride's alcoholism. The people of his birthplace closed ranks too, for MacBride was not only a local boy but a national hero.

When the Irish newspapers eventually started to print accounts of his problems, MacBride began a suit for libel. Distraught and jealous, he also accused Maud of adultery with all her male friends and even vowed to shoot Yeats, a threat Yeats himself managed to shrug off, telling Quinn that MacBride's words were as empty as his pistol. Maud's own difficulties meanwhile were compounded by the law's delay. 'In vain my lawyer tries to get MacBride's lawyer to fix the date for the final hearing,' she wrote to Yeats. MacBride himself was hoping to win his libel action against the *Independent* so that the trial and the verdict could not be reported in the English newspapers, she said, adding that there was no hope of a verdict before the middle of May. 'This waiting is most wearisome,' she continued and, while she waited, she had to reject MacBride's offer of an out-of-court settlement on the condition that she would withhold the most damning evidence against him and leave the question of the child to be arbitrated later. Maud's natural pride would not accept this, and she had to wait until August 1906 before the court finally granted a separation on the ground of MacBride's drunkenness rather than his alleged immorality. Applications for a full divorce were rejected with the argument that, in marrying an Irishman, Maud had taken on MacBride's legal status and, under Irish practice, could not be granted a civil divorce.

MacBride himself meanwhile was awarded visiting rights over his son and, with the lifting of the Coercion Laws against those the English considered trouble-makers, could now return safely to Ireland. Here he quickly made friends with the ageing and increasingly drunken John O'Leary, who had sided with him in the matter of Maud. The old Fenian was now a sad figure from a world which, as James Joyce wrote, had disappeared. Besides drink, only the dusty shelves of the second-hand booksellers seemed to offer O'Leary any delight. 'His plots had gone up in smoke, his friends had died, and in his own native land, very few knew who he was and what he had done.' In 1907 he died, his brand of nationalism now increasingly replaced by a new movement and a new leader: Sinn Fein and its powerful spokesman Arthur Griffith.

Although she had worked closely with Griffith, Maud herself was sometimes to find him 'too suspicious of people's motives', the great misfortune, she declared, of belonging to a conquered country which made its people grow 'narrow'. Quite how narrow was made embarrassingly clear at the end of October 1906 when Maud attended the opening night at the Abbey of Lady Gregory's *The Gaol Gate*. She entered, dressed in black, on Yeats's arm. Instantly a small group in the pit began to hiss loudly and call out 'Up, John MacBride!' Here was the woman they thought had tried to bring degradation on their national hero and had then compounded her villainy by the outrage of seeking a separation. Maud had deeply offended both popular nationalism and popular prejudice about a woman's role. Yeats's look of bewilderment deepened to an expression of gloom, but Maud herself remained smiling and unperturbed, and, as she retained her composure, 'a counter-hissing set up', drowning out the others as the young people in the audience especially realised that they were in the presence of a legend. Maud had already inspired Yeats's new play *Deirdre*, his drama on the greatest of

Irish heroines which would be performed the following month, and now she
appeared to her admirers as a woman 'alive to the last hair of her head'.

VII
The Playboy of the Western World

Dublin audiences were not always so readily appeased, however, and late
in 1906 the Abbey began work on a play potentially so inflammatory
that rehearsals were conducted in secret. Even the ubiquitous Holloway
could find out little about the work, although he 'pooh-poohed the idea'
that there would be organised opposition on the first night. He could
not have been more wrong. When fashionable Dublin crowded into the
theatre for the first night of Synge's *The Playboy of the Western World*,
booing and 'counter-applause' reached such a pitch that the close of the
work was drowned out.[38] Performances on succeeding nights were even
rowdier and Yeats, summoned by a telegram from Lady Gregory which
told him that 'Audience broke up at the word *shift*', hurried back from a
lecture engagement in Scotland to face the crisis in his theatre. Refusing
to give ground before an audience he knew to be motivated by prejudice
rather than aesthetic discrimination, he ordered that the run be continued
and, as commotion mounted to near riot, he and Lady Gregory requested
the presence of the police. This decision to call on the forces of Dublin Castle
to keep the peace in the nation's theatre was deeply resented not only as a
matter of principle but because the police themselves, out of their depth in
so delicate a situation, inflamed the position by such unfortunate actions as
arresting spectators who were trying to leave before the play was over. The
position was not improved when a gang of students from Trinity College
loudly struck up 'God Save the King' from the pit, and by then even the
players were involved in the disturbance.

An appalled Annie Horniman wrote: 'I am informed that low behaviour (I
mean hissing) took place from the stage, and that the hissing was political.
It must be absolutely understood that I will not allow my theatre to be used
for any political purpose whatever, and the players must be informed that
hissing the drunken vulgarity of the stalls is just as bad as the patriotic
vulgarity of the pit.' To Yeats, however, the issue was more importantly
one of free speech, and this he knew must be preserved at all costs
if Dublin and Ireland itself were to maintain even a semblance of an
adequately self-critical public life. When the loathed forces of the alien
English police ensured that the production of *The Playboy of the Western
World* was not brought to a stop, Yeats considered a public debate necessary
if public opinion were to be genuinely free. A meeting was scheduled at the

Abbey for Monday, 4 February 1907. Yeats and Lady Gregory shrewdly charged admission to this, making a profit of £16 but, more shrewdly yet, guessed they were organising an event which would ensure that the world's press, already informing its readers of the fracas, would now carry the fame of the Abbey to the ends of the earth.

They took a gamble on the fact that partisan opinion in Ireland would stand self-exposed in all its narrowness, for *The Playboy of the Western World* is to freer minds a comedy at once extravagant and perceptive in its exposure of lives struggling with the prejudices that blight them. Christie Mahon, the youthful peasant hero of the piece, focusses these aspects of the play. Condemned by his father to marriage with an older woman, he flees to Mayo where, claiming he has killed his father, he briefly enjoys a hero's reputation amid the apparently feisty life about him. Both Pegeen Mike, the publican's daughter, and the wonderfully characterised Widow Quinn are attracted to him, and their rivalry is about to reach a climax when Christie's father, heavily bandaged but very much alive, suddenly appears among them. The moment is a remarkable *coup de théâtre* in which high comedy turns shiveringly to realism as Christie tries once again to kill his father before the now horrified peasant community. He is tied up, discredited and forced to return home where, for all his boasting, he is clearly doomed to the most ordinary of lives while the women he has intrigued return to similarly joyless days and empty dreams.

The objections of the Dublin audience were, as usual, not to the pathos of the life exposed but to the play's alleged profanity and blasphemy.[40] Above all, they believed that the drama was 'an outrageous insult to the West of Ireland and its people'. Underlying such objections was the old prejudice of a repressed nation: its belief in its unassailable moral superiority. As the *Irish Times* observed, the rioters 'founded their objections on a theory of Celtic impeccability which is absurd in principle, and intolerable, when it is sought to be rigidly imposed as a canon of art'. The directors of the Abbey had sought to free themselves and their public from the tyranny of the 'stage Irishman' but, in his place, the audience was baying for 'the pulpit Irishman' and that narrowness of outlook which could be offended by the mere mention of a woman's 'shift'.

Grumbling stagehands condemned Synge as 'a bloody old snot' for using the word, while even the articulate Holloway felt obliged to write in his journal that '*The Playboy* is not a truthful or just picture of the Irish peasants, but simply the outpouring of a morbid, unhealthy mind ever seeking in the dunghill of life for the nastiness that lies concealed there.' Arthur Griffith was predictably outraged, snarling from the pages of *Sinn Fein* that 'this story of unnatural murder and unnatural lust, told in foul language, was told under the protection of a body of police, and concluded to the strains of "God Save the King"'. It seemed that decadents had set up what was supposed to be a national institution and confirmed their presence by summoning the police. It was in vain that Synge, now mortally ill with cancer and normally so reticent in public affairs, wrote to the press in his own defence. He was perfectly clear about the real causes of the attack on his work. He had restored sex to its proper place on the stage, but a prurient audience 'was so surprised they saw the sex only'.

The Dublin audience has been easily condemned for this. Though *The Playboy of the Western World* may seem innocuous now it was, at the time and in the circumstances, one of those advanced works of the century which had to create the audience that would appreciate it. Nor were the production values in the first staging such as to bring out the full range of contrast in the piece. Much of the comedy was lost in what was probably a nervous concern to render the work's realism. The *Leader* described William Fay's Christie as 'a broken-down evil-looking tramp,' and James Joyce, comparing a later production to the first, believed that Fay had presented a much more repulsive and realistic type than Synge had intended. Nor was the arrival of old Mahon the *coup de théâtre* it should have been. When Michael James, the actor playing the role, appeared, 'there stood a man with horribly bloodied bandage about his head, making a figure that took the whole thing out of the atmosphere of high comedy'. As Maire nic Shiubhlaigh wisely observed of *The Playboy*: 'when it was given on the first night it was played seriously, almost sombrely, as though each character had been studied and its nastiness made apparent'. Such production values were bound to offend at the cost of the text itself being fairly evaluated. As one member of that first-night audience later declared, he and his rowdy fellows 'were living, it should be remembered, in 1907, unconditioned to excess in speech and action'.

An immediate and vigorous defence was imperative, and Yeats mounted the stage of the Abbey on 4 February in full evening dress. He had already made clear what he considered the issues involved in his public announce-ment of the meeting a week earlier. 'We have put this play before you to be heard and to be judged, as every play should be heard and judged. Every man has a right to hear it and condemn it if he pleases. But no man has a right to interfere with another man hearing a play and judging for himself.'[41] No man had a right either to dictate to an author what his subject matter should be.

> We have claimed for our writers their freedom to find in their own land every expression of good and evil necessary to their art, for Irish life contains, like all vigorous life, the seeds of all good and evil, and a writer must be free here as elsewhere to ripen weed or flower, as the fancy takes him. No one who knows the work of our Theatre as a whole can say we have neglected the flower; but the moment a writer is forbidden to show the weed without the flower, his art loses energy and abundance.

Having put the argument for aesthetic liberty, Yeats then made clear in an interview the relation of this to national well-being. He was now prepared to state categorically where he thought the enemies of high endeavour skulked.

> When I was a lad, Irishmen obeyed a few leaders, but during the last ten years a change has taken place. Organised opinions of sections and coteries has been put in place of these leaders, one or two of whom were men of genius. Instead of a Parnell, or a Stephens, or a Butt, we must obey the demands of commonplace or ignorant people, who try to take on an appearance of strength by imposing some crude shibboleth on their own and others' necks. They do not persuade, for that is difficult; they do not expound, for that needs knowledge.[42]

This is the refusal of a Cuchulain to bow to weaker men, and 'the country that condescends either to bully or permit itself to be bullied', Yeats declared, 'soon ceases to have any fine qualities.'

Now, on the stage of the Abbey and with a mastery of the situation which showed both his courage and his frank relish of controversy, Yeats announced himself to the audience of his enemies. 'The author of *Cathleen ni Houlihan* addresses you.' Yeats presented himself as the most patriotic of playwrights, and his defiance still has its power to stir and command attention. For a few moments his words silenced a rowdy audience 'with denunciatory speeches ready to deliver' and allowed Yeats himself to interpret Synge's work and explain his own theories of the theatre. JBY was beside him, 'his beautiful mischievous head thrown back,' and what his son gave in passion he gave in wit.[43] JBY knew that Ireland was a Land of Saints, he declared to cheers, 'a land of Plaster Saints', he added to groans. He asserted that Synge's peasant was a real, vigorous, vital man, although a sinner, an insight drowned in uproar when he added that 'unfortunately in this country people cannot live or die except behind a curtain of deceit'. Even his son insisted that he sit down after this, just as he also insisted that a couple of the theatre staff escort some female students to the stalls when an angry young man mounted the stage and made comments that caused the other women in the audience to leave.

Yeats made his own position ringingly and publicly clear:

> Gentlemen of the little clubs and societies, do not mistake the meaning of our victory; it means something for us, but more for you. When the curtain of *The Playboy* fell on Saturday night in the midst of what *The Sunday Independent* – no friendly witness – described as 'thunders of applause', I am confident that I saw the rise in this country of a new thought, a new opinion, that we had long needed. It was not at all approval of Mr Synge's play that sent the receipts of the Abbey Theatre this last week to twice the height they had ever touched before.

The generation of young men and girls who are now leaving schools and colleges are weary of the tyranny of clubs and leagues. They wish again for individual sincerity, the eternal quest of truth, all that has been given up for so long that all might crouch upon the one roost or quack and cry in the one flock. We are beginning to ask once again what a man is, and to be content to wait a little before we go on to ask that further question: What is a good Irishman?[44]

Here is a plea not for a narrow Ireland but for a broader humanity. Yeats joyed and triumphed in the public ferocity of this appeal, permanently impressing many. 'I never witnessed a human being fight as Yeats fought that night,' wrote Mary Colum in her 'Memories of Yeats', 'nor knew another with so many weapons in his armoury.' The triumph of Yeats's 'manly pose' had been asserted and he had given his public definition of his new poise of mind, his new beliefs. 'Manhood is all,' he declared, 'and the root of manhood is courage and courtesy'. It was with such patrician values that he would now outface the narrow standards of the 'mob' and hold down the violent contempt roaring in his heart.

9

The Gifts That Govern Men
(1907–1910)

I
'A Tower of the Apennines'

In May 1907 Yeats, Lady Gregory and her newly engaged son Robert made a trip to Italy, visiting Florence, Urbino, Ferrara, Ravenna and Milan. The visit was to have a profound effect on Yeats, revealing to him not only the hieratic beauty of the Byzantine mosaics preserved in the churches of Ravenna, but the achievements of renaissance patronage fostered by the Medicis in Florence, by Duke Ercole in Ferrara, and most suggestively of all by the Montefeltro family in Urbino. This last, a small and melancholy town perched on its 'windy hill' and dominated by the palace where Castiglione taught Europe its manners, became for Yeats an image of the aristocratic life that was to enter deeply into his thought, giving to his exaltation of Nietzsche's superman the style and self-possession of the courtier. Two prose works from this time – the essay 'Poetry and Tradition' and the pieces collected under the title *Discoveries* – show Yeats absorbing and recreating this aristocratic ethos in terms of his own needs.[1]

The death of John O'Leary and the *Playboy* riots in the weeks before Yeats's departure had revealed to him, he thought, the rectitude Ireland had lost and the less than heroic values that now appeared to replace it. Grief and contempt mingled in his mind, and 'Poetry and Tradition' opens with a lament for the cultured, patrician standards Yeats believed O'Leary and his friend John Taylor (who had also recently died) once embodied. 'They were the last to speak of an understanding of life and Nationality, built up by the generation of Grattan, which read Homer and Virgil, and the generation of Davis, which had been pierced through by the idealism of Mazzini.' That kind of radical and aristocratic feeling for the cause of Ireland, the stoicism which forbade O'Leary ever to describe the hardship of his prison years, appeared with his death as a thing of the past, a lost embodiment of the ideal which had once inspired Yeats and his generation 'to forge in Ireland a new sword on our traditional anvil for that great battle that must in the end re-establish the old, confident, joyous world'.

In the place of such moral assurance Yeats increasingly believed there shuffled a generation which, reading the newspapers rather than the classics and taking their opinions from leader-writers rather than from leaders of men, were content with the unexceptional. The butt of his contempt was what he saw as 'a new class', the Dublin petty-bourgeoisie, the 'mob' Yeats's disdain came close to abusing as he savaged what he considered the levelling and joyless mediocrity around him. Lamenting the change that had come about, he wrote that, with the demise of Parnell, 'power passed to small shop-keepers, to clerks, to that very class who had seemed to John O'Leary so ready to bend to the power of others, to men who had risen above the traditions of the countryman, without learning those of cultivated life or even educating themselves, and who because of their poverty, their ignorance, their superstitious piety, are much subject to all kinds of fear'. Here once again is the horrified recoil from Nietzsche's 'herd', the 'many-too-many', timidly encumbered as they appeared to be with a penny-pinching materialism, a demeaning spiritual life and an urban anonymity unredeemed by even an aspiration to a better existence. Seen by Yeats in terms of bludgeoning generalisations, these people embodied the belief tersely expressed by Kierkegaard (whom Yeats had not read) that the crowd is the lie.

Against this dystopic vision Yeats increasingly set a cultured and intellectual elitism – a belief that value lay in beautiful things – which was at once traditionalist, self-consciously contrived and rooted in irrationalism and doctrines of the will. In this he drew on a range of contemporary prejudices to create his own. 'Three types of men made all beautiful things,' he declared. 'Aristocracies have made beautiful manners, because their place in the world puts them above the fear of life, and the countrymen have made beautiful stories and beliefs, because they have nothing to lose and so do not fear, and the artists who have made all the rest, because Providence has filled them with recklessness.' The archetypes of Yeats's social thought stand revealed and show they belong to the peripheries and the past, to Sligo and renaissance Italy. 'If we would find a company of our own way of thinking,' he wrote, 'we must go backward to turreted walls, to Courts, to high rocky places, to little walled towns, to jesters like that jester of Charles V who made mirth out of his own death; to the Duke Guidobaldo in his sickness, or Duke Frederick in his strength, to all those who understood that life is not lived, if not lived for contemplation or excitement.'

Yeats's exaltation of the aristocratic ideal contains a number of elements that became central to his art. Among the most important of these was a belief in style. The quality Yeats had defined to Russell as the morality of literature now becomes the expression of 'high breeding in words and argument', the revelation of a freedom and force which delights in its power to shape, to give clarity and sophisticated pleasure. The elements of ornament and artifice have an especially important place in 'Poetry and Tradition', for Yeats believed they were an essentially aristocratic abundance far removed from the narrow parsimony of the herd. In late September 1906, Yeats had been reading Donne and the Jacobean dramatists and he clearly took pleasure in their highly wrought contrivance. 'It is in the arrangement of events as in the words,' he wrote, 'and in that touch of extravagance, of irony, of surprise, which is set there after the desire of logic has been satisfied and all that is merely necessary established, and that leaves one, not in the circling necessity, but caught up in the freedom of self-delight.'

Such display was not mere ornamentation, for Yeats saw it as having a moral dimension by which refined delight rounded out the expression of pain to 'tragic joy'. Shakespeare was his chief exemplar of this. 'Shakespeare's persons, when the last darkness has gathered about them,' Yeats wrote, 'speak out of an ecstasy that is one-half the self-surrender of sorrow, and one-half the last playing and mockery of the victorious sword before the defeated world.' Energy and artistry in anguish provide a passion that is never merely self-pity. 'Timon of Athens contemplates his own end, and orders his tomb by the beached verge of the salt flood, and Cleopatra sets the asp to her bosom, and their words move us because their sorrow is not their own at tomb or asp, but for all men's fate.' Such characters attain a universal status because 'shaping joy has kept the sorrow pure'. As Yeats began to deepen his view of tragedy, so the aristocratic nature of artifice created for him that play of contraries, that turbulent energy and stillness, that intersection of the mortal with the immortal, which is where the 'red rose opens at the meeting of the two beams of the cross'. Great tragic art, in other words, is at one with the occult mysteries that unite man to the eternal.

Such qualities are seen as being in direct contrast to what Yeats now felt was the questionable thinness and subjectivity of the Nineties, a twilight poetry that 'drove shadowy young men through the shadows of death and battle'. The merely contemplative was no longer enough for it led to 'the sensuous images through which it speaks,' becoming 'broken, fleeting, uncertain'. Apollonian sunlight and what Yeats was to see as an aristocratic vitalism became imperatives and led him to re-evaluate his own experience. He realised, for example, how he had misinterpreted his meeting with Verlaine. He had been at the time, he now thought, 'interested in nothing but states of mind, lyrical moments, intellectual essences'. He was the poet of *The Rose* and *The Wind among the Reeds*. Only when he had moved beyond this search for something outside himself could he appreciate Verlaine's dictum that a poet should hide nothing of himself and could appreciate how 'it was this feeling for his own personality, his delight in singing his own life, even more than that life itself, which made the generation I belong to compare him to Villon'.

In a similar way, the subjective images of decadence were also to be avoided, and Yeats's drug experiences with the Parisian Saint-Martinists are rediscovered and rejected now. Baudelaire's artificial paradises, Rimbaud's 'disordering of all the senses', collapse less in contempt than in disappointment at what such excess achieves. While those about him in Paris deluded themselves into thinking they had seen God, 'I never forgot myself, never really rose above myself for more than a moment and was even able to feel the absurdity of that gaiety.' And, while aristocratic passion and *élan* disintegrate the folly of decadence, they also wither the tame rationalism of the materialistic imagination and its most baleful expression, 'the play about modern educated people'. This was a genre Yeats condemned, as always, for its inherent weaknesses of feeling, its workaday, lifeless falsity. 'Except where it is superficial or deliberately argumentative', such work 'fills one's soul with a sense of commonness as with dust. It has one mortal ailment. It cannot become impassioned, that is to say vital, without making somebody gushing and sentimental.'

What underlies these comments is a new emphasis on personality, passion and energy. This stemmed in part from Yeats's interest in Nietzsche and in part from those aspects of Blake that had not been so prominent before, the Blake who taught that 'energy is eternal delight and is of the body'. 'Art bids us touch and taste and hear and see the world,' Yeats wrote, 'and shrinks from what Blake calls mathematic form, from every abstract thing, from all that is of the brain only, from all that is not a fountain jetting from the entire hopes, memories, and sensations of the body.' Such euphoria, because it was, as Yeats believed, a fundamental human fact, was not at its extreme purely personal and contemporary. Rather was it part of traditional life. 'Emotion', he wrote, 'grows intoxicating and delightful after it has been enriched by the memory of old emotions, with all the uncounted flavours of old experience; and it is necessarily some antiquity of thought, emotions that have been deepened by the experiences of many men of genius, that distinguishes the cultivated man.' Such an aristocracy of feeling relies on and constantly reanimates received images of its own delight, an art which is at once a discipline and an ecstasy which 'approved before all men those that talked or wrestled or tilted under the walls of Urbino or sat in those great window-seats discussing all things, with love ever in their thought, when the wise Duchess ordered all, and the Lady Emilia gave the theme'. Castiglione's courtier becomes a measure of those who can appreciate the energy and passion of creation.

But the alluring surface of a cultivated minority must not be confused with the entire substance of society, for in Yeats's new aesthetic it was not the mind but the instincts that were sovereign, and these the aristocrat and the artist had in common with the peasant. The aristocrat displays instinct in his freedom from inhibition, while the artist knows it is the foundation of his craft. 'We cannot discover our subject-matter by deliberate intellect,' Yeats wrote in *Discoveries*, 'for when a subject-matter ceases to move us we must go elsewhere.' Again, 'it is our instinct and not our intellect that chooses', he declared and, in so doing, placed himself in the mainstream of one of the fundamental developments of his time. A subordination of deliberate reasoning to the instinctive, the vital, the intuitive and the unconscious – what some called 'the new spiritualism' – was a widely spread interest in the first half of the century and was a way of trying to show the confluence of emotion, thought and action. Yeats himself described this as 'blood, imagination, intellect running together'. And, if this was the foundation of the aristocrat, it was also the virtue of the peasant and the means by which the artist could speak for both.

In this period of revision, Yeats believed that the instinctual drives of the artist might lead him in either of two opposed directions. He could develop 'upward into ever-growing subtlety' or 'downward, taking the soul with us until all is simplified and solidified again'. In Nietzschean terms, this was the choice between the opposing ecstasies of Dionysus and Apollo, and, by choosing Apollo, Yeats believed he could speak for ordinary people, or at least that small number of 'vigorous and simple men' who might be willing to share his vision. 'What moves natural men in the arts', he declared, 'is what moves them in life, and that is intensity of personal life.'

It followed from this, Yeats believed, that complex and sophisticated narrative should be avoided since it threatened the desired simplicity of character and incident. 'The lovers and fighters of old imaginative literature are more vivid experiences in themselves than anything but one's own ruling passion,' he wrote. Malory's Lancelot left a more enduring impression than Tolstoy's Prince Andrei, and Yeats came now to believe that 'the common heart will always love better the tales that have something of an old wife's tale and look upon their hero from every side as if he alone were wonderful, as a child does with a new penny'. One model of the narrator becomes the peasant telling tales of the Great Famine and elaborating them with extravagance and passion; another was those peasant women of Howth recreating for his mother tales 'Homer might have told'. Such narratives, Yeats believed, touch what is eternal, traditional and life-enhancing.

Such stories also offered a world in which the most developed apprehension of the spiritual (or, at least, the supernatural) is at one with the environment from which they spring. They also had about them an awareness of the emotions united each to each by a traditional ordering of their images. It is this quality that some of the greatest poets of the immediate past had lost. Writing of Shelley and, more particularly of that exhilarating masterpiece of synthesis that is Yeats's essay 'The Philosophy of Shelley's Poetry', Yeats himself declared: 'I only made my pleasure in him contented pleasure by massing in my imagination his recurring images of towers and rivers, and caves with fountains in them, and that one Star of his, till his world had grown solid underfoot and consistent enough for the soul's habitation.' The ideal teller of the ideal story is not now a nineteenth-century romantic but a Homer or a Hesiod, for 'a man of that unbroken day could have all the subtlety of Shelley, and yet use no image unknown among the common people, and speak no thought that was not a deduction from common thought'.

Yeats was seeking an image of the artist that was both aristocratic and populist, a form of poetry that would unite his art to his evolving nationalism and his concern with the menace of vulgarity especially. It was entirely typical that he should have also envisioned the fusion of aristocrat and peasant in terms of his third great preoccupation – the occult. Alchemy in particular had shown him that this merging of opposites, the *mysterium coniunctionis*, was the means whereby a man might discover the Philosopher's Stone. The image Yeats had once applied to his mystic marriage with Maud Gonne was now transferred to the union of noble and peasant in the hope that the art which might arise from it would produce a national panacea. As Yeats was to write in a curiously beautiful passage published in *Explorations*: 'to lunar influence belong all thoughts and emotions that were created by the community'. They had, in other words, that ideal simplicity Yeats had sought when, troubled by the sophistication of his art, he had evoked the moon in a secret room above Edward Martyn's chapel. From solar influence, by contrast, derive all those thoughts and emotions 'that come from the high disciplined or individual kingly mind'. The imagination of the true poet was the alembic and marriage-bed where these opposites could combine in occult union. As Yeats wrote: 'I myself imagine a marriage of the sun and moon in the arts I take most pleasure in; and now bride and bridegroom but exchange, as it were, full cups of gold and silver, and now they are one in a mystical embrace.'

In being able to hold the ear of his audience in this quasi-magical way, Yeats's ideal Nationalist poet showed himself not as a seeker after cosmopolitan truth – liberal, pluralist, eclectic – but as a soil-conscious man who believed that the earth of his native country provided him with the compass of his imaginings. At once superman and courtier, patrician and reverer of the folk, driven by blood, instinct and race, he was the figure who taught that 'a man should find his Holy Land where he first crept upon the floor, and that familiar woods and rivers should fade into symbol with so gradual a change that he may never discover, no, not even in ecstasy itself, that he is beyond space, and that time alone keeps him from Primum Mobile, Supernal Eden, Yellow Rose over all'. By the close of the first third of the twentieth century, such extreme aesthetic nationalism was to clothe itself in a variety of ugly uniforms, but it was Yeats's view that its singer should be especially conscious of his mask. A passage in

Discoveries called 'A Tower of the Apennines' provides an interesting image of this.[2]

Yeats describes himself walking towards Urbino, his friends following some way behind in a carriage. 'I was alone amid a visionary, fantastic, impossible scenery,' he wrote. It was sunset and the clouds above the mountains were pregnant with storm. Yeats glimpsed a solitary medieval tower and 'suddenly in the mind's eye an old man, erect and a little gaunt, standing in the door of the tower'. The image penetrated so deeply as to re-emerge in Yeats's mature work to give him what he here describes as his vision of his archetypal poet, the man 'who had at last, because he had done so much for the word's sake, come to share the dignity of the saint'. In his devotion to perfection of form, sought only for its own justification 'or for a woman's praise', the old man has achieved that perfection of body and mind which looks out 'as from behind a mask' or the image of his carefully fashioned artistic completeness.

II

Exit Annie Horniman

If the mask was a means of aesthetic fulfilment, for Yeats the public figure it was also a way of joining his subjective self to a concept of the 'normal active man'. It was a form of self-defence, an aggressive protection from the onslaughts of the world. He had already shown the power of this when confronting the audience that booed *The Playboy of the Western World*, and now, in the acrimonious circles of the Abbey Theatre, donning a mask was to become increasingly necessary.

There were troubles with nearly all of those involved. After Maire nic Shiubhlaigh had signed her contract, for example, her brother rejected an offer of fifteen shillings a week, finding it insultingly small. Maire then discovered that Sarah Allgood was to be promoted to the company's chief actress. When she protested to Yeats she was so severely upbraided, she announced her resignation and sought protection at the hands of John Butler Yeats. Yeats himself threatened to sue for breach of contract and, although he never did so, he regarded Maire's defection with haughty superiority. 'I desire the love of a very few people,' he assured Russell, 'my equals or my superiors. The love of the rest would be a bond and an intrusion.'[3] Other defecting actors then insisted that, as members of the Fays' original group, it was their right to use the name of the Irish National Theatre Society. Yeats carefully marshalled his forces, won the vote at the committee, and let those who wished to secede go off to found the Theatre of Ireland under Edward Martyn. Meanwhile, both Yeats's sales and attendance at the Abbey suffered. The actors found they were playing to nearly empty houses while Yeats's championship of Synge led to the situation where certain people (both in the press and in public) were exalting Synge at his expense. 'The unbaked and doughy youth, semi-educated people who had no standard of comparison, proclaimed Synge to be the master-spirit of the Irish movement'.

In addition, Annie Horniman, as Yeats saw it, continued to meddle ever more keenly in the affairs of the Abbey. Although Yeats himself thought their £400 a year subsidy from Annie would greatly assist the independence of the theatre, Annie had developed an intense dislike for Willie Fay especially. She believed that he exercised inadequate discipline over the company and chided him about rumours of how actresses had talked 'with intoxicated men out of the railway carriage window', and adjusted their hair on station platforms. Willie Fay angrily rejected what she had to say, and Annie wrote to Yeats pointing out that, 'as things stand now, I am in the position of having been told not to interfere in a matter which I am financing'.4

There was much justice in this complaint. Annie was, after all, spending nearly half her annual income on subsidising the Theatre and she was greatly hurt by the fact that 'no one seems to guess the simple fact – that I care for dramatic art'. Although, as she confessed, 'all my pleasure in the scheme was destroyed before the building was first opened', Annie was 'determined not to let my feelings stop my actions'. She was still the *Fortiter et Recte* of the Golden Dawn days, and she wrote to Yeats trying to explain this. 'You often say that I act "by the book" or "by a rule",' she opined. 'I only try honestly to act uprightly, partly because of my own feeling of self-respect. I don't care about money for itself but I have a great sense of responsibility & just because of that strong feeling I will not be really foolish even in regard to small sums.' But she knew this attitude made her unpopular. 'Do what I might,' she wrote, 'I have always felt myself to be an outsider among you & it was a very painful position to be in.' An exasperated Yeats wrote to Florence Farr saying that he had had a bad time with Miss Horniman, whose moon was 'always at the full of late'. Eventually he began to disregard her letters with an arrogance Annie herself thought due to the influence of John Quinn. 'Ever since you were so much with Mr Quinn in America you have got into the way of trying to avoid what you don't like by simply ignoring what is said or written,' she declared.

JBY also realised that much of Yeats's superior behaviour derived from his new interest in Nietzsche and wrote to him condemning this. 'As you have dropped affection from the circle of your needs, have you also dropped love between man and woman? Is this the theory of the overman? If so your demigodship is after all but a doctrinaire demi godship.'5 Yeats, whose annotations in his copies of Nietzsche suggest that he was aware of the philosopher's lack of generosity, responded merely by criticising the quality of the books produced by his sister's press and eventually, in exasperation, resigned. That he was leaving his sisters to an unhappy life was made clear in a letter from his father. 'At present Lily and Lollie only see that they have to work very hard at a dull and slavish kind of work and that they get very little reward for what they do, and possibly or probably after all it may end in ghastly failure.' JBY then drew a pointed contrast between their lives and Yeats's own. 'They see that you live very pleasantly, doing work that is your choice, getting plenty of public and private consideration, everyone anxious to help and make smooth your path.' But Yeats refused to be touched by so humane an appeal.

He and Lady Gregory meanwhile were becoming increasingly dominant in the Abbey's business. Synge had not only fallen in love with an actress whom he believed his fellow directors disapproved of, but was now ill with the lymphatic cancer that would eventually kill him. He also felt he was being deliberately outmanoeuvred. When an American impresario came to Dublin, for example, the man was shown several of Yeats's plays and some half-dozen of Lady Gregory's, but only one of Synge's. Synge was upset and said he might withdraw from the Theatre altogether if it could be proved he was being unfairly treated. He recognised he owed a great deal to Yeats and Lady Gregory, but he threatened to resign again when *The Playboy of the Western World* was withdrawn from the Abbey's programme playing in Birmingham. But, if Lady Gregory was keen to promote Yeats's work over that of his fellow dramatist, she nonetheless regarded his 'subservience' to Annie Horniman as disgraceful. There was a nasty incident when Annie Horniman accused Yeats of cheating with the Theatre's accounts. The letter of complaint arrived at Coole, and Lady Gregory insisted that Yeats either reply to it at once or leave the house. He dictated Annie Horniman a response, but when he signed the letter in Lady Gregory's presence he looked so wretched she decided not to send it.

Annie Horniman still had considerable influence over Yeats, however. At the end of 1906, he sent Synge and Lady Gregory a long report in which he suggested that the Abbey should, as he knew Annie wished, be modelled after the Continental pattern of a National Theatre. He outlined the possibility of creating a wide programme not simply of plays but of training for the actors and the adoption of a repertory system that would include more foreign masterpieces. But the tide was moving against Annie. Lady Gregory saw no possibility of any workable arrangement with her, and acrimony between the two women began to mount. Annie was, Lady Gregory declared, 'like a shilling in a tub of electrified water – everybody tries to get the shilling out'. Lady Gregory was determined nonetheless that Annie's English money should not buy her victory.[6] 'We have the plays & players,' she told Synge. It was essential that Yeats especially did not surrender these. If he did, she warned, 'you will have given Miss Horniman one of our strongest possessions of weapons'. Then she added significantly: 'these plays were our children'. For her part, Annie now thought it necessary to add Lady Gregory to her 'list of truly wicked people'.

Early in 1906 Annie was left a further legacy. Her father died leaving her £25,000, which, since she had not spoken to him for many years after his second marriage, she was determined to spend on the charitable cause of drama rather than on herself. She wrote repeatedly to Yeats inviting him to join her on trips abroad, but he declined to go. She also offered his publishers a guarantee of £1500 towards his *Collected Works*, which were to be issued by the Shakespeare Head Press in eight volumes, and this he accepted.

So comprehensive a review of his entire output was a stressful undertaking, for Yeats himself felt there was much in his past work that was immature and could damage his reputation. More distressing still, revising his past work underlined how far his labours for the Abbey had taken him from the exercise of his lyric genius. Yeats's letters and journals from these years are full of references to his fear that his abilities were being squandered, spread too thin. He often wondered if his talent would ever recover from the heterogeneous labour of these last few years. 'I cry out vainly for liberty and have ever less and less inner life.'[7] He recognised too that there was something self-deceiving in all this work and feared that it was a way of shirking his responsibilities to his art. 'Evil', he wrote, 'comes to us men of imagination wearing as its mask all the virtues.' He had already confessed publicly to a sense of disappointment at what he considered so slight a lyric *oeuvre*. 'It seems to me very little to have been so long about.' Now, unable to add significantly to it, his creativity expressed itself not in new poems but in refashioning his old work. 'Whatever happens I must go on that there may be a man behind the lines already written; I cast the die long ago and must be true to the cast.' The labour he expended in this pursuit was considerable and, realising how powerfully such efforts complemented his refashioning of his public persona, he anticipated the objections of readers such as George Russell by declaring:

> The friends that have it I do wrong
> Whenever I remake a song
> Should know what issue is at stake:
> It is myself that I remake.

Yeats spent much of 1907 working on this project, taking time off from the Abbey to complete it. Annie herself had provided Yeats's publishers with the guarantee partly so he could show his 'twittering imitators in Ireland' his real merit, but snarling Dublin chose to gossip about Yeats being finished as a poet. In addition to such unpleasantness, there were difficulties with his publisher and problems about the portraits that were to adorn the volumes. Not all of these were to Yeats's liking. Sargeant made him into 'a charming aerial sort of thing', which Yeats did not object to, but, while Charles Shannon made him look 'damnably like Keats' and Mancini gave him a Latin air, Augustus John produced a repulsive image which made Yeats look like a gypsy, unwashed and unshaven, 'a melancholy English bohemian, capable of everything except living joyously on the surface'.* The publication of the volumes was a powerful contradiction of such a view and, with the death of Swinburne in 1909, Yeats's position as the supreme contemporary poet in the English language was assured. Meeting his sister in the street on the day the older poet's demise was announced, he stopped her to say, 'I am the King of the Cats.'[8]

The eight volumes of the *Collected Works* with their gold lettering and grey covers are a beautiful production, but they inevitably set jealous Dublin tongues wagging. George Moore caught the tone of this accurately when he wrote that 'if we were not really sorry that Yeats's inspiration was declining, we were quite genuinely interested to discover the cause of it. All his best poems, AE said, were written before he went to London . . . AE was certain that he would have written volume after volume if he had never sought a style, if he had been content to write simply.'[9]

But, while Annie Horniman had helped subsidise the prestigious publication that enabled Yeats's rivals to say this, she realised that if she were going finally to get Yeats himself she would have to act decisively. She now announced that she would, as was her right, discontinue the subsidy to the Abbey after its initial time was up at the end of December 1910. Having thus threatened the existence of his theatre, she then begged Yeats to abandon Dublin for Manchester, where she was proposing to found a new company, telling him that Irish audiences did not appreciate his work. 'You and I', she wrote of the Abbey, 'tried to make it an Art theatre and we had not the living material to do it with. Your genius and my money together were helpless. We must both keep our promises uprightly, but we must not waste our gifts, we have no right to do so.'[10] Annie's anti-Irish feelings became strident. 'They sacrifice you and your work and keep you a bond-slave to them because you are "touched" by that vampire Kathleen ni Houlihan,' she wrote. She also accused Yeats of being 'victimised' by Lady Gregory. He was being manipulated, she declared, 'and you are only let out when you are wanted to get something out of *me*'. The moral and artistic dangers Annie believed she saw in this appalled her. 'All this "diplomacy" will eat into your soul and ruin your genius. That is a sacred thing.'

But Yeats would not submit to such arguments. He wrote to Annie informing her that the proposal she put to him was wholly unsuitable. It

---

* That John himself ebulliently fulfilled this last capacity clearly intrigued Yeats, who wrote to Quinn (one of the artist's major patrons) telling him that he was 'a delight, the most innocent wicked man I have ever met. He wears earrings, his hair down over his shoulders, a green velvet collar. He climbed to the top of the highest tree on the Coole garden and carved a symbol there. Nobody else has been able to get up there to know what it is.'

was essential he show where his true loyalties lay, and he told her he was no longer young enough to change his nationality, which was what her proposal to join her in Manchester amounted to. He went on to say that if the theatre in Dublin did indeed fail he could always return to lyric poetry. But the essential issue was one of national loyalty. 'I shall write for my own people,' Yeats declared, 'whether in love or hate of them matters little – probably I shall not know which it is.' He had accepted Annie's money but preserved his artistic independence. Now he could disparage his benefactor. 'She is a vulgarian,' Yeats declared, and he callously dismissed the remarkable work Annie was embarking on in Manchester's Gaiety Theatre. 'She claims she has lots of plays,' he wrote to Florence Farr in July, '—they must be pretty bad if she has.'

Annie had been rejected and knew she had lost. But, while she largely withdrew from Yeats's life, his father was also to make a decisive move. Knowing that the old man had never been able to visit Italy, Hugh Lane and a group of friends now decided to raise the money to enable him to go. When the funds had been collected, however, JBY suddenly announced he was not going to Italy at all but would visit New York, where Irish-Americans were sure to flock to him, commission portraits and allow him to return to Ireland a wealthy man. Quinn wrote in great agitation arguing that JBY had chosen the worst possible time to come out since there was a slump in the United States. JBY would not be deflected, and, though Sarah Purser complained that the money raised was not being used for the purpose originally intended, everybody else seemed happy enough to let the old artist go to America, and some even provided him with letters of introduction. JBY and Lily, who was going to New York to promote Dun Emer goods at an Irish exhibition, boarded the *Campania* on 22 December 1907, and, when they landed in New York on the 29th, were met by Quinn and escorted to the Grand Union Hotel. Although he probably had not planned this at the time, JBY was never to see Dublin again. From now on he was to know its affairs largely from the letters exchanged between him and his children, as he began to acquire the reputation of 'an old man who ran away from home and made good'.

III

'Theatre Business'

With Annie Horniman moved to the sidelines and Synge increasingly ill, the burden of managing the Abbey Theatre fell largely to Yeats and Lady Gregory. While Synge himself still had the energy to direct *Teja*, a play by Hermann Sudermann translated by Lady Gregory, Yeats directed her translation of Molière's *The Rogueries of Scapin*. Two new dramatists, W. F.

Casey and Lennox Robinson, also started to contribute plays, while a business manager helped with the day-to-day running of the theatre. In his own dramatic work meanwhile Yeats continued his efforts to relate contemporary Ireland to its heroic past and to explore new ways of doing so. In *The Green Helmet* (first written in prose, performed and then privately circulated by John Quinn as *The Golden Helmet*) Yeats attempted to contrast the heroic to the farcical. His disillusion with acrimonious Dublin is suggested by the bickering minor characters in the work whose vigorous if absurd conduct is three times resolved by the heroic Cuchulain. The ancient hero is both a kind of superman rising above the values of those around him and a figure out of Castiglione who eventually offers his life with the reckless abandon of the true aristocrat. Cuchulain emerges as the archetypal hero, while Yeats's recasting of the original play into the ballad-like metre of *The Green Helmet* gave him the opportunity not only to make his satire more vigorous and inclusive but to experiment with those ideas of style and narrative explored in his essays: the union of the aristocratic with the popular, for example, and the creation of a hero who could reveal the intensity of old imaginative literature. In such ways might drama be refashioned as a medium of sharp social criticism.

For this to be effective, however, the Abbey needed commercial success, despite Yeats's own proud hope of running a theatre free from the over-mastering sway of the box-office. He wrote dejectedly that the Abbey was drawing as bad houses as usual, and at the end of 1906 told Florence Farr that 'last winter we played to almost empty houses, a sprinkling of people in pit and stalls'. The first production of Yeats's *Deirdre*, however, brought a measure of success.[11] 'We are beginning to get audiences,' he wrote in a second letter to Florence Farr, and told her that 'last Saturday we turned people away from all parts of the house'. The play itself was 'certainly a success', not only commercially but artistically too. Fashioned from Lady Gregory's version of the popular legend of the doomed and tragic queen, the work went through a substantial number of drafts and, played against Robert Gregory's fine avant-garde set, Yeats felt he could say of it to Katharine Tynan in late 1906 or early 1907:

> it is my best play and the last half of it holds the audience in as strong a grip as does *Kathleen ni Houlihan*, which is prose and therefore a far easier thing to write. The difficulties of holding an audience with verse are ten times greater than with the prose play. [The] modern audience has lost the habit of careful listening. I think it is certainly my best dramatic poetry and for the first time a verse play of mine is well played all round.

Yeats had at first thought of Mrs Patrick Campbell for the leading role but believed that a new actress, Miss Darragh (Letitia Marion Dallas), who proved unpopular with the rest of the cast, had 'more intellectual tragedy in her'. Yeats's patrician aesthetic turned ever more firmly away from the contemporary school of acting which 'finds the scullion in the queen' and sought instead an art which 'seizes upon what is distinguished, solitary, proud even'. Carefully modulated verse-speaking was essential to this, and John Holloway wrote that 'a Yeats play is like a symphony in which the voices are the instruments employed, and if one or more is harsh or over-loudly employed the harmony is slain'. Holloway was nonetheless aware of how these ideals had to be created in the day-to-day conditions of the theatre. He wrote that Yeats's 'attitudes during the rehearsal were a sight to see, as he kept posing unconsciously all the time'. Holloway at least could recognise the ridiculous side of this. 'Yeats's attitudes during rehearsal would have made a fortune for a comic artist,' he declared. 'He is a strange, odd fish with little or no idea of acting, and the way he stares at the players from within a yard or two of them, as they act, would distract most people. You would think he had a subject under a microscope he stares so intently at them.'

Although Yeats himself wanted 'to keep my own people and my own generation till they have brought their art to perfection', he and the Company's manager W. A. Henderson especially were aware of the need for commercial success, especially now that their subsidy was about to be withdrawn, and they knew how much they would be helped in this by 'the advertisement of a performance by Mrs Pat'.[12] When Mrs Campbell finally came to Dublin at the close of 1908 to star in a revival of *Deirdre*, Yeats was offered a dramatic experience he would never forget. Her performance was 'passionate and solitary', and the prestige it conferred on the Theatre itself was considerable. Yeats himself wrote to confirm this in *Samhain*:

> When we and all our players are with the dead players of Henley's rhyme, some historian of the Theatre, remembering her coming and giving more weight to the appreciation of a fellow artist than even to the words of fine critics, will understand that if our people were not good artists one of the three or four great actresses of Europe would not have come where the oldest player is but twenty-six. To the sincere artist the applause of those who have won greatness in his own craft is often his first appreciation, and always the last that he forgets.

Indeed, so impressed was Yeats by Mrs Campbell that he spent much of the summer of 1909 at Coole trying to write *The Player Queen* as another vehicle for her talent.

During this period, and despite Robert Gregory's recent marriage, Yeats retained his honoured place at Coole. Precisely how he was pampered there was described by a fellow guest, the soldier Sir Ian Hamilton. 'No one can ever have heard anyone play up to him like Lady Gregory,' Hamilton wrote.[13] He then went on to describe how the passage leading to 'the holy of holies', Yeats's bedroom, was lined with thick rugs to prevent the slightest noise from disturbing him. Every now and again a maid would tiptoe down the passage bearing a tray of what was said to be beef tea or arrowroot, but Hamilton believed that once at least he distinctly smelt eggs and bacon. When the bluff soldier suggested that a manly chat would cheer the poet up as he groaned in the labours of creation, the idea was met with horror by Lady Gregory. Robert Gregory meanwhile made a chance discovery of precisely how generously Yeats had been treated when he called one evening for a bottle of vintage wine. This wine had been laid down by his father for special occasions, but it was now discovered that it had all gone, Lady Gregory having served it to Yeats over the years while other guests had to make do with lesser vintages.

Lady Gregory herself had been working extremely hard and suddenly, at the beginning of February 1909, the effort took its toll. She was laid low by a cerebral haemorrhage. When Yeats received the news of this from Robert he wrote a letter in which he movingly expressed the depth of his feelings for the woman who had for so many years acted as his patron. At first he thought the letter told him his mother was ill and that his sister was asking him to come at once, then he remembered that his mother had died several years before and that now more than kin was at stake. 'She has been to me mother, friend, sister and brother,' Yeats wrote of Lady Gregory. 'I cannot realise the world without her – she brought to my wavering thoughts steadfast nobility. All day the thought of losing her is like a conflagration in the rafters. Friendship is all the house I have.'[14] Yeats's mind returned constantly to thoughts of the high civilisation he and Lady Gregory had created between them, and memories of Castiglione mixed with his worries. He wrote in his journal: 'all Wednesday I heard Castiglione's phrase ringing in my memory, "Never be it spoken without tears, the Duchess, too, is dead". That slight phrase, which – coming where it did among the numbering of his dead – has moved me till my eyes dimmed, and I felt all his sorrow as though one saw the worth of life fade for ever.'

Despite the seriousness of her illness, Lady Gregory made a remarkable recovery and she was soon able to jot a pencil note to Yeats in which she said she had 'very nearly slipped away'. She was impatient about the speed of her recovery and she wrote again to Yeats: 'I'm still deeply depressed at the prospect of creating work and perhaps am off it altogether.' She was still recovering when, in late March, she got a letter from Yeats tersely informing her of a tragedy. 'In the early morning Synge said to the nurse, "It is no use fighting death any longer", and turned over and died.' Synge was just thirty-eight years old. Lady Gregory was deeply affected. 'This sudden silence is so awful,' she wrote. 'Yesterday you could have asked him his wishes and heard his thoughts – today, nothing.' She even believed she should have died first, a comment she not only made to Yeats but repeated later to John Quinn.

Nonetheless, even in her grief, Lady Gregory could not move Yeats from the centre of her vision. She believed it was Yeats who had made Synge the dramatist he had been. 'You did more than any for him, you gave him his means of expression . . .' Then with typical self-effacement, she added that Yeats had also 'given me mine, but I would have found something else to do, though not anything coming near this, but I don't think Synge would have done anything but drift but for you and the theatre – I helped him far less – just feeding him when he was badly fed, and working for the staging of his plays, and in little other ways – and I am glad to think of it, for he got very little help from any other except you and myself'.[15] By midsummer, Lady Gregory was busy dealing with the details of Synge's will while, together with his girlfriend Molly Allgood and Yeats himself, she helped put together and produce Synge's last, unfinished play, *Deirdre of the Sorrows*.

What Synge's achievement meant to Yeats is powerfully expressed in his preface to the first edition of Synge's *Poems and Translations*, in the diary he kept during Synge's last illness, and above all in the essay 'J. M. Synge and the Ireland of his Time'.[16] Each of these works dwells on Synge's delight in language and his preoccupation with individual life. It was these qualities which, Yeats argued, allowed Synge to present his characters not in terms of photographic realism but of the dreaming and symbolic life he thought was the true essence of the Irish character. It was through these pure and austere gifts that, Yeats believed, Synge the true artist had triumphed over the partisan acrimony that was destroying Ireland's mental life. 'How can one, if one's mind be full of abstractions and images created not for their own sake but for the sake of party, even if there were still the need, make pictures for the mind's eye and sounds that delight the ear, or discover thoughts that tighten the muscles, or quiver and tingle in the flesh?'

Because he was 'a drifting silent man full of hidden passion', the Aran Islands were Synge's spiritual home, while the discipline of his craft made up the whole of his emotional life. In his art, Synge was entirely his own man, Yeats argued, a writer undeflected by the partisanship around him, and therefore able to express himself in a language at once pure, extravagant and imaginative, a language which Yeats himself believed had done much for national dignity, 'for it could not even express, so little abstract is it and so rammed with life, those worn generalisations of National propaganda'. Synge had sought for the truth of the race, Yeats believed, in the depth of the mind, and could therefore touch and bring alive the deepest spiritual realities of the Irish people.

Yeats also gave credit to the contribution of Lady Gregory and her Kiltartan dialect to Synge's achievement. In the Ireland he saw festering about him, Yeats believed Coole and all it represented was an increasingly important symbol of Irish spiritual and artistic dignity. A number of Lady Gregory's own plays from this time take up a similar theme. She still treasured her dream of joining the values of the Ascendancy to those of the people and, in works like *The White Cockade*, showed her wish for a strong and aristocratic hero who could save the people from the false values of the lower-middle classes and return them to the dignity of true national consciousness. A harmonious and hierarchical Ireland still lay close to the centre of her concerns.

Yeats himself meanwhile increasingly believed that the omnipresent vulgarity he saw about him could only be 'conquered by an ideal of life upheld by authority'. He began to think that Protestant social prejudice was something to be admired for its ability to keep 'our ablest men from meddling passions'. Coole especially seemed to offer a locale where the ideals of Castiglione might yet be brought to life and at times, as in the prefatory poem to *The Shadowy Waters*, the landscape there could appear as an image of the Earthly Paradise, a place of 'star-glimmering ponds' and magical inspiration. Two years later, in the poem that gives its title to Yeats's collection *In the Seven Woods*, Coole is again a place of magic where the 'Great Archer' hangs in the skies, and thus provides a refuge from the vulgarity of the world. But that refuge was now thought of as something to be pitted against forces which it may not altogether withstand: the 'commonness' of the world created by Edward VII, the corruption of the aristocratic ideal at the pinnacle of society, along with the vulgarity seen among the milling crowds in Dublin, people happier with celebratory paper flowers hanging in their streets than the rooted organic life of Coole.

But such calamities were not the only danger to the life of aristocratic refinement Yeats envisaged. By the end of the decade, patrician poise and dignity were under legal threat. In July 1909 the Land Court ordered reductions of approximately 20 per cent in the rents paid by fifteen of Lady Gregory's tenants. 'Upon a House Shaken by the Land Agitation', a poem published by Yeats in *The Green Helmet and Other Poems* of 1910, gives expression to what he saw as the futility of this menace:

> How should the world be luckier if this house,
> Where passion and precision have been one
> Time out of mind, became too ruinous
> To breed the lidless eye that loves the sun?
> And the sweet laughing eagle thoughts that grow
> Where wings have memory of wings, and all
> That comes of the best knit to the best? Although
> Mean roof-trees were the sturdier for its fall,
> How should their luck run high enough reach
> The gifts that govern men, and after these
> To gradual Time's last gift, a written speech
> Wrought of high laughter, loveliness and ease?[17]

Yeats was writing here one of the last poems in that tradition of praise for the country house initiated some three centuries earlier by Ben Jonson. Just as Jonson's Penshurst, the home of the poet Sidney, could be extolled as the seat of patriotism, virtue and art, so Coole is praised as the origin of the 'gifts that govern men' (a reference to Lady Gregory's husband's governorship of Ceylon) and of the poetic and dramatic art inspired by a life like that enjoyed by Castiglione's courtiers. Here, Yeats suggests, is that elite munificence which ennobles the world by its self-evident virtue. The power of social amelioration Coole has lies in the values it promotes rather than in the greater fairness that might be gained from redistributing its privileged financial status. The argument is presented as a set of assertions that seem to imply consent to the aristocratic ideal Yeats had made his own. In what was to become an elegy for an ideal increasingly irrelevant to the mass of the Irish people, social hierarchy is here at one with intellectual and moral excellence.

Nor was the Land Court the only threat to Yeats's aspirations. In August 1909, the Abbey Theatre decided to accept George Bernard Shaw's *The Shewing Up of Blanco Posnet*, a play already banned in England for blasphemy but which could be staged in Ireland because the authority of the censor did not stretch there.[18] The proposal to mount the play was not only an anti-British gesture, however. It was also part of Yeats's lifelong battle against censorship of all kinds. As he told his father: 'the real offender is the King who is trying to make England moral and as a means is supporting the Censor by calling actors before him and getting them to speak at the Royal Commission in favour of censorship'. In Dublin, Lady Gregory took over the rehearsals, but Dublin Castle itself, possessed of ancient rights of censorship, once again had its eye on her stage and threatened heavy fines and even the withdrawal of the Abbey's licence if the play were put into performance. Placing all their years of work in jeopardy, Yeats and Lady Gregory crossed Ireland to have a conference with the Lord Lieutenant. An important point of principle was involved. 'We did not give in one quarter of an inch to Nationalist Ireland at *The Playboy* time,' wrote Lady Gregory, 'and we certainly cannot give in one quarter of an inch to the Castle.' Her account of the meeting with the authorities shows both the courage with which she and Yeats faced their problems and the shrewd good manners with which they supported their idealism.

Lady Gregory wrote of 'the courtesy shown to us, and, I think, also by us; the kindly offers of a cup of tea; the consuming desire for that tea after the dust of the railway journey all across Ireland; our heroic refusal, lest its acceptance should in any way, even if it did not weaken our resolve, compromise our principles'. Immediately after the meeting, Yeats and Lady Gregory, having consulted a barrister, believed they would have to bow to the wishes of Dublin Castle. But a rehearsal had already been called; after they had sat through this and left the theatre, they found that during those two or three hours their minds had come to the same decision, 'that we had given our word, that at all risks we must keep it or it would never be trusted again'. As Yeats himself realised, to submit to censorship would be morally and politically disastrous. 'The Lord Lieutenant is definitely a political personage,' he wrote, 'holding office from the party in power, and what would sooner or later grow into a political censorship cannot be lightly accepted.' The decision was a brave and honourable one, and the upshot showed that Dublin Castle had been bluffing. No fines were imposed, and those Nationalist groups such as Arthur Griffith's Sinn Fein who were so often opposed to the Abbey and its policies now enthusiastically gave them their support.

Not all of those on the Unionist side were so broad-minded, however. When Edward VII died on 6 May 1910, the young Lennox Robinson, a promising playwright whom Yeats would place in charge of the Abbey,[19] sent Lady Gregory a telegram asking what he should do.* Unfortunately, her reply, 'Should close through Courtesy', arrived only after the curtain had gone up on the matinée. Since it appeared to Robinson that the damage had already been done, he opened the Theatre for an evening performance as well. A furious Annie Horniman wrote demanding an apology and, when she was not satisfied with the explanation she received, she decided the insult to the Crown was deliberate and threatened to withdraw her subsidy immediately. Arthur Griffith was quick to see an opportunity. Would Yeats capitulate to the Englishwoman for her money? Yeats was in an uncomfortable position: he had to show his patron that his theatre was not politically neutral while also proving to Sinn Fein that it was not subservient to propaganda either. The matter was taken to arbitration, where it was decided that Miss Horniman was under a legal obligation to pay the remaining six months of her grant. Having won his point, Yeats renounced the money.

Although with the greatest generosity Annie Hornimann allowed the directors to take over the lease of the building along with its contents for a nominal sum, she nonetheless threatened legal action again if the first £1000 of this sum was not paid to her promptly. A theatrical tour of England brought in £500 towards this figure, and lectures by George Bernard Shaw and Yeats himself earned a further £2169 for the establishment of an endowment fund. In addition, an invitation came from the American theatrical producers Liebler and Company to perform in America with all expenses guaranteed. The independence of the Abbey had been saved, but

---

* Yeats, who had summoned Robinson from Cork, told him: 'I like your face. I believe you have a dramatic future. I am doing what the man did who took Ibsen from behind the counter in a chemist's shop and set him to manage the Norwegian theatre. He was no older than you, and like you was ignorant of the work he was sent to.' Robinson was to develop into a realist playwright and was to say of Yeats, 'from the day I met him to the day of his death he was the dominant personality in my life'.

as Lady Gregory wrote to Yeats: 'we have certainly seen a good deal of the seamy side of human nature since we began this theatre. E. Martyn's childishness, George Moore's pirating, the seceders' vanity, Miss Horniman's malignant arrogance.'

They had nonetheless achieved an astonishing amount, above all the creation of a distinctively national style of acting and playwriting which was gaining an international reputation. On the tenth anniversary of the founding of the Theatre Yeats himself and Lady Gregory wrote with justifiable pride about this.

> All the laborious building-up, the slow amassing of a large repertory of Irish plays, the training of actors, the making of a reputation with the general public, has been accomplished, or all but accomplished, and there is little needed to make the Abbey Theatre a permanent part of Irish life, the centre of a distinguished school of players, playwrights and translators. We ourselves are ready to accept much or little influence and any arrangement that will make the Theatre intellectual and courageous. We would sooner it came to an end than see the tradition we have created give place to one less worthy.[20]

IV

The Mystic Marriage Revived

While many of the figures involved in Yeats's public existence had now played their parts, others returned to a place in his private life. He was, for example, particularly close to Florence Farr at this time, writing to tell her in early 1906 that he wanted to see her very much and that it would always be a great delight to be with her. Heavily involved in the affairs of the Abbey, Yeats yearned for the intimacy he thought he could share with Florence. 'You cannot think what a pleasure it is to be fond of somebody to whom I can talk,' he declared. 'To be moved and talkative, unrestrained, one's own self, and to be this not because one has created some absurd delusion that all is wisdom ... but because one has found an equal, this is the best of life.' He summed up his feelings, saying 'all this means I am looking forward to seeing you – that my spirits rise at the thought of it.' The couple made plans for a spring lecture tour on their art of the psaltery that year which would take in Leeds, Liverpool, Edinburgh, Oxford and Cambridge.[21]

Yeats confessed to Florence that he thought he had changed, that he could 'move people by power', but he noted a change in Florence too. She had a greater and perhaps more remote spirituality than heretofore which he attributed to her interest in Eastern meditation. Clearly, their tour brought them closer together, and it is possible they became lovers. Certainly, they were sufficiently intimate for Quinn to urge Yeats to allow Florence to come on her own for an American lecture series he had arranged. 'This is, after all, a provincial people,' Quinn wrote. 'For you two to come would be too risky, too easily misunderstood.' Nonetheless, theatre business partly ensured that the relationship faded and that Florence did not help Yeats at the Abbey. In June 1907, she left for the United States without him.

It is possible that they drifted apart because Florence got bored, but a more likely reason was the re-emergence of Maud Gonne. For some time after the failure of her marriage Maud had been unable to enjoy mystic visions, but in May 1907 she wrote to tell Yeats that she had been receiving dreams which prophesied 'some hideous war in which England & France would take part'. She had also developed 'a wonderful power of healing'. As she explained with perhaps only partly unconscious motivation, 'I never fail in taking away pain instantly & even curing coughs & other things.' She added that she had this power of healing to an extraordinary degree and thought it must be the fruit of her work in another life. By the following June, Yeats was again at her side in Paris and it is probable that their reunion had, if only briefly, a physical consummation. There are hints of such closeness in a journal, while a later poem, 'His Memories', also seems to refer to this occasion, juxtaposing age and desire, myth and the physical actuality of sex:

> We should be hidden from their eyes
> Being but holy shows
> And bodies broken like a thorn
> Whereon the bleak north blows,
> To think of buried Hector
> And that none living knows.
>
> The women take so little stock
> In what I do or say,
> They'd sooner leave their cosseting
> To hear a jackass bray;
> My arms are like the twisted thorn
> And yet there beauty lay.
>
> The first of all the tribe lay there
> And did such pleasure take—
> She who had brought great Hector down
> And put all Troy to wreck—
> That she cried into this ear,
> 'Strike me if I shriek.'[22]

But Maud's deep fear of physical contact resurfaced and, in the familiar, agonising pattern of their love, she drew close only to remove their passion to the safety and distance of the astral plane. In June 1908, Yeats recorded in a journal that he had been with her, adding that 'on Saturday evening (20th) she said something that blotted away the recent past and brought all back to the spiritual marriage of 1898 . . . On Sunday night we talked very plainly. She believes that this bond is to be recreated and to be the means of spiritual illumination between us. It is to be the bond of the spirit only and she lives from now on, she said . . . for that and for her children.'[23]

A frustrated Yeats knew how alluring and how dangerous this position could be. As he wrote later: 'she has all my self. I was never more deeply in love, but my desires must go elsewhere if I would escape their poison.' In the past he had sought sexual release with Olivia Shakespear but now, on the very day that Maud told him their love could not be physically consummated on a permanent basis, Yeats wrote to a new woman friend, a young medical masseuse he had met in London called Mabel Dickinson. As he explained to her:

> I have spent my days at the Louvre for the most part. I have seen a good deal of Maud Gonne. She thinks she will not make another attempt to get rid of her husband (as she can in three years) unless he makes more trouble. She is content and I think happy. We have talked over old things sadly perhaps, but always as old things that have drifted away. I shall return to London on Monday morning. . . . I am hoping to hear from you in the morning. It is so long since I have heard. . . . For the moment I am tired of modern mystery and romance and can only take pleasure in clear light, strong bodies – having all the measure of manhood. . . . Ten years ago when I was last in Paris, I loved all that was mysterious and gothic and hated all that was classic and severe. I doubt if I should have liked you then. . . . I wanted a twilight of religious mystery. . . .[24]

Just as in his aesthetic discrimination Yeats was moving towards an Apollonian clarity and vigour so, in his sexual life, he managed to persuade himself he had grown out of his desires of the previous decades and now sought frank physical contact. Mabel Dickinson could offer him this, but the subtlety of passion was altogether more tenaciously rooted in the past than Yeats's letter suggests. If Mabel Dickinson could offer the physical release Yeats craved, Maud still pursued him with a combination of practical advice and mystical allure.

Soon after his departure for London she wrote to him saying that she thought his involvement with the Abbey Theatre was a 'millstone' from which he should try to free himself, at least partially. She understood, she said, that he felt a responsibility towards the actors who depended on him and she admired his recognition of this, for such loyalty was rare in a country like Ireland. Nonetheless, 'for the sake of Ireland, you *must* keep your writing before all else. A great poet or a great writer can give nobler and more precious gifts to his country than the greatest philanthropist ever can give. Your own writing, and above all, your poetry must be your first consideration. Anything that takes you from it, or makes it less intense, is wrong and must be shaken off.'[25] Despite the disagreements they had had about the role of propaganda in art, Maud, especially when she was feeling protective towards Yeats, had a sure appreciation of the depth of his writing, for all she might have disliked the elitist resources on which it continued to draw. She knew, too, how his public interests could threaten his poetry. She reminded him that she had always hated his involvement in politics, even the politics in which she so passionately believed, because it took him away from his true work. She considered the theatre was just as bad or even worse since it brought Yeats 'among jealousies and petty quarrels and little animosities which you as a great writer should be above and apart from'. She realised how harassed he was by such things and she told him that it was just this exasperation with the pettiness about him that made him take up his old class prejudice, which she considered unworthy. She did not realise that her own marriage to MacBride was among the principal causes of this:

> My dear is angry that of late
> I cry all base blood down
> As though she had not taught me hate
> By kisses to a clown.[26]

But, while Maud could offer Yeats what she considered firm and objective practical advice, she could also lure him with the inspiration she believed she derived from the renewal of their mystic marriage. At times she believed she was even on the borders of a new revelation: 'I think a most wonderful thing has happened – the most wonderful thing I have met with in life,' she wrote. 'If we are only strong enough to hold the door open I think we shall obtain knowledge and life we have never dreamed of. The meanings of things are becoming very clear to me.'

Yeats believed that Maud's new vision was in some way a repetition of the Adeptus Minor ritual of the Golden Dawn ceremonies and thought he had to work out the relationship between this and their mystic marriage.[27] A form of astral sex magic also began to preoccupy him. Knowing that he would have to 'pay the price for an inner integrity', he evoked a vision of red and green globes which in their merging supposedly brought together the forces of Mars and Venus. He then apparently had a vision of 'two spirit forms, side by side' climbing to the top of Mount Abiegnus, the mystical mountain of God at the centre of the universe. On 25 July, he repeated the experiment and experienced a 'great union' with Maud (or *Per Ignem ad Lucem* as he always referred to her in his occult writings) in which 'for the first time in weeks physical desire was arrested' amid cascades of roses and apple blossoms.

Maud wrote on the same day that she too had had a vision in which she sent her astral body to Yeats. Conscious that she should not interfere with his work on *The Player Queen*, she wrote to tell him how she had seen an Egyptian form floating over her which resembled Blake's illustration of the soul leaving the body. Her vision was 'dressed in a moth-like garment and had curious wings edged with gold in which it could fold itself up'. This, Maud believed, was the body into which she could project her astral self, and at a quarter to eleven on the night before she wrote her letter she 'put on this body', thought strongly of Yeats and desired to go to him. 'We met somewhere in space. I don't know where – I was conscious of starlight and of hearing the sea below us.' What followed was one of the most mysterious and intimate passages in all of Maud's letters:

> You had taken the form I think of a great serpent, but I am not sure. I only saw your face distinctly and as I looked into your eyes (as I did the day in Paris you asked me what I was thinking of) and your lips touched mine we melted into one another until we formed only *one being, a being greater than ourselves* who felt all and knew all with double intensity – the clock striking eleven broke the spell and as we separated it felt as if life was being drawn away from me through my chest with almost physical pain. I went again twice. Each time it was the same – each time I was brought back by some slight noise in the house. Then I went upstairs to bed and I dreamed of you, confused dreams of ordinary life.[28]

Even the mysteries of astral union were perilously subject to division, but it is clear from her letter that Maud regarded these as something superior to physical sexuality. In her dream of their 'ordinary life' together, for example, she thought they were in Italy and talking of the spiritual union she had just described. Yeats apparently told her that he believed it would tend to the increasing of physical desire, and this troubled Maud since as always she hoped 'there was nothing physical in that union'. Her need for intimacy and her distrust of sex are evident in every line she wrote. Summing up her experience of an astral union with Yeats she declared: 'Material union is but a pale shadow compared with it.' But a pained Yeats was altogether less certain. In the notebook she had given him – a volume bound in white calf and secured with brown leather thongs – he pasted some of the letters she sent him beside records of his own astral experiments and drafts of poems recording his feelings. Among the last is a rough version of 'King and No King' in which he expressed the dilemma of a passionate love refused fulfilment in this world in the hope of spiritual apotheosis in the next:

> how shall I know
> That in the blinding light beyond the grave
> We'll find so good a thing as that we have lost?
> The hourly kindness, the day's common speech
> The habitual content of each with each
> When neither soul nor body has been crossed.[29]

The experiments in astral union continued nonetheless, and in October 1908, when the white notebook was with Maud in Paris, she described an experience which draws heavily on the characters and imagery of *The Shadowy Waters* to present her image of a union that was at once intensely mystical and wholly characterised by the ideal of a heroic and mythical Ireland:

> I was reading this book and other records of old visions last night when suddenly Aileel who was in Liverpool at the time came to me and we became one being with an ecstasy that I cannot describe. The intensity of the spiritual union prevents it lasting long or one would die. I looked at my watch – it was past one. Keeping the books beside me I put out the light and either in sleep or vision I saw Aileel . . . looking very beautiful and happy and triumphant. I dreamed a great deal I think but I can remember little. I was awakened by a great gust of wind blowing through the room. I thought there was some great presence, but could see nothing; half-sleeping, half-waking these thoughts came to me. I saw Aileel's love for me lighting the years like a lamp of extraordinary holiness, and voices said, 'You did not understand so we took it from you and kept it safe in the heart of the hills for it belongs to Ireland. When you were purified by suffering so you could understand we gave it back to you. See you guard it for from it great beauty may be born.' We stood with hands clasped above it in that white radiance and again the white shining bird flew up from it and a voice said, 'It is the image of Forgael's harp which nothing can destroy.'[30]

The passage suggests that, on however unconscious a level, Maud was trying to explain her marriage to MacBride, to picture this as a period of suffering and deprivation caused by a spiritual ignorance from which she had now emerged purified and prepared for a mystical union with her inspired poet. In a journal entry for January 1909, however, Yeats revealed that he realised that Maud's Catholicism had established so strong a grip on her thought that she would not now consider divorcing MacBride. More profoundly, he recognised too that below all of her reactions lay the old dread of physical love. He understood at last how 'this dread has probably spoiled all her life, checking natural and instinctive selection, and leaving fantastic duties free to take its place'. He had penetrated to the core of

Maud's unhappiness and fanatical energy, and, where once she had been able to dominate his emotions, he came to see now that he had established for himself a greater security and a vantage point from which he could look at her with mingled feelings of pity and awe. 'Of old she was a phoenix and I feared her, but now she is my child more than my sweetheart.' Child and phoenix, friend and adviser, a woman of still devastating physical beauty, she had once been his lover and now insisted she could only be his astral bride. Maud harassed Yeats with the very peace she seemed to offer him, and in the first eight poems gathered in *The Green Helmet* he portrayed the anguish and exultation offered by their revived spiritual union.

The poems are grouped under the general title 'Nicholas Flamel and his wife Pernella' (Yeats had to insert an erratum note into the volume when he realised that 'by a slip of the pen' he had at first written down the name of the alchemist Raymond Lully for Nicholas Flamel) and this was an image that for him went back to the earliest days of his and Maud's membership of the Golden Dawn, when he 'began to form plans of our lives devoted to mystic truth, and spoke to her of Nicholas Flamel and his wife, Pernella'. As he had written in 'Rosa Alchemica', he thought of the alchemists as men who 'labour continually, turning lead into gold, weariness into ecstasy, bodies into souls, the darkness into God'. As is always the case in the deepest understanding of the subject, Yeats saw alchemy not as an early form of science, a materialistic search for illusory wealth, but as a programme of spiritual metamorphosis in which the base metal of natural man is transformed into the gold of spiritual enlightenment. In the poems he was now writing, the defeats and anguish of this magical transformation were quite as apparent as its successes.

While 'Reconciliation' suggests that, in the period immediately following Maud's marriage, Yeats had been so devastated that he could write nothing except plays about the remote past, thereby losing the immediacy of personal emotional experience, 'Words' was prompted by a passage in his journal in which he described a different effect Maud had on his work. 'Today the thought came to me that she never really understands my plans, or nature, or ideas,' he wrote in his journal. 'Then came the thought, What matter? How much of the best I have done and still do is but the attempt to explain myself to her? If she understood, I should lack a reason for writing.'

In some of the most powerful of these works, written, as Yeats believed, at a time of confused and debilitating public standards, Homer and classical Greece became the norms by which he hoped to suggest Maud's beauty and power. Maud becomes an embodiment of Helen of Troy. Her beauty is both her glory and her curse. Suffused by the power of a loveliness that is beyond the comprehension of the sterile world of petty-bourgeois Dublin, Maud becomes in Yeats's act of exaltation a force he too can barely comprehend. Noble, beautiful, 'high and solitary and most stern', Maud belongs to the world of primal experience. She is at once a thing of beauty and a thing of terror, awe-inspiring and pitiful in the chaos she wreaks by the power of her presence:

> Why should I blame her that she filled my days
> With misery, or that she would of late
> Have taught to ignorant men most violent ways,
> Or hurled the little streets upon the great,
> Had they but courage equal to desire?
> What could have made her peaceful with a mind
> That nobleness made simple as a fire,
> With beauty like a tightened bow, a kind,
> That is not natural in an age like this,
> Being high and solitary and most stern?
> Why, what could she have done, being what she is?
> Was there another Troy for her to burn?[31]

The sublime woman brings anguish to her poet even as she threatens havoc to the society in which they both live. This is not her fault. Maud moves with high and hapless tragedy through a petty and wretched world, a world whose spiritless and devious manipulations Yeats recorded in the journal, later published in an edited version as *Estrangement*, where this poem is placed on the first page – a challenge to the record of tawdriness that follows it.

V

Estrangement

Yeats felt ever more strongly that true national feeling was collapsing among a people who had no national institutions to revere, no national success to admire, and no genuine imaginative ideal to follow. He believed such models could be created and inspire the race only if those who made them shared with the majority 'some simple moral understanding of life'. But Yeats felt himself far removed from this and sometimes despaired of making the effort. 'If we could create a conception of the race as noble as Aeschylus and Sophocles had of Greece, it would be attacked on some trivial ground and the crowd would follow either some mind which copied the rhetoric of Young Ireland or the obvious sentiments of popular English literature with a few Irish thoughts and feelings added for conscience's sake.'[32]

Much of Yeats's journal is a bitter catalogue of the imaginative and spiritual disaster he believed the new class of the urban petty-bourgeoisie was inflicting on Ireland, and he was particularly worried by the effect of this on young people. When he was asked to speak at the Arts Club, he chose as his subject 'The Ideas of the Young', believing that this title would give him the opportunity to develop the thoughts that were uppermost in his mind. He wrote that he would describe the life of a young Irishman whose mental horizons were gradually being narrowed by the political propaganda around him. He believed that such a young man would meet in Ireland merely crude, impersonal ideas which would make him an anonymous part of the mass. Being ill-educated, such a young man did not even have the beginning of an aesthetic culture, never tried to create a beautiful environment around him, or perfect his sense and his taste.

Even Maud Gonne was not absolved from these bitter attacks. On 20 March 1909, Yeats wrote in his journal that she was learning Gaelic and, believing that she was now about to throw herself into the sort of propaganda work inspired by Douglas Hyde, he was glad that she was committing herself to something he considered almost as harmless as the revival of Celtic decoration in the arts. What he really feared was a revival of her 'opinionated mind', and his concern that she might launch herself into a more active form of politics called forth some of Yeats's most openly sexist comments. 'Women,' he wrote, 'because the main event of their lives has been a giving of themselves, give themselves to an opinion as if [it] were some terrible stone doll.' Being by nature mothers or 'sweethearts', they attached themselves, Yeats believed, to ideas with all the defensive passion and occasional cruelty with which they embraced their lovers or their offspring. Becoming obsessed by notions which were, Yeats thought, a substitute for their true and natural functions, these ideas became at last so much a part of them that their flesh was turned to stone in the stridency of what he only could consider a neurotic passion. Yeats believed that in the past, even when Maud was at her most forceful, she had managed to preserve something of the sweetness of her voice and the play of her humour. Now he could only fear for her. A political woman, he believed, could be nothing more than a sort of hysterical child playing with ideas as with a toy. 'Women', he wrote, 'should have their play with dolls finished in childish happiness, for if they play with them again it is amid hatred and malice.'

George Russell too was swept into this tirade of condemnation, for if Russell was a 'religious genius' it was that very quality which undermined the pursuit of excellence by assuming that all souls are of equal value, that the queen was at one with the apple woman. Yeats believed that this was a profound misunderstanding and raged against it. It was precisely because of the form Russell's nature took that, Yeats thought, he needed more education than anyone else. Intellectual discipline and a wide range of knowledge were the essential ballast to a man who seemed to rely so exclusively on dogmatic intuition. 'With all of the fanaticism of the religious reformer,' Yeats wrote of Russell, 'he has taught many to despise all that does not come out of their own minds and to trust to vision to do the work of intellect.' All that

Yeats could see proceeding from this was the sort of facile arrogance that disparaged anything that did not have an immediate appeal, and the result was 'a luxurious dreaming, a kind of spiritual lubricity', which he believed took the place of logic and will.

Yeats sought for himself qualities altogether more tried and resilient, and the journal suggests that he found these ever more surely embodied in the world of hierarchy and decorum he associated with Coole. Lady Gregory herself naturally personified much of what Yeats was reaching out to, and he wrote approvingly of the way in which she consciously isolated herself from the 'contagious opinions of poorer minds'. He quoted with approval her comment when he told her he was going to stay at Dunsany Castle: 'I am very glad, for you need a few days among normal and simple well-bred people. One always wants that from time to time as a rest to one's mind. They need not be clever.' Lord Dunsany was nonetheless a highly articulate man, and as Yeats became increasingly familiar with the social circles of the Ascendancy families, so he thought he again came to see an analogy between the life of such people and that of the artist and the peasant – traditional peoples to set against middle-class vulgarity. 'We come from the permanent things and create them,' he wrote in his journal, 'and instead of old blood we have old emotions and we carry in our head that form of society which aristocracies create now and again for some brief moment at Urbino or Versailles.'

This was a belief he repeated to E. R. Walsh, a fellow guest at the Nassau Hotel where Yeats stayed when in Dublin. Walsh himself declared that the land reformer 'Captain Shawe-Taylor came nearest to Yeats's ideal gentleman of the Renaissance. Like Hugh Lane, he was a nephew of Lady Gregory, and his remarkable personal beauty and his exquisitely winning way, made him irresistible as a conciliator.' Yeats's essay on Shawe-Taylor elaborates these ideas to portray the embodiment of his ideal.[33] Shawe-Taylor is presented as an aristocrat whose religious life 'concerned itself alone with the communion of the soul with God' and as a man whose instinctual nature expressed the deepest ideas of his race. Yeats wrote of such people that 'it is as though they sank a well through the soil where our habits have been built, and where our hopes take root or lie uprooted, to the lasting rock and to the living stream'. The tragedy lay, however, in Shawe-Taylor's untimely death.

In his attempt to identify himself with the aristocracy as the one sure source of value in Ireland, Yeats had a colleague look up his coat of arms 'for the purpose of a bookplate', and this attempt to ally himself to the nobility occasionally verged on the ludicrous. Told that, on his father's side, he had aristocratic blood in his veins, Yeats saw fit to say that the Duke of Ormonde was not one of the real Butlers and that if matters were properly sorted out he would himself be the Duke. Boasting of this to Russell, the man whom Yeats had condemned for his slap-dash mysticism replied that even if this were the case the title would nonetheless belong to JBY.

Yeats was an increasingly isolated man. For all his praise of the aristocracy, his ardent nationalism excluded him from being publicly associated with the ruling elite, although from time to time Lady Lyttelton, the wife of the Commander-in-Chief, invited him to dinner with carefully selected guests. He remained a lonely individual, separated from the literary circle gathered about George Russell and unable to find agreeable company elsewhere for, as Walsh noted, 'the merely Bohemian company he might have joined, such as that led by Count and Countess Marckiewicz, held no attraction for him'. Even his body seemed to express his restlessness, his impatience, his frustrated energy. His way of hurling himself along the pavement suggested this. As one observer wrote:

> I have seen Yeats in a great many places, bent on various tasks, but I have never seen him walk. He never does walk; he propels himself. Covers a great deal of ground, no doubt, almost every day of his life, and very rapidly, but covers it in a way peculiar to himself and quite undescribable. In all frankness – it isn't pretty. . . . Those long legs shoot him up and down over the ground in a rapid series of leaps which would knock all the breath out of an unpuncturable pneumatic tyre, and if you are trying to walk with him as he hurries along, you will certainly find your ideas getting so knocked about inside your skull, that by the time they emerge in words they are battered out of all recognition.

In addition, the bitterness, dissatisfaction and class-consciousness in the journal are constantly underscored by a sense of the personal and professional strain Yeats was under at this time. He noted frequently the large number of his hours that had to be devoted to theatre business, and he wrote that he cried out continually against his life of sleepless nights and the heterogeneous labour that seemed to deprive him of liberty and any real sense of an inner existence. He was greatly concerned about the time he had to take from writing poetry and he was worried that his 'talent' might not recover from the strain of all the other things on which he was required to expend his energy. Yeats nonetheless felt strongly tempted by the public world, the world of action and conflict, and was made guilty by the fact that while he knew renunciation was the virtue of the artist the lure of victory and administrative triumph was something he felt strongly. The desire to convince and domineer ran deep, yet it was a guilty energy that seemed to exert itself as if in the attempt to hide an essential hollowness.

He knew that he could be difficult and fractious (in several places in the journal he ascribed this to astrological forces), yet at one point in his confessions he felt obliged to write that perhaps he had to 'do all these things that I may set myself into a life of action, so as to express not the traditional poet but that forgotten thing, the normal active man'. Laments about headaches, sleeplessness and the strain on his nervous system are frequent.

At times he even wondered if he had inherited some 'weakness' from his mother's family, and if this expressed itself in an aggressive relationship to the world about him. At other times Yeats felt his energy was 'stopped by a wall, by something one must either submit to or rage against helplessly'. The consciousness of this psychological block sometimes made him ask if he was on the edge of madness, and it is clear that he did have some minor nervous collapse. 'I had been working hard', he wrote in his journal, 'and suddenly I found I could not use my mind on any serious subject. Yet at this moment I cannot tell if the whole thing was not a slight indisposition brought on by too much smoking heightened by that kind of nervous fright I get from time to time: the fear of losing my inspiration by absorption in outer things.'

The stresses imposed upon Yeats both from within and from without were at times so great that it seemed to him he could face them only with a deliberately created personality – a mask. In an important passage in the journal he wrote:

> I think all happiness depends on having the energy to assume the mask of some other self, that all joyous or creative life is a rebirth of something not oneself, something created in a moment and perpetually renewed in playing a game like that of a child where one loses the infinite pain of self-realisation, a grotesque or solemn painted face put on that one may hide from the terrors of judgement, an imaginative saturnalia that makes one forget reality.[34]

In such abject moods as Yeats was currently experiencing, the mask that was sometimes an aggressive means of facing a hostile world, a forced expression of a 'manly pose', was also, by its very artificiality, a means perhaps of apprehending some flickering, tantalising sense of imagined joy. In both cases it was an escape from the burden of the given self, its sterility, its indecisiveness, its bored, rancorous bitterness at its own complaints, its estrangement from its deepest resources. Only later, however, only when that hollow and rigid face had been given life by occult enlightenment, would he be able to know the mask as life indeed: the psyche's completed search for union with its opposite.

Events meanwhile suggested that a period of Yeats's life was drawing to a close even while he waited. By late September 1910, George Pollexfen was clearly dying. Lily was in Sligo to nurse him, and Yeats wrote to her wondering whether he should come over or not. 'I don't like to suggest I should go there to him,' he confessed, 'I have been so long without going that it might make him think that I have heard his state was desperate.' At half-past five on 25 September, Lily heard the wailing of the banshee, and twenty-four hours later George Pollexfen died. Yeats wrote to tell Lily he was glad she had heard the banshee since it seemed a fitting valediction for a man whose instinctive nature had been so close to the supernatural. Yeats himself arrived at Sligo the day after his uncle's death, attended the funeral, and was touched by the masonic service that was also held:

> And Masons drove from miles away
> To scatter the Acacia spray
> Upon a melancholy man
> Who had ended where his breath began.[35]

Yeats then told Lily two important pieces of news. He was about to receive a pension from the Civil List; in addition, he had been asked if he would care to stand as a candidate for the university chair soon to be relinquished by Professor Dowden. A new period of public prestige was, it appeared, about to open before him.

PART FOUR

Ego Dominus Tuus

I call to the mysterious one who yet
Shall walk the wet sands by the edge of the stream
And look most like me, being indeed my double,
And prove of all imaginable things
The most unlike. . . .

10

The Onion Sellers
(1910–1913)

I
'Pensioner Yeats'

Yeats's receipt of a Civil List pension was surrounded with disagreements, misunderstandings and, on his part, a refinement of moral scruple which shows how far he was from being 'the normal active man'. Yeats received his first indication that the government might make such an offer at the close of 1909 when Agnes Tobin informed him that Edmund Gosse, the distinguished man of letters, had sounded her out on the subject, saying: 'We cannot neglect our greatest poet.' Miss Tobin told Gosse she believed that, as an Irishman, Yeats would find it impossible to accept such a gift from the English government, but the issue seemed about to come to nothing when the government was defeated in the House of Lords, parliament was dissolved, and Asquith called a general election.

Gosse was nonetheless still determined to help, and early the following year Yeats accepted his invitation to join a proposed English Academy of Letters. Gosse himself then consulted with Lady Gregory and asked her to provide material for his petition for the pension.[1] Lady Gregory prepared this and, writing to thank her, Gosse recommended that a second letter which she should write to Augustine Birrell, the Chief Secretary for Ireland, needed to state clearly 'the nature and cause of Yeats's poverty'.* All seemed to be proceeding satisfactorily when a misunderstanding developed. On receiving a letter which Lady Gregory had already shown to Yeats, Gosse wrote a reply which caused consternation. 'I cannot express my surprise at the tone of your letter,' Gosse declared. 'If this is your attitude, I wish to have no more to do with the matter, and I am lost in wonder at what can have induced you to interfere in an affair when your opinion was not asked, and when you seem to intend neither to give any help nor to take any trouble.' An offended Lady

---

* Up until his fifties Yeats's books rarely made him more than £200 a year.

Gregory was angered both by this and by Yeats's refusal immediately to draft
an appropriate response. There was, it seems, much 'discussion' on the point
and a parade of moral scruple on Yeats's part which flew in the face of Lady
Gregory's and Robert's code of honour. The poet who was so enamoured
of patrician bearing was shocked to discover the quick and haughty certitude
with which true aristocrats responded to a slight.

Yeats felt he was being propelled by his friends into what he considered an
act of moral crudeness and believed his artistic integrity was being threatened.
He later wrote:

> since I was fifteen and began to think, I have mocked at that way
> of looking at the world, as if it were a court of law where all wrong
> actions were judged according to their legal penalties. All my life I
> have, like every artist, been proud of belonging to a nobler world, of
> having chosen the slow, dangerous, laborious path of moral judgement.
> And yet the moment the code appears before me in the personality of
> two friends, I am shaken, I doubt myself. I doubted because I talked. In
> silence I could have thought the whole thing out, kept my vacillation to
> myself.[2]

Nonetheless, two days after the arrival of Gosse's letter Yeats felt con-
strained to draft what he thought was an appropriately cutting reply which
Lady Gregory eventually declined to post, although for a while Yeats believed
it had been sent.

Unaware of the doubts and difficulties he had caused, Gosse himself
meanwhile wrote to Yeats again on 29 July telling him that the petition for his
pension was now with the Prime Minister and advising him to be 'absolutely
passive'. Lady Gregory, however, was determined to act on her own account.
On the same day that Gosse wrote to Yeats, she wrote to Birrell enclosing
Gosse's 'extraordinary letter' and asking the Secretary to put into 'proper
form' another draft of the material originally prepared for Gosse's petition.
There matters rested for a while as, in an atmosphere already made difficult
by his prevarication, Yeats was left to explain his behaviour to his hostess,
her son and, above all, himself. Eventually, Yeats tried to clear his mind by
writing a remarkable letter to Robert Gregory. In this he confessed that, 'as
I look back, I see occasion after occasion on which I have been prevented
from doing what was a natural and sometimes the right thing either because
analysis of the emotional action of another, or self-distrustful analysis of my
own emotion destroyed impulse. I cannot conceive the impulse, unless it
was so sudden that I had to act at once, that could urge me into action at
all if it affected personal life.'[3]

Faced with a situation where firm if unsubtle behaviour was called for,
Yeats felt bound to write that 'words are with me a means of investigation,
rather than a means of action'. And they remained so. When Gosse wrote a

letter of apology to Lady Gregory it was so faint and inadequate that Yeats and Robert decided they could not show it to her. Yeats himself then tried to square matters with Gosse and wrote a second letter which, however, was probably never sent. But action rather than analysis eventually carried the day, and when Yeats heard on 10 August that the Prime Minister had granted him a Civil List pension of £150 a year he wrote and posted a letter to Gosse thanking him for all his efforts in a way that showed no self-doubt. The whole episode had nonetheless been greatly painful. As Yeats confessed in his journal, the disagreement had 'been the one serious quarrel I have ever had with Lady Gregory, because the first that has arisen from unreconcilable attitudes towards life'. But if Yeats and Lady Gregory eventually made their peace (and it was several years before the incident was wholly forgotten) the verdict of fractious Dublin was swift and deadly. Ireland's greatest poet was now 'Pensioner Yeats'.

Yeats's attempt to win Dowden's chair at Trinity College was equally suffused with difficulties but was finally unsuccessful.4 When Professor Tyrrell approached him about the post, Yeats wrote to the Vice Provost, John Pentland Mahaffy, asking for an interview. This was a difficult letter to write and Yeats prepared several drafts before sending a version in which he unfortunately managed to misspell the title he was seeking. Mahaffy supported him nonetheless, partly because there was bad feeling between himself and Dowden, and, when Yeats further threatened his own case by confessing to his poor eyesight, Mahaffy replied, 'Oh that is all right. There is no work to do. Dowden never did any.' Yeats, however, was determined to prepare himself carefully, and having recently read Spenser, Donne, Ben Jonson and the Jacobean dramatists, he went regularly to the British Museum to immerse himself in the works of Chaucer and other medieval writers. Dowden suggested that the Trinity Board could make arrangements whereby Yeats need not lecture on such subjects as Old English, but he did not whole-heartedly support Yeats's candidature, partly because he did not consider him to be a sufficiently distinguished scholar. JBY in the meantime was greatly concerned that Yeats should not be turned by the university into a mere man of prose and lose his freedom. He need not have worried. Although Dowden was thinking of resigning because of ill-health and indeed took a period of leave of absence, he eventually recovered and resumed his chair. Yeats was to pursue his life not in academe but in the theatre.

II

Edward Gordon Craig and the Abbey Theatre in America

On 7 January 1910, Yeats had a meeting with Edward Gordon Craig which greatly developed his thinking about the staging of plays at the Abbey. Craig himself had returned some months earlier from working with Constantin Stanislávsky on the Moscow Arts Theatre's revolutionary production of *Hamlet*, and now he and Yeats discussed the possibility of using his new ideas in Dublin. Craig by this time had advanced beyond hanging his stage with drapes and had evolved in their place a series of double-jointed folding screens on castors which, painted white or pale yellow, could be used as a subtly lit background. In addition, the screens could be, in Craig's words, 'so arranged as to project into the foreground at various angles of perspective so as to suggest various physical conditions, such as, for example, the corner of a street, or the interior of a building; by this means suggestion, not representation, is relied upon and nevertheless variety is attainable.'[5]

Craig had developed these ideas with the help of a model theatre, and during the spring and summer of 1910 Yeats was experimenting with a version of the Abbey stage built to a scale of one inch to a foot and recording the results in a notebook. The possibility of 'endless transformation' exhilarated him. As he wrote in 'The Tragic Theatre': 'henceforth I shall be able, by means so simple that one laughs, to lay the events of my plays amid a grandeur like that of Babylon; and where there is neither complexity nor compromise nothing need go wrong, no lamps become suddenly unmasked, no ill-painted corner come suddenly into sight'.[6] Here was stimulus and freedom not just for visual effects but for literary ideas as well. 'Henceforth I can all but "produce" my play while I write it, moving hither and thither little figures of cardboard through gay or solemn light or shade, allowing the scene to give the words and the words the scene.'

Nor was it only new works that could be created in this way. Yeats the perpetual reviser could also refashion his previous achievements. *The Land of Heart's Desire*, *The King's Threshold*, *On Baile's Strand* and *Deirdre* were all examined in the light of the new possibilities that had opened up, while Craig himself suggested both staging and costume designs for *The Hour Glass* that were of exceptional importance and interest. The idea for the new set is indicated by one of the four illustrations Craig provided for Yeats's principal edition of his dramatic writings at this time, *Plays for an Irish Theatre*, published in 1911. The Wise Man is shown seated at his desk in a study formed from a circle of screens. A second circle provides a dramatic entrance and the whole suggests both the powerful simplicity and the subtle play of light and shade which pleases the eye by constantly inviting it to explore the interesting use of space.

Craig's costume designs were equally innovatory. Derived from the text, they achieved an authentic sense of being historical without resorting to archaeological verisimilitude. Most interesting was the costume design for the Fool. Craig's acute sensitivity to the visual aspects of character is suggested by the notes made round his design for the costume. The Fool should convey 'a hint of clown a hint of Death and of sphinx and of boy'.[7]

Much of this approach was focussed in Craig's most innovatory idea: the Fool's mask. Yeats, himself a man of masks, was so impressed that, even though no one could yet be found to make the mask, he urged Craig to design another for the Blind Man in *On Baile's Strand*. Craig prepared an etching for this, and when it was exhibited in Dublin during 1913 he wrote a note for the catalogue explaining his purpose. 'The eyes are closed, they are still cross, and I take it that the man sees with his nose. I imagine that he smells his way in the dark, and he seems to keep up an eternal kind of windy whistling with his pursed up lips'. So much of character could a mask convey, and an eerie distance from ordinary life is already clear. Craig then went on to make a more general point. 'The advantage of a mask over a face is that it is always repeating unerringly the poetic fancy, repeating on Monday in 1912 exactly what it said on Saturday in 1909 and what it will say on Wednesday in 1999.' To Yeats, searching for his own idea of the mask, for something at once permanent and poetic to place over his own often vacillating features, Craig's notions were deeply sympathetic. 'Let us again', Craig wrote of the actor, 'cover his face with a mask in order that his expression – the visual expression of the Poetic spirit – shall be everlasting.'[8]

But if ideas in art and life seemed to be drawing close, with the loss of Annie Horniman the Abbey was in urgent need of funds. As Yeats wrote in a public letter:

> our subsidy, including the free use of the Abbey Theatre comes to an end, as well as our patent, in this year. We have saved enough money (about £1,900) to take over the Abbey Theatre and to pay for a new patent, a somewhat heavy expense. Our business advisers tell us that the sum of £5,000, which would hardly support a London theatre for a season, would enable us to keep our theatre vigorous, intellectual, and courageous for another half dozen years.

An appeal for funds was launched, Lady Gregory canvassed donations from her well-to-do friends, and there was a successful season at London's Court Theatre, after which a potentially lucrative four-month American tour was arranged. Yeats agreed to accompany the players from mid-September to mid-October and to lecture on the work of Gordon Craig and Synge especially in talks entitled 'The Theatre of Beauty' and 'The Twentieth Century Revival of Irish Poetry and Drama'.

Having established a secondary repertory company to play at the Abbey in their absence, Yeats sailed with the principal Abbey players from Liverpool on 14 September 1911. They were due to perform in Boston, New York, Philadelphia and Chicago, all cities where there were large populations of Irish-Americans. There were rumours of trouble from the start. News of Yeats's Civil List pension had greatly angered the Anglophobic Irish-Americans, and JBY wrote to Lily that he was sure there would be rows. He was particularly concerned that the Catholic priests would stir up opposition on the grounds of Church and Country, and he was glad that Lady Gregory was accompanying his son. 'Her strong sense and resolute courage', he wrote, 'will be a great aid.'

Despite the fact that many in Boston were prepared to call the plays Yeats brought over anti-Irish in spirit, Yeats could report that they performed 'to an immense crowd and amid great enthusiasm'. Indeed, many of the Bostonians were puzzled about where the supposed offence in the plays lay, and as a result a 'violent' campaign was launched in the newspapers declaring one of Lady Gregory's works anti-Christian and accusing the company as a whole of producing plays aimed at preventing Home Rule. The Theatre was officially denounced by the Irish Society in Boston, and JBY wondered if his son would be pelted with rotten eggs when he was obliged to appear at a debate with one of the Society's members. As the old artist wryly commented, 'it would be unpleasant, but would be *great* – a mild form of lynching disagreeable for the victim, but *disgraceful to the Irish Society*, doing us little harm, but doing them a great deal'.9

Yeats had so arranged matters that he was due to return to Ireland before the players themselves reached New York. He had nonetheless promised to visit his father, and late on the afternoon of 11 October he arrived at the boarding-house where JBY had taken up residence. In the early days of his life in New York, JBY had failed to secure the hoped-for commissions, but he enjoyed the life of the city so greatly that he resolved to stay on. Quinn, although 'the crossest man in the world', remained a staunch friend, but experiences of commissioning oils of himself and his mistress Dorothy Coates were such that Quinn felt he could recommend JBY only as a pencil portraitist. Indeed, JBY was obliged to recognise that it was his son rather than he who had the reputation in the United States. 'You have a great position here,' he wrote. 'The ladies (the next epoch in America belongs to them) meet together to study *Ideas of Good and Evil*. They go through it as if it was an Act of Parliament where every monosyllable is important.'

Yeats himself was cold and dilatory in replying to such correspondence, and JBY was concerned that Yeats's letter to his old schoolfriend Charles Johnston, now resident in New York and loudly singing his praises, was 'rather laconic'. He also had a more delicate matter to deal with. He had received an angry letter from Quinn which contained a 'furious but veiled account' of rumours circulating in Dublin to the effect that, when Yeats had been in Paris seeing Maud Gonne, he had become a close friend of Dorothy Coates and then carelessly boasted back home of his conquest. Miss Coates was careful to picture herself as the wronged party and to paint Yeats as the aggressor, but though the affair developed no further Quinn was so angry that, despite JBY's attempts at conciliation, the lawyer and the poet refused to have anything to do with each other for five years.

Circumstances eventually obliged JBY himself to become a lodger in one of the upstairs rooms of a restaurant on West Twenty-Ninth Street belonging to the three Petitpas sisters.[10] He had dined regularly there for a year and the cosmopolitan atmosphere was greatly attractive to him. The two eldest sisters were 'grim silent people', however and, despite the excellent food and service they provided, so careful about money that JBY often had to sit in his room wrapped in his coat or flee to the warmth of the waiting room at Penn Station. For all that his credit frequently mounted high, the Petitpas sisters were prepared to continue allowing him to live in their establishment for the simple reason that JBY's powers as a conversationalist were such that many guests were attracted to the restaurant. Indeed, dining out with John Butler Yeats became one of the regular features of New York literary and artistic life. JBY had secured for himself a curious but agreeable position in this world, and if he could delight his innumerable companions with the warmth and quality of his talk, he was occasionally nettled by such careless remarks as 'So you're the father of the great Yeats,' a tactless comment which the old man beautifully countered by staring sternly at the speaker and retorting: '*I* am the great Yeats.'

Little information survives to suggest the personal details of the meeting between JBY and his son. A number of minor celebrities had been lined up to meet the poet, and one of JBY's friends reported that he spoke 'a great deal and interestingly'. Certainly, he managed to delight the assembled women for, 'besides all his other charm, "he is such a man of the world". You know the New York ladies.' But if Yeats was a social success on that afternoon, the following morning he went to an appointment of which his father would certainly not have approved. Just as in Boston he had been to see the medium known as Mrs Chenoweth, so now he had a two-hour session with the well-known fortune-teller Mrs Beattie. Although Yeats would continue as a member of the Stella Matutina order of magicians and would even advance through the various grade examinations they offered, his involvement with occult symbolism had begun to wane and an interest in spiritualism was taking its place.

The United States was a particularly appropriate location for this new orientation, since it was there, in 1848, when the daughters of the Fox family of Hydesville, New York State, claimed they could communicate with the spirit of a murdered man buried in their cellar, that the modern spiritualist movement began. The Fox girls themselves became celebrities, and spiritualism soon spread from America to Europe. In its attempt to prove the existence of the soul as an entity that could survive bodily death, it was another effort to combat the rationalism and materialism of nineteenth-century thought. Like the Order of the Golden Dawn, it appeared as an answer to the spiritual problems of contemporary man and, again like the Order, could draw on a wide-ranging and often profound tradition which included such figures as Paracelsus, Swedenborg and Mesmer. Yeats himself would soon be climbing to the garrets of Holloway and Soho to pay his shilling and wait among the servant girls for 'the wisdom of some fat old medium'.

Lady Gregory meanwhile was left in charge of the rest of the American tour.[11] This was to be more stormy and exciting than she could have supposed. Although she herself made a favourable impression on the Americans, she found herself constantly having to defend the art she and Yeats had laboured so hard to produce. Catholic priests joined their opposition to that of the press, condemning the 'hell-inspired ingenuity and a satanic hatred of the Irish people and their religion' which they believed had given rise to these works. When the company eventually arrived in New York, a riot broke out during the first night of *The Playboy of the Western World*. The actress playing Pegeen Mike had a potato thrown at her, while rosaries and stinkbombs rained down on the stage as booing and cries of 'Shame! Shame!' reached such a pitch that Lady Gregory felt she had to go round behind the set and whisper through an opening to the players, telling them they were to continue acting but to spare their voices as the scene would be played again. After the rioters had been removed by the police and the play had come to an end, Lady Gregory gave a speech from the stage which perfectly exemplified her ability to subdue ignorant stupidity with her courteous smile and patrician calm. On the following night, however, she had an even more powerful ally in the presence of Theodore Roosevelt, who joined her in her box, loudly applauded the performance and, at the end of the evening, escorted her from the theatre in triumph.

John Quinn (whom Yeats had carefully avoided seeing) was so impressed by Lady Gregory's poise that he afterwards took her to Tiffany's where he bought her a gold watch. Then, at the end of the tour, he invited her to stay with him in his New York apartment. Here, just turned sixty, Lady Gregory had a brief but passionate affair with the man who was eighteen years her junior and always held her in the highest regard. Trying to analyse her feelings for him, she wrote on her return to Ireland: 'Why do I love you so much? It ought to be for all the piled up goodness of the years. . . . Yet it is not that. It is the call that came in a moment. Something impetuous and masterful about you that satisfies me. This gives me perfect rest. . . . You surrounded me with thought and care.'[12] Lady Gregory had found in Quinn what she never sought from Yeats.

III

Lily and Lollie Yeats

On his return to Ireland, Yeats was to find himself still the victim of public attack. In October 1911, he read *Ave*, the first volume of George Moore's memoirs. Curiously, he did not at first realise how unpleasant some of the descriptions of him were. 'It is not at all malicious,' he wrote to Lady Gregory. 'Of course there isn't the smallest recognition of the difference between public and private life, except that the consciousness of sin in the matter may have made him unusually careful.' Nonetheless, over the coming months, the book was to rankle increasingly and at the end of the year Lily wrote to JBY to say that, although her brother had at first laughed about the work, 'he nevertheless resented it'. In a period when he was strenuously trying to revise his image as a Celt, Moore's mocking presentation of his earlier enthusiasms was particularly offensive, but it was only when the later volumes came out that Yeats was moved to indignation.

While Lily noted her brother's moods in letters to her father, she had difficulties of her own to cope with.[13] When she sailed with her father to New York to display the goods produced by the Dum Emer Industries at the Irish Exhibition there, she had worked on a stall apart from Miss Gleeson and sent the profits (mostly derived from Quinn and his friends) back to Lollie. She was obliged to hurry home, however, when news came that Lollie and Miss Gleeson had quarrelled and Lollie had moved her business out of Dun Emer. Miss Gleeson, whose visit to the United States had not been a financial success, had now seized the press itself and was threatening to sue both sisters. Although JBY urged Lily to fight for her rights, the disagreement resulted in a parting of the ways, the sisters themselves setting up the Cuala Industries, a name taken from the old barony where their house in Dundrum was situated. In December 1908, the Cuala Press issued its first book: *Poetry and Ireland* by Yeats and Lionel Johnson.

The press itself was moderately successful, although it was obliged to carry a worrying burden of debt. But it was Lollie's emotional problems that were the most pressing difficulty, and these were made worse by the presence of the young Ruth Pollexfen. The girl's mother had eventually been obliged to divorce the repellent Fred Pollexfen and, when her daughters were made wards of court, Ruth was assigned to Lily's care. She was an artistic and talented child who grew into a pleasant young woman, but the troubled Lollie felt excluded by the close relationship that grew up between Ruth and Lily. She became suspicious and felt she was being isolated, an anxiety made worse for her by Louis Purser's continuing but increasingly diffident attentions. Lollie was now forty-two and still unmarried, and although Lily wrote Purser a remarkable letter explaining that his behaviour had spoilt years of Lollie's life, 'taking hope and colours out of everything', Lollie seemed condemned to spinsterhood and a slow progress towards breakdown.

Lily's letters to her father firmly but tactfully suggested how painful the situation was for all of those closely involved, and JBY suggested that a short holiday might help Lollie recover her poise. However, when Lollie wrote bitterly and at length from Florence, JBY was obliged to realise that the trip, far from improving matters, had actually made them worse. Lollie returned to Dublin in the middle of May 1911 only to be obliged to watch in bitter suspicion as preparations were made for Ruth Pollexfen to marry Charles Lane Poole. Yeats himself was asked to give the bride away, and JBY, who knew that his son had 'a natural instinct for pomp and ceremony', declared that the poet had been 'admirable' at the job. The occasion caused Lily, however, to reflect on the sadness of her own life. 'I have a birthday this week,' she wrote, 'and have been thinking back and have come to the conclusion that the mistake with my life has been that I have not had a woman's life but an uncomfortable, unsatisfying mixture of a man's and a woman's, gone out all day earning my living, working like a man for a woman's pay, then kept house, the most difficult housekeeping on nothing certain a year.'[14] As she confessed in a passage that sadly decribed her professional life: 'we toil all day and all the year round and only get in at the Industry something over £800 a year – to pay ourselves what no man over 25 would do clerk work for'.

The £500 of debt hanging over the Cuala Industries was a constant worry and this, added to Lollie's condition, meant that from the close of 1910 to the middle of 1912 the press issued only one book, *Synge and the Ireland of his Time*. Discussions with her brother about her financial worries appeared to solve nothing, but, with the death of Edward Dowden in April 1913 and Lollie's agreement to publish a posthumous volume of his poetry, the relationship between Yeats and his sister reached a sour crisis. Yeats feared that his reputation might be sullied by his being associated with what he was sure would be a poor volume. He wrote to Lily saying that if the book was privately printed then little harm would be done but if they decided to issue it commercially 'that is another matter and we shall have to secure some form of circular that will protect me'. By the end of September, three hundred copies of Dowden's poems at ten shillings and sixpence had been run off and Yeats wrote acidly to Lollie on 25 October to say that they were even 'worse' than he feared.[15]

Having rightly declared that Dowden's work was spoiled by 'a general flaccidity of technique', Yeats returned to the important matter of his own reputation. 'Do not forget what I said about the circular. It is entirely necessary that your circular make it plain that I am not responsible for this book. Remember that my critical reputation is important to me. It is even financially important. I cannot have anyone suppose that I am responsible for the selection of this book.' Even in death, it appeared, Dowden was an enemy, and Yeats wrote to JBY complaining about what he considered the underhand trick his sister had played on him. JBY begged him not to make any public remarks about Dowden, who had been, he reminded his son, one of his oldest and dearest friends. Yeats, it seems, did indeed avoid public discussion of Dowden's poems, but he insisted the following year that the Cuala prospectus should print a note declaring: 'This book is not a part of the Cuala series arranged by W. B. Yeats.'

IV

Maud Gonne MacBride and the Nationalist Imagination

While Yeats was immersed in the familiar problems of his family, he continued to see Maud Gonne MacBride. Maud now spent much of her time in France painting, sightseeing and doing charitable work while watching Iseult grow into a young woman and rearing Sean as he prepared to start school. Ireland, however, remained her preoccupation, and visitors from Maud's adopted country kept her in contact with events. She was visited, for example, by Sir Roger Casement, whose portrait she painted and whose ardent nationalism she greatly admired. During the Boer War, Casement had been violently opposed to John MacBride and the Irish Brigade, but now, having seen the brutalities inflicted by Portuguese imperialists in the Belgian Congo, he realised what appalling conditions had been inflicted on the peasants of his native land. Despite being still a civil servant, he praised both MacBride and his Brigade, urging Maud to write an account of them both, saying 'it was a fine fight and should be told'. But, while Maud glowed in the presence of Casement's enthusiasm for her cause, Yeats was altogether more suspicious of him. He had met Casement in the studio of his friend the painter William Rothenstein and, carefully observing him, had come the conclusion that Casement personified 'something new and terrible' for Ireland. With exceptional perspicacity, Yeats defined this as 'the mood of the mystic victim'.[16]

Another visitor to Maud in Paris was Helena Molony, the secretary of the Daughters of Erin. She and Maud decided that their cause would be greatly helped if they issued a newspaper, and early in 1909 the first edition of *Bean na hEireann* ('Women of Ireland') was issued at a penny. The newspaper's emblem of a peasant woman standing before a tower and a rising sun was drawn by another of Yeats's friends, Constance Markiewicz. Taking courage from her sister Eva's example, Constance had begun to see that the life of the great Ascendancy families in Ireland was increasingly irrelevant to the country's deepest needs. Early in 1908, and at the invitation of Helena Molony, Constance arrived at a meeting of the Daughters of Erin dressed in the furs and silk gown she had donned that evening for a Castle ball. Soon, however, the trappings of privilege were put aside, along with her relationship to her charming but feckless husband. Dressed now in patriotic tweed, Constance spoke on public platforms as a committed member of Sinn Fein and busied herself organising a band of Dublin teenage boys into a core of youths trained to fight for Ireland.

Meanwhile, in a little tobacconist's shop on Parnell Street, Tom Clarke, one of the men Maud had helped free from Portland jail, set up the unofficial headquarters of the IRB and drew into his circle people with a deep and even mystical feeling for Irish nationalism. These included Maud herself, MacBride, Constance and a revolutionary young schoolmaster called Patrick Pearse. Maud was especially impressed by Pearse and his school at Rathmines, where the pupils, instructed in the latest Montessori methods, were taught Irish as well as English, Pearse regarding 'the factor of nationality' as of prime importance to the education he was offering. His assistant at the school, Thomas MacDonagh, was a published poet similarly inspired by the idealism of the Irish renaissance, and Maud herself contributed to the imagery of this when she offered the school an allegorical picture of Cathleen ni Houlihan to embellish an establishment where a painting of the young Cuchulain already hung in the hall, its frame decorated with the Gaelic motto 'Though I live but a year and a day, I will live so that my name goes sounding down the ages.' Indeed, so pervasive was the influence of Cuchulain at St Enda's School that pupils sometimes thought of him as a sort of ghostly member of staff patrolling the corridors as a living myth.

Such pagan, Celtic idealism was not the only force to inspire Pearse and his colleagues, however. If Cuchulain was one hero, the missionary saint Colmcille was another, and the Celtic and the Catholic merged for Pearse and others in a vision of blood sacrifice and lives violently surrendered to the cause of Irish freedom. As Pearse himself wrote: 'a love and a service so excessive as to annihilate all thought of self, a recognition that one must give all, must be willing to make the ultimate sacrifice – this is the inspiration alike of the story of Cuchulain and the story of Colmcille, the inspiration that has made one a hero and the other a saint'.[17] To such men as Pearse and his followers, the idea of Ireland's nationhood was now 'holy, a thing inviolate and inviolable'. Like Yeats, they could conceive of nationalism as something essentially spiritual, but where Yeats had rejected Christianity and largely reared his ideas on the poetic inspiration provided by the occult, Pearse and his colleagues found support in images altogether more familiar to the majority of their countrymen. While Ireland itself might be conceived as a 'dark rose', its people were Christ on Calvary 'labouring, scourged, crowned with thorns, agonising and dying', a nation which would nonetheless rise again when it was time for the rose to 'redden into bloom'. Pearse and his colleagues sought less an initiation into mystery than a baptism of blood, and in time this would alter the course of Irish history for ever.

Although Yeats sometimes played down his relationship with Pearse, he had a closer knowledge of the man than he suggested. For his part, it was

Cathleen ni Houlihan which had convinced Pearse that Yeats was far more than the 'English poet of the third or fourth rank' he had once thought him and thus a figure of no interest to a Nationalist. Now, from about 1910, he was to be touched by the interest Yeats took in his school. The distinguished director of the Abbey Theatre was not above attending productions at St Enda's and praising them generously. Yeats told Lady Gregory that the school was 'one of the few places where we have friends', and the depth of that friendship is suggested by his allowing Pearse to stage benefit productions at the Abbey for his school at a reduced rent.

The children mounted plays there in 1910 and 1911, and when, two years later, money for St Enda's was still needed, Yeats was again conspicuously generous. 'We had barely time to frame our project in words when Mr Yeats assented to it,' Pearse recalled, 'and then he did something more generous still, for he offered to produce for the benefit of St Enda's the play of Mr Tagore's to the production of which he had been looking forward as an important epoch in the life of the Abbey – the first presentation in Europe of a poet who, he thinks, is possibly the greatest now living'. Yeats had recently met Rabindranath Tagore in London and he was now keen to promote not only this Indian writer's work but to foster the talent of an Irishman whose educational ideals were similar to Tagore's own. He asked Pearse to write a play for the Abbey, and in May 1913 the Theatre performed Pearse's *An Ri* along with Tagore's *The Post Office*. As Pearse wrote: 'I understood then more clearly than ever that no one is so generous as a great artist; for a great artist is always giving gifts.' Among these gifts was Yeats's time. The Celtic-inspired Pearse had extolled to him that ancient Irish form of education in which children were encouraged by meeting 'men whom their gifts of soul, or mind, or body had lifted high above their contemporaries, – the captains, the poets, the prophets of the people'. Yeats took the hint, and Pearse could boast that now in contemporary Ireland 'we can bring the heroes and seers and scholars to the schools . . . and get them to talk to the children'.

For Maud too at this period it was children who became ever more closely her concern and, while she watched with approval the education offered by Pearse, she organised her own canteen to feed those others who were near to starving on the Dublin streets. These were strenuous activities and, during the summer months, Maud rested from them at Les Mouettes, her house on the Normandy coast which she shared with her own children, her cousin Mrs Clay, and the inevitable menagerie of birds, dogs, rabbits and a black Persian cat called Minnaloushe. The house itself was a gaudy building in Arabic style, but was surrounded by delightful and carefully tended flower and vegetable gardens. In a bedroom upstairs there was alleged to be a haunted portrait, while Maud wrote to Quinn saying that the nearby Mont-Saint-Michel was 'the most magical place in France'. She delighted in telling him that a Druid temple to the sun had once been built there and had been replaced by the church dedicated to the saint, who 'was a sun force too'. The history of the building particularly pleased her for, as she wrote, 'the English tried time after time to take the abbey fortress and left thousands of dead under its walls but never succeeded. It is invincible in its perfection of beauty.'

Maud was also determined that her house should be a sanctuary for her friends as well as her family, and it was while he was staying at Les Mouettes in 1910 that Yeats heard of the misunderstanding whereby Lennox Robinson had kept the Abbey Theatre open on the day that Edward VII died.

Two poems he wrote to Maud in this year show his maturing understanding of their relationship. He suggested in 'Peace' that time had touched and subdued a woman who, in her stormy youth, could never have posed to artists as an ideal form of feminine loveliness precisely because of the violence that raged around her. In 'The Mask', an idea that was preoccupying Yeats in both the personal reflections noted down in his journal and in the theatre now moved to the centre of his lyric poetry. In his journal, the mask was a means of discovering the antithetical personality, a way of avoiding 'the infinite pain of self-realisation' and embracing in its place a joyous and creative sense of psychological release. On the stage, the mask was a means of so wholly disguising the physical personality of the actor that his role could emerge free from the exigencies of continuous self-expression, doing so in a manner that went unerringly to the poetic core of the experience he was portraying. In personal relations, the mask seemed to combine these needs of reaching out to something joyously free of the daily and painfully negotiated self while, at the same time, offering a sense of the essential, enduring delight which the presence of the beloved seems to promise. In other words it was partly a projection.

The lover is attracted to those elements of the beloved which she has discovered in herself and which he in his turn has further fashioned into an image of all that will give him joy. Except in the most elusive moments, however (those moments when the mask so perfectly covers the face that desire and reality seem one), a nagging sense of artifice obtrudes. The lover is unable to trust his imagination and seeks painfully and foolishly for the 'truth':

> 'Put off that mask of burning gold
> With emerald eyes.'[18]

But the beloved is altogether too shrewd to consent and her refusal – the sense the poem conveys of a vividly tantalising sexuality rooted in imaginative understanding – expresses both her conviction that 'It was the mask engaged your mind' and her sense that it is the passion, the 'fire' of their relationship which is the reality rather than prosaic analysis.

While the strong and disquieting sexual charge in 'The Mask' suggests that Maud and Yeats were, in Yeats's view at least, intimately involved in a complex conflict between imaginative desire and the reality of their natural selves, his journal makes clear that politics was as always deeply involved in their relationship too. Yeats was writing the essay he eventually published as *Synge and the Ireland of his Time* and he described how Maud was involved in the composition of this. Because the weather was windy and wet, the household stayed indoors and Yeats and Maud got into an argument about the attacks on Synge and the circumstances that surrounded the first split in the Abbey Theatre. Yeats noticed that this 'old quarrel' was the one difference between them that Maud felt extremely strongly about and, for this reason, he always allowed himself to be drawn into it, hoping he could convince Maud of how fundamental his belief in an elite literature – a literature not made out of popular political slogans – was to his whole way of thinking. Everything he had worked for and his own integrity as a man of letters were involved in this disagreement, and because he thought of Maud as personifying Ireland, 'a summing up in one mind of what is best in the romantic political Ireland of my youth and the youth of others for some years yet', he felt it essential that his essay on Synge should clarify his ideas on national literature. In so doing, he might yet convince Maud of the importance of his purpose.

The journal entries rail against the various types of false national literature Yeats had experienced. He believed that nakedly propagandist writing in the Davisite tradition made a nation slaves in the cause of liberty. Only a literature created for its own sake or in answer to some spiritual need could preserve the imaginative integrity which politicians might one day be able to call on as a true and subtle image of their nation's soul. It was such great poets as Goethe, Shakespeare, Dante and Homer who were the real creators of national character. Any nationalist literature with aims less exalted could only inflict damage by being external and picturesque.

Something altogether more searching was required, and Yeats wrote that the true purpose of a national poet was to create a genuine community of the spirit out of what is 'interior, delicate and haughty'. He wished to fashion for his nation a culture as subtle and unified as that which he saw in the nearby medieval abbey of Mont-Saint-Michel. He was obliged to realise nonetheless that this Unity of Feeling was all but impossible to attain in a world where Unity of Culture had been virtually destroyed, so depriving the people of 'a definite table of values understood by all'. He, Synge and Lady Gregory alone, he believed, had striven for a type of genuine national literature that could help to recreate this ideal, a literature in which the Irish people might one day be able to recognise their true qualities.

But, while the old disagreement between Maud and Yeats over nationalism and literature remained a source of conflict, the strain imposed by her revival of their 'mystic marriage' imposed its own burden. Yeats had found a degree of physical release with Mabel Dickinson, but there is evidence to suggest that his thoughts were returning to Olivia Shakespear. By 1900, the guilt he had felt at their parting was beginning to be assuaged, and by May that year, when Olivia's mother died, the couple were writing to each other. While at Coole in 1910, Yeats turned his attention to Olivia's horoscope, and the details suggest that by June, when he returned from his stay in Normandy, the couple were close and perhaps even intimate. Material even more obscure hints at jealousy on Maud's part, and certainly by January 1911, when Yeats drafted his poem 'Friends,' in which he discussed his relationships with Maud, Olivia and Lady Gregory, his sexual feeling for Maud appears a matter of reminiscence rather than present fact. Her power over him was not, however, something easily relinquished, and visits to Les Mouettes continued through the following two summers.

The effect such a preoccupied but colourful household could have on others was vividly described by James Cousins and his wife, Belfast friends of James Joyce, who had come to look for metaphysical mysteries among the Celtic ruins near Bayeux.[19] The summer of 1912 was an exceptionally wet one and Maud wrote to the young couple: 'as we are all evidently destined to be drowned, you might as well be drowned with friends instead of alone in a strange village hotel. So come over here.' The Cousinses willingly obeyed and were met by a donkey cart at the local railway station. Maud busied herself trying to pack the Cousinses' luggage into the cart while Yeats stood near by looking 'like an elongated rook in rain'. The thin and dreamy form of little Sean loitered somewhere nearabouts, and when the party arrived at Les Mouettes they were greeted by Iseult surrounded by a dog and two cats, while from inside the house came the cooings and chirpings of the various pet birds along with 'a sharp parrot-like exclamation'. Cousins later came across a sleeping dormouse and a family of white rats, while one of the doves alighted with a little gurgle of pleasure on the rim of Mrs Cousins's hat.

The company was later taken to the cathedral at Bayeux in a large farm cart with a hooped canvas covering, Yeats himself being stowed away as conveniently as his inordinate length would permit on the back seat at the end of the canvas tunnel. But such expeditions were for him merely a diversion from more serious concerns. Yeats was often so preoccupied by his thoughts as to appear absent-minded, and once he expatiated over dinner so intensely on his favourite themes that he began to gather all the dishes on the table in front of him, and it took a laughing Maud to point out that the other guests were still hungry. Only partly roused from his reverie, Yeats began indiscriminately to redistribute the plates while offering not a word of apology. At other times he would sit for hours by the kitchen stove chanting in an abstracted monotone the lines of whatever poem he was working on. In the summer of 1912 he wrote the last of his Rosicrucian poems, 'The Mountain Tomb', and by the end of the year had completed 'To a Child Dancing in the Wind', his first evocation of the teenage Iseult.

She had moved him profoundly when he saw her singing by the edge of the sea, chanting words and music she had herself composed. 'She thought herself alone, stood barefooted between sea and sand; sang with lifted head of the civilisations that there had come and gone, ending every verse with the cry: "O Lord, let something remain."' There is a poignant but ambiguous beauty about Yeats's recreation of this scene:

> Dance there upon the shore;
> What need have you to care
> For wind or water's roar?
> And tumble out your hair
> That the salt drops have wet;
> Being young you have not known
> The fool's triumph, nor yet
> Love lost as soon as won,
> Nor the best labourer dead
> And all the sheaves to bind.
> What need have you to dread
> The monstrous crying of wind?[20]

Barely seventeen, Iseult suggested the beauty that had once suffused her mother, as well as having her own hieratic but vulnerable attraction. The agonising hopelessness of a transferred passion was beginning to wake in Yeats.

V

Literary London

With Lennox Robinson looking after the day-to-day business of the Abbey and producing many of its new realist plays, Yeats was able to spend more time in England. Here his life moved in increasingly influential circles, and people recalled him as variously aloof, entertaining or subtly responsive to the needs of others as he focussed on them his concentrated power of attention. At Cambridge, Professor Wedd saw him at his most abstracted.[21] Wedd had been invited to meet Yeats at a lunch,

> but he was then in a sort of trance and found it hard to open his eyes or his mouth. I don't believe he ate or spoke; his followers, a dear simple crowd of hero-worshippers rather nervous at being in a foreign land,

looked and watched for their leader to speak some words of power; but the oracle was dumb. At night . . . he came out of his trance, and then it was the turn of the others to be entranced, for his talk held them all spell-bound.

Unfortunately for Wedd, he could not be there to witness the occasion, but Joseph Hone vividly portrayed Yeats's manner at its most alert. 'In a tête-à-tête conversation Yeats always gave of his best, rarely allowing an otiose remark to pass his lips; and this consideration sprang no less from an inborn courtesy than from a sense of his own dignity and what was due to others. Though sometimes pontifical, he saw the humorous side of things and of an adversary, and would press home an argument with gleeful nodding of the head and rubbing of his clasped hands.'

Yeats was not always in command, however, as his own self-depreciating account written to his father on 29 November 1909 of one of Edmund Gosse's dinner parties when he sat next to the Prime Minister suggests.[22]

Edmund Gosse whispered to me in the few minutes before dinner, 'Mind! no politics,' and then introduced me to Lord Cromer, and Lord Cromer's first sentence was, 'We had a very interesting debate in the House of Lords this afternoon.' I, being still wax under Gosse's finger, replied, 'Ah, I look at English politics as a child does at a racecourse, taking sides by the colours of the jockeys' coats. And I often change sides in the middle of a race.' This rather chilled the conversation.

The Olympian heights from which Yeats was wont to judge people were never far from his mind, however, and, as he told his father: 'I got on better with Asquith; I found him an exceedingly well-read man, especially, curiously enough, in poetry. . . . Not a man of really fine culture, I think, but exceedingly charming.' Asquith himself was considerably impressed by Yeats, and would in time come to value his views on Irish politics particularly. Yeats was prevented from making a similar judgement of Winston Churchill however, who was among the guests at a political weekend Yeats was invited to. Churchill was, Yeats told Lady Gregory, 'obviously the ablest man' there, but, as he confessed, 'I had not much opportunity to talk to him, as he preferred bridge.'

Those who shrank from cards could be rewarded with generous insights. Lady Lyttelton remembered Yeats's still black and uncontrollably swaying hair, his eyes 'burning with vehemence, smouldering with a deeper emotion than he was expressing, and finally a general sense that he did not belong to the life of London, or of England, or indeed perhaps of the life of the Earth itself'. At a weekend houseparty of Lady Desborough's, Yeats and

Edith Lyttelton were thrown together as the only two people who did not want to play whist, and she recalled that:

> We sat side by side on the sofa and plunged into talk. I was tired, and rather fretful because I never seemed to have enough time to read or write. Politics, social service and society swallowed all my energies, and then came the duty of taking my daughter to her first round of balls and parties and I dreaded this interruption to the little spare time I had. I cannot think why I should have poured all this out to Yeats, but I did, and I am glad I did because he said something to me in that dimly-lit luxurious room which I have never forgotten. 'Whenever I have to do something,' he declared, 'like a dull bit of routine business, or enduring the talk of a bore, I always say to myself "Remember, this is an occupation which requires great skill."' It is curious how a few words like these can reverberate in one's being for the whole of life. How often have I admonished myself when starting on some very distasteful job. 'Remember, this is an occupation which requires great skill' – and at once the occasion is invested with dignity.[23]

Yeats's literary friends in London included, besides Edmund Gosse, John Masefield and Robert Bridges, the latter of whom Yeats had known since 1897. Among the many artists he knew were Charles Ricketts and Charles Shannon, Althea Gyles (who designed the cover for *The Wind among the Reeds*) and T. Sturge Moore, who was later to produce some of the most distinguished of Yeats's book-jackets and enter a searching philosophical correspondence with him.* It was yet another artistic acquaintance however, William Rothenstein, who introduced Yeats to a figure who was briefly to impress him, the Indian poet Rabindranath Tagore, whose play *The Post Office* he would produce for the benefit of Pearse's pupils at the Abbey. Rothenstein had met Tagore in India in 1910 and been greatly impressed by his 'inner charm' and refined physical appearance. When Rothenstein returned to London he discovered an English translation of one of Tagore's short stories in the *Modern Review* and was so impressed that he wrote to friends in Calcutta asking if any more of Tagore's work was available in English. He was sent a packet of poems 'of a highly mystical character' which struck him as being even more remarkable than the story. Tagore was then invited to England, where he arrived in 1912. This, his third voyage to Europe, was delayed due to illness, and it was while

---

* There was inevitably an element of coterie politics in this choice of artistic friends. 'There are two artistic camps in England just now,' Yeats told Quinn in 1909, 'the Ricketts and Shannon camp which carries on the tradition of Watts and the romantic painters, and the camp of Augustus John which is always shouting its defiance at the other. I sometimes feel I am divided between them as Coleridge was between Christianity and the philosophers when he said "My intellect is with Spinoza but my whole heart with Paul and the Apostles."' Yeats clearly sided with his heart.

he was recuperating that he translated a large number of his poems for a volume that was later issued under the title *Gitanjali*.

On his arrival, and knowing almost no one else in England, Tagore visited Rothenstein and read him his new work. 'Here was a poetry of a new order, which seemed to me on a level with that of the great mystics,' Rothenstein wrote. So excited was he that he sent word to Yeats about the poet and, although Yeats failed to reply, when Rothenstein wrote again Yeats asked him to send him the translations. 'When he had read them his enthusiasm equalled mine. He came to London and went carefully through the poems, making here and there a suggestion, but leaving the original little changed.' Rothenstein later persuaded the India Society to print a limited edition of Tagore's poems for which Yeats agreed to write an introduction. The brief essay expressed much of Yeats's excitement. 'These prose translations from Rabindranath Tagore', he wrote, 'have stirred my blood as nothing has for years.' Yeats described how he carried the manuscript of the translation about with him for days, reading it in trains, buses and restaurants, and being so moved that he was occasionally obliged to close the little exercise books in which the translations had been made in case he betrayed his emotion to those around him.

Yeats was excited by Tagore's versions of his work because he thought he found in them the sort of poetry he had long thought was merely an ideal in the modern world. The poems were 'the work of a supreme culture', but for all their sophistication 'they yet appear as much the growth of the common soil as the grass and the rushes'. Here was verse that emerged from a tradition 'where poetry and religion are the same thing' and which gathered from 'learned and unlearned metaphor and emotion'. Here, in other words, was that Yeatsian ideal of a poetry which 'carried back again to the multitude the thought of the scholar and of the noble'.

Older friends also inspired him. The mending of his relationship with Olivia Shakespear meant that Yeats could attend the salon she held in her house at 12 Brunswick Gardens, close to Kensington Palace. Olivia was now part of a circle of London hostesses entertaining artists, writers and those interested in the occult, and it was at the Knightsbridge home of her friend Eva Fowler that Olivia had been introduced to the young American poet Ezra Pound. At the close of January 1909, she invited Pound and a friend to tea, and a delighted Pound, ambitious to make his mark on English literary society, wrote to his mother describing Olivia as 'the most charming woman in London'.[24] A little over a fortnight later, on 16 February, Pound was back once again taking tea at Brunswick Gardens. Although he did not know how close Olivia and Yeats's relationship was, her friendship with his hero added immeasurably to her charm, and Pound wrote back to an American friend telling her how he had 'sat on the same hearth rug' on which Yeats himself had stood.

The degree of Pound's interest in Yeats was made evident during the tea party when he began to talk. 'He talked of Yeats, as one of the Twenty of the world who have added to the world's poetical matter – He read a short piece of Yeats, in a voice dropping with emotion, in a voice like Yeats' own – he spoke of his interest in all the Arts, in that he might find things of use in them for his own – which is the Highest of them all.' Olivia's daughter Dorothy was so enraptured by the performance that she fell in love with Pound who, at twenty-three, was just a year older than herself. His slightly unfamiliar first name entranced her, and she confessed to her notebook that he had 'a wonderful, beautiful face, a high forehead, prominent over the eyes; a long, delicate nose, with little, red nostrils; a strange mouth, never still, & quite elusive'. While her mother had passed a mildly critical comment about Pound's 'untidy boots', Dorothy waved such objections aside in her excitement over a young man who was so beautiful to watch and who, she thought, did not know he was so appealing. The presence of a man who was waiting for 'the Great Inspiration' thrilled her too, and, in a social circle where the occult was part of everyday conversation, Dorothy asked him if he had 'seen things in a crystal'. Pound suavely declared he could 'see things' without the help of such supernatural agency and that he was keeping himself 'in readiness, open minded and waiting', for 'the Great Day'.

Pound later wrote that he had known at fifteen 'pretty much what I wanted to do', and had resolved that 'at thirty I would know more about poetry than any man living, that I would know the dynamic content from the shell, that I would know what was accounted poetry everywhere'. The broad if superficial eclecticism of his university education had encouraged such dreams, and Pound early discovered ways of cutting corners in his attempt to pose as a scholar familiar with large swathes of the world's literature. 'It is not necessary', he told his friend William Carlos Williams, 'to read everything in a book in order to speak intelligently of it.' A first-class memory, an ear for jargon and an eye for up-to-date questions helped Pound fashion an appearance of erudition, while his knowledge of languages (a knowledge that experts were often to show as flawed) was based on the idea that 'one NEEDS, damn well needs, to know the few hundred words in the few really good poems that any language has in it'.

In this way the literature of the Old English poets, of the troubadours, of the writers of medieval France and of the dramatists of baroque Spain all came into his purlieu and were added to his acquaintance with Browning, the Pre-Raphaelites and the early works of Yeats. By 1905, Pound was already imitating passages from *The Wind among the Reeds*, and his first volume, *A Lume Spento*, privately printed in Venice, consists of an interesting mélange of passion and pastiche, a young man's ardours finding their expression through voices as various as those of the troubadours and the English and Irish poets of the 1890s. A copy of the volume was posted to Yeats who declared he found the poems 'charming', and Pound was delighted at having 'been praised by the greatest living poet'. It was Yeats and London that now lured him away from Venice.

If Yeats was a principal reason for Pound's decision to visit England, the American was also drawn by his belief that London was 'the *centre* of at least Anglo-Saxon letters and presumably of intellectual action'. With more enthusiasm than precise knowledge, Pound believed there was '*more* going on, and what went on went on *sooner* than in New York'.[25] On his arrival in London, Pound headed for Elkin Mathews's bookshop, the focus of the 'buggers gang', where the works of the poets of the Nineties had been displayed and where James Joyce's only collection of verse, *Chamber Music*, had just been issued. Pound was introduced to some young and very minor literary figures but, determined to take London by storm, he soon met Selwyn Image, Ernest Rhys, the influential writer and editor Ford Madox Ford (still then using his Germanic-sounding name of Ford Madox Hueffer), T. E. Hulme, and those writers who gathered at the Tour Eiffel restaurant in Percy Street. Here Pound read his remarkable and vigorous Provençal pastiche 'Sestina: Altaforte' so enthusiastically that, as one of those gathered there recalled, 'the table shook and cutlery vibrated in resonance with his voice'. Pound was nonetheless rapidly disillusioned with the poetry being produced in London, calling it 'a horrible agglomerate compost . . . a doughy mess of third-hand Keats, Wordsworth, heaven knows what, fourth-rate Elizabethan sonority blunted, half-melted, lumpy'. So far, however, he had failed to meet Yeats or, in his new volume *Personae*, to 'shake off the lethargy of this our time'.

Eventually, in May 1909, when Yeats himself returned to London from Ireland, Olivia and Dorothy Shakespear took Pound to Woburn Buildings to meet his hero. Yeats, Pound wrote, seemed 'inclined to be decent to me', and Pound himself managed to make sufficient of an impression among the throng of Yeats's admirers to be contacted a week after their first meeting and invited to see him the following Monday when Yeats was expecting 'Antonio Cipicco an Italian poet of note', along with some other friends including Florence Farr. Yeats himself returned to Dublin in early July and remained there until November, so the friendship could not at this stage strike a deep root. Pound meanwhile was giving lectures at the London Polytechnic, preparing his prose work *The Spirit of Romance*, receiving the as yet unreciprocated passion of Dorothy Shakespear, and moving to 10 Church Walk, an attractive passageway just off Kensington High Street.

Here he began to perfect his image as a poet, wearing ties loosely knotted like a cravat, spats, a velvet jacket, an overcoat with lapis-lazuli buttons, and a pair of pince-nez perched above a carefully clipped moustache and minuscule goatee. But for all his imitation of the outward appearance of a poet of the Tragic Generation, Pound's admiration for Yeats hid a considerable combativeness. For example, when Yeats returned to London in December 1909, Pound and a friend found themselves sitting close to Yeats and Olivia Shakespear at a performance of Shaw's *The Shewing Up of Blanco Posnet*, and when afterwards Pound took all four of them to tea at Prince's Restaurant in Piccadilly, the two men were soon embroiled in a heated argument about the benefit of knowing several languages besides one's own.

Yeats, who had always found foreign languages difficult to learn, cantankerously dismissed the ability to speak several as merely a bus conductor's knack of memorising strings of words. Pound defended a wide knowledge of vernacular literatures as proof of intellectual power, but Yeats chose not to answer and a stony silence followed. Olivia Shakespear tried unsuccessfully to change the subject, but Yeats merely said it was time for him to go home. Pound, however, calling for the bill, discovered that he did not have the money to meet it and asked in a whisper if he could borrow some cash from his friend who, in her turn, had to be laughingly slipped a sovereign under the table by Olivia Shakespear. All in the party felt sure that Yeats must have been aware of what had been going on and believed they had permanently lost face. Yeats himself left 'after a rather formal farewell', but he was either unaware of what had happened or chose not to notice, and he and Pound were soon friends again.

Pound's often boorish behaviour was more evident on another occasion, when Eva Fowler invited him to dinner along with Ernest Rhys, Ford Madox Ford, D. H. Lawrence and Yeats himself.[26] Yeats apparently became immersed in one of his interminable monologues and Pound, who 'may have felt that he was not getting a fair share of the festivities', took one of the red flowers with which the supper-table was dressed and proceeded to eat it. An absorbed Yeats apparently did not take any notice and the rest of the company was too well bred to comment immediately, though one of them wondered if the flowers were poisonous. Yeats, in fact, was not quite so unaware of what was going on as he seemed, since he reported to Lady Gregory that when the food arrived Pound was no longer hungry, having 'eaten the table-ornaments before the dinner began'. The real triumph of the evening belonged to Mrs Rhys, however, who, watching Pound's behaviour, 'turned to him and said: "Would you like another rose, Mr Pound?"'

Pound was still in awe of Yeats, however, describing him on New Year's Day 1910 as 'the only living man whose work is anything more than a most temporary interest'. He eagerly garnered from others comments Yeats had let drop about him. He believed that 'W.B.Y. says behind my back that I'm one of the few that count.' He had also heard it rumoured that Yeats intended to say something 'decent' about him at a lecture, and, although he was right in his suspicion that Yeats would not do so, in March 1910 Pound wrote to his father to tell him that Yeats was saying that if Pound rhymed like an amateur he had the rhythmic sense of a master and that 'there is no younger generation (of poets). E.P. is a solitary volcano.'

There is little doubt that Yeats was indeed impressed by 'this queer creature Ezra Pound',[27] as he described him to Lady Gregory. He believed he had become 'a great authority on the troubadours' and even considered he had got closer to the right sort of music for poetry than he himself had in his experiments with Florence Farr. Pound had achieved something which was more definitely musical but which nonetheless remained effective speech. Unfortunately, 'he can't sing as he has no voice. It is like something on a very bad phonograph.' Pound had nonetheless managed to impress Yeats in one of the most central and sensitive areas of his own experimentation and Yeats also warmed to a young man who believed poetry should speak to the elect and who was, in the words of William Carlos Williams, 'one of a well recognised group of Americans who can't take the democratic virus'.

Pound's own poetry, the lyrics he published in *Exultations* for example, was still characterised by an imitation of the febrile mannerisms of the 1890s, just as his translations from Guido Cavalcanti, written while he was courting Dorothy Shakespear in Italy, are typified by what Pound himself was later to call 'the crust of dead English'. Pound himself would make determined efforts to chip away at this only when, after a brief trip to the United States, he returned to Europe. Meeting with Ford Madox Ford in Germany, he was made vividly aware of the stylistic offences he had perpetrated. When Pound handed Ford a copy of his new volume of translations, the older man rolled about on the floor in feigned agony at the 'jejune provincial effort' and the stilted language in which he believed Pound was 'fly-papered, gummed, and strapped down'. Pound later claimed that Ford's behaviour saved him at least two years of strenuous self-examination by forcing him 'toward using the living tongue'. While he was not himself impressed by Ford's own poetry, he was nonetheless influenced by his principles, and once he had returned to England he began to ponder the problem of how 'shall the poet in this dreary day attain universality, how write what will be understood of "the many" and lauded of "the few"?'

Both his own and perhaps Yeats's anti-democratic prejudices are evident in this, but Pound himself now went on to argue that precision and beauty were the only ways to 'escape rhetoric and frilled paper decoration'. He argued that it was necessary to call a spade a spade 'in a form so exactly adjusted, in a metric in itself so seductive, that the statement will not bore the auditor'. Pound was looking for a language at once direct, dignified and, above all, unliterary. As he wrote a little later: 'no good poetry is ever written in a manner twenty years old, for to write in such a manner shows conclusively that the writer thinks from books, convention and cliché, and not from real life'. Pound was working towards his doctrine of 'making it new' and was beginning to impress his ideas forcibly on those gathered about Yeats at his Monday evenings. The new prosody was a subject on which he could reduce figures like Sturge Moore to a 'glum silence'. But while Yeats tolerated such treatment of his older friends he nonetheless required Pound to hand round the cigarettes and pour out the chianti. He clearly regarded him as something of an amanuensis, writing to ask him for example to deliver a forgotten parcel and telling him to 'charge me with taxi . . . I do not want to feel I am using up your time'.

VI
Mediums and Messages

Not only had Olivia Shakespear introduced Yeats to Pound, she also played an important part in other areas of his life. Her daughter's best friend at school had been a girl called Bertha George Hyde-Lees. 'George' or 'Georgie', as she came to be known, was born on 17 October 1892, the daughter of William Gilbert Hyde-Lees and his wife Nelly. The marriage was not a happy one. William Hyde-Lees was a wealthy man but his wife's family rapidly came to regard him as 'a most undesirable character'. The couple soon separated and it is probable that William Hyde-Lees died of drink. The year before, George and her mother moved into Drayton Gardens, South Kensington, close to where George first went to school. Although mother and daughter spent much of their time travelling around Europe, their home in London was close to those of Olivia Shakespear and her circle, and in 1909 Nelly married Olivia's brother Harry Tucker in St George's, Hanover Square.

Dorothy Shakespear was one of the witnesses, by which time her friendship with George was well established. Harry and Nelly Tucker themselves then moved to Knightsbridge, and the two families remained sufficiently close for them to take holidays with each other, Harry discovering Stone Cottage at Coleman's Hatch in Sussex, a house that was soon to play an important part in Yeats's life. Yeats himself first met George Hyde-Lees some time in October 1910. She herself had glimpsed the poet in the British Museum rushing past 'like a meteor', and, while taking tea with her mother and Olivia Shakespear, she was formally introduced. Soon afterwards she started helping Yeats to check and collate the large quantity of notes he was making on his experiences of seances and spirit communication.

Yeats's interest in spiritualism developed rapidly after his return from America in 1911 for, with the decline of his involvement with the rituals of the Golden Dawn, he was now urgently seeking a proof for the reality of the immaterial life and thus the foundation of his philosophical position. His meeting in Boston with Mrs Chenoweth had introduced him to a circle of convinced American 'spiritists' who were happy to believe that the true medium was a channel for communication between this and another world of individual souls surviving after death. The chief American proponent of such a view was J. H. Hyslop, sometime Professor of Ethics at Columbia University. At first believing that Mrs Chenoweth's powers merely threw some light on the mind's subliminal processes (a subject of great interest to a number of American academics including the more sceptical William James) a series of experiments eventually convinced Hyslop that Mrs Chenoweth's communications with her 'controls' were a proof of the survival of the soul and its willingness to communicate with the living. Mrs Chenoweth was thus helped to a considerable position in the occult world, and Yeats, setting aside the objections to spiritualism held by Madame Blavatsky and the Golden Dawn, returned from America keen to associate himself with those in London who took a similarly convinced view of the subject.

Among these was W. T. Stead, who in 1909, partly with the intention of setting up an agency to comfort the bereaved, had established Julia's Bureau under the influence of Julia A. Ames, an American woman whose communications with him became the subject of Stead's book *After Death*. Yeats had attended a 'very poor' seance at Cambridge House, Stead's Wimbledon home, on 3 June 1909, going there in the company of Everard Fielding, Honorary Secretary of the Society for Psychical Research.[28] Yeats recorded that 'a Julia' spoke to him through the medium, followed by one Agrippa and a spirit called Leo. When this spirit duly made his presence heard, Yeats asked him if he was 'Leo the writer' and was told by him that he was Yeats's guide. It was only three years later, however, at a seance held at Cambridge House on 9 May 1912, that Yeats and Leo became more closely acquainted.

The medium on this occasion was a Mrs Etta Wreidt of Detroit, who had been recommended to Stead as particularly suited to his purposes of comforting the bereaved and whom he had been going to fetch from America when he was drowned in the sinking of the *Titanic*. Mrs Wreidt later claimed that she received details of Stead's death from one of her controls a couple of days after the loss of the ship and Stead himself became one of the figures who frequently communicated through her. Others included the Indian brave Greyfeather, an eighteenth-century Scottish doctor who had emigrated to the United States, a spirit who claimed that he was the Welsh pirate Henry Morgan, two Amerindian girls called Mimi and Blossom, and Andrew Jackson Davis, who was a control Yeats was later to mention in his essay 'Swedenborg, Mediums and the Desolate Places'. Through these and other controls (and it was this that seemed particularly to establish the truth of her claims) Mrs

Wreidt communicated in a variety of languages which she had never learned. These included Croatian, Arabic, Gaelic, Hindustani, Norwegian and Welsh. Unlike most mediums, it was not Mrs Wreidt's method to fall into a trance. She was conscious throughout the seances she held and was able both to question and to converse with the controls who appeared to her.

Although Miss Harper, the Bureau's secretary and recorder, disparaged the occasion on 9 May 1912 as 'only a very mediocre seance, in comparison with the general order of results', Yeats himself was clearly impressed. He left two records of the occasion, the longer of which, with the accuracy characteristic of his spiritualist records, notes the place, date and time of the experience. He then went on to describe how the room in which they sat was entirely darkened. To begin the seance a long tin trumpet was handed round and later a musical box started playing. This stopped after three minutes or so when the company was suddenly sprinkled with a liquid Yeats felt falling on his hands and face. When asked about this, Mrs Wreidt, who spoke in a strong American accent, said that this was the way her control had of showing he was present and that it was 'a kind of baptism'.

A little later an 'exceedingly loud voice spoke through the trumpet'. Yeats could not understand what it said, but Mrs Wreidt claimed that it had come for 'Mr Gates'. Yeats realised that it was clearly he who was intended, and the spirit went on speaking, loudly and distinctively, saying that it had been in contact with him from his childhood. At this point 'a terrified woman got up and went out', but Yeats continued to hear the spirit, which said that he and his kind wanted to use 'my hand and brain'. This statement made Yeats impatient, since he was repelled by what he considered to be an appeal to his vanity. Indeed, he ceased to listen as carefully as he had before but was aware of the spirit telling him that he possessed 'the key or the key-mind' they wanted. When Yeats asked who was speaking, he was told that he had been contacted by 'Leo, the writer and explorer'. Getting no answer to his question about when Leo had lived, Yeats asked him if he were an eighteenth-century figure. 'Then came some sentence beginning with "Why, man?" or some such phrase implying impatience, certainly containing the word "man" and adding "Leo, the writer, you know Leo, the writer." When I said I knew no such person the voice said: As I thought, "you will hear of me in Rome."'

The medium understood Leo to say that Yeats could find information on him in an encyclopaedia. Again, Yeats later wondered if Leo had really said this, and, although there followed a number of sentences which he could not understand, he noticed that Leo had a strong Irish accent which he did not believe rang quite true. It was, he noted, the 'accent of an Irishman some years out of Ireland, or an Englishman who had a fair knowledge of Ireland'. Indeed, noting again that the medium had a strong American accent, Yeats recorded that Leo seemed to speak in the sort of cod-Irish voice assumed by someone telling an Irish story. Others at the table disagreed, one of them telling Yeats that she considered the accent to be like his own. When Yeats asked the medium why the spirit was using this Irish accent, she replied that Leo had to get his means of expression from Yeats's own mind. Yeats then heard a little click (which was possibly the sound of the trumpet being put down) and his part in the seance appeared over.

Although the company sat for nearly an hour longer, nothing else appeared to happen except that Yeats felt he was touched a couple of times on the top of his head 'as if by the thumb and forefinger of a hand', while he also believed he saw distinctly and without any possibility of being mistaken a little phosphorescent glow burning in front of him that had the size and shape 'of a sixpenny loaf'. Although Miss Harper decided at the end of the session to consult Lemprière's classical dictionary to see if she could find there any reference to the Leo who had appeared for Yeats, the reference she discovered seemed irrelevant and Yeats himself determined not to look up any accounts of Leo until after the next session. With that scepticism characteristic of his attitude to such matters, he did not wish any information he might discover to become 'a suggestion to the control'. He considered it vitally necessary to prove that Leo was a spirit with an independent existence and not a manifestation of his own or the medium's mind. As Yeats himself wrote at the conclusion of his account: 'I have never been quite certain that certain controls who give themselves names of great antiquity do not really select by some process of unconscious affinity from the recorded or unrecorded memories of the world a name and career that symbolises their nature.' He even wondered if Mrs Wreidt herself did not look up such people in *Chambers Biographical Dictionary* before the seances began.

But Yeats was so fascinated by what had happened that he eventually felt he had to break his vow and consult this work before the next seance. Finding only that Leo had been a 'geographer and traveller', he turned to the Hackluyt Society's recent edition of Leo Africanus' *History and Description of Africa*, where to his delight he 'discovered that Leo Africanus was a distinguished poet among the Moors'. A control apparently so sympathetic whetted Yeats's appetite and he began attending the Cambridge House seances regularly. On 5 June 1912, Leo again spoke through the trumpet, more or less repeating what he had said before, declaring that he was in fact Spanish, and telling Yeats that he was trying to teach him 'to write plays in a scientific way'. But Leo resented Yeats's scepticism, and Yeats himself was minded to attribute Leo's truculent behaviour to solar influences. He still believed that the spirit spoke like a stage Irishman, but he concluded that the seance itself was 'not the less interesting to me because I saw nothing in it incompatible with its form being a dream fabrication of the subliminal consciousness of myself & the medium'.

Two further seances in June provided Yeats with a little more information about Leo. He was still doubtful about Mrs Wreidt's methods nonetheless, and wondered if he could persuade her to submit to investigation by such a recognised authority as the famous physicist Sir Oliver Lodge, sometime President of the Society for Psychical Research, a body which Yeats himself joined as an Associate Member early in 1913. But Mrs Wreidt declined, muttering that she was interested in the spiritual world only because it enabled her to 'console the afflicted or some such phrase'. Perhaps because of such comments Yeats's interest in Mrs Wreidt and Leo Africanus seems briefly to have waned, but by this time he had developed a new interest in the automatic writing of a young woman called Elizabeth Radcliffe, whom he had met earlier in the year.[29]

Yeats was probably introduced to Miss Radcliffe through Olivia Shakespear's friend Eva Fowler, at whose Kentish country cottage many of the experiments were conducted. Yeats found that Elizabeth Radcliffe had a remarkable ability to produce automatic handwriting, but, if this skill led Yeats to her in the furtherance of his desire to prove that there was a real basis to his belief in a transcendent world, he was also drawn to her by his need for guidance in a purely personal crisis.

His letters written to Elizabeth Radcliffe throughout June 1913 constantly refer to a matter of 'great importance'. He felt that Elizabeth Radcliffe's scripts might be able to help him in this and he wondered if, when he had interpreted obscure passages in her writings correctly, he could find in them a solution to 'the problem of my life'. He was, he declared, 'living under much strain and anxiety', and, while he was extremely reticent in giving any hint of what this problem might be, his concerns almost certainly related to the fact that in May 1913 he had been telegraphed by Mabel Dickinson and informed that she was pregnant by him. Yeats consulted a number of mediums in the attempt to find out if she could be mistaken, for he was deeply concerned at the prospect of being forced into wedlock with 'an unmarried woman past her first youth'. There was a stormy meeting on 6 June 1913, at the Victoria and Albert Museum, a violent parting and a later truce. Then, presumably because Elizabeth Radcliffe's scripts had helped him to the discovery that his mistress was not after all pregnant, he sent her a profession of his 'profound gratitude' for all that she had done. 'You have changed most things for me,' he wrote, 'and I know not how far that change will go.'

In fact it was to go very far indeed, for Yeats was now beginning to convince himself that Elizabeth Radcliffe's automatic writing provided him with irrefutable proof that the messages she received were the result neither of telepathy nor of a welling up of unconscious memory but were statements delivered from a supernatural world the content and structure of which Yeats would give himself ever more earnestly to exploring. His unpublished

'Preliminary Examination of the Script of E— R—' reveals the extraordinarily detailed care he was prepared to lavish on these matters.

When Yeats began his essay, he had before him copies of nearly all Miss Radcliffe's automatic writing except for that bulk which referred to private matters. He believed they were full of evidence of great value to the psychic researcher, particularly because, while Elizabeth Radcliffe herself knew only English, French and a little Italian, the scripts themselves contained matter in Greek, Latin, Hebrew, German, Welsh, Provençal, Chinese and Coptic, as well as passages in Gaelic and Egyptian hieroglyphics. In the essay itself, Yeats quickly refuted arguments of cheating and the action of either unconscious memory or telepathy. Carefully working his way through the controls who Miss Radcliffe claimed had dictated her messages, Yeats set about systematically eliminating those who might have been influenced by such forces. With this process completed to his satisfaction, he could then write to his father telling him that he knew 'all the rationalist theories, fraud, unconscious fraud, unconscious action of the mind, forgotten memories, and so on and have after long analysis shown that none can account for this case'.

The presence of three communicators in particular seemed to justify Elizabeth Radcliffe's claim that her messengers were indeed genuine spirits of the departed whose previous lives were wholly unknown to her. The messages of the suicide Thomas Emerson, who gave the time and place of his death, seemed to deny the theory that the communicators were the product of unconscious memory since facts about Emerson himself proved extremely difficult to obtain, Yeats eventually seeking help from a reluctant Scotland Yard. The communications of a certain Sister Mary Ellis seemed to confirm his belief, while those of Anna Louise Karsch, a German poetess who spoke in a tongue known neither to Yeats nor to Miss Radcliffe, appeared to contradict the theory that messages given in a language unknown to the medium were a product of telepathic communication with other people in the room who did.

What Yeats felt to be the apparently objective existence of these three spirits led him to 'accept the spiritistic hypothesis' and encouraged him, as he told his father, towards 'elaborating a curious theory of spirit action which may I believe make philosophic study of mediums possible'. What at this stage Yeats's theory amounted to was that in any genuine experiment in automatic writing long-dead spirits who had forgotten how to use language communicated with the medium through the power of the residual memories of those who had died more recently. Much of what they said appeared to take the form of quotations from poetry, the bible and even dictionaries. Yeats was later to achieve a more profound, or at least a more imaginatively satisfying, interpretation of such events, but they already gave him a sense of 'vague loftiness which yet serves its purpose of fixing the thoughts upon spiritual life', and it was this sense of longing for the supernatural, combined with Yeats's desire rigorously to test its factual basis, which led him to draw a willing George Hyde-Lees into the lengthy process of checking the biographical details of Miss Radcliffe's communicators. George's first important contact with Yeats was thus brought about through his interest in how the spiritual world was manifested, an interest that was in time to have the most profound effect on the lives of them both.

VII
'September 1913'

While Yeats was striving to communicate with supernatural voices in England, Irish voices were variously acrimonious and conspiratorial. Yeats listened with deepening distaste and believed that the affair over Sir Hugh Lane's pictures encapsulated the narrow-minded philistinism to which his country and Dublin in particular had sunk. Lane had made it a condition of his gift that the Dublin Corporation build a gallery to house his collection, but negotiations over this were so frustrating that he eventually felt obliged to announce that if a decision were not reached by the start of 1910 he would withdraw his gift. Things seemed to improve when the Corporation voted through a tax which would raise £22,000 to defray the cost of the building provided that a similar amount was raised by private subscription. Fund-raising went ahead, and Lady Gregory in particular made a successful tour of America, raising large sums from wealthy philanthropists. The very success of the campaign ensured opposition, however, and when Sir Edwin Lutyens revealed his plans for a gallery that would span the banks of the Liffey, objections were raised that it was foreign, 'inaesthetic' and ludicrously expensive. It was also argued by some that the fetid river would destroy the pictures, while others urged the Corporation 'not to supply Hugh Lane with a monument at the City's expense'.

Yeats was angered by this reaction, declaring, 'I had not thought I could feel so bitterly over any public event.' What particularly depressed him was the fact that the Dublin Corporation, far from acting with the aristocratic munificence Yeats had seen in the renaissance cities of northern Italy, seemed prepared to be swayed by democratic public opinion and to accept this as the arbiter of excellence in the arts. Yeats was appalled that high patrician ideals should be undermined in this way and gave vent to his feelings in a poem entitled 'To a Wealthy Man who promised a Second Subscription to the Dublin Municipal Gallery if it were Proved the People wanted Pictures'. Ostensibly addressed to an 'imaginary' correspondent, Yeats's poem probably had the actions of Lord Ardilaun in mind when, with an appearance of nonchalant magniloquence –

the 'sprezzatura' praised by Castiglione – he juxtaposed the achievements of an aristocratic elite to the narrow and ill-educated aspirations of the 'mob':

> What cared Duke Ercole, that bid
> His mummers to the market-place,
> What th'onion-sellers thought or did
> So that his Plautus set the pace
> For the Italian comedies?
> And Guidobaldo, when he made
> That grammar school of courtesies
> Where wit and beauty learned their trade
> Upon Urbino's windy hill,
> Had sent no runners to and fro
> That he might learn the shepherds' will.[30]

But Dublin in the early twentieth century was not renaissance Ferrara or Urbino, and the city Corporation eventually decided to reject Sir Hugh Lane's gift. The money raised from private subscription had to be returned, while Lane himself resolved to remove his pictures from Dublin, sending some to Belfast and others to London. It seemed that the 'mob' had won at the cost of depriving their city of a major cultural resource, and there matters might have rested. But Sir Hugh himself, just prior to his departure for America on the *Lusitania* in 1915, drafted but did not sign a codicil to his will which stipulated that his pictures would be left to Dublin. When the *Lusitania* was sunk by a German submarine, Yeats believed it was his duty to campaign for the provision made by Lane in the unsigned codicil, writing many letters to the newspapers and even attempting to raise Sir Hugh's ghost in the hope of being told where a signed copy of the codicil might be found. His campaigns were unsuccessful, however, and the whole issue dragged on until 1952 when a temporary settlement was reached with an agreement that London and Dublin should share the pictures under a continuing loan agreement.

One of those who had been particularly instrumental in opposing the Hugh Lane gallery was the entrepreneur and newspaper proprietor William Martin Murphy. For Yeats, Murphy personified all that he most feared and loathed about the ignorant materialism of the Dublin Roman Catholic middle classes. Here were those people who showed 'how base at moments of excitement are minds without culture'. Not only did they threaten the artistic life of the city and the nation at large, but events were to convince Yeats that they threatened the basic liberties of the people too. This he believed had been particularly clearly shown when Murphy and his fellow members of the Employers' Federation obtained written undertakings from their men that they would not join trade unions such as the Irish Transport and General Workers Union set up by James Larkin in 1909.

Larkin himself, who had enthusiastically supported Yeats in his campaign over Hugh Lane's pictures, believed that he had 'a divine mission' to harness the forces of discontent. In working-class Dublin these were widespread. Unemployment ran at a chronically high level, the average pay packet of a pound a week was well below the poverty line, tuberculosis was rife, while the death rate among children was the highest in Europe. Declaring that he recognised 'no law but the people's law', Larkin together with James Connolly campaigned successfully through their union to secure an improvement of wages and founded a weekly newspaper which urged their twin ideals of socialism and nationalism. As Connolly himself was later to write: 'the cause of labour is the cause of Ireland; the cause of Ireland is the cause of labour. They cannot be dissevered. Ireland seeks freedom. Labour seeks that an Ireland free should be the sole mistress of her own destiny, supreme owner of all material things within and upon her soil.' While such views naturally assured Larkin and Connolly a wide following among the Dublin working people, they were virulently opposed by the Irish Parliamentary Party as well as by Arthur Griffith and the forces of Sinn Fein.

It was Murphy's Employers' Federation that took the most drastic action, however, organising a six months' lock-out during which more than 50,000 people were reduced to destitution. The Catholic Church sided with the employers, Archbishop Walsh issuing a particularly unpleasant public letter in which he told the wives of the workers that if they permitted their children to be fed in the homes of English sympathisers they could no longer be 'held worthy of the name of Catholic mothers'. Yeats was appalled by the threat to liberty posed by this alliance of the Catholic Church and the Dublin middle classes and, as so often, he blamed the newspapers for the degradation and threats to freedom which he believed had resulted. Writing to *The Irish Worker*, he spoke angrily of the other newspapers in the city which, he declared, 'are supposed to watch over our civil liberties, and I charge the Dublin Nationalist newspapers with deliberately arousing religious passion to break up the organisation of the workingman, with appealing to mob law day after day, with publishing the names of workingmen and their wives for purposes of intimidation'.[31]

It seemed to him that the whole of Ireland was gripped by a conspiracy he considered morally reprehensible. 'Intriguers have met together somewhere behind the scenes that they might turn the religion of Him who thought it hard for a rich man to enter the Kingdom of Heaven into an oppression of the poor.' The high patriotic ideals that had once inspired Irishmen – the ideals of Edward Fitzgerald, Robert Emmet, Wolfe Tone and John O'Leary – seemed a thing of the past. The heroic no longer had a place in national life and, in his poem 'To a Shade', Yeats the aristocratic populist turned in disillusioned bitterness to the ghost of Parnell, bidding him return to Glasnevin Cemetery and draw his coverlet of earth about his head 'till the dust stops your ear'. The dead hand of mediocrity held the entire country in its grip, and in 'September 1913' Yeats gave bitter expression to his horror at this state of disillusion and moral paralysis, seeing the lower-middle classes as particularly responsible for it:

> What need you, being come to sense,
> But fumble in a greasy till
> And add the halfpence to the pence
> And prayer to shivering prayer, until
> You have dried the marrow from the bone?
> For men were born to pray and save:
> Romantic Ireland's dead and gone,
> It's with O'Leary in the grave.[32]

As Yeats wrote in a letter to Lady Gregory, he believed that with the decline of standards he saw all around him, Ireland would emerge as merely 'a little greasy huckstering nation groping for halfpence in a greasy till'. The rough and venomous language of his poem inspired by this phrase exactly matches his disillusion and shows how far he had moved from the lyricism of the Nineties. But the cultural pessimism of the political right had partly blinded Yeats to the significance of the events forming around him.

When Asquith was returned as Prime Minister in 1909, it was the MPs of the Irish Party who once again held the balance of power, and in 1912 Asquith introduced the Liberal Party's third Home Rule Bill. In the previous year the Parliament Act had severely curtailed the powers of the House of Lords by reducing its veto on bills to a period of two years. It seemed now that the Home Rule Bill would automatically become law in 1914, and horrified Protestant Unionists in Ulster rallied around Sir Edward Carson (the member for Trinity College and the prosecuting barrister in the case of Oscar Wilde) to protest. On 28 September 1912, Carson led a rally of nearly half a million Unionists in signing 'Ulster's Solemn League and Covenant,' which declared 'that Home Rule would be disastrous to the material well-being of Ulster as well as to the whole of Ireland, subversive of our civil and religious freedom, destructive of our citizenship and perilous to the unity of the Empire'. The Ulstermen were determined to protect their 'cherished position of equal citizenship in the United Kingdom' and declared they would use 'all means' to defeat what they considered a parliamentary conspiracy to press through Home Rule. Soon the whole of Ireland would be in arms.

II

Walking Naked
(1913–1916)

I
Towards Stone Cottage

Yeats was approaching his fifties, and friends and acquaintances watched him closely for signs of ageing. 'His face grew gradually fuller in outline,' wrote Max Beerbohm,

and the sharp angles of his figure were smoothed away; and his hands – those hands which in his silences lay folded downwards across his breast, but left each other and came forth and, as it were, stroked the air to and fro while he talked – those very long, fine hands did seem to have lost something of their insubstantiality. His dignity and his charm were as they always had been. But I found it less easy to draw caricatures of him. He seemed to have become subtly less like himself.[1]

If the outward changes were small and refined, however, the metamorphoses of Yeats's art and the inner man were altogether more considerable, as the three winters from 1913 he spent with Ezra Pound at Stone Cottage in Sussex would show.

Pound himself had been busy establishing his position as the entrepreneur and *enfant terrible* of modern English-language poetry. Enemies were necessary for this, and Pound had in his sights the volumes of *Georgian Poetry* edited by the cultured civil servant Edward Marsh and published by Harold Munro from the Poetry Bookshop.[2] A new friend of Pound's, Richard Aldington, was to describe the Georgians as 'regional in their outlook and in love with littleness'. He wrote disparagingly of how 'they took a little trip for a week-end to a little cottage where they wrote a little poem on a little theme. Ezra was a citizen of the world, both mentally and in fact.' A new movement was also necessary to Pound's purposes, however, and, having introduced Aldington to his friend the poet Hilda Doolittle ('H.D.'), Pound marshalled them into a group he called the Imagists, describing them as 'ardent Hellenists who are pursuing interesting experiments in *vers libre*; trying to attain in English certain subtleties of cadence of the kind Mallarmé and his followers have studied in French'.

Although Pound was later to claim that the Imagist movement was a carefully planned intellectual experiment, he was more honest when he confessed that 'the name was invented to launch H.D. and Aldington before either had enough stuff for a volume'.[3] Pound was determined to publish their work in *Poetry*, whose editor, Harriet Monroe, had invited him in October 1912 to take up the position of 'Foreign Correspondent'. It was for this magazine that Pound also encouraged his friend F. S. Flint to write a piece about the Imagists, 'chiefly at my own dictation'. Flint wrote that 'a few rules' had been drawn up to guide the movement. These included 'direct treatment of the "thing"', the avoidance of any 'word that did not contribute to the presentation', and a resolve 'to compose in sequence of the musical phrase, not in sequence of a metronome'. In an essay of his own which he described as 'Instructions to Neophytes', Pound defined an 'image' as 'that which presents an intellectual and an emotional complex in an instant of time. . . . It is the presentation of such a "complex" instantaneously which gives that sudden sense of liberation . . . which we experience in the presence of the greatest works of art.'

Yeats himself had already made significant advances towards this position. In the notes to *The Wind among the Reeds*, he had written that 'the image – a cross, a man preaching in the wilderness, a dancing Salomé, a lily in a girl's hand, a flame leaping, a globe with wings, a pale sunset over still waters – is an eternal act; but our understandings are temporal and understand but a little at a time'. Just as Yeats's experiments in spiritualism seemed to point to a reality beyond the mundane, so the use of images in art seemed to connect man to the eternal. The image was thus a poetic and spiritual matter, and Pound was in sympathy with this line of approach.

Rigorous stylistic criticism was essential to realising it, however, and Pound wrote to Harriet Monroe that his aims were 'objectivity, and expression; no hind-side-beforeness, no straddled adjectives (as "addled mosses dank"), no Tennysonianness of speech: *nothing* that you couldn't in some circumstance, in the stress of some emotion, *actually say*. Every *literaryism*, every book word, fritters away a scrap of the reader's patience, a scrap of his sense of your sincerity.' Pound had already applied his considerable editorial skills to the works of H.D. and now, having solicited a number of contributions to *Poetry* from Yeats, he decided to use the same process on the works of the older master. He made subtle alterations to 'Fallen Majesty', 'To a Child Dancing in the Wind' and 'The Mountain Tomb'. Yeats was initially angry at a young man taking such liberties with his work, but a number of Pound's changes were substantially adopted by Yeats when he later reprinted these works in his *Collected Poems*.

Pound was resolved, however, not only to purify Yeats's diction but thoroughly to modernise it as well. As he wrote to Dorothy Shakespear about two poems that 'the Eagle', as they both called him, had written for the sequence he was to print as 'Upon a Dying Lady', one of the lyrics is 'rather nice, but he cant expect me to like stale rhyming, even if he does say it is an imitation of an Elizabethan form. Elizabeefan . . . It's just moulting Eagle.' These were, Pound thought, symptoms of stagnation, and, as he had written of Yeats in the January 1913 issue of *Poetry*, 'although he is the greatest of living poets, his art has not broadened much in scope during the past decade'. In fact, Yeats himself was concerned at the pace of his own progress, writing that he had experienced 'a fortnight of gloom over my work'. He felt that Pound in particular 'helps me to get back to the definite and concrete', but if Yeats was grateful for this he was suspicious of his young disciple's efforts. 'In his own work,' he wrote to Lady Gregory, 'he is very uncertain, often very bad though very interesting sometimes. He spoils himself by too many experiments and has more sound principles than taste.'

Some time after Yeats made this criticism, Pound was recommended by Ford Madox Ford and Violet Hunt for the post of literary editor of the *New Freewoman* where, as he told his mother, 'I can amuse myself by drawing comparisons between the intelligence of my friends and the utter imbecility of my enemies.' Among Pound's friends by this time were some of the most distinguished figures of early-twentieth-century poetry, and he was to publish in the *New Freewoman* reviews of work by D. H. Lawrence and Robert Frost, along with poems by H.D. and Richard Aldington. Indeed, with characteristic arrogance, Pound began to treat the magazine as his own territory and, realising that its title was inappropriate to his purposes, persuaded two of its leading figures – Dora Marsden and Harriet Weaver – into having it changed to the *Egoist*. When the publication ran into financial difficulties he also tried to persuade the wealthy Amy Lowell to buy the magazine. The directors were resolved, however, that 'the *Egoist* spark of intelligence is not to be extinguished under Miss Lowell's respectable bulk', and Harriet Weaver eventually decided to manage the business on her own.

Pound himself meanwhile was still contributing occasional material to *Poetry*, although he considered Harriet Monroe a 'bloody fool' and was muttering to Amy Lowell that he felt certain he would soon be compelled to resign his post as foreign correspondent. By the autumn of 1913 he had attempted to do so, but it was at just this time that the magazine decided to award its first annual Guarantors' Prize to the poet who was considered to have published in its pages the most distinguished work of that year. Harriet Monroe wanted the Prize awarded to Vachel Lindsay, but Pound regarded this as an 'insult' and insisted that, for the good of the magazine, the prize should be awarded elsewhere.

'If you give it to Yeats', he wrote, 'you FIRST make the giving of this particular prize serious, you establish a good tradition.' He told Harriet Monroe that if Yeats was 'so dam'd opulent as not to need it, he will probably return it. As for its not being adventurous to offer it to him, I don't see that it is our job to be adventurous in this case but to be just. He has fought a long fight and had damn little reward.'[4] In fact Yeats did turn down the prize, not because he was easily able to but because he was embarrassed. As he wrote to Lady Gregory: 'my first thought was to send it all back but that looked like pride, so much as to say I am too important to take a prize'. In the end he resolved on keeping £10 for himself with which to commission a bookplate from T. Sturge Moore and to return the remaining £40 to Harriet Monroe, suggesting it be given to 'some unknown needy young man in a garret'.

That needy young man of course was Pound himself, and Yeats wrote that he suggested him because 'although I do not really like with my whole soul the metrical experiments he has made for you, I think those experiments show a vigorous creative mind. He is certainly a creative personality of some sort, though it is too soon yet to say of what sort.' Pound himself, who had recently lost the support of an anonymous benefactor, wrote to tell the editors of *Poetry* that he was 'very glad to receive *Poetry's* award at Mr Yeats' suggestion as he is about the only poet now writing in English for whom I have any appreciable respect, or I might say more exactly for whom I have any feeling of deference'. Then, while Yeats commissioned his bookplate, Pound resolved to spend his prize on a new typewriter and 'two statuettes from *the* coming sculptor, Gaudier-Brzeska'.

If the award of the *Poetry* prize was a relatively small incident in the relationship between Yeats and Pound, other of Pound's activities were to prove altogether more important. By the end of September 1913, Pound was writing to his parents to tell them that he had 'seen Mrs Fenellosa (relict of the Fenellosa who has written on Chinese Art, and who had so much to do with the Freer collection) and Sorijini Naidu'. Early the following month he dined with them both and wrote to Dorothy Shakespear that 'I seem to be getting orient from all quarters. . . . I'm stocked up with K'ung fu Tsze, and Men Tsze etc. I suppose they'll keep me calm for a week or so.' In fact, such influences were to keep Pound greatly excited for far longer.

Ernest Fenellosa (whose real surname was Alvarez) had been born in Salem in 1853 and, after graduating from Harvard, had taught economics and philosophy in Tokyo at a time when Japan was opening up to Western influence. Becoming fascinated by Japanese culture, he was appointed manager of the Tokyo Fine Arts Academy, became a Buddhist and was decorated by the Emperor for his services to culture. Fenellosa was then commissioned to travel abroad and enlighten the world about Japanese civilisation. He was appointed curator of the Department of Oriental Art at the Boston Museum of Fine Arts and, when he returned to Tokyo in 1897, became a professor at the Imperial Normal School for three years until he retired to live in London, where he died in 1908. His expertise in his chosen field was far from profound (he could read Chinese poetry only with the help of Japanese interpreters) but by the time of his death he had written a mass of notes for a two-volume book which, with the help of Lawrence Binyon of the British Museum, his wife published as *Epochs of Chinese and Japanese Art*. This work had taken three years to complete, and a considerable quantity of Fenellosa's notes remained unused. Believing that Pound was 'the only person who can finish this stuff the way Ernest wanted it done', Mrs Fenellosa presented the manuscripts to him, promising £40 to cover his expenses.

Some poems by Alan Upwood made up 'out of his head, using a certain amount of Chinese reminiscence' and published in the September 1913 issue *Poetry*, had already suggested to Pound similarities between Chinese poetry and the aims of the Imagists. 'There is *no* long poem in Chinese,' he wrote. 'They hold if a man cant say what he wants in 12 lines he'd better leave it unsaid.' A visit to Upwood himself also touched a deep chord of the esoteric and the elite in Pound and when, in the second week of November 1913, he went to join Yeats as his secretary at Stone Cottage he took with him not only Fenellosa's papers but a belief that 'modern civilisation has bred a race with brains like those of rabbits and we who are the heirs of the witch-doctor and the voodoo, we artists who have been so long despised are about to take over control'. These were attitudes sympathetic to Yeats which both men would explore during the course of that winter.

II
'Responsibilities'

'My stay in Stone Cottage will not be in the least profitable,' Pound wrote to tell his mother.[5] 'I detest the country. Yeats will amuse me part of the time and bore me to death with psychical research the rest. I regard the visit as a duty to posterity.' Yeats's view of the arrangement was altogether more practical. As he had written to Lady Gregory in July: 'I want to arrange for Ezra Pound to act as my secretary this winter. I propose that he take rooms for himself and me an hour out of London and I go straight there after Coole. I shall then do my best not to go anywhere except to London for my Mondays until I start for America . . . Ezra is to do my correspondence and read to me after dark.' These last duties were particularly important since Yeats's eyesight had now become 'practically useless after artificial light begins'. Through the dreary afternoons, therefore, Pound took voluminous quantities of dictation (on 11 January Yeats dictated no less than twenty-one letters) while also embarking on an ambitious programme of reading. In addition, Pound was to help keep Yeats fit. Yeats himself had learned Swedish exercises from Mabel Dickinson, but he was suffering from digestive disorders and Pound taught him to fence, a sport which Pound himself particularly liked because it meant pitting himself against a single opponent rather than a team.

Both men were quickly satisfied by the arrangements in Sussex. Yeats wrote to tell Lady Gregory that 'Ezra is a pleasant companion and a learned one. He never shrinks from work,' while Pound felt able to confess to William Carlos Williams that 'Yeats is much finer *intime* than seen spasmodically in the midst of the world. We are both, I think, very contented in Sussex.' Quite how true this was is suggested by a letter Yeats wrote to Mabel Beardsley, the woman for whom he was composing his sequence 'Upon a Dying Lady' and whom he regularly visited in hospital while he was in London. He told her that 'I am on the border of a great heath and there are woods on the other side and the only village near is scattered about a cross roads with a little old country inn. My walk which is always after dark to save time is to the Post Office or to the inn to order cider, and then out on to the heath and at night when the clouds are not too dark and heavy.' The scattered village was called Coleman's Hatch, while the trees in the Five Hundred Acre Wood which could be seen on the opposite side of the valley from the secluded garden of Stone Cottage were to be made famous in Ernest Shepherd's illustrations to *Winnie the Pooh*.

Stone Cottage itself was an L-shaped building, two storeys high and consisting of six rooms. It belonged to a William Welfare, whose sisters Ellen and Alice were living there at the time of Yeats and Pound's stay. Alice Welfare cooked their meals, kept the house clean and later recalled how hard-working Pound was and how solicitous for Yeats's comfort. 'When breakfast was over they would get to work as if life depended on it. "Don't disturb him," Mr Pound used to say if I wanted to dust, and Mr Yeats would be humming over his poetry to himself in the little room.' Indeed, Yeats himself was so immersed in his work that Alice Welfare recalled how one morning, when Pound was away visiting friends, Yeats came back from the Post Office and said, '"Why, there's nothing doing; all shut up." "But Mr Yeats," I said, "Didn't you know it's Christmas Day!"'

Such moments of absent-mindedness were interludes in the efforts both men were giving to the development of an elite art. Pound had given a half-joking account of these ideas in the *New Freewoman* a few weeks before going to stay with Yeats. An advertisement had appeared in the magazine informing readers of the establishment of a religious order to be called the Angel Club. Pound wrote to the 'Chancellor' of the movement claiming that 'I have longed for some order more humane than the Benedictines who should preserve even the vestiges of our present light against that single force whereof the "ha'penny" press and the present university and educational systems are but the symptoms. . . . I want an order to foster the arts as the church orders fostered painting.'[6] To some extent, the weeks spent with Yeats in Sussex were a trial run for this order of the 'Brothers Minor'.

The poets of the Rhymers' Club could be seen as foreshadowing this and, in his attempt to show how he had advanced beyond them, Yeats had begun to refashion his image of his friends into that explanatory myth of euphoria, high craftsmanship and degradation which would find its final form in the section of his *Autobiographies* he called *The Tragic Generation*. As early as spring 1910 he had delivered a talk called 'Friends of my Youth' as part of his campaign to raise money for the Abbey Theatre, and he wrote in his journal how he would 'read from the books of the Rhymers' Club – Plarr, Johnson, Dowson – and then from Sturge Moore and explain how, coming after the abundance of the Swinburne – Rossetti – Morris movement, we sought not abundance or energy, but preciseness of form. . . . We sought for new subject matter, and many of us were men of passionate living, expressing our lives.'

Yeats would show the generation of the Nineties consisting of men devoted to a fastidious personal lyricism which he would then contrast to the more 'contemplative' verse of their predecessors and the different ideals of those who followed. 'In the generation that came after us', Yeats declared, 'and at the end of the Nineties, the tide changed and our brief movement was over. The young poets, or at any rate the poets younger than myself and my friends, are impersonal, and if their lives are active, or dissipated or vehement they do not sing them.' Pound had hoped that Yeats might mention his own work in the lecture, but was disappointed. His friend William Carlos Williams, brought along to hear Yeats's talk, wrote in his autobiography that Yeats had achieved precisely the effect he intended, however. Writing of the generation of the Nineties, Williams declared: 'what was there left for them to do, then, but to live the decadent lives they did? What else, neglected as they found themselves to be, but drunkenness, lechery or immorality of whatever other sort?'

This interpretation of recent literary history was central to 'The Grey Rock' (the poem with which Yeats had won the Guarantors' Prize), in which he juxtaposed his 'companions of the Cheshire Cheese' against a background of ancient Irish myth. This was a technique that was to be of the greatest importance to the generation of Pound, Joyce and Eliot, for here was a new way of creating a parallel between contemporary experience and ancient traditions which in its turn led to the production of works for a readership capable of appreciating recondite literary allusion. Pound himself acknowledged this when he wrote that '*The Grey Rock* is, I admit, obscure, but it outweighs this by a curious nobility, a nobility which is . . . the very core of Mr Yeats' production.'

The 'old story' Yeats remade for his poem tells how the malignant and supernatural Aoife took a mortal Irish soldier as her lover and, having failed to keep him from fighting in a great national battle, gave him a charm by which he could go invisible. This the victorious warrior eventually rejected out of honour and human sympathy, impulses which led to his death. The mythological part of the poem opens with Aoife's grief and anger at the loss of her soldier, and her cries are a first indication of the fateful relationship in the poem between the mortal and supernatural worlds. It is suggestive, however, of the decisive break Yeats had made from Pre-Raphaelite enchantment that the gods have no languorous grace. Theirs is no Burne-Jones elysium. Feasting at their 'great house at Slievenamon' they are heard to snore, gorged on meat and drowsy with that 'sacred stuff' which is the beer of immortality they have to 'buy' from Goban the smith. With the help of this drink the supernatural powers can live in oblivion, and even Aoife eventually drowns her sorrows in their celestial tavern. But, if alcoholic stupor is the respite of the gods, the lot of humans who yearn for the spiritual world is a discipline eventually wrecked by dissipation and despair. Dowson and Johnson find in alcohol the oblivion which leads to physical death. There is no ready union between heaven and earth, but what the poets have – what their art gives them – is a moral stature altogether more heroic than that the immortals know. Brief lives have sired great poetry:

> *You had to face your ends when young –*
> *'Twas wine or women, or some curse –*
> *But never made a poorer song*
> *That you might have a heavier purse,*
> *Nor gave loud service to a cause*
> *That you might have a troop of friends.*
> *You kept the Muses' sterner laws,*
> *And unrepenting faced your ends,*
> *And therefore earned the right – and yet*
> *Dowson and Johnson most I praise –*
> *To troop with those the world's forgot,*
> *And copy their proud steady gaze.*[7]

Once, in his open letter to the *fratres* and *sorores* of the Golden Dawn, Yeats had envisaged a variously severe and ecstatic intercourse between heaven and earth. Now the two realms are seen to yearn for each other across a terrible divide. The gods can find release in snoring torpor, but the lot of the human visionary is dangerous, tragic and ultimately fatal. Nonetheless, as Yeats turned to his own predicament in the final paragraph of the poem, the true artist's refusal to compromise, his loneliness, stoic heroism and all-justifying intuition of spiritual 'content' give him an elite and even awe-inspiring humanity that places him far beyond the mob.

But the Nineties were over, and Yeats, helping to create modernism in his act of poetic farewell, was the great survivor. While Pound ensured that 'The Grey Rock' won him the Guarantors' Prize, he had as early as 1910 trumpeted the older man's development:

Yeats has been doing some new lyrics – he has come out of the shadows and declared for life – of course there is in that a tremendous uplift for me – for he and I are now as it were in one movement with *aims* very nearly identical. That is to say the movement of the '90'ies . . . for drugs and the shadows has worn itself out. There has been no 'influence' – Yeats has found within himself spirit of the new air which I by accident had touched before him.

Pound knew that such an advance was bound to be uneven and that for some readers there would be loss as well as gain. His letter also shows him prepared to admit, contrary to what has subsequently become the conventional history of this process, that he himself was not the chief instigator of Yeats's new style. As he wrote in 1915:

there is little use discussing the early Yeats, everyone has heard all that can be said on the subject. The new Yeats is still under discussion. Adorers of the Celtic Twilight are disturbed by his gain of hardness. Some of the latter work is not so good as the Wind Among the Reeds, some of it better, or at least possessed of new qualities. Synge had appeared. There is a new strength in the later Yeats on which he and Synge may have agreed between them.

Certainly, Yeats was now ready to show how he had moved on from the sort of Celticism that had become merely a source for imitation:

> I made my song a coat
> Covered with embroideries
> Out of old mythologies
> From heel to throat;
> But the fools caught it,
> Wore it in the world's eyes,
> As though they'd wrought it.
> Song, let them take it,
> For there's more enterprise
> In walking naked.[8]

Yeats had first decisively revealed his new and 'naked' style in the lyrics provoked by the controversy over Hugh Lane's pictures and published in October 1913 as *Poems Written in Discouragement*. Writing later of the proposed gallery itself, Yeats declared: 'one could respect the argument that Dublin, with so much poverty and many slums, could not afford the £22,000 the building was to cost the city, but not the minds that used it'. The insidious influence of middle-class materialism remained and Yeats wrote: 'against all this we have but a few educated men and the remnants of an old traditional culture among the poor'. Now, with the influence of Nietzsche and

Castiglione still yeasting in his mind, Yeats was determined to elaborate an elite and esoteric art, and the reading he and Pound were engaged on during their first winter at Stone Cottage was important to this.

Inspired by his work on the Fenellosa manuscripts, Pound had turned to Frank Brinkley's *Japan and China: Their History, Arts, and Literature*. Here he found a remarkable description of the culture developed by the aristocracy in the imperial court at Kyoto. Flower-arranging, gardening and the tea-ceremony were all described, but two particular activities held an especial fascination. One of these was what Brinkley called 'listening to incense', a mistranslation of an activity which consisted of mixing different types of incense and working out from the combined smell the various constituents and assigning each a name derived from classical literature. This was, as Pound noted, 'a pastime neither for clods nor for illiterates'. Such an elite enjoyment of synaesthesia appealed to Yeats as well. 'When I remember that curious game which the Japanese called, with a confusion of the senses that had seemed typical of our own age, "listening to incense", I know that some among them would have understood the prose of Walter Pater, the paintings of Puvis de Chavannes, the poetry of Mallarmé and Verlaine.'

Here was an insight into a culture of fabulous refinement, but what was particularly to influence both men was Brinkley's description of the Noh drama – the drama as Brinkley called it of 'accomplishment' – which the Japanese aristocracy had evolved into a magnificent formal art. Here was a means of expression deeply appealing to Yeats: 'a form of drama, distinguished, indirect, and symbolic, and having no need of mob or Press to pay its way – an aristocratic form'. One Noh drama in particular made a significant impression at this time, a work called *Nishikigi*. Paraphrasing the plot of this, Pound explained that it showed the ghosts of two lovers kept apart by a hostile woman but reunited through the good offices of a wandering priest. As Pound himself wrote: 'Mr Yeats tells me that he has found a similar legend in Aran, where the ghosts come to a priest to be married.' Yeats had in fact found this legend in Lady Gregory's *Visions and Beliefs in the West of Ireland*, a volume for which he was writing two important essays he and Pound were reading widely in works of spiritualism and magic to research. With his mind full of such diverse material, Yeats could now begin planning out his essay 'Swedenborg, Mediums and the Desolate Places'.[9]

Here, in his attempt to show the universality of spiritualism and a belief in ghosts and apparitions especially, Yeats retold the story of *Nishikigi*. He had already been made aware of the similarities between Irish folklore and his experiences at seances in Soho and Holloway, and now, in a manner typical of late-nineteenth-century syncretist thought, he set out to describe how he lived 'in excitement, amused to make Holloway interpret Aran, and constantly comparing my discoveries with what I have learned of medieval tradition among fellow students, with the reveries of a Neo-Platonist, of a seventeenth-century Platonist, of Paracelsus or a Japanese poet'. Swedenborg, who had had such a profound influence on Blake, was also enlisted, and the essay as a whole is a moving attempt to marshal a wide range of spiritualist material into a work which tries to assert the real existence of the spiritual life through the cumulative weight of evidence. The impression it leaves, however, is less of a case proven than the altogether more beguiling sense of a poet of genius working his way towards the spiritual certainties he so desperately craved. Once again, Yeats was trying to 'hammer his thoughts into a unity', for, if religion was the central topic of the essay, it was also an attempt to assert the imaginative and spiritual riches of Ireland while searching for an esoteric symbolism with which to enrich his poetry.

Yeats was at one with Pound in believing that 'a symbol appearing in a vision has a certain richness and power of energising joy' that was now largely lost in what Pound called the 'literwary' symbol. Both poets also shared the belief that 'perception by symbolic vision is swifter and more complex than that by ratiocination', and when, on 23 November, Yeats wrote his lyric 'The Peacock', he brought together many of his concerns with elite revelation. Presenting himself as a man dispossessed and free of the material world, the poet becomes a visionary who can elaborate fabulous images of internal abundance:

> What's riches to him
> That has made a great peacock
> With the pride of his eye?
> The wind-beaten, stone-grey,
> And desolate Three Rock
> Would nourish his whim.
> Live he or die
> Amid wet rocks and heather,
> His ghost will be gay
> Adding feather to feather
> For the pride of his eye.[10]

The true artist belongs to an esoteric and numinous world which is the antithesis of that inhabited by 'Biddy and Paudeen', Yeats's representatives of the 'mob', with their life-denying ambition to 'toil and grow rich'. The great peacock is, as Pound wrote, a thing of 'aere perennius', that visionary monument which will outlive time and which Yeats himself would later refashion into the 'golden bird' of 'Byzantium'. Pound's recollection of Yeats composing this poem remained one of his profoundest memories, and in the *Pisan Cantos*, written in prison at the end of the Second World War, he offered a vivid portrait of 'Uncle William' composing the work aloud downstairs in Stone Cottage and making 'a great peeeeeeecock . . . in the proide of his oyyee'. The mockery in Pound's lines provides an admirable foil to the accuracy and sense of wonder with which he recreated Yeats's moment of inspiration.

Others too might be recruited into this elite and visionary battle against the forces of materialism. Pound was particularly keen to include James Joyce's apocalyptic poem 'I Hear an Army' in his collection *Des Imagistes*.[11] Yeats himself declared the work 'a technical and emotional masterpiece', and, when Joyce wrote to tell Pound that two publishing houses had backed out of issuing *Dubliners* because Joyce would not allow them to censor his work, Yeats resolved to help him fight what he saw as further proof of the authoritarian mediocrity of the crowd. Indeed, it was Yeats who had first recommended Joyce's poem to Pound, and, although Yeats himself had not brought a copy of *Chamber Music* to Stone Cottage, his praise carried enough weight for Pound to seek it out, open a correspondence with Joyce and devote his considerable energies to help getting published not only *Dubliners* but *A Portrait of the Artist as a Young Man*. So grateful was Joyce for this that he wrote to Yeats: 'I can never thank you enough for having brought me into relation with your friend Ezra Pound who is indeed a miracle worker.'

But during this first winter at Stone Cottage Yeats himself was obliged to face the concerted forces of misunderstanding. Soon after his arrival, a production of *The Playboy of the Western World* at the Liverpool Repertory Theatre provoked disturbances and Yeats felt obliged to write to *The Times* that 'the audience, on the whole, were exceedingly enthusiastic, but from time to time fervid Irish patriots, who are a little old-fashioned in their opinions, interrupted and were thrown out'. That this could be used as an excuse for placing the play under an embargo roused all Yeats's deep-seated hatred of censorship and mass public opinion, and he wrote in his letter that the authorities 'might as well forbid a man whose watch has been stolen to leave his house because of the indignation his complaint had caused among the thieves, as forbid without process of law or public enquiry the production of a famous play which lies under no charge of immorality and is held by most educated Irishmen to be the master-work of the dramatic literature of Ireland'. But, if Yeats still had to fight for Synge's reputation, he was also obliged to preserve his own.

He now discovered that the January 1914 issue of the *English Review* contained a malicious section of George Moore's autobiography entitled 'Yeats, Lady Gregory, and Synge'.[12] In this Moore had refined to a masterly degree his technique of working up half-truth and innuendo into portraits of those he called his friends. Yeats he chose to present as a pampered snob. He gloated over the 'magnificent fur coat' in which Yeats had returned from his first lecture tour to the United States, and took pleasure in describing (albeit at second-hand) a picture of Yeats reclining on a sofa at Coole, 'a plate of strawberries on his knee, and three or four adoring ladies serving him with cream and sugar'. While this could be brushed aside as no more than irksome, Moore's description of Yeats thundering against the middle classes at a meeting designed to raise money for the Hugh Lane picture gallery was altogether more mortifying.

Yeats's erstwhile collaborator wrote that it was 'impossible to imagine the hatred which came into his voice when he spoke the words "the middle classes"; one would have thought that he was speaking against a personal foe'. Seeking to undermine the basis of Yeats's attack on the institutionalised philistinism of Dublin, Moore went on to ask himself 'why Willie Yeats should feel himself called upon to denounce the class to which he himself belongs essentially: on one side excellent mercantile millers and ship-owners, and on the other a portrait painter of rare talent'. The absurdity of Yeats's claims to the Dukedom of Ormonde was thrown in for good measure, and when Dorothy Shakespear wrote to Pound asking how Yeats felt about this attack Pound replied that Yeats 'does nowt but write lofty poems to his ancestors, thinking that the haughtiest reply'.

In fact, damning Moore in verse was about the only response available to Yeats since, as he wrote to Lady Gregory, the statements Moore had made about him were too 'indefinite' for any legal action to be taken. Instead, in 'Notoriety', eventually printed as the last work in *Responsibilities*, Yeats consciously modelled himself on the courtly lyrics of Ben Jonson and declared that provided he still had access to Coole and its Seven Woods this aristocratic resource would protect him from such men as Moore who made all his 'priceless' literary endeavours into nothing more than 'a post the passing dogs defile'.

Moore's attack nonetheless probed a vulnerable spot in Yeats, for the fact that he had been born into the Protestant middle classes rather than to a family on the heights of the Ascendancy nagged him. That there was a strong element of snobbery in this is undeniable, and Oliver St John Gogarty made this clear when he wrote that 'Yeats, though his descent was from parsons, dearly loved a lord. He was at heart an aristocrat, and it must have always been a disappointment to him that he was not born one.' Such snobbery, however, was an irritant that could inspire a nobler social vision. Yeats's praise for aristocratic values went deep into his longing for something permanent, lofty and even spiritual, and as early as 1900 he had written that he used the term 'middle class' to 'describe an attitude of mind more than an accident of birth'. Trying to explain himself fully in his journal, he wrote that 'the word "bourgeois" which I had used is not an aristocratic term of reproach, but, like the old "cit" which one finds in Ben Jonson, a word of artistic usage'. It was, in other words, a term for vulgarity of mind and materialism, in Pound's phrase 'the stomach and gross intestines of the body politic and social, as distinct from the artist, who is the nostrils and the invisible antennae'. Now it was necessary to suggest a pedigree for this idea.

Pound's readings in Confucius helped, providing Yeats with one of the epigraphs he used for his volume *Responsibilities*: 'How am I fallen from myself, for a long time now I have not seen the Prince of Chang in my dreams.' Confucius admired the Prince of Chang (more properly the Duke of Chou) as the founder of a great dynasty and the man who established the rites of ancestor worship in China. Yeats now began consciously to elaborate such ideas for his own family. He had for a long time been urging his father to produce a selection of his letters, which, Yeats believed, would prove beyond doubt that aristocratic sensibilities were indeed a 'state of mind' rather than an accident of birth. JBY had, of course, been dilatory in attempting this project, and Yeats now resolved to hand the material over to Ezra Pound, who, as Yeats told his father, 'is to make a first small volume of selections for Lollie's press'. Yeats also began thinking about writing that first section of his *Autobiographies* he would entitle *Reveries over Childhood and Youth*, but for the moment his most important contribution to ancestral piety was the poem with which he prefaced *Responsibilities*, 'Pardon, old Fathers'.

Here Yeats proclaimed (in the first draft not always accurately) the roll-call of his ancestors, revealing them as men whose inherent qualities showed a natural aristocracy of mind. Yeats wrote in *Reveries over Childhood and Youth* how he was 'delighted with all that joins my life to those that had power in Ireland or with those anywhere that were good servants and poor bargainers'. Patrician values of authority and service are again proclaimed as altogether superior to the parsimony of Biddy and Paudeen 'fumbling in a greasy till'. Benjamin Yeats, for example, the Dublin merchant, is honoured not for his business acumen (which appears as having been far from distinguished) but for being an Irish citizen whose position as an international trader placed him above paying import duties. Somewhat more appropriately, John Yeats ('Parson John' of Drumcliff) is honoured as a philanthropist, as the 'country scholar' who won the Berkeley Medal at Trinity for his proficiency in Greek, and for having been the patriotic friend of Robert Emmet, for which association he was 'suspected and imprisoned though but for a few hours'. The Butler connection is then brought in to give Yeats a military pedigree, the poet at first erroneously thinking his ancestors fought the Battle of the Boyne on the side of James II rather than William of Orange.

Such an inheritance ensures, in Yeats's chilling phrase, that he pulses with blood which 'has not passed through any huckster's loins', and the feats of his Middleton and Pollexfen relatives are cited to illustrate this continuing purity. But the end of the poem has less snobbery than a pathos expressed with a colloquial assurance which is a remarkable achievement. The childless Yeats declares he has nothing to pass to posterity but his work:

> Pardon that for a barren passion's sake,
> Although I have come close on forty-nine,
> I have no child, I have nothing but a book,
> Nothing but that to prove your blood and mine.[13]

Responsibilities is Yeats's only progeny, his only offspring to ensure the continuity of his line. It is, by implication, a noble, Irish and deeply cherished book, and Yeats suggests that the poems placed between this introductory lyric and the concluding 'Notoriety' not only prove his point but illustrate the inherent vulgarity of a George Moore who can only urinate against them like a dog.

Pound characteristically took such ideas of an innate aristocracy of mind to an extreme of what Yeats called 'unrestrained language' (the tempered prosody of Yeats's 'Notoriety' appears to give his own coarseness a traditional sanction). But at the end of their first winter at Stone Cottage Pound was to help arrange an occasion which appeared to both poets as a celebration of the elite values they espoused.

In November 1913, Yeats wrote a letter to Lady Gregory outlining Pound's idea of honouring the Victorian poet and anti-imperialist Wilfred Scawen Blunt with a dinner in London.[14] Lady Gregory approved of the idea, but when Blunt himself was approached he suggested the festivity take place at his Sussex estate, Newbuildings Place. Other poets invited included Sturge Moore, Victor Plarr, Richard Aldington and F. S. Flint. Hilaire Belloc joined them later after a dinner of roast peacock which, Yeats told Lady Gregory, tasted somewhat like turkey. In fact this grand occasion was not without its humorous aspects. Pound had commissioned a 'sarcophagus' from Gaudier-Brzeska which the bemused Victorian Blunt described as 'terribly post-futurist' and which contained, along with Pound's own somewhat inaccurate eulogy of their host's achievements, Yeats's as yet unpublished lament for the failure of artistic endeavour, his lyric 'When Helen Lived'. After the meal a group photograph was taken in which Yeats appeared 'disguised by influenza and glasses' and holding himself in a self-consciously patrician pose, one hand on the lapel of his buttoned-up suit. Of all the figures in the photograph, he is the one with the least obvious spontaneity – the most masked of the poets – and yet incomparably the most powerful. That he dominated his amanuensis was clear to the perceptive Blunt, who declared that Pound made himself 'a sort of understudy of Yeats, repeating Yeats's voice with Yeats's brogue'. The older man passionately searching for new forms had become a model for imitation.

III
The United States, France and Ireland

At the end of January 1914 Yeats left for a tour of the United States.[15] In

New York he booked in at the Algonquin, where he was at once accosted by his father's friend Dolly Sloan with news of JBY, who, she said, was in poor health and straitened circumstances. Regarding such an intrusion as a gross invasion of his family's privacy and honour, Yeats glared down at the unwelcome messenger with 'cold contempt' and, bowing her to the door, merely said 'Good day, madam.' The aristocratic attitude had to be revealed in real life.

When the two men met it was clear that JBY was growing old. Awkward false teeth and increasing deafness made his once brilliant flow of conversation difficult, and friends were saddened by the sight of 'such a fine intellect groping for connections in a conversation'. From time to time JBY relieved his frustrations by drinking a second bottle of cheap wine, but for all his physical debility the essays he now sent his son in the form of letters showed that his intellect was unimpaired. 'The fact is that not only am I an old man in a hurry,' he declared, 'but all my life I have fancied myself just on the verge of discovering the primum mobile.' The letters to his son in which he discussed such topics as 'a distinction between opinions and convictions and beliefs' were no longer a hostile challenge but rather a source of inspiration, and Yeats now felt he could use many of his father's ideas in his lectures.

There remained, however, the problem of JBY's finances and the continuing estrangement between Yeats himself and John Quinn. Quinn had tried to help JBY by commissioning a never-to-be-completed self-portrait, but if he was generous to the father he remained for some time distant from the son. During the Abbey Theatre's 1913 tour of the United States, for instance, Quinn took Lady Gregory on a tour of the historic Armoury Show which he had organised and then, back in his apartment, listened to an outpouring of his guest's venom and her stories of how she considered that Yeats had been disgracefully subservient to Annie Horniman and had merely written a 'milk-and-water' apology to the insulting letter received from Edmund Gosse at the time of Yeats's application for a Civil List pension. Yeats's own arrival in the United States seemed to Quinn, however, to provide the cue for a reconciliation and he wrote to him saying, 'I have always felt that apart from intellect you were always generous in your sympathies and full of humanity and that your heart was in the right place.' Hoping his suggestion would appeal to the poet, he declared: 'I should be glad to shake hands with you and let by-gones be by-gones.' A meeting was held, hands were shaken, and an important friendship was renewed. JBY told his son he was 'more glad than I can tell you that peace is made with Quinn', but the reconciliation was to have effects JBY could not have foreseen.

No sooner had his son left New York than he pursued him with a letter requesting the loan of $250 (about 10 per cent of what Yeats was anticipating making from his lectures) and, on his return to New York, Yeats and Quinn sat down to work out an arrangement mutually beneficial to all three of them. Quinn, who was assembling a great collection of contemporary literary manuscripts, now offered regularly to buy the handwritten drafts of Yeats's work. Although Yeats himself was reluctant to sell these, a confidential agreement was arrived at whereby the sums of money proposed and paid by Quinn for various items of Yeats's work would be used by Yeats for the support of his father. JBY's finances were now on as sound a footing as perhaps they ever could be (particularly because the old artist himself was not allowed to handle large lump sums). After a grand farewell dinner at which Quinn presented the guests with privately printed copies of *Nine Poems* by Yeats as a memento, Yeats himself left for home with sufficient funds to pay his own debt of £500 to Lady Gregory and then attend Ezra Pound's marriage to Dorothy Shakespear.

His travelling continued, however, and by early May 1914 he was in France visiting Maud Gonne MacBride and arranging to investigate a miracle at Mirebeau with her and Everard Fielding, a leading psychical researcher. This was part of Yeats's continuing interest in the paranormal, and he now proceeded to examine the bleeding oleograph of the Sacred Heart with his familiar combination of curiosity and scepticism. Yeats dictated to Maud an unpublished account of events.[16] He also wrote to Lady Gregory telling her that the bleeding picture would offer her 'some strange light on our folklore', as well as to Quinn, who told him that 'an examination by a competent chemist' would show whether what Yeats had seen was human blood or not. Bloodstained handkerchiefs were then sent to the Lister Institute in London, from which Fielding received a 'somewhat discouraging communication' informing him that 'an extract from the handkerchief gave no precipitate with anti-human serum which therefore excluded the possibility of its being human blood'. This apparently convinced Yeats that the whole affair was a hoax, but if such results in his view closed the matter he had nonetheless been obliged to notice the extreme devotion roused in Maud, who 'fell on her knees early in the day and remained on them as far as possible'.

Yeats's helpfulness to Maud herself continued unabated. He listened sympathetically to her complaints about the delicate and moody Iseult, who was now studying Eastern literature with a young brahmin who had fallen in love with her. He recommended one of Iseult's translations to Rabindranath Tagore and tried to find a post for her brahmin in the Indian colonial school system. Indeed, Indian nationalists had now become one of Maud's concerns, but, if she asked Yeats to help in raising legal aid for their cause, Ireland remained the focus of her political concern. At the end of 1913 she had written to John Quinn, who for all his strong disapproval of armed rebellion had been entertaining Patrick Pearse in his New York apartment, to say that 'this Home Rule bill is a step in the right direction and can be improved'. She then went on to express her hope that 'in the future I think we shall see the British Empire, as it exists today, disappear'.

The situation in Ireland meanwhile was approaching its crisis. Early in 1913, a few weeks after signing 'Ulster's Solemn League and Covenant', the Northern Counties set about raising the Ulster Volunteer Force under the command of a retired Indian Army general, Sir George Richardson. Recruitment proceeded apace, but Nationalists continued to regard it as a matter not worthy of serious attention, while John Redmond of the Parliamentary Party was even convinced that Carson and his followers were bluffing. By September 1913, however, letters were appearing in *The Times* urging that cabinet ministers set on Home Rule should be willing to consider proposals for 'accommodation' with the Unionists. Lord Randolph Churchill put forward a similar notion the following month, and at a meeting between Bonar Law and Asquith at the end of the year there was discussion in detail on some form of exclusion for Ulster from the current Home Rule proposals.

This was unacceptable to Redmond, but by March 1914 Asquith had persuaded him that the northern counties could opt out of the Home Rule Act by plebiscite for a period of six years. Redmond's acquiescence in this was a serious weakening of his stature since, if the Nationalists were to abide by their principal of a united Ireland, there was no possibility of an agreement for opting out whatsoever. But Asquith's proposal was even more distasteful to Carson, who, when the second reading of the Home Rule Bill took place, declared: 'we do not want sentence of death with a stay of execution for six years'. Carson himself left stormily for Belfast, while the British government apparently remained committed to the promises it had agreed with Redmond. In this ever more bitterly divided situation, it was now a question of whether parliament would stand by its word.

This could in the end be guaranteed only by an army whose officers in particular were not minded to fire on Northern Protestants. Their harassed and heavy-handed commander gave them the opportunity of obeying orders or dismissal, and in what became known as 'The Mutiny of the Curragh' a large number of them chose the latter. The reliability of the British army in Ireland was now in doubt, and, despite desperate attempts at face-saving on the part of the government, it was clear that the armed forces could no longer enforce the promises made by parliament to Redmond. The position of Carson and the Unionists seemed unassailable, and by April 1914 close on 25,000 rifles and three million rounds of ammunition, secretly purchased in Germany, were landed and dispersed to Unionists throughout Ulster.

Redmond and the Nationalists meanwhile appeared to do nothing, and it was James Larkin and James Connolly especially, responding to the brutality meted out to the Dublin workers during the great strike of 1913, who formed the so-called Irish Citizen Army, a force of a few hundred workers armed only with wooden shafts and hurley-sticks. Despite the failure of his strike, Larkin continued to be an influential voice, claiming that partition was 'a national disgrace' and declaring ever more loudly that 'we have an opportunity given us of achieving much in the near future of our beloved country, to work for, and if needs be to die, to win back, in the words of Erin's greatest living poet, for Catlin ni Houlihan her four beautiful fields'.[17] Yeats's play had indeed given nationalism a voice, and by the time it was raised other groups were expressing similarly strong opinions.

Arthur Griffith, for example, the leader of Sinn Fein, wrote in his movement's newspaper that 'the Irish leader who would connive in the name of Home Rule at the acceptance of any measure which alienated for a day – for an hour – for one moment of time – a square inch of the soil of Ireland would act the part of a traitor and would deserve a traitor's fate'. Alarmed by concessions made to Carson and by the mutiny at the Curragh, such people now resolved to form a force designed to oppose the Ulster Volunteers which named itself the Irish National Volunteers. By May 1914 over 100,000 men had enrolled. Faced with this groundswell of opinion, Redmond made the only move possible to him and took control of the force. The Parliamentary Party and extreme republican elements were now effectively if acrimoniously joined, and a tiny, isolated but rejuvenated IRB resolved to take advantage of this. Determined to advertise their cause, they decided to reopen the initiative of erecting a statue to Wolfe Tone and, at a ceremony by the hero's grave in June 1913, Patrick Pearse, his words quavering with emotion, voiced his resolution to complete Tone's work: 'to break the connection with England, the never-failing source of all our political evils'. From now on Pearse would make increasingly public his extremist mystical views of Irish nationhood. 'We may make mistakes in the beginning and shoot the wrong people,' he declared, 'but bloodshed is a cleansing and a sanctifying thing, and the nation which regards it as the final horror has lost its manhood. There are many things more horrible than bloodshed, and slavery is one of them.'[18]

While Pearse was sounding the yet barely heeded call for a mystical nationalism, others were taking more practical steps to arm the Irish National Volunteers. In particular, two Anglo-Irish supporters of Home Rule – Sir Roger Casement and Alice Stopford Green – believing passionately that Ireland should be able to defend its rights, raised money in London to purchase arms. Erskine Childers and the young writer Darrell Figgis were sent to Hamburg to buy 1500 Mauser rifles and 45,000 rounds of ammunition. Childers, who was an experienced seaman, offered to land these munitions from his twenty-eight-ton yacht, the *Asgard*. The arms were indeed landed, but, when Dublin Castle was informed, the Volunteers were met by a combined force of police and soldiers. The position was uncertain and the police eventually dispersed, but an armed body of soldiers remained to become the butt of a jeering Dublin crowd. When a shot rang out, followed by a volley, three people were killed while thirty-eight more were wounded.

Political tension reached crisis-point, and, although a conference had been held at Buckingham Palace in an attempt to break the deadlock, this failed to reach agreement. The opposed sides in the Home Rule struggle were now armed, the Home Rule Act itself was about to become law, and a struggle seemed all but inevitable. Events far away in Europe, however, were to postpone this. By now Austria had issued an ultimatum to Serbia, and Ireland, along with the rest of Europe, faced the appalling certainty of world war.

IV
'Meditation in Time of War'

Yeats at first wondered if the war would sweep away the mass mediocrity he saw about him. Writing on the day after hostilities were declared, he recalled that 'Nietzsche was fond of foretelling wars for the possession of the earth that were to restore the tragic mind, and banish the mass mind which he hated'.[19] Such a view was rapidly modified as the absurd and the cruel pressed in upon him. Richard Aldington, hoping to enlist, was arrested as a spy, while another friend was sent to the trenches without even being taught how to fire a rifle. As Europe lumbered towards Armageddon, Yeats wrote to Quinn that 'it seems impossible to believe that some day it will be over, and that Sparta and Athens, Prussia and Paris, will ever visit one another'. His response as an Irishman, however, was one of appalled neutrality. Writing to Lady Gregory he wondered 'if history will ever know at what man's door to lay the crime of this inexplicable war? I suppose, like most wars, it is a big man's war, a sacrifice of the best for the worst. I feel, strangely enough, most for the young Germans who are being killed. The spectacled, dreamy faces, or so I pictured them, remind me more of men I have known than the strong-bodied young English footballers.'

By the end of October the realities of civilian existence were beginning to affect Yeats himself, and he wrote again to Quinn telling him that he envied his distance from the war: 'for here people talk war all day and tell each other endless untrue stories. We are given so little news by the censor that we are devoted to rumour as an Irish village.' The fevered uncertainty and coarse jingoism were also oppressive to Yeats's sense of spiritual reality, and in the attempt to preserve some sense of religious experience he turned to the occult rituals of the Stella Matutina, advancing to a new high grade in a ceremony which involved his being placed in a coffin in the Vault of the Adepti and listening to the ringing of thirty-six bells.

Friends had criticised him, however, for his spiritualist interests, saying they led to nothing and were based on little more than self-suggestion. 'To see you on the floor among those papers searching for an automatic script, where one man finds a misquotation among them, while round you sit your guests, shocked me for it stood out as a terrible symbol,' wrote W. T. Horton. 'I saw you as the man with the muck rake in "The Pilgrim's Progress" while above you your Beloved held the dazzling crown of your own Poetic Genius. But you would not look up and you went on with your grovelling.' A few days earlier, in a letter that was to acquire great importance for Yeats, Horton had written to him using an allusion to the *Phaedrus* in the attempt to show him how dangerous it was to let a fascination with a secret world rival his interest in poetry. 'Conquer and subordinate the dark horse to the white one,' Horton declared, recalling Plato's image of the Charioteer of the Soul, 'or cut the dark horse away, from your chariot, and send it adrift.' Such comments express an understandable distaste for the outward signs of Yeats's inner convictions, but the spiritual nourishment he gained from them was made clear on 9 November 1914 when he wrote his first war poem:

> For one throb of the artery,
> While on that old grey stone I sat
> Under the old wind-broken tree,
> I knew that One is animate,
> Mankind inanimate phantasy.[20]

Yeats's work on *Reveries over Childhood and Youth*, the first section of his *Autobiographies*, was another activity which absorbed him at this time and allowed him to explore his abiding fascination with self-recreation. He told Mabel Beardsley that he had never written anything so enthralling to him. The work was 'an apologia for the Yeats family', and, while the genealogical aspects of the work stress those ideas of natural aristocracy which Yeats had explored in 'Pardon, old Fathers', the most pleasing parts are perhaps the contrasts of place (the antithetical worlds of London and Sligo are particularly effective) and the subtly subjective use of time which breaks down strict chronology to link past and present and so suggest the growth of the poet's mind. Many of the portraits are likewise memorable, although Yeats himself was worried that the image he presented of Dowden as the embodiment of all that was imaginatively inert in Anglo-Irish culture would offend his father.

JBY was indeed considerably hurt by the work, for not only had Yeats disparaged one of his own best friends but he had seen fit to include such embarrassing family moments as when JBY pushed him out of a room with such fury that he broke the glass in a picture with the back of my head. In fact, he was so disturbed by the book that for years afterwards, whenever it was mentioned, he would repeat his belief that it was 'as bad to be a poet's father as the intimate friend of George Moore'. Yeats himself was equivocal on these matters, and on Boxing Day 1914 he wrote to his father:

yesterday I finished my memoirs; I have brought them down to our return to London in 1886 or 1887. After that there would be too many living people to consider and they would have besides to be written in a different way. While I was immature I was a different person and I can stand apart and judge. Later on, I should always, I feel, write of other people. I dare say I shall return to the subject but only in fragments.[21]

Now, however, with the first draft of his reminiscences complete, Yeats was keen to get away to Stone Cottage from where, early in 1915, he could write to his father that 'Ezra Pound and his wife are staying with me, we have four rooms of a cottage on the edge of a heath and our back is to the woods.' Here, while the newspapers and even *Poetry* magazine crammed their columns with war verse written in the manner of Newbolt, Kipling and Housman, Yeats and Pound returned to their esoteric studies and the creation of an elite literature. Art had its own purposes to follow, and when Yeats was asked for a war poem he replied with six terse lines:

> I think it better that in times like these
> A poet's mouth be silent, for in truth
> We have no gift to set a statesman right;
> He has had enough of meddling who can please
> A young girl in the indolence of her youth,
> Or an old man upon a winter's night.[22]

Here, in the poem's first title, was Yeats's 'Reason for Keeping Silent'. When he sent the poem to Henry James, he commented that from henceforth he would 'keep the neighbourhood of the seven sleepers of Ephesus, hoping to catch their comfortable snores till bloody frivolity is over'.*

Ezra Pound meanwhile had been widening his circle of acquaintances to include such members of the Vorticist movement as Wyndham Lewis; he had also been developing a friendship with T. S. Eliot and pursuing ideas of a living and vivid use of scholarship which influenced Yeats's enduring indictment of pedantry, his poem 'The Scholars'. Now, at Stone Cottage, Pound himself and Yeats were working their way through a demanding curriculum of reading. Yeats was dictating a revised version of his *Reveries over Childhood and Youth* which Pound typed up for him, the process of revision being partly aided by their study of the autobiography of Lord Herbert of Cherbury, whose family pieties accorded well with Yeats's own. They also read some of the Icelandic sagas translated by William Morris, and it was probably Yeats who told Pound that when his friends wanted to get

---

* The Seven Sleepers of Ephesus, who Yeats may have learned of from Donne's 'The Good-Morrow', were the legendary Christian martyrs who slept period of martyrdom in the early church.

Morris to forget his gout they would praise Milton to him. A furious Morris would then declare that 'Milton was a d—d rhetorician and that "a good poet *makes pictures*".' It seemed to Pound that Imagism in one form or another was a persistent feature of English literature, and, since Yeats had also brought along seven volumes of Wordsworth, partly hoping to shock his companion, Pound decided to read out the well-known passage from *The Prelude* about a boy 'stealing a boat and rowing out onto a dark lake, and then getting very frightened and rowing back breathless. It's an image.'* Pound found a similar confirmation of his beliefs in Browning's *Sordello* and the works of Swinburne and Lionel Johnson. Altogether more influential, however, was his reading to Yeats *Travels in Arabia Deserta* by Charles Doughty.[23]

This was a work that had for Yeats a two-fold appeal. Doughty's interest in the supernatural was particularly agreeable. Here was a work describing a mentality where it was perfectly natural for a learned man to think he had been called out of his house by a friend, only to discover that this man was a jinn in his friend's likeness. Yeats was intrigued that such jinns could possess human minds, while Doughty's description of the Arab practice of 'sand-divination' and the great geometrical figures this required was to emerge later when Yeats presented his philosophical essay *A Vision* as an elaborated version of a manuscript supposedly belonging to a scholar who had spent many years studying among the Arabs. For the moment, however, this world of jinns and mystic geometry lay dormant in Yeats's mind, and it was another aspect of Doughty that exerted its appeal. The complexity of the work's prose demands an elite readership, an audience of people such as Yeats himself. As Pound wrote: 'the number of people who can read Doughty's "Arabia Deserta" is decently and respectfully limited; so much so that the readers of that work tend to form an almost secret society, a cellule, at least of an actual, if almost imperceptible aristocracy'.

Some of the poems Yeats wrote over the next few months aim for a similar audience. They also relate to his continuing autobiographical concerns. Although Yeats had mentioned to his father how wary he was of discussing living people in his memoirs, the writing of *Reveries over Childhood and Youth* had clearly led him to ponder the possibilities, and it is probable that as early as 1915 he was considering writing what he later packaged up and labelled as 'A first rough draft of memoirs made in 1916–17 and containing much that is not for publication now if ever.' The early sections of this

---

* Yeats's own comments were considerably more trenchant and show the level on which his correspondence with his father was conducted. Writing to JBY he developed a line of argument familiar from his schooldays. Wordsworth, Yeats wrote, 'strikes me as always destroying his poetic experience, which was of course of incomparable value, by his reflective power. His intellect was commonplace, and unfortunately he had been taught to respect nothing else. He thinks of his poetic experience not as incomparable in itself but as an engine that may be yoked to his intellect. He is full of a sort of utilitarianism, and that is perhaps the reason why in later life he is continually looking back on a lost vision, a lost happiness.'

work concentrate on Yeats's friendships with the great men of his youth, provide much important information on his early occult activities, and stress particularly his relationship with Maude Gonne. And it was Maud who once again became the subject of a number of his lyrics.

The necessary inspiration to write these was not readily found 'now that I have come to fifty years', and 'Lines Written in Dejection' offers a moving picture of a poet for whom the high moonlit mysteries of youth are memories of a plenitude seemingly gone. 'The holy centaurs of the hills are vanished.' As the poet tells how he must endure in a disenchanted landscape lit merely by a 'timid sun', so Yeats sounds one of the great themes of his mature work: his fear of impotence and decrepitude, his awareness of the ever more painful divide between the light of euphoric vision and the reality of failing powers. Age alone, however, is not the only cause of this visionary occlusion. The tyranny of the abstract mind likewise severs the poet from fruitful responses to the world. Such a mind is 'The Hawk' in the poem of that title, wheeling in self-delighting pride above a world where the larders are bare and human contact strained and artificial. Such discoveries are the barren insight of solecism, and an altogether truer image of the wise man is Solomon, the type of encyclopaedic knowledge whose intellect is saved from desiccation by the sexual energies roused by Sheba. 'On Woman' praises the wisdom Solomon gained 'while talking with his queens', and yet, for the poet 'growing old', such a promise of potency and the attendant pains of love appears as something that must be reserved for a future life, an existence to be found only when the 'Pestle of the moon' has ground him down in preparation for rebirth.

The trio of poems Yeats wrote to Maud Gonne in early 1915 develops these themes. 'His Phoenix' is an expression of the ageing lover's defiance hurled in the face of younger men: 'I knew a phoenix in my youth, so let them have their day.' It may be that the previous amours of the newly married Pound are jocularly alluded to in this work, but the presence of the couple at Stone Cottage can only have enforced Yeats's sense of sexual isolation, and 'Her Praise' is an altogether more moving account of the pathos in this situation:

> I will talk no more of books or the long war
> But walk by the dry thorn until I have found
> Some beggar sheltering from the wind, and there
> Manage the talk until her name come round.[24]

The proud but ageing lover preserves the idealism of youth. In his isolation, however, he is no longer a fit image of the active suitor but a figure who must accept that he is now at one with those poor old men whom 'She' always took pity on. His passion places him with the derelict and, in joining them, the magnanimity of the beloved is exalted in a new, high way.

But, if the poet can find a temporary respite in the companionship of outcasts on the waste moor, Ferrara and Urbino, 'where the Duchess and her people talked', make the true ideal of where he might have lived. Around the lover in reality meanwhile seethes the 'unmannerly town' that had rejected art and culture, spurned Hugh Lane's gift of pictures and defamed his own work. The lover is back in the world depicted in *Poems Written in Discouragement*, and his lot is once again defiant bitterness. Only the beloved can shock him out of this alienation and sterility. She too has been traduced by those she helped, but, as she told the poet, she has never at any time 'complained of the people'. He replies as best he can. His is 'the analytic mind', the hawk, while hers preserves 'the purity of a natural force', and even now, 'nine years' later, he is abashed by her powers.

But the polluting presence of 'the dishonest crowd' remains to harass the poet, and, as a man enamoured of values altogether more transforming, he is obliged to imagine the audience he cannot find. As Yeats summed up his position from the vantage point of 1934:

> I had met much unreasonable opposition. To overcome it I had to make my thoughts modern. Modern thought is not simple; I became argumentative, passionate, bitter; when I was very bitter I used to say to myself, 'I do not write for these people who attack everything that I value . . . I am writing for a man I have never seen.' I built up in my mind the picture of a man who lived in the country where I had lived, who fished in mountain streams where I had fished; I said to myself, 'I do not know whether he is born yet, but born or unborn it is for him I write.'

As Yeats declared in 'The Fisherman':

> Before I am old
> I shall have written him one
> Poem maybe as cold
> And passionate as the dawn.[25]*

But where would such an imagined figure find his place in the political realities fomenting in Ireland after the declaration of war? With the outbreak of hostilities it was agreed by all the major parties that Home Rule was to become law and placed on the statute book with a Suspensory Act which would prevent its coming into force until an amending bill had been introduced allowing for a plebiscite in Ulster. Determined to guarantee the eventual reality of Home Rule, Redmond now emphasised what he believed

---

* Yeats himself remained a keen fisherman, but a story told by Austin Clarke throws an interesting light on Yeats's poem. Clarke was in the Seven Woods at Coole where he saw a glimpse of blue he first thought might be an 'elemental' or a peacock. Creeping forward, 'I saw a tall figure in a marvellous sky-blue watered silk raincoat holding fishing-rods and lines and all that fierce tackle of the country gentleman. . . . Then I looked again, and I recognised dimly from those frontispieces of the books that it was the poet himself, disguised as a great country gentleman and sportsman; as a young romantic poet of the Irish movement, I was shocked and disappointed.'

was Ireland's place within the wider context of Great Britain by promising the government that British troops could be taken out of Ireland, whose coasts would be defended by what he hoped would be a joint force of the Irish National and the Ulster Volunteers. Apart from a small minority of extremists, this position was welcome in Ireland itself, and on 18 September 1914 the Home Rule Act received the royal assent, with the proviso that it was suspended for twelve months or until the end of the war, whichever were the longer period.

In September 1914 it was still believed that the First World War would be over by Christmas. Thousands of Irishmen enlisted for a struggle which, Redmond believed, was 'undertaken in defence of the highest principles of religion and morality and right'. He added that 'it would be a disgrace forever to our country, and a reproach to her manhood, and a denial of the lessons of her history, if young Ireland confined her efforts to remain at home to defend the shores of Ireland from an unlikely invasion, and shrank from the duty of proving on the field of battle the gallantry and courage that has distinguished our race all through its history'.[26] Only a very small minority believed the ancient adage that England's war was Ireland's opportunity. Twenty members of the committee of the Irish National Volunteers resigned and, under Eoin MacNeill, formed a splinter group officially named the Irish Volunteers. It was widely regarded as eccentric. However, as Irishmen joined up in increasing numbers for the Great War, and National Volunteer brigades began to thin out, so voices among the break-away Volunteers became more audible and were increasingly listened to as Carson joined the coalition cabinet and doubts arose about whether England would indeed keep its promise to Ireland and Home Rule.

Unknown to the overwhelming majority of people, the Irish Volunteers were under the control of an extremist Supreme Council of IRB members who did indeed believe that England's war was Ireland's opportunity and had sworn themselves to armed insurrection in the pursuit of an independent Irish republic. Among these extremists was Patrick Pearse, who, by 1915, had joined with Joseph Plunkett and Eamonn Ceannt in a military committee plotting rebellion. These men were a tiny minority within a minority, but their passion was altogether more powerful than their numbers. At the start of August 1915, Pearse himself had given a rousing speech at the funeral of the old Fenian Jeremiah O'Donovan Rossa, declaring that, 'while Ireland holds these graves, Ireland unfree shall never be at peace'. By the middle of the following month he was leading a partly armed demonstration of 1500 Volunteers through the streets of Dublin to a site hallowed in Fenian memory, while, at the end of the year, another celebration was held to commemorate the deaths of the original Fenian Martyrs. The weight of past history was being consciously used for propaganda purposes, but, while Pearse and his friends had their own reasons for this, the majority was unaware of these or of the disastrous efforts made by Sir Roger Casement to secure German backing for their aims. Now, however, with the gradual collapse of Casement's endeavour, Pearse and his companions on the military committee would have to pursue their aims by other means.

V

Masks and Men

Yeats himself, although he was acutely aware of the dangers inherent in the Irish situation now that Home Rule had been postponed in an armed and divided nation, could only observe the situation apprehensively. He was still minded to believe that the British government would honour its promises, but he noted that in London itself the effects of the Great War were seriously wearing down people's nerves. Some form of compensatory activity was necessary, he believed. 'Unless a sufficient number of people read the history of China steadily they will not know what to do if there is a real disaster.' But the effects of the war were inescapable. Maud wrote him letters from the Front telling him that she was 'nursing the wounded from 8 in the morning to 8 at night and trying in material work to drown the sorrow and disappointment of it all – and in my heart is growing up a wild hatred of the war machine which is grinding the life of these great nations and reducing their populations to helpless slavery'. She noted among the majority of soldiers 'a terrible secret bitterness'. Even life at Coole was affected, and at the beginning of October 1915 Maud wrote to Yeats expressing her sorrow on hearing that Robert Gregory had enlisted. 'It seems so outside his life and duty, but one cannot tell how others feel things. It must be a terrible anxiety to Lady Gregory.' In the same month, while he was dictating a letter to Lady Gregory, Yeats himself had an experience of what the Great War meant for Londoners:

> An exciting event has just happened which has put completely out of my head what I was going to say when I dictated the appropriate words 'Owing to threats. There has been a Zeppelin raid.' In the middle of that sentence there came a tremendous noise – series of them. We went down to the door (I am dictating in Miss Jacobs' office opposite the British Museum) – it sounded as if the Museum was bombed. We saw a group of people running past and I shouted, 'Where is it?' and they said right overhead, so I thought it better that we should keep inside the house. However, as nothing happened we went across and stood under the Museum railings where we found four or five other people. We then saw the Zeppelin at a comfortable distance – somewhere over the city I should think – shrapnel bursting round it with tremendous detonations. . . . It has the terrifying effect of thunder

– I mean an emotional effect quite distinct from any consciousness of danger. . . . I have just said to Miss Jacobs, 'Twenty minutes is enough for the day of Judgement so I will take up my letter.' I am so puzzled by those words, 'owing to threats' that I am half inclined to think that they were written automatically by Miss Jacobs.[27]

Amid such incidents Yeats continued to live his literary and social life. Much of his effort was directed towards obtaining a pension for James Joyce from the Royal Literary Fund. The entry of Italy into the war had caused Joyce himself to move from Trieste to Zurich, and Yeats now wrote to Edmund Gosse informing him that 'I have had just heard that James Joyce, an Irish poet and novelist of whose fine talent I can easily satisfy you, is in probably great penury through the war.' Pound was required to gather information so that Gosse could be 'perfectly sure of the *facts*', but war sentiment obtruded even on this, Gosse writing to Yeats that he would not let Joyce 'have one penny if I . . . believed that he was in sympathy with the Austrian enemy'. The pension was eventually granted, but Yeats felt it necessary to write to Gosse not merely thanking him but obliquely pointing out that, in his opinion, artistic merit had nothing to do with political allegiance. 'It never occurred to me that it was necessary to express sympathy "frank" or otherwise with the "cause of the Allies",' he wrote punningly. 'I should have thought myself wasting the time of the committee.'

In addition to such activities as these, Yeats continued to visit the dying Mabel Beardsley, to attend Irish Literary Society dinners and to hold his 'Mondays' at Woburn Buildings. In November 1915, he dined with the intellectual society hostess Lady Cunard, met Arthur Balfour, and learned that he was to be offered a knighthood in the New Year's Honours List. This last he thought he could not accept and he wrote to Lily explaining that 'as I grow older I become more conservative and I do not know whether that is because my thoughts are deeper or my blood more chill, but I do not wish anyone to say of me "only for a ribbon he left us"'.

But, if these were the public aspects of Yeats's life, his interest in spiritualism was leading him into areas altogether more arcane. His fascination with automatic handwriting was still active and had been particularly stimulated by contact with Edith Lyttelton.[28] After the death of her husband in July 1913, Lady Lyttelton had tried communicating with the dead and wrote to ask Yeats for help. He visited her and, soon afterwards, she began to produce scripts referring to him. On 9 May, for example, Lady Lyttelton's control declared that 'Yeats is a prince with an evil counsellor.' This naturally caused some confusion, and five weeks later the control said, 'if this is not understood tell him to think of the double harness – the adverse principle'. Yeats was suddenly 'struck' by the close resemblance between this and the use Horton had made of Plato's Charioteer. The coincidence greatly excited him, and he wrote to Lady Lyttelton enclosing a copy of Horton's statement and saying: 'it is as you will see very nearly what your controls say. Notice their allusion to the horses of Phaeton and to the sign, the sun (Leo). I do not understand it in the least except that you and he speak of a dual influence and bad.' Three years later, and under remarkable circumstances, Yeats would come to believe he had found an answer to this puzzle.

Meanwhile, Leo Africanus repeatedly spoke to him at seances. On 23 June 1913, at a seance held by Mrs Wreidt, Leo 'talked of the theatre as if I had no other interest'. But Yeats remained sceptical. Although 'the spirits excel us . . . in knowledge of fact', he wrote, it seemed that they failed in 'speculation, wit, the highest choice of the mind'. Yeats asked himself 'why has no sentence of literary or speculative profundity come through any medium in the last fifty years, or perhaps ever'. At a seance on 6 June 1915, Leo Africanus informed Yeats that he had foretold his journey to America, but when Yeats asked him for 'something' about his visit with Maud Gonne and Everard Fielding to the bleeding oleograph at Mirebeau, Leo could only repeat some word 'over and over again. It was probably "miracle".' Leo was able to speak about a topic Yeats, Fielding and Maud had discussed over dinner in France, and when Yeats asked him why Elizabeth Radcliffe's automatic writing had ceased he was told that 'she must work once more with her old friends for a time or she will lose her gift'.

The following day, as the manuscript of 'Leo Africanus' shows, Yeats tried to sum up his conclusions about spiritualism. He still considered that 'all the reflective part at these seances seems less convincing than the matter of fact part', but he felt 'sure' that 'minds of some kind can write or speak through a medium in tongues unknown to all present'. He believed that these minds 'know the private affairs of sitters', and that they had a 'strange power over matter'. He believed too that they 'have power of creating luminous substances which can take the human form', and that if their 'abstract reflective power' was limited 'their practical wisdom is often very great'. As if to illustrate this, at a 'remarkable seance at Mrs Wreidt's' on 20 July 1915, there was much discussion about George Pollexfen, Yeats's sisters and the codicil to Hugh Lane's will. When Leo himself then manifested he spoke first about the financial problems of the Abbey Theatre and then went on to prophesy that the war 'would be much longer than we thought'. Finally, speaking in 'what seemed Italian', he foretold Yeats's future, saying: 'when you were young you were a contented man. Life is like that. Then came the thistles, but now you will have the roses. . . . I had done much that would be famous in the record.' Yeats was so impressed that two days later, when he was visited by Sturge More and Miss Scatcherd the medium, he talked about these events with such enthusiasm that Miss Scatcherd offered to call up the spirit of Leo once again. When she had done so, Leo asked Yeats to compose an exchange of letters between them, and in time this was to become an important element in the growth of Yeats's doctrine of the mask.

Yeats had now convinced himself, for the moment at least, that Leo Africanus was 'the person he claimed to be' and that he was also the embodiment of his own antithetical character. One of his profoundest and longest-held convictions was being given new life. As Yeats himself wrote to Leo some months later: 'you were my opposite. By association with one another we should each become more complete; you had been unscrupulous and believing. I was over-cautious and conscientious.' Yeats the spiritualist and antithetical man had, it seemed, discovered supernatural proof for one of his most original insights into the working of the psyche: the idea that energy, completeness and release stem from familiarising oneself with all that is opposite to one's normal, quotidian personality. In an attempt to find new depths in his doctrine, Yeats was obliging himself to face in Leo his shadow side, to confront his antithetical being as an inner and occult reality.

The mask or anti-self it seemed could be a spirit and was no longer a set of fixed features to be worn partly in defiance of the world. It was a living and spiritual means of relating oneself to psychological and cultural abundance, for Yeats believed that, with the reappearance of Leo Africanus, the renaissance traveller and poet, he could identify himself not simply with his complementary being but with an epoch of history where he believed he could find full imaginative existence. As he wrote later, his meditation on Leo and the 'doctrine of "the mask"' was the process that 'convinced me that every passionate man . . . is, as it were, linked with another age, historical or imaginary, where alone he finds images that rouse his energy'. Here were the beginnings of a remarkable expansion of Yeats's philosophy, a development which would in time relate him to the cosmos and the history of mankind.

Meanwhile he was seeking to give poetic expression to his ideas in the philosophical dialogue 'Ego Dominus Tuus', where the antithetical self is shown to be the true poet's master. Yeats was coming to believe, in the words of Leo Africanus, that 'all living minds are surrounded by shades, who are the contrary will which presents before the abstracted [?] mind and the mind of the sleeper ideal images. The living mind could [not] exist for a moment without our succour, for God does not act immediately upon the mind but through meditorial forms.' Leo Africanus, in other words, was a messenger of the divine, a Daimon, and Yeats believed that to deeply intuitive people the ether is thronging with such spiritual embodiments of their own completeness. It is not an inert physical compound to be weighed, measured and mastered by the forces of materialism, but a medium pulsing with spiritual life. For each of such people there exists his own particular guide and teacher, his own visionary form of spiritual completeness, and in 'Ego Dominus Tuus' Yeats sought to summon his to his side:

> I call to the mysterious one who yet
> Shall walk the wet sands by the edge of the stream
> And look most like me, being indeed my double,
> And prove of all imaginable things
> The most unlike, being my anti-self . . .[29]

These closing lines are a remarkable affirmation of visionary courage and draw, as Leo Africanus was to suggest, on some of Yeats's most deeply held religious convictions. The passage seeks to soar free of the commonplace world of common sense and 'the formulas of science', but more than that it seeks the divine. The shade of Leo was to tell Yeats that 'in your heart you know that all philosophy that has lasting expression is founded on the intuition of God, and that he being all good and all power it follows [as] Henry More the Cambridge Platon[ist] so wisely explains that all our deep desires are images of the truth'.

The soul extended may thus touch the threshold of the divine, and yet, even in perceiving this, a man's other self may draw him back to the daily world. 'You are sympathetic,' Leo told Yeats, 'you meet many people, you discuss much, you must meet all their doubts as they arise, and so cannot break away into a life of your own as did Swedenborg, Boehme, and Blake'. As in those euphoric days when Yeats had committed himself to the Castle of Heroes, it seemed that 'invisible gates would open', save now he knew his daily self would struggle with his mystical anti-self in the tussle from which he would make the poetry that is 'Ego Dominus Tuus'. The character in the poem named by Yeats 'Ille' (and mischievously rechristened by Ezra Pound 'Wille') reaches out to the divine, while 'Hic' remains earthbound and sceptical. Hic looks for practical self-knowledge, the easy inspiration of 'impulsive men' and a style formed by 'sedentary toil'. Ille looks for something beyond this half-creative approach. Ille knows that great art cannot be made in this way, that it is a pursuit not of 'deliberate happiness' but of ecstasy won from reaching out after the anti-self, the mask. Dante becomes one model for this, Keats another:

> His art is happy, but who knows his mind?
> I see a schoolboy when I think of him,
> With face and nose pressed to a sweet-shop window,
> For certainly he sank into his grave
> His senses and his heart unsatisfied,
> And made – being poor, ailing and ignorant,
> Shut out from all the luxury of the world,
> The coarse-bred son of a livery-stable keeper—
> Luxuriant song.[30]

Great poets 'own nothing but their blind, stupefied hearts', but Yeats's scepticism of the spiritualist philosophy on which he had reared this insight remained, and during the third of his winters at Stone Cottage with Ezra Pound and his wife he was to explore his ideas further. Partly inspired by his reading of Landor's *Imaginary Conversations*, Yeats began to compose his dialogue with Leo Africanus. Amid the hideously mounting fatalities of the Great War, such communication with the dead had become almost commonplace and makes Yeats's project seem less eccentric. Yeats himself was to write that, 'while the great battle in Northern France is still undecided', he would 'climb to the top of that old house in Soho where a medium is sitting among servant girls', and would be moved to see how 'one would, it may be, ask for news of Gordon Highlander or Munster Fuselier, and the fat old woman would tell in Cockney language how the dead do not yet know they are dead, but still go on amid visionary smoke and noise, and how angelic spirits seek to awaken them but still in vain'.

Meanwhile a curious modern work of spiritualism, Anne Moberly and Eleanor Jourdain's *An Adventure* – at the time an immensely popular and influential work – seemed to confirm that spirits could travel back in history. The two authors of the work, respectively Principal and Vice Principal of St Hugh's College, Oxford, gave a detailed description of how they had been transported to Versailles in the year 1789, and references to this work are frequent in the notes Yeats was preparing for Lady Gregory's *Visions and Beliefs in the West of Ireland*. But, for all the fervour with which he wished to believe such things, Yeats's own spiritualist experiments and his communications with Leo Africanus especially had 'not convinced' him that there was anything in them that had 'come from beyond my own imagination'. Aside from exploring the possibilities such matters raised in his poetry, Yeats was forced to comfort his longings with insights gleaned from anthropology and world literature. As he was to write two years later in *Per Amica Silentia Lunae*:

> spiritism, whether of folk-lore or of the séance-room, the visions of Swedenborg, and the speculation of the Platonists and Japanese plays, will have it that we may see at certain roads and in certain houses old murders acted over again, and in certain fields dead huntsmen riding with horse and hound, or ancient armies fighting above bones or ashes. We carry to *Anima Mundi* our memory, and that memory is for a time our external world; and all passionate moments recur again and again.

That Yeats believed the Noh drama of Japan might be one among these alleged proofs of the enduring spiritual reality of history suggests how, during his third stay at Stone Cottage, he had become immersed in the possibility of a drama revealed to him by Pound's work on the Fenellosa manuscripts. Indeed, Yeats was ever more keen to push at the boundaries of both the composition and the production of his plays. At the start of May 1914, for example, he had commissioned from Charles Ricketts a series of costume designs for *The King's Threshold* which, he considered, gave 'whole scenes . . . a new intensity, and passages or actions that had seemed commonplace became powerful and moving'. Indeed, so impressed was Yeats by Ricketts's work that he commissioned new costumes from him for *On Baile's Strand*, which was due to be revived in the London season of the Abbey Company in June 1915. Among these designs was a magnificent sketch for the costume to be worn by Cuchulain himself, its masterly bold abstracts vividly conjuring up an impression of an heroic age. Now, however, Yeats was to embrace an altogether more radical influence.

As early as 1904 he had prophesied in *Samhain* that 'the hour of convention and decoration and ceremony is coming again'. Now, as Pound worked on the scripts he was to publish through the Cuala Press as *Certain Noble Plays of Japan: From the Manuscripts of Ernest Fenellosa, Chosen and Finished by Ezra Pound*, so Yeats became increasingly aware of a sophisticated, patrician, ritualistic form of drama which, free from factitious realism, might be refashioned to reveal for an elite audience the beauty and truth of Irish myth.* In his essay 'Certain Noble Plays of Japan', written as an introduction to Pound's volume and later reprinted as an essay in Yeats's collection *The Cutting of an Agate*, he made clear the refined and historical background to Noh.[31] 'When for the first time *Hamlet* was being played in London,' he wrote, 'Noh was made a necessary part of official ceremonies at Kioto, and young nobles and princes, forbidden to attend the popular theatre, in Japan as elsewhere a place of mimicry and naturalism, were encouraged to witness and to perform in spectacles where speech, music, song, and dance created an image of nobility and strange beauty.'

What was patrician was also full of artifice. As Yeats had written a decade earlier: 'as long as drama was full of poetical beauty, full of description, full of philosophy, as long as its words were the very vesture of sorrow and laughter, the players understood that their art was essentially conventional, artificial, ceremonious'. The impressive simplicity in the staging of Noh drama emphasised such characteristics. Pound explained this when he wrote of a stage visible from three sides which 'is reached by a bridge which is divided into three sections by three real pine trees which are small and in pots. There is one scene painted on the background. It is a pine tree, the symbol of the unchanging. It is painted right on the back of the stage and, as this cannot be shifted, it remains the same for all plays.' Such hieratic simplicity was greatly appealing to Yeats, who was to declare of his own experiments in such staging

---

* The production of this book was to cause considerable distress to Lollie. She ordered what she considered the right quantity of paper, but Pound added an extra work and so she was obliged to reduce the print run. Yeats then insisted Pound be compensated by a 2 per cent rise in his royalty. Lollie was also to find Pound to be the worst proof reader she ever met.

that it had been 'a great gain to get rid of scenery and substitute for a crude landscape painted upon canvas three performers who, sitting against a screen covered with some one unchangeable pattern, or against the wall of a room, describe landscape or event'.

But it was not only the staging of Noh drama that answered to Yeats's needs. The extreme subtlety of speech required appealed to a poet who for a quarter of a century had been experimenting with techniques for refining the actor's voice and had written that the actor himself 'must understand how to discriminate cadence from cadence and so cherish the musical lineaments of verse or prose that he delights the ear with a continually varied music'. In addition, the language of Noh drama, deriving from the archaic court idiom of fourteenth-century Japan, answered to Yeats's insistence on the traditional and aristocratic. As he wrote in 'Certain Noble Plays of Japan':

> a poetical passage cannot be understood without a rich memory, and like the older school of painting appeals to a tradition, and that not merely when it speaks of 'Lethe wharf' or 'Dido on the wild sea banks' but in rhythm, in vocabulary; for the ear must notice slight variations upon old cadences and customary words, all that high breeding of poetical style where there is nothing ostentatious, nothing crude, no breath of parvenu or journalist.

Again, movement on the Noh stage should have something of the artificial stiffness of a puppet, while the presence of a chorus not only allowed many of the speeches to be sung to instruments but enabled dance to play a vital role in the action. Such dance was again a highly formalised matter. 'The interest', Yeats wrote of the Noh dancers, 'is not in the human form but in the rhythm to which it moves, and the triumph of their art is to express the rhythm in its intensity.' He went on to explain that 'there are few swaying movements of arms or body such as make the beauty of our dancing. They move from the hip, keeping constantly the upper part of their body still, and seem to associate with every gesture or pose some definite thought. They cross the stage with a sliding movement, and one gets the impression not of undulation but of continuous straight lines.'

But what perhaps more than any other convention of Noh drama suggested its distance from the representation of daily life was the actors' use of masks. Disguising the actor's physical personality, the mask allowed him to penetrate the essence of the role he was playing and then to use this emotion to bring the mask to life. Stage convention offered a parallel to Yeats's philosophical enquiries while, as he himself wrote of the aesthetic effect, 'a mask will enable me to substitute for the face of some commonplace player, or for that face repainted to suit his own vulgar fancy, the fine invention of a sculptor, and to bring the audience close enough to the play to hear every inflection of the voice'. He knew that the mask could be a means of conveying profound emotion, and, as he wrote of this paradox, his productions would not 'lose by staying the movement of the features, for deep feeling is expressed by a movement of the whole body'. It was this truth rather than the 'vitality' beloved of the realists that Yeats valued in poetical painting and sculpture, and he wondered if it was 'even possible that being is only possessed completely by the dead, and that it is some knowledge of this that makes us gaze with so much emotion upon the face of the Sphinx or Buddha'.

There are clear elements here of Yeats's communications with the spirit world, while the understanding of the supernatural and the spiritual revealed so often by Noh drama allied its makers, Yeats thought, to the mysterious emotions still familiar to the Irish peasantry. 'These Japanese poets, too, feel for tomb and wood the emotion, the sense of awe that our Gaelic-speaking countrypeople will sometimes show when you speak to them of Castle Hackett or of some holy well.' Noh drama and Irish peasant beliefs were in accord, and, as Yeats wrote in 'Certain Noble Plays of Japan', he loved 'all the arts that can still remind me of their origin among the common people'. Now, in turning once again to the legend of Cuchulain, Yeats believed he had found a typical Noh scenario, an adventure which was 'the meeting with ghost, god, or goddess at some holy place or much-legended tomb'. As he began work on *At the Hawk's Well* (originally entitled *The Waters of Immortality*) so he was creating an elite drama in which he hoped to show that he had 'attained the distance from life which can make credible strange events, elaborate words', while, 'instead of the players working themselves into a violence of passion indecorous in our sitting-room, the music, the beauty of form and voice all come to climax in a pantomimic dance'.

VI

At the Hawk's Well

The composition of *At the Hawk's Well*, which was begun on 4 February 1916, was not without its comic interruptions. Early in that month a policeman arrived at Stone Cottage to tell Pound that he was an alien in a prohibited area and that wartime regulations required him to report to the local police station. This he had failed to do, and an amused Yeats wrote to Quinn telling him how Pound 'after his third visit from a policeman . . . left the house this afternoon with such energy that he tore the coat hook from the wall'. A furious and intimidated Pound wrote to the wife of a cabinet minister asking her to intercede and also persuaded Yeats to write to various influential people, including the Poet Laureate Robert Bridges, who replied with a brilliantly comic letter in response to Yeats's 'asking me to write something to identify Ezra Pound'. Entirely confident that the matter was a trivial one, Bridges adopted a tone of heavy-handed skulduggery. 'You omitted in your letter to show me any *proof* that E.P. was really with you,' Bridges wrote, 'but it happened that he corrected two sentences in the typewritten letter with a pen *and I recognised his hand-writing* before I read the letter. I think it was at first glance, anyhow I have no doubt about its being his writing.'[32] An anxious Pound thought that such foolery 'would have hanged all three of us in any country in Europe', but the summons was eventually withdrawn and Pound and Yeats could continue their work on the elite niceties of Noh drama.

That Yeats himself was seeking only a very small audience for such works was in keeping with the ideas of the poet of *Responsibilities*, but it was also an aspect of his mounting of his own plays at the Abbey. As the poet Austin Clarke recalled, Yeats's poetic dramas 'were a deeply imaginative experience, and, as the poet put on his own plays as often as possible, the experience was a constant one. On such occasions the theatre was almost empty.'[33] The audience usually consisted of no more than twenty or thirty people, and to these devotees Yeats would deliver a lecture, 'telling humbly of his "little play", how he had rewritten it, and what he had meant to convey in its lines'. Mary Colum remembered the passion that went into these expositions:

> I have seen him put such immense emotional and intellectual energy into a talk to an audience of about twenty or thirty, some of them inimical, as would have projected a major scene in one of his verse dramas, and neither for this nor for his work in the theatre did he get any financial return; he did not even at the time get much of any other sort of return, either – little gratitude, and that only from a few.

Austin Clarke, sitting on such occasions in the all but deserted Abbey, 'felt like Ludwig of Bavaria, that eccentric monarch, who sat alone in his own theatre'.

Society London provided the ideal venue for Yeats's new play, however. *At the Hawk's Well* was first played privately in the drawing room of Lady Cunard's house in Cavendish Square on 2 April 1916, and was given a second performance two days later before Queen Alexandra at Lady Islington's home in Chesterfield Gardens, when Beecham conducted the music. Yeats had previously met the Queen at a reception of the Duchess of Sutherland's. She knew his poems, she said, and expressed a wish to see one of his plays. But the Queen soon tired of Yeats's preliminary explanation of Noh drama and asked her lady-in-waiting to tell him to cut it short. Such assembled companies nonetheless appeared to approach Yeats's ideal of 'an audience like a secret society where admission is by favour and never to many', but, though the spectators on the first occasion included a young T. S. Eliot, Pound was critical of the assembled ranks 'of crowned heads and divorcees'.

He had, even so, done much to ensure the play's relative artistic success. In particular, he had introduced Yeats to Edmund Dulac, whose formal style of book illustration was appropriate to the costumes he designed for the play. These included a masked and winged study for the Guardian of the Well, a role performed by another of Pound's friends, the Japanese dancer Michio Ito, who had first come to notice when asked to entertain the company at a party of Lady Ottoline Morrell's. Although Ito himself had not seen a performance of Noh since he was seven, and had even told Pound he thought there was 'nothing more boring' than traditional Japanese theatre, his work on the Fenellosa papers and his Nijinski-inspired training led him to see the correspondence between avant-garde European ideas and the traditions of his homeland.* Yeats himself had seen Ito dance at a society reception, perhaps when he performed five 'dance poems' translated by Pound, and it was partly such experiences which allowed Yeats to write a play 'made possible by a Japanese dancer whom I have seen dance in a studio and in a drawing-room and on a very small stage lit by an excellent stage-light'.

Yeats himself had his play performed 'by the light of a large chandelier', but this can have been the only element of staging familiar to the audience as three Musicians entered in front of a screen and unfolded at an angle a black cloth painted with a gold abstract design of the hawk-headed Guardian. The Guardian herself entered beneath this and crouched beside her well (represented by a square of blue material) as the Musicians sang their chorus of desolation:

> I call to the eye of the mind
> A well long choked up and dry
> And boughs long stripped by the wind,
> And I call to the mind's eye
> Pallor of an ivory face,
> Its lofty dissolute air,
> A man climbing up to a place
> The salt sea wind has swept bare.[34]

Here is the sterile and threatening place among the mountains where the waters of immortality occasionally surge through the leaf-clogged well only to be lost to those who seek them. The Musicians tell how the masked Old Man who now enters through the audience has been watching by the well for fifty years, his life slipping away in hopeless pursuit of immortality. The masked Young Man who then enters reveals himself as Cuchulain (in terms of Noh convention, the *waki*, or questor after a special destiny), who has been led here by a rumour. Although the sinister and pain-riven desolation of the place presses ever more menacingly in on him, he refuses to heed

---

* Ito caused considerable amusement when he went to observe the birds of prey at London Zoo and began prancing about outside their cages in an effort to imitate their movements. Some thought him mad, others decided he was the devotee of an Eastern bird religion.

the Old Man's prophetic warnings as the Guardian of the Well emits her ominous shriek and transfixes him with her hawklike eyes and the frightened Old Man covers his head and falls asleep. Mesmerised by the dance – the climactic moment in the play – the young Cuchulain is now lured from his pursuit of immortality and, as the waters rise and recede unnoticed, rushes off in the fatal pursuit of the queenly Aoife, whose child he will father and who will eventually kill him.

The intense brevity of the play and its sense of the malevolent and the supernatural are so enhanced by its stylisation that the result is far more than an exercise in theatrical genre. It carries a personal charge of sexual menace and spiritual pain. The presentation of Cuchulain hurled by conflicting passions between the equally ruthless and antithetical worlds of the spirit and the body raises a genuine sense of fear, and Yeats's image of a dry and desolate holy well was to have a profound influence. He wrote that he had composed *At the Hawk's Well* to 'delight the best minds of my time' and, after seeing the work performed in Lady Cunard's drawing room, T. S. Eliot wrote that 'thereafter one saw Yeats . . . as a more eminent contemporary from whom one could learn'. Here indeed was an early revelation of modernism, of the world of *Ulysses* and *The Waste Land* where, as Eliot declared, 'the myth is not presented for its own sake, but as a vehicle for a situation of universal meaning'. Yeats was creating twentieth-century literature in an elite London drawing room and before a crowned head of Empire, but, even as he did so, other figures, equally inspired by Cuchulain, were fomenting another revolution. At the end of April 1916, Patrick Pearse and his friends stormed the Dublin Post Office and the centre of the city lay in ruins.

12

Terrible Beauty
(1916–1917)

I
'Easter 1916'

On Easter Monday morning 1916 small detachments of Irish Volunteers and the Citizen Army had threaded their way through an unsuspecting Dublin to seize some two dozen strategic points in the city and so prepare for revolution. One group planned to blow up the Magazine Fort in Phoenix Park, to which they gained entry by pretending they were in pursuit of a lost football. The guards were overcome, telephone wires were cut and a stick of gelignite laid. Unable to find the key to the main munitions dump, however, the Volunteers were obliged to leave with merely a small number of stolen rifles. As they departed, they shot and fatally wounded a youth who was running off to sound the alarm.

Another group resolved to storm Dublin Castle, where, having thrown a bomb into the guardhouse which failed to explode, they were so abashed at what seemed their easy victory that they retreated to occupy some buildings opposite. Further detachments went to seize the Four Courts. Patrick Pearse's friend Thomas MacDonagh occupied Jacob's Biscuit Factory with the support of John MacBride and Maire nic Shiubhlaigh. Constance Markiewicz, dressed in a green uniform and brandishing a revolver, established a temporary outpost in St Stephen's Green, while a detachment of men under the mathematics professor Eamon de Valera occupied Boland's Flour Mills, thereby gaining a strategic advantage over the road from Kingstown Harbour along which the inevitable British troops would march.

The most significant of these small insurrectionary groups was that led by Patrick Pearse. Around noon on Easter Monday, Pearse marched a detachment of some hundred Irish Volunteers and Citizen Army men down O'Connell Street to the General Post Office. This, with the firing of a few shots, he rapidly cleared and made the headquarters of his new 'Republic'. Two flags were then hoisted to declare his intent. One of these was the well-known

371

emblem of a gold harp on a green background, now emblazoned with the words 'Irish Republic'. The other was an unfamiliar tricolour of orange, white and green. With the Post Office thus secured, Pearse himself emerged on the portico steps to read to a largely indifferent crowd his proclamation for the provisional government of the Irish republic: 'Irishmen and Irishwomen: In the name of God and of the dead generations from which she receives her old tradition of nationhood, Ireland, through us, summons her children to her flag and strikes for her freedom.'[1]

In Pearse's imagination myth and history had merged into a vision of the future. The declaration went on to state how well-trained and secret bands of the IRB, the Irish Volunteers and the Citizen Army, 'supported by her exiled children in America and by gallant Allies in Europe', were now confident of a Republican victory. As a consequence, it seemed possible to 'declare the right of the people of Ireland to the ownership of Ireland, and to the unfettered control of Irish destinies'. The long abuse of British rule was at an end, and centuries of Nationalist endeavour had reached their crisis. 'We hereby proclaim the Irish republic as a sovereign independent state, and we pledge our lives and the lives of our comrades-in-arms to the cause of its freedom, of its welfare, and of its exaltation among the nations.'

The nature of the republic envisaged was advanced and tolerant. 'The republic guarantees religious and civil liberty, equal rights and equal opportunities to all its citizens, and declares its resolve to pursue the happiness and prosperity of the whole nation and of all its parts, cherishing all the children of the nation equally, and oblivious of the differences carefully fostered by an alien government, which have divided a minority from the majority in the past.' In Pearse's dream, men and women, Catholic and Protestant, would live side by side in an independent nation state which drew its moral vision from its history. Meanwhile, until open elections had established a parliament, the provisional government would 'administer the civil and military affairs of the republic in trust for the people'. The proclamation then ended with a moving flourish: 'in this supreme hour the Irish nation must, by its valour and discipline, and by the readiness of its children to sacrifice themselves for the common good, prove itself worthy of the august destiny to which it is called'. The longed-for hour of blood sacrifice had arrived, and the proclamation itself was signed by men whose names would enter as surely into Irish history as those of the ancient Celtic heroes who inspired them: Thomas J. Clarke, Sean MacDiarmada, Thomas MacDonagh, P. H. Pearse, Eamonn Ceannt, James Connolly and Joseph Plunkett.

All these men knew that their position was hopeless. Up until a week before the Rising, Eoin MacNeill, the supposed head of the Irish Volunteers, had not even realised that insurrection was being planned and actually heard Pearse deny it. The reading out of a document allegedly stolen from Dublin Castle, but almost certainly forged by Joseph Plunkett and Sean MacDermot,

Annie Horniman circa 1912-13.

William Fay in a portrait by JBY.

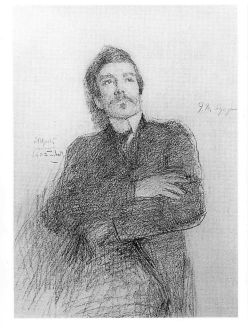

J. M. Synge in 1905 by JBY.

George Moore in 1905 by JBY.

Yeats portrayed with his psaltery by
Charles Shannon.

Exra Pound during his time at Stone
Cottage.

Thoor Ballylee as it currently appears
(photo by Pat Odea).

Iseult Gonne as a young woman.

Masked figure of the Old Man from
At The Hawk's Well.

A portrait of Yeats in 1904.

Yeats at Garsington accompanied (*from left to right*) by Lady Ottoline Morrell's
daughter, Siegfried Sassoon, Ethel Sandys, Eddie Sackville-West and Philip
Morrell.

JBY's pencil portrait of George Yeats drawn in New York during 1920.

Studio portraits of the Yeatses in 1920 by Underwood and Underwood of New York.

Yeats with his family: George, Anne and Michael.

(*Clockwise from top left*)

Yeats at Rapallo with the beard he grew while convalescing.

Yeats in 1932 by Pirie MacDonald.

(*Below and left*) Two portraits of Yeats in the 1930s by Howard Coster.

Maud Gonne in old age.

Lady Gregory in her last years.

Yeats and the Swami in Majorca, 1935-36.

Lady Dorothy Wellesley drawn by
William Rothenstein in 1936.

Yeats with Edith Shackleton Heald
and her sister at Steyning.

Yeats's grave at Drumcliffe, Co.
Sligo (*photo by Pat Odea*).

convinced him nonetheless that the British were determined to suppress the Volunteers and arrest their leaders. This was the one situation which would oblige MacNeill to rouse his forces to action, and he now ordered them to prepare for their own defence. Only on the night of Thursday, 20 April, did he learn of the plan for 'a general scheme for insurrection' and, shocked and appalled, he hurried to see Pearse and tell him he would do all in his power to prevent such a catastrophe, including the issuing of an order to his own men countermanding his instructions that they prepare to fight. However, when he was told that Sir Roger Casement was about to land a large shipment of arms from Germany, MacNeill changed his mind, bowed to what he thought was the inevitable, and said to Sean MacDermot: 'If that is the case I'm in with you.'

Such resolution was brief lived. Worried messengers arrived to tell MacNeill that the alleged Dublin Castle document was a forgery designed to provoke him into readying his men. He was also told that the expected German arms had been captured by the Royal Navy and sunk in Queenstown Harbour. Casement himself meanwhile had been thrown in prison and from there managed to get a message to Pearse informing him of his failure. A horrified MacNeill at once sent orders across Ireland forbidding his Volunteers to take part in any concerted activity whatsoever. When Pearse read the declaration of the new republic from the steps of the Dublin Post Office he was therefore aware that he had neither arms nor men to support him and that the martyrdom for which he longed was now at hand.

The teaching of Pearse's church on such matters was that violent rebellion could be permitted only when the government was a tyranny and rebellion was wanted by so overwhelming a majority that its success was assured. This was far from being the position in Ireland. While Pearse prepared for death, public opinion in Dublin turned strongly against him as the destruction and casualties wrought by British shells mounted and General Lowe and his army moved in. The brave golden words on the green flag turned black from the flames licking round the Post Office. Pearse and a wounded Connolly were obliged to leave the building, still firm in their belief that 'without the shedding of Blood there is no redemption'. On Saturday, 29 April, dressed in his Volunteer uniform, Pearse handed over his sword to General Lowe on the steps of the burned-out Post Office. His other followers surrendered, but the history of Ireland was, in Yeats's words, 'changed utterly'.[2]

Yeats himself was in Gloucestershire staying with the painter William Rothenstein when news of the Rising reached him. He was, Rothenstein recalled, 'much upset'.[3] In fact, Yeats was immobilised by his strong and contradictory feelings, and it would take many months of pained exploration of his emotions before he could finally express them in 'Easter 1916', one of the supreme political poems of the century. Meanwhile, in the days following his learning of the events in Dublin, Yeats could only say how 'these men, poets and schoolmasters . . . are idealists, unfit for practical affairs; they are seers, pointing to what should be, who have been goaded into action against their better judgement'. He felt the all but unbearable coincidence between his long-nurtured dream of heroically romantic Irish nationalism and what had actually occurred on the Dublin streets. 'Pearse and his friends were good men,' he said to Rothenstein, 'selfless but rash, throwing their lives away in a forlorn hope.'

But, if Yeats realised the pathos of their endeavour, other feelings nagged at his conscience, as Rothenstein was aware. 'He obviously felt some discomfort at being safe in England while his friends were risking their lives in Dublin,' he wrote, 'and fretted somewhat that he had not been consulted, had been left in ignorance of what was afoot.' But deeper and more problematic than this was Yeats's knowledge that, as the author of *Cathleen ni Houlihan*, as the architect of the Irish literary renaissance, he had done much to create the climate of feeling in which Pearse and his friends could make their tragic gesture. Yeats had unquestionable evidence of this. *Cathleen ni Houlihan* was actually due to be performed at the Abbey on Easter Monday, 1916, but the players, sensing that its prophecies were coming to pass in the streets around them, abandoned acting for action. Young Seamus Connolly, heading the small party of rebels besieging Dublin Castle, was killed on Easter Monday, 'the first man shot that day'.

As always in moments of great doubt, Yeats wrote to Lady Gregory, wondering if his letter would even reach her now that Arthur Griffith was acting as censor at the General Post Office. He was sure this 'tragic business' would change Ireland, but news was under government embargo and Yeats was left with his pained feelings alone. 'I had no idea that any public event could so deeply move me,' he told Lady Gregory, 'and I am very despondent about the future.'4 A little under a fortnight later he told Quinn he was 'planning a group of poems on the Dublin rising', but confessed he could not write them until he had returned to the city itself. News then came of the execution of the rebels, of the deaths by firing squad of Pearse and MacDonagh, of Joseph Plunkett, of Joseph Connolly so badly wounded that he had to be strapped into a chair as he faced the rifles, and of MacBride, gallantly refusing a blindfold with the assertion that he had stared down British guns before. The heroism of which Yeats had believed Dublin incapable was becoming ever more apparent, and he wrote to Lady Gregory telling her he was 'trying to write a poem on the men executed – "terrible beauty has been born again"'. The lines of his poem were beginning to form, but he still needed to see the place of the tragedy itself, and he crossed to Dublin and dined there with Lady Gregory. He left no record of his immediate feelings, however, and the poem he felt compelled to write still would not come.

Much rode on what he might say. To commit himself whole-heartedly to men who were traitors, however noble their treachery appeared, would be a powerful and dangerous gesture from the country's leading man of letters. As such he had recently declared that he had 'no gift to set a statesman right', and purely propagandist poetry was alien to him. But there was also and inevitably an element of prudence, of calculation even, in Yeats's delay. He knew that open commitment to an apparently futile cause would place his Civil List pension in jeopardy, lose him powerful English friends, perhaps threaten relationships with his new publishers Macmillans, and put at risk his hopes for settling the dispute over Sir Hugh Lane's pictures in Ireland's favour. Besides, England itself might yet 'keep faith', might yet grant Home Rule, and in this context it was far from clear what Pearse's heroic rashness had achieved in solid political terms.

And still there was the question of Yeats's moral responsibility for what had happened. He was forced to ask himself 'if I could have done anything to turn those young men in some other direction'. Again, 'had I helped to create a form of emotion that drove to their death the poet Pearse and the essayist MacDonagh?' If he had, his responsibility both to the past and to the future was considerable. Yeats had been forced into a moral position of the greatest subtlety, and, as Maud Gonne shrewdly declared, 'in 1916, before the magnificent flowering of the seed he had sown with pious exaltation, but left others to water, he stood amazed and abashed'.

As always, Yeats listened with the greatest acuteness to the voices about him. With the execution of the rebels public opinion was beginning to change. Two days before his own death Pearse had prophesied that he and his followers would be 'remembered by posterity and by unborn generations'. What he did not predict was how quickly the Rising would capture the popular imagination, inflamed as it was by the government's response; in Redmond's words, 'the executions, house-searching throughout the country, wholesale arrests . . . have exasperated feeling to a terrible extent'.[5] The relation of Ireland to England was developing into an ever more bitter and complex problem, and Asquith, needing to placate the Unionists, handed negotiations for Home Rule to Lloyd George. With consummate diplomacy, Lloyd George managed to persuade Carson into accepting that six counties of Ulster would be excluded from the immediate imposition of Home Rule (Carson was obliged to surrender Donegal, Cavan and Monaghan), while also persuading Redmond that this was a compromise agreeable to the Nationalists. The question of how long the compromise was to prevail was left vague, but increasingly vocal members of the Conservative Party obliged Asquith to declare the proposed settlement permanent. An embittered Redmond warned the House of Commons that by endorsing Asquith's declaration it had 'taken the surest means to accentuate every possible danger and difficulty in this Irish situation'.

It was the trial and subsequent death penalty imposed on Sir Roger Casement, however, that most patently fuelled the fire. Yeats himself was much concerned by this. He was as yet unaware of the disgraceful proceeding whereby Casement's journal accounts of his homosexual activities had been circulated to those in power to persuade them against clemency. Yeats himself believed so strongly that clemency was essential that he sent a letter to Asquith on the subject and told Eva Gore-Booth he felt 'the argument for clemency is so strong that the government cannot disregard this argument, and I believe also from all I have heard that Asquith is himself human'. He was to be disappointed. Casement was hanged and instantly joined the other Martyrs of 1916.

These men were now passing into popular legend to the detriment of Redmond and the Parliamentary Party, whose inability to deliver Home Rule for the whole of Ireland seemed, by comparison, to make them the shabby upholders of compromise. For all the sacrifices Ireland had made for the Great War, it had received only a slight diminution of the original proposals for Home Rule and these still amounted to a repudiation of the Nationalists' central idea of an undivided land. When, at the end of 1916, Lloyd George ousted Asquith as Prime Minister and appointed Carson to the cabinet, feelings became ever more virulent. But, in the absence of effective leaders to voice these, the Martyrs of the Easter Rebellion became increasingly charismatic figures:

> I write it out in a verse—
> MacDonagh and MacBride
> And Connolly and Pearse
> Now and in time to be,
> Wherever green is worn,
> Are changed, changed utterly:
> A terrible beauty is born.[6]

Yeats here probed to the accumulating psychological truth of the political situation and, in so doing, implied that his embittered analysis of the Dublin of Biddy and Paudeen had been insufficient. As he wrote in the 1916 edition of *Responsibilities*, in partial recantation of his earlier view: '"Romantic Ireland's dead and gone" sounds old-fashioned now. It seemed true in 1913, but I did not foresee 1916. The late Dublin Rebellion, whatever one can say of its wisdom, will long be remembered for its heroism. "They weighed so lightly what they gave," and gave too in some cases without hope of success.' The mixture of attempted impartiality and wonderment in this reflects the stance finally achieved in 'Easter 1916'.

In purely biographical terms, the opening section of the poem is the least authentic. Part of Yeats's purpose in the work was to juxtapose the once 'motley' Dublin of individual caprice with the new, 'green', awe-inspiring city of unified, impersonal sacrifice. His picture of the inconsequential banter, the 'polite meaningless words', exchanged on the streets before the Rising is disingenuous, however. Here was a world Yeats had excoriated for its spiritual vulgarity and whose tiny minority of extremists he knew rather better than he implies. But the newly found passion of the rebels invades the poem with thoughts of the Rebellion itself, deliberately troubling it as, in Yeats's image, the stone in the stream troubles the evanescent and inconsequential natural life flowing about it. Fanaticism has its Medusa-like power to turn the heart to stone, and it is possible that Yeats was influenced here by Shelley's poem on a renaissance painting once attributed to Leonardo da Vinci in which he records his perplexed response to a work whose combined horror and beauty make it 'divine'.

Yeats, however, explores his own complexities of response to the leaders of the Uprising. Like a mother crooning the name of her sleeping child he chants the litany of the rebels' names, but his affection is not for an oblivious infant but for dead men. The contrast is so shocking that he is obliged to turn from wonder to hard political realities. Were the deaths of the rebels 'needless'? There was still the remote possibility that England might 'keep faith' and, in maintaining honour, show the Martyrs to be dreamers and madmen. Such a questioning approach, the refusal of easy conclusions, evokes a mature and flexible mind pondering what it knows to be an as yet unresolved political crisis. 'We sing', as Yeats wrote, 'amid our uncertainty'.

Such uncertainty, however, was not prevarication. It stemmed from Yeats's deeply held convictions about how the true Nationalist poet must avoid rhetoric and propaganda. This was now more than ever important. Yeats had recently written to Lady Gregory to tell her how worried he was that the Rebellion and the events after it would ruin much of what he had worked for, 'all the freeing of Irish literature and criticism from politics'. Now it seemed that crude propaganda would return. However, just as he had fought to save drama from political dogmatism, so, in writing out the names of the Martyrs, Yeats suggests and even creates that almost magical process of thought whereby repetition and incantation acquire something of a talismanic force, that occult power of poetry to enter into events by reflecting on the 'terrible beauty' of what occurred during the five days of Easter 1916. Far from taking a propagandist or rhetorical stand, Yeats the Nationalist poet seems to reflect, to re-enact, the collective mind of the nation moving towards a new awareness.

II
Maud and Iseult

The poem, which was first circulated in a limited-edition pamphlet, was probably completed in France while Yeats was spending the summer with Maud Gonne MacBride. When he eventually sent her a finished copy she was outspokenly critical of what she saw as its lack of wholesale Nationalist commitment.

In May 1916 she had written to Yeats telling him that, at the beginning of the war, she had had 'a horrible vision' which haunted her for days. 'I saw Dublin in darkness and figures lying in the quays by O'Connell Bridge, they were either wounded or dying of hunger – It was so terribly clear it has haunted me ever since. There must have been scenes like that in the streets of Dublin during the last days.'[7] For Maud the Uprising touched the occult, and, as the roll-call of executions became known, so her letters to Yeats provided him with hints for his poem. Maud wrote of the rebels' 'tragic dignity'. She told him she did not 'think their heroique sacrifice had been in vain', and declared that the deaths of the leaders were 'full of beauty and romance'. She condemned Yeats's completed poem, however, saying 'it isn't worthy of you and above all it isn't worthy of the subject'. She believed it was quite wrong to think that sacrifice turned the heart to stone. 'It has immortalised many and through it alone mankind rises to God.' Believing that Yeats had described MacDonagh, Pearse and Connolly as 'sterile fixed minds', she wholly rejected the implication, declaring that 'those three were men of genius, with large, comprehensive and speculative and active brains'. She added that 'the others of whom we know less were probably less remarkable men, but still I think they must have been men with a stronger grasp on Reality, a stronger spiritual life than most of those we meet'.

Naturally, the execution of MacBride stirred Maud most deeply of all, and henceforth she would dress in widow's black. MacBride had left a name for Sean to be proud of, she declared, and Maud wrote to Yeats that 'those who die for Ireland are sacred'. MacBride's heroic gesture had redeemed him. 'Those who enter Eternity by the great door of Sacrifice atone for all.' It was impossible for her, feeling as she did, to approve of the subtlety and sophistication in Yeats's poem, and she wrote frankly to Quinn telling him she thought it 'not worthy of Willy's genius'. She saw his subtlety as prevarication. 'England and Ireland are too far apart for a writer to be able to keep one eye on one and the other on the other without a squint.'

For her own part she wanted desperately to return to Ireland. She hated being away from the country now that its political life had been so deeply stirred. Wartime France was, besides, a hard and dangerous country for her and her two children to live in, and the war was also causing her financial difficulties. Maud rightly believed she would have problems in obtaining a passport, knowing she would fall foul of England's Defence of the Realm Acts, and she wondered if employment as the Irish correspondent for an American newspaper would help with her application. She wrote to Quinn asking for his assistance. She also realised that, as a French citizen, the twenty-one-year-old Iseult was free to travel to London. Maud sent her there, hoping she would be able to persuade Yeats to assist in her purpose. Iseult duly made the dangerous crossing, after which, meeting with Yeats, she told him that Maud was upset, was sleeping badly and felt lonely.

Iseult's courage and beauty made an impression on all who met her. Lady Cunard declared she had never in her life seen 'such a complexion'. Pound thought her a figure from a troubadour romance. Yeats told Lady Gregory that she was 'beautifully dressed though very plainly', and went on to say that when he asked her why she was so pale she told him it was 'too much responsibility'. Stirred, fascinated and made tender by her vulnerability, Yeats confessed to Lady Gregory that Iseult 'makes me sad, for I think that if my life had been normal I might have had a daughter of her age. That means, I suppose, that I am beginning to get old.'[8] Yeats was fifty-one and childless, and Maud Gonne's beautiful daughter stirred complex and difficult feelings in him, for he wanted ever more desperately to marry and have a family of his own.

Lady Gregory as always was sympathetic to this, and while Yeats was at Stone Cottage she had brought a number of what she considered suitable young women to visit him. They were all well connected and well-to-do, but the only young woman in his London circle who interested Yeats was George Hyde-Lees. From the start the relationship between them was rooted in the occult. Like many of those gathered about Olivia Shakespear, George was a proficient reader of the tarot cards. Yeats had seen how useful she could be to him in his work on spiritualism, and it was probably in 1914 that he sponsored her joining the Stella Matutina section of the Golden Dawn under the name *Nemo*. George was also studying astrology, which, as she later told her mother, was 'a very flirtatious business'. For Yeats himself, however, it was an increasingly serious one, and an issue deeply involved in his search for a wife. His studies had suggested to him that late October 1917 was astrologically determined as a period crucial to his hopes. Uranus trining with Saturn and in conjunction with the Moon implied stability, while Saturn in conjunction with Mars in the House of Marriage was a clear indicator of the direction he should take. George, square-faced, handsome, 'awfully intelligent, and . . . alarmingly intuitive', appeared an obvious candidate.[9]

But the political events that had so transformed Ireland seemed to point in a different direction. The execution of MacBride left Maud free to remarry. As always, Yeats consulted Lady Gregory. Ever practical, she realised that the future of the Abbey Theatre and the resolution of the problem over Sir Hugh Lane's pictures now depended to some extent on wealthy Unionists. Knowing how long and complex the relationship between Yeats and Maud was, she urged him to marry her only if Maud 'renounced all politics, including amnesty for political prisoners'. It was bound by this impossible condition that Yeats crossed to Normandy in the summer of 1916. With the imagery of his great poem still working in his mind, he begged Maud 'to forget the stone and its inner fire for the flashing, changing joy of life'. Inevitably, she turned him down. The mystical marriage would not become an astrological union.

Yeats wrote to Sturge Moore from Les Mouettes, 'I am living in a house with three and thirty singing birds which for the most part have the doors of their cages open so that they alight on the table during meals and peck the fruit from the dishes'.[10] Maud's unconventional household maintained its old ways even in the middle of war. Iseult, however, was now of the age when Yeats had first met her mother. Talented, imaginative, but often moody and difficult, her presence prompted in Yeats deep and ambivalent hopes of obtaining the happiness her mother had denied him. Maud watched his growing infatuation with mild amusement, believing it to be something harmless that would rapidly fade. But mysticism and spiritual exploration formed an inevitable bond between the ageing man and the troubled young woman. They both showed a particular interest in contemporary French religious poetry. Maud wrote to Quinn, 'Willie and Iseult are both very interested in reading Péguy and Claudel, and Iseult is translating Péguy into English.' Iseult read aloud a Francis Jammes dialogue between a poet and a bird which made them all cry, and 'a whole volume of Péguy's "Mystère de la Charité de Jeanne d'Arc"'. Yeats began to wonder if such material was something he and Iseult could work on together in order to 'civilise Dublin Catholics'. This was a passing interest, but while it worked on him life at Les Mouettes stirred him in other ways.

He stayed on through the weeks of August and wrote transparently to Lady Gregory:

> I believe I was meant to be the father of an unruly family. I did not think that I liked little boys but I liked Shawn.* I am really managing Iseult very well. The other night she made a prolonged appeal for an extra cigarette. . . . I have stayed on much longer than I intended, but I think you will forgive me under the circumstances – as a father, but as father only, I have been a great success.

The normal round of a seaside holiday was taking on a more than usual ambivalence. Certainly, Yeats impressed Iseult with his strength and ease as a swimmer, who could 'swim for ages under water and reappear after a great distance', but his sexual feelings for her were not something he could easily confess except in his lyrics. He felt, or imagined he felt, Iseult's waking interest in him, and inevitably it stirred memories of how Maud had once slept with him, offering him the sexual comfort she now denied and which, through this painful summer, her daughter seemed to promise:

* Sean MacBride remembered that Yeats was 'very keen on flying kites, and we used to spend hours together on a long strand flying them. He was able to get kites to a marvellous height. He'd apparently always been keen on it, because I remember he told me that his father in Sligo made some kites which he flew.'

> My dear, my dear, I know
> More than another
> What makes your heart beat so;
> Not even your own mother
> Can know it as I know,
> Who broke my heart for her
> When the wild thought,
> That she denies
> And has forgot,
> Set all her blood astir
> And glittered in her eyes.[11]

But if Iseult, with the desperate illogic of the unconscious, seemed to promise a balm for the wounds her mother had opened and a possibility of the domestic happiness Maud had denied him, the position was, as Yeats knew, both troubling and ultimately pathetic. It showed that it was simply not true, in the title of his poem, that 'Men Improve with the Years'. The agile swimmer was not a lover in his youthful prime but a 'weather-worn marble triton'.

The image is an evocative one. Hints of the mysterious, the sinister and the submarine combine with thoughts of a strong and mature torso to suggest power and command. The idea of a triton also suggests the mythological and the untrue, the merely fantastical. A triton is, besides, and necessarily, a work of art – a marble statue by Bernini, for example. He is a man-made figment of the imagination. As such, a triton is something carved from stone, and the image Yeats had used in 'Easter 1916' of a stone troubling the flowing and natural waters of a stream recurs here to suggest once again the dehumanising effect of extreme emotion. The very force of Yeats's feelings emphasises the unnaturalness of fantasy based on deprivation. 'I am worn out with dreams.' And, inevitably, the images of the stone man turn his beloved into something less than human, an illustration from a book pleasing more to his aesthetic imagination than to his heart. In the end, the ageing stone man longs for the palpitating life that reality denies him:

> O would that we had met
> When I had my burning youth!
> But I grow old among dreams,
> A weather-worn, marble triton
> Among the streams.[12]

In September 1916 Yeats could only follow Maud and her family back to Paris, where he left them, returning to England with the promise that he would do all he could to expedite the issuing of a passport from the War Office. Memories of Iseult continued to torment him, however, while memories of her mother's erstwhile beauty reminded him of the unassuaged heartache of his youth. As Yeats persisted in his attempts to gain permission for Maud to visit Ireland (and was eventually rewarded with the cruel promise that she would be allowed to return provided she took no part in politics), so only the occult seemed to offer that hope of union in an afterlife expressed in 'Broken Dreams'.

While Maud felt herself obliged to linger in France, Yeats was free to return to Ireland. Now, as so often, he sought consolation at Coole, where he and Lady Gregory continued with their campaign to have the Hugh Lane pictures brought to Dublin. And it was at Coole too that Yeats wrote one of the most mysteriously beautiful of his lyrics, the poem that was to give its title to his 1919 volume, *The Wild Swans at Coole*:

> The trees are in their autumn beauty,
> The woodland paths are dry,
> Under the October twilight the water
> Mirrors a still sky;
> Upon the brimming water among the stones
> Are nine-and-fifty swans.[13]

The sky mirrored in the lake is a natural emblem of the Hermetic belief 'as above, so below'. Here is the true ordering of the physical and spiritual worlds, and the glorious swans seem equally at home in both, whether in mated happiness on the water or in exultant flight. Only man brings to this perfect scene his intimations of mortality. For nineteen autumns Yeats had enjoyed this marvellous sight, he declares, but the very act of numbering so many years leads him to disquietude and thoughts of death.

But if Coole could prompt such notions, it was above all a place of consolation, of rooted Irish dignity, of belonging and purpose. In the world so violently changing around him Yeats desired these things more than ever. He needed to attach himself to the soil, and the opportunity to do so arose when the Congested Districts Board began to split the Gregory estate into smaller holdings and the little castle at Ballylee, built by the de Burgo family probably in the fourteenth century, came on to the market. The Chief Land Inspector reported that the floors of the castle were as decayed as its roof and that the value of the near ruin as a house was 'sentimental and therefore problematical'. Robert Gregory nonetheless urged Yeats to buy it, and Yeats wrote to Olivia Shakespear telling her that there was a sound cottage at the foot of the castle where he could live while it was being restored. 'If I get it,' he told her, 'I shall plant fruit trees as soon as possible for the sake of the blossoms and because it will make me popular with the little boys who will eat my apples in the early mornings.' The sum of £35 secured Yeats the freehold with vacant possession from April 1917. He had at last found his own home in Ireland, and over the next months and years he worked at restoring the property.

III
Spectral Voices

Thoor Ballylee was a commitment to Ireland during a period when Yeats's feelings against England were hardening. In December 1916, Lloyd George ousted Asquith as Prime Minister and, as a gesture made to appease Irish feeling and persuade the Americans to help in the deteriorating position held by Britain in the Great War, he arranged for the release of 560 Irish prisoners held in England without trial. The return of these men was not treated with any degree of enthusiasm, but among them were two who were to have a profound influence over future events. One was Yeats's old adversary Arthur Griffith, the founder of the pre-war Sinn Fein movement; the other was Michael Collins, a man of whom virtually no one had heard but who had been present at the burning of the Dublin Post Office and had come to realise in his cell how the Rising had been 'bungled terribly' and had suffered from 'a great lack of very essential organisation and co-operation'.

Collins was soon to become a guerrilla leader of the greatest effectiveness, but Yeats himself preferred to believe at this time that the real organisers of public opinion in Ireland were the spectral voices of the executed rebels. Speaking from beyond the grave, their words had a force and clarity which subdued entirely all jabber about compromise and pragmatism. This was an argument he put forward with a vigorous, ballad-like energy in 'Sixteen Dead Men', a poem which he probably wrote at this time (although a dating of a year later is feasible) and whose imagery can certainly be seen in his next drama, *The Dreaming of the Bones*.

Yeats's second Noh-inspired play adopts the Japanese tradition of the ghostly encounter seen in Pound's translation of *Nishikigi*. The nighttime landscape around the Cistercian monastery of Corcomroe in County Clare, desolate even by day, is a haunted place of eerie spiritual power where the sensitive can indulge in what Yeats called 'dreaming back' or imaginative empathy with Ireland's savage history of passion, treachery and defeat. Yeats skilfully creates the 'sense of awe' which in 'Certain Noble Plays of Japan' he declared hovered around the sacred sites of Ireland. Now he brought that ghost-ridden history into confrontation with the violent present in order to underline the 700 years of material, spiritual and cultural devastation wrought by the English in his native land.

A Young Man who is imagined as having been with the Martyrs at the Dublin Post Office is shown fleeing from his pursuers and encountering the ghosts of Diarmuid and Dervorgilla, the adulterous and treacherous couple who were responsible for inviting Henry II to Ireland and so initiating the country's centuries-long history of servitude. It is for this crime against their nation that the pair are punished. They haunt the landscape as spectral lovers doomed to endure a passion that can never be consummated. 'Though eyes can meet, their lips can never meet.' Only an act of forgiveness from the living can redeem them from this purgatory, but as, at the climax of the play, the ghosts and the Young Man ascend a mountain to look down on the devastation wrought by the British, so the Young Man finds himself unable to forgive. His deeply felt speech skilfully combines Yeats's reverence for the Celtic past, his feeling for the high civilisation that could be nurtured in such regions, and his Morris-inspired sense of the beauty of a pre-industrial landscape:

> I can see
> The Aran Islands, Connemara Hills
> And Galway in the breaking light; there too
> The enemy has toppled roof and gable,
> And torn the panelling from ancient rooms;
> What generations of old men had known
> Like their own hands, and children wondered at,
> Has boiled a troopers porridge. That town had lain,
> But for the pair that you would have me pardon,
> Amid its gables and its battlements
> Like any old admired Italian town;
> For though we have neither coal, nor iron ore,
> To make us wealthy and corrupt the air,
> Our country, if that crime were uncommitted,
> Had been most beautiful.[14]

The Young Man cannot forgive such devastation and, indeed, the ghosts of Diarmuid and Dervorgilla will 'never' be forgiven. The genuine bitterness in the play points uncomfortably towards the harsh extremes – the stony-heartedness – that true Nationalist rebels must apparently adopt if their cause is to be successful. Yeats himself was coming to see the necessity for this attitude, along with the moral problems it caused, but as he wrote to Pound: 'England has no business whatever (as I think you put it) to obtrude his affairs on Ireland.' He knew how 'dangerous' such an attitude was if publicly held, however. In a carefully worded letter to Stephen Gwynn giving him permission to print the play in his magazine *Everyman* (an offer Gwynn did not see fit to take up) Yeats declared that 'it might be published with editorial note either repudiating its apparent point of view or stressing the point of view. England once, the point of view is, treated Ireland as Germany treated Belgium.'[15] The rebels of Easter 1916, in other words, were as morally justified in their actions as the Allies were in fighting the Great War against Germany. This was a courageous stance, and when Yeats read the play to a group of friends gathered in Gogarty's house they declared it 'marvellous'. The work was so politically challenging, however, and its Japanese inspiration so revolutionary that *The Dreaming of the Bones* was not performed in Dublin until 1931.

While the ghostly voices of Diarmuid and Dervorgilla are dramatically effective, attempts in real life to communicate with spirits remained inconclusive. Few were more curious than the visits Yeats made at the end of January and on 22 March 1917 to David Wilson's home at St Leonards-on-Sea to converse with his 'Metallic Homunculus'.[16] Among this machine's alleged range of psychic powers was the ability to talk in several languages, but when, late on his second visit, Yeats began to question the Homunculus, all he got were 'incoherent words from an alleged "Leo" who presently said he did not know who he was and that he might be "Yeats". When I said I was "Yeats" he said "no Yeats has gone."' This was hardly encouraging, and although the Homunculus subsequently obeyed commands, it refused to talk any more and Yeats lost interest, concluding that 'the phenomena came from Wilson's own organism'.

Literary occultism as always proved more fruitful, and during this period Yeats composed one of his most obscure and profoundly beautiful meditations on the spiritual life, the work eventually published as *Per Amica Silentia Lunae*.[17] This attempts to expand on the ideas behind 'Ego Dominus Tuus' (the poem is printed as the introduction) but the work is also suffused with Yeats's feelings for Iseult, to whom it is addressed. What he was offering here were his most profound meditations on a lifetime of spiritual experiment. Yeats was literally baring his soul. This was not something that could be done in the daily social world, and the opening paragraphs suggest the contrast between Yeats's public and private lives. He juxtaposes his guilty afterthoughts about how he, always at heart a shy man, succeeded in dominating at a dinner party, to the altogether more powerful world revealed by his solitary meditations. The essential antithesis between the natural man and his visionary opposite is thereby convincingly established.

Yeats then went on to cite Lady Gregory, 'a famous actress' and Synge as three other contemporary artists who had created work out of a state of being wholly opposite to their normal selves. History is then surveyed for other examples. The 'calm nobility' of Landor's *Imaginary Conversations* is contrasted to their author's normally aggressive personality. The image used in 'Ego Dominus Tuus' of an impoverished Keats staring at imagined riches is here developed in prose. Yeats then turned to William Morris, who, 'a happy, busy, most irascible man, described dim colour and pensive emotion, following, beyond any man of his time, an indolent Muse'. Finally, Yeats cites Dante, contrasting him to the dreaming Keats as a tragic poet who fought against both his 'unjust' loathing of his native Florence and the lust that seemed the antithesis of his adoration of Beatrice. The force of this 'double war', it is alleged, created the serenity of the *Paradiso*. Dante was inspired to imagine beatitude because, his passions being his reality, he knew the power of the antithetical self. Yeats as always insists that it is only the passionate who can experience this duality, who can wear the mask and be visited by their Daimon, that 'dazzling, unforeseen, wing-footed wanderer' from the divine world of the *anima mundi*.

Yeats outlines three types of passionate people who are drawn to their mask: the saint, the hero and the artist. The first two 'would always, if they could, resemble the antithetical self'. The artist, however, experiences its power only in moments of inspiration, and 'when it is all over Dante can return to his chambering and Shakespeare to his "pottle-pot"'. In such ordinary moments, these men have no specially active virtue, for authentic morality, like inspiration, comes from the anti-self. Nor can they be divinely inspired at such times for the Daimon can come to a man only when he wears his mask. Passionate desire is one prerequisite for this encounter of opposites, for Yeats writes that 'the Daimon comes not as like to like but seeking its own opposite, for man and Daimon feed the hunger in one another's hearts'. To passionate desire, however, must be added that radical emotional clarity a man can know only when he dons his mask. 'Because the ghost is simple, the man heterogeneous and confused, they are but knit together when the man has found a mask whose lineaments permit the expression of all the man most lacks.' Once known, however, the Daimon becomes a man's destiny, luring him like a beloved woman (and there is surely a passing reference to Iseult here) by his raising that insatiable desire which eventually becomes vision. Such vision, such inspiration, comes 'to our weariness like terrible lightning'. It is evanescent, easily polluted, but ultimately divine.

The second part of *Per Amica Silentia Lunae* begins by describing those spiritual disciplines by which the individual may be readied for such moments of vision. Yeats first evokes, in a sentence of seventeenth-century complexity and grace, the worldwide nature of his beliefs to suggest that they are definingly human. He then cites Goethe on the way in which images may come to the poet by free association. Confessing that he himself has 'no natural gift for this clear quiet', Yeats goes on to describe those talismans he would place on his pillow before going to sleep. Decades earlier, of course, he had placed apple blossom beside him to conjure Maud into his dreams, and 'even to-day, after twenty years, the exultations and the messages that come to me from bits of hawthorn or some other plant seem, of all moments of my life, the happiest and the wisest'.

The fact that occult images could be held in common by different minds in different places and at different times led Yeats, as he had shown in his essay on 'Magic', to 'believe in a Great Memory passing on from generation to generation'. That such images also apparently 'showed intention and choice' and that an overall view of their import could be pieced together only by assembling fragments exchanged by the minds that saw them began to suggest other ideas. 'The thought came again and again before us that this study had created a contact or mingling with minds who had followed a like study in some other age, and that these minds still saw and thought and chose.' Although this 'sense of contact' only came to him two or three times, Yeats now claims it was central to his move from ritual magic to spiritualism. He tells how, in defiance of his masters, he began attending seances and interesting himself in automatic handwriting. He claims that by so doing he acquired a knowledge of the structure of the soul and its after-death experiences.

As far as the structure of the soul was concerned, Yeats now believed that 'all souls have a vehicle or body' called 'the animal spirits'. This vehicle, he thought, could leave body in life as well as at death, and could mould itself 'to any shape it will by an act of imagination'. This shape could then be shown to the mind or even, 'by building into its substance certain particles drawn from the body of a medium', actually appear to the physical eye. Nor was it the possessor of such a soul alone who could mould it. The souls of both the living and the dead could exploit its plastic power. The fact that the images thus created were 'perfect' and artistically satisfying had, Yeats believed, only one explanation. 'Our animal spirits or vehicles are but, as it were, a condensation of the vehicle of *Anima Mundi*, and give substance to its images in the faint materialisation of our common thought, or more grossly when a ghost is our visitor.' Our souls, in other words, are the medium through which the divine mind is experienced, and the thoughts the divine mind creates grow through a process of association.

Yeats's account of the states of the soul after death draw on Henry More and Swedenborg as he describes that process of purification which culminates in the moment when 'the soul puts on the rhythmic or spiritual or luminous body and contemplates all the events of its memory and every possible impulse in an eternal possession of itself in one single moment'. This is the moment of supreme knowledge, 'and from thence come all the passions' and instincts as the purified spirits communicate with mankind and are 'stung to a keener delight from a concord between their luminous pure vehicle and our strong senses'. It is through such 'meditorial shades' that the Daimon also works on the antithetical man and leads him to desire 'whatever among works not impossible is the most difficult'. Mankind thus receives its most profound impulses from the dead, and it is towards the 'condition of Fire' and spiritual serenity that all would rise if they could. In a beautiful passage at the close of the work (many years later versified as one of the lyrics in 'Vacillation') Yeats gave an account of such ecstasy:

Perhaps I am sitting in some crowded restaurant, the open book beside me, or closed, my excitement having over-brimmed the page. I look at the strangers near as if I had known them all my life, and it seems strange that I cannot speak to them: everything fills me with affection, I no longer have any fears or any needs; I do not even remember that this happy mood must come to an end. It seems as if the vehicle had suddenly grown pure and far extended and so luminous that the images from *Anima Mundi*, embodied there and drunk with that sweetness, would, like a country drunkard who has thrown a whisp into his own thatch, burn up time.[18]

Yeats completed *Per Amica Silentia Lunae* in May 1917. The following month he took possession of Thoor Ballylee. The cottage by the side of the tower could be readied for living at a cost of £200, while the medieval tower itself with its 'couple of great rooms' could be restored later. Raftery, the local builder, was invited to submit an estimate and Yeats planned to pay for the refurbishing of his house by giving a series of lectures in America. He wrote to his father extolling the beauty of the place, telling him that there were trout in the river under the window and that Thoor Ballylee would be an economy since he would now need fewer rooms in London. JBY wrote a reply which exactly suggested all that Yeats hoped to achieve by moving to his medieval tower. 'It is all a symbol of the poetical life, a thirst for the soil, and you have it to the centre of the earth. It is in Ireland, another thirst instinctive, and therefore of the poet. And it is old, therefore again a poet's desire.'

Yeats had given physical form to his romantic nationalism and now, as he came into possession of his new home, he wrote a poem describing the Nationalist energies flowing ever more energetically through the country.* 'The Rose Tree' is the most vehement and daring of his poetic meditations on the Easter Rising. Pearse is imagined speaking in his own voice and proclaiming that his doctrine of sacrifice is the one means by which Irish nationalism can be made to flourish. Ghostly voices again inspire, as Pearse declares:

> 'O plain as plain can be
> There's nothing but our own red blood
> Can make a right Rose Tree.'[19]

Nationalist feelings were indeed blossoming with renewed vigour. In February 1917 Count Plunkett (one of whose sons had been killed in the Rising) stood as a parliamentary candidate in opposition to a supporter of John Redmond's and won by a landslide. A little while afterwards, on the first anniversary of the Uprising, a Republican tricolour flew at half-mast over the Dublin Post Office and posters were put up across the city proclaiming

---

* Of the Yeats children, only Jack had throughout committed himself to wholesale Irish independence, having attended Sinn Fein meetings since his return to Ireland in 1910. He disliked the idea of attaining it through violent means, but throughout the period from mid-1915 to early 1917 he was suffering from what appears to have been a depressive breakdown.

that 'The Irish Republic still lives'.[20] Michael Collins noted that the country was now 'ripe for any advancement along the road to salvation', and ten days after Easter Count Plunkett convened an 'Irish Assembly' at which it was affirmed that Ireland was a separate nation, rightly to be set free from foreign domination and to exist in future under its own parliament. Popular opinion had now advanced far beyond traditional calls for Home Rule under the influence of 'what is now know as the Sinn Fein party'.

Precisely how far public opinion had indeed changed was shown when a bye-election was called at Longford. Plunkett's Assembly nominated as their candidate Joe MacGuinness, an IRB man currently serving a term of penal servitude in Lewes prison. MacGuinness himself had no wish to stand since, like the majority of his fellow prisoners, he despised parliamentary methods. But his reluctance was ignored and Michael Collins organised a highly efficient election campaign on his behalf. Remarkably, the Archbishop of Dublin wrote a letter to the newspapers throwing his weight behind MacGuinness's candidacy, and when the prisoner himself won a narrow victory over the Redmond supporter there were exuberant celebrations across the entire country.

Redmond himself and Lloyd George hoped that a convention would reach 'substantial agreement' on the issue of the partition of Ireland, but it soon became clear that their positions were irreconcilable and, when a bye-election was called in East Clare, the new strength of feeling in Ireland was made abundantly clear. The Sinn Fein candidate was the tall, austere young Eamon de Valera, the man who had held Boland's Flour Mills during the Uprising, and whose death sentence had been commuted to twenty years' imprisonment. The day after his candidacy was announced, de Valera was released from prison along with 117 others in a gesture made by Lloyd George in the hope of creating a favourable climate for his convention. Conventions and compromise, however, no longer matched the broad sweep of public opinion in Ireland. De Valera himself campaigned on a platform of the complete independence and liberty of the country, and attracted to his side the immensely influential forces of the church and the now highly efficient Irish Volunteer Organisation. He won a landslide victory and appeared afterwards in Volunteer uniform to tell the excited crowd of his supporters: 'you are worthy descendants of the Claremen who fought under Brian Boru, with the same spirit in your hearts today that your fathers had a thousand years ago!' Myth and politics had coincided once again.

IV
Marriage

It was against this background that in August 1917 Yeats crossed to Normandy to stay with Maud Gonne MacBride and her family. The direction of his thoughts at this time is suggested not only by his dedicating *Per Amica Silentia Lunae* to Iseult but his wondering if he could get a photograph made of Robert Gregory's drawing of Thoor Ballylee and so interest her in his new home. In July 1917 he had written a somewhat disingenuous letter to Lady Gregory in which he said that he was not attracted sexually to Iseult but rejoiced in her youth. He claimed that if his feelings towards her did indeed become sexual he would at once leave Les Mouettes, for he thought that the difference of age between them stood in the way of Iseult's happiness. By the time he arrived in Normandy, however, Yeats had resolved to ask Iseult to marry him. Lady Gregory, believing that Iseult would tie his heart to Ireland, backed his suit and Maud herself raised no objection. Iseult, however, was diffident, and Yeats was obliged to write to Lady Gregory that they were 'on our old intimate terms' but that marriage seemed an unlikely prospect. 'I don't think she will accept. She "has not the impulse".'21

Iseult kept her ageing suitor in limbo and remained undecided when the party returned to Paris in September. Here Yeats delivered an ultimatum. If Iseult would not accept him he would have to marry George Hyde-Lees. The brusque selfishness of this is evident, but less obvious are the pressures working on Yeats as the astrologically determined date for his marriage neared and he found himself no closer to being an engaged man. Maud meanwhile, 'in a joyous and self-forgetting condition of political hate the like of which I have not yet encountered', was resolved to take her family to Ireland, and, as they prepared to board ship at Le Havre, Iseult broke down in tears. She was, as Yeats explained to Lady Gregory, ashamed '"at being so selfish" in not wanting me to marry and so break her friendship with me"'. As the wretchedly unhappy girl crossed the Channel, so Yeats promised her his friendship. Desperate to attain a final answer from her however, he added one last chance for marriage. He told her he must receive a definite reply within a week and that they would meet in an ABC teashop in London to resolve matters once and for all.

At Southampton, the already harassed travellers met further difficulties. Maud and Iseult were served with a notice under the Defence of the Realm Acts forbidding them to proceed to Ireland. The train was held up and the two women were searched as possible spies. Maud was enraged by this and Yeats feared she would 'do something wild'. Finally calming down, Maud resolved she would take a flat in Chelsea and study design for six months at a London art school. Iseult soon made clear that she could not marry Yeats and he, feeling responsible for her as always, eventually found a post for her as an assistant librarian at the School of Oriental Languages. Ezra Pound was then volunteered to be young Sean's tutor and, with the family thus settled, Yeats burst into tears of relief.

The question of marriage nonetheless weighed ever more heavily on him and, determined to resolve the situation one way or another, he had already written to George Hyde-Lees's mother Mrs Tucker from France and was now invited to visit. On 19 September Yeats wrote to Lady Gregory declaring his intention to marry the girl. Their mutual interest in the occult had brought them close, but JBY put his finger on the more self-serving elements in Yeats's plans when he wrote that George's father 'was educated at Eton and Oxford, and that her family own Gainsboroughs and Romneys; which all means money'. In fact, Yeats's Civil List pension along with earnings from his writings meant that his income between 1913 and 1917 only once fell below £500, but it was not the question of money that worried George's mother. She disapproved of what she knew of Yeats's previous amatory entanglements and felt that her innocent daughter had been manipulated into a highly undesirable position. On 30 September 1917 she wrote a frank letter to Lady Gregory in a vain attempt to put an end to the relationship:

> a mutual friend interested him in my daughter, the idea occurred to him that as he wanted to marry, she might do. Fortunately she has no idea of all this unpleasant background, she thinks he has wanted her since the time of the astrological experiments, and when he proposed to come and see us here, I told her he was now free. But it has dawned upon her that there is something amiss, after a long talk with Mr Yeats yesterday. . . . She is under the glamour of a great man 30 years older than herself and with a talent for love-making. But she has a strong and vivid character and I can honestly assure you that nothing could be worse for her than to be married in this manner, so there will be no harm done and a rather unpleasant episode can be closed. She has told no one of the affair, and only a few intimate friends of Mr Yeats (who we do not know) are aware of the matter. Mr Yeats has the kindest heart and I feel that only you can convince him of the entire undesirability of this engagement. George is only 24 and is to begin work at the F.O. in October of a very interesting nature. I am not trying to keep her from marrying, but the present idea seems to me impracticable.[22]

The concerned mother then added a telling postscript. 'If George had an inkling of the real state of affairs she would never consent to see him again, if she realised it after her marriage she would leave him at once.'

The ever resourceful Lady Gregory wrote a now lost reply which apparently allayed these fears, for George's mother wrote again to her saying, 'as long as George has no idea of what I told you I think all will be well now. I am much reassured of your opinion of Mr Yeats's feelings.' Yeats himself had by this time arrived at Coole, where he wrote to tell George that Lady Gregory had advised him that they should get married as soon as possible since this was the best thing that could possibly happen. It is clear, however, that if

Lady Gregory had matters firmly in hand she was determined to be neither sentimental nor indulgent to any of the parties. Certainly, she spoke bluntly to Yeats, disparaging him for the fact that he was now going to be married in the clothes he had bought to woo Iseult in.

Yeats told Lady Gregory that, though his decision might seem coldly calculating, he had reached it only after prayer and many sleepless nights in which he felt his mind was becoming 'unhinged'. He assured her that Iseult seemed content with the arrangement and that he would let nothing break their friendship, but in fact both Iseult and Maud were upset by what now clearly emerged as the manipulative way in which they had been treated, and they were distinctly scornful about what they considered Yeats's prosaic marriage plans. As late as 13 October Yeats himself was still expressing his doubts over his forthcoming marriage, but the date for the wedding had by then been fixed. On 20 October 1917, as the revolving planets moved into a position promising stability, inspiration, children, philosophic friendship and public acclaim for creative endeavour, Yeats and George Hyde-Lees were united in a civil ceremony at the Harrow Road Register Office. Ezra Pound was best man. As the couple left for their honeymoon in the Ashdown Forest Hotel, however, the newly married Yeats was plunged into a state of utter wretchedness, for it suddenly seemed to him that his marriage to George was a terrible mistake.

PART FIVE

Things Fall Apart

❖

Things fall apart; the centre cannot hold;
Mere anarchy is loosed upon the world,
The blood-dimmed tide is loosed, and everywhere
The ceremony of innocence is drowned. . . .

13

The Phases of the Moon
(1917–1919)

I
The Eagle and the Butterfly

In the anguished earliest days of his marriage Yeats believed he had
betrayed three women: George, Maud and Iseult. The physical presence
of his new wife worsened the pain, for Yeats's tormented feelings hovered
with guilty insistence around memories of Iseult particularly. He hoped and
believed that George knew nothing of his turmoil, but on 24 October
(perhaps after receiving a now lost letter from Iseult) his emotions spilled
over into a poem first called 'The Lover Speaks':

> A strange thing surely that my Heart, when love had come unsought
> Upon the Norman upland or in that poplar shade,
> Should find no burden but itself and yet should be worn out.
> It could not bear that burden and therefore it went mad.[1]

The poem concludes with bitter self-reproach, for Yeats was obliged to face
what he thought of as his emotional cowardice: 'I ran, I ran from my love's
side because my Heart went mad.'

The desolation in this is so clear that Yeats's 'blue' mood and its origins
were at once evident to George, who, in her distress, wondered if she should
leave her new husband. Here, in the first days of marriage, was a trial of her
strength and subtlety, and it was characteristic that she should marshal both
to discover that innocently manipulative and self-effacing tact – the devotion
– which played so large a part in her fostering of her husband's genius. The
occult and the practice of automatic writing especially had once brought
them close, and George now wondered if she should fake a sentence or
two to calm her husband's distress. She went to Yeats, and using what had
perhaps already become the private language of their relationship, wrote
out a sentence she later remembered as saying something like: 'what you
have done is right for both the cat and the hare'. Yeats, she believed, would

395

interpret the hare as referring to the fleet-footed Iseult and the domestic cat as herself.

But if George had hoped to lift her husband's gloom by a graceful deception she was only partly successful. So deep a wound was not to be instantly healed, and the process of repair would take a painful course. A second poem, written on 27 October, suggests Yeats's bruised advance from self-recrimination to a more objective but still tortured view of his situation. At first he had blamed himself for running away from Iseult; now he had to confess to the deceits he would have had to force on her in order to persuade her to marry him. In the last stanza of his new poem, reckless pain gives rise to a measure of self-knowledge and a despairing acceptance of the truth:

'Speak all your mind,' my Heart sang out, 'speak all your mind;
  who cares,
Now that your tongue cannot persuade the child till she mistake
Her childish gratitude for love and match your fifty years?
O let her choose a young man now and all for his wild sake.'[2]

At this point George clearly thought she should intervene again. In Yeats's account: 'she said she felt something was to be written through her. She got a piece of paper, and talking to me all the while so her thoughts would not affect what she wrote, wrote these words (which she did not understand) "with the bird" (Iseult) "all is well at heart. Your action was right for both but in London you mistook its meaning."' Perhaps it was now that George really did feel her hand grasped and driven by a force outside her control, for Yeats told Lady Gregory that immediately after George had finished writing, 'I asked mentally "when shall I have peace of mind" and her hand wrote "you will neither regret nor repine" and I think certainly I never shall again.'[3]

Something 'very like a miraculous intervention' had occurred to dispel Yeats's gloom, and its effects were immediate. As he told Lady Gregory: 'the strange thing was that within half an hour after writing this message my rheumatic pains and my neuralgia and my fatigue had gone and I was very happy. From being more miserable than ever I remember being since Maud Gonne's marriage I became extremely happy. That sense of happiness has lasted ever since.' The two poems he had written now belonged to the past and, as if to emphasise this, Yeats sent transcripts to Lady Gregory, telling her that he wanted her to put them safely away 'for they can hardly be published for yet, if ever'. They had served their purpose, and a rejuvenated Yeats prepared for that exhilarating transformation of his life that would occur now that he had apparently realised one of his most persistent ambitions – occult marriage to a seer.

On 5 November, having made a brief visit to London to see the dentist and, at George's suggestion, to place the troubled Iseult in the care of George's mother, the Yeatses returned to the Ashdown Forest Hotel, where they resumed their communication with the spirits. Four pages of script were produced on this occasion and they were to have such a profound importance for Yeats that they were preserved by him and dated. They were the first papers in a massive spiritualist enterprise which was to extend over seven years and which, losses notwithstanding, amounts to a record of 450 sessions, 8672 questions and 3627 pages of automatic script. This archive was then augmented, after March 1920, with 270 pages recording communications transmitted by George during 164 of her 'sleeps'. From this prodigious quantity of material, and with the help of an immense card-index system, Yeats was to create that work of psychic, historical and philosophic synthesis first published in 1926 as *A Vision* and which underpins the greater part of his mature thinking.

The Yeatses' occult progress towards their vision was far from straightforward, and from the start it was to embrace not simply Yeats's exploration of his personal conflicts but his work and his day-to-day plans, matters often deflected by psychic 'frustrators' and the sheer intractability of the messages received. Important revelations came from the start nonetheless. When Yeats and George resumed their communications on 5 November, the control at once made clear that a negative period of sterility was over. 'End of enmity in your evil influences thats why.' The control repeated his message and began to hint that emotional well-being was astrologically related to the balance a man achieved between the influence over him of the sun and the moon. Puzzled and intrigued by this, Yeats tried to find out something of the nature of the control himself and learned that his name was Thomas of Dorlowicz, that he communicated with George 'by chance', and that he was 'here for a purpose and must go when that is done'.

That evening the Yeatses sat down to resume their task, but the relative clarity of the earlier session was clouded. Thomas began to complain about 'Frustrators' who tried 'to control me and influence my communications'. Chief among the culprits, perhaps unsurprisingly given that the Yeatses were now making a fresh occult start, was one Leo, who was 'not to be trusted'. Then, with earlier rivals seemingly out of the way, George delivered a message from Thomas which seemed wholly unrelated to anything that had gone before: 'one white one black both winged both necessary to you'. The horses drawing Plato's Chariot of the Soul were apparently racing across the astral plane and were showing Yeats, as he came to believe, the state of his inner man, his conscious and unconscious mind.

Because that mind 'cannot see its own state objectively', the control could not use anything produced by it – could not use Yeats's own thoughts – and instead had to latch on to ideas given to him by somebody else. In this case, Thomas had picked up on that confusing but fascinating coincidence of Horton's and Lady Lyttelton's use of an image from the *Phaedrus* and was, Yeats eventually believed, trying to show him 'a bundle of images' symbolic of his state of mind. He was being told, in other words, that he needed to achieve a position of balance, of psychic or psychological integration, between the warring parts of his divided self. He had to achieve an equal mastery over the black horse and the white, reconcile the influence of the sun and the moon, harmonise his self and anti-self, and bring into amity the subjective and the objective man. In a phrase that is fundamental to *A Vision*: 'the dark unruly horse of the moon is equated symbolically to the inner, subjective, and "antithetical self"; the white horse of the sun to the outer, objective, and daily or "primary self"'.[4] Soon Yeats was being told that he was too much under the influence of the moon, that the sun 'is too little emphasised'. As if to underline that what he was submitting to was a process of psychological self-discovery which had as its end the integration of his personality, Thomas now told him that the visionary truths he delivered 'were taken from the inner wisdom of your own consciousness by selection'.

Such ways of thinking are less obtuse than may at first appear, particularly given the wide interest in spiritualism at this time. Since the existence of 'spirits' themselves – the ontological reality of Thomas of Dorlowicz for example – can neither be proved nor satisfactorily refuted, a more productive procedure than enquiring into origins is to examine the use Yeats made of communicators whose reality he mostly believed in. These uses were firstly and most obviously therapeutic, as a later communication of Thomas's was to make clear:

Yeats. Is clearing the sub-conscious the principle element in your ethic.

Thomas. Yes because to clear the subconsciousness is the basis of the realisation of good and evil forgiveness and understanding and of all moral or ethical virtues

Yeats. Is clearing sub-conscious the getting rid of memory.

Thomas. Nothing can ever be forgotten in one incarnation It is the anodyne of memory

Yeats. What form of life most clears the sub-conscious.

Thomas. A life of intimacy with a few people or friends who trust and are trusted that is to say unless there are very considerable numbers of concealments in the subconscious[5]

This is kindly and wise, and shows perhaps something of George's knowledge of current psychoanalytic theory, but the Yeatses' experiments with the occult had other interesting parallels with the discoveries of psychology. This was true even of their methods. By the time Yeats and his wife began their automatic writing in earnest, both were widely familiar with its techniques as generally practised. For their own purposes, however, they made a number of significant modifications. Above all, they allowed no observers to be present. George was particularly insistent on this and consistently refused her husband's requests that others be allowed to watch or participate. George at least knew that what was happening between them was uniquely private. Nor were these occasions, as other seances claimed to be, wholly a matter of automatism. The communications of the spirits and, very soon, the questions that prompted them were scrupulously recorded by the Yeatses themselves along with date, time and place. Blacked-out rooms and much of the melodramatic paraphernalia of conventional seances were avoided (although the couple may have used a crystal ball from time to time) and, as the initially rebarbative records of their communications become slowly more familiar, so it it possible sometimes to observe the subtle and very human tact with which George moved in and out of mediumship, gently crossing the boundary between the inspired and the common-sensical. She was involved, as she was surely aware, in an exercise of the utmost delicacy and, in the course of time, as confidence was gained, as the communication became more familiar, so the wild scrawls of the early days in which she ran all her words together were replaced by a more orderly hand, a more systematic punctuation.

The occult quality of what was communicated was not lessened by this, and the greater regularity suggests that both Yeats and George were growing more comfortable with what analysts sometimes call the use of the 'active imagination'. That the Yeatses were so scrupulous about recording their encounters was important in this respect for it allowed their communications to become far more than an evanescent series of impressions. Shape, narrative and development became apparent and, for Yeats especially, there came also the growing awareness that this unfolding drama was something happening to him in the depths of his being. If he was helping to create a script, he was also one of the actors. Indeed, in time he would realise that he was playing the principal role. Thomas of Dorlowicz had told him early on that revelation came from the 'inner wisdom' of Yeats's own awareness, his unconscious mind, and confirmation altogether less occult for this idea is provided by those psychoanalysts who believe that what 'spirits' communicate are actually projections of their auditors' deep-seated unconscious energies. Analysts sometimes consider that these projections of the concerns of the living through what are taken to be the voices of the dead are in fact efforts made by the living to become fully conscious, to be more completely aware of the repressed and dispossessed parts of their psyche.[6]

In this respect, spiritualism was a natural development of Yeats's doctrine of the mask and, indeed, of his interest in occult research from the time of his involvement with Theosophy. As with those earlier endeavours, spiritualism was also and obviously a cry of revolt against an omnipresent scientific materialism. But what was protest was also self-discovery and, as Yeats realised while he moved towards creating *A Vision*, the translation of his unconscious concerns into a communicable language had a powerful redeeming effect, a sense of assurance gradually won and, with this, some measure of content. That this was already proving to be the case is borne out by his letters. The happiness that descended on him when George's automatic writing became emotionally significant deepened, and by 8 November, writing from Stone Cottage where they were now staying, he could tell a friend that 'my wife and I are fellow students in all my interests so I think we should prosper'.

The strain on George herself was nonetheless considerable. The sustained use of her powers was taxing in the extreme and gradually she would evolve techniques for achieving a respite both for herself and for her demanding and even greedy husband. She had at all costs to avoid the imaginative inertness of extreme fatigue, a sense of permanently threatened potency and failure. She had, as she surely realised, the vulnerable and hungry psyche of the leading poet of the day in her cure, and he was also her husband. That he had chosen her, a woman young enough to be his daughter, spoke to one sensitive enough to hear it not of lust but of deep-seated sexual insecurity and the fear manifest in many of his works. The flagellations, crucifixions and executions of the poetry and prose Yeats produced in the Nineties spoke of an inner terror and deprivation. If George was, at this time, a young woman who would never (or hardly ever) compete with his ego, he had allowed her nonetheless to become the chatelaine of all that was most vulnerable in his soul.

There would inevitably be moments, for all his declared happiness, when Yeats would project on to George his bitterness about the deprivation they were both trying to assuage. Equally difficult, but quite as essential to the unfolding of their task, was Yeats's need to talk openly about the other women on his mind. Pages of the script are given over to discussions of Maud and Iseult, and this was a process that was to bear fruit in Yeats's play *The Only Jealousy of Emer*, which was even now being constructed in the light of the answers he was receiving from George's controls.

But what is so profoundly remarkable about this hardest worked of all the muses is the generosity of George's attention – that and the intellectual stamina with which she faced an almost daily onslaught of questions from one of the most active minds of her time. No quarter was given by Yeats in his efforts to build the script into a philosophic system capable of encompassing his world view. And some of the questions he asked as he dived and wheeled from the intensely personal to the grandly metaphysical were extremely tough. What was the best way to construct a talisman so that George's intuitions would be deepened in her sleep? Why did the 'too great strength of Iseults antithetical self' cause her attacks of melancholy? 'In the dream life after death does not the primary self produce itself in many dreams?' Maud Gonne inevitably became a subject of enquiry too, and George and the control suggested that a man does not 'actually fall in love with a woman who *was* really his ideal'. After a while it becomes clear that the questions Yeats posed grew out of the previous answers received and that George and her controls were responsible for creating many of the technical terms which were to become increasingly important.

It was already evident, however, that some measure of order had to be imposed on this plethora of insight and, believing that they might have been specially selected to chart 'the way of the soul', Yeats and George began to think about preparing a typescript of their communications in which personal details would be edited out to give an appearance of universality. Thus the control's answer to the question why Iseult's antithetical self caused her such distress was reduced to the simple, gnomic statement 'the antithetical self is the source of creative power'. Yeats, it seemed, now had occult proof of some of his most treasured ideas and, keen to tell his friends about the 'very exciting mystical philosophy' he and his wife were discovering, they left Stone Cottage on 13 November to return to London.

The newly married poet was regarded with a deal of metropolitan irony, and Arthur Symons, active again after his mental collapse, may have expressed a not uncommon view when he wrote to Quinn: 'wish you had heard Maud laugh at Yeats's marriage – a good woman of 25 – rich of course – who has to look after him; she might either become his slave or run away from him after a certain length of time'. Others, while welcoming George into their circle, were dubious of her encouraging her husband's spiritualist experiments. These Yeats himself clearly discussed with relish, even if George always tried to insist that their methods and the part she played should be kept a secret. Indeed, his enthusiastic chattering may well have been annoying to her and in time she would nickname him 'William Tell'.

In the days before the Yeatses decided to preserve their scripts the controls had suggested to George that they appeared in order to give Yeats images for his poetry. Others were distinctly suspicious of this. W. T. Horton, for example, was still adamantly opposed to the whole business. 'I have given up all spiritualist things and all things automatic or unconscious,' he declared, 'for I have found them all unreliable, foolish or dangerous'. He believed nothing new could come from them and that they were, in fact, positively destructive. 'Automatism etc. leads to obsession, depletion, hallucination, utter lack of self-reliance and self-control, weakness and moral disintegration.' In an argument that Yeats was bound to reject, he urged that spiritualism 'robs the Creative Artist of all and makes him of non-avail and instead of increasing in wisdom like Goethe he becomes vague and incomprehensible like Blake in his prophetic books'.[7] The designer Edmund Dulac and his wife seem to have been more sympathetic, however, as were those members of the Society for Psychical Research with whom Yeats probably discussed these issues. Certainly, when he and George returned to Stone Cottage, their enthusiasm for their script was undiminished.

They now recorded their questions in one book and their answers in another. This second period of intense communication began on 20 November with a long series of questions about Iseult's problems which suggests the Yeatses' familiarity with the thought of Freud. On a different level, Yeats's Cuchulain plays and *The Only Jealousy of Emer* in particular were now revealed to him as being 'a symbolism of the growth of the soul'. In addition, the script was taking on a more philosophical, a more universal character, even if Yeats's questions often veiled personal concerns about Iseult, Maud and himself. George too remained a natural focus of attention, and during a lengthy session on the evening of 22 November Yeats asked: 'why were we two chosen for each other?' The answer was elliptical, beautiful, delicate. The image of Yeats as 'The Eagle' was a long-established one, but earlier that afternoon the control had shown him and George how a butterfly was a 'symbol of innocence of emotion' which helped clear the subconscious of destructive anger. George now became the Butterfly to Yeats's Eagle, and the idea so moved him, seemed such an apt expression of her youthful wisdom and 'the crooked road of intuition', that he was soon to write in a poem:

And wisdom is a butterfly
And not a gloomy bird of prey.[8]

Yeats came to number these lines among his personal favourites and from then on, whenever he signed for someone a copy of one of his books, he often inscribed it with a version of this beautiful tribute to the psychological and artistic content he was now for the first time beginning to learn.

II
The Great Wheel

The Butterfly brought her Eagle far more, however, than the consolations of trust and intimacy, although these were much for a man whose long loneliness had been full of deprivation and pain. In addition to personal comfort, the Butterfly gathered for Yeats those images which his intellect would, over the next seven years, fashion into a psychological and historical system of cosmic proportions. This process began almost as soon as Yeats and George left London for their second stay at Stone Cottage.

The late afternoon session of 24 November had not been particularly fruitful, although, perhaps under the influence of Blake, it had produced some remarkable apophthegms, including 'human wrath represents divine Beauty'. They had been trying to relate these and other abstractions to the cardinal points of the circle, but with little success. Near the close of the session Yeats asked a question about 'the 28 stages' but Thomas balked at providing an explanation there and then and promised he would 'give their meanings later'. He was as good as his word. When the Yeatses sat down to resume their work at 8.30 that evening, Thomas asked George to 'draw a circle for me into 28'. This she did, and then, in minutes that must have strained her faculties to the utmost, she began to write down those characteristics of the human personality she and Yeats would thenceforth relate to the twenty-eight days of the cycle of the moon as it is pictured circling round the Great Wheel.

Just as a man's perception of the waxing and the waning of the moon is determined by the sun, so, in the Yeatsian system, his perception of himself is determined by the proportion of lunar to solar influence in his make-up. As Yeats himself explained:

> the Sun is objective man and the Moon subjective man, or more properly the Sun is *primary* man and the Moon *antithetical* man. . . . Under the Sun's light we see things as they are and go about our day's work, while under that of the Moon we see things dimly, mysteriously, all is sleep and dream. All men are characterised upon a first analysis by the proportion in which these two characters or *Tinctures*, the objective or *primary*, the subjective or *antithetical*, are combined.[9]

Phase One of the cycle, being completely objective, is unpopulated since no human life can be fully objective, just as its complementary Phase Fifteen is also barren since no man can be wholly subjective. As Yeats explained in his poem 'The Phases of the Moon': 'there's no human life at the full or the dark'.

So far this is an essentially static description of the range of character types. What gives each phase its dynamic, its suffering and exultation, is the opposition and discord imagined existing between four fundamental Faculties. The first of these is what Yeats called the Will, which is a man's given personality. Opposed to this is the Mask, by which 'is understood the image of what we wish to become, or that to which we give our reverence'. The second pair of contrasted faculties consists of Creative Mind or the intellect as it was 'understood before the close of the seventeenth century – all the mind that is consciously constructive', and the Body of Fate which is 'the physical and mental environment, the changing human body, the stream of Phenomena as this affects a particular individual'. It is the interplay of these four Faculties which gives a man his individual character and destiny. 'The being becomes conscious of itself as a separate being, because of certain facts of *opposition* and *discord*, the emotional *opposition* of *Will* and *Mask*, the intellectual *opposition* of *Creative Mind* and *Body of Fate*, discords between *Will* and

Creative Mind, Creative Mind and Mask, Mask and *Body of Fate, Body of Fate* and *Will.*'[10]

As Yeats himself confessed, only long familiarity with the system could make it wholly intelligible, but since, exercising his creator's privilege, he placed himself with Dante and Shelley at Phase Seventeen of his system – one of the most favourable positions – an account of this phase may go some way to explaining the whole.[11] For a man at Phase Seventeen 'mental images . . . flow, change, flutter, cry out, or mix into something else . . . without frenzy'. His Will seeks such 'images rather than ideas', but because his Creative Mind is essentially antithetical it cannot synthesise them and the Man of Phase Seventeen consequently seeks to hide his confusion and disorder from himself and others by yearning for a Mask which provides 'simplification through intensity'. This Mask is derived from Phase Three of the cycle, which is described as being a state 'almost without intellect . . . a phase of perfect bodily sanity'. It is a place of rest, delight and simplification where a man 'seems to move among yellowing corn or under over-hanging grapes'. This was a psychological state where many of Yeats's heroes also found their solace. It:

> gave to Landor his shepherds and hamadryads, to Morris his 'Water of the Wondrous Isles', to Shelley his wandering lovers and sages, and to Theocritus all his flocks and pastures; and of what else did Bembo think when he cried, 'Would that I were a shepherd that I might look daily down upon Urbino.' Imagined in some *antithetical* mind, seasonal change and bodily sanity seem images of lasting passion and the body's beauty.

This pastoral idyll is nonetheless constantly under threat from the Body of Fate, the destructiveness of the real physical world. In a passage of thinly disguised autobiographical significance Yeats declared that the Creative Mind of a man at Phase Seventeen might well seek to personify in 'some woman perhaps' an image of the intensity and simplification which his Mask desires. The Body of Fate nonetheless 'snatches away the object' – Maud Gonne married John MacBride while her daughter refused to give herself to Yeats in marriage – with the result that the Creative Mind 'must substitute some new image of desire; and in the degree of its power and of its attainment of unity, relate that which is lost, that which has snatched it away, to the new image of desire'. In purely personal terms, what Yeats was here confessing to was his need to fashion George into the sort of woman who could, in his imagination at least, fill the void left by the loss of the women he had previously adored.

It is not only private life that is affected by this painful play of the four

Faculties, however. The public life of a man at Phase Seventeen also exists under the strain of contradiction.

> Because of the habit of synthesis, and of the growing complexity of the energy, which gives many interests, and the still faint perception of things in their weight and mass, men of this phase are almost always partisans, propagandists and gregarious; yet because of the *Mask* of simplification, which holds up before them the solitary life of hunters and of fishers and 'the groves pale passion loves,' they hate parties, crowds, propaganda.

Here, described in terms of his own system, is a picture of Yeats the lyric poet battling in public against the crude forces of mass opinion.

The particular glory of Phase Seventeen is that it is here that 'the *Daimonic* man' finds himself. Yeats described this character type in a particularly complex yet fascinating section of *A Vision*. While the Will and the Creative Mind are essential characteristics of the light, of objective man, his Body of Fate and his Mask belong to the dark and subjective world over which he has no rational control. His Daimon also haunts this nighttime landscape, and in this world of continuous conflict and antithesis a man's Daimon is seen as taking a female form. Yeats had hinted in *Per Amica Silentia Lunae* that the passionate affinity between a man and his Daimon was analogous to the erotic relationship between a man and a woman, and now, in a passage that clearly refers to his thinking about his marriage, Yeats expanded on this idea.

'Man and *Daimon* face each other in a perpetual conflict or embrace,' and this relation 'may create a passion like that of sexual love. The relation of man and woman, in so far as it is passionate, reproduces the relation of man and *Daimon*, and becomes an element where man and *Daimon* sport, pursue one another, and do one another good or evil.' A man 'in the right of his sex' is a particular combination of the four Faculties, while his woman 'in the right of her sex' is a wheel which reverses the masculine one. Yeats portrays this relationship as being something far more subtle than a clockwork interplay of cogs, however. He was trying to explain the extraordinary power George now had over his deepest feelings and perceptions, and he wrote that 'the *Daimon* carries on her conflict, or friendship with a man, not only through the events of life, but in the mind itself, for she is in possession of the entire dark of the mind. The things we dream, or that come suddenly into our heads, are therefore her *Creative Mind* . . . through which her energy, or bias, finds expression.'

Such indeed was the influence of George over Yeats's instincts at this time and he sought to account for how this passion brought regularity and balance to his existence. What he was trying to explain was how George gave him inspiration that drew deeply on his unconscious energies without adversely affecting his intellect. He wrote that when the antithetical man allowed his daimonic influence 'to flow through the events of his life . . . and so to animate his *Creative Mind,* without putting out its light, there is Unity of Being'. The presence of George, in other words, allowed Yeats to find his psychological integrity and wholeness. He was no longer a man in whom blocked and frustrated parts of the psyche brought disharmony and pain, but a man who could, instead, rejoice in the radiance of emotional health. This was a state he described thus: 'a man becomes passionate and this passion makes the *daimonic* thought luminous with its peculiar light – this is the object of the *daimon* – and she so creates a very personal form of heroism or of poetry'. Here is an admission that the extraordinarily potent blend of therapy, spiritualism and astrology which the Yeatses were indulging had indeed brought Yeats himself a significant degree of content which allowed him to write to Lady Gregory that he felt he now understood life for the first time.

Such work was extremely taxing and George at least was well aware of the importance of rest. It was probably on 8 December that they left Stone Cottage for London, where, under instructions from Thomas, they conducted no experiments pertaining to the system for nearly two weeks. There were, however, other occult matters to deal with. The question of Sir Hugh Lane's pictures was still unresolved and Yeats now attended one of the many seances at which he tried to raise Lane's spirit in the hope of locating a signed version of the codicil to his will which would prove that it really had been his intention to leave his collections to Dublin. Although the spirit who was summoned had 'the nervous excitability' that had characterised Lane during his lifetime, nothing of any substance was achieved and Yeats and George turned to more practical matters.

In particular, 18 Woburn Buildings had to be turned from a bachelor residence into somewhere suitable for a newly married couple. George bought some furniture, changed the crockery and, with the help of a maid, gave the rooms the thorough cleaning that many of Yeats's female friends at least realised they needed. But the problem of Iseult still remained to be faced. In the safe remoteness of Stone Cottage, George had had to deal with the young woman as an important aspect of her husband's unhappiness. Now she had to face her in her own right. Once again she revealed her generosity and tact. There was no question in her mind of forcibly ousting a rival, and she took the altogether shrewder course of making Iseult her ally. 'They made friends for my sake,' Yeats declared, 'but now it is for each other's.' They spent mornings 'talking dress' and, as intelligent women, discussing weightier matters too. Both, 'according to the new fashion for young girls,' were interested in serious study. Each, for example, was learning Sanskrit, and Yeats looked on with delight, hoping that in such ways the relationship between two women who were so important to him would ripen into something that would sustain them all. Indeed, matters progressed so amicably that Iseult was invited to spend Christmas with the Yeatses at Stone Cottage.

George and Yeats himself returned to Sussex around 20 December and at once resumed their spiritualist studies, hoping to cover as much ground as possible before the inevitable interruption of the holidays. Many of Yeats's questions concerned Cuchulain and his work on *The Only Jealousy of Emer*, but new and fundamental insights would not be fully revealed until the Yeatses moved to Oxford at the start of 1918. This change of location was prompted in part by a letter from Frank Pearce Sturm, a doctor, poet and occultist, who had told Yeats of his belief that Oxford was about to become a great centre in the revival of spiritualist learning. George, with anticipatory shrewdness, wondered whether she would be more surprised by the minds or the hats of the dons' wives, and Yeats wrote to John Quinn that he thought she would give herself over to extravagance out of a desire for contrast.

Oxford was now to become an important centre in their lives, and, regardless of whether the city itself was about to undergo an occult revival, the Yeatses' rooms in Broad Street certainly became a centre of active spiritualism. As Yeats wrote to Lady Gregory: 'a very profound, very exciting mystical philosophy – which seems the fulfilment of many dreams and prophecies – is coming in strange ways to George and myself'. He was already 'writing it all out in a series of dialogues about a supposed medieval book, the *Speculum Angelorum et Hominum* by Giraldus'. This elaborate farrago of well-intentioned deception was eventually to form the introduction to the first version of *A Vision*, but for the moment the format of the book had not yet matured in Yeats's mind. He was still being inundated with material – in the first three months of 1918 he and George recorded the answers to some 1850 questions on more than 600 pages of script – and it was only gradually that Yeats himself came to realise that casting this as a platonic dialogue between two of his invented characters from the Nineties, Michael Robartes and Owen Aherne, would not automatically solve the problem. By 14 January, however, the results of his persistent questioning of Thomas about *The Only Jealousy of Emer* had allowed him to complete that work.

This, the most elusive of Yeats's Noh plays, presents Cuchulain suspended between life and death. Emer his wife and Eithne Ingubar his mistress confront each other, and Emer encourages her rival to win her husband back to life with a kiss. It is not Cuchulain, however, but his anti-type, Bricrui the god of discord, who appears, causing Eithne to flee. Bricrui then explains that the 'real' Cuchulain must either be awakened from his dream and released from the guilt of his infidelity or be lost to Fand, the Woman of the Sidhe. The cost of his redemption is Emer's surrendering all hope of his love. Fand's dance of seduction is the central action of the play and is her effort to win for herself a hero who will complete her perfection.

Cuchulain recognises her as the erstwhile Guardian of the water from *At the Hawk's Well* and is, as in the earlier work, inspired to follow her. At the last moment, Emer's heroic renunciation saves him from unworldly oblivion, but at the cost of having Eithne Ingubar claiming him for her own. Heroism goes unrewarded, and the autobiographical references in the play – Yeats's long-standing assimilation of himself to Cuchulain and the similarities of Fand to Maud, Eithne to Iseult and Emer to George – make the work a disquietening one. Despite the fact that Emer, in the occult symbolism of the play, represents the eternal, Celestial Body of fire, Yeats's dramatic solution to his feelings of having betrayed these women could have brought little comfort to any of them.

III
Oxford

For all the occult fecundity of the Yeatses' first stay in Oxford, neither the spirits nor those humans who may reasonably have been assumed to have had an interest in them were altogether helpful. On 22 January, for example, Leo appeared saying that he 'hates medium' and wanted to 'displace' Yeats's mind. He then went on to tell him that he disliked him for his learning and his knowledge about the spirits and also because he had 'a degree of initiation' into the rituals of the Golden Dawn. A week later Yeats asked the control if he wished 'us to find certain mystic associates here in Oxford'. He was particularly keen to know if he should seek out Charlotte Moberly and Eleanor Jourdain, the authors of *An Adventure*, but, although Yeats was told that Miss Moberley 'expects you both', the lady showed herself unresponsive to Yeats's approaches and to experiments which she clearly considered undesirable.

The session on 29 January was not altogether negative, however. Aymor announced his appearance as a new control and told the Yeatses that of three stages of their occult work 'one is past' and 'the second *begins*'. On being asked by Yeats to define this second stage Aymor explained that it consisted of two parts: 'firstly of man and the spirits – secondly of the spirits and God'. The state of the soul after death was now to move to the centre of the Yeatses' enquiries, and life after death and reincarnation became central issues. This change of interests was in part prompted by the news that on 23 January Robert Gregory's plane had been shot down in Italy by, as it was later revealed, an Italian pilot, and that he had been killed. Yeats now felt obliged to focus both his spiritualism and his poetry on this tragedy.

In the postscript to a letter she sent him on 2 February, Lady Gregory wrote: 'if you feel like it some time – write something down that we may keep

– you understand him better than many'. Writing to him again, she added an appeal from Robert's wife Margaret. 'If you would send even a paragraph – just something of what I know you are feeling – to the Observer – or failing that the Nation – she would feel it a comfort.' With the subtle persistence that characterised her dealings in such matters, Lady Gregory also sent Yeats 'typed notes . . . not to use but to waken your memory to different sides of him'. Yeats's 'Note of Appreciation' duly appeared in the *Observer* on 17 February. Here, despite his reservations about the real nature of Robert's achievements, Yeats concentrated on the outward reputation of the dead hero, presenting him as a modern embodiment of the renaissance man:

> I have known no man accomplished in so many ways as Major Robert Gregory, who was killed in action a couple of weeks ago and buried by his fellow-airmen in the beautiful cemetery at Padua. His very accomplishment hid from many his genius. He had so many sides: painter, classical scholar, scholar in painting and in modern literature, boxer, horseman, airman – he had the Military Cross and the Légion d'Honneur – that some among his friends were not sure what his work would be. To me he will always remain a great painter in the immaturity of his youth, he himself a personification of handsome youth. I first came to understand his genius when, still almost a boy, he designed costumes and scenery for the Abbey Theatre.[12]

This was generous but, to a poet so deeply involved in the occult, insufficient. At the session on 31 January Yeats had asked a number of excited questions about the spiritual state of 'the newly dead'. He learned that at the moment of death itself there is a period of unconsciousness when 'the soul is wrapt away by the guides and angels to a momentary vision of future life then as consciousness returns it returns to its own life'. The soul then remains with the body for some days and, although seeing and hearing as if incarnate, is alone and isolated. In this state it meditates on 'the dissolution of the passionate body'. The period of meditation usually ends with burial (for Yeats an important ritual in his consideration of death and afterlife states), following which the Celestial Body can dream back until, reaching its pre-natal state, it can then go forward once again. In the metaphysical lyric from 'Shepherd and Goatherd', the first of Yeats's verse elegies for Robert Gregory, the elderly goatherd voices this idea:

> Jaunting, journeying
> To his own dayspring,
> He unpacks the loaded pern
> Of all 'twas pain or joy to learn,
> Of all that he had made.[13]

Yeats imagines the 'outrageous war' fading from Gregory's memory as he becomes an adolescent shepherd courting his girl to the sound of a flute and then, going backwards through boyhood games, eventually recovers his cradle, where he finally loses all experience in a state of innocence.

The Yeatses' communications with the spirits at this time did not only concern the dead, however. Those who might be brought into life were of equal importance. It is clear that George was thinking of motherhood, and the way in which her communicators broached this subject is disturbing. On 23 February, a control appeared insisting that he 'must give a message from a spirit who has been very persistent for some time . . . She calls herself Anne Hyde Duchess of Ormonde and gives you both her dear love.'[14] At the time of Anne Hyde's appearance, George 'dreamed of her and that her child had lived three days and that she died very young'. Wondering if there were occult connections in a turn of events so obviously flattering to Yeats's ancestral preoccupations, he hurried to the Bodleian* where, after some inaccurate research, he discovered in Clarendon's *Diary* and Thomas Carte's *An History of the Life of James, Duke of Ormonde* that Anne was in fact the Countess of Ossory (her husband did not become Duke of Ormonde until three years after her death) and that she had died a short while after the birth of her child. Intrigued by this and working late into the night of 5 March, Yeats eventually received a communication which assured him that 'Ann wishes her boy to reincarnate because she cannot leave him until he [?is] – she will not want you to reincarnate herself only her boy because she looks on you as on her husband and on medium as on herself'.

Such aristocratic occultism was bound to appeal to Yeats, but the script itself shows the altogether more human and natural impulses underlying George's concern in the matter. At the start of the session on the previous day all their communicators had again made clear George's worries that Yeats would talk irresponsibly about the personal nature of the communications: 'never mention *any* personal message – these . . . are the most important of all our communications'. Having yet again emphasised this important point, George went on to write out a sentence of touching directness: 'her happiness will always depend on you only but the child would only give her happiness in being your child she does not want a child for its own sake'. Quite how true this might have been is disputable, but Yeats was told that 'the important thing is for you to know if you want a son'. George's feelings were apparently considerably less important than her husband's. 'She will on the whole be equally happy during your life whether you want a child or no It will always be you she will love in the child . . . but the decision on your part must be honest and unbiased.' Then, aware how vacillating Yeats could

---

* Yeats loved the Bodleian deeply, telling Lady Gregory that if ever she were to do 'any work that needs a library you must come and stay with us here, for it is well understood that the Bodleian is the most friendly comfortable library in the world, and I suppose the most beautiful'.

be in a matter of such profound personal importance, the control told him that 'you must not wait till you are growing old – remember a child will not make her any more happy now'. A new matter had been broached and, with these very personal concerns in place, the Yeatses prepared to make their first journey as a married couple to Ireland, sending a telegram to announce their arrival on Saturday, 9 March.

IV
The Yeatses in Ireland

When they arrived in Ireland, George had first to be introduced to Yeats's brother and sisters. Lollie in particular was charmed by her. 'We like George *greatly*,' she wrote to JBY. 'You feel that she has plenty of personality but that her disposition is so amiable that she does not often assert herself – not from inertness, but because she is happiest in agreement with the people about her.' Tea at the Abbey Theatre reinforced this impression, and Lily later declared that George 'is that comfortable and pleasant thing, a good woman with brains, and no axe of her own to grind. After all, this is the best mixture to make a good wife and the best of mothers.' The newlyweds spent only a few days in Dublin, however, Yeats being determined to show George as much of his particular Ireland as possible.

By 13 March they were staying in the Royal Hotel at Glendalough, an ancient centre of Celtic Christianity whose atmosphere prompted the Yeatses to continue with their spiritualist investigations and, in particular, to research the mysteries of death and the afterlife of the soul. Yeats was still working on 'Shepherd and Goatherd', a poem he was to finish on 19 March, and the idea of 'dreaming back' naturally played a large part in the Yeatses' seances. The existence of a nearby ancient round tower was also important to them, and the spirits seemed to give their assent to Yeats's proposition that occult forces had led them to be close to this building. Certainly, the spiral staircase in the tower itself began to fascinate Yeats, and 'the image of the shuttle, spiral and funnel' started to take its place in his imagination as a powerful symbol of the spiralling, ascending movement of the spirit. One of the controls had told George that the medium must meditate on such images and had informed them that the tower itself was a symbol of 'abundant flowing life'.

Such images helped shape one of the first poems Yeats wrote in celebration of his marriage. 'Under the Round Tower' shows the beggar Billy Byrne lying below the monument and dreaming of a golden king and a silver lady, a sun and a moon, who dance in erotic and astrological celebration about the obviously phallic suggestiveness of the ancient Irish tower. George was now the theme for lyric, and in 'Solomon to Sheba' (borrowing imagery he had once used to celebrate Maud Gonne) Yeats portrayed the fructifying effect of a woman and erotic passion on the analytical mind of an essentially intellectual man. In this poem, as the sun goes down and the world is transfigured by the subjective light of the moon, so the exultant lover apostrophises his relationship as one in which passion can bring the whole world into its circle.

By the end of March the Yeatses had moved on to Glenmalure, where, perhaps in an attempt to regain that sense of balance and integration which was so important a part of their seances, George's communicators told Yeats that he should become more active and primary, and that he should also be more critical of the information he was receiving and the ideas he deduced from it. By the end of the first week of April, however, the couple were preparing to face the rigours of Coole.

At the time of his engagement Yeats had written to Lady Gregory asking her if he should bring George to the house. Realising that his marriage meant that she would in part at least lose him, Lady Gregory had somewhat haughtily replied: 'I'd rather you didn't come till you were married and nothing could be done about it.' Now nothing could. The visit must nonetheless have made both Yeats and George apprehensive. For all the pleasure his marriage had brought him and the intense occult excitement he was finding in the automatic script particularly, Coole and Lady Gregory carried with them the weight of years of shared experience, of literary endeavour, and deep and subtle friendship. All of this had been supported by a relationship between a middle-aged bachelor and a widow of mature years. Now that rich and delicate balance had been irreversibly changed and Yeats would have to assert both to George and to Lady Gregory herself his new independence.

There had always been much of the mother in Lady Gregory's proprietorial attitude towards Yeats, her not always obedient son, and this was oddly and tellingly confirmed by the boyish prank Yeats now felt obliged to play. He and George had recently acquired a cat they called Pangur (their later homes were to be filled with an ever increasing menagerie) and, as Yeats well knew, Lady Gregory had long placed an embargo on pets in the house. Yeats was determined to break this. As Frank O'Connor told the story, Pangur was brought to Coole but, halfway up the drive, 'the famous public man suddenly got cold feet at the thought of the frosty visage of that old lady in the big house, and he tapped the driver on the shoulder and said, "Drive to the stables," and Pangur was put into the stables'.[15] Yeats then waited until Lady Gregory had gone to bed before bringing the cat into the house, taking it out the following morning. When George later told Lily that 'the Gregories don't like pets unless they are useful', the mildly hurt and dismissive tone in her voice is evident. Certainly, the cat itself was required to live in the stables at Coole, and since George and Yeats never knew whether it had been fed or not, they had to feel it round the waist to make sure.

The unbending dignity of Lady Gregory now had much of pathos about it. The remorseless reduction of rents and the growing burden of taxes meant that her financial position was more than ever under threat. The money she received as an annual income from the estate, granted her at the time of her marriage, had halved. She occasionally augmented it by renting Coole out for the Christmas shooting season, she earned money from her lecture tours in America and, like Yeats himself, she now received a small royalty payment from the performance of her plays at the Abbey. Robert and his wife, however, having lived both in London and in Paris, had been a drain on the family finances, and Robert himself had earned little or nothing from his painting. But now Robert was dead.

Lady Gregory had, of course, feared for him from the time of his enlistment, and on the back of a receipt for clipping hedges she had written after his death: 'what shall I do?' As always, she listed her priorities and stuck by them. She resolved to hold on to the house and to keep it 'healthy and peaceful for the children'. She was also determined to 'keep the Abbey going', not to give up its ideals, and to continue with her own work 'as far as will can do it'. She was above all resolved to 'keep courage and patience through all'. But the pain of Robert's death ran very deep. 'The awakening every morning is the worst,' she wrote to Quinn. 'I try to keep myself asleep – to hold onto dreams – to believe the weight of sadness is a dream. I am just doing all I can for his wife and his children.' Yeats had known that this was how she would react, and in 'Shepherd and Goatherd', a poem whose most deeply felt passages relate to Lady Gregory rather than to her son, he had depicted the defiant fortitude of a great lady wholly devoted to her domain:

> She goes about her house erect and calm
> Between the pantry and the linen-chest,
> Or else at meadow or at grazing overlooks
> Her labouring men, as though her darling lived,
> But for her grandson now. . . .[16]

This was an attitude of which Lady Gregory herself was well aware. Writing to Quinn immediately after Robert's death, she said that last month she had been planting the grounds for her son but now she was planting for her grandson Richard. More than ever the trees at Coole were her consolation. 'These woods have been well loved, well tended by some who came before me, and my affection has been no less than theirs. The generations of trees have been my care, my comforters. Their companionship has often brought me peace.' She thought an elegy from Yeats might crown her grief, however, and hoped for a poem which had 'the intensity and crystallisation of thought' that would 'go best' with her memory of Robert.

'Shepherd and Goatherd' could not be that poem. The antithetical pastoral mode brought Yeats the simplicity he desired from his mask but not the 'intensity' both he and Lady Gregory in their different ways insisted upon. Nor were its occult speculations of much comfort to a practical widow and orthodox Christian. Although her reactions to the poem are not known, it is likely Yeats showed it to her during this period and that she began persuading him towards the creation of another work over whose composition she hoped to have more control, particularly of its philosophical content. Yeats himself was finding Coole inimical to the occult, Aymor complaining 'conditions not good' and instructing the Yeatses that they should reread and codify what had already been given to them, thereby encouraging them 'to wait until you are alone again' to get 'a full exposition' of new material. With the occult thus circumscribed, Yeats was obliged to approach 'In Memory of Major Robert Gregory' from another angle and to find different means of tackling what he had all along faced as his distinctly ambivalent feelings about the true nature of Robert's achievements.

Yeats had harboured these uncertainties for at least half a dozen years, and they went close to the heart of what he felt that he and Lady Gregory had achieved at Coole. At the close of 1912, for example, he had written a poem called 'The New Faces' in which he had imagined Lady Gregory's descendants playing 'what tricks they will' in the old house but still being less intensely alive than the ghosts of Yeats and Lady Gregory themselves roving the gravelled paths in the garden. Lady Gregory had understandably found the work mildly offensive and she required Yeats to suppress it for at least ten years. Nagging doubts about Robert's determination and will power remained nonetheless, and Yeats felt sufficiently strongly about this to tell Lady Gregory rather meanly that Hugh Lane considered that Robert would never work unless he needed the money. Yeats also confided his doubts to his journals, writing there of how he imagined Coole 'slowly perfecting itself and the life within it in ever-increasing intensity of labour, and then of its probably sinking away through courteous incompetence or rather sheer weakness of will'. When Robert himself died, Yeats wrote frankly to both John Quinn and Iseult that he was far more moved for Lady Gregory's sake than for Robert's.

Circumstances at Coole itself had often seemed to confirm Robert's marginal position there. From his sixteenth year onwards he had returned to the house to find Yeats sitting at the head of the table, occupying one of the master bedrooms, giving advice about the estate and, at Lady Gregory's insistence, drinking the finest wine in the cellars. Both Robert and later his wife Margaret felt they were treated somewhat patronisingly in the house, and Robert confessed that he believed Yeats had usurped his rightful position. Lady Gregory did not think, as her son did, that Robert had the right to live in possession at Coole when he attained his majority, and, although a fortnight after his death she offered to leave the house immediately, Margaret did not take this offer up. She had remarked, perhaps somewhat acidly, that while the sedum was in flower Yeats was sure to be at Coole. Now he was there in the early spring and, grieving and perhaps jealous, Margaret treated both the Yeatses rather abruptly. She took to contradicting everything Yeats said at dinner, and Yeats, losing patience, 'turned on her'. This was a deliberate rather than a spontaneous response since Yeats had come down to table 'in the highest spirits with this wicked intention' in mind. Afterwards he went upstairs well satisfied, and, though George told him that he had behaved badly, she 'had so much sympathy with me, that we omitted our usual precaution against conception' and George was soon to find that she was pregnant.

It was for this uneasy household that Yeats now had to create a great elegiac poem. His and George's moving out of Coole itself to Ballinamantiane Cottage provided distance and inspiration for the poem but did not lessen Lady Gregory's active interest in how the work was proceeding. When George decided to spend a few days away from the estate, Yeats wrote to her in some exasperation:

> I have done nothing but . . . discuss with Lady Gregory the new stanza that is to commend Robert's courage in the hunting field. It has been a little thorny but we have settled a compromise. I have got from her a list of musical place-names where he has hunted and hope for a new representation of the place. I have firmly resisted all suggested eloquence about aeroplanes 'and the blue Italian sky'. It is pathetic for Lady Gregory constantly says it is his monument – 'all that remains'. I see that she feels that his pictures are as it were his thought but not himself.

In the final version of the poem, Robert's ability as a painter is treated with some measure of ambiguity. Yeats wrote that the community at Coole had 'dreamed' that a major artist had come among them, a choice of verb which points to the limited scale of Robert's achievement, cut off prematurely as it appeared to have been, while also hinting perhaps that the talent itself may have been something of an illusion. For all that Yeats wished to present Robert as a renaissance man, an *uomo universale* out of Castiglione, artistic ability alone cannot bind him to that representative company of greatly talented in the poem which includes John Synge. Similarly, Robert's scholarship could not compete with Lionel Johnson's, also brought into the elegy as a memorable and now dead Irish acquaintance. In fact, Robert Gregory comes most vividly to life in Yeats's descriptions of him as a man of the soil and a reckless horseman. Indeed, it is the stanza about Robert's equestrian prowess (the stanza with which his mother had particularly interfered) in which Yeats most nearly attains the much desired 'intensity' of response:

When with the Galway foxhounds he would ride
From Castle Taylor to the Roxborough side
Or Esserkelly plain, few kept his pace;
At Mooneen he had leaped a place
So perilous that half the astonished meet
Had shut their eyes; and where was it
He rode a race without a bit?
And yet his mind outran the horses' feet.[17]

It is this intensity of action, a virtue rather more athletic than aesthetic or intellectual, that underlies Yeats's third poem on Robert Gregory: 'An Irish Airman Foresees his Death'. Perhaps taking his inspiration from Lady Gregory's comments, Yeats here presented a concise but evocative image of the war in the skies. To achieve this, a number of facts had again to be suppressed. Yeats chose to ignore, for example, the fact that Robert was a committed imperialist, and presents him instead as an Irishman led to his moment of intensity and death purely by 'a lonely impulse of delight'. There is a feeling that the speaker of the poem is already a partly disembodied spirit, a soul about to begin its 'dreaming back'. The sense of exaltation and tragedy in the work is powerful and dignified, and carries a sufficient emotional charge to make Robert's imagined assertion that his previous efforts were as nothing compared to this last, glorious moment entirely convincing.

V

'The Growing Murderousness of the World'

If the solitary, aristocratic intensities of Robert Gregory's death were, in 1918, a forceful reminder of 'the growing murderousness of the world', they were nonetheless a matter for elegy, the concern of the dead. Nationalism in Dublin was taking other forms, and in February of that year the correspondent of the *Irish Nation*, reporting on a Sinn Fein meeting, wrote: 'two new forces made their appearance on the platform at the Mansion House on Monday night week. Mrs Maud Gonne MacBride may not be responsible for the Bolshevik incursion, and the Bolshevik ideal may not be responsible for Mrs MacBride's return to Ireland, but the advent of either or both is – to say the least – significant.'[18]

For weeks before this, Maud, who was staying in Yeats's lodgings in Woburn Place, had haunted the corridors of the War Office demanding her right to return to Ireland. When not hunting down harassed civil servants, she attended meetings of the radical Women's Social and Political Union and the Women's Freedom League, where she met Mrs Charlotte Despard, the extreme and eccentric sister of Lord French, field marshal at the Battle of

Ypres. Dressed in black and wearing sandals and a lace mantilla, Mrs Despard was an ardent socialist whose views not only had caused great embarrassment to her brother but eventually resulted in her being ostracised by her class. Passionately involved in the struggle for human rights and confirmed in her belief that Ireland should be an independent nation, she and Maud were naturally drawn to each other, and the passing of the Representation of the People Act at the end of 1917 confirmed the belief of both that women, permitted now to vote for the first time, could play a real and active part in politics.

To be prevented from doing so in Ireland was extremely irksome, and Maud wrote to Quinn lamenting that she was 'still held up in London, and longing to be among all my friends in God's own country'. The War Office proving intransigent, other means of escape had to be adopted. Maud, who had once convinced intellectual and artistic Dublin that she was the very embodiment of Cathleen ni Houlihan, now determined once again on disguise. With a shawl over her head and her imperious figure artificially broadened by rags stuffed under her skirt, she hobbled up the gangplank at Hollyhead carrying a couple of poor-looking suitcases tied with string. The police and secret service were evaded, and fellow passengers were so convinced by her appearance that they made a space for her on the crowded deck, where Maud sat mumbling over her rosary with a beating heart. Having got so far, she still feared that the port authorities in Dublin would recognise her, but 'I might not have worried so much, because I was so well disguised that my friends were unable to recognise me'. Once arrived in Dublin she rented a house at 73 St Stephen's Green and, reunited with old acquaintances, started again working for her favourite causes: amnesty for prisoners, meals for poor children, freedom for Ireland. It is also probable that she found time to visit Coole, where she offered her condolences to Lady Gregory and met with Yeats and George.

Maud embodied an Ireland pullulating with hope and anger. Soon after his election, de Valera had declared that, until another mode of administration was found more suitable, 'the Irish Republic is the form of government that the Sinn Feiners will give allegiance to'. The landslide victory of William Cosgrave at the polls in Kilkenny seemed to confirm the influence of the movement, which was widely supported by a young population swollen to greater numbers than ever before because of the war and the consequent steep decline in emigration. Efficiently organised by Collins's secret society at its core, Sinn Fein, for all the apparent vagueness of its political programme, seemed headed for success. Its violent and anarchic tendencies were nonetheless a cause for great concern. While the larger part of the population felt that Ireland would be able to assert its independence not through armed revolution but by resort to the Peace Conference that was to be held at the end of the world war, many in the Volunteer movement believed that physical force would probably be necessary. To this end they began organising concerted raids for arms and commandeering acres of private land for the growing of essential supplies against the possibility of famine. A degree of lawlessness was once again becoming apparent, and such activities – enhanced by the Volunteers' conspicuous and illegal military-style drilling – resulted in a large number of arrests.

If the British government hoped such actions would placate those wavering in their support of Sinn Fein they were grievously disappointed. The Volunteer prisoners in Mountjoy jail refused to be treated as common criminals, to do prison work or to wear prison uniform. There was some organised violence, but altogether more powerful was their decision to adopt protest by hunger-strike. An unavoidably brutal regime of forced feeding was instituted and, when Thomas Ashe died of heart failure and congestion of the lungs as a result of this, Michael Collins organised a massive public funeral for him in September 1917. Dublin went into mourning, some 40,000 followed the coffin including members of the clergy, the unions, the Irish Volunteers, the Irish National Volunteers and Citizen Army led by Constance Markiewicz. Three volleys were fired over the grave and Michael Collins, addressing the crowd in Irish, declared: 'nothing additional remains to be said. That volley which we have just heard is the only speech which it is proper to make over the grave of a dead Fenian.'

Such a groundswell of public opinion would have been disturbing to the authorities even in more settled times, but in the early months of 1918 the British government was facing what appeared to be international disaster and potential annihilation. A massive German offensive had pushed the Allies in Europe back to within forty miles of Paris, and the loss of life was so catastrophic that on 9 April the war cabinet announced that conscription would be introduced into Ireland. In his desperation, Lloyd George hoped to make this move more palatable by offering what to all Nationalists was the wholly unacceptable sop of instant Home Rule based on partition. Members of a meeting of Nationalists of all shades of opinion at the Mansion House consulted with the clergy gathered in conference at Maynooth and issued a unanimous declaration: 'the attempt to enforce conscription will be unwarrantable aggression which we call upon all true Irishmen to resist by the most effective means at their disposal'.

Yeats immediately realised how dangerous the situation was and, along with Lady Gregory, James Stephens, George Russell and Douglas Hyde, signed a motion of public protest in which all declared they felt 'compelled to appeal and protest against the enforcement of conscription in our country, believing, as we do, that such action will destroy all hope of peace in Ireland and good will towards England in our lifetime'.[19] An insensitive and desperate English government had played into Sinn Fein's hands, and, in a last-ditch attempt to stem the tide of outraged Irish opinion, despatched Lord French as viceroy, aware no doubt that five days after his landing he would issue a proclamation about a supposed 'German Plot' in Ireland and claim then that the current leaders of Sinn Fein were in league with the enemy. Such rumours had little more basis than the fact that the Martyrs of 1916 had indeed made futile attempts to win German support, but allegations of widespread treason allowed for widespread arrests. Seventy-three Sinn Fein activists were immediately imprisoned, including Griffith, de Valera and Maud Gonne.

Ireland seemed menaced by the anarchy of massive and materialistic forces no one could control. In western Europe a war that was tearing down an old civilisation threatened to swallow uncountable numbers of young Ireshmen and destroy the nation's last chance of political stability. To the east, a violent Marxism posed an ideological threat which Yeats greatly feared was impinging on Ireland too now that radicals like Maud Gonne had apparently interested themselves in communism. The murder of the Czar and his family reinforced this fear, while the fact that the English royal family had been persuaded not to offer their Russian relatives shelter again underlined what Yeats believed was the moral bankruptcy of British imperialism. 'I have been told that King George V asked that the Russian royal family should be brought to England. The English Prime Minister refused, fearing the effect on the English working class. . . . We . . . would think that he showed lack of personality, of manhood even, because he did not abdicate.' As the war in Russia between the Red and White armies deepened into prolonged brutality, Yeats's concern about the communist threat grew. 'What I want', he declared, 'is that Ireland be kept from giving itself (under the influence of its lunatic faculty of going against everything which it believes England to affirm) to Marxian revolution or Marxian definitions of value in any form. I consider the Marxian criterion of values as in this age the spear-head of materialism and leading to inevitable murder.'

Confronted by so much horror, Yeats felt a deep need for some form of historical explanation which would give him perspective and understanding. He believed that for some time now the communicators had been providing material which could be synthesised into a theory which pitted occult insight against dialectical materialism. These concerns now moved to the centre of his interest as he continued to work on *A Vision*.

Yeats's first intimations of his cyclical theory of history came to him at the session of automatic writing he and George held on 21 November 1917. Early in the next month he was presented with the symbol he would henceforth use to explain his ideas. This symbol consisted of two interpenetrating and revolving cones or 'gyres' which represented (among other things) the so-called subjective and objective periods of history. Subjective periods were deemed to be antithetical and aristocratic, while objective or primary periods were democratic. Each of these contrasted types was seen as rising to its climax only to be violently replaced as an Initiate or New Messiah heralded the coming of its opposite. These revolutions happened over great cycles of time which, in their turn, could be divided into the familiar twenty-eight phases of the moon. As Yeats somewhat crudely described his system: 'history is very simple – the rule of the many, then the rule of the few, day and night, night and day forever'.[20]

What this meant in specific terms was that modern man lives, according to the Yeatsian system, in the primary and democratic Christian era which replaced the aristocratic civilisation of the ancient world. That two-thousand-year period was now coming to its climax, however. Indeed, its second half had already reached Phase Twenty-Two, a moment of crisis in which primary energies were at their widest and most diffuse and hence showing those characteristics of terminal decline which would allow for the birth of the new dispensation. In particular, the enfeebled democratic nature of the primary phase had, as philosophers from Plato to Mill feared it would, led to anarchy and tyranny. These fearful possibilities were, Yeats believed, visible both in the mounting chaos in Ireland and in the materialistic, soul-destroying nature of Soviet communism in which all men were equal and all men were slaves.

The late May and early June of 1918 saw the Yeatses working with particular concentration on these ideas. As George's pregnancy became an established fact, so the Initiates who heralded the new cycles of history – Christ, Buddha and the New Messiah especially – became particularly important to them, for they were beginning to believe that their own child might be the latest of these figures. If it was somewhat foxing that the New Messiah was apparently to be born before the end of the Christian cycle, Thomas was perfectly clear that astrologically his birth would be positioned in the centre of the cycles of Libra and Scorpio, in other words at the mid-point of Yeats's and George's own cycles. His characteristics would, of course, be lunar, antithetical and aristocratic, the anti-type of Christ.

Although Yeats himself had now completed 'The Phases of the Moon' and 'The Double Vision of Michael Robartes', two poems in which ideas from *A Vision* are expounded, work on the script itself was intensely demanding and George in particular was growing tired. The communicator suggested that Yeats set to work on synthesising the matter he had already received rather than searching for new material. By 15 July, he had written thirty pages in the first of three projected dialogues, his attempt to 'survey all arts and letters under the glare of my mathematical lightning'. But this was not a sufficient respite for George. There were more sessions in mid-July, but a session held on 5 August (the last for three weeks) revealed her as touchy and impatient. She was particularly irked by Yeats's sometimes muddled and apparently random questioning, and went so far as to write 'accept no when I say it'.

By September, however, the script was once again revealing fruitful insights, and the concept of Unity of Being particularly moved once again to the centre of Yeats's attention. Thomas now told him that this ideal state 'cannot exist in separation from the body' and could be experienced only by those whose Will placed them between Phases Sixteen, Seventeen and Eighteen, points on the Great Wheel where Yeats and George, along with many of their friends and favourite authors, were placed, and where both Thomas and the Giraldus of the *Speculum* could also be found. It was these people alone who could know, in an important revelation, that Unity of Being consisted of 'complete harmony between physical body intellect and spiritual desire – *all may be imperfect* but if harmony is perfect it is unity'.

There were more very involved sessions when Yeats took George to see Rosses Point and the scenes of his childhood, but when they met on 21 September it was in Thoor Ballylee.* The creation of his new home was naturally a matter of deep emotional importance to Yeats. He was determined that the ancient building should preserve an uncluttered simplicity and be furnished only with those life-enhancing things 'the great and passionate have used'. He feared strongly that the aura of his castle might be spoiled by new houses 'planned in a government office', but he was above all resolved that Thoor Ballylee should be, as Thomas insisted towers were, a place of flowing images and vision.

Practical matters had to be attended to first, however, and Yeats wrote describing how he and George 'had bought the whole contents of an old mill – great beams and three-inch planks, and old paving stones; and the local carpenter and mason and blacksmith are at work for us'. To celebrate this work Yeats also composed a memorable expression of marital pride in possession to be inscribed 'on a great stone beside the front door':

> I the poet William Yeats,
> With old mill boards and sea-green slates,
> And smithy work from the Gort forge,
> Restored this tower for my wife George;
> And may these characters remain
> When all is ruin once again.[21]

Although the slates were never used, the proposed roof being deemed unable to stand up to the Atlantic winds, and although the top level was never made habitable, Thoor Ballylee was in time to become the central symbol of one of the supreme volumes of twentieth-century poetry, a tower as central to Yeats's thought as Duino was to Rilke's or Bollingen to Jung's. For the moment, however, this wealth of suggestion was not apparent. The early

---

* While visiting Rosses, Yeats also took George to see his childhood sailing friend Henry Middleton in his 'small forgotten house' set on its 'storm-bitten green'. Henry had turned into an eccentric recluse. Yeats found him in the sitting room beside a butter-churn and surrounded by cheap novels. 'You see', said the immaculately dressed Henry after a while, 'that I'm too busy to see anyone.'

sessions of automatic writing held there were unproductive, and Thomas complained that the tower was 'very *cold*'. The Yeatses also found that it was extremely damp, and on 24 September they moved on to Dublin.

The tiring journey across Ireland did not prevent them from having a further session of automatic writing that evening, and this was to prove one of the most remarkable occasions in the whole enterprise. For the first time the spirits told them directly that their child was to be 'in some way connected with an "avatar"'. Just as in the early days when Thomas of Dorlowicz, unable to use Yeats's own thoughts, had picked up on the curious coincidence of the use made by Horton and Lady Lyttelton of the central image from the *Phaedrus*, so now the unknown communicator reached back to Yeats and George Russell's correspondence of 1896 in which Russell had enthused about the return to Ireland of the Celtic gods. 'The gods have returned to Erin,' Russell had told him, 'and have centred themselves in the sacred mountains and blow the fires through the country. They have been seen by several in vision, they will awaken the magical instinct everywhere, and the universal heart of the people will turn to the old druidic beliefs.'[22] Yeats had been distinctly disparaging about this at the time, but now he saw possibilities in Russell's old enthusiasms. In particular, Russell had written: 'out of Ireland will arise a light to transform many ages and peoples. There is a hurrying of forces and swift things going out and I believe profoundly that a new Avatar is about to appear and in all spheres the forerunners go before him to prepare. It will be one of the kingly avatars, who is at once ruler of men and magic sage. I had a vision of him some months ago and will know him if he appears.' Yeats now believed that he had been given spiritualist confirmation that that Avatar would be the child ripening in George's womb.

He nonetheless felt he needed to tie this extraordinary promise more closely to his family, and the hints of Confucian ancestor worship seen in *Responsibilities* were given an occult cast. Russell himself had laid a particular emphasis on the fact that the birth of his Avatar was related to the existence of 'sacred mountains' in Ireland, and George's communicators confirmed that 'the actual mountains are . . . spiritual centres'. It thus seemed desirable to relate the Yeats family to a particular mountain, and Ben Bulben conveniently fitted the bill. Another coincidence seemed only to confirm this occult relationship. The spirits had told Yeats that 'the avatar is or will be the fifth generation from the mountain'. A simple exercise in family history at once revealed that Yeats's son would be the fifth in descent from 'Parson John' of Drumcliff, whose male heirs 'had all lived at some time or other in shadow of Ben Bulben'. The beautiful mountain of Yeats's childhood was becoming as sacred in his adult mythology as was Mount Abiegnos, the burial place of Father Christian Rosenkreutz, to the Golden Dawn.

The world into which the Irish redeemer would be born, however, was an ever more desperate and dangerous one. By October 1918 the issue of conscription in Ireland was again being raised in Westminster, and Yeats remained aware of the dangers the issue dragged in its wake. Writing to Viscount Haldane, he made it clear that 'if conscription is imposed upon Ireland it will be neither imposed or met in cold blood'. Speaking sensitively and accurately about the long Irish memory, Yeats wrote that 'there will be incidents that will become anecdotes and legends according to whether they are told by the educated or by the poor, and the legends of the poor never die. Each side will have its wrongs to tell of and these will keep England and Ireland apart during your lifetime and mine. England will forget the anecdotes in a few years, but the legends will never be forgotten.' In fact conscription was not to be introduced into Ireland, but the knowledge that it lurked as a threat helped greatly to increase the popularity of Sinn Fein. When, in August 1918, Britain, as part of a now victorious Allied army, introduced a voluntary recruiting campaign to swell the forces pushing the Germans back to their frontiers, Sinn Fein managed to break up the meeting held to support it.

Much of this success was due to the initiative of the now fugitive Michael Collins, who was working to ensure that Sinn Fein itself would be victorious in the general election called for December 1918. The Representation of the People Act was to play a crucial role in this, for by extending the vote to all males over twenty-one and to all women over thirty it virtually trebled the size of the Irish electorate, many of whom were young and poor and felt they stood to gain far less from England than from Sinn Fein's proposal that elected candidates would refuse to attend Westminster and, from a National Assembly in Dublin, would appeal to the forthcoming international Peace Conference to arbitrate their claim for their nation's independence.

Yeats looked on contemptuously at this surge of democratic fervour. First from the windows of his club and then from the house at 73 St Stephen's Green rented to him by the imprisoned Maud Gonne, he watched the workings of 'The Leaders of the Crowd'. Here he thought was personified much of what he most feared and loathed: the lethal crudities of propaganda and bigoted demagoguery, the craving for a mass following, and the rejection of intellectual integrity in the effort to cajole a willing herd of 'primary' people into an anonymous, identically thinking mass.

Such naked contempt was made more complex by the imprisonment of Maud, herself one of the leaders of popular opinion. For all that she had the companionship of Constance Markiewicz, Kathleen Clarke and Hanna Sheehy-Skeffington, the prison regime and diet at Holloway nearly broke her. 'All she'd do was talk to her canary,' Kathleen Clarke commented. 'She was like a caged wild animal herself, like a tigress prowling endlessly up and down. We were given the chance to apply to the Sankey Commission for release, and in her misery, she said she would – said she'd point out she hadn't been in Ireland during the war. Con said: "If you do that, you need never come back to Ireland," and she tore the application up.'[23] Maud grew thin and her hacking cough kept her cell-mates awake at night. Yeats asked Lady Cunard and others to use what influence they had, but it was Maud's illness – 'a recrudescence of her former pulmonary tuberculosis' – that was decisive.

The specialist who was eventually allowed to examine her recommended immediate transfer to a more congenial climate. John Quinn was informed of this and not only promised her money for expenses but contacted the English newspapers to inform them that her 'death or serious illness while detained in English prison' would have a disastrous effect. After five and a half months in Holloway, Maud was eventually released and sent to a nursing home, but she refused to stay there and, five days later, was back at Woburn Buildings, where she was reunited with Iseult as well as with Sean, whom she had last seen running after her Black Maria as she was carried off to prison. As London celebrated the Armistice, Maud was delighted to watch rebellious young people tearing down a poster of the King in Trafalgar Square. Now, however, she felt her return to Ireland was imperative. Technically, she was still held under the Defence of the Realm Acts and was 'somewhat scared at the risk she was about to take'. She had resolved once again on disguise, however, and now, dressed as a Red Cross nurse and accompanied by her children, she made her way to Dublin and her house at 73 St Stephen's Green.

Yeats, furious and alarmed, refused to let her in. Upstairs, now seven months pregnant with the New Messiah, George was lying ill with pneumonia. Maud was far too dangerous and demanding a figure to be allowed anywhere near her, and, besides, her presence in the house posed a severe threat to Yeats's own psychological well-being. Her illegal presence also brought with it the threat of police raids, and a terrible row broke out which soon became public property. Maud accused Yeats of being unpatriotic and a coward, while he accused her of having a 'pure and disinterested love of mischief'. Dublin gossip accused Yeats of having meanly conspired with the Chief Secretary to ensure that Maud stayed locked up in a London nursing home while he lived on at her house. The Chief Secretary himself refused to have anything to do with these ridiculous allegations, and eventually, while Maud herself went off to the Wicklow Mountains to live with a small colony of artists gathered there, Yeats prepared to vacate her home.

The friendship was eventually resumed, and the young artist Cecil Salkeld noted that Maud received Yeats 'with the gay good-humour characteristic of her. I fancied the place she occupied in his verse had placed them both beyond possibility of any prolonged quarrel.' Yeats started to attend Maud's At Homes and took a keen interest in anyone who was close to her; Brendan Behan later remembered that he would even chat to his mother, who was the housemaid there. But, though Maud made 73 St Stephen's Green into a Republican salon, the recent months had taken a terrible toll. 'She looks ghastly,' Yeats told Quinn. 'I heard a young English officer speak of her the other day as a tragic sight.'

Yeats's feelings for Maud were at this time too complex and too ambivalent to inspire him to poetry, and it was Constance Markiewicz, still held in Holloway, whom he chose to portray as a once beautiful and aristocratic free spirit now supposedly demeaned by her immersion in those democratic enthusiasms which, at the general election of 1918, had ensured the electoral success of Sinn Fein. Beauty and dignity had been destroyed by slumming in the 'abounding gutter' of Dublin political life. Yeats imagines the humiliated Constance feeding a gull at her cell window and asked:

> Did she in touching that lone wing
> Recall the years before her mind
> Became a bitter, an abstract thing,
> Her thought some popular enmity:
> Blind and leader of the blind
> Drinking the foul ditch where they lie?[24]

Yeats was lamenting the apparent collapse of his aristocratic and antithetical ideal, the destruction of those forces which he once hoped might work to Ireland's benefit. The contempt in the poem suggests his established mastery of poetic hatred, but a letter to Constance's sister Eva Gore-Booth tempered his public outrage. 'Will you permit me to say', he wrote, 'how much I sorrow over the misfortune that has fallen upon your family? Your sister and yourself, two beautiful figures among the great trees of Lissadell, are among the dear memories of my youth.'

Constance Markiewicz, however, was but a single example of the destructiveness roaring through Yeats's world now that the primary gyre of the Christian era was apparently approaching its climax. The whole world, it seemed, was raging with cruelty and anarchy. In January 1919, speaking at a debate on 'Socialism and the War', Yeats declared that 'Russia had, in the name of progress and in the name of human freedom, revived tyranny and torture of the worst description – had, in fact, resorted to such a medieval crime as burning men for their opinions'. But it was not merely the prospect of war in distant countries that was so appalling. Ireland too was moving ever closer to violence and chaos.

Sinn Fein had been elected on a mandate promising a National Assembly in Ireland made up of members absenting themselves from Westminster. It had also offered the hope of establishing the independence of the country through an appeal to the Paris Peace Conference. This last proved vain. The great powers gathered in France were there to settle the affairs of defeated peoples and had resolved not to interfere in each other's internal affairs. Now, while the new Dail Eireann filled its ministerial posts, proclaimed a constitution and issued an Irish Declaration of Independence, Lloyd George insisted that Irish problems were solely a British concern and that the Peace Conference could give no support to the claims of the indigenous Irish population. These claims were backed, however, not only by a democratically elected body but by a secret machinery of influence wholly different in its approach to the public statements of the Dail. Many of those, like the Finance Minister Michael Collins, who were members of the Dail were also members of the Volunteers or even the IRB, and what they could not achieve by peaceful persuasion they might yet obtain by other means.

While Collins and a colleague staged the spectacular feat of freeing their president, de Valera, from Lincoln prison, thereby permitting him to go to America and there canvass support for the cause, Collins himself organised raids for arms across Ireland and began an efficient and terrible campaign of murder against the English forces stationed there. This was a course of action far outside the mandate on which he had been elected, and such democratic sanction as it had lay less in the fact that the Dail had described 'a state of war' as existing between England Ireland than in the clear evidence that Westminster had chosen wholly to ignore the will of the people as expressed in the December election. From this position of mutual intransigence abounding blood and horror would flow. The correspondent of a London newspaper, writing from Sligo, told of the mounting contempt of Collins and the 'physical force men' for those urging 'moral force' alone.[25] Collins himself declared that 'Ireland was likely to get more out of a state of general disorder than from a continuance of the situation as it then stood'. Over the succeeding months, as murders multiplied and the British resorted to the iron fist of military rule, so 'moral force' became increasingly irrelevant. Men like Collins, the *Daily News* reporter declared, 'are never in the ascendant except at times of extraordinary national emotion'. The long history of Ireland showed this to be true, but present events made clear that 'such a time it is only too plain to see we are rapidly approaching now'. Yeats too was convinced of the truth of this. His knowledge of his homeland, his view of the world stage and the insights of his occult studies all persuaded him of the imminent collapse of civilisation:

> Things fall apart; the centre cannot hold;
> Mere anarchy is loosed upon the world,
> The blood-dimmed tide is loosed, and everywhere
> The ceremony of innocence is drowned;
> The best lack all conviction, while the worst
> Are full of passionate intensity.[26]

The pitiless turning of the gyres has brought the democratic and self-effacing Christian period to a terrible climax. Now 'the Second Coming is at hand'. Far from being, as Christians believe, the period which will see the thousand-year rule of the godly, this era would be, Yeats thought, drawing on the deepest resources of his imagination, an aristocratic, physical, assertive and occult period of frightening primeval energies. Images drawn from across his career went into creating it: the magical Armageddon he had half welcomed and half feared in the Nineties, his first tattwa vision of 'a desert and a black Titan raising himself up by his two hands from the middle of a heap of ancient ruins', later images of 'a brazen winged beast that I associated with laughing, ecstatic destruction'. All of these gathered round the nightmarish imagining of the 'rough beast' slouching towards Bethlehem to herald the year 2000 and the millennium of the antithetical gyre. The occult, the political and the poetic had once again coincided in an understanding of life mystically ordered by forces beyond man's intellectual control. The innumerable automatic scripts Yeats was still working on indeed begin to justify their eventual title: *A Vision*. Yeats had entered on his greatness by seeing the omnipresent, ineluctable violence at the heart of the twentieth century.

VI
'The Spreading Laurel Tree'

It was into such a world, in Dublin on 24 February 1919, that George gave birth to a daughter, named Anne after Anne Hyde. As Thomas was later to tell them, the communicators could not influence gender. They could, however, provide something of the visionary material for the poem Yeats began two days after Anne's birth. But the strength of paternal feeling that flows through 'A Prayer for my Daughter' is above all a human one, an immense assertion of love, hope and a conservative sense of dignity maintained in the face of chaos.

The poem begins with storm. At first Yeats had imagined this as something metaphorical, a popular tempest of strident voices screaming in their creation of the last destructive days of the primary, democratic gyre. In a revision of genius, he turned such matters to symbol. The Atlantic sea-storm howling about Thoor Ballylee is above all the wildness of nature able in its sheer elemental might to suggest the appalling power of forces beyond the reach of moral judgement and roaring into terrible life from what, in an old symbol, we may choose to think of as the sea of materialism. Only 'one bare hill' and 'Gregory's wood' – the landscape around the tower itself with its suggestions of natural and aristocratic defences – protect the poet as he imagines the future, a state beyond this screaming madness, emerging 'out of the murderous innocence of the sea'.

These opening stanzas are a sublime evocation of a world at once physically real, politically tormented and spiritually understood through the power of symbol. As they close, and as Yeats imagines Anne's young womanly beauty, so storm gives way to tranquillity, madness to decorum, primary and democratic to antithetical and aristocratic. Chaos has indeed produced its opposite: 'love of order in the people', authority and tradition. But the price of this desired state, Yeats believed, was dreadfully high. 'Everywhere', he would write, 'one notices a drift towards Conservatism, perhaps towards Autocracy. I always knew that it would come, but not that it would come in this tragic way.' It appeared that it had to be fashioned out of universal destruction, and its creation, he believed, had to be a 'conspiracy of the few', the advance guard. 'When the new era comes bringing its stream of irrational force it will, as did Christianity, find its philosophy already impressed upon the minority who have, true to phase, turned away at the last gyre from the *Physical Primary*.' It is as one of this elite band, a member of these 'organic groups, *covens* of physical or intellectual kin melting out of the frozen mass', that the poet now imagines his daughter.[27]

The virtues of an aristocratic gentlewoman – modest beauty, courtesy, the serenity of a mind so without rancour that the soul can discover its rightful joy – embody much of what he wishes for her. To establish this patrician comeliness and give it force, Yeats contrasted it, with all the mastery of malice at his disposal, to the evils imagined in a Maud Gonne he never mentions by name. The vices of a woman blown by the winds of democratic fervour to the very doorway of the house where the mother of a new image of perfection lay dangerously ill is excoriated here with an imagery and language drawn from classical legend, personal experience and the naked brutality which gives rise to phrases such as 'an old bellows full of angry wind'. It is a vertiginous assemblage of the embittered, the angry and the unnatural.

It is also a magnificent contrast to the poem's images of the abundance and decorum that inspire art – the closing stanza imagining Anne's wedding, for example, or the beautiful image of her as a bird living in innocent delight in the branches of the laurel, the poet's tree:

> May she become a flourishing hidden tree
> That all her thoughts may like the linnet be,
> And have no business but dispensing round
> Their magnanimities of sound,
> Nor but in merriment begin a chase,
> Nor but in merriment a quarrel.
> O may she live like some green laurel
> Rooted in one dear perpetual place.[28]

Michael Robartes and the Dancer, the volume which contains this poem, is a collection full of occult elaboration and political terror, but it is also one in which the newly married poet can celebrate domestic tranquillity. 'A Prayer for my Daughter' orchestrates all these themes with unique richness as, in imagining a revived aristocratic Irishness, it creates a new fusion of Yeats's poetry with his occult and Nationalist interests. Future months would show, however, that this was an imagining of human potential under dire threat.

14

In Time of Civil War
(1919–1923)

I
'Under Saturn'

Yeats completed 'A Prayer for my Daughter' at Thoor Ballylee in June 1919. The summer passed agreeably with Yeats himself writing in the ground-floor room of the tower or on the river bank, where he could watch the otters fishing for trout. A seventeenth-century cradle had been found for Anne, while George busied herself painting the rafters of their new Irish home. 'In Ireland,' Yeats was to declare, 'the country life has for us the . . . fascination that it is the only thoroughly Irish life.'[1] Autumn nonetheless pointed to the hardships of winter. The second and third floors of the tower were still open to the wind, while there was also the threat of flooding. Many years later, Anne was to recall that 'the floods could nearly always be counted on'. When they invaded, George would 'come down, sweep out the worms and things,' and, when the place was once again habitable, Yeats himself would appear 'and life would resume as usual'. In the couple's early days at Ballylee, Thomas of Dorlowicz had also complained how cold the tower was and, with a new baby to look after, it was imperative the Yeatses find alternative winter accommodation.

Dublin and much of the rest of Ireland, however, were becoming increasingly dangerous. The repressive measures taken by the British government as the campaign of killing accelerated proved to many moderate supporters of Sinn Fein that the struggle for independence would indeed be a violent one. The arrival of an American Commission for Irish Freedom enhanced this sense of embattled national identity, and the *Irish Times* commented that 'three weeks ago none save fools and fanatics believed in the possibility of an Irish Republic. Today a large number of Irish Nationalists hope, and a still larger number fear, that in the near future an Irish Republic may come to birth from the grotesque union of British folly and American sentiment.' These forces would certainly play their part, but Michael Collins's initiatives were to be vital as well. While gathering his finest marksmen into the 'Squad', Collins simultaneously developed a sophisticated intelligence system and organised boycotts and a campaign of intimidation which varied between the maiming of victims and the murder of culprits whose corpses would then be left with a label tied to them marked 'Spy – killed by IRA'. Meanwhile, in the absence of a more constructive British policy, troops and armoured cars hourly suggested to Dubliners that they were still allegedly subservient to an alien power.

If Dublin held few attractions for a family, London was equally uncongenial to Yeats and he had, besides, recently given up his lodgings in Woburn Buildings. In October 1919 he decided to move to Oxford, where he rented rooms at 4 Broad Street, furnishing them with items brought from London, to which were added pewter dining plates and a green parrot. The move was not without its emotional pressures, however. Despondency set in, and, if the opening lines of 'Under Saturn' suggest that George thought this was due to memories of Maud Gonne, the rest of the work shows that Yeats was facing his guilty feelings about leaving his homeland. Circumstances were now to prevent him from living permanently in Ireland for over two years.

Yeats was also growing aware of how far his dramatic art was diverging from the current achievements of the Abbey Theatre. In the the late November and early December issues of *The Irish Statesman* he published his essay 'A People's Theatre, a Letter to Lady Gregory', in which he praised the Abbey for drawing its energies from the talents and traditions of the Irish people in a way that had set an international standard of quality. He feared, however, that for all its evident success the new roots of the Theatre drew their nourishment from an objective and realistic world of history and verifiable fact – from the energies of the primary gyre – and this was for him 'a discouragement and a defeat'.[2] He wrote to Lady Gregory that Lennox Robinson 'represents the Ireland that must sooner or later take over the work from us . . . the sooner some young man, who feels that his own future is bound up with the Abbey, is put in charge the better'. Yeats believed that such energies as Robinson and the Cork realists showed were on the point of passing away, but he did not think that the world was yet ready for the type of drama he himself envisaged and, indeed, had gone some way towards creating.

'I desire a mysterious art,' Yeats wrote,

> always reminding and half-reminding those who understand it of dearly loved things, doing its work by suggestion, not by direct statement, a complexity of rhythm, colour, gesture, not space-pervading like the intellect, but a memory and a prophecy: a mode of drama Shelley and Keats could have used without ceasing to be themselves, and for which even Blake in the mood of *The Book of Thel* might not have been too obscure.

May 1919 had seen an English production of Yeats's *The Player Queen* (when it was produced again at the Abbey in December Holloway wrote that 'though its purport is wrapt in mystery its beauty won home'), but his Noh plays *The Dreaming of the Bones, The Only Jealousy of Emer* and *Calvary* failed to reach the stage and were issued along with *At the Hawk's Well* as *Four Plays for Dancers* in 1921. Yeats had pushed his dramatic writing beyond the bounds of likely production and he was now, he confessed, 'rather tired of the theatre'.

December was to bring further disappointments. The systematic campaign of terror and murder in Ireland was continuing to accelerate as the IRA became an ever more practised guerrilla force, murdering policemen and punishing in hideous ways those Irish people who defied its orders. In Clare, for example, a man peppered with three hundred shotgun pellets in his thighs, groin and lungs provided a hideous warning to those who would not obey. Lloyd George announced that he was determined to make 'a real contribution towards settling this most baffling of problems', but what he proposed was largely a rehash of the old idea of partition. This remained hateful to Nationalists. As the *Irish Times* declared: 'they know that national ideals and the ancestral spirit of a common patriotism cannot persist in a divided country. They know that the fantastic homogeneity which the government proposes for the Ulster Unionists would be an excrescence on the map of Ireland, and would be ruinous to the trade and industry of the Northern Protestants.' As the *Irish Times* continued: 'we yearn for peace, but in Mr Lloyd George's proposal we see not peace but a sword'.[3]

This was to prove all too true. By the start of 1920 fourteen Irish policemen had been killed, twenty others had been wounded, and when the forbearance of the Royal Irish Constabulary eventually snapped the police embarked on an 'orgy of violence'. Other disillusioned constables, shunning such behaviour, chose to resign. These resignations were so substantial that the authorities realised that drastic measures would have to be taken if they were still to be able to impose law and order, and by April 1920 four hundred English recruits had been gathered from men recently demobilised from the British army. The dreaded 'Black and Tans' had arrived.

II
Sato's Sword

Despite the mounting horror, Yeats was still keen to complete the renovation of Thoor Ballylee, and to pay for this he arranged another lecture tour across the United States. Pound snidely commented that he would make enough out of this 'to buy a few shingles for his phallic symbol on the Bogs. Ballyphallus or whatever he calls it with the river on the first floor.' In January 1920, having left little Anne in the care of Yeats's sisters, he and George set sail on the *Carmenia*.

George knew that she would be on display in America and she handled matters with a delightful combination of tact, kindness and resilient humour. JBY was her first challenge, and no sooner had she and Yeats settled into the Algonquin than she phoned the old man and introduced herself. In fact, JBY was quite as apprehensive as she. 'First impressions are always important,' he told Lily, and he was so worried that his shabby overcoat would reveal the poverty of his bohemian life that he spent dollars he could ill afford on having it repaired. This proved an unnecessary expense since Quinn, quietly determined that all should proceed as smoothly as possible, made sure he was provided with a 'magnificent' new coat to face both the harshness of the New York winter and the meeting with his son and daughter-in-law.

Informed by JBY that George had phoned him, Quinn went round to the Algonquin to accompany Yeats and his wife to the Petitpas' boarding house. The old man, dressed in his best clothes and a pair of dancing slippers, shook hands with his son and was introduced to George who, after a moment's hesitation, kissed him. Her searching gaze threw him for a few seconds until he realised that 'she was really wanting to find out what I thought of her'.[4] JBY was fully aware that '*liking needs time*', but he was resolved to be carefully sympathetic. Although he thought George good-looking and even capable of being 'very good-looking', his artist's eye immediately detected 'a certain *drawn* look that slightly disfigures her mouth'.* He found her frankness refreshing but felt himself obliged to be cautious, just as he thought she did. They were testing each other out, but over the course of the next weeks JBY was to come to appreciate the remarkable strengths of the woman his son had married so late in life.

If JBY was one hurdle, New York literary society was another. On 29 January the Poetry Society of America held a dinner for Yeats at the Hotel Astor. George surveyed the diamond-hung princesses of the world's greatest democracy with a degree of amusement. Scribbling in her programme, she noted that Margaret Widdener was 'a dreadful woman' and that Jessie B. Rittenhouse was 'another dreadful woman'. She had already marked out Julia Ford as 'a ghastly bore', and she was soon to discover that she was one of those most irksome of people, a collector of the great. Obliged to attend one of Mrs Ford's At Homes, George listened to her hostess going about mentioning her 'in her shrill strident voice' until she 'got sick of her own name'. She later told JBY she thought Mrs Ford's breath smelt of whisky and joked that even in those prohibition days, when men would do anything

---

* In fact, at this time or a little later, she was worrying about Anne, who had not been putting on weight. She was later reassured that all was well.

for the sake of that smell, Mrs Ford would be unable to tempt even the most desperate.

JBY relished what he called 'the salt of malice' in George, and when Yeats himself left to lecture in Toronto and Quebec, he was to come to appreciate the qualities of a daughter-in-law who would walk eighteen blocks through a snow storm to visit him. As he drew her portrait, so he learned how invaluable was this devoted woman who answered his son's telephone calls, arranged his schedules, took letters at his dictation, and saw it as her duty generally to protect him from the disagreeable. 'I like George more and more,' he confessed to Lily. 'There are no vast depths in her, but endless kindness and sympathy and I fancy a lot of practical talent.' His pencil portrait was altogether more penetrating. George sits in a gracefully alert posture, a self-confident woman, her large, intelligent eyes surveying a world at which, for all the 'drawn' quality of her mouth, she chooses to smile. More than this, her large earrings and the slightly raffish veiling of her headdress perhaps unwittingly suggest her occult powers. Here is a portrait of a daughter-in-law, a wife, a muse and a seer.*

On his return from Canada, Yeats collected George and embarked on a lecture tour that was to last until mid-April and take in a chain of cities and universities including Washington, Pittsburg, Chicago, Illinois, San Francisco, New Orleans and much of Texas. Yeats included on this tour a new lecture called 'My Own Poetry with Illustrative Readings'. This was naturally popular, partly because it concentrated mainly on his early work and 'everyone assures me that the older I grow the more unintelligible I become'. He would start with 'The Lake Isle of Innisfree' so as 'to get it over' and then recite such works as 'Cap and Bells' and 'Had I the Heavens' Embroidered Cloths'. His delivery was sometimes criticised, an expert in voice production asking 'Will you kindly tell me, Mr Yeats, why you read your poetry in that manner?' 'I read my poetry as all the great poets from Homer downwards have read their poetry,' came the reply. The lady was not to be silenced by such a rebuke. 'Will Mr Yeats give me his authority for saying that Homer read his poetry in that manner?' 'The only authority I can give you', he replied, 'is the authority that a Scotsman gave when he claimed Shakespeare for his own country, "The ability of the man justifies the assumption."' This apparently achieved the desired effect. But, despite invariably being asked, Yeats always refused to read out his more intimate lyrics. 'Under no circumstances will I read you a poem that may be taken as a personal utterance.' 'Quite right,' came a nasal woman's voice from the audience, 'I will always say that in future.'[5]

---

* What the sketch could not capture, of course, was George's colour, what Yeats described as her 'red-brown hair and a high colour which she sets off by wearing dark green in her clothes and earrings'.

But, if such was the public face of Yeats's communications, the journey round the United States was significantly to change the way in which he and George received messages from the spiritual world. George now began the series of her 'sleeps'. As Yeats later explained: 'we had one of those little sleeping compartments in a train, with two berths, and were somewhere in Southern California. My wife, who had been asleep for some minutes, began to talk in her sleep, and from that on almost all communication came in that way.'[6] Yeats then tried to explain what this implied. 'My teachers did not seem to speak out of her sleep but as if from above it, as though it were a tide upon which they floated. A chance word spoken before she fell asleep would sometimes start a dream that broke in upon the communications, as if from below, to trouble or overwhelm, as when she dreamed she was a cat lapping milk or a cat curled up asleep and therefore dumb.' Indeed, this cat, which may have been a projection of George's self-consciousness, became a considerable nuisance. 'The cat returned night after night, and once when I tried to drive it away by making the sound one makes when playing at being a dog to amuse a child, she awoke trembling, and the shock was so violent that I never dared repeat it. It was plain therefore that, though the communicators' critical powers were awake, hers slept, or that she was aware of the idea the sound suggested but not of the sound.' From now on, feline frustrators notwithstanding, George's 'sleeps' were to be an important source of spiritualist communication for Yeats and his preparation of *A Vision*.

It was Portland, Oregon, that was to prove one of the most poetically fruitful stops on their tour. Here Yeats's lecture was attended by the Japanese Consul Junzo Sato, who, already knowing his poetry, came to visit Yeats bearing a present wrapped in pale, flower-embroidered silk. 'He untied the silk cord that bound it and brought out a sword which had been for 500 years in his family. It had been made 550 years ago and he showed me the maker's name upon the hilt.' Yeats was abashed at such generosity and he sent for George hoping she might help him find some way of refusing the gift. Surely, she said, so venerable an heirloom should stay in Sato's family. With supremely practised courtesy, Sato replied: 'My family have many swords.' The gift was accepted, although Yeats later put Sato himself 'under a vow' to tell him when his first child was born so that the sword could be returned to the family under the terms of Yeats's will. Meanwhile, he had acquired a poet's fetish, something that the great and passionate had used, and whose 'moon-luminous' beauty would inspire him profoundly.

In fact, thoughts of Japan had greatly preoccupied Yeats over the preceding months. Not only had he prepared a collection of Noh-inspired drama for the press, but he had wondered about the possibility of taking a lectureship in Japan to support his wife and family. He would be living in a country which was far from the turmoil of his own and which embodied, he believed, those values of aristocratic hierarchy and refined beauty which were the prerogatives of the antithetical gyre. Slowly the idea became less appealing, although news from Ireland continued to be discouraging. Yeats wrote to Lady Gregory trying to imagine the privations that had descended on Galway, while a meeting with de Valera failed to convince him that Irish politics were in the hands of the type of Celtic hero he admired. 'I was rather disappointed,' Yeats confessed. De Valera was 'a living argument rather than a living man, all propaganda, no human life, but not bitter, or hysterical, or unjust. I judged him persistent, being both patient and energetic, but that he will fail through not having enough human life to judge the human life in others.'[7] This was a poet's assessment of a politician of consummate guile and, while perceptive, was not wholly accurate. 'He will ask too much of everyone, and will ask it without charm. He will be pushed aside by others,' Yeats declared. Time would show this to be only partly true. Meanwhile, in de Valera's absence, Ireland itself continued to hurtle towards anarchy.

During the course of 1920, 182 policemen and 50 soldiers were killed, while a further 387 people were wounded. The battle-hardened Black and Tans, set down in a country about which they knew little and cared even less, were faced day and night with open hostility and the prospect of murder at any time or place. Inevitably they turned to a brutal campaign of reprisals. While Lloyd George pursued his sterile and unpopular belief in partition, his Black and Tans murdered often innocent civilians, while the IRA began to develop into a hideously proficient guerrilla force. Violence variously spectacular and mean-minded gripped the land as the murder of such figures as the Lord Mayor of Cork alternated with the burning of those small creameries on which the livelihoods of many poor country people depended. By the middle of 1920, it was becoming clear that the rule of law in Ireland was breaking down.

The Yeatses returned to New York in mid-April, where they stayed with Quinn for the remaining weeks of their time in the United States. This was an enjoyable period and Yeats, able to domineer at Quinn's dining table, declared that he had never felt better in his life. Quinn himself now delicately raised an important topic – the issue of the ageing JBY's return to Ireland – but failed to persuade Yeats to take his father with him. Realising the immense importance of placing half a world between himself and his father, Yeats told Quinn that he could not insist on JBY's return when he had offered personally to guarantee the old man's expenses in New York. It might, he slyly declared, look as if he was merely trying to save money. In compliance with his host's insistence, however, Yeats did later suggest to his father that he might accompany him home, but the invitation was made with such diffidence that JBY managed to refuse without upsetting any of those concerned. The Yeatses then left for Montreal (crossing the Canadian border at half-past four in the morning in a successful attempt to evade a United States tax of 8 per cent on Yeats's earnings) and sailed to England. In all respects their expedition had been, as George confided to Lily, a considerable success.

III
'All Souls' Night'

Lily herself came to stay with the Yeatses in Oxford during the high summer of 1920. She and her brother had tea with Edwin Ellis's sister, who read aloud from her brother's poems, while on 16 August Lily and Yeats visited Robert Bridges at Boar's Hill and then 'walked the whole way home and were two hours over it and lost our way'. Such pleasant idling was interrupted, however, when a message arrived from Maud Gonne MacBride summoning Yeats to Ireland. Iseult was in trouble.

After an affair with Ezra Pound, Iseult had been pursued by a handsome, hypersensitive and inexperienced boy of seventeen who would later make his name as the novelist Francis Stuart. Yeats's poems had provided the vocabulary of their courtship, and the nearness of both Iseult and her mother to the poet encouraged Stuart to believe he might be able to enter the Yeats circle, for all that the women's repeated disparagement of 'poor Willie' was irksome to him. Iseult herself rightly perceived that their relationship could only be a passing one, and she told Stuart that she was 'the willow rooted on the riverbank and you're the black swan gliding past'.[8] To the temperamental difficulties caused by the frequent collisions of these two over-wrought people, however, was added the further problem that Stuart and Iseult's mother loathed each other. Maud believed that Stuart was a wholly unsuitable figure for her daughter to interest herself in, while Stuart found his future mother-in-law's rigid political views absurd. The young couple conducted their courtship in the greatest secrecy, but Maud inevitably impinged, breaking into the flat Stuart had rented from Lennox Robinson for example and shrieking at him 'like a fishwife'. Yeats already knew something about these problems and had even suggested that Iseult marry Robinson, who, despite being homosexual, had fallen in love with her, proposed and been turned down.

In such circumstances, Iseult and Stuart decided to elope to London. Terrified of the sexual implications of what he had done, however, Stuart spent much of their first night alone in a café where he mulled over the to him horrible fact that Iseult not only had slept with Ezra Pound but in childhood had had to fend off the advances of her step-father. After three months it was clear that the relationship was failing, but the pressure from Maud was such that, despite her continuing disapproval of Stuart, she considered a marriage necessary for her now compromised daughter. The ceremony took place a few weeks before Stuart's eighteenth birthday, and on 13 April 1920 Lady Gregory confided to her diary that she saw in it 'nothing but disaster – the boy's father having died in a mad house'.

Settled in the remote and inaccessible house at Glenmalure which had featured in Synge's *The Shadow of the Glen*, and which Maud herself had purchased with money raised by selling her home in France, Iseult's marriage rapidly moved towards disaster. Stuart in particular could not cope with the pressure he was under and one afternoon ran into the glen where, with tears streaming down his face, he set fire to the gorse bushes while jumping from rock to rock so clumsily that he stumbled and dislocated his knee. Soon afterwards, Iseult informed him she was pregnant. Rows and reconciliations followed until Maud called on a reluctant Yeats to intervene. As he told Lady Gregory, he could not 'go into the details now but you can imagine with what a heavy heart I am setting out'.

He went straight to Glenmalure, where, with Maud and Iseult, it was decided that the young mother should spend some days in a nursing home. Perhaps giving more credit to Maud's fevered imagination than he should, Yeats then wrote to Lady Gregory telling her how Iseult 'has been starved, kept without sleep and several times knocked down by her husband who is mad'. He went on to detail how Stuart had failed to provide Iseult with any money, how he kept her on what were virtually starvation rations, and how he had obliged her to pay the rent for the house. Yeats himself was exasperated by Iseult's tendency to 'defend her husband through all and minimise all his wrongs', and even came to see Stuart himself as a sadist, a judgement he later retracted. Iseult responded by saying that 'if he is mad he but needs me the more . . . what good was I doing with my life? I may as well spend it this way.' Besides, Stuart had 'charm and certain gifts of poetical fantasy'.

Yeats wondered if a stay in Oxford might enable him to help the young man develop his literary plans but meanwhile more drastic action would have to be taken to save the marriage. Stuart would have to pay Iseult a reasonable settlement and be made to understand that she would leave him for ever at the first signs of another scene. It was then agreed that the young husband should be allowed merely one visit to the nursing home, where he was to avoid all painful subjects and consent 'to such settlements as will save Iseult and her child from starvation'. To make assurance double sure, Iseult was frightened into believing that if she allowed Stuart to continue behaving in the way he had then her child might die. Eventually, a measure of paper reconciliation was achieved, although the couple remained largely apart until they met again in Dublin, determined to try and rebuild their relationship.

During this troubled period at Glenmalure, Yeats was also composing, a fact made clear to Cecil Salkeld one morning when Maud said to him: 'Willie is booming and buzzing like a bumble bee . . . that means he is writing something.'[9] A preoccupied Yeats then appeared and, asking Salkeld to accompany him for a walk up the glen, proceeded to thread his way around the rocks while murmuring under his breath. Suddenly he stopped short and said: 'Do you realise that eternity is not a long time but a *short* time. . . ?' Salkeld said he did not understand, and Yeats continued: 'Eternity is the glitter on the beetle's wing.' Salkeld said he could well envisage infinity in such a way. 'Yes,' Yeats said, adding with apparently complete irrelevance, 'I was thinking of those Ephesian topers . . .'* He then showed Salkeld a tiny piece of paper 'on which he had written 8 lines which had been perhaps ten times corrected'. All the young artist could make out was an obsession with the phrase 'Mummy wheat', but Yeats's mention of the Ephesian topers inspired Salkeld to make a watercolour of them that evening which he showed to Yeats the following day. Yeats's composure that night suggested that his poem was now complete and, when he and Salkeld were on their own, he brought out a pigskin-covered brandy flask and 'a beautifully written manuscript'. He then told Salkeld: 'Your picture made the thing clear,' and added that he was going to dedicate the poem to him and call it 'The Black Centaur'. Salkeld was 'impressed and gratified. But when printed in 1928, in *The Tower*, the poem was altered; it was corrected and it was entitled: "On a Picture of a Black Centaur by Edmund Dulac"'.

Iseult herself eventually told Yeats that she would meet him in Dublin, where he was due to have his tonsils removed by Oliver St John Gogarty, an operation performed with the surgeon's 'usual exuberant gaiety', despite a haemorrhage and talk of dying speeches. As Yeats recovered, it seemed for a while at least that Iseult's marriage had been saved, but the letter Yeats wrote to her giving his interpretation of the situation provides a vivid example of the sort of conversation now to be expected from a convinced occultist. Yeats believed that the people around him were going through one of their astrologically inspired 'initiatory moments'. He told Iseult that he had 'looked up your dates' and went on to confirm that:

> when you accepted Francis, Venus and Saturn were in conjunction and when you decided to go to the Nursing Home Venus and Neptune were in conjunction. This should mean that the worst is over and as the object of all such moments is to compel a too subjective nature into objective action and in the case of your phase into action implying practical expediency and prudence . . . it gives you some guidance also. To you it may mean the start of a new and stronger life.

Unfortunately, it did not.

---

* Yeats was probably rejecting an idea of eternity as duration for seeing it as a Blakeian intensity. He had compared himself to the Ephesians at the start of the Great War, see p. 439.

The agonies and disasters befalling Yeats's friends were mirrored in the public life of Ireland as a whole, and Maud was privy to both. Dressed in the dramatic mourning gowns she designed for herself, she was accused by many of capitalising on her status as the widow of a Martyr, but she ignored opprobrium as always and threw herself into the relief of Irish suffering. She suggested to Arthur Griffith that the women of the country band together to help victims of atrocities. She organised the feeding of starving schoolchildren and the provision of employment for their parents where industries had been destroyed. She learned how a drunken English soldiery had wrecked the school founded by Pearse, and, when the two children of Pearse's friend MacDonagh were left orphans, Maud helped to look after them. On 21 November, after the police had opened fire on a crowd gathered to watch a football game and Tommy Whelan had been arrested for complicity in the disturbance, Maud stood with his mother outside Mountjoy prison as the youngster was hanged.

Her own son's life was in constant danger too. On 26 September, when Sean was driving Constance Markiewicz and a French writer through Dublin, the police stopped the car and, recognising Constance, arrested all three passengers. Sean was soon released, but Constance was tried and sentenced to two years' hard labour. Sean himself, at a mere sixteen, had already been appointed leader of an IRA squad. This was no honorary position given to him because of his father. While hiding Ernie O'Mally in Lennox Robinson's flat and watching the 'steel plated lancias and armoured cars with swinging turrets' roll through the streets, Sean was taught how to use an automatic rifle. Even men lying wounded in hospital were now being rounded up by the British and, fearful that one of his own gunmen whose leg had recently been amputated might be treated in this barbarous way, Sean led a raid on Mercer's Hospital, held up the medical staff, carried his comrade to a car and drove him to the safety of a private house. 'The English may batter us to pieces but they will never succeed in breaking our spirit,' wrote Maud.[10] Her sorrows deepened, however, when Iseult's baby died of spinal meningitis three months after its birth. She was plagued with insomnia, while her anguished nights were further disturbed by the endless sound of shooting and the all-pervasive threat of sudden death.

Other deaths were altogether less random. On 31 October 1920 Terence MacSwiney, the Republican Lord Mayor of Cork, who had replaced the murdered Thomas MacCurtin, died in Brixton prison after a hunger strike lasting seventy-four days. Yeats inevitably recalled his own bard Seanchan starving himself in his play *On the King's Threshold* and resolved now to make a decisive revision to the work. 'I shall give it the tragic end it has always needed and make some other changes. Events this autumn may make it very appropriate.' The audience who saw the play presented in its revised form at the Abbey in November 1921 could not fail to have been reminded of MacSwiney when, at the end of the work, the Oldest Pupil describes Seanchan's death:

> some strange triumphant thought
> So filled his heart with joy that it has burst,
> Being grown too mighty for our frailty,
> And we who gaze grow like him and abhor
> The moments that come between us and that death
> You promised us.[11]

For all Yeats's current disillusion with the theatre, the Abbey itself remained what he always wanted it to be, the active centre of a high poetic Irish nationalism.

Yeats's summer absence during 1920 had nonetheless placed a great strain on George. She herself had come down firmly on Iseult's side in the marital dispute, but in her husband's absence the presence of Lily in the Oxford house became so aggravating that she was obliged to pretend she was going to the Bodleian to read when, given that her eyes were sore, she was really going there to be on her own. She was, besides, anxious about her new state of pregnancy and the fact that her astrological aspects were negative. A letter from Yeats made her cry with relief, but there are hints in the automatic script that the Yeatses' sex life at this time was not free from intimate and painful difficulties. In particular, Yeats had for a year now been harbouring doubts about his virility, doubts which in time would become obsessive.

At a session of automatic writing on 31 July 1919, the control told him that he was 'unaccustomed for some time to twice – therefore *gradually* try twice as always once will increase fatigue'.[12] Yeats was puzzled and concerned as to why this should be and was told 'because you cease to be able to do more – it is like not taking enough exercise and a long walk exhausts you'. George was concerned gently to reassure her husband, and wrote out, 'you must accustom yourself to gradually declining power and rest assured your power will always be amply sufficient'. Yeats himself suggested that they should make love twice a month, but even his sex life it seems was to be regulated by the stars. George resisted Yeats's somewhat mechanical suggestion of fortnightly intercourse and felt inspired to write that it should take place only when the 'configurations' the control had told them about had occurred, 'and *never* more than once for every three times of *once*'. Yeats was being gently persuaded away from a nervous and domineering assertion of his masculinity that had its roots in a fear of impotence. But at other times he needed reminding that George too had legitimate demands to place on their lovemaking. 'Both the desire of the medium and her desire for your desire should be satisfied – that is to say her desire and you as the image of her desire must be kept identical.'

It was not just the intimacies of the bedroom that were a concern to George, however. She may have guessed at this time (and certainly came to know later) that the comparatively elderly father often found a spontaneous and generous paternal feeling difficult to express. While Yeats treasured fantasies of fatherhood prolonging his life, and even imagined himself living to 1970 or the millennium, the state of childhood itself could move him to blank indifference. He could be amused when George tried to teach Anne the Lord's Prayer and she made 'such interjections as "Father not in heaven – father in the study"', but when he returned to Oxford after his tonsillectomy he found himself looking out of the window and, watching Anne in her perambulator, wondering which was more boring, convalescence or infancy. Eventually he was reduced to asking George to tell the little girl how much he loved her provided she was old enough to understand.* More tragically, George's current pregnancy was terminated by a miscarriage that August.

While revolving these dismal thoughts, his father's problems also weighed on Yeats's mind. Despite earning a $400 fee for a portrait, JBY's debts to the Petitpas were mounting beyond the limits of his funds, while, on 26 July 1920, the sisters sold their boarding house, the two eldest ones returning to France with a handsome profit. A bewildered JBY resolved to go home to Ireland, and Quinn was keen to encourage him. He wrote to Yeats that the old man would be unable to 'stand another winter in New York' and had besides only $71.18 in his account. Believing that JBY would indeed return to Dublin if he were found 'a comfortable room, with fairly good light and heat', Quinn told Yeats that such a life 'would be heaven in comparison with the dingy, ill-lighted and often unheated and cold room that he has two flights up in the rear'.

An enfeebled Yeats telegraphed Quinn that he agreed to all that the lawyer said, but Quinn himself replied irritably that the idea of JBY's return to Dublin 'must come from you and must be based upon the reasons and promises suggested in my letter'. Yeats dutifully dictated a letter to George in which he told his father that 'when you return to Dublin I shall see to it that you have a studio. I think Lily has written to you about this. It may possibly be at the Arts Club but one cannot settle details yet. I am quite clear in my mind that you ought to return.' JBY's reply to this has been lost, but when Yeats wrote again he told his father that he realised the old man had 'no present intention of returning'. Yeats himself was far from willing to force the issue, telling him that 'it is for you to decide. I can say no more.' But he then went on to utter the threat that he might have to organise another lecture tour in the United States if the old man ran out of money. This was a blunder, since it appeared to hold out to JBY

---

* Yeats appears as an often remote but never an unkindly father. He did not, for example, believe in corporal punishment and he would play games, especially croquet, with both his children. As Anne Yeats commented: 'He was rather awe-inspiring, I think, on the whole. You always had to stay rather quiet.' Both children went on to pursue successful careers.

the possibility, however remote, of his continued stay in New York being financed.

If such decisions could for the moment be postponed, Oxford provided Yeats with a vivid and satisfying social life. John Masefield and Robert Bridges lived on Boar's Hill. Yeats became friendly with Percy Simpson and the luminously gifted and gregarious Maurice Bowra, then an undergraduate, while he also held Monday At Homes in 4 Broad Street which were open to students. A shy man himself, Yeats could be sensitive to younger people and was perceptive in his encouragement of their abilities. These occasions could be alarming, nonetheless. Both Yeats and George conspired in asking their guests questions designed to relate their personalities to the twenty-eight phases of the moon. When each was satisfied that the unsuspecting victim had been accurately assessed, they would then mumble a number to each other, seldom disagreeing about the balance of lunar and solar elements they had detected. Yeats was also prone to monologuing, and when a cousin of George's, an undergraduate at St Hugh's, presumed to ask a question at the close of one of these performances, she was not invited back and George had to meet her secretly at a tea room in the city.

Other undergraduates were more fortunate. L. A. G. Strong, for instance, tactlessly asking what qualities in George Moore's writing made 'one read on eagerly', was told: 'I never did read on, so I don't know.'[13] Strong blushed, Yeats proceeded to soften the blow and eventually asked the young man regularly to attend his 'Mondays'. These occasions left a permanent impression, Strong recalling that 'I seldom left the house till midnight or after, and would walk up the Banbury Road to the school where I was teaching, exhilarated, walking on air, upheld and inspired by the knowledge, which rapidly became incredible during the week, that life could be lived on such a plane of thought and at such a pitch.' The tone was not always so exalted, however. Yeats, who willingly dined with undergraduates at their tables in hall, could vary high discourse with Rabelaisian anecdotes, while the occult frequently made its presence felt, a smell of incense suffusing the rooms once when India was under discussion. On another occasion Yeats told the story of an Oxford house where he had been investigating 'phenomena' but, as he described them, he became rigid, his veins swelled and his jaw so stiffened that he could barely speak and then only wild words. 'They are trying to stop me,' he said. On another occasion he took such advice. He was strolling with his friend Sturm when both men heard a shrill whistling. Sturm said it came from some passing boy, but Yeats refused so simple an explanation. 'Not at all, Sturm,' he said, 'not at all. I was just on the point of revealing to you a magical formula which would enable you to remember your past incarnations, when your daimon gave that whistle to warn me not to do so. It would be dangerous for you to know.'

The most vibrant intellectual and social life, however, was not to be found in Oxford itself but at the nearby home of Lady Ottoline Morrell in Garsington.[14] Although the friendship between Yeats and Lady Ottoline was to end in bitterness, it was for many years something each was to value greatly. Ireland was a particular bond. Ottoline first visited her mother's country in September 1919. It made a lasting impression on her, awakening sensibilities of which she had previously been only half aware. The Irish too warmed to this tall and grandly eccentric woman with her outlandish clothes and warm human interest in all about her. With introductions provided by Desmond MacCarthy, she met such figures as George Russell, Maud Gonne MacBride and James Stephens, but it was Yeats who became one of her closest Irish friends. He was, she said, 'such a relief to me after these dry English'. Both were formidable conversationalists and 'we talked by the hour and I enjoyed him enormously'. Nor was Ottoline's interest in Ireland solely literary. She found she was deeply stirred by the Nationalist cause and even attended Sinn Fein meetings in London escorted by Bertrand Russell.

Such interests ensured Yeats a leading place among the gathering of geniuses at Ottoline's beautiful, time-worn seventeenth-century Oxfordshire house. Garsington Manor became something like an English Coole, and contemporary photographs show a tall and elegantly suited Yeats wholly in sympathy with the panelled rooms, their antique dignity offset by the Morrells' collection of the finest contemporary British art. The marvellous Italianate garden would also become an inspiration, a complete contrast to the violence-menaced Ireland hostess and poet both cared so greatly about.

But Garsington was above all the meeting-ground of genius. Remote from her neurotic and demanding husband, Ottoline made the house a place where the most promising and ambitious undergraduates of their day could meet the lions of English intellectual society: Eliot, Woolf, Russell, John, Yeats and a score of others. As David Cecil recalled, 'the lions were there all right – Yeats, Sassoon, and the rest – but they were not on show, not caged. Rather I saw them in their natural haunt, relaxed, unobserved, at play; or, if they wanted to work, free to go and do so.' Joseph Hone described how returning undergraduates would take a bus to Oxford from nearby Cowley and remembered how one evening Yeats and Ottoline led the party: 'Yeats tall and stately, gesticulating, his hair ruffled in the wind, and Lady Ottoline, in period lilac silk, large picture-hat and shoes with high red heels, listening to him and nodding, her long face alight with animation. They looked like beings from some pageant outside time.' For some, however, such proximity with the great was overwhelming, and Ottoline, who for all her generosity of spirit had a patrician regard for good manners, was intensely annoyed when a young Eddie Sackville-West was placed beside Yeats at dinner and never said a word to him.

Yeats himself was sufficiently close to Ottoline to be one of the few to whom she confided the great secret of her life: her affair with the local builder and odd-job man Lionel Gomme, familiarly known as 'Tiger'. This was a relationship which briefly brought Ottoline deep emotional and sexual satisfaction along with lasting tragedy. Ottoline was one day summoned from London by a telegram informing her that Tiger, always a highly strung young man, was seriously ill. She arrived back at Garsington to find him lying in the stable yard unconscious after a second brain haemorrhage. Half an hour later he died in her arms. In the desolation of her grief she turned to Yeats and George, and, to the dismay of many of her other friends, took to tarot readings and seances. 'I feel Tiger's spirit all the time with me,' she wrote.

But Yeats had his own dead to summon. In November 1920, he completed 'All Souls' Night', later printed as the epilogue to *A Vision*, the great poem in which he evoked the spirits of his erstwhile occult friends, Horton, Florence Farr and MacGregor Mathers.

The pain and eccentricity in the lives of those seeking occult exaltation become one focus of Yeats's concern in this invocation, thereby enhancing his suggestion of the world all three of his central figures had hoped to transcend. Horton, living on the perilous edge of platonic desire where the erotic and the divine become confused, is shown yearning for death. Florence Farr had tackled a comparable theme in her novel *The Solemnisation of Jacklin*, which contains a partial portrait of Yeats as the troubled Dorus alchemically awakened to his highest awareness by Susanna's chaste but ecstatic 'kiss of peace'. A short while after completing this work, Florence herself left England for Ceylon, where she became principal of the country's first girls' school. She gave Yeats her psaltery as a parting gift. Yeats somewhat uncharitably portrayed Florence in the poem as fleeing abroad to hide from her friends the humiliating signs of ageing. He also payed tribute, however, to her continuing mystical research in a stanza which seems to fuse Florence's speculations with the actual fate of her soul itself after her death from breast cancer in April 1917:

> Before that end much had she ravelled out
> From a discourse in figurative speech
> By some learned Indian
> On the soul's journey. How it is whirled about
> Wherever the orbit of the moon can reach,
> Until it plunge into the sun;
> And there, free and yet fast,
> Being both Chance and Choice,
> Forget its broken toys
> And sink into its own delight at last.[15]

An invocation to MacGregor Mathers was altogether more problematic. Yeats admitted openly to his erstwhile master's arrogance, his lack of balance, his charlatanism. Although this is partly softened by his mentioning spontaneous memories of the 'generous things' Mathers did, even in his ghostly form Mathers is a perturbing spirit. Moina Mathers, who was left after his death to live in considerable poverty, objected to such a portrayal of her husband (she particularly disliked the portrait of Mathers in Yeats's autobiographical reminiscences) and wrote to tell him that Mathers was only for one brief, three-month period seriously disturbed, and that was during the world war when Yeats himself was barely in contact with him. 'But this illness in no way ever interfered with his superb mental work,' Moina insisted, 'which revealed its height on the day of his death in 1918.' For the purposes of posterity, however, Yeats chose to portray Mathers as being as potentially fractious in his ghostly life as in his fleshly one. By so doing, he managed to juxtapose the turbulence of the occult to its longing for the disembodied in a way that powerfully suggests the menace he frequently recognised as lurking near the heart of the supernatural.

IV
'Herodias' Daughters'

While 'All Souls' Night' is partly imbrued with the sinister and with an existence 'where the damned have howled away their hearts', the ever present tragedy of Ireland revealed a nation rapidly becoming a hell on earth. The Government of Ireland Bill was effectively a dead letter as far as solving the country's problems was concerned, and many parts of the land had now descended into wholesale lawlessness. British strong-arm policies worsened the bitterness, and the *Galway Express* wrote of the disgraceful behaviour of the Black and Tans that: 'when they throw petrol on a Sinn Feiner's house, they are merely pouring paraffin on the flames of Irish nationality'. In these circumstances, Irish reprisals began to gather about them an aura of moral justification, and, for all Winston Churchill's defiant threats that 'we are going to break up this murder gang', it was precisely the barbarity of the struggle which consolidated national feeling.

Through the last quarter of 1920 and into the spring of the following year, Black and Tans were recruited at the rate of nearly a thousand a month. Between January and July 1921, four hundred Crown agents were killed and seven hundred were wounded, while the same period saw the death of 707 civilians and the wounding of 756 more. What these numbing statistics meant in human terms was poignantly evoked in Lady Gregory's journals. Honing her ear for dialect even in the midst of a national tragedy, she wrote on 20 March 1921 how she had met Old Niland, who told her:

> Bartley Hynes that was living up the road from Kinvera to Galway had his house burned, and the furniture and the hay and corn, by the Black-and-Tans. And there is a woman, an O'Donnell, over there in Peterswell, and she having but the one son, and they pulled him out of the bed and brought him abroad in the street and shot him, and they brought her out that she'd see him shot. And she took the son in her arms and he died in her arms. About twelve days ago that happened. They didn't give no reason at all for what they had done.[16]

The dismay and incomprehension in this account were the experience of thousands across the country.

Lady Gregory herself was so angered and so moved that between October 1920 and January 1921 she wrote a series of anonymous articles for the *Nation* detailing the atrocities. These articles were a significant contribution to the Nationalist propaganda effort, while her description in 'Murder by the Throat' of the shooting of the pregnant mother of three children as she stood by the gate of her house nursing her baby so horrified Yeats that he would soon work it into his poetry. Lady Gregory had reservations about the way in which Yeats expressed his nationalism at this period, however. In particular, he had drafted a poem called 'Reprisals' which, reversing the political neutrality of 'An Irish Airman Foresees his Death', urges the ghost of Robert Gregory to return to Ireland and play his part in the struggle against the terrorism inflicted by a 'half-drunk or whole-mad soldiery'. His mother found this distasteful. 'I cannot bear the dragging of Robert from his grave to make what I think not a very sincere poem – for Yeats knows only by hearsay while our troubles go on . . . I hardly know why it gives me extraordinary pain, and it seems too late to stop it.' In fact, she did prevent the work's publication, and on the envelope in which she filed the carbon copy of the poem Yeats sent her she wrote: 'I did not like this and asked not to have it published.' Although Yeats himself was satisfied with the work, he complied with Lady Gregory's request, and 'Reprisals' was not finally published until after the deaths of both of them.[17]

Yeats was nonetheless determined to muster such influence as he could and was somewhat surprised by the extent of this. He wrote to erstwhile Prime Minister Asquith, possibly suggesting Dominion status for Ireland, and requesting an interview. He told Lady Gregory that, to his amazement, Asquith himself 'came to see me – this was some days before he wrote to *The Times* – and stayed some time talking of Ireland to George and myself. As I do not know where this letter will go I will not say what was said. He said of my suggestion, "I will bear it in mind, Mr Yeats," but I don't suppose he will act on it now.' Certainly, the suggestion of Dominion status for Ireland was soon to be placed on the political agenda. Meanwhile, to make clear his anti-British feelings, Yeats refused to write a tribute for those Englishmen who had served in the British army because it would lack sincerity. While he could indeed honour those like Robert Gregory who had fought and died in Italy or France, the ever swelling ranks of violent Black and Tans recruited among British ex-servicemen were a force he could look on only with disgust.

The degree of Yeats's anger was made public when he was invited to speak at the Oxford Union on the motion 'That This House Would Welcome Complete Self-Government in Ireland and Condemns Reprisals'.[18] Both the house and the gallery of the Union were crowded for a debate that kindled more passion than any since the end of the war. Yeats himself reportedly strode up and down the aisles waving his arms and shaking his fists as he told his audience 'that not law, only English law, has broken down in Ireland. Sinn Fein brought real justice into his part of Ireland for the first time for centuries. The only complaint was that they protected property perhaps a little too vigorously.' The *Freeman's Journal* noted the tremendous applause that arose when Yeats suggested an independent inquiry be set up, but more daring still was his use of some of Lady Gregory's stories of barbarity with which he condemned the English, saying that they had done in Ireland what Germany had done in Belgium. Such comments were highly inflammatory, but more courageous yet was Yeats's publication in the same month of *Michael Robartes and the Dancer* with its outspoken poems on the influence of the Martyrs of the Easter Uprising. In such ways, no one was left in any doubt about where Yeats's sympathies lay.

It seemed unwise for him actually to return to Ireland with his baby daughter and newly pregnant wife, however, despite George's evident enthusiasm for doing so. 'I had proposed Oxford as a place to live in because I thought it unfair to George to live wholly in Ireland,' he told Lady Gregory, but: 'I now find she would have preferred Ireland from the start.' The restoration of Thoor Ballylee was proceeding slowly, however, while the money Yeats had set aside from his United States lecture tour for his Irish projects was being rapidly eaten into by the expense of living in the centre of Oxford. In April 1921, he and his family moved to Minchin's Cottage in nearby Shillingford, hoping they would make 'a pot of money' out of letting Broad Street, and from there to Cuttlebrook House in Thame.

Here they lived constantly surrounded by phenomena. Warm breath seemed to come up from the ground at a particular corner of the road. Once, when Yeats was about to tell George a story of a Russian mystic, forgetting that it might make her misunderstand an event in her own life, 'a sudden flash of light fell between us and a chair or table was violently struck'. Whistling sounds told of the presence of the communicators, who were about to give revelations through George's 'sleeps', and these came so frequently that the servants complained and Yeats had to ask his spiritual advisers to choose some other sign. But sweet smells were the most constant phenomena: 'now that of incense, now that of violets or roses or some other flower, and as perceptible to some half-dozen of our friends as to ourselves, though on one occasion when my wife smelt hyacinth a friend smelt eau-de-cologne'.

It was here in August, his arrival greeted by a smell of roses filling the house, that George gave birth to the son the Yeatses were to call Michael. John Quinn and Lennox Robinson were asked to be godfathers, and while both mother and child were well (the doctor commenting that the boy had a beautifully shaped head) Yeats's laboured jocularity reveals once again that distressing element of coldness sometimes to be seen in his attitude to his children. 'All I can say', he wrote, 'is that he is better looking than a new-born canary (I had four hatch out in my bed-room a little while ago) and nothing like as good-looking as the same bird when it gets its first feathers.' The 'Prayer' Yeats wrote to celebrate Michael's birth has little of the stature of the poem he had written to celebrate the birth of Anne, but 'Nineteen Hundred and Nineteen' horri-fyingly portrays the violent world into which both his children had been born.

Yeats wrote of the poems which make up this sequence that they 'are not philosophical but simple and passionate, a lamentation over lost peace and lost hope. My own philosophy does not make brighter the pros-pect'. The modesty here is slightly disingenuous even if the pessimism is not, for what the poems offer, in a recondite and allusive manner that recalls other supreme works of these years – *The Waste Land* among them – is a view of the destruction of European civilisation in which agonised images and fractured form are at one with their terrible sub-ject. 'Nineteen Hundred and Nineteen' is Yeats's wider exploration of themes broached in 'The Second Coming': anarchy and the violent destruc-tion of culture, innocence and decorum in a world lusting for degrada-tion.

Only the black arts can survive in such a time, and Yeats takes the widest historical perspective to place his view. Just as the loss of Phidias' gigantic statue to the goddess of wisdom in the Parthenon stands for the destruction of Periclean Athens in the Peloponnesian War, so the horrors in Ireland underline what Yeats, in his role as the Thucydides of the contemporary world, reveals as the complacency burrowing under the high Edwardian afternoon of the Pax Britannica. Multiplying horrors have exposed the falseness of this world, the failure of its apparently matchless justice, the erroneous belief that its armies were marshalled for show, and the facile optimism of its faith in progress and its ignorance of 'that most momentous of events, the return of evil'. One death in Ireland reveals the lie:

> Now days are dragon-ridden, the nightmare
> Rides upon sleep: a drunken soldiery
> Can leave the mother, murdered at her door,
> To crawl in her own blood, and go scot-free . . .[19]

So much for justice, parade-ground armies and progress, but Yeats's answer is less anger than despair, the recognition by a profound mind that in such a world as this there is no adequate syntax for outrage, no hieratic form for nightmare. The strict decorum of the first section breaks under the strain as Yeats produces for his readers a troop of Chinese dancers whose airborne dragons of whirling silk replicate the 'dragon-ridden' days of the first section and so make art itself a terrible intimation of a world hurrying towards evil. The glories of nature and the spirit also depart (the swan, in Yeats's image, 'has leaped into the desolate heaven') leaving the poet with disillusion and impotent anger which, exposing the falsity of his erstwhile hopes, reduces him first to the perverse and self-delighting baseness of 'the weasel's tail, the weasel's tooth', and then to the merest cynicism.

There follows the last and most terrible section, the final recognition that in such a world as this Yeats's lifelong aim of forging a unity between nationalism, the occult and poetry results not in exultation but in an art that is forced to describe a specifically Irish witches' sabbath of the black magic and sexual squalor. The little boy in Sligo who once sensed a living world of spirits when he watched a peasant lift his cap as the Sidhe swept by in a swirl of leaves has here become the ageing man imagining that the breeze is a whirlwind propelled across his entire country by the lascivious dancing of evil powers. 'Herodias' daughters have returned again.' In their wake come the basest figures: the medieval Kilkenny devil worshipper Robert Artesson, the arrogant and stupid object of the witch Lady Kyteler's lust. Their fornication is a sort of cultural black mass, and it is a measure of Yeats's achievement that he had the courage to force his art to face this nadir of national and occult depravity.

In addition to analysing the violent present, Yeats was also proceeding with his autobiographical works, in particular 'Four Years', which was to form the first book of *The Trembling of the Veil*. He was examining, in other words, the period between 1887 and 1891 when, as a very young man, he set out to meet the luminaries of literary and occult London: Henley, Wilde, Morris, Madame Blavatsky and MacGregor Mathers among others. Here can be seen the formation of Yeats's ideas of the mask and the antithetical man, along with their application to the characters he was describing. 'My mind began drifting vaguely towards that doctrine of "the Mask" which has convinced me that every passionate man (I have nothing to do with the mechanist, or philanthropist, or the man whose eyes have no preference) is, as it were, linked with another age, historical or imaginary, where alone he finds images that rouse his energy.' But, despite its success as a means of characterisation, not all of the observation in 'Four Years' was either accurate or kind.

Werner Laurie had offered Yeats an advance of £500 for the right to issue the work in a privately printed edition, and Yeats was resolved to set this money aside to pay JBY's bills and finance what increasingly appeared to be his necessary return to Ireland. JBY himself had previously been upset about family secrets being openly displayed in his son's autobiographical writings, but now, when he read Yeats's description of how he had returned to his 'enraged family' from Oxford, where he had been copying rare editions, he was hurt by the slight and resolved to take his son to task. He wrote to him vividly describing the family hardships at that time, but, finding this insufficient to purge his anger, returned to the subject the following day, complaining that the phrase 'enraged family' was merely a 'chimera of the imagination' which his son had put in to heighten the dramatic effect of his writing. He shrewdly guessed that the phrase would 'delight all his young lady friends in America and elsewhere and will please Lady Gregory and evoke that smile'. Indeed, Lady Gregory became a particular butt of JBY's anger since he felt he could blame her for what he considered the fundamental faults in Yeats's entire approach to literature. 'Had you stayed with me and not left me for Lady Gregory and her friends and associations you would have loved and adored concrete life for which as I know you have a real affection. What would have resulted? Realistic and poetical plays, and poetry in closest and most intimate union with the positive realities and complexities of life. And that is the world that waits, so far in vain, its poet.'[20]

This was a stinging rebuke and roused Yeats's defences of haughtiness and disdain. When he returned the proofs to Lollie for the Cuala Press edition he told her that she might change the word 'enraged' to 'troubled' provided this could be easily done, and a cruel family slight was made crueller by being thus diminished to the status of a mere question of book production. However, underlying the resentment on both sides lay the vexed matter of JBY's return to Ireland. The insistence of Quinn and his own son that he return home caused JBY to look at both men with embittered suspicion. There were some grounds for this since Yeats had sent Quinn a 'stern letter' and asked the lawyer to book an autumn passage for the old man. JBY himself prevaricated and talked of returning when his never to be completed self-portrait was finished, but Quinn himself, pressured, over-worked and by now thoroughly bored with JBY's failure to finish his masterpiece, placed a deposit for the ticket with the offices of the Cunard Line. So threatened did JBY now feel that he fell ill and vehemently told Quinn that his sickness was entirely due to the nervous exhaustion inflicted on him by the manipulation of others.

Yeats himself, embarrassed, angry and realising that he was involved in a situation he would probably fail to resolve, wrote bitter letters about his father to Quinn. All his youthful resentment, stirred no doubt by memories brought to the surface by the writing of his memoirs, boiled over in missives to the United States. 'It is this infirmity of will which has prevented him from finishing his pictures and ruined his career. He even hates the sign of will in others. It used to cause quarrels between him and me, for the qualities I thought necessary to success in art or in life seemed to him "egotism" or "selfishness" or "brutality".' This flow of sour correspondence continued while the old man himself remained intransigent. He ran through a gamut of excuses for staying in the United States and eventually declared boldly: 'I will not leave America.' Quinn, realising that he had lost, reclaimed his deposit from the Cunard shipping offices and wrote with exasperation to Yeats that 'it was not infirmity of will that made his decision this time. It was strength of will, sheer stubbornness,' that and the fact that JBY almost certainly realised he was dying.

Partly to escape from the bitterness caused by those on whom he was most dependent, and partly perhaps to convince himself that there was life in him yet, JBY threw himself into a hectic last round of social activity and portrait drawing. But Dolly Sloan managed to convince him to see a doctor, who pronounced the old man to be suffering from 'a tired heart'. He was now in great pain and breathing only with difficulty. A morphine injection allowed him to sleep for an hour, and when he woke he found his friend Mrs Foster and Quinn at his bedside. 'I thought I was in hell,' he muttered, 'and I awakened to find myself in heaven and you are all here with me.' The doctor whom Quinn insisted attend the patient found weakness of the lungs as well as of the heart, and prescribed camphor and morphine. JBY lingered for several days, still conversing brilliantly, and Quinn was to write that 'his brain was clear to the end'.

That end was, however, lonely and sad. Early on the morning of 3 February 1922, his last moments had come. The only person present was the nurse, who wrote that 'he woke up and tossed restlessly back and forth for a few minutes. As his pulse was very weak I was just about to give him some heart stimulant (which he had had several times during the night) when he suddenly turned over on his right side, closed his eyes and went into his last eternal sleep. It was then 6.50 a.m.' As Yeats wrote to Lily: 'he has died as the Antarctic explorers died in the midst of his work and the middle of his thought, convinced that he was about to paint as never before'. Beside the corpse lying in the squalid New York room stood the unfinished self-portrait of John Butler Yeats, the most poignant testimony to the life he had lived.

The position in the Ireland to which JBY had so successfully avoided returning had meanwhile reached another crisis. At the close of 1920, de Valera returned from America to an embittered and disillusioned country where it was clear that the forces of the British Crown were now involved in a losing battle. The ghastly round of killings was continuing, and early in the following year martial law was extended across many counties along with nationwide powers for internment without trial. By the close of January 1921, 1463 civilians were in camps where they were given prisoner-of-war treatment without prisoner-of-war status. The sheer ruthless persistence of the IRA had begun to suggest that a negotiated peace was the only certain way of ending the conflict, and, as a first sign of concession, the cabinet decreed that the newly returned de Valera was not to be arrested unless indisputably involved in criminal activities. It was the May elections, however, that were central to the subsequent moves towards a truce and negotiations.

The elections were held under the terms of Lloyd George's 1920 Government of Ireland Act. This had laid down that North-east Ulster was to be given its own Home Rule legislature, subordinate to Westminster, while a separate Southern parliament was also to be created. When the results were counted, forty Unionists and twelve Nationalists were returned to the Northern parliament, while there were returned to the Dail 124 Sinn Fein candidates and four Unionists representing Trinity College. Although the Government of Ireland Act itself had proposed a Council of Ireland consisting of twenty members of each parliament which would have powers to unite both sides without reference to Westminster, the result confirmed the inevitability of the first tragedy that was now to engulf the country – partition. The Nationalists' highest aim of a free and united Ireland was destroyed, and when Lloyed George asked de Valera 'as the chosen leader of the great majority in southern Ireland' to negotiate terms with him in London, the possibility of a comprehensive solution to the Irish problem was irrevocably compromised.

The Treaty negotiations and their aftermath were to precipitate the second tragedy, civil war. Arthur Griffith and Michael Collins led an Irish delegation whose members were aware that it was the Anglo-Irish War which had persuaded the British to treat their erstwhile enemy as a nominal equal. Griffith and Collins were, in addition, the properly elected representatives of the overwhelming weight of Irish opinion, and public opinion in England required that the dreadful hostilities be brought to an end with the recognition of what it was hoped would be acceptable demands from both sides. All the Irish delegates were agreed that, for the purposes of negotiation at least, demands for a fully fledged republic were 'out of the question,' and this remained a view acceptable to the greater part of Irish and English opinion alike.

But Lloyd George's proposal to offer Dominion status to the South while preserving the autonomy of the North proved unacceptable, and de Valera urged the Dail unanimously to reject it. Such an impasse threatened the very existence of the discussions, and delicate negotiations ensued which led to Lloyd George issuing a second invitation for Ireland to come to the negotiating table 'with a view to ascertaining how the association of Ireland with the community of nations known as the British Empire can best be reconciled with Irish national aspirations'. De Valera himself had by this time worked out a principle of External Association which, rather in the manner adopted later by the countries of the Commonwealth, suggested the voluntary association under the Crown of a fully independent Irish state with the British Empire.

On 6 December 1921, after weeks of negotiation, the delegates completed their Articles of Agreement for a Treaty between Great Britain and Ireland. This document was inevitably a compromise, but the very word 'Treaty' implied the historic recognition of what was now to be called the Irish Free State. It also affirmed the Dominion status of the country under a 'representative of the Crown in Ireland', and committed members of parliament to swearing an Oath of Allegiance. A masterpiece of diplomatic drafting, the Oath required Members to 'swear true faith and allegiance to the Constitution of the Irish Free State as by law established' while simultaneously requiring them to 'be faithful to H.M. King George V, his heirs and successors by law, in virtue of the common citizenship of Ireland with Great Britain and her adherence to and membership of the group of nations forming the British Commonwealth of Nations'.[21] Such a wording subtly evaded a precise definition of the place of the Crown in Irish affairs, and to Griffith and Collins at least was a tolerable compromise which, as Collins himself declared, gave the Irish the freedom to achieve freedom. Yeats was in agreement, writing that he had 'never thought they would get so much out of Lloyd George and so am pleased'.

His pleasure was short-lived. Despite the agreeing of terms apparently acceptable to most moderate people, it now became apparent that some members of the Dail who had supported the negotiations had at the same time nurtured in their hearts an altogether more extreme and mystical view of Irish freedom. Chief among these was de Valera. Distancing himself from the delegates who had negotiated the Treaty, he published a letter denouncing its terms as unacceptable to the mass of the Irish people. Yeats at once saw the dangers lurking in the threat posed to the compromise so delicately reached. 'I am in deep gloom about Ireland,' he wrote, 'for although I expect ratification of the treaty from a plebiscite I see no hope of escape from bitterness, and the extreme party may carry the country. When men are very bitter, death and ruin draw them on as a rabbit is supposed to be drawn on by the dancing of the fox.'[22]

Such forebodings proved justified. Although the Treaty was indeed ratified by the Dail after an acrimonious debate, the narrow margin of sixty-four to fifty-seven in favour encouraged de Valera and his supporters to announce that they could not swear the Oath of Allegiance, thereby disqualifying themselves from the publicly agreed forms of legitimate political life. The presidency of the Irish Free State passed to Arthur Griffith, who worked closely with Michael Collins, himself chairman of the provisional government. A number of other pro-Treaty ministers supported them, while Collins, who was also president of the Supreme Council of the IRB, recommended acceptance of the terms of the Treaty to its members, about half of whom accepted them.

Yeats remained for a while cautiously optimistic. In part this was a matter of personality. The prospect of seeing his old enemy Arthur Griffith in a position of responsibility in the new provisional government was altogether less alarming than it once might have been. Griffith had ceased his onslaughts against Yeats after the Easter Rising and, realising the contribution the Irish literary renaissance had made to the changing political fate of the country, had even suggested that the poet's birthday be honoured as a day of national importance by Sinn Fein internees. Yeats in his turn was prepared cautiously to modify his opinion of his old adversary. 'I expect to see Griffith, now that he is the musical target, grow almost mellow and become the fanatic of broad-mindedness and accuracy of statement.' It was just possible perhaps that the narrow and bigoted partisanship Yeats had so disparaged among the Dubliners of 1913 might now be replaced by something altogether more acceptable. 'Griffith isolated from the "impossibilist" people may be better for our purposes than the old Griffith.' Indeed, it seemed that his presence was one of those forces which had obliged the 'impossibilist' minority to exclude themselves from the provisional government by their refusal to swear the Oath of Allegiance.

Among these fanatical followers of extreme nationalism were all the female members of the Dail, including Constance Markiewicz. Yeats claimed that he was not unhappy to see Constance and 'other emotional ladies among the non-jurors', but his sympathies in this most fraught and complex period were altogether more subtle and perhaps more calculating than the adoption of a merely crude stance. Might not the loss of such feelings as these women embodied 'unbalance things for a time on to the side of hard-headedness and the man of business' – the very forces that Yeats had always most deeply feared? The way of feeling could not be abandoned, nor, as it now emerged, could a path to potential personal influence. Just before de Valera's secession from the Dail, Yeats had been asked by Sinn Fein to go as a delegate to the Irish Race Congress in Paris. There he gave 'a truly beautiful address on Irish literature', tracing 'the literary and dramatic revival from its beginning up to the present time, concluding with a moving recitation of Pearse's "Wayfarer" written the night before his execution'. The implication was that Pearse, as a member of the IRB, had given his ghostly blessing to those members of that organisation who had now been persuaded to the pro-Treaty side. The Easter Uprising, in other words, had reached its culmination in the representative and democratic provisional government.

Certainly, the invitation itself was a sign that the provisional government wished to recognise Yeats, and it was possible that he might even become minister for the fine arts. Partly in the effort to futher these ambitions, George, who was increasingly dissatisfied with their life in Oxfordshire, crossed to Ireland, where she managed to obtain at a reasonable price 82 Merrion Square, a dignified house in that part of Dublin which is 'to Dublin what Berkeley Square is to London'. They felt that they would be able to afford to live there if they let the stables and the top floor, and by spring 1922 the Yeatses had returned to Ireland. Any hope Yeats might have nursed of returning to a settled country was premature, however, for if elected power lay with men like Griffith and Collins, violence was in the hands of the IRA, its numbers swollen by new young recruits and its heart still given over to the Republican cause. What this meant for Ireland would soon become agonisingly clear. The dance of the daughters of Herodias was not yet done.

V

'The Heart's Grown Brutal'

The Yeatses settled themselves first in Thoor Ballylee. 'George makes at every moment a fourteenth century picture,' Yeats wrote. 'And out of doors, with the hawthorn all in blossom all along the riverbanks, everything is so beautiful that to go elsewhere is to leave beauty behind.' Beauty was little protection, however, in a country moving inexorably towards civil war.

The anti-Treaty members of the IRA whom Collins had been unable to carry with him were organising themselves as an autonomous force with their headquarters in the Dublin Four Courts. The army that Collins had done so much to create was now a threat to his political survival, and, while rioting in Ulster led to an ever deepening and more bitter divide between the Protestants of the North and the Catholics of the South, Collins had to face the dreadful prospect of violence among those so recently freed from British imperial rule. Both he and de Valera were anxious to avoid hostilities and, when a general election was called to give democratic status to the provisional government and the new constitution, the two men agreed on an electoral pact by which the once united Sinn Fein party was to present itself as a single panel of candidates divided on the issue of the Treaty in exactly the proportion which had earlier voted for or against it.

Collins frankly told the British government that he believed such manipulation was necessary if the election were to take place at all, since the split in the IRA had already led to sporadic outbreaks of violence in the South over which he and his government had little or no control. Post offices were robbed, goods were seized from the railways, the lines themselves were seriously damaged, the crews were prevented from running the trains, and telephone and signal wires were cut. Murders settled old scores, while armed anti-Treaty men tried to bully public opinion out of supporting the Treaty which the vast number wanted. That this last was indeed so was proved by the electoral returns. Despite the pact, 94 out of the 128 new members of the Dail were pro-Treaty candidates, who now had a clear democratic mandate. But events were soon to be propelled towards their awful crisis by forces that had little to do with the will of the people.

On 22 June the arch anti-Nationalist Sir Henry Wilson was murdered on his London doorstep by two IRA men. The British government, deeply concerned that the violence in this the newest Dominion was now spreading to the heart of the Empire itself, immediately put the blame for Wilson's death on the anti-Treaty Republicans ensconced in the Four Courts and issued an ultimatum to the provisional government, ordering it to take action against these men if it did not wish to see the Treaty abrogated. At 3.40 on the morning of 28 June the Irish government complied, requiring the anti-Treaty men's surrender within twenty minutes. The order was ignored and the government had no other option but to ready the inexperienced gunners of the Free State Army and command them to open fire. So untrained were these men that it took them two days of shelling across the Liffey to reduce the Four Courts to rubble, but by 30 June they had succeeded. The first actions of the new Irish government thus consisted of violence against other Irishmen and, as the anti-Treaty leaders in Dublin were thrown into prison, so those in the rest of the country consolidated themselves into forces known as the 'Irregulars'.

Soon they were wreaking havoc across the land, and during the high summer of 1922 some 500 men were killed. With savage irony, these included Collins himself, ambushed at Bealnamblath, where, after a fight lasting half an hour, a ricocheting bullet hit him in the back of the head. Ten days earlier, Arthur Griffith, his health destroyed by over-work, had died of a cerebral haemorrhage in a Dublin nursing home. Leadership of the Free State government passed into the hands of Kevin O'Higgins and a veteran of the Easter Uprising named William Cosgrave. These men were aware of the appalling responsibilities they now had to address, which were nothing less that the preservation of the Free State itself. 'We are faced with eradicating from the country the state of affairs in which hundreds of men go around by day and by night to take the lives of other men.' They offered an amnesty and then, equipping themselves with the sternest emergency powers, resolved to end the guerrilla war at all costs.

The anti-Treaty propagandist Erskine Childers was arrested, court-martialled *in camera*, and shot, one of eight men judicially murdered in November 1922. The anti-Treaty members of the IRA immediately issued an order stating that any members of the Dail who had voted for the emergency powers would be shot on sight, and the government reluctantly agreed to a ghastly show of force. At the close of November 1922 it ordered that the men it had interned in Mountjoy jail should be shot without trial. Such barbarities continued into the early months of 1923, and came to an end only when de Valera ordered the Irregulars to lay down their arms. As O'Higgins lamented, the earliest months of the new Free State government had not been spent in constructive efforts at building up a country with which one day even Northern Protestants might wish to be associated. Instead 'we preferred to burn our own houses, blow up our own bridges, rob our own banks, saddle ourselves with millions of debt for the maintenance of an Army and for the payment of compensation for the recreations of our youth'. His confession continued in this searingly honest vein. 'Generally, we preferred to practise upon ourselves worse indignities than the British had practised on us since Cromwell and Mountjoy.'[23]

During the summer months of 1922 spent at Thoor Ballylee, Yeats became the poet of this inferno. He wrote to Sturge Moore in August telling him he was working on 'a series of poems about this Tower and on the civil war at which I look (so remote is one here from all political excitement) as if it were some phenomenon of nature'. The poems were eventually gathered into the sequence 'Meditations in Time of Civil War', and the second of these, 'My House', suggests that Thoor Ballylee did indeed offer Yeats an apparently secure and withdrawn atmosphere for contemplation. Here is an ancient, natural world where the 'symbolic rose' can flower and the poet himself can nightly pursue his scholarship by the light of a candle whose gleam is at once physical and metaphorical.

Such illusory permanence is constantly undermined, however. What the poet seeks to offer are 'befitting emblems of adversity', and their fitness lies in the fact that they offer no abiding defence against a mutable world hurtling towards anarchy. Sato's 'changeless sword', a great work of art from an ancestral culture, appears to rise above flux, but its blade is like a crescent moon and so reminds the poet of a world conceived as constantly changing under lunar influences. A family too may 'lose the flower' of its inherited traditions of intellectual vigour and that natural aristocracy of mind Yeats had praised since the days of *Responsibilities*. The commonplace is a constant threat even to the stone securities of the tower, and, just as the owls fly in circles above it, so the gyres of history turn and bring changes that offer little cause for joy.

Sometimes their presence brought barbarism uncomfortably close. Yeats wrote to Sturge Moore that he had heard the explosion as a local bridge was blown up. He witnessed a car pass 'with a National soldier and a coffin up on end'. The Nationalists were, he said, in control of the area and the local people were with them, 'but the Irregulars come out at night'. From time to time the war even marched up 'The Road at My Door', bringing variously an 'affable Irregular' with his ghastly jokes about bloodshed, or a 'brown lieutenant' of the Nationalists with whom Yeats could discuss the disasters wrought by the weather on his garden – the garden of Ireland where the wind has blown the petals from the 'symbolic rose' and left only 'common greenness' behind. For all his sympathy with the Nationalist cause, however, these poems strive to avoid the openly partisan. As Yeats wrote to Lady Gregory: 'I will never take any position in life where I have to speak but half my mind and I feel that both sides are responsible for this whirlpool of hate. Besides only action counts or can count till there is some change.' But the man of reflection can merely turn impotently away, his mind blinded and chilled by the hatred eddying meaninglessly about him.

'One felt an overmastering desire not to grow unhappy or embittered, not to lose all sense of the beauty of nature,' Yeats wrote. But, again, the natural world offers no easy comfort. The birds and bees build their nests around the 'loosening masonry' of the tower, obeying a natural and instinctual order, but man lives otherwise than by instinct:

> We had fed the heart on fantasies,
> The heart's grown brutal from the fare;
> More substance in our enmities
> Than in our love . . .[24]

The result is claustrophobic uncertainty, war, burning, murder. From fantasy come division and death, the 'whirlpool of hatred' stirred up especially by those who still followed the absolutist convictions of Pearse and the Easter Martyrs. Many of the poems gathered in *Michael Robartes and the Dancer* had celebrated these men, seen their blood sacrifice as fructifying, their ghosts as inspirational voices. Now, in the midst of national horror, Yeats was forced to reconsider his position. 'Perhaps there is nothing so dangerous to a modern state, when politics take the place of theology, as a bunch of martyrs,' he wrote. 'A bunch of martyrs (1916) were the bomb and we are living in the explosion.' His own responsibility for the language and emotion which helped send Pearse and his kind to their deaths became more onerous than ever before.

Certainly, Yeats claimed no visionary Nationalist privilege now. From the apparent securities of 'My House' with its mystic Irish rose blooming by the door, he has moved to exposing the fragility of art, family and nature. As he does so he has also moved his poetry from apparently meaningful intellectual effort, through 'the cold snows of a dream', to facing the evils of political delirium. In the last poem of the cycle, Yeats turns his attention to the dreadful heart of the phantasmagoria of unintelligibility. Even the title of the work is terrible. 'I see Phantoms of Hatred and of the Heart's Fullness and of the Coming Emptiness'.

As a poem about the collapse of meaning, this work strains at the limits of the comprehensible. Nature and the mind of the poet are both misted, frenzied, and dominated by an unnaturally 'unchangeable' moon. Society too has collapsed in an anarchy of armed violence and mass hysteria, and blindly 'plunges towards nothing'. Even the poet himself has been briefly tempted by the furore of populist hysteria and his visionary world no longer offers him meaningful images. The once lovely ladies on their magical unicorns* now form merely an effete and blinded procession which 'gives place to an indifferent multitude', the hawks of the primary gyre and their 'innumerable clanging wings that have put out the moon'. Yeats shows himself as old and powerless, and the poem offers perhaps the most alarming moment of personal disillusion in the whole of his work. Far from being able to hammer his thoughts into a unity, he is obliged to confess that, with the collapse of Ireland into civil war, his nationalism has rocked on its foundations and can find no abiding relationship with his occult interests, which, in their turn, can express themselves only in a poetry where meaning itself hovers on the edge of incoherence.

Events seemed to confirm this with a fatuous and even comic nihilism that was entirely appropriate. At midnight on 19 August the Irregulars blew up the bridge at Ballylee. 'They forbade us to leave the house, but were otherwise polite, even saying at last "Good-night, thank you", as though we had given them the bridge.' The river, dammed by the debris, rose so high that in September the Yeatses were obliged to leave their tower because the kitchen was now under two feet of water. They had planned to stay with Lady Gregory and to superintend from Coole the work that still needed to be done, but this plan had to be abandoned when someone shot and wounded their builder.

The family returned instead to Dublin, and Yeats revived his 'Mondays' at Merrion Square, telling friends that Dublin was largely placid, although bursts of gunfire could be heard at night. Certainly, the situation seemed sufficiently stable for Yeats himself to leave George and the children there in November 1922 while he went to visit Lady Ottoline Morrell at Garsington. George wrote to him there detailing the worsening situation, in particular the general horror felt at the execution of Erskine Childers and the other Irregulars in Mountjoy jail. She told Yeats that there had been an eleven-hour delay before the relatives of the dead men had been informed of their murder. She told him too that she had gone out to the pictures and returned home to

* These figures were derived from a print by Gustave Moreau which Yeats had hung in Thoor Ballylee.

the sound of machine-gun fire. Precisely how lawless Dublin had become, however, was suggested by the headline carried by the *Freeman's Journal* on 13 November: 'Bonfire of Papers, Sequel to Search of Madame MacBride's House'.[25]

To avoid the daily turbulence of the city, Maud had moved out with Mrs Despard to a house in Clonskeagh, some ten miles from the centre of the city. The soldiers of the Free State now raided the house in St Stephen's Green and reporters described the devastation they caused, writing how 'in the upper rooms, presses and cupboards were pulled open and the contents left lying about. The military were on the scene for some time, and before leaving they piled up a heap of papers on the centre of the road and set them ablaze.' Among these papers were letters from Yeats, records of their occult experiments, drafts of poems, the memorabilia of a three-decade love affair between two remarkable people. The permanent loss of such details is heart-rending, but in the immediate context of 1922 it posed a particularly bitter threat to Yeats. His name was already being mentioned in connection with Cosgrave's new government, which was to be officially sworn in on 6 December, and George was worried that Maud might appeal to him for help. In fact, as she gradually became aware, Maud was rancorously accusing Yeats of being willing to accept honours from men she herself considered traitors to the deepest traditions of Irish nationalism, and rumours were common in the group gathered about Maud's friend Mrs Despard that Yeats was a pro-English traitor. Concerned by the dangers that the violence of a rumour-mongering Dublin posed to George, Yeats wrote to tell her to stay indoors at night until the crisis was over.

Meanwhile, he was reconsidering his own political ideas, deepening his authoritarian views in the light of present events, and trying to weld his love of traditional decencies to what appeared to be the most advanced contemporary thought. In a poem written some time earlier and subsequently placed first among Yeats's 'Meditations in Time of Civil War', he had written of Garsington where he was now staying as one of those 'Ancestral Houses' whose traditional and ceremonious glory provided an albeit insecure protection against the rampant barbarism of the present:

> O what if gardens where the peacock strays
> With delicate feet upon old terraces,
> Or else all Juno from an urn displays
> Before the indifferent garden deities;
> O what if levelled lawns and gravelled ways
> Where slippered Contemplation finds his ease
> And Childhood a delight for every sense,
> But take our greatness with our violence?[26]

Yeats at once apostrophises and laments the passing of what such houses as Coole and Garsington personified: wealth, abundant and overflowing life, decorum, 'inherited glory'. Above all, he was beginning to admire what he thought of as the power and even the violence of the men who could commission and build these monuments of aristocratic magnificence. Yeats wondered where, in the modern world, he could find a comparable expression of authority.

The newspapers appeared to provide him with what he sought. At the close of October 1922, Mussolini completed his triumphant march on Rome and persuaded the King of Italy to accede to his demand to be made premier. Newspapers in England praised him as the heir of Garibaldi, the restorer of order in Italy, a man of judgement and even of humour. He embodied for figures as diverse as Chamberlain, Churchill and Yeats himself, blind to the element of thuggery in his politics, a resolute fascism which stood opposed to Marxist totalitarianism and praised order, hierarchy and discipline. As Mussolini himself trumpeted of the world he saw rising out of the devastation of the First World War:

the orgy of licence has come to an end, the enthusiasm for social and democratic myths is over. Life is flowing back to the individual. A classical revival is taking place. The soulless, drab egalitarianism of democracy, which had . . . crushed all personality, is on its death-bed. New kinds of aristocracy are arising, now that we have proof that the masses cannot be protagonists but only the tools of history.[27]

To Yeats as a man who believed he had seen the collapse of civilisation into a witches' sabbath of barbarism and crude violence, and who was, besides, a poet convinced by his own occult philosophy that the primary and democratic gyre was bringing about the destruction from which would arise something altogether more elite and magnificent, Mussolini provided a focus of hope and a proof that the Second Coming was indeed at hand. 'When I was under thirty,' he wrote, 'it would seem an incredible dream that 20,000 Italians, drawn from the mass of the people, would applaud a politician for talking of the "decomposing body of liberty", and for declaring that his policy was the antithesis of democracy.' Here indeed was that 'drift towards Conservatism, perhaps towards Autocracy,' which Yeats 'always knew' would come. Its implications for ravished Ireland seemed clear. 'We are preparing here, behind our screen of bombs and smoke, a return to conservative politics as elsewhere in Europe, or at least to a substitution of the historical sense for logic. The return will be painful and perhaps violent, but many educated men talk of it and must soon work for it and perhaps riot for it.' As Yeats told Lady Gregory: 'all talk here is conservative and eyes are turned full of enquiry towards Italy'.

Yeats would soon be able to give public expression to this accelerated drift to the right. On 6 December 1922, members of the Dail met and, while the Republican deputies boycotted the occasion, swore the Oath of Allegiance whose slippery clauses had propelled their country into civil war. Later, Oliver St John Gogarty hurried excitedly round to 82 Merrion Square, where, finding no one at home, he chalked on the grand Georgian front door the simple words 'Senator W. B. Yeats'.

VI
The Senator

The next day Gogarty telephoned George to tell her that Yeats's appointment to the Senate had less to do with his poetry or his work for the Abbey Theatre than with his former association with the IRB, a political interest of which George had up to now been unaware.

The Senate itself had been set up under the terms of the Treaty partly to protect the interests of Southern Unionists. It was designed to consist of sixty men who had 'done honour to the nation by reason of useful public service', or who 'because of special qualifications or attainments . . . represent important aspects of the nation's life'. Although the Senate's principal purpose was the revision of bills, which it could only delay rather than veto, Yeats believed that the chamber could exert considerable influence. 'We are a fairly distinguished body,' he wrote, 'and should get much government business into our hands.'[28] Indeed, the senators were determined to show their power and, somewhat to the annoyance of the Dail, made numerous changes to the legislation presented to them. Yeats himself was determined that the Senate should be given time to do its work in a professional manner and be accorded proper dignity.

Membership was, however, accompanied by a real degree of personal danger. 'Here one works at the slow exciting work of creating the institutions of a new nation – all coral insects but with some design in our heads of the ultimate island. Meanwhile the country is full of arms and explosives ready for any violent hand to use.' In particular, those sections of the IRA which opposed the Treaty believed that the Senate was designed to placate Protestant loyalists and declared the senators themselves to be the enemy. Their members were under orders to burn the houses of senators, and Yeats wrote to Olivia Shakespear that he had 'for near neighbours two senators, one of whom has had his house bombed for being a senator, and one is under sentence of death because he owns the *Freeman's Journal*'. There was even an attempt to kidnap Gogarty while he was taking a bath, and the distinguished surgeon escaped only by a daring night plunge into the swollen Liffey. Gogarty was later to release two swans on to the river as a gesture of thanks for his life, but between 8 January and 2 February 1923 no less than twenty-four houses were destroyed, including those of President Cosgrave, Stephen Gwynn and Horace Plunkett.

Yeats himself had been in Plunkett's house shortly before it was attacked and believed he received a psychic intimation of the violence about to be wrought there. It seems that such dangers briefly so perturbed him that he wondered if he should take his place in the Senate at all, and it appears that it was George who eventually persuaded him that he owed his country a duty of public service. He was provided with bodyguards, to whom he gave detective stories 'to train them in the highest tradition of their profession', and in time he could boast to Olivia Shakespear that 'I have two bullet holes in my windows but one gets used to anything.' Yeats was thus perfectly serious when he wrote that his income as a senator would 'compensate me somewhat for the chance of being shot or my house being burned or bombed', but as he became familiar with Senate business, so he vowed that he would 'speak very little but probably intrigue a great deal to get some old projects into action'.

These 'old projects' went to the complex core of Yeats's nationalism. Above all he was resolved to avoid compromising with materialistic and imperial England, to maintain the moral and spiritual integrity of Ireland, and to seek the attainment of his dream of Unity of Being. He wrote to George Russell that this last idea in particular had 'been forced again into my mind, after a long interval of apparent individualism, by my present philosophy'. He urged Russell to draw up a 'cultural economic political policy of national unity', telling him that the 'conception of unity and culture has become a cardinal principle in all exposition of the future in my system'. Unity of Being was a particular quality of the antithetical gyre and, by associating his spiritual beliefs with his political convictions, Yeats was once again trying to hammer his thoughts into a unity. At times he wondered how such 'abstract studies' as he was pursuing in *A Vision* could have a practical effect on his attempts to steer the ship of state, but a powerful image convinced him that they could indeed be of help. 'Though the ship crosses the world,' he wrote, 'the helmsman never takes his eyes from a disk covered with letters and lines that is perhaps some eighteen inches across.'

Poetry inevitably helped inspire this imaginative fusion of Yeats's ideas. Believing that man was now in Phase Twenty-Two of the second Christian millennium, Yeats looked back across history to the end of the first thousand years of the Christian epoch and to the collapse of the empire of Charlemagne. Surely that tumultuous event would now be recapitulated in the dissolution of the British Empire, a matter of immense historical importance in which Ireland itself might play a decisive part. Indeed, the fall of empires as the gyres turned increasingly preoccupied Yeats's imagination, and, looking back to Phase Twenty-Two of the Greek era, he noted that it had seen the end of Alexander's empire. Such moments of historic change prompted his great sonnet 'Leda and the Swan'.

This powerful and disturbing picture of mythological rape was partly inspired by a painting attributed to Michelangelo, a photograph of which Yeats kept on his desk while he was writing the poem. Yeats pictured the moment when Zeus in the form of a swan seduced the mortal Leda, who presently laid three eggs, from two of which hatched Castor and Clytemnestra (the wife of the Greek leader Agamemnon), and Pollux and Helen of Troy. From this ghastly moment emerged a terrible human destiny:

> A shudder in the loins engenders there
> The broken wall, the burning roof and tower
> And Agamemnon dead.[29]

Yeats believed that a similarly violent epoch was about to come to pass in the contemporary world, and, explaining that he wrote the poem in answer to a request from George Russell, he developed his ideas by saying that '"after the individualist, demagogic movement, founded by Hobbes and popularised by the Encyclopedists and the French Revolution, we have a soil so exhausted that it cannot grow that crop again for centuries". Then I thought, "Nothing is now possible but some movement from above preceded by some violent annunciation." My fancy began to play with Leda and the Swan for metaphor, and I began this poem.'

The relation of Yeats's political thinking to his spiritualist interests is clear, but, as he himself was obliged to confess, the horror of the sexual element in the poem is its dominant and shocking note. Indeed, so powerful is this assertion that Russell felt obliged to turn the sonnet down, saying that his 'conservative readers would misunderstand the poem', and the offence it could indeed cause to contemporary sensibilities is suggested by the fact that Yeats's typist burst into tears when she read the lines and refused to copy them for him. Yeats himself remained convinced that he had accurately evoked the dynamics of cultural and historical change, and insisted in an interview that 'everything seems to show that the centrifugal movement which began with the Encyclopedists and produced the French Revolution . . . has worked itself out to the end. Now we are at the beginning of a new centripetal movement' – a movement which, he believed, led to what he called 'authoritative' government.

The poet, the Nationalist and the occult experimenter had once again powerfully coincided and, in his role as a senator, Yeats believed that this combination would help him play his part in what he regarded as his and his fellow senators' duty to 'govern this country well'. He believed that 'we can do that, if I may be permitted as an artist and a writer to say so, by creating a system of culture which will represent the whole of this country, and which will draw the imagination of the young towards it'.

But Yeats had not only his own convictions to guide him in this process of creating national consciousness. Just as in his early years he had turned to the immense resources of Celtic mythology and literature to establish the imaginative and spiritual basis of Irish national feeling, so, especially after he had completed *A Vision*, he turned to another great period of Irish cultural endeavour which heretofore he had largely ignored – the literary and philosophical achievements of the Irish eighteenth century and, in particular, the work of Berkeley, Swift and Burke. With his powerfully eclectic and selective imagination, Yeats began to build from the ideas of these men a view of national consciousness which was at once rooted in tradition and agreeable to his own anti-liberal and anti-materialist ideas.

The works of Berkeley in particular presented Yeats with a distinctly Irish tradition of philosophical anti-materialism, a system of thought wholly opposed to the mechanistic traditions which Yeats believed had so disastrously contributed to the now waning influence of the primary gyre and its denial of imaginative and spiritual life. 'The mischief began', he wrote, 'at the end of the seventeenth century when man became passive before a mechanised nature.' Just as Blake had seen Bacon, Newton and Locke as the figures pre-eminently embodying this disastrous attitude, so Yeats now turned to Berkeley, who had likewise disparaged these men in his *Commonplace Book*, saying, '"We Irish do not hold with this." That was the birthplace of the national intellect and it caused the defeat in Berkeley's philosophical secret society of English materialism, the Irish Salamis.'[30]

In Berkeley, Yeats found a figure to oppose a materialistic world 'separated from taste, smell, sound, from all the mathematician could not measure'. He believed ever more vehemently in his boyhood insight that the scientific world of statistical analysis produced an inert and repetitious universe of false values where everything was the same because it did not have the spiritual insight to relish difference and diversity. Its inevitable end was what Yeats considered the barren plane of democracy. 'Instead of hierarchical society where all men are different, came democracy; instead of a science which had rediscovered *Anima Mundi* . . . came materialism. Science spelt the death of the individual soul and of society.' With what was to become an ever more characteristically sweeping grandiloquence, Yeats at once asserted his beliefs and suggested that the world had already taken them up. The passion of his conviction appears to compel assent. 'No educated man to-day', he declared, 'accepts the objective matter and space of popular science, and yet deductions made by those who believed in both dominate the world, make possible the stimulation and condonation of revolutionary massacre and the multiplication of murderous weapons by substituting for the old humanity with its unique irreplaceable individuals something that can be chopped and measured like a piece of cheese.'

Yeats believed that Swift in particular had foreseen the political damage that was bound to ensue from such ways of thinking. Just as he himself had once been impressed by Kropotkin's telling him that the French Revolution, by sweeping away the ancient traditions of the French peasantry, had exposed them to the merciless exploitation of the world of capitalism, so Swift had foreseen 'the ruin to come, democracy, Rousseau, the French Revolution'.[31] And what 'Swift stared on till he became a raging man', Burke excoriated in works which became the foundations of modern conservatism. 'When the democratic movement was in its beginning,' Yeats wrote, 'Burke opposed it in speeches and essays.' For Yeats, Burke was pre-eminently a man who stood against mechanical political theory. He held that the constitution of a nation, far from being 'a problem of arithmetic', a matter of democratic head-counting, was actually an ancient, growing, organic body spreading slowly like a broad oak tree, its roots deeply planted in ancient traditions of aristocracy.

Here were ideas having a profound appeal to the poet and the visionary Nationalist who, believing that the world was passing to authoritarianism, wished to create strong government in his country based on traditional values. In the Irish eighteenth century, Yeats believed he had found a source of themes that answered his needs. In particular, here were ideas through which the nation could rediscover its national consciousness in opposition to England.

> Berkeley with his belief in perception, that abstract ideas are mere words, Swift with his love of perfect nature, of the Houyhnhnms, his disbelief in Newton's system and every sort of machine, Goldsmith and his delight in the particulars of common life that shocked his contemporaries, Burke with his conviction that all States not grown slowly like a forest tree are tyrannies, found in England the opposite that stung their own thought into expression and made it lucid.[32]

Supported by ideas culled from the finest intelligences of the Anglo-Irish eighteenth century, Yeats found his natural position among the Independents in the Senate led by his father's erstwhile friend Andrew Jameson. Many in Dublin regarded this group of lawyers, bankers and peers who met in the Kildare Street Club as revanchist members of the establishment. Yeats, however, admired these men while respecting and even feeling awed by their practised grip on the reins of power. Here, he felt, were men of substance to set against the democratically elected. He wrote later that 'in its early days some old banker or lawyer would dominate the House, leaning upon the back of the chair in front, always speaking with undisturbed self-possession as at some table in a boardroom. My imagination sets up against him some typical elected man, emotional as a youthful chimpanzee, hot and vague, always disturbed, always hating something or other.'[33] Although he was on visiting terms with these men, Yeats felt he had to be on his guard. As he wrote to Olivia Shakespear: 'a new technique which I am learning is silence – I have only spoken once and then but six sentences and shall not speak again perhaps till I am (if I shall ever be) at ease with it'.

Yeats recognised that, in the absence of de Valera and his followers, self-excluded from government by their refusal to swear the Oath of Allegiance, the Independents formed a necessary element of opposition. He was fully aware of the dangers of one-party rule and, with President Cosgrave's blessing, sounded out leading English figures about the possibility of abolishing the Oath altogether. He hoped in this way to avoid violent conflict, but it is suggestive of the atmosphere in which he was working that the government itself had set its mind to crushing the Republicans by force. The idea of abolishing the Oath of Allegiance was something the majority party would consider only once more violent measures had succeeded, and Yeats wrote that 'my plans are still government policy but are postponed till peace has come by other means. They will be used not to bring peace but to lay war's ghost. At least so I am told officially. Unofficially I hear that the War party carried the day.' This was a situation that distressed Yeats considerably, and in his maiden speech he had urged conciliation, arguing that 'the past is dead not only for us but for this country. . . . I suggest we are assembled here no longer in a Nationalist or Unionist sense, but merely as members of the Seanad.'

Cosgrave believed, however, that political initiatives came more properly from the Dail than from the Senate, 'from the House in which popular feeling is more generously represented'. That the senators had not been elected Yeats considered, made their moral responsibility to their country the more clear. He thought it 'very important to this Seanad, because of the very nature of its constitution, that we should show ourselves as interested as the Dail is in every person in this country. We do not represent constituencies; we are drawn together to represent certain forms of special knowledge, certain special interests, but we are just as much passionately concerned in these great questions as the Dail.'

Such ideas show Yeats once again in his role as the aristocratic popularist. He was a man of the right determined to preserve the unity of his country, a man deeply concerned with authority and order but determined nonetheless to preserve liberty. That this stand meant opposition very soon became clear to him. It also meant frequent disappointment. For example, Yeats seconded an amendment to the Indemnity Bill of 1923 which aimed to effect a fully reciprocal amnesty between England and Ireland, only to see it defeated. The independence of Ireland was of paramount importance to him and he strongly but unsuccessfully resisted attempts to join the country to the League of Nations, a move which he believed might find Ireland in the position of having to fight as an ally alongside the English. Similarly, although he admired the Justice Minister Kevin O'Higgins for his autocratic strength, Yeats was determined that the internal affairs of Ireland should be run in a manner that did not compromise its moral integrity. He was appalled, for example, by the execution of Republican leaders as a reprisal for their assassination of a deputy, and wrote sadly that the ministers 'made terrible decisions, the ablest had signed the death warrant of his dearest friend'.

Indeed, Yeats constantly urged the protection of the rights of the citizen against the state and campaigned continuously against moves which arbitrarily enhanced the power of government officials and ministers. Even when public fears about the conduct of imprisoned Republicans was running high in the country, Yeats spoke in the Senate about the conditions under which these men were kept, and resisted government attempts to set up a Prison Inspection Committee, which he did not believe could be adequately independent. The matter was eventually left to subside, but Yeats would not let it rest. He rose to speak on the issue in January 1924, and his words suggest the cogency with which he could address the house. 'I have felt for some months considerable curiosity as to the fate of that clause, and I think our labour Senators have also felt some curiosity. I shall be very glad if that curiosity could be satisfied, to know whether these persons have been appointed, whether they have inspected the prisons; and, if they have not been appointed, if they are going to be appointed, and when.'[34] His enquiry was, however, left unanswered.

Aware that increasing age posed a threat of his losing contact with the young, Yeats made conspicuous efforts to keep in touch with them. 'I know something of the opinions of those who will make the next generation in this country,' he told the Senate. 'I know it, perhaps, better than most members of this House.' Indeed, his contacts were such that he was aware that a disgruntled Free State Army was planning a coup, and he was deputed as the man best able to convince the government of the serious issue they were facing. He supplied O'Higgins with both the names and the information which, when the militia eventually sent an ultimatum to the government, allowed the Dail to repress the mutiny without loss of life.

Issues of justice also greatly concerned him. Yeats believed that, with the coming of independence, the people should realise that 'the law is now their own creation, their own instrument', and he not only supported those who wished the courts to substitute Irish robes for British gowns and wigs but, more importantly, was determined to resist Cosgrave's efforts to subordinate the judiciary to the executive. When the Dail threatened this vital principle, Yeats spoke out fearlessly. 'We want to judge these amendments in an abstract way, in the light of history, keeping in mind the fact that all civilised Governments that we know of, have found it necessary to ensure the independence of the Judges from the Executive.'

In addition to attending to the present and the future, Yeats was also concerned to protect that past. The preservation of ancient monuments particularly concerned him since he realised that these were not only a focus for national identity but an attraction to foreign tourists and thus a source of much-needed revenue. One of his favoured parliamentary techniques was to demand the setting up of a select committee on any difficult issue, and by this means he managed to have meetings of the Senate itself transferred from the National Museum (where he was worried about the fire risk posed to the treasures stored there) to Leinster House. Similarly, confessing that 'the greater proportion of my own writings have been founded upon the old literature of Ireland', he was determined to preserve ancient manuscripts and chaired a committee which put forward proposals analogous to those he had once hoped to see issuing from the work of Sir Charles Gavan Duffy and the New Irish Library. However, despite the fact that the proposals were carefully drafted, nothing came of the idea, for all Yeats's declarations that it was just this literature and the emotions it inspired which had led to an independent Ireland. Again, when the Dail proposed that Gaelic should be made a compulsory subject in schools, Yeats was deeply concerned by the issues of state intervention this implied, and a dialogue essay he wrote on the question shows that, despite his belief in strong and authoritative government, he was reluctant to give it overweening power. 'I am not sure that I like the idea of a State with a definite purpose, and there are moments, unpractical moments, perhaps, when I think that the State should leave the mind free to create.'[35] Here, once again, was the politician speaking as an artist and a writer.

And it was as an artist and a writer that Yeats was now to be honoured. He had recently received honorary degrees from Queen's University, Belfast, and Trinity College, Dublin, but in November 1923 he was awarded the supreme accolade of the Nobel Prize for literature. He had already had an intimation that either he or Thoman Mann would be made laureate that year, and it was Bertie Smyllie, the editor of the *Irish Times*, who eventually telephoned him to confirm the award.

I said 'Mr Yeats, I've got very good news for you, a very great honour has been conferred on you,' and I was rather enthusiastic and gushing at the time, and I said, 'This is a great honour not only for you but for the country,' and I could tell that he was getting slightly impatient to know what it was all about, so I said, 'You've been awarded the Nobel Prize, a very great honour to you and a very great honour to Ireland,' and to my amazement the only question he asked was, 'How much, Smyllie, how much is it?'[36]

15

Public Man

(1923–1927)

Nobel Prize

S ome ten minutes after Smyllie's call, Yeats received telephone con-
firmation from the Swedish Ambassador that the Nobel Prize would
indeed be awarded to him, and at half-past midnight, when he had
finally answered all the questions posed to him by the journalists who visited
Merrion Square, he and George, left alone, searched for a bottle of wine.
Finding the cellar empty, they celebrated the new honour by cooking some
sausages.

On 6 December, they left Harwich for Esbjerg in Denmark on a steamboat
whose cabins were panelled in pale birchwood and where the elaborate
smorgasbord suppers confused them by their astonishing plethora of cold
food, 'most of which we refuse because we do not recognise it, and some,
such as eels in jelly, because we do'.[1] Yeats was convinced that he had
been awarded the prize as an honour as much to his new nation as to
himself, and throughout his journey to Sweden thoughts of national identity
preoccupied him. Questioned by journalists at Copenhagen about Ireland
and the British Empire, he declared 'that if the British Empire becomes
a voluntary Federation of Free Nations, all will be well, but if it remains
as in the past, a domination of one, the Irish question is not settled. That
done with, I can talk of the work of my generation in Ireland, the creation
of a literature to express national character and feeling but with no deliberate
political aim.'

Yeats felt it was his expressing such ideals in his plays for the Abbey
Theatre that was particularly responsible for his name being put forward for
the prize, and in his acceptance speech, 'The Irish Dramatic Movement', he
was resolved 'to tell the Royal Academy of Sweden of the labours, triumphs
and troubles' this had involved.[2] He provided a deft, synoptic view of the
progress of the Irish literary renaissance from the death of Parnell in 1891

through to the current realistic work now being produced for the Abbey by such writers as Lennox Robinson, but he dwelt particularly on the influence of John Synge and Lady Gregory, saying that, as he accepted the prize, so he 'felt that a young man's ghost should have stood upon one side of me and at the other a living woman sinking into the infirmity of age'.

The Royal Theatre in Stockholm staged *Cathleen ni Houlihan*, but while he was pleased by this it was the presentation ceremony on 10 December that impressed Yeats especially. The self-possession and the intelligent, patrician kindness of the Swedish royal family in particular confirmed his preference for a nation united by a regard for natural aristocracy. The formal courtesy of the life they expressed appealed to him, and 'I who have never seen a Court, find myself before the evening is ended moved as if by some religious ceremony, though to a different end, for here it is Life herself that is praised.' His mind began to run on those Irish gentlemen of previous centuries who had sought employment in foreign courts, on Castiglione's commendations of Urbino, and on Ben Jonson's praise of the Jacobean court as 'a beautiful and brave spring' which watered all the noble plants of England. Here, Yeats believed, in the patrician world of the Swedish court, was something to bind old and young together in a tradition that seemed altogether richer and more fruitful than any modern democratic 'dream'. Such he believed was how nature intended things to be, and he thought once again that, through a respect for past forms, culture and society were preserved at a high and constantly refreshed level.

The 'Jacobin frenzy' of those who deplored such a world seemed, by contrast, merely vulgar, while the art produced by people like the Swedes impressed Yeats as a fulfilment of ideals he had cherished since he had first discovered cultural nationalism in his early twenties. In 'The Bounty of Sweden' he gave particular praise to the Stockholm Town Hall as an architectural expression of these beliefs. Here was a building 'decorated by many artists, working in harmony with one another and with the design of the building as a whole', something in marked contrast to what he considered the tyranny of public opinion exercised over such matters in England and Ireland. In Sweden, enlightened aristocratic patronage had 'made possible the employment of the best. These myth-makers and mask-makers worked as if they belonged to one family'. Aesthetic merit and social cohesion were one, and, with something of a flamboyant compliment to the Swedes, Yeats underlined his theme. 'No work comparable in method or achievement has been accomplished since the Italian cities felt the excitement of the Renaissance, for in the midst of our individualistic anarchy, growing always, as it seemed, more violent, have arisen once more subordination, design, a sense of human need.' Unity of Culture had here been achieved.

To encounter his ideal inevitably caused Yeats to reflect on the current state of Ireland, and 'The Bounty of Sweden' ends with a passage that points towards ideas which would increasingly preoccupy him as he sought to create what he thought of as a strong basis for his newly formed homeland. The fact that the Swedish court had 'gathered about it not the rank only but the intellect of its country' suggested that Sweden enjoyed a cultural life superior to that provided by democracy alone. 'No like spectacle will in Ireland show its work of discipline and of taste,' he thought, and such a concern with the place of a cultural and social elite would involve Yeats ever more deeply as he returned to Ireland to resume his work as a Nationalist and man of letters.

II
Five Women

The £7500 that came with the award of the Nobel Prize was a welcome addition to the Yeatses' finances. Promising Quinn that none of the money would be spent on Thoor Ballylee, Yeats invested £6000 and reserved a further £500 to complete the furnishing of 82 Merrion Square and pay off the sums still owing on the house.

There was, however, a further and unexpected demand on Yeats's prize money.[3] On a visit to England in July 1923, Lily had suffered a sudden and complete physical collapse. Consumption was at first suspected; then, as Lily passed her days in the expensive Roseneath nursing home, so a variety of diagnoses were developed, all of them ignoring the thyroid condition that was the real cause of her distress. At first it was believed that Lily was suffering from a possibly fatal numbing of the nerves that controlled her breathing. A throat specialist was brought in who, seeing matters in an altogether less serious light, recommended cough syrup and a course of retraining to correct an asymmetry of Lily's vocal cords. Then Lollie arrived. Her volatile temperament immediately diagnosed the cause of her sister's illness: she was neurasthenic, her illness all in her mind. So convincingly did Lollie make her case (her own instability perhaps suggesting a family trait) that one at least of Lily's doctors was convinced and declared that what the deluded woman needed was hard work and an adopted baby. His fellow consultant strongly disagreed, but, when the diagnoses were presented to Yeats himself, he opted at once for the psychological explanation as something fitting with his own intuitions. 'The whole family are exceedingly nervous and suggestible,' he declared. 'I remember once being crippled with rheumatism and my instant cure by an unexpected half hour's animated conversation. We are not a normal family.' Such insights carried the day, and the steadfast Lily was now designated the family neurotic.

As a result of this it at once became apparent not only that a wholesale reordering of the sisters' affairs in Dublin was necessary but that Yeats himself would have to take the initiative and foot the bill. For the remaining sixteen years of his life, sometimes sternly but always selflessly, he gave his sisters his practical, moral and financial support. The problems that faced him were considerable and trying. The most serious was the £2000 overdraft his sisters' business had managed to accumulate. In addition, new workspace had to be found and someone would have to take over Lily's place as head of the embroidery section. Beneath such difficulties meanwhile, poisoning all, ran the problems caused by Lollie's temperament and the pained relationship between the sisters that resulted from them. Yeats would have to find ways of dealing with all of these issues. New premises and the management of the embroidery section were the easiest problems to solve. The Cuala office was moved, rent free, into Merrion Square for eighteen months, where George, 'who knows what people wear and has seen modern art', took over Lily's supervisory role. From now until her death in 1968, George would be irreversibly involved in her sister-in-laws' affairs.

With extreme generosity, Yeats used a significant portion of his Nobel Prize money to pay off his sisters' overdraft. He then reconstructed the company so that its two divisions were separate. In such ways might acrimony between Lily and Lollie be partly avoided, but while this was a relief to the slowly recuperating Lily (whose medical expenses Yeats also paid), Lollie soon discovered that her brother was now not only her eagle-eyed literary adviser but her financial backer with powers altogether greater than those he had previously enjoyed. Lollie continued to insist on her editorial independence, thereby helping to sour her brother's relations with Padraic Colum and the poet Monk Gibbon. New taxes and British and Free State curbs on exports meanwhile restricted sales, while business practices at Cuala did not improve. An audit in 1925 concluded that 'it may come as a surprise to the partners to learn that their goods are being sold at less than cost'. Despite his protestations that he would help them only once, Yeats again felt he had to attend to a large overdraft. George meanwhile, drawn into this difficult situation, showed a loyalty and determination that were constantly tested. She helped organise sales of Cuala products at Merrion Square and, through the next two decades, took on, as her son explained, the taxing role 'of intermediary and general peacemaker between my father and his sisters'.

With what was left over from the prize money after these expenses, Yeats began to assemble a reference library for himself, buying, along with a selection of art books, a set of the *Encyclopaedia Britannica*, the *Cambridge Histories* and Gibbon's *Decline and Fall*. Such purely cultural interests could not for long be separated from his occult enquiries, however, and 1924 saw him labouring to complete the first version of *A Vision*.

Partly because George was adamant that her great contribution to this work should not be made public, Yeats led his readers into the first version through an elaborately playful series of framing devices involving himself, Michael Robartes and Owen Aherne. The first of these figures from Yeats's occult short stories of the Nineties tells Aherne that after the riot at the end of 'Rosa Alchemica' he went to Cracow, where he came across a book entitled *Speculum Angelorum et Hominorum*, which contained a portrait of its author Giraldus (reproduced in *A Vision* as a woodcut version which is partly an image of Yeats himself) and then travelled through the Middle East in search of an explanation of its occult teaching. Now, returned to London, Robartes wants to show Yeats this bundle of notes describing 'the mathematical law of history . . . the adventure of the soul after death . . . the interaction between the living and the dead and so on'.[4] Yeats agreed to write an exposition of its contents, but perhaps the most suggestive part of the ruse is the supposed origin of the occult wisdom found by Robartes among the Judwali bedouin, a people whose religious beliefs are at one with those of *A Vision* itself.

The origin of these beliefs lies in the innocent communications offered by a young bride who, some say, was given by the Caliph Harun Al-Rashid to his friend the philosopher Kusta-ben-Luka. This information was conveyed during the bride's 'sleeps', and there are clear analogies here with George's later means of communicating her occult insights to Yeats. The whole scenario, however, is suffused in ambiguity. The motives of the Caliph are far from straightforward, while Kusta himself seems to veer between asceticism and sexual indulgence.

> The only thing upon which there is general agreement is that he was warned by a dream to accept the gift of the Caliph, and that his wife, a few days after the marriage, began to talk in her sleep, and that she told him all those things which he had searched for vainly all his life in the great library of the Caliph and in conversation of wise men. One curious detail has come down to us in Bedouin tradition. When awake she was a merry girl with no more interest in matters of the kind than other girls of her age, and Kusta, the apple of whose eye she had become, fearing that it would make her think his love but self-interest, never told her that she talked to him in her sleep. Michael Robartes frequently heard Bedouins quoting this as proof of Kusta-ben-Luka's extraordinary wisdom.

To compound such Borges-like complications: 'all these contradictory stories seem to be a confused recollection of the contents of a little old book, lost many years ago with Kusta-ben-Luka's larger book. . . . This little book was discovered, according to tradition, by some Judwali scholar or saint between the pages of a Greek book which had once been in the Caliph's library. The story of the discovery may however be the invention of a much later age.'5

A false trail has been elaborately laid and even more cunningly confused. Occult inspiration is apparently arbitrary, indefinite, a puzzling reflection in a maze of mirrors. At the heart of the fiction, however, lies the possibility of a profound and beautiful truth: the idea that occult inspiration is intimately connected with love and sexual desire. In his versified narrative of these events, 'The Gift of Harun-Al-Rashid', Yeats offers a moving sense of the wonder that engulfed him in the earliest days of his occult marriage to George. The relation of youth to age, it is suggested, need not necessarily be the disharmonious union of January to May but rather an altogether more tentative coming together of different but mutual needs.

This was an obvious personal preoccupation. At his Nobel Prize presentation ceremony, Yeats had been able to examine his medal itself and he later explained that:

> it shows a young man listening to a Muse, who stands young and beautiful with a great lyre in her hand, and I think as I examine it, 'I was good-looking once like that young man, but my unpractised verse was full of infirmity, my muse old as it were; and now I am old and rheumatic, and nothing to look at, but my Muse is young. I am even persuaded that she is like those Angels in Swedenborg's vision, and moves perpetually "towards the dayspring of her youth".'

Kusta-ben-Luka himself goes further than this and wonders if he won the love of his young bride and muse by her hearing imaginary stories of his past with the result that she loved him the more for his apparently age-worn experience. Was it fascination with his love of mysteries that drew her, or was it the flickering light of those mysteries themselves playing over his elderly face which caused her to be moved by his physical frailty and powerful mind? The poet raises these delicate questions to throw a net of suggestive possibilities around his apparently unlikely happiness.

These musings of the elderly husband are as touching as they are honest, and the tender wondering of Kusta is especially clear in the lovely passage where he describes the wisdom his wife gave him, all unaware, in her sleeps. But more engaging still are Kusta's doubts about his relation to his wife now that the period of occult communion is over and he fears that she will see his love merely as an expression of gratitude. Kusta knows very well that if his relationship were to fade into the light of common day then all his 'fine feathers' would be plucked and he would be left to shiver in the cold. There is a genuine and not unreasonable fear here, but the poem nonetheless concludes on an exultant note describing the apparently absolute dependence of occult vision on physical love:

> The signs and shapes;
> All those abstractions that you fancied were
> From the great Treatise of Parmenides;
> All, all those gyres and cubes and midnight things
> Are but a new expression of her body
> Drunk with the bitter sweetness of her youth.[6]

To those readers wearied or even repelled by what at times seem the arbitrary yet rigid categories of human behaviour set out in *A Vision*, this passage is a moment of solace.*

It is also a moment of revelation. Yeats's system now appeared complete, and its origins in erotic love have been confessed to. Yeats was no longer obliged to see himself as the occult equivalent of a Vorticist painter reducing nature to rule and line, a man 'absorbed in some technical research to the entire exclusion of the personal dream'. The body had reasserted its complementary wisdom, and Yeats could claim that the whole elaborate structure of his vision could be regarded as a crystallisation of something altogether more fluid. Viewed in this light, the Great Wheel and the sexually suggestive interpenetration of the gyres are 'stylistic arrangements of experience comparable to the cubes in the drawing of Wyndham Lewis or to the ovoids in the sculpture of Brancusi'.[7] They are, in other words, the occult and philosophical equivalents of movements like Cubism and its derivatives: new attempts to express the multi-dimensional subtlety of nature in a world deadened by old perspectives.

But, for all the radiant confidence of the conclusion to 'The Gift of Harun Al-Rashid', real life often belied the relationship the poem celebrates. Writing to George in April 1924, when she was ill from what Yeats himself believed was over-work, he told her that he would come to Dublin and stay at his club rather than at Merrion Square, fearful

---

* Precisely how arbitrary some of the ascriptions of leading figures to the lunar phases could be is suggested by an anecdote narrated by Bertie Smyllie. He told how Yeats and Conor Cruise O'Brien were once in the Arts Club where Yeats was holding forth on the subject. 'He said, "Number One – the highest phase – is perfect beauty." With a respectful silence for a few seconds we all listened, and then he said, "Number Two was Helen of Troy – the nearest approximation to perfect beauty." And he went right round the twenty-eight, or rather twenty-seven, phases and finally he came to the last, and then he said that the lowest form of all is Thomas Carlyle and all Scotsmen.' The company was somewhat shaken and Cruise O'Brien piped up: '"WB," he said – he'd a very mincing voice, Cruise – "have you ever read a word of Carlyle? You say Carlyle is the lowest form. Oh come! Have you ever read a word of Carlyle?" "Carlyle, Cruise, was a dolt," said WB. "But I insist, WB, did you ever read one single word of Carlyle?" "Carlyle, I tell you, was a dolt." "Yes, but you haven't read him." "No, I have not read him, my wife, George, has read him and she tells me he's a dolt."'

that George might think her discomfort made him uncomfortable. That she may have needed her husband by her seems to him to have been of little account. In the day-to-day life of an occult marriage there was the same impenetrable privacy of concern and selfishness as in relationships altogether more mundane.

Yeats wrote his letter to George from Coole. Despite the honesty of Lady Gregory's articles during the Black and Tan War, the chief threat to her estate came not from the military but from her daughter-in-law. Margaret had resolved, as was her right, to sell both the house and the land, but a compromise was eventually agreed whereby Lady Gregory would keep the house and 350 acres, the income from which would go to Margaret. In November the rest of the estate was sold for £9000. Although there was an unpleasant incident involving Margaret during the Anglo-Irish War, Lady Gregory was told that she herself would be safe 'as long as there is a Gregory in Coole'. She believed she owed this immunity to her articles, but with the departure of the Black and Tans local hostilities emerged, and Lady Gregory was threatened by a disgruntled tenant. With her habitual courage she 'showed him how easy it would be to shoot me through the unshuttered window if he wanted to use violence'. Yeats was impressed by this example of patrician courage, and fifteen years later would remember it as one of the most precious of the 'Beautiful Lofty Things' by which he sustained his own ideals:

> Augusta Gregory seated at her great ormolu table,
> Her eightieth winter approaching: 'Yesterday he threatened my life.
> I told him that nightly from six to seven I sat at this table,
> The blinds drawn up' . . .[8]

A little while later Yeats arranged for Free State officers to patrol the grounds at Coole, and both Lady Gregory and the estate remained unmolested during the Civil War despite the fact that her family house at Roxborough was razed to the ground. It was not the militia or disgruntled tenants that were the chief threat to her physical person, however, but her 'finding a hard lump under my left breast' on 27 May 1923.* Once again showing her imperturbable determination, she submitted to an operation under a local anaesthetic during which, until she fainted, she 'was able to keep a face of courage'.

Long association and these particular incidents confirmed Yeats in a judgement of his great patron and her patrician code which finally caused him to place her in Phase Twenty-Four of *A Vision*, that point on the Great Wheel where 'all is sacrificed to this code; moral strength reaches its climax'. Aristocratic pride and the humility of service characterise this balance of lunar

---

* In July 1924, John Quinn was to die of liver cancer, aged fifty-four.

and solar energies, along with what Yeats rather harshly saw as an atrophying of the higher imaginative faculties:

> There is no philosophic capacity, no intellectual curiosity, but there is no dislike for either philosophy or science; they are part of the world and that world is accepted. . . . They submit all their actions to the most unflinching examination, and yet are without psychology, or self-knowledge, or self-created standards of any kind, for they but ask without ceasing 'Have I done my duty as well as So-and so?' 'Am I as unflinching as my fathers before me?' And though they can stand utterly alone, indifferent though all the world condemn, it is not that they have found themselves, but that they have been found faithful.

Yeats also attributed such qualities to Queen Victoria, and a bemused Lady Gregory commented that she did not think the English Queen could have written *Seven Short Plays*.[9]

Lady Gregory's remark on her place on the Great Wheel indicates that, while their relationship was marked by a continuing degree of deference on Yeats's part and her own invariable recognition of his genius, their friendship was kept fresh by a constant sparring affection based on years of acquaintanceship. Quite how frank this could be is suggested by an incident recorded by Lady Gregory while she was writing her memoirs. These she read out to Yeats, chapter by chapter, and when she wondered aloud if she was placing too many compliments to herself in the work Yeats told her he could 'make a list of your faults if you like. You are autocratic.' While this was undeniably true, Lady Gregory swiftly turned the accusation to her advantage. '"I suppose when you say that," I said, "you are thinking of such a case as when I found you and Synge shivering disconsolately in the Abbey scene dock, because you were kept out of the Green Room by the uncleanly habits of the stage-manager's little dog, and you were waiting for me to come and turn it out."' Put on his mettle, Yeats parried, 'If you argue like that over every fault I give, how can I give any more? And I have plenty more on the list.' With a great hostess's disarming subtlety, Lady Gregory put an end to the conversation. '"Oh," I said, "and when you first came here in your youth you said that I had but one fault, and that was my enmity towards squirrels."'[10]

Lady Gregory did not always get her way, however. When she read in his draft of his Nobel Prize acceptance speech that Yeats had described her as 'an old woman sinking into the infirmities of age', she had, at seventy-one, just taken a train across Ireland to Dublin and a taxi to the Abbey, where both she and Lennox Robinson were afraid that Yeats's description might damage her power to fill the house by suggesting that she had 'gone silly'. Yeats prevaricated, agreed to change the phrase, then, confessing that copy had already been sent to the newspapers, said he would moderate his description only to the degree of describing Lady Gregory as 'a living woman sinking into the infirmity of age' – the version that was eventually used.

If these were relatively trivial matters, there had been a more serious cause of quarrel between Yeats and Lady Gregory earlier in 1923 when 400 Republican prisoners went on hunger-strike. The government refused to submit to their demands for release or trial, and Lady Gregory and Lennox Robinson wrote a letter of protest to the newspapers. Yeats himself believed that the government should hold firm as this was a matter affecting national security (he was already appraised of the mumblings of discontent among the junior officers of the Free State army) and, since Lady Gregory herself was staying in Yeats's house, this placed her in a difficult position. She told Yeats what she had done and suggested, because he might not approve, that she should move out to a hotel. 'He would not allow that, and after talking for a while thought perhaps we had done right.' In fact, the hunger-strike was eventually called off and the prisoners were released, with the result that Lady Gregory felt herself 'more than ever a Republican though "without malice"'.

While the political differences between Yeats and Lady Gregory were indeed without serious rancour, the same could not be said of his relationship with Maud Gonne MacBride. Yeats's appointment to the Senate and his attitude to the Republican prisoners in particular were sources of conflict. Maud herself later declared that Yeats had turned away from both her and the Irish people 'when he became a Senator of the Free State which voted Flogging Acts against young republican soldiers still seeking to free Ireland from the contamination of the British Empire'.[11] Maud organised a Prisoners' Defence League to support those the government had imprisoned and was in her turn arrested and thrown into Kilmainham jail without charges. Here, in heroically defiant mood, she at once joined those of her fellow Republicans on hunger-strike, and when a bemused prison doctor wondered why she remained so cheerful, she replied: 'Why wouldn't I laugh when I won either way?'

Iseult, however, could not accept the situation with such bravado and, as so often, appealed to Yeats for help. He, as always, complied. He went to see Cosgrave, arguing that Maud had always had delicate health, but, when the President told him that women, doctors and the clergy should keep out of politics since their business was with the sick, Yeats wrote to Olivia Shakespear saying: 'I am afraid my help in the matter of blankets, instead of her release (where I could do nothing), will not make her less resentful. She had to choose (perhaps all women must) between the broomstick and the distaff and she has chosen the broomstick – I mean the witches' hats.'

The cynicism in this suggests the power Maud still had over the deepest recesses of Yeats's imagination, but her actions when, after twenty days, she was released from prison and carried out on a stretcher posed a challenge that was more than merely personal. Maud and Mrs Despard had led the Women's Prisoners' Defence League in a highly organised and efficient campaign in which detailed administration was matched by considerable courage. For example, when a bomb was planted near Mrs Despard's house, 'Madame Gonne-MacBride brought it to Rathdrum Police Station and handed it in, saying, "I return your property. You will be able to send it on to the particular force that placed it in Mrs Despard's outhouse."' Mrs Despard herself was away from Dublin at the time, speaking at election meetings in the south, but as one of Maud's closest friends she was part of a group of women politicians – among them Helena Molony, Hanna Sheehy-Skeffington and Constance Markiewicz – who personified two of the forces Yeats most feared in the new Ireland forming around him: Roman Catholicism and extreme socialism.

Maud never wavered in her religious conviction, and she was now expressing her socialist commitment strongly. She was firmly convinced that the Free State was but a continuation of the old British tyranny under a new name, and argued publicly and passionately for the adoption of a new political vision:

> In Ireland an obscure prejudice, born of slave teaching, surrounds the words Socialism and Communism, which even the clear thought and noble life and death of James Connolly failed to entirely dispel. Humanism in this case would be a true title, for Communism is the apotheosis of Christ's teaching of the brotherhood of man and the upraising of humanity. As a triumphant world wave, it will eventually reach Ireland and will find no contradiction in the Republican ideal.[12]

For Yeats, such ideas were anathema. The woman with whom he had once hoped to save the soul of Ireland through the magical force of a mystic marriage was now living proof that the democratic and Christian era was at its hysterical end, and that the world could expect the return of the antithetical gyre foreshadowed in 'Leda and the Swan'.

III

'From Democracy to Authority'

That poem had, however, been rejected for publication, and Yeats now sought editors other than George Russell through whom he could publicise the work. Iseult's husband Francis Stuart appeared to provide him with an opportunity. Stuart himself had been one of the Republican prisoners who had gone on hunger-strike, but he was released with the Christmas amnesty and was accompanied by members of the Women's Prisoners' Defence League back to his mother-in-law's home at Roebuck House. While in prison Stuart had fallen under the spell of Jim Phelan, an ardent Republican who believed not only that Collins had betrayed his ideals when helping to set up the Free State, but that Yeats too had lied in his poetry and that a truth-telling Irish poet would have been hanged rather than honoured with the Nobel Prize. Phelan also impressed upon Stuart the sovereign importance of avoiding conformity and second-hand experience so that a writer especially could preserve his integrity.

While in prison, Stuart had written a number of poems gathered together in a volume called *We Have Kept the Faith*, an advance copy of which was sent to Yeats as a Christmas present in 1923. Before Stuart's release, Harriet Munroe's magazine *Poetry* offered him its annual prize for the work of a promising young poet, and Yeats claimed to be similarly impressed by Stuart's writing. Stuart himself found Yeats a 'strange and rather chilly figure with his eagle glance', but both men were passionately concerned about issues of national culture, the idea that Ireland should build an intellectual life for itself that was not modelled on English examples. Stuart lectured and published a pamphlet on *Nationality and Culture*, and was soon persuaded by a Dublin bookseller to issue a monthly literary magazine called *To-morrow*.

Yeats was intrigued by this, believing it would stir 'an admirable row', and when Stuart and his fellow contributors came to see him, he loftily suggested they found their magazine on the 'doctrine of the immortality of the soul, most bishops and all bad writers being obviously atheists'. Here, in Stuart's magazine, there appeared to Yeats a means of confronting an increasingly materialistic world with his own most deeply held beliefs, and he went so far as to draft an editorial for the first issue. The Nobel Laureate would not slip into complacent mediocrity, but he would not be merely rash either. Appearing under the names of Stuart and Cecil Salkeld, the editorial was a declaration of support for Yeats's aristocratic and spiritual values which praised the great artists of the Italian renaissance for exuberantly reuniting pagan energies with Christian beliefs. Having created this atmosphere of defiant spiritual imagination, Yeats then proceeded to publish 'Leda and the Swan' in the second issue. It was less this work, however, than a blasphemous short story by Lennox Robinson which caused the magazine's rapid demise, but Yeats soon found other forums where he could propound his ideas.

In the attempt to recreate an authentically Celtic atmosphere in Ireland, the government had proposed the revival of the Tailtean Games, at which, on Yeats's suggestion, the Royal Irish Academy was to sponsor awards for Irish writers whose recent work had conferred 'honour and dignity upon Ireland'. Yeats, along with George Russell and Lennox Robinson, chose Stuart's poems for the prize. Although Stuart himself claimed that he 'felt little of that touch of the ridiculous that Yeats's solemnity could so easily evoke, in having to go up to a dais and kneel while he placed a laurel crown on my head', he did not in fact miss the element of the absurd in the occasion, noting that as he knelt down Yeats seemed to be 'enveloped in one of the clouds that seemed occasionally blown across his path', and that he was short-sightedly groping about for the laurel wreath lying on the table.

That Yeats was in fact in a serious and deeply preoccupied mood is suggested by a photograph of him taken at a garden party given by Gogarty at Ely Place to celebrate the revival of the Games. The photograph shows Compton Mackenzie, Augustus John, Edwin Lutyens, G. K. Chesterton, James Stephens and Lennox Robinson variously posturing in attitudes of tweedy ebullience. Yeats himself sits in the left-hand corner, an isolated figure withdrawn into the carapace of top hat and tails, his face frozen into a gesture of worried earnestness. In so far as he was preoccupied by political concerns, these were matters to which he was to give vent in a speech delivered at the Tailtean Banquet on 2 August 1924.

It is clear from the draft of this speech that Yeats was preparing a wholesale onslaught against the forces of socialism, materialism and mass opinion – against the false idea 'that the world was growing better and better, and could not even help doing so owing to physical science and democratic politics'.[13] Urging the energies of a contrary argument, he asked, 'Is it not possible, perhaps, that the stream has turned backwards and that a dozen generations to come will have for their task, not the widening of liberty, but recovery from its errors: that they will set their hearts upon the building of authority, the restoration of discipline, the discovery of a life sufficiently heroic to live without opium dreams?'

The reversal of Marx's most famous adage in the last clause clearly reveals one of the main enemies Yeats had in his sights, while the title of an earlier interview given on 16 February 1924 in the *Irish Times* suggests what Yeats considered to be the positive influences from which he was deriving his ideas: 'From Democracy to Authority: Paul Claudel and Mussolini – A New School of Thought'. Here he argued that 'the modern State is so complex that it must find some kind of expert government – a government firm enough, tyrannical enough if you will, to spend years in carrying out its plans'. Although Yeats was careful to hint at a separation between his own thought and his French mentor's royalist, Catholic and anti-semitic views, he stressed that he was sympathetic towards the belief that the state should be seen not as a scientifically created automaton but as a living entity, 'a growing child or an old man'.

Yeats believed that he could see 'the same tendency here in Ireland towards authoritative government' as he thought he could glimpse in France and Italy. The question was, he argued, whether this movement towards authoritarianism was merely a brief reaction to be expected in the aftermath of the Civil War, or, 'as I think, a part of a reaction that will last one hundred or one hundred and fifty years'. He believed that such an impetus would not preserve the same levels of intensity throughout this time but that it nonetheless indicated 'a steady movement towards the creation of a nation controlled by highly trained intellects'. The thinkers of the French right seemed to support his ideas, and Yeats claimed that 'psychologists and statisticians in Europe and America were also attacking the foundations of the nineteenth century liberal belief in progress'. Yeats already believed he had found his principal voice of authority in Mussolini and wrote enthusiastically that 'a great popular leader has said to an applauding multitude "We will trample upon the discomposing [*sic*] body of the Goddess of Liberty"'.[14]

IV
'We Are Not a Little People'

Circumstances now obliged Yeats to expose himself more closely to Mussolini's political experiment. Nineteen-twenty-four was the last year in which he was to experience a tolerable degree of physical health. His eyesight, always poor, was now considerably impaired, he was growing a little deaf as well as stout, and when out walking for his exercise found that he had high blood pressure and suffered from a loss of breath. It was clear that he needed to recuperate, and in November he and George set out on a three-month holiday during which they would visit Sicily, Capri and Rome.

In Rome, Yeats discovered books which had influenced Italian fascism. Croce's *Philosophy of Vico* led him to the root of these ideas, and he was pleased to find in Vico's theories confirmation of his own cyclical view of history. 'Students of contemporary Italy,' Yeats wrote, 'where Vico's thought is current through its influence on Croce and Gentile, think it created, or in part created, the present government of one man surrounded by just such able assistants as Vico foresaw.' Although Croce himself was soon to turn away from Mussolini, realising the barbarism that underlay the Duce's praise of aristocracy, discipline and anti-materialism, Gentile was to influence Yeats particularly. The Italian philosopher's belief that elites rose from and fell back into the mass of the people who themselves could not influence history, appealed to Yeats as 'the converse of Marxian socialism', but it was Gentile's ideas on education that Yeats was to find particularly important.[15]

He took from them what he found most humane: a belief in stimulation rather than a discipline of fear, an acknowledgement of the concrete over the abstract, and the idea that 'the whole curriculum of a school should be as it were one lesson and not a mass of unrelated topics'. Gentile's national emphases were important too, and from them Yeats derived the idea that Irish schools should 'feed the immature imagination upon that old folk life, and the mature intellect upon Berkeley and the great modern idealist philosophy created by his influence upon Burke who restored to political thought its sense of history'. Do this 'and Ireland is reborn, potent, armed and wise'. Yeats was nonetheless well aware of the dangers in such an approach, and for all that he urged a nationalist curriculum he insisted that 'the child itself must be the end in education'. He was concerned that such a view might be lost sight of and warned that 'there is a tendency to subordinate the child to the idea of the nation. I suggest whether we teach either Irish history, Anglo-Irish literature or Gaelic, we should always see that the child is the object and not any of our special purposes.'

So interested did Yeats become in education that, on his return to Ireland, he spent much time visiting primary schools throughout the land, talking to teachers and inspectors and forming his own opinions about what was happening. The position appeared a bleak one. Yeats thought that in the wake of the Great War children across Europe had become ill disciplined, but that in Ireland:

it is worse than elsewhere, for we have in a sense been at war for generations and of late that war has taken the form of burning and destruction under the eyes of the children. They respect nothing. One teacher said to me, 'I cannot take them through Stephen's Green because they would pull up the plants.' Go anywhere in Ireland and you will hear the same complaint. The children, everyone will tell you, are individually intelligent and friendly, yet have so little sense of the duty to community and neighbour that if they meet an empty house in a lonely place they will smash all the windows.

Eventually, Yeats was made Senate spokesman on the School Attendance Bill, and, far from urging repression in the face of the depressing circumstances he had made himself so familiar with, he constructed an argument which placed education close to the centre of national life and declared that 'we ought to be able to give the child of the poor as good an education as we give to the child of the rich'. School buildings would have to be improved, poor pupils fed, and all should be provided with books, washing facilities and, if necessary, clothes.

As part of this interest in Ireland's education system Yeats paid a visit early in 1926 to St Otteran's School in Waterford to see the Montessori principles and the ideals of the Parents' National Education Union that were practised there. Precisely how depressing such experiences could be is suggested by one of George's letters:

We lunched with Mother de Sales on Sunday . . . terrible O terrible . . . pale green washed walls and sacred pictures of the late eighteenth century, a dreadful plaster – very whitened plaster – Christ in the centre of the mantelpiece, draped in red plush with tassels, flanked on either side by two oriental and purely mundane figures, one of each sex, very markedly so, and these in turn flanked by two of the worst vases I have ever seen.[16]

George and Yeats were treated to an appalling lunch heavily laced with alcohol ('the brazen William drank two large glasses after refusing whisky and brandy that were urged on him'), whereupon they went down to inspect the classrooms, which were empty and freezing. Yeats apparently spent nearly two hours discussing the curriculum, Montessori methods and the Parents' National Education Union, besides closely questioning the 'blushing nuns' about how often the floors were washed and whether the children came to school clean. For George, the visit ended with a melancholy sense of self-deprecation, but for Yeats it issued in one of the great poems of his maturity, 'Among School Children'.

The tone of this work is partly suggested by a short note written after his visit to St Otteran's: 'Topic for poem. Schoolchildren, and the thought that life will waste them, perhaps that no possible life can fulfil their own dreams or even their teacher's hope. Bring in the old thought that life prepares for what never happens.' The poem begins in the dimity world of a primary-school classroom where the dutiful children learn to be neat 'in the best modern way' as they stare with mild surprise at the slightly portentous presence of Yeats, the 'sixty-year-old smiling public man'. But this outwardly conventional figure is inwardly a visionary. Perhaps it is the very smallness of life in a primary-school classroom that triggers thoughts at once despairing and euphoric: memories of a moment of emotional intimacy with Maud Gonne MacBride in the period of her majestic beauty and the corresponding realisation of the bitter decrepitude of old age which 'means that even the greatest men are owls, scarecrows, by the time their fame has come'. This last theme was to become one of the great subjects of Yeats's mature poetry, but here, out of his sense of physical decline, arises one of his most radiant passages – a vision of energy, completeness, wonder and Unity of Being:

> Labour is blossoming or dancing where
> The body is not bruised to pleasure soul,
> Nor beauty born out of its own despair,
> Nor blear-eyed wisdom out of midnight oil.
> O chestnut tree, great-rooted blossomer,
> Are you the leaf, the blossom, or the bole?
> O body swayed to music, O brightening glance,
> How can we know the dancer from the dance?[17]

The Ireland in which Yeats's schoolchildren were growing up was far removed from such ecstasy. Throughout the country unemployment was running at chronically high levels and was alleviated less by government policy than by large-scale emigration. Many of those remaining lived in appallingly over-crowded conditions, the slums in Dublin especially being responsible for a terrible rate of infant mortality. Patrick Pearse had believed that an independent Ireland would solve these problems. 'A free Ireland', he declared, 'would not, and could not, have hunger in her fertile vales and squalor in her cities.' He went on to promise that:

a free Ireland would drain the bogs, would harness the rivers, would plant the wastes, would nationalise the railways and waterways, would improve agriculture, would protect fisheries, would foster industries, would promote commerce, would diminish extravagant expenditure (as on needless judges and policemen), would beautify the cities, would educate the workers (and also the non-workers who stand in direr need of it).[18]

To the ministers of the Free State, however, such idealism had, it seemed, to yield to harsh daily practicalities. In the place of erstwhile revolutionary utopianism there emerged the grim necessity of balancing the books.

Considerable and successful efforts were made to rebuild the nation's infrastructure (the Shannon scheme to provide a national electricity supply was a spectacular example of this), while a Land Act and a Land Law hastened the process of transferring farms to the possession of their tenants. An efficient civil service was also maintained, but as this was run along lines similar to those during the days of British imperialism it seemed but one more example of the belief that, as de Valera and the IRA were keen to point out, Cosgrave's government, rather than creating a genuinely Irish community, was essentially 'West British'.

Nothing seemed to confirm this more bitterly than the division of the nation into North and South. On the day that the Irish Free State formally came into being, the powers in Belfast informed both Westminster and Dublin that the North was determined to remain separate. Under the terms of the Treaty this meant that a Boundary Commission had to be appointed, but, when this sat in 1925, it dashed Free State hopes that its findings would reduce Northern Ireland to a mere four counties, which, being too small to create a viable economic or political unit, would inevitably merge with the South. The Commission ruled that the size of Northern Ireland was not its concern and, concentrating on the detailed arrangements of the border, declared that the six counties should remain substantially as they were. It had already been agreed that such findings would be legally binding, and the Free State, desperate to save face, entered into tripartite discussions which eventually resulted in the South being freed from its obligation to sustain part of the United Kingdom's national debt in return for the effective removal of the Treaty's moribund Council of Ireland and the acceptance by all parties of the fact of partition. With what later emerged as grotesque irony, it was agreed that North and South would now discuss matters of common interest 'in a spirit of neighbourly comradeship'. Both de Valera and the IRA saw this as an appalling setback to Nationalist aspirations and, by holding fast to an indivisible ideal of a united republic, helped to maintain the idea that physical force rather than negotiation offered the likeliest means of ending partition.

The Southern Ireland thus created was overwhelmingly Roman Catholic, a position that had been greatly reinforced in the third quarter of the nineteenth century by the powerful influence of Cardinal Cullen. The church drew its bishops and priests from the people, an extensive campaign of church building was followed, and a large number of devotional practices including pilgrimages, the use of the rosary and reverence for the Sacred Heart and the Immaculate Conception helped inspire a deep and widespread belief which easily left the impression that the Catholic Church was the national church of Ireland.

In this atmosphere it was a matter of intense embarrassment to the Free State government that it had inherited from the imperial parliament the power to grant divorce. This was a function it intended to renounce, and Yeats was appalled by the many dangers he foresaw. In March 1925 he published his 'Undelivered Speech' outlining his objections. Here he showed that he particularly opposed state interference in matters of conscience, declaring that 'we put our faith in human nature, and think that if you give men good education you can trust their intellects and their consciences without making rules that seem to us arbitrary. Some rules there have to be, for we live together in corporate society, but they are matters of practical convenience.'[19]

He saw too that the decision of the Free State parliament to surrender its power to grant divorce was conditioned in part at least by a blinkered and obsessive desire to make itself (for all de Valera's caveats) appear as different from the government at Westminster as possible. In the past, such attitudes had helped promote the cause of Irish freedom (although Yeats himself had always been wary of the degree of fanaticism involved in this), but he believed that now, with the achievement of independence, matters were different:

> For the last hundred years Irish nationalism has had to fight against England, and that fight has helped fanaticism, for we had to welcome everything that gave Ireland emotional energy, and had little use for intelligence so far as the mass of the people were concerned, for we had to hurl them against an alien power. The basis of Irish nationalism has now shifted, and much that once helped us is now injurious.

Yeats was particularly aware that such old-fashioned government attitudes would alienate the Ulster Protestants, who 'can be won, not now, but in a generation, but they cannot be won if you insist that the Catholic conscience alone must dominate the public life of Ireland'.

This was perhaps true, but the Dail's attitudes were bound to harden the differences already caused by partition. To attack Catholic culture in such a situation was dangerous, but Yeats insisted on opposing the influence of a rigid and international dogma over the 'living, changing, advancing human mind' and, when he actually spoke on this issue in the Senate, his attack on the historical veracity of the Gospels was so extravagant as to cause outrage.[20] Equally notorious was his assertion that divorce did not increase immorality. He despised the narrow-mindedness of those who supposed it did, and in a passage of reckless daring (later reworked into his poem 'The Three Monuments') he argued that the very landmarks of Dublin itself proclaimed a spirit of sexual tolerance. He was referring in particular to the statues of O'Connell, Parnell and Nelson. 'It was said about O'Connell in his own day', Yeats declared, 'that you could not throw a stick over a workhouse wall without hitting one of his children, but he believed in the indissolubility of marriage, and when he died his heart was very properly preserved in Rome.' With the irony of a considerable orator, Yeats then declared that 'we had a good deal of trouble about Parnell when he married a woman who thereby became Mrs Parnell'. He then turned to the Protestant Bishop who would have denied the loose-living Nelson his right to a statue and 'would have preferred to give him a gallows because Nelson should have been either hanged or transported'. Drawing general conclusions from these particular instances, Yeats turned to the house and declared: 'I think . . . we have in our midst three very salutary objects of meditation which may, perhaps, make us a little more tolerant. . . . I do not think that the memories of these great men of genius were swept away by their sexual immoralities.'

Above all, Yeats was determined to show that the proposal to abrogate the government's right to grant divorce was an attack on the rights of the minority Protestants in the South to whom he himself belonged. To infringe such people's liberties in the name of a supposedly unifying Catholic dogma would not be to bind the nation together but to create an embittered faction within it. Yeats produced two general ideas with which to buttress this notion. He argued first that 'once you attempt legislation upon religious grounds you open the way for every kind of intolerance and for every kind of religious persecution'. This was undoubtedly a valid warning, if exaggerated, but Yeats was also determined to show that it was precisely the minority group under attack which had produced the glories of eighteenth-century Irish culture.

In a peroration that became notorious, Yeats declared: 'We against whom you have done this thing are no petty people. We are one of the great stocks of Europe. We are the people of Burke; we are the people of Grattan; we are the people of Swift, the people of Emmet, the people of Parnell. We have created the most of the modern literature of this country. We have created the best of its political intelligence.'[21] The effects of this on Yeats's reputation were, of course, disastrous. He was accused of being reactionary, divisive and a snob, even if he did tell Lady Gregory that he got 'constant congratulations on my speech'. Knowing that he could not possibly win, Yeats had opted for the histrionic, but he came in time to realise that he could not 'match those old lawyers, old bankers, old businessmen, who, because all habit and memory, have begun to govern the world'. As he confessed to Pound: 'No, Ezra, those generalities that make all men politicians and some few eloquent are not as true as they were. You and I, those impressive and convinced politicians . . . are as much out of place as would be the first composers of sea-shanties in an age of steam.'

On some matters, however, Yeats remained 'an incendiary', and the long-drawn-out issue of the Hugh Lane pictures could still inspire a blazing passion. Yeats had explained the position to the Senate in 1923 and had appeared with Lady Gregory and Hugh Lane's sister as a witness on the British government commission of enquiry set up to investigate the question. Victory had seemed all but assured until 1925, when Sir Joseph Duveen offered to build a new wing for the Tate Gallery provided the Lane collection were housed in it. The offer was accepted, the wing was built and, despite the ownership of the pictures being still a *sub judice* matter, King George V offered formally to open the new building. By the time Yeats spoke in the Senate the London gallery had indeed been opened and the commission had rejected Ireland's claim to Lane's pictures. An angry Yeats cast doubts in the Senate on the English King's loyalty to his Irish peoples and was furious at his failure to take advice from the Irish executive. Hoping to win inflamed Republican and Labour support for his exposure of what he considered an insult, Yeats declared that Ireland would, along with Canada, 'seek at the next Imperial Conference for some clarification or modification of the relations between the Crown and the Dominions. I think that this recent experience of ours shows that one or the other is necessary.'

But such activities and their strong undertow of nationalism were none-theless increasingly repellent to George, and she was concerned about what she thought of as the deleterious effect they had on her husband's art. 'I have been reading nothing but poetry just lately,' she wrote to a friend, *not* his!! and it has made me realise how damnably national he is becoming. Nationality throws out personality and there is nothing in his verse worth preserving but the personal. All the pseudo-mystico-intellecto-nationalistico stuff of the last fifteen years isn't worth a trouser button. . . . As long as there was any gesture in it, as long as there was a war on and so on and so on, it was worth it, but really now to spend hours listening to rubbish in and out of the Senate and going to committees and being visited by fishermen's associations, and Freddy Ryans and nincompoops and miaows and bow-wows of all sorts mostly mongrels is a bit too much. However.[22]

Sometimes such differences of opinion boiled over into argument, and in March 1926, when Yeats had been crying up the Abbey's style of acting against what he called 'the English Stage Cliché', George 'bit Willie's head off'. So irked was she by nationalism that she had been 'cock-a-hoop' when Ireland failed to win a sporting Triple Crown, and she declared that Yeats himself 'was most abusive and he was being really very cross and unpleasant coming home from the Abbey and going on like a thorough-paced Irish-anti-Englishman'.

V
'Cease to Remember the Delights of Youth'

Although George was realising that she would have to stand up to her husband if she were to preserve her independence, Yeats's poetry of the middle 1920s was altogether wider and more profound than George in a tetchy moment cared to confess. Two masterpieces in particular reveal the antithetical man as he faced the realities of advancing age. In 'Sailing to Byzantium', the elderly poet moves in imagination at least from the 'sensual music' of the natural world to a culture where all is artifice, anonymity and permanence. As Yeats had suggested in *A Vision*, the Byzantium of Justinian was a civilisation where Unity of Being had been almost completely achieved.

I think that in early Byzantium, and maybe never before or since in recorded history, religious, aesthetic and practical life were one, that architect and artificers – though not, it may be, poets, for language had been the instrument of controversy and must have grown abstract – spoke to the multitude and the few alike. The painter and the mosaic worker, the worker in gold and silver, the illuminator of Sacred Books, were almost impersonal, almost perhaps without the consciousness of individual design, absorbed in their subject-matter and that the vision of a whole people.[23]

To be gathered into this 'artifice of eternity', however, the poet is obliged to renounce his physical and sexual being. This was made explicit in an early prose draft of the poem where Yeats wrote, 'for many loves have I taken off my clothes, for some I threw them off in haste, for some slowly and indifferently . . . but now I will take off my body'. Only in this state can the poet realise that ambiguous dream of fulfilment:

> Once out of nature I shall never take
> My bodily form from any natural thing,
> But such a form as Grecian goldsmiths make
> Of hammered gold and gold enamelling
> To keep a drowsy emperor awake;
> Or set upon a golden bough to sing
> To lords and ladies of Byzantium
> Of what is past, or passing, or to come.[24]

The pain of age – the recognition of passion amid physical decrepitude – receives an altogether different treatment in 'The Tower'. Abstract philosophy alone, it seems, can provide an antidote for the poet's vigorous but inappropriate feeling. It appears that truth can only be derived from reason, and that in an ageing man passion is somehow something unsuitable, indecorous and even pathetic. The second part of the poem rejects such lifeless pessimism, however, assembling a range of anecdotes and reviving once more the figure of Red Hanrahan from *The Secret Rose* to suggest how the imagination can win life from poverty and desolation. The final part of the poem glorifies this experience and defiantly rejects mere abstraction to suggest that the whole of man's experience of this world and the world to come is and can only be created by the power of his vision. In a mood of defiant assertion (a mood that was increasingly to characterise Yeats's mature work) he declares his faith:

> I mock Plotinus' thought
> And cry in Plato's teeth,
> Death and life were not
> Till man made up the whole,
> Made lock, stock and barrel
> Out of his bitter soul,
> Aye, sun and moon and star, all,
> And further add to that
> That, being dead, we rise,
> Dream and so create
> Translunar Paradise.[25]

Art alone is the true expression of this discovery, and Yeats concludes the poem with an assertion of art's impersonal power. However, for all that

Yeats's poetry from this period celebrates an art which rises above the turbulence of mortal existence, circumstances were to make him aware that in contemporary Dublin literature remained a focus for bitter conflict.

By 1923 Sean O'Casey had unsuccessfully submitted two plays to the Abbey Theatre, but in that year the management accepted *The Shadow of a Gunman*, which was mounted in a production Lady Gregory declared to be 'an immense success, beautifully acted, all the political points taken up with delight by a big audience'. The following year *Juno and the Paycock* was even more enthusiastically received, and Lady Gregory turned to Yeats on the first night and said: 'This is one of the evenings at the Abbey that makes me glad to have been born.' A deep friendship developed between the ageing aristocrat and the forty-year-old working man, who was invited to Coole in June 1924. There, far from feeling overwhelmed, O'Casey was put at his ease by what he shrewdly called Lady Gregory's 'serving eagerness'. As he later recalled, 'he hadn't been ten minutes at the table before he felt he had often been there, to eat soberly, and talk merrily of books and theatre, and of the being of Ireland; she in simple and most gracious ways showing how things were handled; pointing out that dese things were done, not because of any desire for ceremony, but because dey made one more comfortable, and things easier to eat'.[26]*

The production in 1926 of O'Casey's *The Plough and the Stars* was to show, however, that 'the being of Ireland' was a volatile existence easily stirred to hatred. The Abbey itself was now in receipt of a government subsidy of £800 (subsequently raised to £1050), which had saved it from bankruptcy after the lean years of war. This made the Irish National Theatre the first state-subsidised theatre in the English-speaking world, but the price was a government nominee on the board. This man, George O'Brien, had strong reservations about the language used in O'Casey's play. He was not alone. Michael Dolan, the Abbey manager, was equally concerned by language that went 'beyond the beyonds', and he wrote to Lady Gregory, 'I respectfully beg of you to pause and think what it will mean. As you know, we cannot afford to take risks.' Some of the cast too were perturbed, but when O'Brien made it plain that he believed the play might offend 'so seriously as to provoke an attack on the Theatre of a kind that would endanger the continuance of the subsidy', Yeats and Lady Gregory publicly declared for freedom. Behind the scenes, however, they negotiated with a practised subtlety and firmness. They had already decided that certain passages would have to be removed, and at a meeting Lady Gregory gave an account of the Abbey's past battles with censorship and 'Yeats also spoke in the same sense. O'Brien sat up in his chair reiterating at intervals, "that song is objectionable," (we had already decided that it must go, but left

* O'Casey probably exaggerated Lady Gregory's lisp.

it as a bone for him to gnaw at).' Lady Gregory could declare afterwards that the directors' meeting had been 'easy' and that O'Brien had behaved 'like a lamb'.

The same could not be said of the audience, and following the outbursts which had greeted the second and third nights there was an eruption of violence on the fourth. There was much in the unheroic presentation of the Easter Uprising to offend committed Nationalists, but O'Casey was probably correct when he wrote that 'the attack was born of no sudden impulse, but was thought of long before the cry came. In it there was no tint of fear for Ireland's honour, the integrity of art, or the dignity of the Irishman. It was aimed at Yeats.' The women of the extreme Republican group were particularly vehement, and these of course included Maud Gonne MacBride. As so often, she was opposing Yeats and the production of great literature for the sake of political ends, but O'Casey's portrait of her is touched with tragedy. 'Here she sat now, silent, stony; waiting her turn to say more bitter words against the one who refused to make her dying dream his own. There she sits stonily silent, once a sybil of patriotism from whom no oracle ever came; now silent and aged . . . never quite at ease with the crowd, whose cheers she loved; the colonel's daughter still.'

As the tumult in the theatre itself rose, Yeats called for silence but could not be heard. Anticipating that this might happen, he had earlier given the text of his prepared speech to the *Irish Times*. Just as with the riots that had greeted *The Playboy of the Western World*, when Yeats had defiantly presented himself as the patriotic author of *Cathleen ni Houlihan*, so now, as history repeated itself, he reminded the people of Ireland of that long-gone conflict.

> You have disgraced yourselves again. Is this to be an ever-recurring celebration of the arrival of Irish genius? Synge first, and then O'Casey! The news of the happenings of the past few minutes will go from country to country. Dublin has once more rocked the cradle of genius. From such a scene in this theatre went forth the fame of Synge. Equally the fame of O'Casey is born here tonight. This is his apotheosis.[27]

This was true, but the bitterness of the controversy was such that O'Casey, like many brilliant Irishmen, eventually left the country for good.

In April, Yeats was ill with measles and a mild rupture. While he recuperated, he deepened his awareness of contemporary thought by reading Whitehead's *Science and the Modern World* and Spengler's *Decline of the West*, as well as studying (despite his protestations in 'The Tower' against this ancient author) Stephen MacKenna's translation of Plotinus. He spent the early spring regaining his strength at Thoor Ballylee, where a small incident occurred that seemed symbolic of the modern Ireland Yeats was coming increasingly to disparage. A paralysed old beggar who had once been a piper visited and lamented the passing of the life lived in the now gutted or deserted great houses of the land. 'The gentry have kept the shoes on my feet, and the coat on my back and the shilling in my pocket – never once in all the forty and five years that I have been upon the road have I asked a penny of a farmer.' The appeal of this was such that Yeats felt constrained to give the man five shillings, which, he supposed, he spent on drink in the nearest town.

But, if the traditional arts were in decay, Yeats's own inspiration was still greatly productive, stirred to creativity by his obsession with his failing physical powers. 'A Man Old and Young' is a series of sparse and moving lyrics on his sexual career. Maud Gonne MacBride, Olivia Shakespear and Iseult are all evoked, and a letter Yeats wrote to Olivia Shakespear suggests the disillusioned tone of the whole: 'I came upon two early photographs of you yesterday . . . who ever had a like profile? – a profile from a Sicilian coin. One looks back to one's youth as to [a] cup that a mad man dying of thirst left half tasted. I wonder if you feel like that.' The last poem in the sequence is a translation from Sophocles' *Oedipus at Colonus* and is particularly apt in this context:

> Endure what life God gives and ask no longer span;
> Cease to remember the delights of youth, travel-wearied aged man;
> Delight becomes death-longing if all longing else be vain.[28]

The power and directness of this are impressive, and illustrate Yeats's claim that in his translations 'the one thing that I kept in mind was that a word unfitted for living speech, out of its natural order, or unnecessary to our modern technique, would check emotion and tire attention'. As Yeats told Olivia Shakespear, he had made his language 'bare, hard, and natural like a saga', and this was the fruit of many years of intermittent pondering over the problem of translating Greek tragedy. Gogarty had drafted for him a version of *Oedipus* as early as 1904, and Yeats had considered staging the play at the Abbey in 1910 to flourish Irish freedom in the face of English censorship which had declared the play immoral and banned it from the stage. During the winter of the following year Yeats had tried his hand at turning Jebb's translation into 'speakable English' but had decided not to continue with this because the ludicrous ban on Sophocles' work in England was lifted. George, however, was impressed by what Yeats had achieved and now she urged him to take up the work again.

This time Yeats used a French translation, and he soon became deeply interested in the work. Indeed, *Oedipus* itself was barely completed before Yeats went on to produce his version of *Oedipus at Colonus* and, as he told Olivia Shakespear, 'I have but one overwhelming emotion, a sense as of the actual presence in a terrible sacrament of the god, but I have got that always, though never before so strongly from Greek Drama.' He felt that when Oedipus enters the Wood of the Furies he experienced that same sense of awe and terror as an Irish countryman feels in 'certain haunted woods in Galway and Sligo'. The resulting productions were a tumultuous success. As the *New York Times* wrote: 'one does not expect to see an audience, drawn from all ranks of life, crowding a theatre beyond its capacity and becoming awed into spellbound and breathless attention by a tragedy of Sophocles. Yet that is exactly what happened at the Abbey Theatre.'

VI
'Blood and the Moon'

Yeats's enthusiastic translation of Sophocles was one impediment to the 'last great effort' with which he was hoping to complete his *Autobiographies*. Another was the immense amount of work he felt obliged to put in after May 1926 when he was appointed chairman of the Senate committee set up to design a new Irish coinage. Yeats characteristically interested himself in all aspects of this project, and the result was a national coinage of great aesthetic distinction. Yeats himself had suggested that the coins should 'tell one story' by representing Irish birds and animals. This highly practical proposal nonetheless gave rise to acrimony. The Republicans objected to the appointment of an Englishman as designer, while Catholics criticised a 'pagan' coinage that was wholly without religious symbolism.

While Yeats's work on the coinage committee was probably the most concrete achievement of his career in the Senate, Catholic criticism of his work especially pointed to the narrowing culture of the newly independent Irish state. The church was determined to lay on it its crushing hand of morality. A joint pastoral of the Irish Hierarchy issued in 1927 suggests the atmosphere they were creating:

> These latter days have witnessed, among many other unpleasant sights, a loosening of the bonds of parental authority, a disregard for the discipline of the home, and a general impatience under restraint that drives youth to neglect the sacred claims of authority . . . the evil one is ever setting his snares for unwary feet. At the moment his traps for the innocent are chiefly the dance hall, the bad book, the indecent paper, the motion picture, the immodest fashion in female dress – all of which tend to destroy the virtues characteristic of our race.[29]

Such attitudes would soon involve Yeats once again in a bitter struggle with the menace of censorship, but now two deaths were to make starkly clear the nature of the new nation forming around him.

Constance Markiewicz died in August 1927. Hers had been the remarkable career of a remarkable woman. She had not merely left the ranks of the Anglo-Irish Ascendancy, understanding that as a class it could have little political relevance in a modern Ireland; she had also been actively involved in the Easter Uprising and had played a significant part in events subsequent to that. Yeats, however, yearning for old order and decorum as things which might give dignity to his country, chose to see Constance's achievements as a deformation of her inherited beauty. Her sister, the ardent socialist Eva Gore-Booth, had died the year before, and in his poem to the women Yeats chose to see their politics as an image of their ageing bodies now 'withered old and skeleton-gaunt'. This was deeply unfair, and it is significant that Yeats, in some of the most beautiful lines he ever wrote, chose to praise and memorialise that now irrecoverable period when, as a young and tortured writer, he had found some measure of consolation in the graciousness of their ancestral home:

> The light of evening, Lissadell,
> Great windows open to the south,
> Two girls in silk kimonos, both
> Beautiful, one a gazelle.[30]

Constance Markiewicz had, Yeats thought, capitulated to a mob against whom he wished to oppose the rule of educated and able men. He believed in particular that Kevin O'Higgins, the Minister for Justice, embodied these qualities, calling him 'the one strong intellect in Irish public life'. Yeats had become his friend and admired the determination of the politician who, during the Civil War, had argued for the execution of some seventy-seven people captured with arms in their possession. For Yeats himself, the existence of the death penalty, while a fearsome thing whose use he wished to see contained, had considerable symbolic and national importance. The people's assent to it, he thought, was a fundamental way of showing that they considered the government legitimate. Yeats argued that the English had had no such mandate and five years after the executions following on the Easter Uprising had been rightfully expelled. 'The Government of the Free State', on the other hand, 'has been proved legitimate by the only effective test; it has been permitted to take life.'[31] Such a contract, Yeats believed, implied 'moral unity'. What in the present situation it could not guarantee, however, was safety. The chthonian law of an eye for an eye was, as O'Higgins himself knew, a daily threat. 'Nobody', he declared, 'can expect to live who has done what I have.' On 10 July 1927, on his way to Mass in a Dublin suburb, O'Higgins was shot dead.

The event inspired two poems. In September, Yeats wrote the terse and gnomic 'Death', in which O'Higgins, as a 'great man in his pride', is seen confronting his murderers armed with the superior, liberating assurance of those who know that the cycles of reincarnation make a mockery of death. A month earlier, Yeats composed 'Blood and the Moon', an altogether more troubled reflection on contemporary Ireland. Here, the symbolic Thoor Ballylee is no longer a place of flowing life and images. Reared as other ancestral houses had been, the 'bloody, arrogant power' that fashioned it mocks the debilitated, contemporary world. As in real life, the winding stair at the tower's core (which was to give itself as the title to Yeats's next great volume of poetry) is a turning, spiralling gyre that leads not to the assurance of an antithetical and lunar age but merely to uncertainty and incompleteness. Just as the upper storeys of Thoor Ballylee were never renovated by Yeats and led only to a waste room at the top, so the great political and spiritual vision of eighteenth-century Ireland Yeats had been studying with such enthusiasm appears to peter out into nothing. It was possible to imagine Swift, Goldsmith, Berkeley and Burke once mounting the steps of the tower, and it was possible to think of their power: of Swift rooting out the folly of the world in the bitterness of his indignation, of Goldsmith delighting in the elegance of his prose, of Burke, who proved 'that the State was a tree, no mechanism to be pulled in pieces', and of:

> God-appointed Berkeley that proved all things a dream,
> That this pragmatical, preposterous pig of a world, its farrow that so
>   solid seem,
> Must vanish on the instant if the mind but change its theme. . . .[32]

The civilisation of eighteenth-century Ireland once led from cleansing rancour to vision, but now all is weakness and uncertainty, contemporary men in Ireland have no real authority and are seen as weakly clamouring 'in drunken frenzy for the moon'. They have neither moral, political nor visionary certainty and can merely watch impotently as the souls of the dead (in a familiar image of metamorphosis after death) beat at the windows of the unfinished tower, just as the butterflies and moths did in real life. There are, it seems, no heroes to inspire the country, and underlying the poem is Yeats's fear of an Ireland ever more disastrously trapped in narrow philistinism, a new nation emasculated by its reneging on old vision.

PART SIX

Under Ben Bulben

Cast a cold eye
On life, on death.
Horseman, pass by!

16

The Last Romantics
(1927–1932)

I
Illness

The burden of Yeats's many years of unremitting search for occult vision, a vigorous national life and an art in which to express these was beginning to take its toll. By October 1927, his physical health had so far deteriorated that George later wondered if he was undergoing a breakdown, and confessed that if she had anticipated he would become so fragile she would never have agreed to have children. A cold, probably exacerbated by Yeats's heavy smoking, turned to congestion of the lungs which was accompanied by a high temperature and delirium. Yeats himself 'hardly expected to recover', and was advised to seek the sun. By November 1927, George had arranged for them to travel to Algeciras where, amid 'the rich midnight of the garden trees', an exhausted Yeats determined to revise the proofs of *The Tower* and struggle with his forebodings.

'At Algeciras – A Meditation upon Death' uses landscape and memory to convey the burden of his feelings, the flight of the 'heron-billed pale cattle-birds' across the 'narrow Straits' to the hotel garden suggesting the passage of the soul from this world to the next. A childhood memory of carrying shells from the Rosses beach to one of his Pollexfen relatives prompts thoughts of the artist offering his life's work to God, but, for all the sense of immanent beauty and majesty, the poem ends with an honest recognition that the greatest of mortal problems remained for Yeats unsolved. His poetic imagination seems constantly to have returned to his childhood and youth, however, and in 'Mohini Chatterjee' – intended as a companion poem to the earlier 'Meditation' – he brought to mind his teenage interest in Theosophy and Eastern religion. The first part of the poem versifies Chatterjee's doctrine of reincarnation and his belief in preserving an absolute passivity, along with his idea that all life is 'a stream which flows on out of human control, one action or thought leading to another, that we ourselves are nothing but a mirror and that deliverance consists of turning the mirror away so that it reflects nothing'.[1]

Such a philosophy had had a considerable fascination for the adolescent Yeats, but the mature, antithetical man could not accept it uncritically, and the second part of his poem to his early mentor suggests the human value of a life of strenuous and passionate acceptance. This was a theme more powerfully developed in 'A Dialogue of Self and Soul,' where Yeats captures the gyring energies of the Soul dwindling from intensity as the Self emerges into so full an acceptance of life that 'a sweetness flows into the breast' even as the body learns to laugh and sing and bless a world in which man is bound to endure 'that toil of growing up' and all the ignominy and suffering of life from boyhood to maturity.

'I am content to live it all again.' The spiritual resilience of this, marvellously suggestive as it is of the heroic defiance and tragic joy of the mature Yeats, had nonetheless to be accompanied by a physical forbearance which in the short term must have been difficult to sustain. Yeats's congested lung did not recover, and, when he and George moved on to Seville in the hope of more sunshine, it began to bleed. After ten days it was decided that they could perhaps find better medical help in France, and they moved to the Hôtel Saint Georges at Cannes. The doctor was adamant that Yeats should have complete rest. He was to stay in bed or lie on a couch, coming downstairs only for lunch. He was not to read too much and so avoid over-excitement, and was even told to turn his head slowly so as to calm the pace of his thoughts. It would be three or four months before he was able to work again, but it was during their time at Cannes, as Yeats slowly recuperated, that he and George experienced one of their most spectacular visitations from the supernatural world.

Yeats had returned from his walk at a quarter to five one afternoon to hear George locking the door of her room. After a while she rose and began to walk in her sleep, coming into Yeats's room through the connecting door and lying down on the sofa. 'The communicator had scarcely spoken before I heard somebody trying to get into her room and remembered that the nurse brought our daughter there every afternoon at five. My wife heard and, being but half awakened, fell in trying to get to her feet, and though able to hide her disturbance from the nurse and from our daughter, suffered from the shock.'[2] Unperturbed, the communicator reappeared the next day at a later time, the first of many visitations in which he discussed what Yeats had written.

He was clearly very angry that Yeats's questions showed the influence of his philosophical reading and this led to a fierce spiritualist argument, 'one of those quarrels which I have noticed almost always precede the clearest statements'. This indeed proved to be the case. In a few minutes the spirits 'drew that distinction between what their terminology calls the *Faculties* and what it calls the *Principles*, between experience and revelation, between understanding and reason, between the higher and lower mind, which has engaged the thought of saints and philosophers from the time of Buddha'.

Thus fortified, the Yeatses had, by mid-February 1928, moved on to Rapallo on the Italian Riviera, attracted there partly by the presence of Ezra and Dorothy Pound. It seems that Yeats's health had indeed improved by this time. George, who was due to take the children to school in Switzerland, told Dorothy that Yeats needed to read or have read to him a least four detective novels a week: 'apart from them he has histories of Indian philosophy and various english parasites in that line . . . to say nothing of the works of Saint Theresa. . . . Quite horrid, the latter, *I* think!' Pound himself noted that Yeats arrived in Rapallo 'not so delapidated'. He was 'still able to complain about being gaga, and be disgusted with favourable notices in the British press, which he takes to be sign of his final passing. Prepared to be starred as last victorian etc. Hears his early work was more poetic etc.'[3]

Despite his weak state, Yeats's response to Rapallo was radiant. 'This is an incredibly lovely place,' he told Lady Gregory, 'some little Greek town one imagines. . . . Here I shall put off the bitterness of Irish quarrels and write my most amiable verses.' Yeats was later to give public expression to his delight in 'houses mirrored in an almost motionless sea, mountains that shelter the bay from all but the south wind', and in the mixed and cosmopolitan society that gathered in the town, writers and painters such as Thomas Mann, Gerhard Hauptmann, Max Beerbohm and Oscar Kokoshka, passing Italian peasants and impoverished princes 'on the broad pavement by the sea'.

Pound's apartment was an inevitable focus of social life and complications. He had recently befriended the young George Antheil in Paris and declared him 'possibly the salvation of music. He has been causing riots in Budapesth; I think by playing Strawinsky.' Intrigued by his protégé, Pound persuaded him to compose two sonatas for Olga Rudge, a concert violinist with a strong and resourceful personality who in July 1925 became the mother of Pound's illegitimate daughter. Both Pound and Dorothy maintained an appearance of outward respectability, although their marriage was no longer a happy one, and in June 1926 Dorothy returned pregnant from a solo visit to Egypt. Yeats himself wrote to Olivia Shakespear that 'I hear that you are to be a grandmother and that the event is taking place in the usual secrecy . . . I congratulate you upon it. Dorothy . . . will make an excellent mother.' But by September 1926 he was writing again: 'I divine that you have already adopted the grandchild.' Dorothy indeed took the newly named Omar Pound to England, where she stayed for a year, and where Omar himself was brought up at first by a retired nanny living in a village near Bognor Regis.

Pound himself meanwhile was pursuing his musical enthusiasms. He had recently written an opera and attended the première of George Antheil's *Ballet Mécanique*, a work for eight grand pianos and two large aeroplane propellers which caused outrage on its first performance in Paris. Back in Rapallo, Pound, with his sombrero, cape and yellow scarf, was also completing the seventeenth of his *Cantos* – a luminous description of Venice which Yeats would later want to reprint in his *Oxford Book of Modern Verse*. Yeats was particularly intrigued, however, by Pound's regularly going out at night to feed the Rapallo cats, and he later shrewdly moralised this strange compulsion into a wider understanding of Pound's nature and his embittered place in contemporary literary politics. 'Cats are oppressed, dogs terrify them, landladies starve them, boys stone them, everybody speaks of them with contempt,' Yeats declared. 'If they were human beings we could talk of their oppressors with a studied violence, add our strength to theirs, even organise the oppressed and like good politicians sell our charity for power. I examine his criticism in this new light, his praise of writers pursued by ill-luck.'

Pound's embattled position had earlier been made clear in Wyndham Lewis's *Time and Western Man*, a book which Yeats had been reading and enjoying when his French doctor ordered him to rest. The book contained a strenuous attack on Pound, Lewis pointing out that Pound's real interest was in ancient and medieval poetry, which he was able skilfully to imitate, and that this suggested that his conspicuous and angry modernism was essentially something false, a parasite's enthusiasm disguised his own lack of originality. This was not wholly accurate, and Yeats wrote some paragraphs on the assault which he later destroyed, but during the course of the year it was to become evident that an increasingly bitter and distorted Pound believed that Yeats had been drawn to Rapallo by the irresistible pull of his own superior genius.

The publication of *The Tower* in February 1928 showed how otiose such a judgement was. Sturge Moore's subtle and harmonious cover design offers an indication of the poetic world to be found in the volume. Yeats had asked for 'something in the nature of a woodcut' and insisted that the representation of the tower itself 'should not be too unlike the real object, or rather that it should suggest the real object. I like to think of that building as permanent symbol of my work plainly visible to the passer-by. As you know, all my art theories depend upon just this – rooting of mythology in the earth.' The upper half of the completed design certainly suggests this, for the tower is impressively solid. The remarkable quality of the work, however, lies in the way Sturge Moore, by reflecting the rootedness of the real tower in the waters around it (in strictly geographical terms an impossible view), managed to convey its immaterial, visionary qualities, a sense both of reality and of transformation, a visual equivalent perhaps of the hermetic maxim 'as above, so below'.

The difficulties, the agonies even, of that relationship are a central element in the range of the verse itself. Of all Yeats's carefully ordered volumes, *The Tower* most powerfully suggests his ability to arrange the vast scope of his lyric genius into a sequence so compelling that poems magnificent in isolation gain in stature, in drama, from their being juxtaposed to each other while being gathered up into the greater artifice of the whole. The ordering of the poems, the progress from the yearning to escape into imaginative permanence seen in 'Sailing to Byzantium' and on to the concluding intimations of an afterlife glimpsed in 'All Souls' Night', is deepened throughout by the presence of Yeats's *Vision* philosophy which, barely obtruding as an abstract system, is nonetheless, as its name implies, an imaginative means of grasping historical change and exploring the agonies of its human consequences. In nothing is the volume more courageous, however, than in its recognition that the intuitions on which it is founded break down under the stress of evil and despair. The would-be artificer of the golden bird and the occultist peering into the afterlife is also the nationalist forced to the recognition that inexplicably powerful forces of evil have shattered the decorum of art, turned vision to despair and national endeavour to a black-mass of self-delighting destruction. Bewildered and visionless in a world too terrible to sustain coherence, the poet of *The Tower* becomes one of the supreme voices of the twentieth century, his Ireland a personal image of universal confusion.

The greatness of *The Tower* nonetheless lies to some large extent in its refusal of abject pessimism and mere materialist despair. For all the pained reflection on sexual passion in 'A Man Young and Old', it is the old man in 'The Gift of Harun Al-Rashid' who discovers the possibility of transcendent meaning in physical passion, and the old man also who, among schoolchildren, has an intimation of this world seen in terms of euphoric delight, energy, a homesick affirmation of a right to joy. The poet of *The Tower* is as always, but here most powerfully, magus, poet and politician forging and failing to forge his thoughts into a unity, searching for a world and an afterworld adequate to his intuitions and surveying a life often inadequate to his deepest needs. Across the volume, the sheer scale and human fullness of his engagement leave that impression of greatness – of myriad suffering and exultant life – that very few artists can achieve, and those the greatest. These were qualities immediately recognised. Yeats was, the *Criterion* declared, 'what we moderns mean by a great poet'.

The search for political stability so painfully evident in *The Tower* and Yeats's interest in the rise of Mussolini (which partly inspired such poems as 'Ancestral Houses') was matched by Pound's growing fascination with Italian fascism. The Duce's features had for several years been regularly stencilled on the walls of Rapallo, and in early 1927, two years before Mussolini himself suspended Italian parliamentary government, Olga Rudge had an audience with him, hoping to play on his avowed interest in contemporary art. Pound himself was naturally interested in an authoritarian government that seemed to concern itself with such things, and at the end of 1926 he wrote to Harriet Munroe, 'I personally think extremely well of Mussolini.' Pound was already beginning to move towards that position from which he would soon make those disastrously clumsy generalisations about politics and economics that would eventually lead him to personal tragedy. Even now he could write of Mussolini, 'if one compares him to American presidents (the last three) or British premiers etc., in fact one can NOT without insulting him. If the intelligentsia don't think well of him, it is because they know nothing about "the state", and government, and have no particularly large sense of values. Anyway, WHAT intelligentsia?'

Rapallo was, however, a backwater in a Europe largely innocent of the appalling forces that were slowly being unleashed within it. As Giuseppe Bacigalupo, the son of the local doctor, recalled: 'it was an unproblematic world, not yet bombarded by daily news of catastrophes. The radio had only just started; newspapers were read absent-mindedly because they always promised fair weather. And they were usually right.' Pound could imagine Yeats himself staring out across the bay and murmuring, 'Sligo in heaven' – a mood that determined him and George to move back there in the autumn.

On 18 April 1927, Yeats and George returned to Dublin by way of Switzerland, resolved either to sell their house in Merrion Square or to keep the top floor and rent out the rest. The burden of these domestic arrangements fell to George, who organised the sale of the house and the removal of the furniture while complaining that she also had to put up with Lady Gregory, whose increasing age was making her a somewhat tiresome house-guest. Yeats himself was still frail, however, and he wrote to Olivia Shakespear telling her how 'two Dublin doctors have sat upon me; the Cannes man said, "Lungs and nervous breakdown can be neglected, nothing matters but blood pressure" and gave me a white pill. The Monte Carlo man said, "Blood pressure and lungs can be neglected, nothing matters but nervous breakdown," and gave me a brown pill. The Dublin men say, "Blood pressure and nervous breakdown can be neglected, nothing matters but lungs," and have given me a black pill.' Yeats was to need all of the energy he could muster, however, to throw himself into the conflicts that now awaited him.

Among the most difficult of these was the rejection of O'Casey's latest play, *The Silver Tassie*. This was a study of the effects of the Great War on ordinary Irishmen and women which veered wildly from realism to a sort of expressionistic collage. All the directors of the Abbey expressed reservations about its effectiveness, but it was left to Yeats to write the letter of rejection. This was, as he confessed, 'a hateful letter to write', but its firmness and clarity is of a piece with that refusal to make concessions to what he considered bad writing which he had shown since his early dealings with Edward Martyn. 'I had looked forward with great hope and excitement to reading your play,' Yeats wrote, 'and not merely because of my admiration for your work, for I bore in mind that the Abbey owed its recent prosperity to you.'[4] These were not, however, reasons to compromise artistic standards.

While Yeats could admire the first Act of *The Silver Tassie*, the rest saddened and discouraged him. O'Casey had written the work not out of his own deepest concerns but from the mere force of his opinions. The play was, in other words, a species of dramatic journalism. As Yeats complained: 'there is no dominating character, no dominating action, neither psychological unity nor unity of action'. This was sweeping and hard, if justified. The comments Yeats then went on to make are the result of years of matured experience. 'The mere greatness of the world war has thwarted you; it has refused to become mere background, and obtrudes itself upon the stage as so much dead wood that will not burn with the dramatic fire. Dramatic action is a fire that must burn up everything but itself . . . the whole history of the world must be reduced to wallpaper in front of which the characters must pose and speak.' The sensitive O'Casey, newly married and about to become a father, was wounded by these comments (as well as by Lady Gregory's tactlessly telling him that he could withdraw the play and offer it to a London management) and proceeded to publish the Abbey directors' letters in the *Observer*. Yeats called on the Society of Authors to take action and replied to O'Casey's move through the columns of the *Irish Statesman*. The row was deeply regrettable, not least because, as Yeats told Lady Gregory, O'Casey was 'now out of our saga'.

If Yeats's refusal of *The Silver Tassie* was based on the highest aesthetic principals, two bills that came before the Senate kindled his lifelong concern with artistic freedom. A Copyright Act proposed that Irish authors must print in Ireland if they were to preserve their rights over their work. Yeats argued that the lack of specialist presses in the country meant that many authors were obliged to publish their work abroad, which thus made the Bill's proposals unfair. He declared that the Bill smacked of censorship, but it was the Censorship of Publications Act itself which roused his full fury at the bigotry which he believed the church was imposing upon Ireland. 'Holy Church – no, the commercial tourist agency that conducts the annual Lourdes pilgrimage, and the Catholic Truth Society, and The Society of Angelic Welfare have pressed on the Government a bill which will enable Holy Church to put us all down at any moment.'[5] The Cosgrave government had, he believed, capitulated to such forces, and the passing of the Censorship Bill marked the nadir of Yeats's respect for Irish public life. His attempts to fight for artistic liberty were unavailing, and, by the time the Bill had been passed, Yeats had left the Senate, a disappointed man.

II

'Words for Music Perhaps'

Although the Chairman of the Senate had told Yeats he would be re-elected whenever he wished, the poet's health was now so poor that rest was essential.

The Merrion Square house had been exchanged for a flat at 72 Fitzwilliam Square, but by October 1928 Yeats was keen to return to Rapallo. The correspondent of the *Daily Mail* met him at the Savile Club as he was on his way through London and found the occasion sufficiently interesting to provide his readers with a vignette of the great man. 'Mr Yeats, who is an Irish Senator, is no more the lanky, sombre poet of 35 years ago,' he wrote. 'Instead he has a comfortable figure, rather suggestive of an English country magistrate.' Yeats's conversation belied this impression, however. He was, readers of the newspaper were told, 'one of the best talkers of our time'. Informing them that they ought to hear Yeats tell one of his short stories, the correspondent went on to say that 'he recites his own delicate verses in a magnificent booming tone, but his thoughts are not always in the clouds. His worldly talk is very racy and very pungent.' There was no comment on Yeats's enfeebled health, merely the suggestion that 'he spends the winter at Rapallo, choosing that spot because (he says) there is another poet there with whom he can argue'.[6] That poet, of course, was Pound.

Pound continued to fascinate Yeats, and Richard Aldington, who was also staying in Rapallo, recalled that he 'used to worry himself a lot about Ezra, who seemed to support one of Yeats's numerous fads, the theory of the antithetical self'.[7] Aldington's description of the older poet's concern is also a remarkable portrait of Yeats himself. Yeats had been invited to dine with Aldington at his hotel. 'It was a cold night; and Yeats arrived with his hands thrust into a pair of grey woollen socks, because he had lost his gloves. Recovering from this shock, we went to dinner.' Further small embarrassments ensued:

> With the spaghetti a long thin lock of Yeats's hair got into the corner of his mouth, and the rest of us watched with silent awe his efforts to swallow his hair with a strand of spaghetti. Giving this up in dudgeon, he suddenly turned to me and said to me in portentous tones: 'How do you account for Ezra? . . . Here is a man who produces the most distinguished work and yet in his behaviour is the least distinguished of men. It is the antithetical self.'

In fact, though Yeats did have a high regard for Pound's work, he was also considerably puzzled by it and by the *Cantos* in particular. Thirty of these had now been printed, but, while Yeats told Pound that he often found in them 'some scene of distinguished beauty', he could find no overall structure. Others had been similarly bewildered, and Pound gave Yeats the reply he always made, 'He explains', that the work would, 'when the hundredth Canto is finished, display a structure'. The structure would be 'that of a Bach fugue. There will be no plot, no chronicle of events, no logic of discourse, but two themes, the descent into Hades from Homer, a metamorphosis from Ovid, and mixed with these medieval or modern characters.' Pound also offered another interpretation. As Yeats wrote in 'A Packet for Ezra Pound': 'he had scribbled on the back of an envelope certain sets of letters that represent emotions or archetypal events ... ABCD and then JKLM, and then each set of letters repeated, and then ABCD inverted and this repeated, and then a new element XYZ, then certain letters that never recur and then all sorts of combinations'.[8] As Yeats himself felt bound to declare: 'it is almost impossible to understand the art of a generation younger than one's own'. Pound was nonetheless delighted by the effect he had managed to produce, crowing that 'Unc. Wm. came to lunch to express profound impression produced by effort to comprehend cantos. etc.'.

Yeats tried to explain his own thoughts in 'A Packet for Ezra Pound', also offering there much information on George's 'sleeps' especially. Meanwhile, as he recuperated, 'life returned to me as an impression of the uncontrollable energy and daring of the great creators ... I wrote ... almost all that group of poems, called in memory of those exultant weeks *Words for Music Perhaps*.' Yeats's sense of excited fecundity spilled over into his letters to Olivia Shakespear. He had written to her in the previous year, delighted by the success of *The Tower*, and telling her that it had sold two thousand copies in the first month, 'much the largest sale I have ever had'. Nonetheless, looking back over the book, Yeats felt bound to confess, 'I am astonished at its bitterness and long to live out of Ireland that I may find some new vintage.' For Yeats that bitterness gave the book its power and 'it is the best book I have written'. The greater ease of Rapallo would, he hoped, now allow him 'to write verse again', a verse free from 'bitter passion'. He was searching, as always, to recreate himself, to set aside his immediate past and reach out to its antithesis with that vigour of mature genius which is one of the most astonishing qualities of Yeats's old age. The constant refashioning of himself and his art in his middle sixties is exhilarating and, in the deepest sense of that word, wonderful. Yeats thrust himself into new life ever more fully with a sure if reckless trust in his own unfailing abundance. 'I am writing "Twelve Poems for Music" – have done three of them (and two other poems) – not so much that they may be sung as that I may define their kind of emotion to myself. I want them to be all emotion and all impersonal. . . . They are the opposite of my recent work and all praise of joyous life, though in the best of them it is a dry bone upon the shore that sings the praise.'

Yeats's reaching out to opposites is clear even in his euphoria. 'I am full of doubt.' He sensed that his current work was slighter than what had gone immediately before (which was true even as early spring is slighter than the depth of winter) and mistrusted his content. But 'I am writing more easily that ever I wrote and I am happy,' he told Olivia Shakespear. 'Whereas I have always been unhappy when I wrote and worked with great difficulty.'

Now lyrics spilled from him with an abandon that matches their subject matter. 'Sex and the Dead', he would declare, 'are the only things that can interest a serious mind.' Death had encircled the tower; now Yeats turned to the praise of sex. A new figure, Crazy Jane, exalts the uncontrollable energies of her body, which defies the life-hating theology of the church and so has a true knowledge of the divine. She was founded, Yeats confessed, on a 'local satirist' near Gort who had 'an amazing power of speech. One of her great performances is a description of how the meanness of a Gort shopkeeper's wife over the price of a glass of porter made her so despair of the human race that she got drunk. The incidents of that drunkenness are of an epic magnificence.' Contraries meet in Crazy Jane and, in their fullness, redeem her from the ghostly existence foredoomed for the unfulfilled dead. She expresses herself in this world and in the vigour of her sexuality, so evading Yeats's threat that 'if you don't express yourself . . . you walk after you're dead. The great thing is to go empty to your grave,' sure in the shocking knowledge that truth and completeness lie in the union of opposites:

> 'A woman can be proud and stiff
> When on love intent;
> But Love has pitched his mansion in
> The place of excrement;
> For nothing can be sole or whole
> That has not been rent.'9

Despite his long stay in Rapallo, Yeats still maintained his directorship of the Abbey Theatre, and events were now to inspire him to take a fresh interest in his Noh dramas. A friend sent him some photographs of the 1926 revival of Albert van Dalsum's 1922 Amsterdam production of *The Only Jealousy of Emer*. These made so great an impression on him that he set about revising the play with a less elite audience in mind:

I wrote *The Only Jealousy of Emer* for performance in a private house or studio, considering it . . . unsuited to a public stage. Then somebody put it on a public stage in Holland and Hildo van Krop made his powerful masks. Because the dramatist who can collaborate with a great sculptor is lucky, I rewrote the play not only to fit it for such a stage but to free it from abstraction and confusion. I have retold the story in prose which I have tried to make very simple, and left imaginative suggestion to dancers, singers, musicians.10

The dancer who inspired Yeats was Ninette de Valois. An Irishwoman trained by Diaghilev, she founded her own school of dancing in England in the 1920s, and Yeats was impressed with her work. She herself described how she first met Yeats when she was producing a work at the Festival Theatre in Cambridge:

I put on some dances there and he happened to be in the audience and he asked the Director of the theatre could he meet me because he was very thrilled with the evening. I met him at the back of the theatre the next morning, or rather in the front, in the foyer, and it was terribly dark. I saw this great figure sitting in a chair there in profile, and he started a marvellous conversation with me. I was too terrified to notice anything really. The conversation was about the evening before and suddenly at the end he said to me, 'I want you to come to Dublin and help me revise my plays for dancers which must be restaged and put back into the Dublin scene.'

By November 1927, Yeats had arranged a space suitable to his new dramatic needs. The library of the Mechanics' Institute had fallen vacant and Yeats commissioned Michael Scott to convert it into the tiny Peacock Theatre. Joseph Holloway described how 'a big room in the front building of the Abbey has been converted into a tiny theatre seating 100. It has been named The Peacock Theatre, and seats and decorations have all been carried out in peacock blue – even the front of the building facing Abbey Street has been painted a similar colour. A blue lookout truly, but I hope not for the little playhouse.' Eventually the rehearsal room became the home of the Abbey School of Ballet, founded and directed by Ninette de Valois.

With his mask-maker, his dancer and his theatre in place, Yeats needed to find a musician to write a score for the play he was now revising as *Fighting the Waves*. George Antheil was the obvious choice, and Yeats wrote excitedly to Lady Gregory on 9 March, 1929 about his discovery. He hoped that Antheil would write music not only for *Fighting the Waves* but for *At the Hawk's Well* and *On Baile's Strand* as well.

If he persists, and he is at present enthusiastic, it means a performance in Vienna in the autumn. He has a great name there since his setting of *Oedipus* a few months ago. He is a revolutionary musician – there was a riot of almost Abbey intensity over some of his music in America. There will be masks and all singing within the range of the speaking voice – for my old theories are dogmas it seems to the new school. The setting of *Fighting the Waves* should be ready for Miss de Valois to do in Dublin in May. He is about 28 and looks 18 and has a face of indescribable innocence. His wife, a first violinist from somewhere or other, looks equally young and innocent. Both are persons of impulse and he may or he may not get through his month of toil upon the three plays. He promises to keep the instruments required for *The Fighting of the Waves* within the range of the Abbey. During the fight in *Oedipus at Colonus* (he did both plays) there were twelve pianos played at once.

Antheil himself was equally fascinated by Yeats. He described in his memoirs how Yeats was 'always getting messages from spirits' and was an expert in seeing ghosts in broad daylight – 'a rather difficult feat, as I am told by those who are authorities on this subject'.[11] The two men would sit together discussing their work on Yeats's play when suddenly Yeats himself would interrupt the conversation and say, 'Hallo, William,' and tip his soft felt sombrero. Antheil, looking round and seeing that there was nobody anywhere near their table, asked in astonishment where 'William' was. '"Right in the chair alongside of you; he's the ghost of my indigestion," Yeats would say.' Sometimes Yeats would hold fairly prolonged conversations both with William and with other Irish spirits 'who had been kind enough to come all the way from Dublin to see him'. This habit began to unnerve Antheil, who had previously visited the poet at night but now decided to see him only in the daytime because he had become afraid of walking home alone in the dark. In fact, these ghostly colloquies helped Antheil's inspiration, and he wrote that 'the secret of my success in writing such true Irish music is contained in the fact that Yeats's play is entirely about Irish ghosts. With "William" sitting there alongside of me at the café every day, what else could have happened but that William soon became quite visible and even audible, giving me not only most valuable tips on ancient Irish music, but also singing old Irish melodies (in a rather cracked voice, I admit) while I hastily wrote them down in my notebook.' Antheil's very demanding music was finally scored for a small chamber orchestra: flute, clarinet, trumpet, trombone, bass drum, piano, first and second violin, cello and contrabass.

The Yeatses returned to Dublin via London in early May 1929. Much of the summer was spent in the new Fitzwilliam Square flat, which overlooked a pleasant garden and where Yeats had a delightful study, its blue walls and ceilings painted by George, who enhanced this scheme with the addition of gold-coloured curtains. Part of Yeats's time, however, was spent at Coole, where Lady Gregory was becoming an increasingly infirm old woman. In September 1926 she had had to undergo a second operation for breast cancer, and, although this time she was given a general anaesthetic, she begrudged having to spend £100 on 'my poor body'. She was also growing a little deaf, and her eyesight was failing along with her memory. When visitors arrived she did not always recognise them, but, with her customary courtesy, invited them to tea and, 'by degrees I made them out, a nice woman next to me was Lady Susan Dawney, and a pretty, bright girl Lady Blanche Beresford, engaged to one of the young men'. It transpired that they were all 'Yeats enthusiasts', and Yeats read to them from *The Tower* and afterwards presented one of the women in the party with a signed copy of some recent work as a wedding present.[12]

It was not only physical decrepitude that was troubling Lady Gregory, however; she was also increasingly pressed for money. Royalties from her plays and her collections of Irish myths were a welcome source of income (in 1924 she had earned £467 'as an authoress'), but rising income taxes especially forced her to small economies. She rode in third-class railway carriages across Ireland, and her embarrassed granddaughters noticed how, when they were having a meal in a restaurant, 'Grandma took a used envelope out of her purse, and tipped all the sugar left in the sugar basin into it, folded it up, and put it back in her purse.' Lady Gregory justified this by saying she had paid for the sugar and, since she never took sugar in her tea, 'she didn't see why she should leave it all for them to sell to someone else'. At the beginning of April 1927, however, she was obliged to sell Coole – 'all – house, woods, gardens' – to the Ministry of Lands and Agriculture, whose Forestry Department would now take care of her extensive plantings while renting her back the house and gardens for £100 a year. She would not be obliged to leave the house that had been her lifelong passion, and Lady Gregory now began *Coole*, her account of her long affair with the property and the grounds with their copper-beech tree engraved with the initials of the famous visitors she had entertained.

These and Lady Gregory's influence as a great literary hostess are also the subject of Yeats's 'Coole Park, 1929'. As so often, Yeats first drafted the work in prose. 'Describe house in first stanza. Here Synge came, Hugh Lane, Shaw Taylor, many names. I too in my timid youth. Coming and going like migratory birds. Then address the swallows fluttering in their dream like circles. Speak of the rarity of the circumstances that bring together such concords of men. Each man more than himself through whom an unknown life speaks. A circle ever returning into itself.' In the published work Yeats returned gloriously to the poem on the Great House. Coole is seen as a place where the intellect of man fashions a high, timeless civilisation that is as one with nature and yet superior to it. Lady Gregory's great literary guests are attracted there like the birds, but it is Lady Gregory herself, a figure analogous to Nature and yet superior in the range of her intellect and understanding, who made the house what it was:

> They came like swallows and like swallows went,
> And yet a woman's powerful character
> Could keep a swallow to its first intent;
> And half a dozen in formation there,
> That seemed to whirl upon a compass-point,
> Found certainty upon the dreaming air,
> The intellectual sweetness of those lines
> That cut through time or cross it withershins.[13]

The theatre had been at the heart of Yeats's relationship with Lady Gregory, and nearly a year after completing his poem to Coole his *Fighting the Waves* was presented at the Abbey before a distinguished audience which included the Governor General and the American Ambassador. The work was described on the programme as a 'Ballet-Play' and the note Yeats wrote for it succinctly describes the new form of the work and the changes he had made:

> In this dance play I have brought together 'The Only Jealousy of Emer' and another Irish story. At the opening Cuchulain is shown fighting the waves in a frenzy of grief for he has killed his son. Then we see him lying in a bed, a seemingly drowned man, attended by his wife Emer and another. He is not dead but entranced. The goddess Fand who loves him comes seeking to entice him away; she is defeated by the love of Emer and Cuchulain awakes. The play closes with Fand's dance among the waves, the dance of her despair.

Ninette de Valois danced the role of Fand, and Yeats declared that the play was his greatest stage success since *Cathleen ni Houlihan*. Certainly, the theatre was full every night, but Holloway was far from certain that George Antheil's collaboration was of artistic value and was particularly concerned about the performance of J. Stevenson as the Singer:

> Oh, the harsh, discordant notes he had to sing. I said when I heard that Yeats liked the music that was enough for me – as he has no ear for sound! Those on the stage worked wonders against the braying. . . . There was an augmented orchestra to interpret the noisy discords – drums, flutes, cornets etc., and Miss Grey was at the piano. Dr Larchet conducted and couldn't extract head or tail out of the score. The principals wore masks and also some of the dancers. It was a pity to waste such talent on such strange materials. . . . Fancy having to engage a full orchestra of musicians to try to play such stuff that could be as well interpreted by children on tin cans![14]

Yeats now received an offer of a year's professorship in Japan which George, returning from Switzerland with the children, insisted he turn down. He visited Coole again that summer, and also had his last holiday at Thoor Ballylee. For all the romantic allure of the place and its profound symbolic significance for his art, the tower was an increasingly impractical place in which to live and rear a family. The building was remote and George had to cycle four miles to Gort for provisions, while the general dampness contributed to Yeats's rheumatism. It proved impossible to maintain the place adequately during their absence, and rather than allowing it to remain a drain on the family finances it was resolved that the tower should be sold.

III
'That Gong-Tormented Sea'

Yeats's health was still giving him considerable trouble. A winter visit to

London showed him how careful he had to be. 'I can't at present do a great deal,' he wrote. 'I overtired myself yesterday – a lunch with Mrs Hall and a tea with Gerald Heard – and today I have coughed up blood again. . . . I caught the cold that undid me at *The Apple Cart*, and perhaps it was the cold coming on, but I hated the play.' Yeats was obliged to rest in bed for several days, after which he and George left for Rapallo. When he arrived on the Italian Riviera, Yeats complained about sleepiness and tired himself further by finishing the beautiful brief lyric 'After Long Silence', again working it up from a prose version. It was clear however that he was becoming increasingly unwell, his temperature rising at night and his body showing all the signs of nervous prostration. The doctors who called were unable to diagnose his complaint, but concern was such that on 21 December he wrote a three-line will which was witnessed by Ezra Pound and Basil Bunting, after which he collapsed and lay in a raging fever attended by a nurse. Eventually a Dr Pende of Genoa, an expert in tropical diseases, was summoned and he decided that Yeats had contracted Malta fever. Medicines were ordered and the danger gradually passed, but for the next nine weeks Yeats was obliged to spend much of his time in bed, drinking a daily half-bottle of champagne provided for him by Gerhard Hauptmann and so exhausting all available supplies of detective stories that he was eventually obliged to turn to Westerns.

But he remained very feeble and, during the long course of his convalescence, he 'had the further entertainment of growing a beard and had for a time a magnificent appearance with the beard and hair of St Peter out of a Raphael cartoon, and after that the local barber called every week and after several weeks produced a masterpiece, and I have now hair brushed upward and a small beard running down into a point'. Pound, who would only meet Yeats at an open-air café because of his fear of catching Malta fever from him, was particularly impressed by the beard, saying that Yeats should be sent by the Free State government as their minister to Austria since 'Austria would alone perfectly appreciate my beard'. George decided, however, that what her husband really needed was mountain air and she took him to the hotel at Portofino Vetta, high above the Gulf of Genoa, where his health rapidly began to improve to the extent that he was able to give a little time each morning to his revised version of *A Vision*.

On 16 April, Yeats received a letter from Sturge Moore criticising the fourth stanza of 'Sailing to Byzantium'. The idea of escape into art troubled Moore and he wrote that he was 'sceptical as to whether mere liberation from existence has any value or probability as a consummation. I prefer with Wittgenstein, whom I dont understand, to think that nothing at all can be said about ultimates, or reality in an ultimate sense.' Such responses reflect the influence on Sturge Moore of his brother, the philosopher G. E. Moore, and his fellow empiricist Bertrand Russell. Both men had early rejected idealist thought – the belief that reality ultimately consists of minds and ideas and that matter cannot exist independently of them – for the conviction that philosophy needed to be brought as close as possible to logic and mathematics. Both thinkers were intolerant of subjectivism and system-building and came, in Russell's words, to 'confess frankly that the human intellect is unable to find conclusive answers to many questions of profound importance to mankind, but . . . refuse to believe that there is some "higher" way of knowing, by which we can discover truths hidden from science and the intellect'.[15] To Yeats, this was anathema. 'I go back to Calderon,' he told Sturge Moore. 'Not only things, but dreams themselves are a dream.'

Yeats nonetheless decided that Moore's letter about his poem showed that its ideas 'needed exposition', and materials for a masterpiece began to be accumulated. 'Subject for a poem . . . Death of a friend . . . Describe Byzantium as it is in the system towards the end of the first Christian millennium. A walking mummy. Flames at the street corners where the soul is purified, birds of hammered gold singing in the golden trees, in the harbour [dolphins], offering their backs to the wailing dead that they may carry them to Paradise.' This prose note was then slowly but miraculously transformed into 'Byzantium', Yeats's attempt to suggest the state of the soul as it approaches a world after death where physical existence unwinds as the immortal part of man approaches what Yeats called the 'condition of fire' where all is music and rest:

> At midnight on the Emperor's pavement flit
> Flames that no faggot feeds, nor steel has lit,
> Nor storm disturbs, flames begotten of flame,
> Where blood-begotten spirits come
> And all complexities of fury leave,
> Dying into a dance,
> An agony of trance,
> An agony of flame that cannot singe a sleeve.[16]

It is, however, profoundly typical of the antithetical man and the consummate poet that the vision of 'Byzantium' is altogether more rich and humanly complex than an attempt to picture a form of transfiguration. The 'condition of fire' is inevitably related to the symbolism of water and its ancient associations with materialism. Yeats refuses wholly to separate these, and the last stanza of the poem, helped by its suggestively oblique grammar, appears to emphasise the lure of the physical and the sexual even as it seems to propel the reader's attention and the disembodied souls themselves towards eternity:

> Astraddle on the dolphins' mire and blood,
> Spirit after spirit! The smithies break the flood.

The golden smithies of the Emperor!
Marbles of the dancing floor
Break bitter furies of complexity,
Those images that yet
Fresh images beget,
That dolphin-torn, that gong-tormented sea.[17]

The richness of the poem is finally a human richness – the experience of antimonies rather than the rigour of dogma. As Yeats wrote of the contrary worlds of fire and water:

that conflict is deep in my subconsciousness, perhaps in everybody's. I dream of clear water . . . then come erotic dreams. Then for weeks perhaps I write poetry with sex for theme. Then comes the reversal – it came when I was young with some dream . . . with a flame in it. Then for weeks I get a symbolism like that in my Byzantium poem . . . with flame for theme. All this may come from the chance that when I was a young man I was accustomed to a Kabbalistic ceremony where there were two pillars, one symbolic of water and one of fire.[18]

It is the acceptance of such oppositions, its affirmation woven deep into the subtlety of the language and startling nature of its imagery, which is a measure of the poem's true scale.

While Yeats was meditating on this triumphantly affirmative poem, he was also reading Swift, who would inspire his altogether different play *The Words upon the Window-Pane.* Then, after he had come down again to Rapallo he lay on the balcony of his apartment in the Via Americhe reading to his children and teaching them chess. 'We are all brown like old meerschaum pipes,' he told Olivia Shakespear. By 3 July, Yeats was strong enough to begin the long sea journey north, travelling via London to Dublin, and, in the last weeks of June, Gogarty brought him and Augustus John together in Connemara, where John once again expressed his wish to paint a portrait of Yeats. Yeats examined his ageing face in the mirror 'noticing certain lines about my mouth and chin . . . and have wondered if John would not select those very lines. . . . In those lines I see the marks of recent illness, marks of time, growing irresolution, perhaps some faults that I have long dreaded, but then my character is so little myself that all my life it has thwarted me. It has affected my poems, my true self, no more than the character of a dancer affects the movements of a dance.'

Yeats sat for his portrait in the open air, his feet covered by a fur bag, his hair blowing in the wind. The portrait was not, however, a great success, nor were the sittings wholly agreeable to John. He thought his subject had become 'a mellow, genial and silver haired old man', and he complained that Yeats's stories both at the dinner table and while John was at his easel bored him. As Gogarty described the finished work, Yeats 'is seated with a rug round his knees and his broad hat on his lap, his white hair is round his head like a nimbus, and behind him the embroidered cloths of heaven are purple and silver'. There is little suggestion, however, of the intellectual force and passion that were to propel Yeats into his old age, and Virginia Woolf was an altogether more accurate portraitist when she described meeting him at Garsington.[19]

She noted that he was now putting on weight, that the thin poet of legend was becoming a stout elderly man. Yeats had 'grown very thick', and she felt that he looked like a solid wedge of oak. 'His face is too fat,' she wrote, 'but it has its hatchet forehead in profile, under a tangle of grey and brown hair; the eyes are luminous, direct, but obscured under glasses; they have however seen close.' Walter de la Mare was also present, and having told a long dream story Yeats took up the subject with vehemence, analysing soul states in dreams 'as others talk of Beaverbrook and free trade'. Conversation then moved on to painting, de la Mare having recently visited the National Gallery. Yeats declared he could get nothing from El Greco and Rembrandt. Milton he similarly disparaged for having 'Latinised poetry'. As for his own work, Yeats said, he could only write 'thumbnail' poems rather than epic 'because we are at the end of an era'. He then discoursed on symbolism and, as he did so, Woolf wrote: 'I got a tremendous sense of the intricacy of the art; also of its meanings, its seriousness, its importance, which wholly engross this large active minded and immensely vitalised man.' Like others, she was impressed 'by his directness, his terseness. No fluff or dreaminess. He seemed to live in the middle of an immensely intricate briar bush, from which he would issue at any moment; and then withdraw again. And every twig was real to him. Indeed he seemed in command of all his systems, philosophies, poetics and humanities; not tentative any more. Hence no doubt his urbanity and generosity.'

IV

'Vacillation'

With the John portrait finished, Yeats moved on to Coole, where he worked on his play *The Words upon the Window-Pane*. The drama is one of Yeats's most successful and shows not only his mastery of the stage but the continuing fertility of his invention and the way in which this emerged out of his earlier concerns. In a period when many plays at the Abbey showed the influence of the Cork realists, *The Words upon the Window-Pane* adopts their techniques to create a setting for a seance which then eerily suggests the influence of spiritualism over the contemporary world. The house in which the seance takes place belonged to Swift's friend Stella, and his 'hostile' influence still haunts it, an example of that 'dreaming back' familiar from Yeats's earlier experiments with Noh drama and here used again to explore the spiritual and moral dilemma of modern Ireland.

Art, spiritualism and national identity once more come into a powerful relation, a relation that partly focusses on Yeats's hatred of materialism, the merely mechanical or what, in this borrowed eighteenth-century context, he chose to call Whiggery. In 'The Seven Sages', Yeats had identified Swift as one of those great Irish intellects 'that hated Whiggery', which he defined as 'a levelling, rancorous, rational sort of mind'. As he wrote elsewhere: 'how convenient if men were but . . . dots, all exactly alike, all pushable, arrangeable. . . . Instead of hierarchical society, where all men are different, came democracy; instead of a science came materialism: all that Whiggish world Swift stared on till he became a raging man.'[20]

In the play itself the young research student John Corbet is imagined interesting himself in precisely this tragic dilemma. As he tells the others at the seance: 'I hope to prove that in Swift's day men of intellect reached the height of their power – the greatest position they ever attained in society and the State, that everything great in Ireland and in our character, in what remains of our architecture, comes from that day; that we have kept its seal longer than England.' Corbet knows, however, that such a vision as Swift's sees the democratic 'ruin' to come, and that Swift's greatness was also the cause of his insanity. But it is the role of Mrs Henderson the medium which most frighteningly embodies the emotional weight of this insight. In a virtuoso's role which moves from voicing the words of her infant control, 'a dear little girl called Lulu', through to being the mouthpiece for the tragic grandeur of Swift and his relationship with Stella and Vanessa, Mrs Henderson suggests the range of Yeats's themes and the frightening, unillusioned intensity of his preoccupation with his eighteenth-century hero.

The prominent place given to the young intellectual John Corbet in the play is not without its significance. Yeats learned that many of the young men living in 'the garrets and cellars' of Dublin were either communist or Catholic or both, and it was these people whose attention he now wished particularly to attract. Here were the two forces most dangerous to contemporary Ireland as Yeats saw it, and he was resolved not to isolate himself from them since, with the plummeting popularity of Cosgrave's government especially, IRA support of de Valera suggested that socialism was in the ascendant. It offered what many thought was the best means of working for a revived and truly Gaelic Ireland. An IRA mission was sent to Moscow, where some of its officers even received military training, while in 1931 the IRA were to found Saor Eire, a socialist organisation of workers and farmers. This devoted itself to the overthrow of the inheritance of British imperialism and capitalism by establishing the revolutionary leadership of the working classes who, along with the small farmers, would own the land and the means of production, distribution and exchange. With a socialist republic thus established, Saor Eire then hoped to restore a truly Gaelic nation, fostering the Irish language, its culture and its traditional games.

For all Yeats's increasingly hieratic manner he was determined to be open to the talents of the younger generation and, in addition to appointing F. R. Higgins and Walter Starkie as directors of the Abbey Theatre, he surprised Dublin by telling an audience at a banquet that 'the future of Irish literature was with the realistic novel'. Sean O'Faolain and Liam O'Flaherty were singled out for praise. As early as 1927 Yeats had written to Olivia Shakespear asking her if she had read O'Flaherty's novels and telling her that he thought they were great works 'and too full of abounding natural life to be terrible despite their subjects. They are full of that tragic farce we have invented. I imagine that part of the desire for censorship here is the desire to keep him out.' Yeats would have none of this, and when Cecil Salkeld brought O'Flaherty to one of Yeats's Monday evenings the difficult young writer was confused when Yeats's approach to him and proved to be 'not only most courteous but assumed a humility which was almost disconcerting. When we rose to go Yeats accompanied us down the stairs, saying to O'Flaherty: "So good of you famous young men to look up an old man."'

Celebrations nonetheless made Yeats aware of his increasing age, and in November 1930, when he took a short holiday in England, John Masefield organised a private festival to celebrate the thirtieth anniversary of their first meeting. 'I had a rather moving experience at Masefield's,' Yeats wrote to George. 'He made a long eulogy of my work and myself, very embarrassing, and then five girls with beautiful voices recited my lyrics for three quarters of an hour. I do not think the whole audience could hear, but to me it was strangely moving and overwhelming.'[21] Another indication of Yeats's status as a grand old man of letters was Macmillans' proposal to issue an Edition de Luxe of his works. Partly to find the necessary solitude in which to prepare this and partly because he wanted to be in comparatively easy reach of the ailing Lady Gregory, Yeats and George quit their Dublin flat for a furnished house overlooking the Bay of Killiney, ten miles south of Dublin. 'I have a great sense of abundance,' Yeats told Olivia Shakespear. 'Months of re-writing! What happiness!' In addition to revising his previous output, however, Yeats had to ready unpublished work for the autumn, and this would include not only his revised version of *A Vision* but his plays and essays collected into a volume called *Wheels and Butterflies*, along with a new book of verse provisionally titled *Byzantium* but later issued as *The Winding Stair and Other Poems*.

It is a sign of Yeats's undiminished creative energy that, while undertaking this considerable body of editorial work, he was also redrafting his play *The Resurrection*, which he had originally composed in 1927. The drama is influenced by his reading in anthropology and while being, as the original cast complained, more of a debate than a dramatic action, it nonetheless interestingly focusses on Yeats's preoccupation with the place of the supernatural in human history. The biblical event is imagined as taking place during a period when, for intellectuals at least, a season of extreme rationality has come round. While the ordinary people celebrate the rites of Dionysus – the annual resurrection myth of a class whom, Yeats thought, could never make history – a learned Greek and a Hebrew discuss the nature of Christ in a manner drained of wonder. 'Man becomes rational,' as Yeats wrote to Olivia Shakespear, 'no longer driven from below or above.' Through the miracle of 'the slain god, the risen god,' however, by the appearance of the resurrected Christ in other words, miraculous intervention destroys inert reason, gives exhausted men a new vision, and ushers in a new historical era.

During this period of concentrated work in Ireland the Yeatses' flat in Rapallo had been let to Ezra Pound's father, while it seemed desirable to bring the children back from Switzerland to have them educated in Dublin. Yeats wrote a letter to an imaginary schoolmaster in which he described the ideal curriculum he had imagined for Michael. A thorough grounding in Greek was Yeats's principal aim, the father hoping that his boy would be taught by the Berlitz method so that 'he may read as soon as possible that most exciting of all stories the Odyssey from the landing in Ithaca to the end'. In an attempt to arm the boy against Yeats's own philosophical enemies, he wished him to be thoroughly grounded in mathematics, since 'I know that Bertrand Russell must, seeing that he is such a feather-head, be wrong about everything but as I have no mathematics I cannot prove it. I do not want my son to be as helpless.'

Other educational ideas clearly drew on notions put forward by JBY decades before. While Yeats's condemnation of Latin literature as 'the classic decadence' was probably his own, his distaste for a theoretical knowledge of geography and of history stripped of literary inspiration clearly echoes the thoughts of his father. Similar biases are revealed when Yeats wrote: 'don't teach him one word of science as he can get all he wants in the newspaper, and in any case it is no job for a gentleman'. When he and George went to inspect the chosen school, however, Yeats himself set aside such impractical and high-falutin ideals for questions familiar to him from his days working on the School Attendance Bill. The Warden's wife was impressed by Yeats's insistent enquiries about sanitation, ventilation, heating and so on, but an embarrassed George called out: 'Don't mind him, he's only showing off.'

If his son's education was one of Yeats's concerns at this time, another was the continuing problems of his sisters.[22] Lily's ill-health was such that she had to make repeated visits to Dublin doctors, and by early 1929 she appeared so run down that it was decided to X-ray her. The results at last showed what had been her physical problem all along: an abnormally shaped thyroid gland pressing down in her throat and chest and responsible for all her symptoms of difficult breathing, flushing, chills and constant fatigue. This last was now so marked that it was clear she could no longer carry on as an active member of Cuala and instead she continued her embroidery at home on her own account, working a book-jacket for Yeats's copy of William Morris's Kelmscott Chaucer and, when she could or thought she should, embroidering her larger decorative panels. 'The Garden' was one of these, and a twelve-guinea commission for a version of it proved irresistible. But she had barely begun work when, on 2 April 1931, she had another serious physical collapse and was obliged to stay with the Yeatses for a fortnight to rest.

It was clear that she would never recover her full strength and Yeats (chastened perhaps by the knowledge that her condition had proved to be physiological rather than psychological as he had once sweepingly supposed) suggested she slowly close down the embroidery business. Early in December 1931 Lily held her last Cuala embroidery sale and George, who had been extremely understanding throughout, wrote to her husband, 'Cuala is wound up – the Embroidery I mean. I have paid all the bills except the overdraft at the bank.' This had now risen to £1800, a thousand of which was the debit in the embroidery account. Once again, Yeats was called upon to be selflessly generous and he took out a further £1000 of his Nobel Prize money to settle matters at the bank while offering another £200 in cash to enable the rest of the business to pay its daily expenses. In addition, Yeats and his wife offered Lily a guaranteed income of £7 a month provided that she tried to equal this sum with her own work, Yeats suggesting that she embroider 'little pictures of famous houses'.

This was both practical and kindly, but, if Lily was suitably grateful for the help she had received, Lollie continued to be thoroughly exasperating. The press was 'going through a bad time', partly because of mounting world-wide recession, but Lily, realising that her sister 'never grows', attributed this to the fact that 'she never puts her teeth into the work, barely reads the proofs, fiddles and fritters away her day'. When her brother tried to discuss business matters with her on the telephone bickering was the inevitable result, and a diplomatic Lily suggested that one of the employees bring proofs to Yeats so that he could avoid a face-to-face confrontation with his ungracious sister.

There were, however, rewards outside the family. In May 1931 Yeats travelled to Oxford to receive an honorary doctorate. Maurice Bowra, now a proctor, had put Yeats's name forward, and recalled that he looked magnificent in his scarlet gown, with his white hair, and his eyes like an eagle's.[23] Yeats himself was delighted by the beauty of the Sheldonian Theatre and the large audience gathered there not, as he thought, to see a great poet, but to attend a debate on the abolition of the Divinity Moderations. After the ceremony, Bowra threw a small but Olympian dinner at Wadham for

Yeats to which he invited Kenneth Clark and Livingstone Lowes and their wives along with Elizabeth Bowen, John Sparrow and Nancy Mitford. Bowra himself made a short speech in which he said that 'the University which had expelled Shelley had now tried to make amends by honouring the greatest poet of the age'. Yeats nodded but chose not to make a formal reply, saying that he had had no warning. 'This was agreed to be right.'

After the dinner the company moved on to Bowra's rooms, where Yeats read some of his poems, introducing them with short explanations and comments so that they should be fully understood. As he was leaving, Yeats said to John Sparrow, 'No emperor does himself so well as an Oxford don,' and the following day over tea Sparrow was treated to a further epic conversation in which Yeats uttered such memorable phrases as 'The tragedy of sexual intercourse is the perpetual virginity of the soul' and 'Damn Bertrand Russell. He's a proletarian. He has a wicked and vulgar spirit.' Bowra himself felt that the 'more material side of the evening had at least been a success', but when Yeats wrote his letter of thanks he told Bowra how reassured he had been that his poems had been understood and valued, adding: 'I have not written verse for some months, and it may be owing to you and your friends that I am eager to write it. I thank you and thank them.'

In London Yeats presented Macmillans with six of the seven volumes of edited material for the Edition de Luxe of his works and then returned to Dublin, where in July he began working with the young Italian scholar Mario Rossi, who had agreed to collaborate with Joseph Hone on a study of Berkeley.[24] Rossi was warm and outgoing, and the Irish poet with his interest in Italian political thought found an agreeable companion in him, declaring that 'we shall send him back to Italy with a faultless Dublin accent'. A frail Lady Gregory invited Rossi to Coole, where he was one of the last guests encouraged to carve his initials on the famous copper beech tree. The beauty of Coole impressed Rossi deeply and in his *Viaggio in Irlanda* (subsequently translated as *Pilgrimage to the West*) he apostrophised the house and its tutelary deities. Of Coole itself he wrote, 'the impression is of something intimate, something retired yet cordial. It is as though the house, not wishing to be directly seen, wished to hide itself in the depth so that only friends should find it.' With a young man's conspicuous deference he wrote of Lady Gregory herself,

> you have never pretended to be a guide, to be a chief, to be a mother of Ireland and therefore you have been more than a guide, more than a national chief; you have created what did not exist, a common soul for the Catholic and the Protestant, for the poets and artists, for diverse and hostile spirits, and the living reality of the Irish soil – because all these could be your friends.

Rossi watched Yeats closely too (despite getting the colour of his eyes wrong when he came to write up his memories) and recalled him particularly 'striding patiently' about Coole 'with bowed head and enquiring about philosophy'. Rossi declared that he had never met a more eager interest in metaphysics outside of Coole and he was particularly impressed by the sincerity of Yeats's enquiries, since it was clear he wanted '*to know*. He was searching again and again for an explanation.' That Yeats was not attracted by 'abstruse speculation' or the harsh technical difficulties of the subject impressed Rossi particularly. Here was a man needing the support of ideas just as he needed the sustenance of food. 'He wanted to solve his problems. He wanted to come in clear about his own mind.'

Rossi was impressed equally by Yeats's enthusiasm and his humility. He saw that Yeats wanted to know 'how his poetical problems could be shaped as logical problems'. He realised how 'he wanted to connect thing and image; to prove that the poet's expression goes further than usual vision, reaches – beyond sensation and word – the intimate transempirical nature of the world, to assure himself that the poet's way of dealing with reality is in fact a metaphysical description of it'. Yeats was searching, in other words, for an idealist justification of his deepest insights. 'He asked and listened and asked and listened again. His slow voice, which he had deliberately trained on the psaltery, might have seemed pontifical. But he was not proud of himself. He was proud of poetry, of the great things to which he gave voice.' Berkeley was a common bond, and in the introductory essay Yeats composed for Hone and Rossi's book he wrote that his experience of reading the philosopher was such that 'we feel perhaps for the first time that eternity is always at our heels or hidden from our eyes by the thickness of a door'. Vision, as always, remained paramount.

Intimations of ecstasy were seized, however, amid the sadness of human decrepitude. Lady Gregory was failing, her physical frailty a *memento mori* among the patrician values she represented:

> Sound of a stick upon the floor, a sound
> From somebody that toils from chair to chair;
> Beloved books that famous hands have bound,
> Old marble heads, old pictures everywhere;
> Great rooms where travelled men and children found
> Content or joy; a last inheritor
> Where none has reigned that lacked a name and fame
> Or out of folly into folly came.[25]

Yeats stayed beside her during the winter of 1931 and the spring of the following year, helping her sometimes with her correspondence as she had once helped him. 'He is', she was able to write, 'so kind, and makes his tea, and talks pleasantly – carries his kindness through the day.' Yeats declared that she was 'indomitable to the last, seeing to all her household duties and weekly charities', despite being racked by arthritis. How painful this process of watching an old friend die could be was suggested, rather scornfully, by George. She told Dorothy Pound that Lady Gregory's mind was going but added that her husband 'doesnt seem to mind the re-iterations. Personally they send me nearer lunacy than anything I ever met.' That Yeats's patience must have been as tried as his compassion is clear, yet he stood by her with all the fastness of a great friendship and filled the vacant hours with an exhaustive programme of reading.

'Can you send me Balzac *Harlot's Progress* – vol. II. I have just finished vol. I. I want to go right through Balzac again: he has fascinated me as he did thirty years ago. In some ways I see more in him than I did thirty years ago. He is the voice of the last subjective phases, of individualism in its exaltation.' The result of so prodigious an undertaking (hardly something to be lightly considered by a man with deteriorating eyesight, even if Lady Gregory did continue her habit of reading aloud to him when she could) was the eventual issuing of the essay 'Louis Lambert'.

In these winter months of 1931, however, the abounding spiritual and sexual certainties of the Crazy Jane poems seemed wholly out of place and Yeats, ever the antithetical man, began to assemble the lyrics eventually gathered under the title 'Vacillation'. Although at their centre stands his lyric reworking of that passage of mystical intensity he had first composed for *Per Amica Silentia Lunae* – that moment in a crowded London teashop when he had experienced 'twenty minutes more or less' of the transforming fire of spiritual happiness – the poems as a whole offer no certainties, no final truths. The fire of illumination is experienced only through the suppression or death of the body. Perhaps, Yeats suggests, with another bow to his anthropological reading, only the self-castrated priests of Attis can be suspended between the bodily and spiritual worlds, but then 'in a state of equilibrium there is neither emotion nor sensation'. Besides, man must work, the artist exalt life, and everyone must suffer moments of painful self-recrimination in a world where 'all things pass away'. The temptations of a conventional religious belief which, his letters to Olivia Shakespear suggest, seem to have lured Yeats at this time, must finally be set aside, however. The creative artist at least must accept the altogether more difficult idea that it is just the vacillations, the veering between exultation and daily doubt which these poems record, that make up his true theme. An old man pottering between the beatific vision and the daily round, he must finally accept a fallen world. 'What theme had Homer but original sin?'

Yeats also reread *Prometheus Unbound* at this time, but the greatest new impression made on him came from the autobiography of an Indian holy man called Shri Purohit Swami, and for this work, in which the soul once more seeks certainties and health, Yeats eventually wrote an introduction. Yeats had first met the Swami at Sturge Moore's house and had been impressed by the aristocratic sensitivity of 'a man of fifty, broken in health by the austerities of his religious life.'[26] But he soon became attracted less by his outward demeanour than by 'something much simpler, more childlike and ancient'. His religious discipline had preserved that 'spontaneity of the soul' which seemed to Yeats 'Asia at its finest and where it is most different from Europe'. The Swami's mystical insight and power rekindled Yeats's interest in Eastern mysticism and he was enthused by its lack of concern with original sin, its trusting to vision, and its love of nature – qualities which seemed to set it apart from the modern Christianity of the West. In a faith like the Swami's, Yeats believed, he could find something that could repair the damage of centuries and bring back to European thought the spiritual spontaneity he believed belonged to Byzantine theologians and Irish monks.

> The Indian . . . approaches God through vision, speaks continually of the beauty and terror of the great mountains, interrupts his prayer to listen to the song of birds, remembers with delight the nightingale that disturbed his meditation by alighting upon his head and singing there, recalls after many years the whiteness of a sheet, the softness of a pillow, the gold embroidery upon a shoe. These things are indeed part of the 'splendour of that Divine Being'.

Yeats felt that such qualities were being threatened in an Ireland where the repressive grip of Catholicism seemed to grow ever tighter, and in an attempt to assert intellectual and poetic values in national life he resolved to found an Academy of Letters and invited George Russell to Coole to discuss the project. Russell did indeed draw up a constitution for the Academy but did so under a cloud of deepening pessimism. For him, the spiritual state of Ireland was something that induced near-despair. 'There is nothing to interest me in a nation run by louts,' he wrote to Yeats, 'and your Academy of Letters will not have the slightest effect in a country where all the papers are united in fears of clerical denunciation. I may think differently later on, but just now I feel alien to everything except the earth itself and if it was not for that love I would leave Ireland.' Such pessimism was deepened by the election on 16 February 1932 of de Valera and the Fianna Fail party to government.

Despite the foreign policy successes of the Cosgrave government and, in particular, the leading role its members had played at Imperial Conferences in asserting the sovereign rights of the Dominions – an initiative that led to the Statute of Westminster, which formally recognised the equality of the Dominions with the United Kingdom and their right to reject British legislation – domestic political failure pointed to the Cosgrave government's rapid demise. De Valera had long been taunting the opposition for being merely the 'Commonwealth Party', but it was an austerity budget introduced in the face of chronic world recession on the eve of the 1932 general election, along with high unemployment and falling exports, which assured its defeat. Although the new ministers went to the Dail with guns in their pockets, a smooth transition of power symbolised the maturity of the new state, but Yeats, who had naturally voted for Cosgrave, was now to be shown how narrow the new government would prove to be.

When he learned that a number of Irish-American societies were pressuring de Valera to exercise censorship over the Abbey, his worst fears were confirmed. He went to see the new President, and, although personally impressed by his probity, he nonetheless realised again the importance of maintaining a concerted literary opposition to censorship. That spring, however, he was to lose the one person who had stood steadfastly by him in all his attempts to protect the new literature of Ireland from unwarranted political interference. In February 1932, while Yeats himself was briefly away from Coole, Lady Gregory had written him a letter instinct with valediction and patrician poise. 'Dear Willie,' she wrote:

> I don't feel very well this morning, rather faint once or twice. It may be the time has come for me to slip away – and that may be as well – for my strength has been ebbing of late, and I don't want to become a burden and give trouble. I have had a full life and except for the grief of parting with those who are gone, a happy one. I do think I have been of use to the country and for that in great part I thank you.
>
> I thank you also for these last months that you have spent with me. Your presence made them pass quickly and happily in spite of bodily pain, as your friendship has made my last years – from first to last fruitful in work, in service. All blessings to you in the years to come!
>
> A. Gregory[27]

Yeats sent her pain-killing drugs from Dublin, 'guaranteed not to contain morphia or to affect the mind', but he had been about Abbey business when he had a late-night telephone call from Lady Gregory's solicitors which told him that she had died during the night of 22 May 1932. He returned to Coole the next day and noticed among those who came to pay their respects 'a queer Dublin sculptor dressed like a workman'. He watched him as 'he walked from room to room and then stopped at the mezzotints and engravings of those under or with whom . . . the Gregories had served, Fox, Burke and so on, and after standing silent said "all the nobility of the earth". I felt he did not mean it for that room alone but for lost tradition. How much of my own verses has been but the repetition of those words.' Now Coole and all it represented seemed to have gone:

> We were the last romantics – chose for theme
> Traditional sanctity and loveliness;
> Whatever's written in what poets name

> The book of the people; whatever most can bless
> The mind of man or elevate a rhyme;
> But all is changed, that high horse riderless,
> Though mounted in that saddle Homer rode
> Where the swan drifts upon a darkening flood.[28]*

Yeats had once again outlived the great figures of a literary epoch, and although he later believed that he saw Lady Gregory's arm at the edge of a door waving up and down in a spectral farewell, the end of this great friendship meant that he would now have to discover new ways, new sources of energy, new inspirations, in his quest to unite occult and Nationalist aspirations in the crucible of his art. This he would have to do, however, in an Ireland that was for him an ever deepening source of pessimism.

---

* The house itself was demolished for building stone nine years after Lady Gregory's death. The autograph tree was preserved, however, and may still be seen at the site.

17

Bitter Furies of Complexity
(1932–1935)

I
'Rich Life and Vigour'

In May 1932, still grieving for the loss of Coole and its chatelaine, Yeats decided to take a thirteen-year lease on a plain but attractive eighteenth-century farmhouse called Riversdale, situated at Rathfarnham by the foot of the mountains outside Dublin. The house itself was surrounded by a well-planted, four-acre garden which included not only beds for flowers, fruit and vegetables, but a croquet lawn which Yeats soon learned to enjoy, becoming a proficient if erratic player.* The rooms of the house itself were small, and two of them off the hallway were knocked into one to create for Yeats a study and a sitting room. From a corner of this a glass door led out to a conservatory where he kept his pet canaries, while the lemon-yellow walls were lined with his books and pictures. Joseph Hone recalled that 'Sato's sword lay across the great oak writing-table'.[1] Yeats's bedroom was on the floor above and looked out in one direction towards the mountains while the other window opened on to the orchard and occasionally had a meatbone hung from it to attract the birds.

Money was of course needed to create so attractive a home, and on 21 October Yeats set out on his final American lecture tour to raise resources both for Riversdale itself and for the Irish Academy of Letters, which had been launched the previous month. He took Alan Duncan with him as his secretary on an exhausting schedule that included giving twenty lectures. He travelled, however, in great comfort, Henry Ford providing him in each major city with cars and drivers previously lent to Winston Churchill. There were occasions when Yeats lectured twice in a single

---

* Anne Yeats commented of her father's game later: 'he was a very good croquet player and he used to hit a ball at the far end, seemed to concentrate a lot on it, and I don't think he played to win, but I think he liked winning the game like anybody else. I remember somebody came to tea and cheated to let him win, and he never played with her again.'

day, but his physical resilience was constantly evident despite his recent illnesses, and he would even give his chauffeur permission to go home during the cold autumn nights, telling the man that he would get a taxi. The Abbey players were also on tour in New York at this time, and Yeats wrote to George telling her how he had 'just come from the theatre where *The Words upon the Window-Pane* was played before a vast audience, every seat sold and people standing'. Drawing-room lectures meanwhile raised some £700 for the Academy, which would now be able to offer a prize for the best book by an Irish writer under the age of thirty-five.

Yeats returned to Riversdale on 28 January 1933. While he had been away, his sister had issued *Words for Music Perhaps and Other Poems*, a collection later added to *The Winding Stair*. Yeats's prodigious fertility was as evident as ever, and Edmund Dulac's wife wrote to him that it was 'good to see that you have come thro the Tower and discovered another passion on the other side. This must be very exciting news for all writers – indeed all men. No other poet I have ever heard of has done this. One "passion of life" they always have of course or they would not be poets; to go on with rich life and vigour and fullness of power to a third is I think unknown except to you.'[2] Yeats himself, however, was beginning to have doubts about his creativity, since he had written no verse for some months after Lady Gregory's death. He also began to think often about his own demise.

Spiritualist beliefs inevitably mingled with such painful reflections, and, when the poet Louis MacNeice visited with his fellow classics scholar E. R. Dodds, Yeats confined the conversation to such matters. At one point the rapaciously questioning Dodds asked Yeats if he had ever seen the spirits. 'Yeats was a little piqued. No, he said grudgingly, he had never actually seen them . . . but – with a flash of triumph – he had often *smelt* them.'[3] Now, however, apparitions began to make their presence felt even in broad daylight. 'As I woke,' Yeats wrote to Olivia Shakespear, 'I saw a child's hand and arm and head – faintly self-luminous – holding above – I was lying on my back – a five of diamonds or hearts I was [not] sure which. It was held as if the child was standing at the head of the bed. Is the meaning some fortune teller's meaning attached to the card or does it promise me five months or five years? Five years would be about long enough to finish my autobiography.'

The deaths of Lady Gregory, and earlier of George Moore and Edward Martyn, meant that Yeats could now extend his autobiographical writing to the period of his earliest involvement with the theatre in Ireland. These days he recalled in *Dramatis Personae*, an engaging piece of revenge from which Moore particularly emerges vigorously caricatured as a gauche and parvenu intellectual with a coarse interest in sex:

On a visit to Coole, during some revising of *The Bending of the Bough*, or to begin *Diarmuid and Grania*, its successor, he behaved well till there came a long pause in the conversation one night after dinner. 'I wonder', said Moore, 'why Mrs — threw me over; was it because she wanted to marry —' – he named a famous woman and a famous peer – 'or was it conscience?' I followed Moore to his room and said, 'You have broken the understanding.' 'What understanding?' 'That your conversation would be fit for Robert.' Robert, Lady Gregory's son, was on holiday from Harrow. 'The word conscience can have only one meaning.' 'But it's true.' 'There is a social rule that bars such indiscretions.' 'It has gone out.' 'Not here.' 'But it is the only thing I can say about her that she would mind.' Mrs — had been much taken with Moore, I had heard her talk of him all evening, but was of strict morals: I knew from the friend who had listened to Moore's daily complaints and later to his contradictory inventions, that he had courted her in vain. Two or three years after his Coole transgression, he was accustomed to say: 'Once she and I were walking in the Green Park. "There is nothing more cruel than lust," she said. "There is," I said. "What is that?" "Vanity," and I let her go a step or two ahead and gave her a kick behind.'[4]

Now all the named characters in the tale were, with the exception of its teller, dead. In its way this passage too is a life amid ghosts.

II
Blueshirts

But if there were old scores to settle there were new battles to fight. Not only did Yeats's Academy face opposition from Catholic Action, he was also obliged to watch the social unrest consequent upon de Valera's election. In particular, de Valera's determination to abolish the Oath of Allegiance and his refusal to pay Land Annuities to England led to severe economic attrition between the two countries which was particularly painful for Ireland since virtually all its exports went to England. The idea that the country could be self-sufficient was a nonsense. Although huge efforts were made to increase food production, agricultural prices slumped, unemployment soared and a road-building programme was introduced to help alleviate this, while, once again, emigration took its toll on the country's more able young people.

Ireland was in a state of deepening crisis, and Yeats now swept up de Valera into his belief in government by strong men who could mould public opinion rather than slavishly follow the democratic views Yeats himself had so long feared. 'There is Hitler in Germany, Stalin in Russia, Mussolini in Italy,' he wrote, 'and now we have Ireland passing into a similar [era] in its intensity, in [its] fanaticism.'⁵ De Valera, who had famously declared that he had only to look into his own heart to be told 'straight off what the Irish people wanted', seemed to Yeats to be cast in the same mould as other European tyrants. Here, apparently, was a leader who might impose on the Irish masses those eighteenth-century political values nurtured by Swift particularly. As Yeats wrote in July 1933: 'De Valera has described himself . . . as an autocrat expressing the feeling of the masses. If we must have an autocrat let him express what Swift called the "bent & current" of a people not a momentary majority.'

Throughout 1932, however, the presence of de Valera, far from appearing to weld the nation together, seemed to many to be fracturing it. The IRA were breaking away from him, while worried supporters of Cosgrave, fearful that de Valera and his party would not look favourably upon erstwhile members of the Free State army, began what was first named the Army Comrades Association. This was a volunteer force allegedly devoted to freedom of speech and attacking what they feared as the communist tendencies of the IRA. The ACA itself claimed to be above party loyalties, and in its attempt to establish its identity soon began to borrow the motifs of Continental fascism, including drilling, saluting and the wearing of the blue shirts which later provided a name for the forces of Irish fascism. Their numbers swelled greatly while Yeats himself was in America, and by the closing months of 1932 clashes between the ACA and the IRA had become so fierce that the breakdown of civil order appeared a worrying possibility. If de Valera were to be 'torn in pieces', then the communism espoused by the IRA might become a real threat in Ireland. By March 1933 Yeats was trying 'in association with [an] ex-cabinet minister, an eminent lawyer, and a philosopher, to work out a social theory which can be used against Communism in Ireland – what looks like emerging is Fascism modified by religion'.⁶

It is far from clear what such an alliance might have meant, but the general direction of Yeats's political thought at this time is clear. 'In politics I have one passion and one thought, rancour against all who, except under the most dire necessity, disturb public order, a conviction that public order cannot long persist without the rule of educated and able men.' This was an old belief heightened by the current situation, which appeared to be reaching a climax over the summer months of 1933. On 13 July Yeats wrote that 'politics are growing heroic. De Valera has forced political thought to face the most fundamental issues. A Fascist opposition is forming behind the scenes to be ready should some tragic situation develop. I find myself constantly urging the despotic rule of the educated classes as the only end to our troubles.' Yeats genuinely believed that the actions of the IRA and the distress caused by the economic war with England might bring chaos, and he thought that democratic politics would, as a result, 'be discredited in this country and a substitute will have to be found'. Looking to Germany and feeling 'emulous' of what Hitler's Brownshirts appeared to be achieving, Yeats associated himself with shirts of a different hue. 'Our chosen colour is blue, and blue shirts are marching all over the country. . . . The chance of being shot is raising everybody's spirits enormously.'

So far, however, Yeats had had very little contact with members of the Blueshirt movement. It was only when his friend Captain Dermot MacManus, 'his head full of vague Fascism, got probably from me', determined to introduce Yeats to the newly appointed Blueshirt leader General Eoin O'Duffy that the absurdity of trying to maintain high civilisation through the support of marching thugs gradually became apparent to him. The meeting was arranged so that Yeats could 'talk my anti-democratic philosophy. I was ready, for I had just rewritten for the seventh time the part of *A Vision* that deals with the future.' As a consequence, O'Duffy was treated to a lecture. 'Talk went in the usual line: the organised party directed from above. Each district dominated through its ablest men. My own principle is that every government is a tyranny that is not a government by the educated classes and that the state must be hierarchical throughout.'[7]

MacManus had hoped that Yeats might be the philosopher of the Blueshirt movement and such an idea may have had an appeal for him. However, as Yeats expatiated on his views, so the difference between the visionary poet and the fascist leader became ever more evident. That Yeats actually appeared more absurd than dangerous was not at first obvious to him.

> I urged the getting of a recent 3 volume description of the Italian system . . . and putting some Italian scholars to make a condensation of it. I urged also that unless a revolutionary crisis arose they must make no intervention. They should prepare themselves by study to act without hesitation should the crisis arise. Then, and then only, their full programme. I talked of the 'historical dialectic', spoke of it as proving itself by events as the curvature of space was proved (after mathematicians had worked it out) by observation during an eclipse. O'Duffy probably brought here that I might talk of it.

If this last idea was true, the end of the meeting proved its futility. Yeats, who wore blue shirts partly under the influence of William Morris and partly to show off his magnificent mane of white hair, was utterly incomprehensible to O'Duffy, who wore a blue shirt for reasons altogether more degrading, reasons which suggested to Yeats that he was merely an uneducated lunatic. Although for a little while after the meeting Yeats still hoped that O'Duffy would stand against democracy and for the rule of hierarchy and educated men, he was already beginning to have his doubts. O'Duffy 'seemed to me a plastic man but I could not judge whether he would prove plastic to the opinions of others. . . . The man plastic to his own will is always powerful. The opposite kind of man is like a mechanical toy, lift him from the floor and he can but buzz.' That O'Duffy was barely capable even of buzzing soon became clear. When he boasted that 20,000 Blueshirts would march through Dublin to commemorate such strong Irish leaders as Griffith, Collins and O'Higgins, the government took the normal precautions, filled the city with policemen, banned the march and eventually saw it cancelled. O'Duffy adroitly moved himself into parliamentary politics, heading the Fine Gael coalition working in support of the Treaty.

Quite how absurd matters could become when feelings were running so high is suggested by a story of Frank O'Connor's. O'Connor told how Yeats decided that some neighbours with a dog were Blueshirts like himself. 'Mrs Yeats, who was democratic in sympathies, kept hens, and the Blueshirt dog worried the democratic hens. Naturally, Yeats supported the dog.' Unfortunately, one of George's hens one day disappeared and she was sure that it was the dog who had stolen it. She wrote to complain and the neighbours replied, by return, that the dog had been destroyed. 'Mrs Yeats, who was very fond of animals, was conscience-stricken, but Yeats was delighted by what he regarded as a true Blueshirt respect for law and order. One evening he called at my flat in a state of high glee,' O'Connor continued. 'The democratic hen had returned safe and sound and Mrs Yeats was overwhelmed with remorse. Another victory over the democracies!'[8] The whole episode of Yeats and the Blueshirts was however nothing more than what Yeats himself at the end of the summer was calling 'our political comedy'.

Yeats's Blueshirt involvement had, however, produced a number of poems. 'Three Songs to the Same Tune' were not published until February 1934, and both then and at their reprinting at the end of the year Yeats's attached notes showed him carefully distancing himself from the Blueshirt movement. 'Some months ago that passion laid hold upon me with the violence that unfits the poet for all politics but his own,' he declared. 'While the mood lasted, it seemed that our growing disorder, the fanaticism that inflamed it like some old bullet embedded in the flesh, was about to turn our noble history into an ignoble farce.' Yeats was still passion-ately seeking a political affiliation that might provide 'unity of culture not less than economic unity, welding to the purpose museum, school, university, learned institution,' but, eventually realising 'there is no such government or party today', offered his public heavily revised versions of works in which the Blueshirts themselves appear as the embodiment of fanaticism. In the revised version of 'Parnell's Funeral', for example, the poet laments the collapse of intellectual freedom in a country that has succumbed to 'the contagion of the throng'. The nation's leaders, in an image Yeats borrowed from his anthropological reading, have failed to nourish themselves from Parnell's sacrificed heart, and so have betrayed the people.

As O'Duffy's Fine Gael party became ever more evidently 'the mob that howls at the door', so Yeats turned to lament the dwindling of contemporary Irish politics from the high and heroic standards once set by Parnell. A deeply disillusioned Yeats, rejecting Blueshirt fascism, was obliged to look on the contemporary world with increasingly isolated and rancorous disillusion. He saw public life in Ireland moving from violence to violence or merely to an apathy in which parliament disgraced itself and those who entered it, so creating a country in which men of letters would live like outlaws in a world of darkening ignorance and mounting cultural despair. He believed that the party that could save the country from this would have to be forceful and rely on marching men, but O'Duffy was not the leader of such a group.

Precisely how Yeats's political ideas had been running at this time was made evident to a young Diarmuid Brennan when he called on the poet in the high summer of 1934 to discuss an anthology of the poetry 'that had come out of those six revolutionary years in Ireland, 1916–1922. The shimmering jewel was to be Yeats's 'Easter 1916'.[9] Brennan arrived at Riversdale clutching copies of *The Winding Stair* and a volume of *The Prison Letters of Constance Markiewicz* edited by Esther Roper. George told the young man he was 'in beautiful time for tea' and led him into Yeats's study, introducing Brennan as 'our young correspondent' and telling her husband that he was a poet too. Yeats was wearing a porridge-coloured suit and 'a soft butterfly tie', and Brennan, already mortified with embarrassment, 'had the illusion Yeats towered over me like a column of honey and cream. I did not know what to do with Con Markiewicz's prison letters. I had the book in my right hand and tried to transfer it, fumblingly, but Yeats stretched out a Japanese hand and took the book and sat down.' He began to leaf through the pages and, when George reappeared with the tea things, asked (perhaps mischievously) if she had seen the volume of letters their young friend had edited. Then, warming to his theme, Yeats began to talk vehemently of the Famine and the English treatment of the Irish.

'I did not grasp it at the time,' Brennan wrote, 'but I was passing in and out of the life of William Butler Yeats at a moment when a hard, fierce nationalism was replacing the romanticism of half a century before.' As he listened he was dazzled and astonished as Yeats 'insisted there could be no boundary to the advance of a nation once its intellectual forces were properly harnessed'. Brennan reasonably wondered how unity of culture could be achieved except through democratic government. 'By militants,' Yeats said; 'and he said it so passionately a look of youngness transformed his face. "By marching men."' Although he had been disappointed by the Blueshirts, Yeats's energies would soon seek to express themselves in other ways.

<h1 style="text-align:center">III</h1>

'A Full Moon in March'

It was not only the political situation in Ireland that Yeats looked on with a pained combination of impotence, anger and underlying fear. His art seemed to him equally in decline. 'I found that I had written no verse for two years; I had never been so long barren. . . . Perhaps Coole Park where I had escaped from politics, from all that Dublin talked of, when it was shut, shut me out from my theme; or did the subconscious drama that was my imaginative life end with its owner?'[10]

Deeply concerned about what he considered this waning of his lyrical genius, Yeats set about drafting in prose a new play called *The King of the Great Clock Tower* in the hope that this might inspire him to write lyrics for the characters. The form of the work itself reverts to Yeats's experiments with Noh drama, while its ideas and images reach deep into his insecurities and his own past work, revitalising themes from the Nineties in which creativity is closely associated with intimations not just of immortality but of sex and physical destruction. The King of the Great Clock Tower's beautiful wife – a role created by Ninette de Valois – ends the play dancing with the poet's severed head. Time and death are powerfully connected to those who fashion art out of 'heroic wantonness'. It is the fear of impotence, however, which provides the play with one of its most powerful undercurrents. As Yeats himself wrote of the Queen's dance, it 'is a long expression of horror and fascination. She first bows before the head (it is on a seat) then in her dance lays it on the ground and dances before it, then holds it in her hands.' This concluding Salomé-like performance was seen by Yeats himself, continuing to exploit his anthropological interests, as a sort of fertility rite. 'It is part of the old ritual of the year: the mother goddess and the slain god,' he wrote, thereby suggesting that the ambiguous association between sex, creativity and death has a universal dimension. But it also had a personal character, for Yeats was privately worried that what he thought of as his declining poetic inspiration was related to age and his fears of sexual impotence.

Others were not encouraging about his work. Although Yeats himself declared that the first production of *The King of the Great Clock Tower* was a great success, Ezra Pound had been far from enthusiastic about the work. The Yeatses had travelled to Rapallo partly to dispose of their flat in the Via Americhe and to bring back their furniture and pictures. Yeats took the opportunity of presenting the draft of his newest play to Pound, clearly anxious to get the approval of a leading member of the younger generation. As Yeats himself explained:

> when I had written all but the last lyric I went a considerable journey partly to get the advice of a poet not of my school who would, as he did some years ago, say what he thought. I asked him to dine, tried to get his attention. 'I am in my sixty ninth year' I said, 'probably I should stop writing verse, I want your opinion upon some verse I have written lately.' I had hoped he would ask me to read it but he would not speak of art, or of literature, or of anything related to them. . . . He took my manuscript and went away denouncing Dublin as 'a reactionary hole' because I said that I was re-reading Shakespeare, would go on to Chaucer, and found all that I wanted of modern life in 'detection and the wild west'. Next day his judgement came and that in a single word 'Putrid'.[11]

After the first production of *The King of the Great Clock Tower* on 30 July 1934, however, Yeats sent a favourable review to Pound via Dorothy telling her that 'he may have been right to condemn it as poetry but he condemned it as drama. It has turned out the most popular of my dance plays.'

Such moods of happy vindication nonetheless alternated with disturbing personal doubts about some of the issues *The King of the Great Clock Tower* had incorporated. The phallic implications of the play's title are evident enough, but by 1934 Yeats was sufficiently concerned about his own sexual potency to speak despondently of it to a friend, who told him, partly in jest, that as long ago as 1918 the Austrian physiologist Eugen Steinach had developed an operation supposedly able to rejuvenate failing sexual prowess.[12] The operation had been widely performed in Vienna, and in 1924 the London surgeon Norman Haire wrote his book *Rejuvenation*, which purported to describe the more or less successful results of twenty-five Steinach operations he had himself performed. The operation itself, which was essentially a vasectomy, took a mere quarter of an hour but was unfortunately backed up by a now falsified theory which held that the process would increase the production of male hormones and reinvigorate the patient's whole body. Yeats told Haire that he felt he had lost his inspiration over the last three years and was clearly desperately keen that the operation should revive both his art and his private life.

Yeats underwent his Steinach operation in the first week of April 1934, and it would soon emerge that this was an extraordinary case of the finest poetry being produced by false science, since there is a quantity of anecdotal evidence to suggest that after the operation Yeats was still unable to have erections. His imagination, however, was liberated. George subsequently told the biographer Richard Ellmann that the effect on her husband was 'incalculable', and Yeats himself believed that, as a result of it, 'he had written new poems which, in the opinion of those whose opinion he valued most, were among his best work'. Yeats was undergoing the traumas and delights of what he called his 'second puberty', and the results were the poems included in the volume he called *A Full Moon in March*.

Works from this time include 'A Prayer for Old Age', Yeats's refusal of stately senilities and his choice of passion and folly:

> God guard me from those thoughts men think
> In the mind alone;
> He that sings a lasting song
> Thinks in a marrow-bone . . .[13]

The 'Supernatural Songs' deepen this determination and spiritualise it, for here Yeats's principal concern is with the relation between sexual desire and divine revelation. The erotic is shown as the origin of all revealed wisdom and thus becomes the basis for the totality – the inclusiveness – of human experience. Yeats's aim is to celebrate the potency of body and spirit, and to do so in a series of intense and often recondite lyrics which daringly adapt Christian imagery to their purpose. He described the first of these lyrics, 'Ribh at the Tomb of Baile and Aillin', to Olivia Shakespear, saying that in it 'a monk reads his breviary at midnight upon the tomb of long-dead lovers on the anniversary of their death, for on that night they are united above the tomb, their embrace being not partial but a conflagration of the entire body and so shedding the light he reads by'. As Yeats declared in the next lyric in the series: 'Natural and supernatural with the self-same ring are wed'.

These poems are not only visionary, but have a challenging Irish element to them, since Ribh is portrayed as an early Irish Christian who, far from being just a devout and mostly conventional Catholic, is in Yeats's view a man associated with the primary religious experiences of the world. Yeats believed that one of the characteristics of early Irish Christianity was that 'Christ was still the half-brother of Dionysus', and declared that he also associated early Christian Ireland with India since he believed with Hegel that all civilisation began on the Indian sub-continent. Other cultures played their part too, for Yeats declared that 'Saint Patrick must have found in Ireland, for he was not its first missionary, men whose Christianity had come from Egypt, and retained characteristics of those older faiths.' Early Celtic paganism also contributed its riches for, as Yeats wrote, 'I am convinced that in two or three generations it will become generally known that the mechanical theory has no reality, that the natural and supernatural are knit together . . . Europeans may find something attractive in a Christ posed against a background not of Judaism but of Druidism.' Irish religious experience encapsulated in Ribh thus drew to itself all the most ancient and potent religious beliefs of mankind and pointed the way towards a liberating and visionary future.

A number of these lyrics also present Yeats's astrological thought in an extremely concentrated form, but if the predominant accent is one of celebration – the exaltation of the unity between sexual desire and the beatific vision – the close of the sequence offers something profoundly and painfully characteristic of Yeats's late poetry, a terrible sense of emptiness, meaninglessness, energy rendered pathetic by a universe that has no abiding coherence:

> Civilisation is hooped together, brought
> Under a rule, under the semblance of peace
> By manifold illusion; but man's life is thought,
> And he, despite his terror, cannot cease
> Ravening through century after century,
> Ravening, raging, and uprooting that he may come
> Into the desolation of reality:
> Egypt and Greece, good-bye, and good-bye, Rome![14]

Placed at the end of so concise and exultant a series of lyrics, this poem, 'Meru', is deeply shocking. A series of works that begins in radiance ends in the blackness of a seemingly absolute doubt. The poem challenges all that has gone before it and suggests a vision of life in which passionate mankind stretches out body and soul towards the beatific vision even while acknowledging that such experiences may have no meaning whatsoever. Here, in miniature, is the terrifying awareness of the late Yeats.

In addition to this remarkable extension of his lyric output, Yeats also maintained his interest in the theatre and the world of European contemporary drama. In particular, he was invited to Rome as a guest of the Royal Academy of Italy to speak at the Congress of Dramatic Theatre held by the Alessandro Volta Foundation between 8 and 14 October 1934. The President was that year's winner of the Nobel Prize for Literature, Luigi Pirandello, and Yeats was chairman of the fourth session which took as its topic 'Drama in the Moral Life of the People'. The final two days of the Congress were given over to discussing state support for the theatre, and Yeats gave an address which traced the history of his own and others' involvement in 'the rise and achievement of a small, dingy, impecunious theatre, known to Irishmen all over the world because of the fame of its dramatists and its actors, because of the riots that had accompanied certain of its performances, because of its effect upon the imagination of Ireland'. He outlined the work of Synge and Lady Gregory, and, placing himself with these people as representatives of the Protestant Ascendancy that was now passing away, declared, 'it was right that we should give to the new Catholic Ireland that was about to take its place, a parting gift, the Irish National Theatre'.[15]

Yeats concluded his address with a passage that was both factual and optimistic. 'For a few years,' he declared, 'the theatre had a great prosperity, but now the tide has sunk again, and it must every two or three years tour the United States. It is a repertory theatre, changing its bill every week, and the repertory is now immense, but its whole repertory seems to rise or sink in popular favour according to that granted to or withheld from some one dramatist.' The theatre was, he thought, waiting for new blood. 'I await with confidence our next popular dramatist. Ireland has won its political freedom; the struggle for intellectual or imaginative freedom, for an escape from the tyranny of the second-rate, whether it come from the commercialised art of the contemporary stage, or from the nightmare in our own souls, must, in some measure, be fought out upon the stage.'

Drama remained for Yeats an essential aspect of his nationalism, but, while this was respected, others wished to pay tribute to Yeats's strength as a dramatic poet. Among these was Edward Gordon Craig, who, in a discussion which followed the giving of papers on developments in stage design, rose to praise a man whose influence on him had helped allow him change the whole course of the modern staging of plays. 'The remarkable fervour shown by most of the speakers who have insisted on the prime importance of the Dramatic Poet, the written word, the part which lives when all else is forgotten,' Craig said, 'urges me to remind the delegates and all present, that we have had in our midst for three or four days a great Dramatic Poet and no one till now even mentioned his name. . . . I refer to W. B. Yeats, of Ireland.'

IV
New Friends and Old

So much strenuous activity had an inevitable effect on Yeats's health, and in February 1935, when a lawyer came to see him about Lady Gregory's papers and read him 'document after document' for an hour, he collapsed shivering, panting and spitting blood from his congested lungs. While he was recuperating he worked on the proofs of *Dramatis Personae* in an upstairs room lit by two candles in great sconces which, he said, had once stood beside a bier. Those who wanted to celebrate his forthcoming seventieth birthday were deeply concerned, and not for Yeats alone. The Secretary of the Pen Club called at Riversdale and said to George: 'Oh, Mrs Yeats, don't let him slip away before June!'

By the time his birthday came round, however, Yeats was sufficiently recovered to entertain the Masefields and others at a lunch party, where he told the young Julian Bell to write poetry out of his emotions rather than his ideas. Bell, soon to be killed in the Spanish Civil War, was deeply impressed, telling another of the guests that he had at last seen a poet who looked like a poet. Edith Sitwell had sent Yeats a bunch of flowers from

Paris, while a little bound volume of goodwill messages arrived, signed by more than a hundred distinguished people, including Shaw, Hugh Walpole, Sir John Lavery and Augustus John. There was a dinner that evening where John Masefield and Desmond MacCarthy spoke, while the next day tributes appeared in the newspapers.

The *Irish Times*, publishing a supplement on Yeats and his work, declared: 'it must suffice that he undoubtedly is the greatest poet writing in the English language, that his work will endure while the English tongue is spoken, and that in an age which has produced a large number of brilliant writers – men of the calibre of Shaw, of Synge, of Moore, of Joyce, and of O'Casey – the name of William Butler Yeats stands unapproached and unapproachable'.[16] The article then went on to place Yeats in that eighteenth-century tradition with which he so wished to identify himself, thereby pointing out the relationship he had forged between literature and national consciousness. 'From the national point of view W. B. Yeats occupies an almost unique position in Irish life; for he is virtually the first man since Swift who has been able to bring the Anglo-Irish tradition into line with positive nationalism.'

Others were chary of such tributes. Yeats and Maud Gonne MacBride had been apart for a decade, but she continued to shine for him as 'almost the sole surviving friend of my early manhood, protesting in sybiline old age, as once in youth and beauty, against what seems to her a tyranny'. The presence of Maud's friend Mrs Despard, whom Yeats could not abide, had been a particular barrier to the renewal of their friendship, but when, in 1933, Mrs Despard left Roebuck House to campaign for civil rights in Belfast, a rapprochement seemed possible. In addition, Yeats's vigorous opposition to the establishment also pleased Maud, even if he was fighting from a position wholly contrary to her own. They began occasionally to meet again, but, if Yeats's attempts to avoid confrontation by insiting on merely chatting about light topics annoyed Maud, their meetings were always and necessarily charged with emotion. They met, for example, at the Kildare Street Club for tea, where the rules against women obliged the couple to sit in the hall. There the uncomfortable Yeats introduced Maud to an Anglo-Irish peer, an insult to her political convictions which resulted in a disagreement and their parting in a huff. But more serious matters also divided them. At the end of 1935, Maud followed Charlotte Despard to Belfast, where both hoped that the next move in Irish revolutionary politics would be made. Although Yeats admired Maud's energy, he was quite unable to share her enthusiasms. 'He found the inhabitants of the lost province of Ulster so disagreeable that he hoped that they would never reunite with the rest of Ireland.'[17]

There were problems too with Lady Gregory's daughter-in-law, now remarried to a Captain Gough, who was determined to keep Yeats at arm's length from Lady Gregory's literary estate. Lady Gregory herself had added a codicil to her will insisting that Yeats's decision in such matters should be 'final', but ironically in view of the long-drawn-out battle both she and Yeats had fought over the Hugh Lane pictures, this codicil was made invalid by having merely one witness. Margaret consequently felt she was within her rights to turn down the idea that Yeats should write her erstwhile mother-in-law's life until at least the time that Lady Gregory's autobiography had appeared. The fraught relationship gradually mellowed, however, and was certainly repaired by late 1934.

But the ageing poet now had to face the sadness of the loss of others of his contemporaries and lifelong acquaintances. George Russell, so deeply disillusioned with contemporary Ireland that he had left the country, died in Bournemouth. At the end he was desperate for a word from Yeats, and a letter happily arrived just in time to be read to him. Russell's body was then brought back to Ireland. For a while, Yeats was sunk in utter dejection, but when the cortège reached the cemetery he took his place behind the hearse and walked proudly to his friend's graveside. Russell was, he wrote a few days later, 'my oldest friend. I constantly quarrelled with him but he never bore malice, and in his last letter to me, a month before his death, he said that generally when he differed from me it was that he feared to be absorbed by my personality.'

Other life now had to be found, new self-transformations to be made, and as Yeats progressed towards what would be his last period younger women began to kindle the artistic and erotic excitement he had hoped would be awakened after his Steinach operation. His recent dramatic writing had renewed his interest in the musical speaking of verse, a subject he discussed with F. R. Higgins and which was to lead him to start the publication of a series of *Broadsides* from the Cuala Press. In September 1934, however, he received an invitation to meet the actress Margaret Ruddock with a view to creating a poet's theatre in London. The idea attracted him, since it seemed to provide the possibility of an outlet for poetic dance plays which the current realistic tastes of the Abbey did not encourage, and Yeats travelled optimistically to London. He found Margaret Ruddock (whose stage name was Margot Collis) to be a highly strung, beautiful and newly remarried divorcee of twenty-seven with deep, limpid eyes and a rich contralto voice. Margaret Ruddock was also trying to be a poet, and Yeats was 'amazed by the tragic magnificence of some fragments and said so'. Her beauty, her voice, her talent, Yeats's own dejected memories of his physically starved youth, stirred desires he believed had been released by his operation, the longing to be 'a foolish passionate man', 'a wild old wicked man', the poet writing out of 'an old man's frenzy'.

Such hopes of potency went hand in hand with pathos. Gazing on a past that seemed to be made out of 'lost opportunities to love', Yeats knew himself to be 'famine struck', old, but certain that when stirred by the beauty of Margot's half-closed eyes 'a sort of hidden glory' fell about his 'stooping shoulders'. The ageing man is at one with the starved youth, save that he is deprived of youth's cruel advantage of seemingly limitless time:

> The Age of Miracles renew,
> Let me be loved as those still young
> Or let me fancy that it's true,
> When my brief final years are gone
> You shall have time to turn away
> And cram those open eyes with day.[18]

Yeats recommended that as an actress Margot work on developing her vocal powers. She had stirred both his desire and his creativity, and when he was in Rome for the Congress of Dramatic Theatre he wrote to her saying that he was rewriting *The King of the Great Clock Tower* for her, that the old version was 'bad because abstract and incoherent'. He wanted something 'poignant and simple – lyrical dialogue all simple. It takes years to get my plays right.' Margot Ruddock was beginning to establish herself in Yeats's imagination as one in that series of much younger women who could stir his fertility. 'O my dear, my mind is so busy with your future and perhaps you will reject all my plans – my calculation is that, as you are a trained actress, a lovely sense of rhythm will make you a noble speaker of verse – a singer and sayer.' Her voice, imagined in its perfection, took on for Yeats an erotic significance. 'You will read certain poems to me, I have no doubt of the result.' It was planned with Frederick Ashton, Ashley Dukes, Edmund Dulac, T. S. Eliot and Rupert Doone of the Group Theatre that Margaret would play the leading role in *The Player Queen*. Tyrone Guthrie might have produced the work, but Dukes let them down and the project became a Yeats Festival playing at the Little Theatre from 28 to 31 October 1935. In this season Yeats had the pleasure of seeing Margot perform excellently as the True Queen in his play.

Other women friends Yeats made at this time included the novelist Ethel Mannin.[19] On the surface their friendship was a curious one 'in view of the wide disparity in our ideas, Yeats with his innate mysticism, and I with my then inveterate materialism'. Ethel Mannin was partly attracted by Yeats's sheer vitality, and she wrote of a 'Yeats full of Burgundy and racy reminiscence', a 'Yeats released from the Celtic Twilight and treading the antic hay with abundant zest. In the latter years of his life because of his health he took only a little white wine and weak whisky and was less racy, but his tremendous Irish wit remained unimpaired.'

A painful incident between them nonetheless showed the direction in which Yeats's political thought was moving. Ethel Mannin had been to a party at the Soviet embassy where she had met Ernst Toller, the German poet, playwright and political figure. Toller asked her to dine with him but she explained that she had arranged to meet Yeats at the Savile Club. Toller immediately seized on what he saw as an opportunity. 'There was a movement afoot to get Ossietsky, the German writer, imprisoned in Germany, the Nobel Peace Prize. If he should be awarded this he would most certainly be released from gaol, but to get it he must have a recommendation from some other Nobel-Prize winner. Yeats had the Nobel Prize for Literature – why should he not be the one to recommend Ossietsky for the Peace Prize?' Although Yeats had asked Ethel Mannin that she should not bring other people to meet him, Toller was so insistent that he eventually got his way, and he and Ethel Mannin found Yeats waiting in the entrance of his club 'wearing the cloak he sometimes affected in the evening'. Since women were not allowed into the Savile, the trio crossed to Claridge's, where, over drinks, Toller pressed his argument.

'I knew before Toller had finished that Yeats would refuse. He was acutely uncomfortable about it, but he refused. He never meddled in political matters, he said; he never had. At the urging of Maud Gonne he had signed the petition on behalf of Roger Casement, but that was all, and the Casement case was after all an Irish affair. He was a poet, and Irish, and had no interest in European political squabbles. His interest was Ireland, and Ireland had nothing to do with Europe politically; it was outside, apart. He was sorry, but this had always been his attitude'. All three were deeply upset, but Yeats persisted that 'he knew nothing about Ossietsky as a writer; that he could not be involved in a matter of this kind; that it was no part of an artist's business to become involved in affairs of this kind. He was sorry. He was very sorry.'

This picture of Yeats refusing to help save a man from the Nazis is a depressing one, and if it cannot be excused it can at least be explained, and the explanation casts a light on the development of Yeats's political thought in his last years after his disillusion with O'Duffy, the Blueshirts and Irish fascism. As he was at pains to point out in a long letter of self-justification sent to Ethel Mannin, his refusal to help Ossietsky had nothing whatsoever to do with anti-semitism or Nazi sympathies. 'I am not callous,' he wrote, 'every nerve trembles with horror at what is happening in Europe, "the Ceremony of innocence is drowned".' Yeats had now developed a profound mistrust of the coercive state, of any regime based on an ideology. 'Do not try to make a politician of me,' he begged Ethel Mannin, 'even in Ireland I shall never I think be that again – as my sense of reality deepens, and I think it does with age, my horror at the cruelty of governments grows greater, and if I did what you want, I would seem to hold one form of government more responsible than any other, and that would betray my convictions. Communist, Fascist, nationalist, clerical, anti-clerical, are all responsible according to the number of their victims.'

Yeats felt himself above all an Irish poet, and believed ever more passionately that Ireland alone, isolated on the western coast of Europe, should be kept free from the organised brutality goose-stepping its way across almost every other part of the Continent. Great individuals alone could stand against the encircling horror and assert the values of a full humanity. Ireland needed and possessed such men, and in a Europe hastening towards organised barbarism the country had to preserve its neutrality. 'Do not try to pour Ireland into any political system. Think first how many able men with public minds the country has, how many it can hope to have in the near future, and mould your system upon those men. It does not matter how you get them, but get them. Republics, Kingdoms, Soviets, Corporate States, Parliaments, are trash, as Hugo said of something else, "not worth one blade of grass that God gives for the nest of the linnet". These men, whether six or six thousand, are the core of Ireland, are Ireland itself.'[20] Everywhere Yeats looked for the evidence that seemed to justify his ideas and point to the political decadence. 'I am alarmed at the growing moral cowardice of the world, as the old security disappears – people run in packs that they may get courage from one another.' Again: 'all over the world men are turning to Dictators, Communist or Fascist. Who can keep company with the Goddess Astrea if both his eyes are upon the brindled cat?'

In such a world it seemed ever more important to Yeats to preserve the integrity of Irish nationalism as he envisaged it. The Irish should retreat inside themselves to find their own real strength, and for Yeats, as he repeated in his own person the search that he believed his nation should undergo, so an image from his youth rose constantly before him to suggest all that was finest in Irish nationhood – John O'Leary exercised over the ageing Yeats the influence he had exerted over him as a young man. 'Damn Toller,' he wrote to Ethel Mannin, 'but you should know that no nationalist of the school of John O'Leary has ever touched international politics.' Here was an image of sanity to cling to in a world increasingly gone mad. 'Why should I trouble about Communism, Fascism, liberalism, radicalism, when all, though some bow first and some stern first but all at the same pace, all are going downstream with the artificial unity that ends every civilisation?' Fascism he could now dismiss with an image that disparaged the *fasces* themselves, those bundles of tied rods which gave rise to the word: 'only dead sticks can be tied into convenient bundles', he declared. Socialism too could be similarly disparaged: 'I remember old O'Leary saying "no gentleman can be a socialist though he might be an anarchist".'[21] And here was a position the elderly Yeats felt he could sincerely adopt. In a world of hideously competing ideologies he would stand apart as a gentleman of the right and an anarchist. As he wrote to Lady Gerald Wellesley, later Duchess of Wellington, 'my dear I am as anarchic as a sparrow'.

Yeats had been introduced to Dorothy Wellesley by Ottoline Morrell in May 1935. Now, with the loss to him of Coole, Dorothy Wellesley's magnificent Sussex home, Penns-in-the-Rocks, became a centre of aristocratic culture and that sense of patrician decorum which was for Yeats so fundamental a need. Dorothy Wellesley was also a poet, and Yeats had read her work in connection with his editing the *Oxford Book of Modern Verse*. The editorship of this book was a great honour from which Yeats could expect both money and enhanced reputation, but it was also a challenge. As he himself explained: 'I can never do any kind of work (apart from verse) unless I have a problem to solve. My problem this time will be "How far do I like the Ezra, Auden, Eliot School, and if I do not, why not?" Then this further problem. "Why do the younger generation like it so much? What do they see or hope?"'

V
The Oxford Book of Modern Verse

Yeats put an enormous amount of work into trying to solve these problems. A severe attack of congestion of the lungs in the early months of 1935 had confined him to the ground floor of his and George's temporary home at 17 Lancaster Gate Terrace for more than five weeks, but by July he had set to work on the anthology, asking his agent to arrange that its starting date should be fixed at around the time of the death of Tennyson. He worked either in the British Museum, where in one day he 'read or smelt' forty-five books of poetry, or at home, where he cut out lyrics he liked from the books he had bought. George too put a great deal of work into the anthology, in particular taking over the onerous task of typing poems, collating texts, arranging acknowledgements and seeing that authors were paid. She also helped Yeats choose fourteen of his own poems, the greater part of which were comparatively recent works, including 'Sailing to Byzantium' and his two great tributes to the world created by Lady Gregory: 'Coole Park, 1929' and 'Coole and Ballylee, 1931'. The volume remains, however, notoriously unsatisfactory. This is partly because some poets like Kipling and Pound proved too expensive to be adequately represented, while others, such as Robert Graves and Laura Riding, declined to be included at all.

Yeats's own prejudices and editorial practices were responsible for other sometimes displeasing aspects of the collection. Yeats saw the volume as representing 'the revolt against Victorianism', which he defined as 'a revolt against irrelevant descriptions of nature, the scientific discursiveness of *In Memoriam* – "When he should have been broken-hearted," said Verlaine, "he had many reminiscences" – the political eloquence of Swinburne, the psychological curiosity of Browning, and the poetical diction of everybody'.[22] Yeats saw Walter Pater as the man who had headed this revolt, and 'that is why I begin this book with the famous passage from his essay on Leonardo da Vinci. Only by printing it in *vers libre* can one show its revolutionary importance.' Yeats then moved on to the poets of the Nineties, Count Stenbock, 'scholar, connoisseur, drunkard, poet, pervert, most charming of men,' standing as his synecdoche of the movement, before declaring, in a famous phrase: 'then in 1900 everybody got down off his stilts; henceforth nobody drank absinthe with his black coffee; nobody went mad; nobody committed suicide; nobody joined the Catholic church; or if they did I have forgotten'.[23] This is all sufficiently amusing, but the anthology barely justifies Yeats's claim that 'I think England has had more good poets from 1900 to the present day than during any period of the same length since the early seventeenth century. There are no predominant figures, no Browning, no Tennyson, no Swinburne, but more than I have found room for have written two, three, or half a dozen lyrics that may be permanent.'

A search for who these might be quickly reveals curious partialities for the frankly mediocre (Dorothy Wellesley, for example, is represented by no less than eight pieces, some of them of considerable length) along with extraordinary lacunae and judgements of great figures that verge on the ridiculous. Thomas Hardy is represented merely by four poems, none of which suggests that profound and profoundly moving lyric genius which places him among the great poets of his own or any age. Hopkins gets similarly short shrift, but if the seven poems by which he is represented display him more adequately than the Hardy selection, two sentences from the Introduction are distastefully dismissive. 'Fifty-odd years ago I met him in my father's studio on different occasions, but remember almost nothing. A boy of seventeen, Walt Whitman in his pocket, had little interest in a querulous, sensitive scholar.' Half a century had not changed Yeats's opinion. 'I read Gerard Hopkins with great difficulty, I cannot keep my attention fixed for more than a few minutes; I suspect the bias was born when I began to think. He is typical of his generation where most opposed to mine. His meaning is like some faint sound that strains the ear, comes out of words, passes to and fro between them, goes back into words, his manner a last development of poetical diction.'

Such errors of judgement were further compounded by Yeats's habit of editing other people's poems with a view to improving them. Even Oscar Wilde was not immune from such high-handed treatment. Writing of the *Ballad of Reading Gaol*, Yeats declared that 'I plucked out even famous lines because, effective in themselves, put into the Ballad, they become artificial, trivial, arbitrary; a work of art can have but one subject.' Yeats declared of his amputation: 'I have stood in judgement upon Wilde, bringing into the light a great, or almost great poem, as he himself had done had he lived; my work gave me that privilege.' Other poets, when they were not cavalierly dismissed, were again simply rewritten.

Many of the judgements of modern figures in the Introduction are quixotic.

'While T. S. Eliot has produced his great effect upon his generation because he has described men and women that get out of bed or into it from mere habit,' Dorothy Wellesley is presented as a poet of profound, exciting and thoroughly modern passion to whom 'nature is a womb, a darkness; its surface is sleep, upon sleep we walk, into sleep drive the plough, and there lie the happy, the wise, the unconceived'. Similarly, despite the fact that Yeats claimed to admire the work of Auden and his followers, he could not resist a slighting, witty comment on their politics, although time has justified his views. 'Communism', he wrote, 'is their *Deus ex Machina*, their Santa Claus, their happy ending, but speaking as a poet I prefer tragedy to tragi-comedy.' Some might have been able to brush aside such comments, but others were deeply offended by the anthology. In particular, Yeats's decision to include the work of W. J. Turner and to mention his novel *The Aesthetes* in his Introduction infuriated Ottoline Morrell, who had been cruelly lampooned in it. Although Yeats himself tried to make amends, Lady Ottoline was too upset to forgive him, scribbling on his last letter to her, 'Yeats fini'.

The most notorious aspect of the anthology, however (and to some its most offensive), was Yeats's outright dismissal of the poets of the First World War.

> I have a distaste for certain poems written in the midst of the great war; they are in all anthologies, but I have substituted Herbert Read's *End of a War* written long after. The writers of these poems were invariably officers of exceptional courage and capacity, one a man constantly selected for dangerous work, all, I think, had the military cross; their letters are vivid and humorous, they were not without joy – for all skill is joyful – but felt bound, in the words of the best known, to plead the suffering of their men. In poems that had for a time considerable fame, written in the first person, they made that suffering their own. I have rejected these poems for the same reason that made Arnold withdraw his *Empedocles on Aetna* from circulation; passive suffering is not a theme for poetry.

Yeats was judging and dismissing these men in terms of his own evolving aesthetic: 'In all the great tragedies, tragedy is a joy to the man who dies.'

Inevitably, the anthology faced 'universal denunciation from both right and left', even if it sold briskly. To Yeats, to be in the heart of such controversy was to be alive, but it was Sean O'Casey who exposed the pathos underlying the cantankerousness and combativeness of the ageing poet.[24] He had visited him at Lancaster Gate Terrace when Yeats was 'in the centre of strife, selecting poems for his *Oxford Book of Modern Verse*'. O'Casey noticed the piles of modern poetry littering the room, interspersed here and there with detective novels and Wild West stories but, refusing to be drawn into a controversy about Yeats's work, saw instead how ill the poet was. 'The teeming thoughts of Yeats turned suddenly into himself as a tremulous stoppage of breath started an outburst of coughing that shook his big, protesting body, stretching his wide chest on a wrack of straining effort to rid itself of congestion, or end the effort by ending life.' He was a large man in great physical discomfort, and O'Casey noticed that as Yeats's hands 'gripped the sides of his chair, his fine eyes began to stare and bulge, showing the storm within, as he leant back and leant forwards to sway with the waves of stuffy contortion that were forcing resistant life from his fighting body'. The pathos and the humiliation were clear. 'The whole stately dignity and courage of the poet was crinkling into a cough,' O'Casey wrote. But he could see further than this. 'He has caught an everlasting cold, thought Sean. His own black oxen are treading him down.'

18

Why Should Not Old Men Be Mad?

(1935–1939)

I

'A Crazed Girl'

On 28 November 1935, Yeats and the Swami sailed from Liverpool to Majorca where Yeats planned, among other things, to work with his friend on a translation of the Upanishads. But Yeats was clearly a sick man. Four days of violent storm during the voyage strained his heart, and at the Hotel Terramar in Palma the plump and pink-robed Swami walked slowly in front of him when he went up and down stairs so that he should not further injure himself by excessive exertion.

For all this, Yeats threw himself into a demanding routine of work. He took breakfast early and then wrote in bed for four hours, composing his new play *The Herne's Egg*. This difficult and elusive drama, in part derived from Samuel Ferguson's long poem *Congal*, reworks many of Yeats's philosophical ideas and favourite images. We are shown life as a battle between man and man, as well as between man and the divine. Although the last scene in the play shows Congal's death and curious reconciliation with all the opposites in his nature, much of the play is concerned with sexuality and, in particular, with the relationship between Attracta, or the eternal and subjective feminine; godhead embodied in the Great Herne; and the heroic Congal himself. Attracta believes she is the Herne's rightful bride, but Congal sees this as an illusion and is determined to penetrate her, thereby satisfying the reality of her virginal desire as he understands it. In fact, Attracta is raped that night by seven men, and her belief that she has actually slept with the Great Herne is probably to be accounted for on a symbolic level by suggesting that the seven rapists correspond to the seven fundamental essences which Madame Blavatsky taught make up all living things. They can thus perhaps be seen as an image both of Congal the perfected man and of the cosmos or Great Herne.

The belief that human sexuality is profoundly related to the spiritual secrets of the universe – the subject of many of the 'Supernatural Songs' – is again suggested in Yeats's essay on 'The Mandukya Upanishad', a work supplementary to the introduction he wrote for the Swami's book *The Holy Mountain*. Here, writing of Tantric philosophy, Yeats described the state 'where a man and woman, when in sexual union, transfigure each other's images into the masculine and feminine characters of God, but the man must not finish, vitality must not pass beyond his body, beyond his being'. In a passage which almost certainly carries an autobiographical suggestion, Yeats wrote, 'there are married people who, though they do not forbid the passage of the seed, practise, not necessarily at the moment of union, a meditation, where in the man seeks the divine Self as present in his wife, the wife the divine Self as present in the man. There may be trance, and the presence of one with another though a great distance separates. If one alone meditates, the other knows; one may call for, and receive through the other, divine protection.'[1]

That sense of occult union which Yeats had experienced since the days of his mystic marriage with Maud Gonne preoccupied his old age, but the physical facts of his life were altogether more painful and disturbing. By the end of January 1936, he was again seriously ill. He himself put his breathlessness down to asthma, but the position became so serious that eventually the Swami and the hotel proprietor decided to telegraph George, who came out to Majorca at once to make sure that Yeats had proper medical supervision. He convalesced through February and March, his heart slowly getting back to normal, and by April he was sufficiently better to start working again at the Casa Pastor, the hillside bungalow rented for the family. News of his illness had reached London, however, and St John Ervine (one time temporary manager of the Abbey Theatre) cruising the Mediterranean, took advantage of his ship's calling at Majorca to go ashore and see Yeats. 'I could not have found him more perfectly posed,' Ervine wrote in an article for the *Observer*. 'He was seated at a table with a Yogi! . . . The Yogi, dressed in bright pink and looking like a bright carnation, sat with his hands folded on his ample paunch. . . . Yeats sat back in his chair and began to fumble for words but could not find them until a chance remark of mine unloosed his tongue and, with extraordinary recovery of spirits, he began a very entertaining discourse.'[2] Yeats, who was working on the *Aphorisms* of Patanjali, was taken aback by Ervine's sudden appearance. His surprise was nothing, however, compared to that when, at 6.30 one morning, Margot Ruddock walked uninvited into the Casa Pastor.

As Yeats wrote describing the incident to Olivia Shakespear: 'the girl, who is quite a beautiful person, came here seven or eight days ago. She walked in at 6.30, her luggage in her hand and, when she had been given breakfast, said she had come to find out if her verse was any good.' Yeats had known her for some time, during which he had watched the 'tragic magnificence' of her early verse fragments disintegrate with her technique. Now she was clearly having a nervous breakdown. 'She went out in pouring rain, thought, as she said afterwards, that if she killed herself her verse would live instead of her, went to the shore to jump in, then thought she loved life and began to dance.' In this state she went to call on the Swami. 'She was wet through so the Swami gave her some of his clothes; she had no money, he gave her some. Next day she went to Barcelona and there went mad, climbing out of a window, falling through a broken roof, breaking a knee-cap, hiding in a ship's hold, singing her own poems most of the time.'[3]

Almost inevitably it was left to George to sort matters out. The British Consul in Barcelona had appealed to Yeats for help, and George crossed over to the city, where she found Margot Ruddock 'with recovered sanity sitting up in bed at a clinic writing an account of her madness'. But the problems were not yet over. 'It was impossible to get adequate money out of her family,' Yeats told Olivia Shakespear, 'so I accepted financial responsibility and she was despatched to England and now I won't be able to afford new clothes for a year.' The notoriety that quickly gathered round the incident was extremely embarrassing. Margot's husband wrote to congratulate her on 'the magnificent publicity'. Yeats himself suspected that the man was also responsible for describing the incident in the newspapers. The inconvenience was considerable, and Yeats told Olivia Shakespear that 'when I am in London I shall probably hide because the husband may send me journalists and because I want to keep at a distance from a tragedy where I can be no further help'. On his return to London Yeats indeed concealed himself for a while in the recesses of the Savile Club before going on to stay with Dorothy Wellesley at Penns-in-the-Rocks. The poem Yeats wrote on the incident, however, 'A Crazed Girl', suggests themes that were increasingly to preoccupy him. Margot Ruddock, the 'crazed girl improvising her music', dancing, maiming herself, wound in the ecstasy of her mad art, her whole being given over to extreme experience, personifies that 'tragic joy' which lies at the heart of Yeats's final poetic vision.

II
'Lust and Rage'

Yeats imagined and dismissed the deceptive tranquillities of old age. Conjuring to mind a poet of advancing years, he wrote:

> surely, he may think, now that I have found vision and mask I need
> not suffer any longer. He will buy perhaps some small old house,

where, like Ariosto, he can dig his garden, and think that in the return of birds and leaves, or moon and sun, and in the evening flight of the rooks he may discover rhythm and pattern like those in sleep and so never awake out of vision. Then he will remember Wordsworth withering into eighty years, honoured and empty-witted, and climb to some waste room and find, forgotten there by youth, some bitter crust.[4]

Now, with a reckless vigour that refused compromise and nicety, and which was sometimes coarse and sometimes sublime, Yeats threw himself into 'the brutality, the ill breeding, the barbarism of truth'. What matter that others looked on appalled:

> You think it horrible that lust and rage
> Should dance attendance upon my old age;
> They were not such a plague when I was young;
> What else have I to spur me into song?[5]

With Yeats adrift on what he imagined was the hormonal floodtide of his 'second puberty', Dorothy Wellesley became a beacon on which he could focus the wildness and complexity of his sexual imaginings, her lesbian tendencies heightening his fevered longings with exhilarated shocks of polymorphous desire. 'My dear, my dear – when you crossed the room with that boyish movement, it was no man who looked at you, it was the woman in me. It seems that I can make a woman express herself as never before. I have looked out of her eyes. I have shared her desire.'[6] Even the pictures in Yeats's bedroom at Riversdale became for him a phantasmagoria of passion uninhibited by conventional restraint. Over the mantelpiece was 'a large lithograph by Shannon, boys bathing, the most conspicuous boy drawn with voluptuous pleasure in back and flank, as always with Shannon'. But the waterside pleasures of adolescence were juxtaposed to images of terror. Hanging under the Shannon lithograph was a charcoal study by Burne-Jones which showed 'sirens luring a ship to its doom, the sirens tall, unvoluptuous, faint, vague forms flitting here and there'. Gustave Moreau's *Women and Unicorns*, which had helped inspire one of the nightmare images in *The Tower*, also retained its problematic suggestiveness, 'the mystery that touches the genitals, a blurred touch through a curtain'.

Dorothy Wellesley's own poems, as their over-representation in the *Oxford Book of Modern Verse* suggests, carried for Yeats their complex charge of eroticism and creativity, a fascination which could become akin to that of intercourse itself when he set about remodelling them and collaborating with her. 'Ah my dear how it added to my excitement when I re-made that poem of yours to know it was your poem. I re-made you and myself into a single being. We triumphed over each other and I thought of *The Turtle and the Phoenix*.' Dorothy Wellesley's original poem, which became the basis of 'The Three Bushes', drew on the myth of Cupid and Psyche to discuss the ambiguous relation and division of body and soul in the acts of love and sex. The completed poem is a series of lyrics inspired by the triangular relationship between a poet and a lady so spiritually in love with him that the carnal becomes disparaged and the lady's chambermaid has to substitute for her in the poet's bed. The lady's three songs explore the ambivalence of her own incomplete response to her poet, while the lover's song suggests, how, after sexual intercourse, mind and body seem equally satisfied, as content as a bird exhausted after flight. It is the chambermaid's songs, however, that most daringly explore the relationship of the sexual to the spiritual:

> From pleasure of the bed,
> Dull as a worm,
> His rod and its butting head
> Limp as a worm,
> His spirit that has fled
> Blind as a worm.[7]

Limp penis and spent soul are briefly as one but, as the first song suggests, it is only in death that these antimonies can be finally and symbolically reconciled. All three characters – lady, lover and chambermaid – eventually lie beside each other in the graveyard, and the three bushes of the title (on one level clearly suggestive of pubic hair) are three intertwining rose trees growing inextricably over the three graves, their visionary flowers drawing their sustenance from it matters not which of the bodies below.

That Yeats did not wish to think his late-flowering passion for Dorothy Wellesley was merely an old man's sentimental infatuation is suggested by the sixteen-line poem dedicated to her in which he associates her with the landscape around Penns-in-the-Rocks, recreating her as an embodiment of sensuous, contented indolence who is nonetheless aware of the antithetical forces flickering in her unconscious mind. For all Dorothy Wellesley's serenity as she sits in her room, what she is imagined as hearing approaching her are not the commonplace satisfactions of the morally upright, but the terrible step of the 'Proud Furies each with her torch on high'. As always, it is the antithetical soul which bears the full burden of truth, drawing together opposites to create both wholeness and struggle. 'We have all something within ourselves to batter down and get our power from this fighting,' Yeats wrote. He became obsessed by 'the stirring of the beast underneath,' along with the 'completeness' with which it was held down. Struggle was the condition of a great soul. 'Even my poem "To D.W." should give this impression. The moon, the moonless night, the dark velvet, the sensual silence, the silent room and the violent bright Furies. Without this conflict we have no passion only sentiment and thought.'

And it was passion, as always, that Yeats sought. His mask was now that of 'The Wild Old Wicked Man', the brother of Crazy Jane, frank in his exultant lewdness and suffering, his all but daily experience of tragic joy. Indeed, so insistent were Yeats's sexual desires that, he claimed, he would be unable to travel to India with the Swami's friend Lady Elizabeth Pelham since his Steinach operation 'though it revived my creative power . . . revived also sexual desire: and . . . in all likelihood will last me until I die. I believe that if I repressed this for any long period I would break down under the strain as did the great Ruskin.'⁸ But these fires of passion were also a tempering flame. Yeats was convinced that it was passion fulfilled that had changed and hardened his art. He had emerged out of the darkness of frustration, he told Dorothy Wellesley, 'a man you have never known – more man of genius, more gay, more miserable. . . . I have recovered a power of moving the common man I had in my youth.'

Outwardly at least George refused to be troubled by these late affairs, realising perhaps with wifely shrewdness that they presented her with no challenge and that what was really required of her was a mature, dispassionate concern for her husband's well-being. Certainly, this was the side of her feelings that she chose to show to Yeats himself, saying with just a sufficient twist: 'When you are dead people will talk about your love affairs, but I shall say nothing, for I will remember how proud you were.'⁹ But if George was capable of this, Yeats's insistence that his 1937 revised edition of *A Vision* should make clear the manner in which he had received his intimations of spiritualist truth infuriated her. She saw no reason why the book should not be published without an explanation of how its insights were gained, and Yeats's determination to expose his domestic sybil caused the most painful and perhaps the most serious quarrel that ever threatened their marriage. Nonetheless, Yeats inevitably carried the day, and the major poems he was now writing clearly owe their ideas to his long and strenuous efforts to hammer his insights into a coherent whole.

What *A Vision* cannot entirely explain, however, is the fierce celebration of anarchic ecstasy, the tragic joy, with which Yeats stared on a world which his philosophy told him was hurtling towards destruction, and which his political experiences suggested could not be saved by any modern creed. Looking at a world going to ruin, Yeats cried with the Delphic oracle: 'Rejoice!' Hideous destruction becomes an exhilaration in its own right because out of it will supposedly emerge creativity, the antithetical era of order and hierarchy.

Aloof in the certitudes of hate and philosophical conviction, Yeats can wildly celebrate cataclysm:

> Conduct and work grow coarse, and coarse the soul,
> What matter! Those that Rocky Face holds dear,
> Lovers of horses and of women, shall,
> From marble of a broken sepulchre,
> Or dark betwixt the polecat and the owl,
> Or any rich, dark nothing disinter
> The workman, noble and saint, and all things run
> On that unfashionable gyre again.[10]

'What matter!' What matter if Hitler's troops were moving into the Rhineland and that people across Europe were growing increasingly terrified that aeroplanes and zeppelins would once again become the angels of death hovering with their bombs over great aggregations of people until 'the town lies beaten flat'. Coventry, Dresden, Hiroshima – those tragedies of a few years hence – are in this mood of exultation merely the harbingers of a great age to come. For Yeats, they are scenery on the world's stage, and what is required of their citizens is what was required of the Abbey players – the proper decorum of tragic joy. Only 'hysterical women' will vainly fuss about trying to put things right. A triumphalist historicism means that the peacemakers can be swept aside for the heroic who will perfect history as a work of dramatic art. They alone will know the cold passion and tragic joy that will transfigure them. A literary insight from the world of the theatre supposedly becomes an apt response to history.

As Yeats explained his theatrical idea: 'the heroes of Shakespeare convey to us through their looks, or through the metaphorical patterns of their speech, the sudden enlargement of their vision, their ecstasy at the approach of death: "She should have died hereafter," "Of many thousand kisses, the poor last," "Absent thee from felicity awhile."' For Yeats, Shakespeare's anthropology and spiritualism combine to suggest the timeless and transcendent rightness of this elite heroism. Lear, Hamlet and the rest 'have become God or Mother Goddess, the pelican "My baby at my breast," but all must be cold; no actress has ever sobbed when she played Cleopatra, even the shallow brain of a producer has never thought of such a thing. The supernatural is present, cold winds blow across our hands, upon our faces, the thermometer falls, and because of that cold we are hated by journalists and groundlings. There may be in this or that detail painful tragedy, but in the whole work none. I have heard Lady Gregory say, rejecting some play in the modern manner sent to the Abbey Theatre, "Tragedy must be a joy to the man who dies."'[11]* And who should be the observers of the cosmic drama? In 'Lapis Lazuli', a poem

---

* Yeats had earlier attributed the remark to himself.

inspired by a Chinese stone carving given to Yeats for his seventieth birthday by Harry Talbot de Vere Clifton, Yeats suggests that an appropriate audience is a small and elite group of refined men sitting remotely on a mountain and listening to 'mournful melodies' while:

> Their eyes mid many wrinkles, their eyes,
> Their ancient, glittering eyes, are gay.[12]

Such vehement assertions as Yeats made in 'The Gyres' and 'Lapis Lazuli' suggest by their sheer fury that they spring less from confidence than from doubt and even fear. The greatness of *New Poems*, the volume in which both 'The Gyres' and 'Lapis Lazuli' are printed, is that it frankly admits this. Impotence, unhappiness, pessimism, a sort of defiant, cynical energy roused as a defence against the perception that the world might indeed be meaningless, are clear in many of the poems. As always with Yeats, but here in a more violent manner than anywhere else in his work, the juxtaposed lyrics dramatise each other, their contrasts offering a picture altogether more complex and humane than the impression presented by any one poem in isolation.

The rewriting of *A Vision* had obliged Yeats to face some troubling problems about man's relationship to the spiritual world and the apparently rigid determinism which his historical thought seemed to imply. He had tried to solve or at least palliate the latter problem by introducing into the revised version of his book his concept of the Thirteenth Cone or Sphere, which he invested with the power to change everything, thereby exposing certainty to flux. There could be no final answers. As a result, the triumphalist poet of 'The Gyres' is also the penitent of 'The Pilgrim', seeking truth at 'Lough Derg's holy island'. The only answer to his urgent questioning, however, is the horrible, insistent meaninglessness of a ballad refrain, 'fol de rol de rolly O'. There is in many of these final works a despairing bleakness, a fear of ultimate emptiness, a recognition of physical and spiritual impotence, which is altogether more truly terrifying than the violent swagger of Yeats's historicism and which goes, indeed, some way to explaining it.

'What Then?', for example, suggests that the little boy who sixty years earlier had sat in a tree at the edge of his playground and knew that he might fashion himself into a famous man, could now, his achievements completed, oblige himself to face the desolation of a world where there are no certainties, no assurances of the beatific vision, and finally only the image of an old man facing death:

> 'The work is done,' grown old he thought,
> 'According to my boyish plan;
> Let the fools rage, I swerved in naught,
> Something to perfection brought';
> *But louder sang that ghost 'What then?'*[13]

This was, as Yeats recognised, a 'melancholy biographical poem', and his eventually agreeing to send it as a contribution to his old school magazine *The Erasmian* was an action not without its irony. But Yeats had never surrendered to the weakness of mere sentimental pessimism. He knew its allure but he rejected it. 'My temptation is quiet,' he could write, and at moments he guessed that neither 'loose imagination' nor, more intolerably, 'the mill of the mind' forever mechanically working on and on could 'make the truth known'. But quiet was not enough, surrender was insufficient. Defiance, self-recreation, vision, were all preferable:

> Grant me an old man's frenzy,
> Myself I must remake
> Till I am Timon and Lear
> Or that William Blake
> Who beat upon the wall
> Till Truth obeyed his call. . . .[14]

And madness and vision, when they were not spurred by 'lust', could yet be inspired by 'rage'. The tempestuous political furies of Yeats's last years are remarkable in their vehemence.

For instance, Yeats was visited by Henry Harrison, 'an old decrepit man', who fifty years before had joined Parnell's party at Oxford and had now written a book to defend his memory. He begged Yeats to write something to convince all Parnellites that Parnell had nothing to be ashamed of in his love for Kitty O'Shea. The resulting ballad, 'Come Gather round me Parnellites', was Yeats's late tribute to 'Proud Parnell', and his own belief that 'a proud man's a lovely man' is wholly in keeping with his political thought and its belief in strong individuals. Such phrases could not be used, however, of Roger Casement, whom Yeats was obliged to describe as 'not a very able man but he was gallant and unselfish, and surely had his right to leave . . . an unsullied name'. In 1936 Yeats had read an argument to prove that Casement's diaries and their descriptions of his homosexual activities were forged. The argument itself was almost certainly false but Yeats was for a while convinced and made so angry by what emerged as the 'public insincerity which was about to bring such discredit upon democracy' that he was inspired to write two ballads to Casement's memory. Here again his purpose was to attack the institutionalised hypocrisy of the state and defend an individual against it.

'I am fighting in those ballads for what I have been fighting all my life,' he wrote, 'it is our Irish fight though it has nothing to do with this or that country. Bernard Shaw fights with the same object. When somebody talks of justice who knows that justice is accompanied by secret forgery, when an archbishop wants a man to go to the communion table when that man says he is not spiritually fit, then we remember our age-old quarrel against gold braid and ermine, and that our ancestor Swift had gone where "fierce indignation can lacerate his heart no more", and we go stark, staring mad.'[15] Joseph Hone recalled meeting Yeats just after he had written on Casement and being astonished by the ferocity of his feelings. 'He almost collapsed after reading the verses and had to call for a little port wine.' Rage, rage against corruption, rage against the defamation of the individual, all inspired Yeats as he asserted that it was precisely the need for such outstanding figures as humiliated Parnell that was the most obvious requirement of his country.

Indeed, his fury was such that he felt he had to explain himself to both Dorothy Wellesley and Ethel Mannin. Dorothy Wellesley in particular had been so astonished by the vehemence of Yeats's anti-English outbursts that she accused him of encouraging 'hate between nations', and Yeats felt obliged to write, 'of course I don't hate the people of England, considering all I owe to Shakespeare, Blake, Morris – they are the one people I cannot hate.' His venom against England at the time of the abdication crisis was strongly felt nonetheless, his long-held contempt for the British monarchy rising to a crisis in 'A Model for the Laureate', where he satirised 'cheers that can be bought or sold' and the whole paraphernalia of monarchy, which is castigated for being a mere nothing if it keeps a man from his beloved. As Yeats wrote to Dorothy Wellesley, the poem was 'the kind of thing I would have written had I been made Laureate, which is perhaps why I was not made Laureate'.[16]

But it was less rage against Britain that truly inspired Yeats than his need to assert what he considered the necessary moral force of great men. As he himself wrote: 'these ballads of mine though not supremely good are not ephemeral, the young will sing them now and after I am dead. In them I defend a noble-natured man, I do the old work of the poets but I will defend no cause.' As he told Dorothy Wellesley: 'I want to stiffen the backbone of the high hearted and the high-minded . . . so that they may no longer shrink and hedge when they are facing rag merchants.' This may well have been true, but the inspiration of the ballads was as much personal as political. 'Before all I want to strengthen myself,' Yeats declared. He was drawing on images of the recent past to prepare himself for his last bitter engagement with Irish nationalism.

III

'The Circus Animals' Desertion'

During 1937 Yeats's interests turned to the broadcasting of poetry on the radio. Early experiences at home might have suggested that these experiments would not be as successful as they ultimately proved. Anne Yeats recalled how the family eventually acquired a wireless. Yeats himself had been resistant to this for a long time but 'when we acquired one, the first evening it was turned on, he was listening to it, and he couldn't hear very well, so he put his hand to his ear, and said, I beg your pardon?'[17] By October 1936, however, Yeats was planning programmes in which he would experiment with a drum or other musical instrument to heighten the intensity of spoken rhythms. By December, W. J. Turner, Hilda Matheson and George Barnes were rehearsing with Ronald Watkins and Margot Ruddock as readers.

Because Yeats could not make his intentions entirely clear, the programme was postponed and when, the following February, a programme similar to that originally intended was broadcast from the Abbey, it was, as Yeats had to confess, 'a fiasco'.[18] Yeats included his recent ballads on Parnell and Roger Casement, but while the actor who sang the Parnell poem created an effective impression in the theatre by clapping his hands in time to the music, Yeats had to admit that the broadcast wholly destroyed this, giving merely the impression of 'a schoolboy knocking with the end of a penknife or spoon'. He was clearly shaken and wrote modestly to George Barnes that he would 'attend what rehearsals you ask me to, but it is quite plain that all I can do is to choose the poems and make certain general suggestions. . . . Perhaps my old bundle of poet's tricks is useless.'

Barnes persisted nonetheless, and during 1937 Yeats took part in four programmes: 'In the Poet's Pub' (2 April); 'In the Poet's Parlour' (22 April); 'My Own Poetry' (3 July); and 'My Own Poetry Again' (29 October). V. C. Clinton-Baddeley and Margot Ruddock joined Yeats as his readers, and Barnes left a telling description of how exquisitely attuned to the finest nuances of recital Yeats remained. The fruits of his years of experiments with the psaltery were now being applied to the radio. 'His ear for the sound of speech was so sensitive that it outran comprehension,' Barnes recalled.

> His sensitiveness to the sound of words made rehearsals long and exacting. Knowing exactly what he wanted himself, he found it difficult to express because he noticed nuances which we could hardly hear. Nor was he helped by his own voice, an instrument inadequate (when I knew him) for conveying his meaning accurately. Margot, perhaps by intuition, could get what he wanted but could not be depended upon to reproduce it later. Baddeley's professional training enabled him to do what he was told over and over again once he had got the effect desired.

Indeed, so concerned was Yeats with the correct speaking of verse that he expressed his ideas to his listeners in 'Modern Poetry: A Broadcast', where he declared:

> a poem is an elaboration of the rhythms of common speech and their association with profound feeling. To read a poem like prose, that hearers unaccustomed to poetry may find it easy to understand, is to turn it into bad, florid prose. If anybody reads or recites poetry as if it were prose from some public platform, I ask you, speaking for poets, living, dead, or unborn, to protest in whatever way occurs to your perhaps youthful minds; if they recite or read by wireless, I ask you to express your indignation by letter. William Morris, coming out of a hall where somebody had read or recited his *Sigurd the Volsung*, said: 'It cost me a lot of damned hard work to get that thing into verse.'

The clever use of the direct appeal and anecdote in this passage shows that Yeats quickly mastered radio technique, but the effect of the broadcasts on Margot Ruddock was so extreme that she had to return to a mental home after working on them.

Such intensity inevitably triggered quarrels between all of those involved, and Yeats realised that such situations, properly contrived, could actually lead to extremely interesting programmes. He proposed to debate with either James Stephens or Edmund Dulac the idea 'that it is not the duty of the artist to paint beautiful women and beautiful places is nonsense. That the exclusion of sex appeal from poetry, painting and sculpture is nonsense (are the films alone to impose their ideas upon the sexual instinct?). That, on the contrary, all arts are an expression of desire – exciting desirable life, exulting desirable death.' Themes so close to Yeats's heart would indeed have made a fascinating programme, and he wrote that it was his idea 'to work it all up into a kind of drama in which we will get very abusive, and then one or the other of us will say with a change of voice "Well, I hope they will have taken all that seriously and believe that we shall never speak to each other again." The other will say "Stop, the signal is still on us. They can hear us." Then the first speaker will say "God", or if that is barred by the BBC – "Hell".' From barely knowing how a radio worked, Yeats had progressed speedily to envisaging programmes which deconstructed their own appearance of spontaneity.

Yeats's talks on his own poetry were, Hone recalled, 'very moving and he read with great feeling'. The effort nonetheless tired him, and when plans were made to revive 'In the Poet's Pub' and another programme, Yeats felt obliged to write to the BBC that 'I have no chance of being able to fix dates ahead. My broadcasting is finished. I am sorry considering all the trouble you have taken with me.' In fact, the BBC authorities had been greatly impressed by Yeats, and Lennox Robinson recalled that 'every time they loved him more and more, and they gave him more and more money, and in the end they wanted to give him the best battery, the best whatever they could do to his home in Rathfarnham, and they said, "Have you got electric light in the home?" He had to wire back to his wife to find out whether they had electric light in the home – he hadn't.'[19]

Yeats's social life meanwhile continued as active as ever. He was, for example, elected a member of the Athenaeum under Rule Two, which meant that he did not have to pay an entrance fee and, passing under the classical entrance and on to the gracious library, he not only fulfilled a long-treasured desire but had ready access to such luminaries as Maurice Bowra, as well as the possibility of entertaining his women friends in the ladies' annexe. These now included not only Dorothy Wellesley and Ethel Mannin, but the successful journalist Edith Shackelton Heald, whose charming house at Steyning in Sussex, where she lived with her sister, became somewhere Yeats regularly stayed on his visits to England.[20] Here he could enjoy Edith Shackelton Heald's careful hostessing, which protected him from bores and kept him in contact with such friends as the Dulacs and R. A. Scott-James, who now published his poems in the *London Mercury*.

Letters between Yeats and Edith Shackelton Heald suggest that by the close of 1937 Yeats, now in his early seventies, and Edith herself, now in her early fifties, were very close if not intimate. She had long admired him, writing eight years before of Yeats as a man 'whose grave manners and melodious conversation seem to take one back to a more spacious ancient world, who can be as practical as any other Irishman (which is saying a lot) and yet sees the fairies and has dealings with spirits'. Their friendship appears to have matured in the wake of Dorothy Wellesley suffering a period of mental collapse, and certainly advanced to the point where they could consider going on holiday with each other. George meanwhile, as so often, was forbearing, suggesting some sadness when Yeats was not with her for his birthday but nonetheless wishing him well in Sussex where, she knew, he was prone to tire himself. She even wrote to Edith Shackelton Heald herself pointing this out and giving advice about his medicine, as well as comparing what were clearly the delights of southern England to the restrictions of Dublin.

On 7 August 1937, after his return to Ireland, the Irish Academy of Letters held a dinner for Yeats at which he announced that an American Testimonial Committee formed under James A. Farrell, the retired President of the United Steel Corporation, had assured him a fund which would allow him a moderate income for the rest of his life. Both the subscribers to the fund and the guests at the dinner were promised a new poem, and the result was 'The Municipal Gallery Revisited'. Yeats touchingly described the origin of this poem:

for a long time I had not visited the Municipal Gallery. I went there a week ago and was restored to many friends. I sat down, after a few minutes, overwhelmed with emotion. There were pictures painted by men, now dead, who were once my intimate friends. . . . It is said that an Indian ascetic, when he has taken a certain initiation on a mountain in Tibet, is visited by all the Gods. In those rooms of the Municipal Gallery I saw Ireland in spiritual freedom, and the Corots, the Rodins, the Rousseaus were the visiting gods.[21]

As so often, Yeats first drafted the poem in prose form and then wrote up the verses, creating these at about the rate of a stanza a day. The result is a fine and beautiful poem, at once intimate and stately, private and public. Amid the violently clashing feelings of *New Poems* as a whole, it provides a sustained moment of calm reflection, a dignified meditation on Yeats's lifelong attempt to work for Ireland:

> You that would judge me, do not judge alone
> This book or that, come to this hallowed place
> Where my friends' portraits hang and look thereon;
> Ireland's history in their lineaments trace;
> Think where man's glory most begins and ends,
> And say my glory was I had such friends.[22]

Yeats wrote to Dorothy Wellesley on 5 September 1937, 'I have just finished a poem which for the moment I like exceedingly. It is on the Municipal Gallery. . . . It is very much what my speech foreshadowed – perhaps the best poem I have written for some years unless the "Curse of Cromwell" is.' This last was another of Yeats's political ballads, and precisely the sort of audience these works found was suggested by him when he told Dorothy Wellesley that 'after I had left the Academy banquet somebody called for the "Curse of Cromwell", and when it was sung a good many voices joined in'.

The poem once again rails against an Ireland that has disastrously fallen away from the high and noble standards of nationalism Yeats evoked in 'The Municipal Gallery Revisited'. The poet expresses himself 'through the mouth of some wandering peasant poet' who moves through a disillusioned and spectral world where Cromwell, 'the Lenin of his day', has destroyed the old and hierarchical ancestral securities to create a country where 'money's rant is on'. Even when the singer encounters the ghosts of a greater past, daylight brings disillusion as he wakes to find himself in a ruined house. The social bitterness here is as deep and as pessimistic as it was when Yeats held Biddy and Paudeen up to national scorn. 'My poetry is generally written out of despair,' he said, 'I see decreasing ability and energy and increasing commonness. . . . What can I do but cry out, lately in simple peasant songs that hide me from the curious?' Sometimes this seemed an inadequate mask, however, and Yeats wrote that 'there were moments when hatred poisons my life and I accuse myself of effeminacy because I have not given it adequate expression. It is not enough to have put it into the mouth of a rambling peasant poet.'[23] Art contained possibilities of self-deception, and it was this theme that Yeats now explored in one of his supreme poems, 'The Circus Animals' Desertion'.

The ageing man of masks, unable to find new themes for his poetry, is here obliged to review his career. To do this at all was to some degree an expression of the fear of impotence which is so strong throughout Yeats's later work, but it is precisely this feeling of failure which leads him (in the revised version of the work) to an extraordinary and profound modesty in which Yeats comes to a new understanding of the processes of his art. He had always sought for high contrivance rather than mere self-expression, which was something which even now filled him with distaste. He went some way to explaining this in the 'General Introduction for My Work', prepared for a complete edition which was in fact never produced.[24] In the opening section of this essay, 'The First Principle', Yeats considered the relationship between personal experience and high art, showing that the movement is always away from the purely personal and subjective towards the general and deeply experienced. The great poet 'is more type than man, more passion than type'. Yeats declared that 'a poet writes always of his personal life, in his finest work out of its tragedy, whatever it be, remorse, lost love, or mere loneliness; he never speaks directly as to someone at the breakfast table, there is always a phantasmagoria'. But the process of creation, working on deep personal feeling, is also a rebirth. As the poet labours to complete his work, so 'he has been reborn as an idea, something intended, complete'. In this lies his power, for by the continuous exercise of his craftsmanship and inspiration 'nature has grown intelligible, and by so doing a part of our creative power'. The poet, in other words, touches the deepest essence of shared humanity; his element is the *anima mundi*.

In 'The Circus Animals' Desertion', Yeats reverses the direction of this argument without denying its validity. His emphasis is on the personal distress from which art springs, whether in his case it be the starved sexual fantasising that led him to create the Pre-Raphaelite beauty of Oisin's Nimah, or his pity for Maud Gonne's fanatical heart and his wish to redeem her misery. There is danger, however, at the root of this profound personal feeling. It deflects the artist from his purpose. The sexual allure of Nimah could become more important to the poet than the themes of the poem in which she appears. The 'dream' of healing the psychic torment of Maude Gonne could become more involving than the wider ideas Yeats was seeking to treat in *The Countess Cathleen*. Such enchantment is indeed a perpetual temptation to the writer, and Yeats confessed that in all his dramatic writings the lure of the stage itself could prove more powerful than 'those things' that actors and 'painted stage' were supposed to represent.

Powerful ideas could nonetheless be given real life by drawing on the mind and the life-energies of the poet, but, with a beautiful and deeply moving modesty, it is not the power of these 'masterful images' with which Yeats chooses to end the poem but rather the recognition of the sad and now failing human mess from which they drew their strength. As Yeats surveys this, so he returns to his abject humanity. The real world from which art is created is:

> A mound of refuse or the sweepings of a street,
> Old kettles, old bottles, and a broken can,
> Old iron, old bones, old rags, that raving slut
> Who keeps the till. Now that my ladder's gone,
> I must lie down where all the ladders start,
> In the foul rag-and-bone shop of the heart.[25]

The poet who throughout his career had sought the union of the disparate parts of his antithetical self, here, in a moment of magnanimous tenderness, knows in his apparent impotence that the sublimities of creation are rooted in the pitifully mundane.

IV
'I Am an Old Fenian'

Yeats had told Dorothy Wellesley in the autumn of 1937 that he wanted to 'get to a warm climate with friends and dig myself into some inexpensive spot until spring'. He chose Menton, where he corrected the proofs of *New Poems* which the Cuala Press was due to publish the following April. Menton suited him admirably. Writing to Edith Shakelton Heald from the Carlton Hotel, he told her that 'the life is good for my mind and body – my life is fixed henceforth, the winter here or near here'. He was, he told her, writing poetry, but he was also greatly excited by a 'big essay' which he was eventually to issue as *On the Boiler*, a work originally intended as a periodical publication. Perhaps nowhere in Yeats's late work is his search for 'the brutality, the ill breeding, the barbarism of truth' more evident than in this problematic and often frankly distasteful work. Yeats's title derives from early Sligo memories of 'a mad ship's carpenter' named McCoy who was wont to climb on to a rusting boiler left to decay in the Sligo quays and from there read the scriptures and denounce his neighbours. Yeats thus put on the mask of a crazed bigot in order to express his extreme political views.

As always, his concern was with Ireland and with Irish national integrity. His growing mistrust of the state and his refusal to accept either communism or such organised fascism he knew as valid solutions to contemporary problems meant that he had to found his ideas in his old interest in a race philosophy. 'Race, which has for its flower the family and the individual, is wiser than Government, and is the source of all initiative,' he wrote in an unpublished diary.[26] Surveying a Europe that was rushing ever more frantically towards world war, Yeats believed that it was essential for Ireland to preserve its neutrality, its independence, and to do so by asserting national unity based on individual and internalised discipline. Returning ever more determinedly to his Fenian roots and the example of John O'Leary, Yeats thought that one of the great threats to this national strength was the insidious power of the British Empire, and many of his views on international politics were based around this fear.

Not only was Ireland itself in dispute with England over the constitution and the Land Annuities (a dispute that was wreaking economic havoc across the country), but Yeats feared that Ireland might be drawn into international conflicts through its proximity to England. For example, when the League of Nations decided to impose sanctions against Italy after Mussolini had invaded Abyssinia, Yeats was appalled that de Valera had voted in favour of these and so 'ranged Ireland on the side of England'. The position seemed to him to grotesque. 'It is assumed here that Ireland will send an armed force. Ireland upon the side of England and against the country of the Pope!' Although Yeats's sympathies lay entirely with the beleaguered Abyssinians, he resented the fact that his feelings were being manipulated by forces outside his control. 'All through the Abyssinian war my sympathy was with the Abyssinians, but those feelings were chilled by my knowledge that the English government was using those feelings to help an Imperial policy I distrusted.'[27]

To be truly Irish as he saw it and to escape the contamination of English imperialism, Yeats took up positions which on the surface at least often appear unacceptable. Despite the fact he was appalled that Irishmen under the influence of O'Duffy expressed their sympathy for Franco during the Spanish Civil War, Yeats could see advantages in a fascist victory.[28] While nobody 'wanted to see General O'Duffy back in Ireland with enhanced fame helping "the Catholic front"', an institution which was still attacking Yeats himself, a fascist victory in Spain might yet, Yeats thought, help limit the world-wide damage caused by the British Empire. 'I am an old Fenian,' he declared, 'and I think the old Fenian in me would rejoice if a Fascist nation or government controlled Spain, because that would weaken the British empire, force England to be civil to the Indians, perhaps to set them free and loosen that hand of

English finance in the Far East of which I hear occasionally.* But this is mere instinct. A thing I would never act on.' And indeed it was not. When the Second International Writers' Conference was held in Madrid in 1937 amid reports of mounting fascist atrocities, Pablo Neruda wrote to Yeats requesting a public declaration of his support. This was sent, and Neruda could proudly report that 'Ireland's national poet' had 'rallied to the defence of the Spanish Republic'. It was a wholly uncharacteristic gesture from a writer usually firm in his conviction that he would not take part in political matters that did not affect Ireland, but it was, nonetheless, a clear and public repudiation of the known face of organised fascism.

Now, however, in Ireland itself, Yeats hoped that an aristocratic life would filter down to the people. *On the Boiler* shows that race and patrician excellence were more than ever his touchstones. If Yeats had repudiated the territorial ambitions of European fascism, he was violently possessed by much of the imagery that nourished its nationalist ideals. The Ireland he wanted would be confined within its borders, but there its strength would be the strength of its strong men, its permanence a racial ideal, an 'indomitable Irishry' exemplified in its supermen and, occasionally, its superwomen. 'I write with two certainties in mind,' Yeats declared.

> First that a hundred men, their creative power wrought to the highest pitch, their will trained but not broken, can do more for the welfare of a people, whether in war or peace, than a million of any lesser sort, no matter how expensive their education, and that although the Irish masses are vague and excitable because they have not yet been moulded and cast, we have as good blood as there is in Europe. Berkeley, Swift, Burke, Grattan, Parnell, Augusta Gregory, Synge, Kevin O'Higgins, are the true Irish people, and there is nothing too hard for such as these.[29]

It is noticeable that this list includes Catholics as well as Protestants (Yeats's views were pan-Irish rather than sectarian) and he went on to say that 'if the Catholic names are few history will soon fill the gap'.

On the Boiler was designed to shock its readers into a recognition of Yeats's position and it does so through a style of studied outrageousness. 'The whole State', Yeats wrote, 'should be so constructed that the people should think it their duty to grow popular with King and Lord Mayor instead of King

---

* Yeats had discussed Indian affairs when Professor Bose visited him at Riversdale with Dr Wilbraham Trench. Yeats had then inveighed against 'an absence of tragedy in Indian poetry', citing Tagore especially. Indians, he said, should express themselves in their native languages rather than English. Conversation turned to the conflict of Moslem and Hindu. Could Yeats give a message to divided India? 'Let 100,000 men of the one side meet the other. That is my message to India, insistence on the antimony.' Then seizing Sato's sword and waving it in the air, he shouted: 'Conflict, more conflict!'

and Lord Mayor growing popular with them.' Right rule, he argued, came from the example of the best, 'a company of governing men'. Such people emerged to prominence through their natural strength and not through the ballot box. The decline of Irish political life seemed to prove this. 'Our representative system has given Ireland to the incompetent,' Yeats declared and, looking back to his days as a senator, felt that he was in a position to declare that 'as the nominated elements began to die out – almost all were old men – the Senate declined in ability and prestige'. As a result, the country was everywhere in retreat, high culture and good breeding giving way to ranting popularism and what Yeats saw as a terrifying rise in 'the uneducatable masses'. The bitter indignation of Swift, an indignation running to insanity, appeared at times to be the only appropriate response:

> Why should not old men be mad?
> Some have known a likely lad
> That had a sound fly-fisher's wrist
> Turn to a drunken journalist;
> A girl that knew all Dante once
> Live to bear children to a dunce;
> A Helen of social welfare dream
> Climb on a wagonette to scream.[30]

Most of these figures are readily identifiable, for all the appearance of anonymity. Maud Gonne MacBride and Iseult and Francis Stuart are here made cruelly to personify national decadence.

It was, however, the children of the so-called dunces that called forth Yeats's most notorious arguments in *On the Boiler*, for he now put the case for eugenics, believing that he and pseudo-science alone possessed the answer to a grave potential crisis.[31] Here were facts, he suggested, which others had sought dishonestly to obscure. 'Though well-known specialists are convinced that the principle European nations are degenerating in body and mind, their evidence remains almost unknown because a politician and newspaper that gave it adequate exposition would lose, the one his constituency, the other its circulation.' Bolstering his prejudices with a lengthy quotation from Burton's *The Anatomy of Melancholy* and statistics culled from such recent works as Raymond Catell's *The Fight for Our National Intelligence*, Yeats painted a lurid picture of Irish decline in which ancient standards were increasingly smothered under the torpor of mass mediocrity. 'Since about 1900,' he wrote, 'the better stocks have not been replacing their numbers, while the stupider and less healthy have been more than replacing theirs. Unless there is a change in the public mind every rank above the lowest must degenerate, and, as inferior men push up into its gaps, degenerate more and more quickly.'

Yeats then cited what he imagined to be his evidence for this. 'The results are already visible in the degeneration of literature, newspapers, amusements (there was once a stock company playing Shakespeare in every considerable town), and, I am convinced, in benefactions like that of Lord Nuffield, a self-made man, to Oxford, which must gradually substitute applied science for ancient wisdom.' Oblivious to the fact that this last was exactly what he was here doing himself, Yeats proceeded to argue that nature was always more powerful than nurture, and he luridly reproduced the results of experiments made by various leading eugenicists to prove this. He contended that, if the 'gangrel stocks' continued to multiply, radical intervention would become an absolute necessity. The educated classes would have to seize control of agriculture and industry to ensure that the less gifted were deprived of the necessities of life.

While Yeats thought that 'the drilled and docile masses' might submit to such an outrage, he believed that 'a prolonged civil war seems more likely, with the victory of the skilful, riding their machines as did the feudal knights their armoured horses'. This was a deeply unpleasant response to an important social problem in a poor and Catholic country where, of course, contraception was forbidden, but even where Yeats tempered his arrogant language his argument remains repellently autocratic:

> Sooner or later we must limit the families of the unintelligent classes, and if our government cannot send them doctor and clinic it must, till it get tired of it, send monk and confession box. We cannot go back as some dreamers would have us, to the old way of big families everywhere, even if the intelligent classes would consent, because that old way worked through lack of science and consequent great mortality among the children of those least fitted for modern civilisation.

Given Yeats's belief in the superiority of nature over nurture, he now argued, in a cruel reversal of the enlightened educational ideas he had once put forward, that it was a waste of time trying to teach the children of the masses. He then went on to suggest that those who were capable of academic achievement should be taught 'nothing but Greek, Gaelic, mathematics, and perhaps one modern language'. Families should be responsible for teaching all other subjects. 'English, history, and geography and those pleasant easy things which are the most important of all should be taught by father and mother, ancestral tradition, and the child's own reading, and if the child lack this teaching let father, mother and child be ashamed, as they are if they lack breeding and manners. I would restore the responsibilities of the family.'

In particular, Yeats wanted families of soldiers.[32] 'The formation of military families should be encouraged.' He argued that such families were essential if the country were, as he believed it must, 'to take over the entire defence of its shores'. Britain still preserved rights over the the Treaty ports in Ireland, and, although de Valera was to secure the return of these under the London Agreements of 1938, rumours that England might have to be prepared to invade Ireland in order to defend itself against the Germans suggest that Yeats's fear of encroaching enemies was not wholly without foundation.* The Irish army he envisaged would protect his country from both physical and moral danger. 'I know enough of my countrymen to know that, once democratic plausibility has gone, their small army will be efficient and self-reliant, highly trained though not highly disciplined. Armed with modern weapons, officered by men from such schools as I have described, it could throw back from our shores the disciplined uneducated masses of the commercial nations.' Materialism, as always, was the enemy.

It is characteristic of the wild veering of Yeats's last period, however, that, printed after the depressing prose sections of *On the Boiler*, is the text of one of his late and most perfectly modelled plays, the short and terrible masterpiece *Purgatory*. This work presents Yeats's concern with eugenics and national decline in the context of his perennial fascination with the theme of 'dreaming back', offering thereby a picture of an Ireland in which hierarchical and ancestral virtues have been betrayed, so leaving the country in a seemingly hopeless agony, its people in a spiritual crisis that achieves genuine tragic intensity. The pity the play inspires and its sense of terror when the beatific vision does not appear – does not redeem – make this one of the greatest of all Yeats's dramas, a work that transcends and exposes the impure roots of its thought.

An old man and his oafish son appear before a ruined house and a blasted tree. The old man confesses that he is the son of the domain, the child of an aristocratic mother and a dissolute, low-born father. His mother died in giving birth to him but his father lived on to squander the great inheritance of the house in dissipation. Eventually, the drunken man burned the house down, thereby destroying the actual and symbolic world of aristocratic Irish values. For this deed, his once youthful son murdered him with his knife, but because he himself belongs fully neither to the aristocracy nor to the mass he has been obliged to live a wretched, divided life, earning his living as a pedlar. Seen in terms of the eugenicists, his is the personal and social calamity of an ill-considered alliance.

Degeneration is cumulative, however, and has reached its fullest development in the old man's son, a bastard begotten on 'a tinker's daughter in a ditch'. Education, the old man declares, would have been wasted on the boy who, at a mere sixteen, shows the horrifying abasement of the herd, of a people obsessed merely with money and drink. Now, as these characters symbolic of the moral collapse of Ireland stand before the ruined ancestral house, so the ghosts of the couple who initiated this decline appear, forced

* The Cabinet in fact often discussed the forcible occupation of Irish ports in 1940.

like other ghostly couples in Yeats's plays to live out time and time again the scenes of their wickedness in an agonising process of 'dreaming back'. Both the old man and the boy watch this scene in horror. Its tragic consequences, however, are ineluctable. The old man has already explained to the boy that ghostly suffering may be relieved when the 'consequence of those transgressions' committed by the ghosts have been brought to an end. In a terrible moment, the old man now turns and knifes his son to death, hoping thereby to end a ruined line and so free his parents from the consequences of their misdeeds.

Dead, the boy cannot pass 'pollution' on, but nor, it seems, can his murder redeem suffering either. As the ghosts remain lingering in the house, the old man realises that the sacrifice of his son has not saved the ghostly couple from the spiritual consequences of their sin. Only God may do that, and here God is remote, invisible, even perhaps uninterested. Man on his own is powerless to atone for the sins that man has committed, and the play closes with a sense of the hopeless agony of trapped and wicked individuals acting out their spiritual dramas in a world shut off from the beatific vision. Yeats's lifelong attempt to hammer his occult interests into a unity with his nationalism and poetry is here magnificently and sombrely successful.

V

'Golden Codgers'

Yeats returned to Ireland in May 1938, where, although he had hoped to discuss the controversial ideas in *On the Boiler* with Maud Gonne MacBride, he found himself too ill to meet with her. By the summer, however, he had recovered his strength, and while he was staying with Edith Shakelton Heald at Steyning he received a letter from Maud asking him if she could reprint some of his work in her autobiography. 'Yes, of course,' he replied, 'you can quote those poems of mine, but if you do not want my curse, do not misprint them. People constantly misprint quotations.' By the late summer of 1938 Yeats had returned to Riversdale, where there took place a scene of the greatest pathos: the last meeting between Yeats and Maud.[33] She remained even in age one of the 'Beautiful Lofty Things' Yeats apostrophised as symbols of the spiritual force of Ireland. For all her political and religious views, she was still at one in his imagination at least with John O'Leary, Standish O'Grady and Augusta Gregory, the greatest of Ireland's noble people and of these, she was the most beautiful:

> Maud Gonne at Howth station waiting a train,
> Pallas Athene in that straight back and arrogant head:
> All the Olympians; a thing never known again.[34]

Much had divided them in recent years, as Maud was well aware. 'The whirlpool of life had sent the current of our activities wide apart. We had quarrelled seriously when he became a Senator of the Free State which voted Flogging Acts against young Republican soldiers still seeking to free Ireland from the contamination of the Bitish empire, and for several years we had ceased to meet.' Now, as she came into the room, she saw Yeats sitting in an armchair from which he could rise only with great effort. But all the intensity of their past hovered over this fragile moment. They were, in their different ways, still ardently Irish and mystic to the core, still driven by those powerful influences which had made her Cathleen ni Houlihan and he the greatest poet of his land. He looked at her and, with the pathos of old age, half memory and half hope, said: 'Maud, we should have gone on with our Castle of the Heroes, we might still do it.' She stood speechless before him, so surprised that he should remember such things that she could not reply. Lines from his poems echoed through her mind. Art, the occult and nationalism still exerted their power 'and I realised that Willie and I still "bent low and low and kissed the quiet feet" and worshipped Her, who is "purer than a tall candle before the Holy Rood"'.35

As if to prove this, a few weeks later Yeats read in the newspapers that a letter signed by Maud had been found by the police on a suspected IRA captive. Throwing up his arms in wonderment, he cried out: 'What a woman! What vitality! What energy!' Perhaps Rothenstein would make a drawing of her to capture something of her unbowed personality. 'No artist has ever drawn her, and just now she looks magnificent.' No drawing was ever made, however, and it was left to Yeats himself to create in 'A Bronze Head' his most profound and disturbing poem on the woman whose complex mixture of violence, tenderness and extraordinary, inspiring physical beauty had preoccupied him throughout much of his adult life. Yeats took as his starting point for the poem a bronze-painted plaster cast of a bust of Maud by Lawrence Campbell in Dublin's Municipal Gallery. This far from idealised work, 'withered and mummy-dead', allowed Yeats to speculate on the mystery of Maud's personality, that magnanimous and 'most gentle woman' who yet seemed to him to be possessed by the fury of some supernatural agent, the Grey Woman perhaps whom years before he had tried to exorcise. Suspended between the natural and the supernatural, between political Ireland and occult powers, Maud remained that enigma at once terrible and pitiable who had harassed Yeats and inspired some of the greatest love poetry in the language.

Works of art, indeed, now prompted some of Yeats's most profound poetical meditations. In 'Long-legged Fly', he explored the paradox that artistic geniuses, like the heroes and heroines that transform history, must meditate their turbulent, world-changing images in the silence of reclusive thought. 'The Statues' explores the action of art on the consciousness of a period. Man creates his image of the divine and changes his world, Phidias' rigorous Apollos inspiring the ancient Greeks to their victory over the undisciplined Persians at Salamis, even as the lithe Cuchulain inspired Pearse and thus the creation of a modern Irish state which even now seems to be threatened by the 'formless spawning fury' milling through it. Mankind aspires to images of godhead which transfigure him with their perfection but, as Yeats suggested in 'News for the Delphic Oracle', the divinities can also be seen as 'golden codgers' adapting themselves to human weakness, the Isles of the Blessed where the gods live in eternity becoming an ever more vibrant place as the immortals begin to behave with a life-giving human lubricity. Yeats's image of the nymphs and satires copulating in the foam, taken from a Poussin in the Dublin National Gallery which was then believed to represent the marriage of Peleus and Thetis, is a glorious moment of erotic celebration, but 'Man and the Echo' powerfully suggests that agonised pessimism, that doubt in the beatific vision, that sense of the mill of the mind endlessly shuffling its guilts without any hope of redemption, which is the terrible antithesis to the celebration and defiance that mark so many of these late poems.

Meanwhile, Yeats was gathering ideas for a second and never completed number of *On the Boiler*. Writing to Dorothy Wellesley on 22 June 1938, he told her that he was 'full of life and not too disturbed by the enemies I must make. This is the proposition on which I write: There is no overwhelming evidence that man stands between eternities, that of his family and that of his soul. I apply those beliefs to literature and politics and show the change they must make.'

In August, Yeats made his last public appearance at the Abbey for the opening of *Purgatory*, which was mounted as part of a celebration of the Irish Dramatic Movement. After the performance he addressed the audience, telling them that he had put into the work 'his own convictions about this world and the next'. He retired to bed, too tired by his efforts to answer the questions of a Boston Jesuit who believed his theological ideas were confused, but he nonetheless found the energy to write to the newspapers to repeat that *Purgatory* was indeed an expression of his deepest convictions.

By September he had sufficiently recovered his energy to visit friends in Oxford and Sussex and to discuss his own recent work and that of Stephen Spender, Charles Madge and George Barker with R. A. Scott-James at his cottage in Berkshire. His vitality remained impressive, but a short while after his return to Dublin in October he was saddened by news of the death of Olivia Shakespear. He wrote in his grief to Dorothy Wellesley, telling her that 'for more than forty years she has been the centre of my life in London, and during all that time we have never had a quarrel, sadness sometimes, but never a difference. When first I met her, she was in her late twenties but in looks a lovely young girl. When she died she was a lovely old woman. You would have approved her.'

Yeats's own age and frailty were increasingly evident. The Japanese academic Shotaro Oshima, visiting Riversdale in the summer of 1938, noticed that although Yeats continued to talk vigorously and attractively, he 'now and then . . . repeated himself and I could not help feeling the gloomy presence of old age in him'.[36] Certainly, he easily tired, and George recognised that it was her duty to protect him from unnecessary effort. As Oshima was preparing to leave the house he stood hesitating for a moment in the front garden and then asked George if he would be allowed to take a photograph of her husband. 'If you want to take his picture so much,' she said, 'why didn't you say so before he went upstairs. He has been very ill of late and has not even seen his brother and sisters. It was with a great effort that he saw you. He is very tired.' George spoke in an intense tone which made Oshima realise 'how far I had been availing myself of their generosity', and he made a humble apology. But courtesy forbade Yeats from failing to gratify the wishes of a man who had come so far to see him. Oshima was taking snapshots of the house and the beautiful gardens around it when Yeats appeared at the front door and sat down on a bench in front of the ivy growing over the wall. 'He took out his monocle from his pocket and applied it to his left eye. Rather surprised I hastily took two snaps of him. After a while I said good-bye to Mr and Mrs Yeats and left the house still feeling the warmth of the old poet's hand in my palm.'

Beneath the graciousness, however, there ran a deepening preoccupation with death. In August Yeats wrote to Dorothy Wellesley telling her that he had been so annoyed by Rilke's ideas on mortality which he had discovered in a book of critical essays that he had written (although not in the margin of the work as he claimed) the following lines:

> Draw rein, draw breath.
> Cast a cold eye
> On life, on death.
> Horseman, pass by.[37]

A week later Yeats was writing to Ethel Mannin to tell her that he was arranging for his burial place in the Sligo churchyard where his great-grandfather, Pastor John, had been rector a century before. The last three lines of the poem he had copied out for Dorothy Wellesley would serve as his epitaph. By 4 September he had completed the major poem in which they appear, 'Under Ben Bulben'.

Written in a metre appropriate to spells and incantations, 'Under Ben Bulben' draws together Yeats's occult and Nationalist interests, his certainty of the immortality of the soul and his desire for a strong, eugenically cleansed nation, into a work of powerful and sometimes bludgeoning assertion. Race and soul are once again Yeats's preoccupation, and the visionary hordes of the Sidhe, immortal and heroically energetic in their completeness, provide his image of perfection. The man of action, the artist and the poet must all celebrate this and so provide the people of Ireland with an ideal of heroic and spiritual national endeavour that is at once timeless and free from both materialism and what Yeats regarded as the false compromises of democracy. The vigour is unquestionable, yet terrible too:

> Irish poets, learn your trade,
> Sing whatever is well made,
> Scorn the sort now growing up
> All out of shape from toe to top,
> Their unremembering hearts and heads
> Base-born products of base beds.
> Sing the peasantry, and then
> Hard-rising country gentlemen,
> The holiness of monks, and after
> Porter-drinkers' randy laughter;
> Sing the lords and ladies gay
> That were beaten into the clay
> Through seven heroic centuries;
> Cast your mind on other days
> That we in coming days may be
> Still the indomitable Irishry.[38]

The night before Yeats left Ireland for the last time he read 'Under Ben Bulben' aloud to F. R. Higgins. The evening came to an end and 'we parted', Higgins-recalled, 'on the drive from his house. The head of the retiring figure, erect and challenging, gleamed through the darkness as I turned back; while on the road before me my thoughts were still ringing out with the slow powerful accents of his chanting.'[39]

VI
'The Dark Grows Blacker'

Yeats travelled first to England where, at the Sussex home of Edith Shakelton Heald, he wrote the prose scenario for his last play, *The Death of Cuchulain*. With that completed, he and George journeyed south to the Riviera, taking rooms at the Hôtel Idéal Séjour at Cap Martin. He had both friends and family around him. Dorothy Wellesley was staying at La Bastide, a villa in the hills above Beaulieu, and when she went down to see Yeats she was astounded 'at what seemed a miraculous return to health'. He appeared strong and 'his brain was more active than ever, if such a thing could be possible'.[40]

Yeats was half sitting up in bed when she arrived, and he was greatly excited, saying to her: 'I want to read you my new play.' For all the tangle of corrections on the manuscript, Yeats read out 'with great fire' *The Death of Cuchulain*. Into this dense and enigmatic work he had poured both reminiscences of his earlier dramas on the great Irish hero and ideas wrested from the deepest parts of his visionary philosophy. As Cuchulain declines as a physical man, so he develops triumphantly towards a spiritual existence. He is shown moving towards the phase of the saint, towards renunciation, expiation, passivity and acceptance of his need to become his own opposite, his anti-self symbolised by the Blind Man who kills him. Dorothy Wellesley was deeply moved by this affirmation of tragic joy and the transcendence of the merely human. She was, she wrote, 'half aware that it was in some sense a premonition of his own death, though I did not know it was to come so soon'.

There were dinner parties at La Bastide, where W. J. Turner and the great pianist Arthur Schnabel were guests, and conversation turned to the work of Stefan Georg and Rilke, about whom the poet and the musician strongly disagreed. Christmas too was celebrated at Dorothy Wellesley's villa. 'W.B. seemed very gay,' she wrote. 'He was full of charming stories: the little monkey god who threw down mangoes from the tree; the holy man embedded in the block of ice. He told me afterwards with great pride, knowing that it had been a good performance, that the stories had been especially for Michael.'

Other delightful evenings followed. Yeats and George, W. J. Turner and Dorothy Wellesley's friend Hilda Matheson lunched one afternoon 'at that strangely charming and pagan place, La Turbie', after which they drove into the hills behind Menton to look on the snow-covered mountain peaks in the bitter, sunlit, winter cold. 'A great exhilaration seemed to be upon us,' and, as they returned to Yeats's hotel, he talked enthusiastically 'about his theories of words for songs'. Dorothy Wellesley showed him her own recent composition, a little song called 'Golden Helen', which was to be printed in the Cuala *Broadsides*. '"Yes, Yes," he said, "It has great poetical profundity."' By this time they had arrived back at the hotel itself, and Dorothy Wellesley noticed how Yeats, sitting under the lamp in his light-brown suit and blue shirt and handkerchief, seemed a beautiful man as the radiance of the lamplight fell on his white hair, transfiguring it to a pale sapphire. He turned to Hilda Matheson and asked her to make a tune for Dorothy Wellesley's poem, and the two women then went outside, walking up and down in the rain and the darkness until they had composed the air which Hilda Matheson proceeded to sing. Yeats seemed pleased by it.

He too was composing, finishing on Saturday, 21 January his last poem,

'The Black Tower'. He had partly dictated the work from his bed, his mind returning to the themes that had preoccupied him throughout his life. The haunted tower itself, partly Thoor Ballylee, is a last bastion of Irish integrity where, as the vulgar forces of the contemporary world vainly wave their trivial banners, supernatural forces await resurrection, new energy, the antithetical gyre:

> *There in the tomb the dark grows blacker,*
> *But winds come up from the shore,*
> *They shake when the winds roar,*
> *Old bones upon the mountain shake.*[41]

But, for all his imaginative power, Yeats knew his health was failing. Earlier in the month he had written to the Swami's friend Lady Elizabeth Pelham, 'I know for certain that my time will not be long.' He was resting in preparation for writing his 'most fundamental thoughts and the arrangement of thought which I am convinced will complete my studies. I am happy, and I think full of an energy, of an energy I had despaired of. It seems to me that I have found what I wanted. When I try to put all into a phrase I say, "Man can embody truth but he cannot know it." I must embody it in the completion of my life'.[42]

That completion was now close. By Tuesday, 24 January, Yeats was too tired to spend the evening with Dorothy Wellesley as arranged. Two days later, she called on him and saw that he was now very ill, 'in fact I saw he was dying, and I saw that he knew it'. She stayed for only five minutes, fearing to tire him, but in the afternoon she and Hilda Matheson called again, George having said to them: 'Come back and light the flame.' Now, as she returned to the dying man's bedroom, Dorothy Wellesley sat on the floor by his side, holding his hand as Yeats struggled to speak: 'Are you writ . . . are you writing?' 'Yes, yes,' she said. 'Good, good,' he replied and kissed her hand. She kissed his in return, but now his mind was wandering a little as he murmured scraps of poetry. Late that evening he rallied sufficiently to dictate to George corrections for *The Death of Cuchulain* and 'Under Ben Bulben'. The following day, however, his condition had greatly deteriorated and he passed into a coma. The intense pain in his heart was relieved by shots of morphia, but at two in the afternoon of the next day, Saturday, 28 January 1939, Yeats died, his last works corrected, a table of contents drawn up for his posthumous *Last Poems*.

Canon Tupper was brought from Monte Carlo to repeat some prayers over the body which, by Sunday, was too changed for the artist Dermod O'Brien to make a drawing of it. Yeats himself had said that if he died in France he thought that the cemetery at the little town of Roquebrune overlooking Cap Martin and Monaco would be a suitable resting place and that, if the family wished to, they could 'dig him up later' and return his body to Sligo. George, Dorothy Wellesley, Edith Shackelton Heald and her sister, Hilda Matheson and Dermod O'Brien and his wife all walked up the long stony path to the cemetery, where the Anglican burial service was read. Meanwhile, tributes and condolences flooded in. James Joyce sent a wreath, and T. S. Eliot in his letter of condolence described Yeats as the leading modern poet. O'Casey wrote that 'his greatness is such that the Ireland which tormented him will be forced to remember him for ever'.[43] Later, there were memorial services at St Patrick's Cathedral in Dublin and at St Martin's-in-the-Fields.

The Irish government, in its telegram of condolence, had expressed the hope that Yeats's body would be brought back for burial in Ireland, and the Dean of St Patrick's offered an interment in the Cathedral, something that had not happened for a century. The French government proposed the use of a destroyer to carry the coffin back to Ireland, but the outbreak of the Second World War seven months later eventually made this impossible, and it was not until September 1948 that an Irish corvette, the *Macha*, returned Yeats's body to Galway. George, Jack, Anne and Michael went on board as the coffin was piped ashore to be laid in state in front of the Sligo town hall. The cortège then wound its way to Drumcliff churchyard, where it was met by Sean MacBride, Minister for External Affairs, and other members of the government and local dignitaries. A Church of Ireland service was then held as Yeats was finally laid to rest in that ancestral Sligo which his genius had throughout a lifetime fashioned into one of the supreme and often troubling countries of the mind.

Notes on Sources

PREFACE

1 *If I Were Four and Twenty*, p. 1.
2 Sean O'Casey, *Autobiographies*, vol. II, p. 347.
3 *Collected Letters*, vol. I, p. 303.
4 A letter to Lady Elizabeth Pelham quoted in Joseph Hone, *W. B. Yeats*, p. 480.

1
THE IGNOMINY OF BOYHOOD

1 For John Butler Yeats's early life see his *Early Memories* and William M. Murphy, *Prodigal Father: The Life of John Butler Yeats*, pp. 19–124.
2 *Autobiographies*, p. 53.
3 *An Address Delivered before the Law Students' Debating Society . . . November 21, 1865*, quoted in Murphy, op. cit., p. 47.
4 See especially Richard Ellmann, *Yeats: The Man and the Masks*, pp. 7–21.
5 *Autobiographies*, p. 11.
6 The house still stands and is marked with a blue plaque.
7 Quoted in Murphy, op. cit., p. 57.
8 Sir Charles Trevelyan, 1846, quoted in John O'Beirne Ranelagh, *A Short History of Ireland*, p. 117.
9 Quoted in ibid., p. 120.
10 Quoted in Murphy, op. cit., p. 54.
11 For the correspondence between JBY, Dowden and Todhunter, see ibid., esp. pp. 66–71.
12 *Autobiographies*, p. 5.
13 WBY's early reminiscences of Sligo are in ibid., pp. 5–26 and 49–55.
14 Lily Yeats, 'Grandmother Yeats', quoted in Murphy, op. cit., p. 89.
15 *Autobiographies*, p. 8.
16 Quoted in Murphy, op. cit., p. 94.
17 Lily Yeats, quoted in ibid., p. 92.
18 'Swedenborg, Mediums and the Desolate Places', in *Explorations*, p. 56.
19 See *Autobiographies*, pp. 25–6.
20 For WBY's return to London see ibid., pp. 27–31.

21 *Collected Letters*, vol. I, p. 4.
22 See *Autobiographies*, pp. 31–42.
23 Charles Adderley, quoted in Elie Halevy, *A History of the English People in the Nineteenth Century: Victorian Years, 1841–1895*, vol. IV, p. 411, and cited in Karl Beckson, *London in the 1890s*, p. 344
24 JBY quoted in Murphy, op. cit., p. 118.
25 See *Autobiographies*, pp. 42–6, for WBY's early memories of Bedford Park.
26 See ibid., p. 62, and *Memoirs*, pp. 71–2.
27 See *Autobiographies*, pp. 55–65.
28 Ibid., p. 64.
29 Quoted in Joseph Hone, *W. B. Yeats*, p. 67.
30 JBY, *Early Memories*, p. 29.

2
GROWING INTO MAN

1 For contemporary views of WBY at the Erasmus Smith School see E.H. Mikhail, ed., *W. B. Yeats: Interviews and Recollections*, vol. I, pp. 1–13; for WBY's own memories see *Autobiographies*, pp. 56–9.
2 Quoted in Richard Ellmann, *Yeats: The Man and the Masks*, p. 30.
3 Ibid.
4 See *Autobiographies*, pp. 67–75.
5 Ibid., p. 76.
6 *J. B. Yeats: Letters to his Son W. B. Yeats and Others 1869–1922*, pp. 52–3.
7 See *Autobiographies*, pp. 79–83.
8 'The Stolen Child', ll. 8–11.
9 See *Autobiographies*, p. 80.
10 'The Stolen Child', ll. 13–23.
11 A. P. Sinnett, *Esoteric Buddhism*, p. viii.
12 Ibid., p. 12.
13 *Autobiographies*, pp. 115–16.
14 See P. S. Sri, 'Yeats and Moihini Chatterjee', *Yeats Annual*, ii, pp. 60–76.
15 'The Song of the Happy Shepherd', ll. 1–10.
16 See *Autobiographies*, pp. 93–102.
17 Quoted in Joseph Hone, *W. B. Yeats*, p. 46.

18 Quoted in D. George Boyce, *Nationalism in Ireland*, p. 216.
19 For John O'Leary see *Autobiographies*, pp. 94–102, and Marcus Bourke, *John O'Leary: A Study in Irish Separatism*, passim. For Standish O'Grady see David Pierce, *Yeats's Worlds: Ireland, England and the Poetic Imagination*, pp. 80–5.
20 See 'The Poetry of Sir Samuel Ferguson', in *Uncollected Prose*, vol. I, pp. 87–103.
21 Ibid.
22 See *Autobiographies*, pp. 103–5.
23 For Father Russell, see Hone, op. cit., p. 55. Hopkins is quoted in William M. Murphy, *Prodigal Father: The Life of John Butler Yeats*, 7. 146.
24 'Down by the Salley Gardens', ll. 5–8.
25 See *Autobiographies*, pp. 139–54.
26 Ibid., pp. 173–81.
27 *The Wanderings of Oisin*, Book I, ll. 20–30.
28 Quoted in *W. B. Yeats: The Poems*, p. 397.

3
THE TROUBLING OF HIS LIFE

1 Henry James, *The Princess Casamissima*, quoted in Malcolm Bradbury, 'London 1890–1920', in Malcolm Bradbury and James McFarlane, eds *Modernism*, p. 172.
2 Lollie Yeats quoted in William M. Murphy. *Family Secrets: William Butler Yeats and his Relatives*, p. 61.
3 See *Autobiographies*, pp. 139–54.
4 William Morris, 'What I Mean by Socialism'.
5 See 'The Happiest of the Poets', in *Essays and Introductions*, pp. 53–64.
6 See *Autobiographies*, pp. 124–9.
7 Oscar Wilde, *A Woman of No Importance*, Act II.
8 See *Autobiographies*, pp. 130–9.
9 See *Memoirs*, p. 31.
10 See *Autobiographies*, pp. 189–95.
11 See Murphy, *Family Secrets*, pp. 59–85.
12 See ibid., esp. pp. 71–5.
13 Quoted in William M. Murphy, *Prodigal Father: The Life of John Butler Yeats*, p. 529.
14 'The Lake Isle of Innisfree', ll. 1–4.
15 Quoted in Karl Beckson, *London in the 1890s*, pp. 78–9.
16 Maud Gonne MacBride, *A Servant of the Queen*, p. 97. See also *Memoirs*,
pp. 40–7, and Nancy Cardozo, *Lucky Eyes and a High Heart: The Life of Maud Gonne*, pp. 1–105.
17 See Richard Ellmann, *Yeats: The Man and the Masks*, pp. 67–8.
18 See *Autobiographies*, pp. 183–8, *Memoirs*, pp. 26–7, and 'Magic', in *Essays and Introductions*, pp. 28–36.
19 The rituals, symbols, lectures etc. of the Golden Dawn are given in Israel Regardie, *The Golden Dawn*, passim. The Neophyte Ceremony is given in ibid., pp. 114–33.
20 See *Autobiographies*, pp. 162–5, and *Memoirs*, pp. 28–31.
21 Quoted in Joseph Hone, *W. B. Yeats*, p. 77.
22 For WBY's essays on Blake see 'William Blake and the Imagination' and 'William Blake and his Illustrations to the *Divine Comedy*', in *Essays and Introductions*, pp. 111–45.
23 See *Autobiographies*, esp. pp. 299–304, and 'The Tragic Generation', ibid., pp. 279–349 for individuals.
24 Quoted in Hone, op. cit., p. 84.
25 There is a useful discussion of WBY's response to Todhunter's plays in Liam Miller, *The Noble Drama of W. B. Yeats*, pp. 17–18.
26 *John Sherman* in *Short Fiction*, p. 36.
27 *Memoirs*, p. 45.
28 See *Autobiographies*, pp. 236–49.
29 *If I Were Four and Twenty*, p. 1.
30 'To the Rose upon the Rood of Time', ll. 1–12.
31 *Autobiographies*, p. 559.

4
CELTIC TWILIGHT

1 See *Memoirs*, pp. 59–68.
2 See *Autobiographies*, pp. 199–228.
3 *Memoirs*, p. 71.
4 The Portal Ceremony is described in Israel Regardie, *The Golden Dawn*, pp. 35–6.
5 *Collected Letters*, vol. I, p. 303.
6 'The Rose of Battle', ll. 25–36.
7 'To Ireland in the Coming Times', ll. 17–32.
8 'To the Rose upon the Rood of Time', ll. 15–21.
9 *The Celtic Twilight*, reprinted in *Mythologies*, pp. 1–141.
10 Ibid., pp. 54–6.
11 Ibid., p. 56.

12 See *Uncollected Prose*, vol. I, pp. 266–75.
13 Maud Gonne MacBride, *A Servant of the Queen*, p. 178.
14 See *Autobiographies*, pp. 120–1 and 280–3.
15 See ibid., pp. 279–80.
16 See ibid., pp. 335–9.
17 See 'Verlaine in 1894', in *Uncollected Prose*, vol. I, pp. 397–9.
18 'A Symbolical Drama in Paris', ibid., pp. 320–5.
19 *The Land of Heart's Desire*, in *Collected Plays*, p. 69.
20 George Moore, *Ave*, pp. 45–6.
21 See *Autobiographies*, pp. 304–10.
22 See *Olivia Shakespear and W. B. Yeats: After Long Silence*, passim.

5
ROSA ALCHEMICA

1 For this visit, see *Memoirs*, pp. 15–77.
2 See 'Magic', in *Essays and Introductions*, pp. 28–52.
3 The intricate processes of Yeats's revisions to his lyrics are comprehensively charted in *The Variorum Edition of the Poems of W. B. Yeats*, ed. Peter Allt and Russell K. Alspach. For the sake of convenience I have, unless stated, quoted the final versions of works.
4 See *Memoirs*, p. 77.
5 Olivia Shakespear is referred to under the name of Diana Vernon in the *Memoirs*, see esp. pp. 85–9.
6 See *Autobiographies*, pp. 253–5.
7 Ibid., p. 254.
8 See *Memoirs*, pp. 79–80, and *Autobiographies*, pp. 284–91.
9 See *Memoirs*, pp. 80–1.
10 'He bids his Beloved be at Peace', ll. 9–12.
11 Quoted in Joseph Hone, *W. B. Yeats*, p. 104.
12 See *Memoirs*, pp. 86–7.
13 See George Moore, *Ave*, pp. 47–53.
14 See *Autobiographies*, pp. 318–29.
15 Wagnermania is described in Karl Beckson, *London in the 1890's*, pp. 272–91.
16 See *Autobiographies*, pp. 322–6, and *Memoirs*, pp. 90–2.
17 *Memoirs*, p. 91.
18 See *Essays and Introductions*, pp. 116–45.
19 *Letters of W. B. Yeats*, p. 286.
20 *Mythologies*, p. 290.

21 'The Secret Rose', ll. 27–32.
22 *Memoirs*, p. 100.
23 See E. H. Mikhail, ed., *W. B. Yeats: Interviews and Recollections* vol. I, pp. 44–8.
24 See *Autobiographies*, pp. 385–7.
25 *Ibid.*, p. 343.
26 See *Memoirs*, p. 100.
27 See *Autobiographies*, pp. 388–95.

6
THE PATH OF THE CHAMELEON

1 'The Valley of the Black Pig'.
2 The phrase is Mary K. Greer, *Women of the Golden Dawn*.
3 'He reproves the Curlew'.
4 For WBY's meeting with Synge, see *Autobiographies*, pp. 343–6.
5 See *Memoirs*, p. 89.
6 'The Lover mourns for the Loss of Love'.
7 See *Memoirs*, pp. 111–21.
8 *Gonne–Yeats Letters*, p. 72.
9 Lady Gregory, *Seventy Years*, pp. 309–10.
10 Quoted in Mary Lou Kohfeldt, *Lady Gregory: The Woman behind the Irish Renaissance*, p. 106.
11 For the Prospectus, see Lady Gregory, *Our Irish Theatre*, p. 20.
12 See *Memoirs*, pp. 125–8.
13 See *Autobiographies*, pp. 388–91.
14 Ibid., p. 364.
15 See William M. Murphy, *Prodigal Father: The Life of John Butler Yeats*, pp. 194–9.
16 Quoted in ibid., p. 195.
17 Quoted in Joseph Hone, *W. B. Yeats*, pp. 155–6.
18 See Greer, op. cit., p. 190.
19 Ibid., pp. 217–19.
20 'He thinks of those who have Spoken Evil of his Beloved', ll. 3–6.
21 Quoted in Nancy Cardozo, *Lucky Eyes and a High Heart: The Life of Maud Gonne*, p. 146.
22 *Gonne–Yeats Letters*, p. 89.
23 'He hears the Cry of the Sedge'.
24 *Essays and Introductions*, pp. 189–94.
25 'He wishes for the Cloths of Heaven'.
26 See Cardozo, op. cit., pp. 153–67.

27 See *Memoirs*, pp. 131–4.
28 *Gonne–Yeats Letters*, pp. 99–100.

31 'The Folly of Being Comforted', ll. 6–12.
32 *Gonne–Yeats Letters*, pp. 164–6.

7
CATHLEEN NI HOULIHAN

1 See George Moore, *Ave*, pp. 69 ff.
2 See Liam Miller, *The Noble Drama of W. B. Yeats*, pp. 85–6.
3 See *Memoirs*, p. 120.
4 'Who goes with Fergus', ll. 1–6.
5 See Joseph Hone, *W. B. Yeats*, p. 169.
6 Quoted in A. Norman Jeffares, *W. B. Yeats: A New Biography*, p. 210.
7 *The Arrow*, 24 November 1906, quoted in S. B. Bushrui, *Yeats Verse-Plays: The Revisions 1900–1910*, p. 2.
8 See *Ave*, pp. 241 ff.
9 See *Autobiographies*, pp. 425–38.
10 For the background to the Boer War see Karl Beckson, *London in the 1890s*, pp. 372–7. See also Nancy Cardozo, *Lucky Eyes and a High Heart: The Life of Maud Gonne*, pp. 171–84.
11 Quoted in Cardozo, op. cit., p. 184.
12 See ibid., pp. 181–93.
13 See Mary K. Greer, *Women of the Golden Dawn*, pp. 234–73.
14 See Israel Regardie, *What You Should Know about the Golden Dawn*, pp. 189–96.
15 Ibid., p. 196.
16 Maud Gonne MacBride, *A Servant of the Queen*, p. 280.
17 See *Memoirs*, pp. 115–16.
18 Ibid., p. 123, and *Autobiographies*, pp. 434–6.
19 See Miller, op. cit., pp. 49–52.
20 'At Stratford-on-Avon', *Essays and Introductions*, pp. 96–110.
21 Quoted in Miller, op. cit., p. 65.
22 Ibid., p. 60.
23 See Mary Lou Kohfeldt, *Lady Gregory: The Woman behind the Irish Renaissance*, pp. 143–6.
24 *Collected Plays*, p. 86.
25 'Adam's Curse', ll. 1–14.
26 Ibid., ll. 34–8.
27 Maud Gone MacBride, op. cit., p. 318.
28 Louise Morgan, in E. H. Mikhail, ed., *W. B. Yeats: Interviews and Recollections*, vol. II, p. 200. For Gogarty, see ibid., p. 305. For Masefield, see ibid., pp. 44–8.
29 Maud Gonne MacBride, op. cit., pp. 318–19.
30 See Cardozo, op. cit., pp. 218–21.

8
A MANLY POSE

1 For John Quinn, see B. L. Reid, *The Man from New York: John Quinn and his Friends*.
2 *Collected Letters*, vol. III, p. 372.
3 See Liam Miller, *The Noble Drama of W. B. Yeats*, pp. 86–7.
4 For a full account see Mary K. Greer, *Women of the Golden Dawn*, pp. 278–91.
5 See article on 'The Psaltery', in 'Biographical and Historical Appendix' to *Collected Letters*, vol. III, pp. 725–8.
6 'The Players ask for a Blessing on the Psalteries and on Themselves', ll. 1–7.
7 See Greer, op. cit., pp. 321–2.
8 For Evelyn Gleeson, see William M. Murphy, *Prodigal Father: The Life of John Butler Yeats*, pp. 231–7.
9 See William M. Murphy, *Family Secrets: William Butler Yeats and his Relatives*, pp. 84 ff.
10 See Nancy Cardozo, *Lucky Eyes and a High Heart: The Life of Maud Gonne*, pp. 239–56.
11 *The Shadow of the Glen*, Nora's last speech.
12 Quoted in Cardozo, op. cit., p. 238.
13 See Greer, op. cit., pp. 282–5.
14 See *Collected Letters*, vol. III, pp. 439–44 and 445–9.
15 See S. B. Bushrui, *Yeats's Verse-Plays: The Revisions 1900–1910*, pp. 73–119.
16 Quoted in Joseph Hone, *W. B. Yeats*, pp. 198–9.
17 Ibid., p. 204.
18 *Letters of W. B. Yeats*, p. 413.
19 Quoted in Elizabeth Cullingford, *Yeats, Ireland and Fascism*, p. 25.
20 *Letters of W. B. Yeats*, p. 424.
21 Quoted in Murphy, *Prodigal Father*, p. 264.
22 E. H. Mikhail, ed., *W. B. Yeats: Interviews and Recollections*, vol. II, pp. 302–5.
23 Ibid., p. 301.
24 Ibid., p. 249.
25 See ibid., pp. 395–403.
26 See Murphy, *Prodigal Father*, p. 263.
27 See Murphy, *Family Secrets*, p. 120.
28 Synge to Stephen MacKenna, c. January 1904, quoted in Murphy, *Prodigal Father*, pp. 268–9.

29 'The Fascination of What's Difficult', ll. 8–9.
30 See Bushrui, op. cit., pp. 1–38.
31 See Miller, op. cit., pp. 103–12.
32 Quoted in Murphy, *Prodigal Father*, pp. 277–8.
33 For WBY and tragedy see Bushrui, op. cit., pp. 24–5, 42–6, 115–17.
34 *Collected Plays*, p. 255.
35 See Miller, op. cit., p. 120.
36 See Mary Lou Kohfeldt, *Lady Gregory: The Woman behind the Irish Renaissance*, pp. 180–2.
37 See Cardozo, op. cit., pp. 246–56.
38 See Miller, op. cit., pp. 130–2 and Kohfeldt, op. cit., pp. 192–5.
39 Miller, op. cit., and Mikhail, op. cit., vol. I, pp. 54–68.
40 See James Kilroy, *The 'Playboy' Riots*, passim.
41 *Uncollected Prose*, vol ii, p. 349
42 Kilroy, op. cit., p. 32
43 See Murphy, *Prodigal Father*, p. 317.
44 Uncollected Prose, vol. ii, p. 352.

9
THE GIFTS THAT GOVERN MEN

1 For 'Poetry and Tradition' and *Discoveries*, from which the following quotations are taken, see *Essays and Introductions*, pp. 246–60 and 261–97 respectively.
2 Ibid., pp. 290–1.
3 *Letters of W. B. Yeats*, p. 466.
4 For Annie Horniman, see James Flannery, *Miss Annie F. Horniman and the Abbey Theatre*, pp. 21–3.
5 Quoted in A. Norman Jeffares, *W. B. Yeats: A New Biography*, p. 153.
6 See Mary Lou Kohfeldt, *Lady Gregory: The Woman behind the Irish Renaissance*, p. 192.
7 WBY's Journal is printed in *Memoirs*, pp. 137–278.
8 Quoted in Joseph Hone, *W. B. Yeats*, p. 232.
9 Ibid., p. 227.
10 See Mary K. Greer, *Women of the Golden Dawn*, pp. 324–7.
11 For the productions of *Deirdre* see Liam Miller, *The Noble Drama of W. B. Yeats*, pp. 124–9.
12 For Mrs Patrick Campbell, see ibid., pp. 144–5.
13 Quoted in Hone, op. cit., pp. 227–8.
14 *Memoirs*, pp. 160–1.
15 Quoted in Kohfeldt, op. cit., p. 208.
16 The Preface and 'J. M. Synge and the Ireland of his Time' are in *Essays and Introductions*, pp. 306–10 and 311–42. The Journal is in *Autobiographies*, pp. 497–527.
17 'Upon a House Shaken by the Land Agitation'.
18 See Kohfeldt, op. cit., pp. 211–12.
19 Ibid., p. 221.
20 WBY and Lady Gregory, *Paragraphs Written in Nov. 1909, with Supplement and Financial Statement*, quoted in Miller, op. cit., p. 146.
21 See Greer, op. cit., pp. 309 ff.
22 'His Memories'.
23 See Nancy Cardozo, *Lucky Eyes and a High Heart: The Life of Maud Gonne*, pp. 257–66.
24 Ibid., p. 261.
25 *Gonne–Yeats Letters*, pp. 255–6.
26 An unpublished poem quoted in ibid., p. 266.
27 Ibid., pp. 259–60.
28 Cardozo, p. 260.
29 'King and No King', ll. 11–16.
30 Quoted in Cardozo, op. cit, pp. 262–3.
31 'No Second Troy'.
32 *Memoirs*, p. 184.
33 See *Essays and Introductions*, pp. 343–5.
34 *Memoirs*, p. 191.
35 'In Memory of Alfred Pollexfen', ll. 9–12.

10
THE ONION SELLERS

1 See Mary Lou Kohfeldt, *Lady Gregory: The Woman behind the Irish Renaissance*, pp. 218–19.
2 *Memoirs*, pp. 256–7.
3 Ibid., p. 252.
4 See William M. Murphy, *Prodigal Father: The Life of John Butler Yeats*, pp. 377–8.
5 Craig's patent application is in Liam Miller, *The Noble Drama of W. B. Yeats*, pp. 150–3.
6 Ibid., p. 153.
7 For Craig and the mask, see ibid., pp. 163–5.
8 Ibid., p. 165.
9 Murphy, *Prodigal Father*, p. 388.
10 See ibid., pp. 363–4.
11 See Kohfeldt, op. cit., pp. 223–32.
12 Ibid., pp. 232–3.
13 See William M. Murphy, *Family Secrets:*

William Butler Yeats and his Relatives,
pp. 135–8.

14 Ibid., p. 191.

15 Ibid., pp. 192 ff.

16 Nancy Cardozo, *Lucky Eyes and a High Heart: The Life of Maud Gonne*, p. 264.

17 For Pearse's ideology, see F. S. L. Lyons, *Culture and Anarchy in Ireland, 1880–1939*, pp. 85–95.

18 'The Mask', ll. 1–2.

19 See Cardozo, op. cit., p. 285.

20 'To a Child Dancing in the Wind'.

21 See Joseph Hone, *W. B. Yeats*, p. 209.

22 Ibid., p. 237.

23 Ibid., pp. 263–4.

24 For Pound and Olivia Shakespear, see Humphrey Carpenter, *A Serious Character: The Life of Ezra Pound*, pp. 103–6.

25 For Pound in London, see ibid., pp. 97–101.

26 Ibid., p. 134.

27 For the relationship between WBY and Pound see James Longenbach, *Stone Cottage: Pound, Yeats, and Modernism*, passim.

28 For Yeats's experiments in spiritualism, see especially 'The Manuscript of "Leo Africanus"', ed. Steve L. Adams and George Mills Harper, in *Yeats Annual*, no. I, pp. 3–47.

29 For WBY and Elizabeth Radcliffe, see George Mills Harper and John S. Kelly, '"Preliminary Examination of the Script of E[lizabeth] R[adcliffe]"', in George Mills Harper, ed., *Yeats and the Occult*, pp. 130–71.

30 'To a Wealthy Man who promised a Second Subscription to the Dublin Municipal Gallery if it were proved the People wanted Pictures', ll. 9–19.

31 See Elizabeth Cullingford, *Yeats, Ireland and Fascism*, pp. 80–2.

32 'September 1913', ll. 1–8.

II
WALKING NAKED

1 Max Beerbohm, *Mainly on Air*, p. 101, quoted in David Pierce, *Yeats's Worlds: Ireland, England and the Poetic Imagination*, p. 3.

2 See Humphrey Carpenter, *A Serious Character: The Life of Ezra Pound*, pp. 176–80.

3 For Imagism see Carpenter, op. cit., pp. 196–98

4 Ibid., p. 28

5 Quoted in Carpenter, op. cit., p. 220.

6 See James Longenbach, *Stone Cottage: Pound, Yeats and Modernism*, Longenbach, op. cit. p. 26

7 'The Grey Rock', ll. 52–64.

8 'A Coat'.

9 *Explorations*, pp. 30–70.

10 'The Peacock'.

11 See Longenbach, op. cit., p. 43 and 54.

12 Ibid., p. 60–1.

13 'Pardon, old Fathers', ll. 19–22.

14 See Carpenter, op. cit., pp. 228–30.

15 See Murphy, *Prodigal Father*, pp. 414–18

16 See George Mills Harper, '"A subject of Investigation": Miracle at Mirebeau' in George Mills Harper ed. *Yeats the Occult*, pp 172–89.

17 Quoted in Robert Kee, *The Green Flag*, vol. II, p. 200.

18 See F. S. L. Lyons, *Culture and Anarchy in Ireland, 1890–1939*, pp. 85–95.

19 See Longenbach, op. cit., p. 108.

20 'A Meditation in Time of War'.

21 Longenbach, op. cit., p. 161

22 'On being asked for a War Poem'.

23 See Longenbach, op. cit., p. 143–6

24 'Her Praise', ll. 11–14.

25 'The Fisherman', ll. 37–40.

26 For Ireland and the First World War, see Kee, op. cit., pp. 217–33.

27 Quoted in Longenbach, p. 179–80.

28 For Yeats and Lady Lyttelton, see *Yeats's 'Vision' Papers*, vol. I, pp. 7–10, and 'The Manuscript of "Leo Africanus"', ed. Steve L. Adams and George Mills Harper, in *Yeats Annual*, no. I, pp. 3–47.

29 'Ego Dominus Tuus', ll. 70–4.

30 Ibid., ll. 54–62.

31 See *Essays and Introductions*, pp. 221–37.

32 See Longenbach, op. cit., pp. 261–2.

33 Quoted in E. H. Mikhail, ed., *W. B. Yeats: Interviews and Recollections*, vol. II, p. 381.

34 *Collected Plays*, p. 208.

12
TERRIBLE BEAUTY

1 The 'Proclamation of the Republic' is printed as an appendix in R. F. Foster, *Modern Ireland, 1600–1922*, pp. 596–7.'

2 'Easter 1916', l. 15.

3 E. H. Mikhail, ed., *W. B. Yeats:*

Interviews and Recollections, vol.
II, p. 282.
4 *Letters of W. B. Yeats*, p. 613.
5 Robert Kee, *The Green Flag*, vol. III,
pp. 9–10.
6 'Easter 1916', ll. 74–80.
7 For Maud Gonne and the Easter
Uprising, see Nancy Cardozo, *Lucky
Eyes and a High Heart: The Life of Maud
Gonne*, pp. 297–310.
8 Ibid., p. 310.
9 Omar Pound, ed., *Ezra Pound and
Dorothy Shakespear: Their Letters,
1909–1914*, p. 58.
10 See Cardozo, op. cit., p. 313.
11 'To a Young Girl'.
12 'Men Improve with the Years', ll. 14–18.
13 'The Wild Swans at Coole', ll. 1–6.
14 *Collected Plays*, p. 443.
15 *Letters of W. B. Yeats*, p. 654.
16 See *Yeats's 'Vision' Papers*, pp. 8–9.
17 *Mythologies*, pp. 317–69.
18 Ibid., pp. 364–5.
19 'The Rose Tree', ll. 16–18.
20 See Kee, op. cit., vol. III,
pp. 17–29.
21 *Letters of W. B. Yeats*, p. 628.
22 Quoted in David Pierce, *Yeats's
Worlds: Ireland, England and the Poetic
Imagination*, p. 196. For the astrological
background to the marriage, see
Elizabeth Heine, 'W. B. Yeats's Map
in his Own Hand', *Biography*, 1, no. 3
(1978), pp. 37–50.

9 *A Critical Edition of Yeats's 'A Vision'
(1925)*, p. 13.
10 Ibid., p. 24.
11 Ibid., esp. pp. 75–9.
12 *Uncollected Prose*, vol. ii. pp. 429–30.
13 'Shepherd and Goatherd', ll. 95–9.
14 For Anne Hyde, see *The Making of
Yeats's 'A Vision'*, pp. 209–11 and
218–26.
15 Quoted in E. H. Mikhail, ed., *W. B.
Yeats: Interviews and Recollections*, vol.
II, p. 326.
16 'Shepherd and Goatherd', ll. 35–42.
17 'In Memory of Major Robert Gregory',
stanza VIII.
18 See Nancy Cardozo, *Lucky Eyes
and a High Heart: The Life of Maud
Gonne*, p. 323.
19 See Elizabeth Cullingford, *Yeats, Ireland,
and Fascism*, p. 103.
20 For Yeats's theory of history and
contemporary politics, see ibid.,
pp. 115–43.
21 'To be Carved on a Stone at Thoor
Ballylee'.
22 *The Making of Yeats's 'A Vision'*, p. 131.
23 Cardozo, op. cit., p. 327.
24 'On a Political Prisoner', ll. 7–12.
25 Robert Kee, *The Green Flag*, vol.
III, p. 56.
26 'The Second Coming', ll. 3–8.
27 *A Critical Edition of Yeats's 'A Vision'
(1925)*, pp. 213–14.
28 'A Prayer for my Daughter', ll. 41–8.

13
THE PHASES OF THE MOON

1 'Owen Aherne and his Dancers',
I, ll. 1–4.
2 Ibid., II, ll. 9–12.
3 *Letters of W. B. Yeats*, p. 633. For
background material and transcripts
of the Yeatses' occult experiments, see
George Mills Harper *et al.*, eds, *The
Making of Yeats's 'A Vision': A Study of
the Automatic Script*, and *Yeats's 'Vision'
Papers*.
4 *A Critical Edition of Yeats's 'A Vision'
(1925)*, p. xvii.
5 Quoted in *The Making of Yeats's 'A
Vision'*, p. 38.
6 This is particularly so for analysts of the
Jungian school.
7 Quoted in *The Making of Yeats's 'A
Vision'*, p. 39.
8 'Tom O'Roughley', ll. 7–8.

14
IN TIME OF CIVIL WAR

1 See David Pierce, *Yeats's Worlds:
Ireland, England and the Poetic
Imagination*, pp. 207–10.
2 Liam Miller, *The Noble Drama of W. B.
Yeats*, pp. 248–9.
3 Robert Kee, *The Green Flag*, vol.
III, p. 91.
4 William M. Murphy, *Prodigal Father:
The Life of John Butler Yeats*, pp. 505–8.
5 See Joseph Hone, *W. B. Yeats*,
pp. 325–7.
6 'Introduction' to *A Vision*, pp. 9–10.
7 Quoted in Elizabeth Cullingford, *Yeats,
Ireland and Fascism*, p. 104.
8 For Iseult Gonne and Francis Stuart at
this time see Geoffrey Elborn, *Francis
Stuart: A Life*, pp. 33–55.
9 See Hone, op. cit., pp. 330–2.
10 See Nancy Cardozo, *Lucky Eyes*

and a High Heart: The Life of Maud Gonne, p. 343.

11 *Collected Plays*, pp. 141–2.

12 *Yeats's 'Vision' Papers*, vol. II, p. 487.

13 See Hone, op. cit., pp. 335–42.

14 See Miranda Seymour, *Ottoline Morrell: Life on the Grand Scale*, esp. pp. 419–40.

15 'All Souls' Night', ll. 51–60.

16 Lennox Robinson, ed., *Lady Gregory's Journals, 1916–1930*, p. 152.

17 See Mary Lou Kohfeldt, *Lady Gregory: The Woman behind the Irish Renaissance*, pp. 267–8.

18 See Cullingford, op. cit., pp. 108–9.

19 'Nineteen Hundred and Nineteen', ll. 25–8.

20 Murphy, *Prodigal Father*, pp. 526–30.

21 See Kee, op. cit., vol. III, pp. 152–3.

22 *Letters of W. B. Yeats*, p. 675.

23 Kee, op. cit., p. 171.

24 'Meditations in Time of Civil War', VI, 'The Stare's Nest by My Window', ll. 16–19.

25 See Cardozo, op. cit., pp. 354–5.

26 'Meditations in Time of Civil War', I, 'Ancestral Houses', ll. 25–32.

27 Quoted in Cullingford, op. cit., p. 147.

28 For Yeats and the Senate, see ibid., pp. 165–96.

29 'Leda and the Swan', ll. 9–11. See also *W. B. Yeats: The Poems*, pp. 663–4.

30 *Explorations*, p. 435.

31 *The Words upon the Window-Pane*, *Collected Plays*, p. 602.

32 'Bishop Berkeley', *Essays and Introductions*, p. 402.

33 *On the Boiler*, p. 12.

34 Quoted in Cullingford, op. cit., p. 173.

35 *Uncollected Prose*, vol. II, p. 448.

36 Quoted in E. H. Mikhail, ed., *W. B. Yeats: Interviews and Recollections*, vol. II, pp. 323–34.

15
PUBLIC MAN

1 See 'The Bounty of Sweden', in *Autobiographies*, pp. 531–58.

2 'The Irish Dramatic Movement', in ibid., pp. 559–72.

3 For Lily's illness see William M. Murphy, *Family Secrets: William Butler Yeats and his Relatives*, pp. 220–37.

4 See *A Critical Edition of Yeats's 'A Vision' (1925)*, pp. xv–xxiii.

5 See *The Variorum Edition of the Poems of W. B. Yeats*, pp. 828–9.

6 'The Gift of Harun Al-Rashid', ll. 181–6.

7 *A Vision*, p. 25.

8 'Beautiful Lofty Things', ll. 181–6.

9 For Lady Gregory at this time, see Mary Lou Kohfeldt, *Lady Gregory: The Woman behind the Irish Renaissance*, pp. 256–89.

10 Lady Gregory, *Seventy Years*, p. 365.

11 Quoted in E. H. Mikail, ed., *W. B. Yeats: Interviews and Recollections*, vol. II, p. 281. See also Nancy Cardozo, *Lucky Eyes and a High Heart: The Life of Maud Gonne*, pp. 356–72.

12 Quoted in Cardozo, op. cit., p. 149.

13 Quoted in Elizabeth Cullingford, *Yeats, Ireland and Fascism*, p. 149.

14 Ibid.

15 Ibid., pp. 190–1.

16 Quoted in David Pierce, *Yeats's World: Ireland, England and the Poetic Imagination*, p. 222.

17 'Among School Children', stanza VIII.

18 Quoted in John O'Beirne Ranelagh, *A short History of Ireland*, p. 215.

19 *Uncollected Prose*, vol. II, p. 452.

20 For Yeats's speech, see Cullingford, op. cit., pp. 182–5.

21 Quoted in ibid., p. 184.

22 Cited by Ann Saddlemeyer in 'George Hyde-Lees: More Than a Poet's Wife', in A. Norman Jeffares, ed., *Yeats the European*, p. 192.

23 *A Vision*, pp. 279–80.

24 'Sailing to Byzantium', stanza IV.

25 'The Tower', ll. 26–36.

26 O'Casey, *Autobiographies*, vol. I., p. 187.

27 Quoted in Gerald Fay, *The Abbey Theatre: Cradle of Genius*, pp. 147–8.

28 'From *Oedipus at Colonus*', ll. 1–3.

29 Quoted in O'Beirne Ranelagh, op. cit., p. 231.

30 'In Memory of Eva Gore-Booth and Con Markiewicz', II. 1–4.

31 See Cullingford, op. cit., p. 188.

32 'Blood and the Moon', ll. 13–15.

16
THE LAST ROMANTICS

1 *W. B. Yeats and T. Sturge Moore: Their Correspondence, 1901–1937*, pp. 67–8.

2 *A Vision*, pp. 20–2.

3 For WBY and Pound in Rapallo at this time, see 'A Packet for Ezra Pound', in *A Vision* and Humphrey Carpenter,

A Serious Character: The Life of Ezra Pound, pp. 424–36 and 443–79.
4 Quoted in James Simmons, *Sean O'Casey*, pp. 94–5.
5 *Letters of W. B. Yeats*, p. 746.
6 See illustration in David Pierce, *Yeats's Worlds: Ireland, England and the Poetic Imagination*, p. 233.
7 Quoted in ibid., pp. 232–3.
8 *A Vision*, pp. 4–5.
9 'Crazy Jane talks with the Bishop', ll. 13–18.
10 See Liam Miller, *The Noble Drama of W. B. Yeats*, pp. 272–7.
11 Quoted in ibid., pp. 278–9.
12 See Mary Lou Kohfeldt, *Lady Gregory: The Woman behind the Irish Renaissance*, pp. 290–4.
13 'Coole Park, 1929', ll. 17–24.
14 Quoted in Miller, op. cit., p. 284.
15 Quoted in Michael P. Biddis, *The Age of the Masses*, p. 93.
16 'Byzantium', ll. 25–32.
17 Ibid., ll. 33–40.
18 See *W. B. Yeats: The Poems*, p. 720.
19 *A Moment's Liberty: The Shorter Diary of Virginia Woolf*, p. 289
20 *On the Boiler*, pp. 25–6.
21 See Joseph Hone, *W. B. Yeats*, p. 423.
22 See William M. Murphy, *Family Secrets: William Butler Yeats and his Relatives*, pp. 237–47.
23 E. H. Mikhail, ed., *W. B. Yeats: Interviews and Recollections*, vol. II, pp. 398–400.
24 See Hone, op. cit., pp. 426–8.
25 'Coole Park and Ballylee, 1931, ll. 25–32.
26 For WBY and the Swami, see 'An Irish Monk' in *Essays and Introductions*, pp. 426–37.
27 Quoted in Kohfeldt, op. cit. pp. 301–2.
28 'Coole Park and Ballylee, 1931', ll. 41–8.

17
BITTER FURIES of COMPLEXITY

1 See Joseph Hone, *W. B. Yeats*, pp. 435–6.
2 Ibid., p. 437.
3 E. H. Mikhail, ed., *W. B. Yeats: Interviews and Recollections*, vol. II, p. 205.
4 *Autobiographies*, p. 429.
5 'Modern Ireland', p. 256.
6 *Letters of W. B. Yeats*, p. 808.
7 See Donald Torchiana, *Yeats and*

Georgian Ireland, p. 161. For a discussion of WBY and the Blueshirts, see Elizabeth Cullingford, *Yeats, Ireland and Fascism*, pp. 197–214.
8 Mikhail, op. cit., vol. II, pp. 220–3.
9 Ibid.
10 Quoted in *The Variorum Edition of the Poems of W. B. Yeats*, p. 750.
11 Preface to *The King of the Great Clock Tower*, quoted in Liam Miller, *The Noble Drama of W. B. Yeats*, p. 294.
12 For WBY's Steinach operation, see 'W. B. Yeats's Second Puberty', in Richard Ellmann, *Four Dubliners*, pp. 27–9.
13 'A Prayer for Old Age', ll. 1–4.
14 'Meru', ll. 1–8.
15 'The Irish National Theatre', quoted in Miller, op. cit., pp. 297–9.
16 Quoted in Hone, op. cit., p. 445.
17 See Nancy Cardozo, *Lucky Eyes and a High Heart: The Life of Maud Gonne*, pp. 375–85.
18 Quoted in A. Norman Jeffares, *W. B. Yeats: A New Biography*, p. 324
19 For Mannin's account of the friendship, see Mikhail, op. cit., vol. II, pp. 271–6.
20 *Explorations*, p. 414.
21 *Letters of W. B. Yeats*, p. 869. For the influence of O'Leary on WBY at this period, see Cullingford, op. cit., pp. 215–33.
22 See 'Introduction', *The Oxford Book of Modern Verse*, pp. v–xlii.
23 Ibid., p. xi.
24 See Mikhail, op. cit., vol. II, pp. 212–18.

18
WHY SHOULD NOT OLD MEN BE MAD?

1 *Essays and Introductions*, p. 484.
2 Quoted in Joseph Hone, *W. B. Yeats*, pp. 449–50.
3 Ibid., p. 450.
4 *Memoirs*, p. 342.
5 'The Spur'.
6 *Letters on Poetry from W. B. Yeats to Dorothy Wellesley*, p. 108.
7 'The Chambermaid's Second Song'.
8 Quoted in A. Norman Jeffares, *W. B. Yeats: A New Biography*, p. 320.
9 Richard Ellmann, 'W. B. Yeats's Second Puberty', in *Four Dubliners*, p. 29.
10 'The Gyres', ll. 17–24.
11 Quoted in A. Norman Jeffares, *W. B. Yeats: A New Biography*, p. 332.
12 'Lapis Lazuli', ll. 55–6.

13 'What Then?', ll. 16–20.
14 'An Acre of Grass', ll. 13–18.
15 *Letters of W. B. Yeats*, p. 876.
16 Quoted *W. B. Yeats: The Poems*, p. 795.
17 E. H. Mikhail, ed., *W. B. Yeats: Interviews and Recollections*, vol. II, p. 323.
18 For WBY's broadcasting, see Hone, op. cit., pp. 457–62.
19 Mikhail, op. cit., vol. II, p. 323.
20 For WBY and Edith Shakelton Heald, see David Pierce, *Yeats's Worlds: Ireland, England and the Poetic Imagination*, pp. 260–4.
21 Quoted in *The Variorum Edition of the Poems of W. B. Yeats*, pp. 839–40.
22 'The Municipal Gallery Revisited', stanza VII, ll. 3–8.
23 *Letters of W. B. Yeats*, p. 886.
24 See *Essays and Introductions*, pp. 509–26.
25 'The Circus Animals' Desertion', III, ll. 3–8.
26 'Genealogical Tree of Revolution', quoted in Elizabeth Cullingford, *Yeats, Ireland and Fascism*, p. 216.
27 For WBY and the Abyssinian War, see ibid., p. 220.
28 For WBY and the Spanish Civil War, see ibid., pp. 220–2.
29 *On the Boiler*, pp. 16–21.
30 'Why should not Old Men be Mad?', ll. 1–8.
31 See *On the Boiler*, pp. 16–21.
32 Ibid., pp. 29–30.
33 See Mikhail, op. cit., vol. II, p. 281.
34 'Beautiful Lofty Things', ll. 10–12.
35 Mikhail, op. cit., vol. II, p. 281.
36 Ibid., pp. 233–8.
37 'Under Ben Bulben', VI, ll. 9–11.
38 Ibid., V, ll. 1–16.
39 Mikhail, op. cit., vol. II, p. 293.
40 For Dorothy Wellesley's account of WBY's last days, see ibid., pp. 239–41.
41 'The Black Tower', ll. 7–10.
42 Quoted in Hone, op. cit., p. 480.
43 *Autobiographies*, vol. II, p. 347.

Bibliography

Yeats's Writings

Ah, Sweet Dancer: W. B. Yeats, Margot Ruddock: A Correspondence, ed. Roger McHugh, London, Macmillan, 1970

Autobiographies, London, Macmillan, 1955

A Book of Irish Verse Selected from Modern Writers, London, Methuen, 1895

The Collected Letters of W. B. Yeats, vol. 1, 1865–95, ed. John Kelly and Eric Domville, Oxford, Clarendon Press, 1986; vol. 3, 1901–4, ed. John Kelly and Ronald Schuard, Oxford, Clarendon Press, 1994

The Collected Plays of W. B. Yeats, 2nd. ed., London, Macmillan, 1952

The Correspondence of Robert Bridges and W. B. Yeats, ed. Richard Finneran, London, Macmillan, 1977

A Critical Edition of Yeats's 'A Vision' (1925), ed. George Mills Harper and Walter Kelly Hood, London, Macmillan, 1978

Essays and Introductions, London, Macmillan, 1961

Explorations, selected by Mrs W. B. Yeats, London, Macmillan, 1962

Fairy and Folk Tales of the Irish Peasantry, London, Scott, 1888

Florence Farr, Bernard Shaw, W. B. Yeats: Letters, ed. Clifford Bax, London, Home & Van Thal, 1946

The Letters of W. B. Yeats, ed. Allan Wade, London, Rupert Hart-Davis, 1954

Letters on Poetry from W. B. Yeats to Dorothy Wellesley, intro. Kathleen Raine, London, Oxford University Press, 1964

Letters to the New Island, ed. Horace Reynolds, Cambridge, Mass., Harvard University Press, 1934

Memoirs, ed. Denis Donoghue, London, Macmillan, 1972

Mythologies, London, MacMillan, 1959

On the Boiler, Dundrum, Cuala Press, 1938

The Oxford Book of Modern Verse, 1892–1935, chosen by W. B. Yeats, Oxford, Clarendon Press, 1936

The Secret Rose and Other Stories, London, Macmillan, 1962

The Senate Speeches of W. B. Yeats, ed. Donald R. Pearce, Bloomington, Indiana University Press, 1960

Short Fiction, ed. G. J. Watson, London, Penguin, 1995

The Speckled Bird with Variant Versions, ed. William H. O'Donnell, Toronto, McClelland & Stewart, 1976

Uncollected Prose by W. B. Yeats, vol. 1, ed. John P. Frayne, London, Macmillan, 1970; vol. 2, ed. John P. Frayne and Colton Johnson, London, Macmillan, 1975

The Variorum Edition of the Plays of W. B. Yeats, ed. Russell K. Alspach, London, Macmillan, 1966

The Variorum Edition of the Poems of W. B. Yeats, ed. Peter Allt and Russell K. Alspach, New York, Macmillan, 1957

A Vision, London, Macmillan, 1962

W. B. Yeats: Letters to Katherine Tynan, ed. Roger McHugh, London, Burns Oates & Washbourne, 1953

W. B. Yeats and T. Sturge Moore: Their Correspondence, 1901–1937, ed. Ursula Bridge, London, Routledge & Kegan Paul, 1953

W. B. Yeats: The Poems, ed. Daniel Albright, rev. edn, London, J. M. Dent, 1994

W. B. Yeats: Prefaces and Introductions, ed. William H. O'Donnell, London, Macmillan, 1988

The Works of William Blake: Poetic, Symbolic, and Critical, 3 vols, ed. Edwin J. Ellis and W. B. Yeats, London, Quaritch, 1893

Yeats's 'Vision' Papers, 3 vols, ed. George Harper Mills *et al.*, London, Macmillan, 1992

Biographies, Background and Critical Studies

Beckson, Karl, *Arthur Symons: A Life*, Oxford, Clarendon Press, 1987

—— *London in the 1890s: A Cultural History*, New York and London, W. W. Norton, 1992

Biddis, Michael P., *The Age of the Masses*, Harmondsworth, Penguin Books, 1977

Boyce, D. George, *Nationalism in Ireland*, 3rd. ed. London, Routledge, 1995

Bradbury, Malcolm and James McFarlane, eds, *Modernism 1890–1930*, London, Penguin Books, rev. edn, 1991

Brennan, J. H., *Discover Astral Projection: How to Achieve Out-of-Body Experiences*, London, Aquarian, 1989

Bushrui, S. B., *Yeats's Verse-Plays: The Revisions 1900–1910*, Oxford, Clarendon Press, 1965

Cardozo, Nancy, *Lucky Eyes and a High Heart: The Life of Maud Gonne*, London, Gollancz, 1979

Carpenter, Humphrey, *A Serious Character: The Life of Ezra Pound*, London, Faber & Faber, 1988

Cullingford, Elizabeth, *Yeats, Ireland and Fascism*, London, Macmillan, 1981

Elborn, Geoffrey, *Francis Stuart: A Life*, Dublin, Raven Arts, 1990

Ellmann, Richard, *Yeats: The Man and the Masks*, 1948, rev. edn, London, Oxford University Press, 1979
—— *The Identity of Yeats*, London, Macmillan, 1954
—— *Eminent Domain: Yeats among Wilde, Pound, Eliot and Auden*, London, Oxford University Press, 1967
—— *Four Dubliners: Wilde, Yeats, Joyce, Beckett*, London, Hamish Hamilton, 1987
—— *Oscar Wilde*, London, Hamish Hamilton, 1987
Fay, Gerald, *The Abbey Theatre: Cradle of Genius*, Dublin, Clonmore & Reynolds, 1958
Finneran, Richard, George Mills Harper and William M. Murphy, eds, *Letters to W. B. Yeats*, 2 vols, London, Macmillan, 1977
Flannery, James, *Miss Annie F. Horniman and the Abbey Theatre*, Dublin, The Dolmen Press, 1970
Foster, R.F., *Modern Ireland, 1600–1972*, London, Allen Lane, 1988
—— *Paddy and Mr Punch: Connections in Irish and English History*, Harmondsworth, Allen Lane, 1993
Greer, Mary K., *Women of the Golden Dawn: Rebels and Priestesses*, Park Street Press, Rochester, Vermont, 1995
Gregory, Augusta, Lady, *Seventy Years 1852–1922: Being the Autobiography of Lady Gregory*, ed. T. R. Henn and Colin Smythe, London, Oxford University Press, 1974
Gwynn, Stephen, *Scattering Branches: Tributes to the Memory of W. B. Yeats*, London, Macmillan, 1940
Hardwick, Joan, *The Yeats Sisters: A Biography of Susan and Elizabeth Yeats*, London, Pandora, 1996
Harper, George Mills, *The Making of Yeats's 'A Vision'*, 2 vols., London, Macmillan, 1987
—— *Yeats's Golden Dawn*, London, Macmillan, 1974
—— *W. B. Yeats and W. T. Horton: The Record of an Occult Friendship*, Atlantic Highlands, New Jersey, Humanities Press, 1980
Harper, George Mills, ed., *Yeats and the Occult*, London, Macmillan, 1976
Harwood, John, *Olivia Shakespear and W. B. Yeats: After Long Silence*, London, Macmillan, 1989
Heine, Elizabeth, 'W. B. Yeats's Map in his Own Hand', *Biography*, 1, no. 3 (1978), pp. 37–50
Henn, T. R., *The Lonely Tower: Studies in the Poetry of W. B. Yeats*, London, Methuen, 1950
Holroyd, Michael, *Augustus John: A Biography*, rev. edn, Harmondsworth, Penguin Books, 1976
Hone, Joseph, *W. B. Yeats: Man and Poet*, 1949, rev. edn, London, Routledge & Kegan Paul, 1962; repr. Penguin Books, 1971

Hone, Joseph, ed., *J. B. Yeats: Letters to his Son W. B. Yeats and Others 1869–1922*, London, Faber & Faber, 1944

Howe, Ellic, *The Magicians of the Golden Dawn: A Documentary History of a Magical Order*, London, Routledge & Kegan Paul, 1972

Jeffares, A. N., *W. B. Yeats: Man and Poet*, 1949, rev. edn, London, Routledge & Kegan Paul, 1962

—— *A New Commentary on the Poems of W. B. Yeats*, London, Macmillan, 1984

—— *W. B. Yeats: A New Biography*, London, Hutchinson, 1988

Jeffares, A. N. and K. G. W. Cross, eds, *In Excited Reverie: A Centenary Tribute to W. B. Yeats, 1865–1939*, London, Macmillan, 1965

Jeffares, A. N. and A. S. Knowlands, eds, *A Commentary on the Collected Plays of W. B. Yeats*, London, Macmillan, 1975

Johnson, Josephine, *Florence Farr: Bernard Shaw's 'New Woman'*, Gerrards Cross, Colin Smythe, 1975

Kee, Robert, *The Green Flag*, London, Weidenfeld & Nicolson, 1972; repr. Penguin Books, 3 vols, 1989

Kelly, John, '"Friendship Is the Only House I Have": Lady Gregory and W. B. Yeats', in Ann Saddlemeyer and Colin Smythe, eds, *Lady Gregory Fifty Years After*, Gerrards Cross, Colin Smythe, 1987

Kermode, Frank, *Romantic Image*, London, Routledge & Kegan Paul, 1957

Kilroy, James, *The 'Playboy' Riots*, Dublin, The Dolmen Press, 1971

King, Francis, *Modern Ritual Magic: The Rise of Western Occultism*, rev. ed, Bridport, Dorset, Prism Press, 1989

Kohfeldt, Mary Lou, *Lady Gregory: The Woman behind the Irish Renaissance*, London, André Deutsch, 1985

Longenbach, James, *Stone Cottage: Pound, Yeats, and Modernism*, Oxford, Oxford University Press, 1988

Lyons, F. S. L., *Ireland since the Famine*, London, Fontana, 1963

—— *Culture and Anarchy in Ireland, 1890–1939*, Oxford, Clarendon Press, 1979

MacBride, Maud Gonne, *A Servant of the Queen*, London, Gollancz, 1938

Mikhail, E. H., ed., *W. B. Yeats: Interviews and Recollections*, 2 vols, London, Macmillan, 1977

Miller, Liam, *The Noble Drama of W. B. Yeats*, Dublin, The Dolmen Press, 1977

Moore, George, *Ave*, London, Heinemann, 1911–14

Moore, Virginia, *The Unicorn: William Butler Yeats's Search for Reality*, London, Macmillan, 1954

Murphy, William M., *Prodigal Father: The Life of John Butler Yeats (1839–1922)*, Ithaca and London, Cornell University Press, 1978

—— *Family Secrets: William Butler Yeats and his Relatives*, Dublin, Gill & Macmillan, 1995

O'Beirne Ranelagh, John, *A Short History of Ireland*, Cambridge, Cambridge University Press, 1994

O'Casey, Sean, *Autobiographies*, 2 vols, London, Macmillan, 1963

Pierce, David, *Yeats's Worlds: Ireland, England and the Poetic Imagination*, New Haven and London, Yale University Press, 1995

Pound, Ezra, *The Letters of Ezra Pound, 1907–1941*, ed. D. D. Paige, London, Faber & Faber, 1951

Rajan, Balachandra, *W. B. Yeats: A Critical Introduction*, London, Hutchinson, rev. edn, 1969

Regardie, Israel, *What You Should Know about the Golden Dawn* (previously issued as *My Rosicrucian Adventure*), Phoenix, Arizona, New Falcon Publications, 1993

—— *The Golden Dawn: A Complete Course in Practical Ceremonial Magic*, St Paul, Minnesota, Llewellyn Publications, 1994

Reid, B. L., *The Man from New York: John Quinn and his Friends*, London, Oxford University Press, 1968

Robinson, Lennox, ed., *Lady Gregory's Journals*, 1916–1930, London, Putnam, 1946

Seymour, Miranda, *Ottoline Morrell: Life on the Grand Scale*, London, Hodder & Stoughton, 1992

Simmons, James, *Sean O'Casey*, London, Macmillan, 1983

Smith, Anthony D., *National Identity*, London, Penguin, 1991

Taylor, Richard, *A Reader's Guide to the Plays of W. B. Yeats*, London, Macmillan, 1984

Sinnett, A. P. *Esoteric Buddhism*, London Trubner & Co, 1884.

Thuente, Mary, *Yeats and Irish Folklore*, Dublin, Gill & Macmillan, 1981

Torchiana, Donald, *Yeats and Georgian Ireland*, Oxford, Oxford University Press, 1966

Tynan, Katharine, *Memories*, London, Eveleigh Nash & Grayson, 1924

Vendler, Helen, *Yeats's 'Vision' and the Later Plays*, Cambridge, Mass., Harvard University Press, 1963

White, Anna MacBride and A. Norman Jeffares, eds, *The Gonne-Yeats Letters, 1893–1938: Always your Friend*, London, Pimlico, 1993

Wilson, Edmund, *Axel's Castle: A Study in the Imaginative Literature of 1870–1930*, New York and London, Scribner's, 1931

Woolf, Virginia, *A Moment's Liberty: The Shorter Diary of Virginia Woolf*, London, Chatto & Windus

Yeats, John Butler, *Early Memories: Some Chapters of an Autobiography*, Dundrum, Cuala Press, 1923

Yeats: An Annual of Critical and Textual Studies, ed. Richard Finneran, Ann Arbor and London, UMI Research Press, 1983–

Yeats Annual, ed. Warwick Gould, London, Macmillan, 1982–

Index

JBY denotes John Butler Yeats; Y denotes William Butler Yeats

595

Index